APPLIED PRINCIPLES OF FINANCE

Preliminary Edition

J. Randall Woolridge, Ph.D
Gary Gray, Ph.D
Penn State University

KENDALL/HUNT PUBLISHING COMPANY
4050 Westmark Drive   Dubuque, Iowa 52002

Contents

CHAPTER 1

INTRODUCTION TO APPLIED PRINCIPLES OF FINANCE

In recent years, executives, politicians, and the general public have shown an intense interest in the economy and the capital markets. Round-the-clock broadcasts of business news on CNBC and other financial networks turn CEOs, market strategists, stock analysts, and mutual fund managers into television personalities. Retirees and teenagers alike channel surf to see how the markets performed that day. The stock market provides a daily barometer on the health of the financial world. In turn, this focus on the economy has elevated the position of finance in business and society.

This book is designed for undergraduates as a first course in finance. It may be used as an introductory text for finance majors, or as a self-contained text for the only finance course that a general business student will ever take. We assume that you are familiar with elementary accounting and statistics, along with basic algebra, which are what you will need to know to apply the concepts and principles underlying finance and to use the few equations that are in the book.

The text addresses each of the areas of finance that are so important in today's business world: corporate finance, capital markets and institutions, valuing future cash flows, and investments and valuation.

The book is structured around three analytical pillars of finance—the time value of money, the valuation of assets, and the assessment and management of risk. At the foundation of these pillars are basic principles, rules and theories of finance that should guide corporate managers, individual investors, and students in making intelligent financial decisions. We discuss these principles in depth in Chapter 2 of the text.

In this chapter we help you to develop:

- A knowledge of the expanding role of finance in business and the economy;
- An understanding of the three areas of finance—corporate finance, capital markets and financial institutions, and investments and valuation;
- An introduction to ten important principles that underlie the theory of finance;

- A discussion of the three basic sets of decisions that corporate managers face—the investment decision, the financing decision, and the dividend decision; and
    - A familiarity with the tools in your financial toolbox.

1.1   Finance

Finance involves the management of money. Included in the study of finance are the principles involving how money should be invested and how money should be raised for investment. From either the perspective of an individual or a company, this includes why, how, and whether to invest in projects, ventures, or stocks that have *risky* payoffs to be received in the future.

The decision to make an investment should be based upon three cash related criteria: a conservative projection of the *amount* of the money that you expect to receive on the investment, the probable *timing* of the money that you expect to receive, and a reasonable assessment of the probability or *risk* associated with receiving the money. Once you estimate the amount, timing, and risk of the cash flows associated with an investment, you use financial techniques to determine the true **value** of the project, investment or stock.

Finance involves the management of money.

We can think of the field of finance as a set of contractual arrangements and economic decisions made among a complex web of entities, such as: governments (United States, Spain, Japan, Germany), government agencies (the Federal Reserve, SEC, FDIC), financial institutions (banks, insurance companies, investment firms), financial markets (the NYSE, the NASDAQ, the bond, currency, and commodity markets), companies (major corporations, small businesses), and individuals (you and your family). Finance involves how each of these different groups raises, invests, and manages its money.

SEE BOX ENTITLED 'GAMBLERS, MASTERS AND SLAVES' FOR A PERSPECTIVE ON THE CHANGE IN ROLE OF FINANCE IN ORGANIZATIONS

As highlighted in Exhibit 1-1, the study of finance is generally broken down into three areas: corporate finance, capital markets and financial institutions, and investments and valuation.

- *Corporate finance* involves how companies raise and invest money and manage their financial resources.

- *Capital markets and financial institutions* examines the structure of capital markets, the role of financial institutions, the process of financial intermediation, and how money flows in the economy.
- *Investments and valuation* focuses on valuation techniques and how to value alternative investment opportunities that are provided primarily through financial markets and institutions.

Exhibit 1-1

Finance

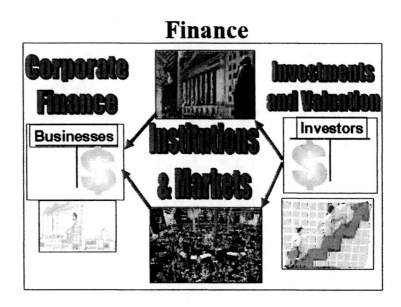

Capital markets are the financial markets where issuers and investors buy and sell debt and equity securities.

In order to invest in plant and equipment, technology, and other assets, companies raise capital through transactions with financial institutions or by issuing securities directly in the capital markets. Companies can raise capital in the financial markets by selling debt instruments (which usually have a fixed or variable interest payment and the repayment of principal) or equity (also known as stock, which represents ownership in the company) to investors.

In the United States, companies can go either directly to the stock and bond markets to raise capital, or may go through financial institutions (such as banks and insurance companies) for funds. In most countries, financial institutions provide the bulk of the capital to companies. To provide this capital, these institutions must in turn raise money by offering attractive investment opportunities and financial services, such as checking and savings accounts, life, health, and casualty insurance, or pension programs, to individuals, households and firms.

Debt represents an obligation to repay borrowed moneys.

Stock represents ownership in a company.

As we examine the areas of corporate finance, capital markets and financial institutions, and investments and valuation, we place each area into the context of the broader world of finance that includes financial instruments, institutions, markets, and investors.

1.2   Ten Principles of Finance

In this section we list ten important principles that underlie the theory of finance. We describe these principles in Chapter 2 and apply them in the chapters that follow as we examine corporate finance, capital markets and financial institutions, and investments and valuation. The principles of finance and areas to which they relate are:

- **Return versus Risk:** *Higher Returns Require Taking More Risk*—There is a positive relationship between risk and return.
- **Market Efficiency:** *Efficient Capital Markets are Tough to Beat*—The prices of stocks and bonds in the capital markets react very quickly to new information.
- **Risk Preference:** *Rational Investors are Risk Averse*—Individual investors are risk averse and prefer less risk to more.
- **Supply and Demand:** *Supply and Demand Drive Asset Prices in the Short-run*—On a day-to-day basis, security prices in the markets are driven by short-term supply and demand conditions.
- **Corporate Finance and Governance:** *Corporate Managers Should Make Decisions that Maximize Shareholder Value*—The goal of management should be to maximize the value of the firm's common stock.
- **Minimizing the Cost of Investing:** *Transaction Costs, Taxes and Inflation are your Enemies*—To the extent possible, minimize your transaction costs and the negative effects of taxes and inflation on investment returns.
- **The Time Value of Money:** *Time and the Value of Money are Inversely Related*—A dollar a dollar today is worth more than a dollar tomorrow.
- **Asset Allocation:** *Your Asset Class Allocation is a Very Important Decision*—The decision to invest in stocks, bonds, or cash is critical in determining your success.
- **Diversification:** *Asset Diversification Will Reduce Your Risk*—Don't put all your eggs in one basket.
- **Investment Valuation:** *Value Equals the Sum of Expected Cash Flows Discounted for Time and Risk*—The value of any financial investment is the sum of its expected cash flows discounted for timing and risk.

1.3   Corporate Finance

Finance is a continually evolving field and information technology has contributed significantly to its pace of change and complexity. Computer processing power has increased the accuracy and speed of information flow so that new information can be immediately incorporated into business planning and decision-making. Technology has reduced the cost of transactions, which in turn leads to more transactions and trading. Improved technology allows the increased trading volume on stock exchanges, the creation by financial engineers of new financial instruments, and the implementation of sophisticated hedging and investing practices around the globe.

The world's capital markets include a wide variety of organized exchanges where financial claims are traded. These claims include debt and equity capital (the bond and stock markets) as well as currencies, commodities and other financial assets. For a country, the level of government interest rates, relative currency values, and the performance of the country's stock markets are the primary gauges of the health of its economy. For a business or a company, the ultimate indicator of its success or failure is the market value of its common stock.

During the past twenty years, a wave of international deregulation has swept over the financial markets thereby opening new sources of capital for companies throughout the world. Financial markets tend to function most efficiently in a deregulated environment. However, the recent breakdown in accounting and corporate governance at Enron, WorldCom, and Adelphia has shown that regulation and oversight are necessary to reduce corruption and fraud in the financial markets.

With the internationalization of finance, the increased speed of trading, and the low cost of transactions, capital flows freely and rapidly around the globe. The downside of the free flow of capital is the volatility that may be associated with it. This volatility occurs in the stock market as well as with interest rate movements, currency fluctuations, and other variables that directly impact the economy. Today, global financial markets are more interdependent than ever before.

1.4.1   *The Role of Corporate Finance*

Corporate financial managers are the interface between the providers of capital (institutional and individual investors) and the financing of the firm. Corporate financial managers face three basic sets of decisions:

- **The Investment Decision:** Investing funds of the company in working capital, tangible and intangible assets to buy or build projects and investments that will be worth more than they cost;

- **The Financing Decision:** Raising money for the company from institutional and individual investors through the sale of debt and equity claims to finance the investment projects of the firm; and
- **The Dividend Decision:** Deciding how much of the company's cash from operations should be reinvested in the business and how much should be returned to the company's shareholders in the form of dividends.

Financial managers are responsible for raising and investing capital for new projects that will create additional value for the firm and its investors. Finance professionals access the capital markets to issue debt and equity on behalf of the firm. Once a company raises capital it then must invest it successfully. As stated in the principle relating to corporate governance, **Corporate Managers Should Make Decisions that Maximize Shareholder Value**. Each of their investing, financing, and dividend decisions should be made in a way that creates the maximum value for shareholders. A company achieves this goal by investing in projects that create a positive *net present value* (*NPV*) for the firm.

Net present value is the value (positive or negative) associated with investing in a project or venture.

Capital budgeting is the valuation, planning and managing of corporate investments for a firm. A project with a positive NPV is an investment in a new product, an acquisition, or other asset that provides a return on investment to the firm in excess of the company's weighted average cost of capital. The *cost of capital* for a firm is the cost of raising debt and equity capital for the business. Minimizing the cost of capital by using the right mix of debt and equity, often called the *capital structure decision*, is an important role for the finance function of the company.

Cost of capital is the cost of raising debt and equity for the firm.

The primary business functions relating to the operations of a firm include: finance, marketing, management, logistics, and accounting. All of the functions of the modern corporation are interrelated. For example, if the firm is launching a new product:

- *Finance* assesses the financial viability of the product and, if needed, raises the capital to fund it;
- *Marketing* researches and determines where, when, and how to sell the product;
- *Management* assesses the strategic and human resource aspects relating to the production and marketing of the product;
- *Logistics* handles procurement of raw materials and other inputs, internal operations and transportation of the product; and
- *Accounting* measures the performance of the product and provides timely information to other departments.

Finance concentrates on the monetary aspects of a company, including: the daily cash flow requirements, financial planning, and short and long-term investment and financing decisions. The marketing department generates revenue by pricing, marketing, and selling the products and services of the firm. Management monitors the production and resource allocation and makes decisions regarding the business. Logistics oversees the daily operations to keep the business running smoothly. Accounting is used to measure and monitor the operations of the firm and to calculate the profits or losses associated with the product.

1.5   Capital Markets and Financial Institution

In Chapter 7 we discuss the capital markets. The *primary markets* are capital markets in which governments, agencies and municipal entities issue debt securities and corporations issue stocks and bonds to investors, and the issuer of the securities receives the proceeds from the sale of securities. The process, in which issuers receive funds directly from the purchasers of stocks and bonds in the markets, is called *direct finance*. We also discuss *secondary markets* in which stocks and bonds are traded after their initial issuance.

Another function of financial markets is to provide investors with *liquidity*—the ease with which an owner of a security can sell an investment to another investor or trade it in the securities markets. Securities markets provide a marketplace where buyers and sellers of securities can complete transactions quickly and efficiently, and save investors from a costly search for potential buyers and sellers of a stock or bond. Financial markets also provide information about the current market value of securities to investors, issuers and other economic participants. The markets in which the current owners of securities receive the funds from the buyers of securities are called secondary markets.

In Chapter 8 we examine financial institutions and the role of financial intermediation. Financial institutions provide important services to the economy of the United States and the world. We describe *indirect finance*—the process of funds moving from investors through financial intermediaries to borrowers. Financial institutions and financial markets exist so that excess monies from investors can be transferred cheaply and efficiently to businesses, governments, individuals and other entities that have profitable investment opportunities and a shortage of funds.

A financial intermediary borrows funds from savers/investors by issuing a claim—a savings or checking deposit, or a contract such as an insurance policy or pension obligation—and uses those funds to make loans or to purchase higher yielding securities. This process is called *financial intermediation*. Financial institutions, such as commercial, investment and savings banks, life, property and health insurance companies, pension funds and mutual funds, act as middlemen in the capital markets. They perform numerous functions for their clients, but in general, financial institutions link lenders and borrowers in the economy through financial intermediation.

Financial intermediation involves the creation and sale of *secondary securities* by financial institutions, which then uses those proceeds to purchase primary securities. Secondary securities include: savings and checking accounts, annuities, insurance policies and pension plans, and mutual funds. Secondary securities are designed to fulfill one or more needs of the clients of the financial institution—the individuals, households, corporations, retirees, and entrepreneurs—that deposit moneys with and borrow funds from the financial institutions.

Financial institutions sell these secondary securities or services to their clients and use the funds provided by their clients to purchase what are know as *primary securities*—stocks, bonds, loans, mortgages, and other financial assets. The interest, dividends, principal, and gains from the primary securities, along with the other assets of the FI, pay the cash flows associated with the secondary securities—the monthly pension checks, or the claims under a casualty policy, or the life insurance payment—whatever products the FI has created and the payments under which they are obligated to honor.

1.6   Investments and Valuation

Each business day millions of investors around the world trade stocks and bonds in the financial markets. Those same investors watch stock and bond prices go up or down—often it seems for no specific reason. Perhaps you've wondered, what are the principal factors that propel daily price changes?

The economics underlying the movements of the stock and bond markets are a mystery to most people. At the end of trading each day, analysts on financial news networks attribute price movements to any number of factors: government reports on consumer or wholesale prices, changes in interest rates, the increasingly bullish or bearish sentiment of investors, or company earnings reports exceeding or falling short of expectations.

During the decade of the 1990's, the stock markets in the United States performed spectacularly. Fueled by the birth and growth of the Internet and the significant reduction of transactions costs, the Dow Jones Industrial Average rose from a level of 2,753 at the end of 1989 to 11,453 at the end of the Millennium. Likewise, the S&P 500 moved from 353 points to 1,469, and the NASDAQ Index rocketed from 454 to 4,069—a nine-fold increase. However, the Internet stock market bubble burst and markets retreated severely in 2000, 2001 and 2002—the NASDAQ plummeting a total of 75%, the S&P 500 down 40%, and the DJIA dropping 27%. In 2003, stock markets around the world rallied by an average of from plus 25% to 55%. And in 2004, the DJIA rose 3%, the S&P 500 rose 9% and the NASDAQ increased by 8%. Investors familiar with the stock markets know that stock returns and prices can fluctuate substantially.

In this book we describe what drives stock and bond prices and why. In Chapters 9 and 10 we begin to dig into the process of valuation and the time value of money. We discuss the art of compounding to future value and discounting to present value. We explain the discounted cash flow approach to valuation and learn how to value investments that have level cash flows and then investments with uneven cash flows. Chapter 11 visits the subject of capital budgeting and the measures of investment return including net present value, internal rate of return and the payback period.

The final five chapters of the book examine what we consider to be the most important area of finance—investments and valuation.

- Chapter 12 addresses the issues relating to what determines the required and expected rates of return associated with an investment. We see from the principle relating to return versus risk—**Higher Returns Require Taking More Risk**, that there is a direct trade-off between the expected rate of return on an asset and its risk. We see how that trade-off is represented in an asset valuation model.
- Chapter 13 focuses on the existence of efficient capital markets and tests of the efficient market theory. We learn how prices and returns of financial assets adjust quickly to the receipt of new information. We see from the principle relating to market efficiency—**Efficient Capital Markets are Tough to Beat**, that it is very difficult to outperform the strategy of buying and holding a diversified portfolio. However, we also discuss some exceptions or anomalies that shows it is possible to beat the market.
- In Chapter 14 we discuss bonds—debt securities that are sold to investors in order to raise long-term funds for the U.S. Government, corporations, municipalities, agencies or other entities. We discuss the types and structures of bond issues, the risks associated with bonds; the term structure of interest rates; and we value par, premium and discount bonds. In the valuation of bonds we see at work the principle relating to the time value of money, that **Time and the Value of Money are Inversely Related**.
- In Chapter 15 we value common stock, which represents an ownership interest in a corporation. We see that the value of a stock is crucially dependent upon two variables: the amount of future profits or cash flows that the firm is expected to generate; and the interest rate or required yield that is expected from the investment. In valuing a stock we use the principle relating to investment valuation, that **Value Equals the Sum of Expected Cash Flows Discounted for Time and Risk**, and we closely examine the Capital Asset Pricing Model.
- Chapter 16 focuses on the management of risk. We discuss three risk transfer techniques: diversification, hedging, and insurance and the relative strengths, costs, and benefits of each of these techniques. We also describe and

discuss derivative securities, their types, characteristics, and valuation procedures. We learn from the principle relating to diversification, that **Asset Diversification Will Reduce Risk**, and it will do so without cost.

1.7   The Financial Toolbox

Financial decision-making incorporates elements of economics, accounting, and statistics. As finance has become more analytical and quantitative, numerous tools have been developed to assist in making strategic financial management decisions. These tools include:

- Financial statements and ratio analysis;
- Present value concepts;
- Models of risk and return; and
- Spreadsheet modeling methods.

Financial statements and ratios analysis. Decision-making in finance is forward looking. Investing and financing decisions require projecting sales and expenses, as well as fixed and working capital requirements. The firm's current financial position is the base from which these projections are made. The company's financial statements—the balance sheet, income statement, and statement of cash flow—measure this position. For forecasting purposes, financial ratios are commonly used to establish relationships between key financial variables.

Present value concepts. Whereas decision-making in finance is forward looking and requires future projections, decisions are made in the present. There is a time value to money (a dollar today is worth more than a dollar tomorrow), and comparability requires that projected future dollars be discounted back to the present for decision-making purposes. The farther into the future is the expected cash flow, the lower is its present value—Time and the value of money are inversely related. Present value concepts are an essential element of the financial toolbox.

Models of return and risk. The trade-off between return and risk is a principle of finance. An investor requires a higher expected rate of return to invest in riskier investments (a safe dollar is worth more than a risky dollar). Various models of risk and return have been developed to assist in measuring risk, and to assess the return requirements associated with accepting additional risk. These models are used primarily in financial decision-making to discount expected cash flow streams for valuation purposes.

Spreadsheet modeling methods. Decision-making in finance has clearly benefited from computer-based spreadsheet software. Spreadsheet programs have become an essential planning tool for modeling investing and financial decisions.

These programs allow you to make projections and then to perform statistical and sensitivity analysis on data.

1.8   Overview of the Book

This book is designed to provide an overview of the world of finance. It is oriented around the three primary areas of finance: corporate finance, capital markets and financial institutions, and investments and valuation. Exhibit 1-2 provides a conceptual overview, with four reference points:

1.   Strategic decisions on investments in working capital and long-term assets produce operating cash flows;
2.   A firm's capital structure decisions in terms of its financing mix between debt and equity capital determine its cost of capital;
3.   Financial institutions and capital markets stand between companies and investors and serve as conduits for firms to raise capital; and
4.   Investors evaluate a company's operating cash flows and cost of capital to determine the firm's market value.

Exhibit 1-2
Corporate Finance, Capital Markets, and Valuation:
The Big Picture

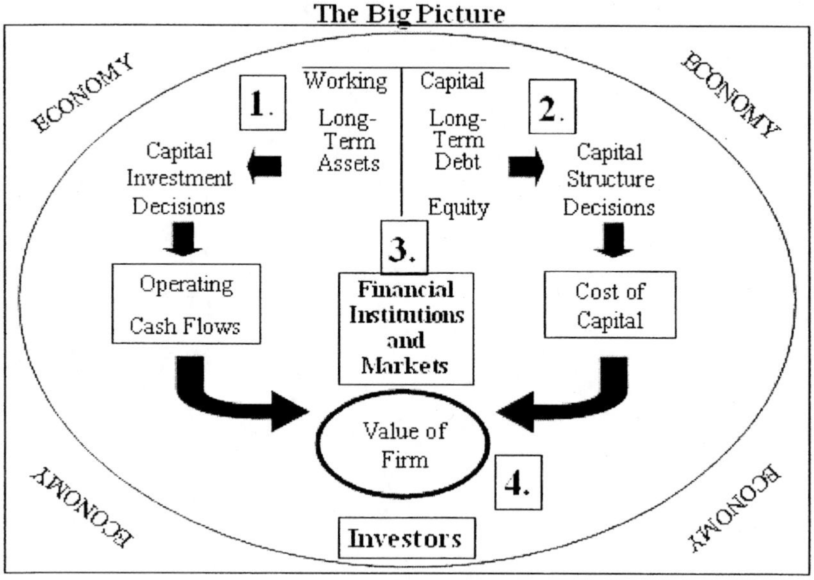

The principles of finance—relating to creating shareholder value and corporate governance; the time value of money and valuation; risk and return; and market efficiency, among others—are recurring themes in the book. In addition, the elements of the financial toolbox—financial statements and ratio analysis, present value concepts, models of risk and return, and spreadsheet modeling methods—are covered and employed in financial decision-making applications.

Part 1 of the book is an introduction to finance and a discussion of ten important principles of finance. Part 2 of the book focuses on corporate finance, primarily from a strategic perspective. Part 3 provides an overview of financial institutions and capital markets. The essentials of cash flow valuation are covered in Part 4. Finally, valuation principles and their use in investment and financing decisions are presented in Part 5.

List of Terms

1. Finance
2. Corporate Finance
3. Capital Markets
4. Debt
5. Stocks
6. Market Efficiency
7. Asset Allocation
8. Diversification
9. Risk
10. Markets
11. Financial Intermediaries
12. Investment Decision
13. Financing Decision
14. Dividend Decision
15. Net Present Value
16. Cost of Capital
17. Primary Markets
18. Secondary Markets
19. Liquidity
20. Direct Finance
21. Indirect Finance

Questions

1. What is finance?
2. Broadly speaking, who is affected by finance? Are you? Why? Explain where you fit into the "big picture."
3. How has the growing importance of capital markets affected the role of finance in organizations?
4. How has the financial landscape changed in the past decade?
5. What are the three major areas of the study of finance?
6. Describe the basic steps involved in the process of investment valuation.
7. Describe the basic functions of finance in a business firm.
8. Explain how the five primary business functions interrelate: finance, marketing, management, logistics, and accounting.
9. Briefly define the four pillars of corporate finance.
10. Describe the differences between the capital budgeting decisions and the capital structure decisions that face corporate managers.
11. Explain the concept of risk and return. Why is it important when investing in a project?
12. What three cash criteria should an investment decision be based upon?
13. What determines short-term security prices? Long-term prices?
14. What are the three basic decisions that corporate financial managers face?
15. How does the principle of asset allocation differ from the principle diversification
16. Why would one expect to receive a higher yield from a corporate bond than from a government security?
17. Why are financial markets and financial intermediaries vital to our economy?
18. What are the elements of the financial toolbox?
19. List and briefly describe the three primary financial statements.

CHAPTER 2

TEN PRINCIPLES OF FINANCE[i]

During the inflating of the high-tech stock market bubble of the 1990s, many market players believed that stock prices moved only upward, and that the Dow Jones Industrial Average would climb to 36,000. Speculators subscribed to the *greater fool theory*—if they bought Internet Capital Group (ICGE) at $200.94 per share, they thought they could sell it the next day to someone else for $225. These gamblers did not understand risk or the tradeoff between risk and expected return. Nor did they realize how quickly a stock's price plummets in response to bad news, and how interest rates and a corporation's earnings affect a stock's value.

The bubble popped! Over the period from 2000 to 2003, the NASDAQ index declined 75%, at the end of 2002 the Dow was at 8,341.63; ICGE traded at $0.36 per share—down 99.9%; and investors desperately needed a rational and informed approach for investing in stocks.

This chapter introduces ten principles, which anchor rational financial decision-making relating to corporate finance, capital markets and financial institutions, and the valuation of assets. Some principles, such as minimizing the cost of investing, should be obvious—even to newcomers in the area of finance. Others, such as principles relating to market efficiency and diversification, are subtle and are supported by the results of rigorous academic research and testing. Each of the principles, however, should eventually become intuitive to you as you read and reason through them, and as you learn about finance.

2.1 Return Versus Risk:
Higher Returns Require Taking More Risk

Finance theory assumes that a rational investor prefers to receive a higher percentage return on an investment to a lower return, and would rather accept less risk than more risk in earning that return. The proverbial free lunch does not exist in the investment world. A trade-off occurs between a higher expected return and greater risk of an investment. Safe investments have low returns. High returns require investors to take big risks.

The tradeoff between return and risk is such an important principle that we devote Chapter 12 to explaining and developing this concept. In this section we introduce you to the risk/return trade-off. It's extremely important that we all start on the same page when discussing expected returns and risk. And you might want to read Section 12.2 where we define terms relating to risk and return.

2.1.1   The Ibbotson & Sinquefield Study

In an extensive study,[ii] Professors Roger Ibbotson and Rex Sinquefield calculated annual percentage rates of returns and examined the distributions of those returns over the time period from 1925 until 2004 for the following classes of investments:

- U.S. Treasury bills with a three-month maturity;
- U.S. Government bonds with an average 20-year maturity;
- High quality corporate bonds with an average 20-year maturity;
- A portfolio of large cap common stocks as represented by 500 of the largest companies in the U.S.; and
- A portfolio of small cap common stocks as represented by the smallest twenty percent of the companies listed on the NYSE.

The results of the I&S study are important and show the direct relationship between the expected return of an asset and the risk associated with receiving that return. Table 2-1 presents the summary statistics for percentage returns on the five investment classes. The average percentage return is calculated on a compound average and simple average basis. For reasons that we describe in Chapter 13, we use compound annual returns as our preferred measure of return. The risk associated with an asset class is measured by how widely the annual returns vary over time as recorded by the standard deviation of the annual return distribution.

Table 2-1
Ibbotson & Sinquefield Study

Asset Class	Compound Annual Return	Simple Average Annual Return	Std. Dev. of Return
U.S. Treasury Bills	3.70%	3.80%	3.10%
U.S. Treasury Bonds	5.40%	5.80%	9.40%
Corporate Bonds	5.90%	6.20%	8.60%
Large Company Stocks	10.40%	12.40%	20.40%
Small Company Stocks	12.70%	17.50%	33.30%

The I&S Study demonstrates the direct trade-off between return and risk. An investment in a Treasury bill with no default risk and very little price volatility has a lower expected average return (3.7%) than a portfolio of large cap stocks (10.4%). The Treasury bill also has a lower risk measure of 3.1% relative to the returns of a portfolio of large company stocks with a standard deviation of 20.4%. Returns on individual stocks can swing even more wildly than the portfolio returns shown in Table 2-1. For example, the price of Internet Capital Group fell from $200.94 per share to $0.36 per share in a brief period of time. On average, when investing in common stocks and accepting risk, investors have increased returns significantly.

When we think about risk, we mainly focus on negative outcomes—losing a job, breaking a leg while skiing a double black diamond on Ajax Mountain, being gored while running with the bulls in Pamplona. In economics and finance, however, *risk means uncertainty*. Risk is measured by assigning *equal probability to both negative and positive outcomes*. As we discussed, we typically calculate the risk of an investment by its standard deviation. The measure of risk or uncertainty is the same if the observed return on the asset we own exceeds the average return by 10%—an outcome that we prefer, or if the observed return is 10% below the average return—a more onerous result.

Risk means Uncertainty!

2.1.2 Return Versus Risk

When deciding whether to buy or sell an investment such as a stock or a bond, you should assess whether the probabilities of positive or negative surprises are equal, or whether the probabilities of reward or risk are skewed in a particular direction. Over time, there is a tendency for the returns and the risks of the financial markets to revert to their average levels, a concept known as *reversion to the mean*.

Reversion to the mean is the tendency for measures of performance such as percentage rates of return to revert to their historical averages.

For example, the returns on the S&P 500 over the 1995-1999 period were as follows: 37.4%, 23.1%, 33.3%, 28.6%, and 21%. The average annual return over this 5-year period was a remarkable 28.7%—the best 5-year run in the history of the stock market! However, the compound average annual return for a stock over the long run, as we can see from Table 2-1, has been about 10.7%. Mean reversion suggests that the return levels associated with the stock market run of the late 1990s were not sustainable and it was likely that much lower or negative returns were on the horizon that would eventually bring average stock returns back into line with historic returns.

When stock prices are at relatively low levels as measured by price-to-sales, price-to-book value, or price-to-earnings ratios (we'll define all of these ratios later in the book), the chance for a very good stock return increases significantly, and you may want to consider buying a stock or a stock mutual fund. Conversely, when price-to-book values and price-to-earnings ratios approach levels of irrational exuberance (are at historically high levels), you might want to sell overvalued stocks, flee to the sidelines and invest in bonds or in money market instruments. For instance, during the late 1990s the prices of technology stocks were at levels far higher than their profits from operations could ever support. The downside risk of stocks appeared to be significantly higher than the upside potential. It would have been wise for investors to reduce exposure to the equity market.

Likewise, the same caveats exist when investing in fixed income securities such as bonds. At the end of 2002, the 10-year U.S. Treasury rate was at a 40-year low of 3.82%—not the time to buy long-term fixed rate investments. Be prepared to take on additional risks to earn increased returns, but first make sure that the odds are in your favor. This is part of the asset allocation decision that we discuss in the principle relating to asset allocation later in this chapter.

2.2   Market Efficiency:
Efficient Capital Markets are Tough to Beat

2.2.1   Efficient Capital Markets

Introduced by Professor Eugene Fama of the University of Chicago, the *efficient capital markets* (ECM) hypothesis states: the stock market is brutally efficient; current stock prices reflect all publicly available information; and stock prices react completely, correctly, and almost instantaneously to incorporate the receipt of new information. In simple terms, an efficient capital market is a market that efficiently processes information. Prices of securities fully reflect available information and are based on an accurate evaluation of all available information. We discuss stock market efficiency in greater detail in Chapter 13.

Efficient capital markets, along with the *random walk hypothesis* of stock prices and the *capital asset pricing model*, form the cornerstone of modern portfolio theory (*MPT*). The capital asset pricing model (CAPM) is a theory about the pricing of assets and the trade-off between the risk of the asset and the expected returns associated with the asset. In the CAPM two types of risk are associated with a stock: unsystematic or firm-specific risk; and market or systematic risk, measured by a firm's beta. (We discuss CAPM and beta in greater detail at the end of this chapter, and in Chapter 12.)

If the stock market is efficient, it would be useless to analyze patterns of past stock prices and trading volume to forecast future prices—which are what stock market technicians do in technical analysis. It also would be useless to analyze the economy, industries, and companies, and study financial statements in an effort to find stocks that are undervalued or overvalued—which are what most Wall Street research analysts do in fundamental analysis.

> *Random Walk Hypothesis states that changes in stock prices are random.*

Many investment professionals think that the concept of efficient capital markets is just the musing of some ivory tower academics and that the ECM hypothesis doesn't properly describe the real life action of the stock market. Many academics disagree and point to studies that support the notion that the stock market is efficient. The good news for Wall Street professionals is that some chinks exist in the armor of proponents of efficient capital markets.

A number of assumptions about investor behavior and the structure of capital markets underlie modern portfolio theory and the efficient capital market hypothesis. Investors are assumed to be rational and calculating, to have identical beliefs and expectations of how the market works, and to have equal access to new information. Investors are assumed to be intelligent and so well informed that the prices they establish, based on new information, are correct (equilibrium) prices. In recent years academicians who specialize in the field of behavioral finance have challenged the assumptions underlying modern portfolio theory. We discuss behavioral finance and its implications for the efficient market hypothesis in Chapter 13.

Various studies have been undertaken to test the notion of efficient capital markets. The goal of many of the studies is to find trading rules that would consistently produce investment returns, adjusted for risk, that are greater than a buy and hold a diversified portfolio strategy. Most of the studies have found results that were consistent with the assumptions of efficient capital markets. One very important study, conducted by Professors Fama and Kenneth French, found that stocks with a high book equity to market equity ratio consistently outperformed stocks with low book equity to market equity ratios. We discuss the Fama and French study and its implication for efficient capital markets, and other similar studies, in great detail in Chapter 13.

2.2.2 ECMs--Our Belief

Even if some exceptions or anomalies exist, we feel that the United States financial and capital markets are reasonably efficient. Stock prices react quickly to new information, and it is very difficult for an investor to consistently beat the investment returns associated with a buy-and-hold a diversified portfolio strategy.

Investment opportunities that produce excess returns do exist, however, such as investing in low (P/E) or high book value to market value stocks—strategies that we discuss further in Chapter 13. We love to take advantage of these types of opportunities. However, investing in these "undervalued situations" is not always for the faint of heart, particularly if the ratios are attractive because of a recent decline in stock price due to an accounting scandal (Enron or WorldCom) or a corporate governance fiasco (Adelphia). A stock's price can go to zero, and bankruptcy proceedings frequently leave stockholders with worthless stock certificates—suitable only for the recycling bin.

We use the results of fundamental research of a stock, such as its book-to-market value and its price earnings ratios, as an initial signal that the company warrants additional analysis. We then run the company through a stock valuation model (described in Chapter 15) to determine its intrinsic stock value. If intrinsic value is greater than the stock's price, and the value/price ratio is greater than 1.0, the stock is undervalued and a buying opportunity may exist. If intrinsic value is less than the stock's price and the value/price ratio is less than 1.0, the stock is overvalued and we would sell it or avoid buying it.

We then assess the cause of this favorable value/price relationship. If the cause is related to an event that is associated with extreme financial distress, we would not purchase the stock. If the cause is due to a temporary problem or a concern for a situation that has a high likelihood of being corrected by the company, it may be a buying opportunity. Once we're comfortable that the company will remain viable, we then determine if the value/price relationship indicates a purchase. If the odds are in our favor, we pull the trigger and buy!

2.3   Risk Preference:
Rational Investors are Risk Averse

In finance and economics, risk is defined as the *uncertainty of future outcomes*, and there is a great deal of concern relating to risk and how individual and institutional investors react in risky or uncertain situations. When it comes to risk taking behavior and the manner in which finance and economic theory predict that investors will act under uncertainty, risk preferences of investors are generally classified into one of three categories—risk averse, risk neutral, or risk taking.

Risk-aversion means that an investor prefers less risk to more risk. "A bird in the hand is worth two in the bush." This common expression along with, "A safe dollar is worth more than a risky dollar," reflects the concept of risk-averse behavior. To a risk-averse investor, the pain of losing a dollar is greater than the pleasure of winning a dollar. If a risk-averse investor is given the choice between two investments with the same expected rates of return, she will select the investment with the lower level of risk or uncertainty.

To a *risk-neutral* investor, the pain of losing a dollar is equal to the pleasure associated with winning a dollar, and he shows no particular concern about risk. In economic theory, a *risk-taker* is an investor who enjoys taking risks. For a risk-taker, the pleasure of winning a thousand dollars exceeds the pain of losing a thousand dollars.

Finance theory and how it predicts investors will act under uncertainty is based upon the assumption that most investors generally exhibit risk-averse behavior, and that investors make rational decisions.

A risk-averse investor does not avoid risk at all costs. She may gamble with small percentages of her wealth in hopes of attaining a significant but unlikely payoff. She can make the occasional trip to Las Vegas or Atlantic City and feed the quarter slot machines or take a seat at the $2 blackjack table. She also may participate in the Power Ball lottery in hopes of striking it big, even though she knows that the odds are greatly against her. With a small portion of her assets, she even may have purchased Internet stocks at their height in hopes of latching onto the next Microsoft or Dell.

For the principle relating to risk aversion to hold, it's not necessary for investors to make intelligent risk/return decisions at all times—only when they are deciding how to invest a significant amount of their assets.

2.3.1 *Risk Aversion—What Does it Mean?*

What does risk aversion mean in real life? Let's assume that an investor has decided to buy one of the following two hypothetical stocks: stock ABC that has an annual expected return of 10%, and a risk measure—the standard deviation of return—of 10%, or stock XYZ that has an annual expected return of 10%, and a standard deviation of 20%.

Exhibit 2-2
Return-Risk Bell Curve for Stock of ABC versus XYZ

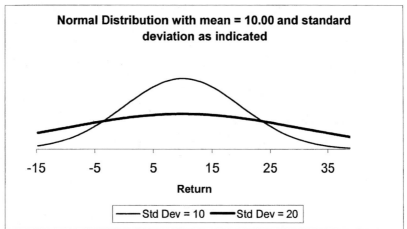

As you can see from Exhibit 2-2, both stocks have the same expected return of 10%. The dispersion of the returns of stock ABC is much more concentrated around the average and the probability of the return being closer to the average return for ABC is much higher than the returns for stock XYZ.

- A *risk-averse* investor, given the symmetric nature of the returns, would always prefer to buy stock ABC because of the lower risk associated with stocks that have the same expected return.
- A *risk neutral* investor would be indifferent between the purchase of the two stocks.
- And a *risk taking* investor would prefer to buy stock XYZ because XYZ has a greater probability of generating an abnormally high return (and abnormally low return—the distribution has more volatility) than stock ABC.

2.3.2   *Risk Aversion—Implications for Investing*

Risk aversion is a good thing—we are very risk averse—we enjoy making money by investing wisely and despise losing money because of a foolish investment decision. It's important that you realize the type of investor you are and how much risk you can stomach in the way of investment losses. If you can't afford to lose money—meaning that if you lose money on your investments you won't be able to eat or pay the rent this month, don't invest in highly volatile stocks. Keep your money in Treasury Bills or in a bank savings account. If you have some excess savings and you want to test your stock picking abilities, then carefully research your choices and invest in stocks that your believe are undervalued and have a higher probability of increasing in value than decreasing.

As far as your own degree of risk aversion, several websites have free online tests that help you to determine your risk/return profile. We list them in Appendix 2-A, along with a description of their quizzes. Make sure that you understand the risks involved in the asset in which you are investing. If the odds aren't in your favor or the extra return isn't sufficient to compensate you for the additional risk, take a pass and find an investment with more favorable risk/return characteristics.

2.4   Supply and Demand:
Supply and Demand Drive Asset Prices in the Short-run

2.4.1   *The Law of Supply and Demand*

The stock market performs like all markets in a competitive economy. The market price of a stock is determined by the interaction of the supply of stock by sellers and the demand for stock by buyers. Current price is where the supply of stock intersects with the demand for stock.

On the demand side, a substantial reduction in transaction costs helped to fuel the bull market of the 1990s. Lower costs greatly increased demand for stocks, thereby driving up prices. Investors, who during the 1980s had to pay a full-service broker several hundred dollars in commissions to buy 100 shares of Microsoft, can now buy 1,000 shares for an $8 Internet brokerage fee. These low costs make it possible for day-traders to buy and sell stocks and garner substantial net profits, even from small moves in a stock's price.

Additionally, the price performance of Internet stocks in the late 1990s spurred an almost insatiable demand for stock of companies in the Internet arena. This excess demand drove price to sales (P/S) and price to earnings (P/E) ratios for these stocks to levels that were unprecedented in the history of the United States' stock markets. On the supply side during the Internet heyday, investment bankers and corporate issuers moved quickly to create new companies that could sell initial public offerings (*IPOs*) to investors to help satisfy demand. The supply during the Internet bubble followed the demand for stock with a slight lag.

As we discuss in Chapter 6, the performance of Internet IPOs in the late 1990s was extraordinary—V.A. Linux Systems soared 733% on the day it was issued. FreeMarkets, Webmethods, Akamai, and CacheFlow all had first-day closing prices over 400% above their IPO offering price. CEOs of Internet companies didn't worry about revenues, products, or employees. Rest assured, if investor demand for a type of company exists, investment bankers will partner with entrepreneurs to create the companies that will issue stock to meet the demand. Eventually, supply will catch up to demand. When that occurs, demand inevitably falls.

2.4.2   What Does Current Stock Price Tell the Market?

A stock's current price multiplied by the number of its shares outstanding determines the market capitalization (market cap) or total value of the common stock of a company. Think about that statement! Does the fact that a share of ICGE traded at $200.94 on January 3, 2000, mean that Internet Capital Group with 287.7 million shares outstanding was truly worth $57 billion? Would some investor or group of investors have ever paid $57 billion for an Internet incubator whose underlying portfolio of assets was not worth one-tenth that amount? It's doubtful!

Market Capitalization = Current Stock Price * Amount Shares Outstanding (Eq. 2-1)

In reality, a company's current stock price only indicates the amount that the marginal investor, given supply and demand considerations, is willing to pay to acquire as little as 100 shares of the company's stock. In the short-run, this current price may or may not have anything to do with the true long-term value of a company. The current price may be heavily influenced by a very temporary and extreme supply and demand imbalance, or by the stock market's reaction to the receipt of new information.

An example of a temporary supply and demand imbalance occurred for the stock of EntreMed (ENMD), a biotech firm that specializes in cancer research. Short-term demand for the stock drove the price to stupid and unsustainable levels. On Friday May 1, 1998, a total of 19,100 shares of ENMD stock changed hands on the NASDAQ market and its price closed at $12-1/16 per share. On May 3, the company was the subject of a very favorable front-page article in the *New York Times*. The article contained no new information regarding the company, but described its cancer research in glowing terms. It also gave the company exposure to potential new investors who wanted to be owners of the next Microsoft of biotech. The article greatly influenced the short-term demand for EntreMed's stock.

On Monday May 4, faced with a tremendous increase in demand, the stock opened at $84.87 per share—a jump of over $72—six times the closing stock price on the previous trading day. The closing price of ENMD on May 4th was $51.87, down $33 from its opening price. ENMD's trading volume on May 4 was 23,432,500 shares—a huge increase from the 19,100 shares traded on May 1. The upward momentum of ENMD's stock price and the short-term excess demand for shares couldn't last. On December 31, 2004, ENMD closed at $3.24 per share.

2.4.3 Supply and Demand and Publicly Available Information

Most publicly traded companies have an investor relations (IR) department that is responsible for distributing information about the company to investors and to the media. The IR department usually pushes the positive news that increases the demand for the company's stock and drives up its price, and tries to sweep any bad news under the rug. We have noticed the tendency for good news, such as a patent award or a new oil discovery, to gush freely and in minute detail from the company's investor relations department. Conversely, IR departments downplay negative news regarding a company, such as accounting irregularities and SEC investigations (Enron, Adelphia, WorldCom, Computer Associates, Tyco). Bad news seeps out slowly over time and in sketchy detail.

The short-term imbalance of supply and demand in the stock market is the arena for technical analysis, which we describe in Chapter 15. Momentum traders buy a stock simply because its price has risen due to excess short-term demand. Conversely, they sell a stock simply because its price has fallen due to excess short-term supply. Absent the possession of insider information or clairvoyance, it is impossible to predict the flow of information that will positively or negatively affect the short-run performance of a stock or an investment. The actions of these traders affect stock prices in the short-run. We tend not to be momentum purchasers. When we buy a stock, we buy it because we believe it's undervalued based on fundamental analysis, and that the price will move to its intrinsic value in the long-run.

2.5 Corporate Finance and Governance:
Corporate Managers Should Make Decisions that Maximize Shareholder Value

2.5.1 Maximizing Shareholder Value

What is the appropriate goal for the management of a corporation? Managers should make decisions that benefit the owners of the firm—its stockholders. What is the most desirable goal associated with owning a stock? If we assume that stockholders purchase stock in order to receive the greatest financial return, then the answer is obvious—Good decisions increase the value of the stock, and poor decisions decrease value. The financial manager acts in the shareholders' best interest by making decisions that increase the value of the company's stock.

The appropriate goal of the financial manager, which we examine more fully in Chapter 3, is to maximize the current value of the company's stock. This goal avoids the problems of how to book profits, whether management should have a short-term or long-term horizon, or to focus on accounting income or economic profits. There is no ambiguity in the criterion of maximizing shareholder value, and we explicitly mean that the goal is to maximize the *current* value of the company's stock.

What is the appropriate goal when the firm has no traded stock? Corporations are not the only type of business entity, and the stock of many privately held corporations rarely changes hands, so it's difficult to say what the value per share is at any given time. As long as we are dealing with for-profit businesses, only a slight modification is needed. The total value of the stock in a corporation is simply equal to the value of the owners' equity. Therefore, a more general way of stating the goal of creating shareholder value is to:

Maximize the market value of the existing owners' equity.

Strategic financial management decisions that affect shareholder value relate primarily to three areas of corporate finance: capital budgeting, working capital management and capital structure. Exhibit 2-3 depicts these decisions from a balance sheet perspective. We discuss these three areas in the sections that follow.

Exhibit 2-3

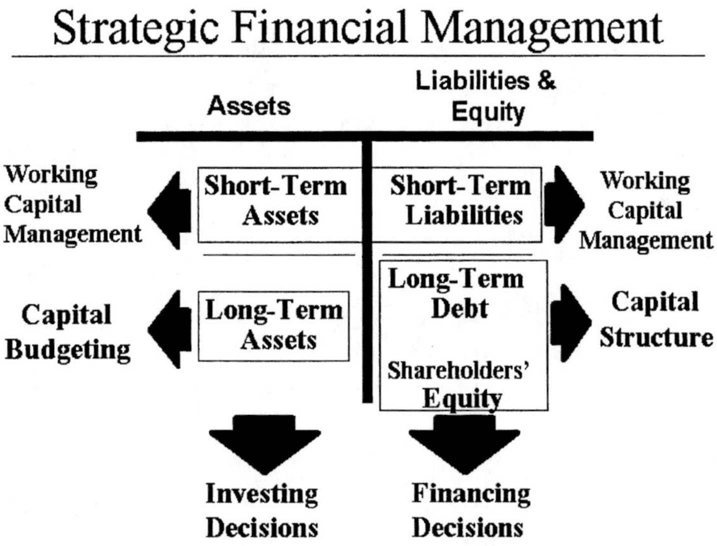

Strategic Financial Management

2.5.2 *Capital Budgeting Decisions*

Capital budgeting is the process of planning and managing a firm's long-term investments in projects and ventures. The financial manager tries to identify investment opportunities that are worth more than they cost to acquire or to fund, so that the present value of the future cash flows generated by an asset exceeds the cost of that asset. Capital budgeting decisions are the most important financial decisions that the management team of a corporation makes—they define the company. Capital budgeting decisions relate to the fixed assets of the firm—what it does, what it makes, and the industries in which the firm is involved.

Regardless of the specific investment, financial managers must be concerned with how much cash (amount) they expect from the investment, when (timing) they expect to receive it, and how likely (risk) they are to receive it. Evaluating the amount, timing, and risk of future cash flows is the essence of capital budgeting. In fact, whenever you evaluate a business decision, these factors should be your most important considerations. We discuss the capital budgeting decision and techniques in great depth in Chapter 11.

The goal of financial managers in the capital budgeting process is to create additional value for stockholders by investing only in projects or ventures that have a *positive net present value*. Financial managers should make capital budgeting decisions that offer the firm the highest risk adjusted return, and that:

Maximize the net present value of the investments that are
financed by the firm's capital budget

2.5.3 *Working Capital Decisions*

Working capital management is another significant responsibility of the firm's financial managers. Working capital refers to the firm's short-term assets, such as accounts receivable and inventory, and its short-term liabilities, such as loans due within one year and accounts payable that are owed to suppliers. Managing the structure and amount of the firm's working capital is a day-to-day activity that should insure that the firm has sufficient resources to continue its operations and to avoid costly financial interruptions.

Some questions relating to working capital are:

- How much cash and inventory should the firm keep on hand?
- What credit terms are appropriate for its products and services? And,
- How and where will the firm obtain any needed short-term financing?

There is a trade-off between liquidity and profitability in working capital management. Capital invested in cash on hand, inventories, and accounts receivable do not earn as high a return for the firm as moneys invested in its fixed assets and projects. Because of this trade-off, financial managers try to reduce the costs associated with financing inventories and accounts receivable. Relating to working capital management, the appropriate goal for the financial manager is to:

Minimize the cost of maintaining the net working capital position
of the company

2.5.4 *Capital Structure Decisions*

Capital structure refers to a firm's specific mixture of long-term debt and equity that it uses to finance its operations and investments. The financial manager has two concerns in this area. What is the least expensive source of funds? And, how much should the firm borrow?

In addition to determining the financing mix, the financial manager has to decide how, when and where to raise the money. The expenses associated with raising long-term capital can be considerable, so the different possibilities must be evaluated carefully. The firm can issue ownership or equity claims by selling common or preferred stock to investors. The firm also can issue debt through the sale of bonds to investors, or through borrowing funds from a financial institution such as a bank or an insurance company in the form of a loan. From the perspective of a shareholder of a company, the optimal capital structure decision is to create a financial structure that will minimize the company's cost of capital. The appropriate goal for the financial manager is to create a capital structure that will:

*Minimize the weighted average cost of capital (WACC)
of the company*

2.6 Minimizing the Cost of Investing:
Transaction Costs, Taxes and Inflation are your Enemies

Transaction costs and the effects of taxes and inflation can greatly reduce the real returns on your investments. Transaction cost comes in many forms: brokerage commissions when you execute a trade; sales loads, 12b-1 fees and redemption fees when you purchase or sell a mutual fund; and yearly asset management fees paid to a mutual fund, stockbroker, or investment adviser. Transaction costs can significantly decrease the returns on your investment portfolio.

It should be every investor's mission to reduce her transaction costs to the lowest possible level. A stockbroker or financial planner can tell you what stocks to buy, how to allocate your investments among asset classes, and how to make your investment program tax efficient. If you benefit from his advice and services be prepared to pay a reasonable commission or fee. However, if you purchase a mutual fund and pay a 5.25% commission to an investment advisor, you have wasted a huge chunk of your money. You have paid far too much for handholding. You can purchase a similarly managed no-load fund with no sales charge.

If you make your own investment and asset allocation decisions, you should search for the lowest brokerage fees or investment management charges available from reputable financial institutions. You should despise paying any unnecessary costs. Make it your goal to minimize transactions costs!

Taxes and inflation are also enemies. Exhibit 2-4 shows the long-term effect of taxes and inflation on investment returns for common stocks, long-term government bonds, Treasury Bills, and municipal bonds over 1926-1999. The results are dramatic. Common stocks provided a 5.0% compounded annual return after taxes and inflation. However, taxes and inflation wiped out the returns on government bonds and Treasury Bills. Given their exemption from federal income taxes, municipal bonds provided a 2.5% positive return after inflation.

Exhibit 2-4

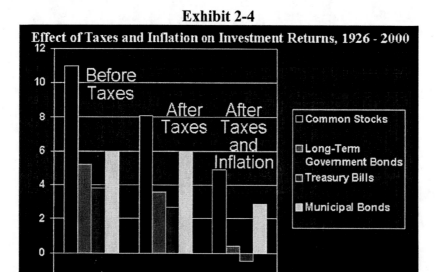

As shown in Exhibit 2-4, taxes can have a negative effect on investment performance. Each year when you receive dividends, interest income and short-term capital gains, you pay a portion of that income to Uncle Sam at current federal income tax rates of up to 35%. Long-term capital gains are taxed at rates up to 20%. Tax payments greatly decrease the after-tax return on your investments, if they are held in a taxable account. Investors can establish tax-advantaged accounts to accumulate retirement assets. Three types of accounts are individual retirement accounts (IRAs), Roth IRAs, and 401(k) retirement accounts.

An investor's annual contribution to an IRA is tax deductible, if the investor's taxable income does not exceed a certain level. The current maximum tax-deductible contribution to an IRA is $2,000 (which is scheduled to increase to $5,000 over time). Tax on the income received on the IRA is deferred until money is withdrawn from the IRA account. Such moneys are then taxed as current income.

Contributions to a Roth IRA are not tax deductible, but the Roth IRA allows dividend, interest and capital gains on the investments to compound on a tax-exempt basis. If the investor is at least 59½ and has invested for at least 5 years, he may withdraw money on a tax-free basis. This is similar to the treatment of interest on a municipal bond, which is generally exempt from federal income taxes and often exempt from state income taxes as well.

Many employers establish 401(k) plans for their employees, allowing them to make tax-deferred investments to a retirement account. Contributions to a 401 (k) plan may be matched by the employer. As with IRAs, tax on the 401(k) is deferred until the money is withdrawn and then is taxed as ordinary income. Self-employed professionals may have substantial pension programs that allow taxes to be deferred until distributions are made to the pensioners.

Inflation decreases the real rate of return on the investment. Needless to say, inflation is beyond the control of the investor. There is a special type of bond issued by the U.S. Treasury called Treasury inflation-protected securities (TIPS) that provides some relief against the effects of inflation, but be prepared to invest in riskier asset classes to help overcome the negative effect that inflation has on fixed-income assets. You should understand how inflation affects your resources and your future consumption requirements. In an inflationary environment, all financial assets become less valuable.

2.7   The Time Value of Money:
Time and the Value of Money are Inversely Related

One of the basic ideas underlying finance is that a dollar today is worth more than a dollar tomorrow. We invest today's dollars with the hope they will grow over time and will buy tomorrow's greater cash flows. In fact, any financial or investment decision involves spending money today and receiving cash payments in the future. For you to assess if an investment is a diamond or a dog, you must be able to compare the value of money that you invest today with the value of the money that you expect to receive in the future. To make this comparison effectively you must understand the simple math that underlies the time value of money—compounding and discounting. We describe compounding and discounting in depth in Chapter 9.

When we value an asset, we first estimate the future cash flows or profits that the asset will generate. The projection of profits involves multiplying earnings by a series of inputs that estimate growth over a period of time—a process that's known as *compounding*. Once we estimate those future profits, we use another math concept to bring those future dollars back to today's values—a process known as *discounting*.

2.7.1   *Compounding and Future Value*

A key to the pricing of any investment is to understand the concepts of discounting and compounding. If the dollar invested today is worth more than the dollar received in the future, how much more depends on the rate of return, the method of compounding, and the length of time between today and when you expect to receive the dollar.

Compounding is the process of going from today's value, or present value (*PV*), to some expected but unknown future value (*FV*). Compounding also means to multiply by a number greater than 1.0 over a number of time periods. You'll see what we mean by this statement in a minute.

Future value is the amount of money that an investment will grow to at some future date by earning interest at a certain rate. Let's look at an example to see how compounding and future value works.

Suppose Jane buys stock at $10 per share in GHI Steady Growth Company (it pays no dividend), and the shares increase in value (miraculously and exactly) at the rate of 8% per year. If Jane holds the stock for five years, what is the ending value of a share? Table 2-2 below shows how the stock price of GHI has grown over time, compounding by 8% per year over the five-year period. The five-year future value of the GHI compounded at a rate of 8% is $14.69.

Table 2-2
GHI Steady Growth Company
Compounding and Future Value Schedule

Year	Beginning Stock Value	Growth In Value	Ending Stock Value
1	$10.00	$0.80	$10.80
2	$10.80	$0.86	$11.66
3	$11.66	$0.93	$12.60
4	$12.60	$1.01	$13.60
5	$13.60	$1.09	$14.69
Total Growth in Value		$4.69	

In this example, when we compound we multiply the beginning stock value by 1.08 over five periods:

*$10 * (1.08) * (1.08) * (1.08) * (1.08) * (1.08) = $14.69*

When we compound, if *r* is the compounding rate (also called a *growth rate, interest rate* or *yield*), *n* is the number of years, *PV* is the present value of a single payment investment, then the future value (*FV*) of the investment is:

$$FV = PV * (1.0 + r)^n \qquad \text{(Eq. 2-2)}$$

In math terms, this says that when you compound the number *PV* at a rate *r* for *n* periods, the future value is equal to the present value times (1.0 plus the compounding rate), raised to the *n*th power. Jane's GHI Steady Growth Stock example looks like this:

$$\$14.69 = \$10 * (1.0 + .08)^5$$

2.7.2 *Discounting and Present Value*

The math underlying discounting and the calculation of present value is the exact flip side to compounding and future value. Discounting is the process of going from an expected future value to a present value. Discounting also means to multiply by a number less than 1.0, over a number of time periods. Present value is what an investment is worth today, if an expected future value is discounted at a certain rate and for a period of time. Let's look at an example to see how discounting and present value works.

Today is your birthday and Aunt Gertie promises you a present—$100 to be given to you at some time in the next five years. What is the present value of Aunt Gertie's $100 promise? This is a tough one. Aunt Gertie is usually reliable but she's a tad overweight and is not in great health. There's a slight chance that she may die before she pays off, so some risk is involved. You're also not sure exactly when that $100 is going to flow to you. With the uncertainty of both risk and timing, this sounds like a problem for a present value table. In Table 2-3 we lay out the possibilities, with the number of years, n, ranging from 0 to 5, and the discounting rates ranging from 6% to 8% to 10%.

Table 2-3
Aunt Gertie's $100 Gift
Present Value Factors

Year (n)	R = 6%	r = 8%	r=10%
0	1.0000	1.0000	1.0000
1	0.9434	0.9259	0.9091
2	0.8890	0.8573	0.8264
3	0.8396	0.7938	0.7513
4	0.7921	0.7350	0.6830
5	0.7473	0.6806	0.6209

The numbers listed in Table 2-3 are known as *discount or present value factors*. These factors give the present value of a dollar that you expect to receive at some time, n, in the future, discounted at a rate, r. As you can see in Table 2-3, as n increases and the payment is expected further into the future, the present value factor decreases—meaning the future payment is worth less today. For example, if Aunt Gertie pays today, it doesn't matter what the discount rate is—the value is $100. If Aunt Gertie's health risk increases to the 10% level and you do not expect the $100 for five years, the present value factor is where row $n = 5$, intersects with column $r = 10\%$—equal to (0.6269). The $100 promise is worth $62.69 today. Likewise, as the discounting rate, r, increases, the present value factor decreases—meaning that the future payment is worth even less today. If time to payment increases or risk increases, the present value of an investment decreases.

The equation for a discount factor for the payment of $1 to be received *n* years from now with a discounting rate of *r* is:

$$Discount\ Factor = 1/(1 + r)^\wedge n \qquad (Eq.\ 2\text{-}3)$$

Let's see what happens when r = 8%, and n = 3. The number $[1/(1 + .08)] = (.9259)$. And $(.9259) * (.9259) * (.9259) = (0.7938)$; just like Aunt Gertie's present value factor table promised.

2.7.3 The Importance of the Time Value of Money

If you are serious about investing, it is essential that you understand how to properly value stocks and bonds. This requires that you know the basics regarding the time value of money—the math underlying compounding and discounting.

The math is not difficult but does require you to understand the relationship between present and future values, how to use exponents, and how to compound to future value and discount to present value. Inexpensive calculators have built-in financial programs that quickly churn out future and present values. We strongly recommend that you take the time necessary to understand compounding and discounting and learn how to use a financial calculator for those functions.

2.8 Asset Allocation:
Your Asset Class Allocation is a Very Important Decision

It's important to periodically examine your assets and investment policy to determine the best way to invest to meet your life's goals—putting children through college, taking vacation trips to foreign countries, earning a pilot's license, learning how to hang glide, owning a home in Key West for the winter and a ranch on the Yellowstone River for the summer. Along with your goals you may also have some constraints, such as liquidity needs, tax considerations, or unique health concerns.

In short order, the volatile markets of the new millennium have demonstrated some valuable lessons about risk and return in managing a portfolio of assets. Modern finance theory teaches us that if we are to achieve the highest level of return for the amount of risk we can stomach, we should diversify our investment holdings over an array of assets classes.

The diversification process begins with asset allocation—dividing investment funds among different asset classes. The most basic classes are cash and short maturity deposits or securities, fixed income securities and bonds, and common stock. Conservative investors tend to put more of their funds in cash and fixed income securities, while more aggressive investors will have a larger portion of their wealth in common stock.

Within the asset classes are subclasses. Bonds include subclasses related to security type (Treasury, corporate, municipal, and foreign) and maturity (short-term—1 to 3 years, medium-term—3 to 7 years, and long-term—over 7 years). For common stock, there are many different subclasses. The most general relate to market value: large cap—over $5 billion, mid cap—$1 to $5 billion, and small cap—under $1 billion stocks; and investment style—value versus growth stocks.

The trade-off of risk and return that we discussed in the first principle int his chapter also applies to asset classes, as illustrated in Exhibit 2-5 below. Fixed income asset classes have less risk (as measured by the standard deviation of returns) and provide lower expected returns than equity asset classes. Among equity asset classes, large cap stocks tend to be less risky than small cap stocks, and value stocks generally tend to be less risky than growth stocks. International equities over time have exhibited greater risk and return than domestic stocks.

Exhibit 2-5

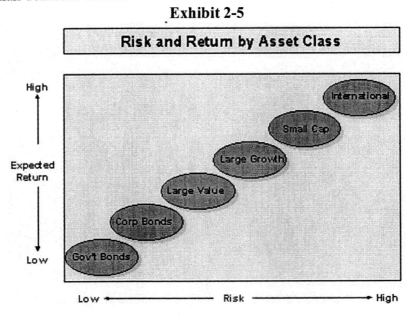

2.8.1 Typical Asset Allocation Mixes

Some investors maintain a fixed percentage of their funds in asset classes (say 20% cash, 30% bonds, and 50% stocks), and others prefer to change their asset allocations based on their expectations of risk and return. Wall Street firms employ market strategists who recommend an asset allocation mix for clients. *The Wall Street Journal* periodically polls the brokerage firms to determine their preferred asset allocation levels. Recommended allocations in a recent poll ranged from 80% stocks, 10% bonds, and 10% cash for one firm, to 40% stocks, 55% bonds, and 5% cash for another. The standard Wall Street benchmark for asset allocation is 10% cash, 35% bonds, and 55% common stocks.

Asset allocation levels should reflect beliefs about the anticipated risk and return of asset classes. If you believe the stock market is going to crash, you should lower your stock allocation, shifting moneys to bonds or cash. If you believe that long-term interest rates are going to rise substantially, you should shift money from bonds into cash. In this way, there may be an element of *market timing* involved in your asset allocation. Market timing—the moving into and out of different asset classes because of beliefs about their expected performance—is frowned upon by followers of modern portfolio theory. Nonetheless, it is a practice that many Wall Street professionals embrace.

Asset allocations should be tailored to an investor's particular circumstances and risk preferences.

Exhibit 2-6

2.8.2   *Studies of Asset Allocation*

The importance of asset allocation in explaining the investment performance of mutual funds and pension funds was highlighted a decade ago in two studies[iii] by Dr. Gary Brinson and his colleagues. Their research showed that more than 90% of the variability in fund performance over time was attributable to asset allocation, as shown in Exhibit 2-6. This means that from a total rate of return perspective, the decision of the asset classes in which to invest is more important than the specific securities that are selected for investment.

What Drives Portfolio Performance

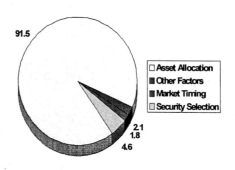

2.8.3   *Optimal Asset Allocations*

Your investment portfolio should be divided between stocks, bonds, and cash reserves. We recognize that risky stocks have a higher expected return than bonds, which have a higher expected return than cash reserves. Let's assume that you are 50 years old, have been successful in business, have significant funds to invest, and have decided on an aggressive Wall Street asset allocation recommendation—55% stocks, 35% bonds, and 10% cash.

You must decide your desired asset allocation and in what asset classes you want to focus. Your allocation will be a function of your risk/return profile—how much risk you can stomach when it comes to volatility and potential losses in your stock allocation. Your risk/return profile should also be a function of where you are in your financial life cycle. As you approach retirement, you may want to lower your stock exposure and increase your bond allocation.

2.9   Diversification:
Asset Diversification Will Reduce Your Risk

As we discussed in the principle relating to risk preference, rational investors are risk averse. As such, risk-averse investors require additional compensation in terms of expected return to take on more risk. We also discussed the principle on return versus risk and the direct trade-off between expected return and risk. Over time, if you want to achieve a higher return, you are going to have to take on more risk.

How much risk can you deal with in your investment portfolio? Could you sleep at night knowing that your retirement nest egg could be cut in half due to any number of social, political, and economic factors that could rile the world's financial markets? This is a perplexing problem. We all want to earn a higher return. But, can we deal with the higher risk that we must take to earn that expected return? What if disaster strikes? An assessment of your risk tolerance is an important first step in the investment process. A number of online investment personality quizzes address the issue of individual risk tolerance. Appendix 2-A provides a summary of online risk assessment resources, as well as their URLs.

The first step to reduce the risk of your portfolio is to diversify your holdings. *Diversification* means to spread your wealth among a number of different investments. The goal of diversification is to invest in a group of assets that provides you with the best return possible given a level of risk. Your assets are everything that has value to you: your family, home, career, health, cars, furniture, clothing, and financial assets, such as insurance policies, stocks, bonds, and cash reserves.

When you make decisions affecting risk and return, consider the total amount of your assets—your career, house, and all of your tangible and financial assets as being held in one portfolio, one pool. Protect against having too much concentration of your assets in one financial institution that could conceivably fail. We suggest that you maintain financial accounts at different commercial banks, brokerage firms, and mutual fund companies. Within these accounts, allocate your assets efficiently to minimize taxes in the manner that we discuss in the principle relating to asset allocation.

2.9.1   Career, Home and Employer

First, take an inventory of your assets. If you are young and intend to work for a number of years, in all probability your biggest asset is your human capital—the ability to earn income by selling your skills or labor. A large portion of the cash flow that will finance your lifestyle and enable you to purchase investments will come from your job.

Since the goal of diversification is to reduce the downside risk of your asset base, avoid investing a substantial amount in the stock of the company for which you work. Also avoid investing in companies in related industries. For instance, if you work in the relatively volatile financial industry for an investment bank such as Merrill Lynch, you shouldn't invest a large portion of your assets in the stock of Goldman Sachs.

From a risk perspective, it usually is a bad idea for an employee to sink a significant portion of his investment portfolio in the stock of his employer, whether in a retirement account or through holdings in other accounts. We felt the pain for what happened to employees/pensioners/shareholders of Enron. Employers often make it financially attractive for employees to purchase shares of the company, sometimes at a steep discount. If the discount is significant enough, purchase the stock; but at your earliest opportunity liquidate the shares and deploy the money into other assets.

Likewise, many American families, especially younger families, have a large percentage of their wealth tied up in a house. If you live in an area that is dependent upon one industry, such as high-tech in Silicon Valley, the entertainment industry in Los Angeles, or the finance industry in New York, avoid investing a large portion of your financial assets in that industry. You don't want an economic event that crushes your investments to also negatively affect the value of your house, giving you a double dose of pain.

For a first shot at diversification, try to separate your career assets from your investment assets. Also, don't over-invest in a house if its value is closely tied to the well-being of your employer.

2.9.2 *Financial Assets*

We assume that you have enough liquid assets to finance six months of expenses and some unforeseen emergencies, and that you have insurance coverage to cover tragedies. In the principle relating to asset allocation, we noted that the diversification process begins with asset allocation. Spreading your funds over alternative asset classes reduces the overall risk of your portfolio. We describe the diversification process and get a better understanding of diversification and risk in Chapter 12.

Achieving the highest return for each level of risk is known as investing efficiently—investing on the *efficient frontier*. Efficient frontiers are portfolios that are designed with the help of computer modeling and are beyond the scope of this book. This type of investing is normally accomplished by investing in different asset classes. The most general asset classes for stocks are value and growth stocks, and large and small capitalization stocks. If you have decided to increase your expected return on your assets by investing a portion of your portfolio in common stock, how should you diversify to reduce your risk?

Stockholders face two types of risk: systematic risk and unsystematic risk. Systematic risk represents the risk of the stock market. Changes in stock prices are caused by changes in the economy, taxes, and other market factors. When these factors change, it affects the entire market. Although systematic changes in the market affect each stock to a different degree, all stocks are impacted. As discussed in the principle relating to return versus risk, we measure the systematic or market risk of a stock by its beta.

Unsystematic risk is specific to a company. It is risk inherent to a particular stock due to decisions made by a corporation relative to the industry in which it operates. While unsystematic risk is unique for all firms, it can be similar for firms in related industries.

Total Risk = Systematic Risk + Unsystematic Risk   *(Eq.2-4)*

Diversification reduces the unsystematic risk of a portfolio. On average, the negative stock-specific surprises affecting companies in a diversified portfolio are offset by positive surprises.

Table 2-4, summarizes the results of a study[iv] performed by Meir Statman in 1987. The study looked at randomly grouped portfolios of stocks of various sizes to determine the marginal amount of diversification achieved by adding additional stocks to a portfolio. Volatility of individual stocks is measured by the standard deviation of their returns. The average standard deviation for an individual stock was found to be 49.24%—a significant amount of volatility and risk. According to the findings, if ten randomly selected stocks are combined into a portfolio, its volatility and risk dropped by more than 50% to an average of 23.93%. The volatility of a ten stock portfolio was not significantly less than the volatility of a 1000 stock portfolio.

Based on these results, we see that diversification is easy to obtain in a portfolio. It does not require hundreds of stocks to adequately diversify a portfolio—most studies suggest that 20 to 25 stocks are sufficient. It does, however, require that stocks within a portfolio be selected from different industries to reduce the correlation among the assets. Diversification occurs in a portfolio only if the stocks selected have different types of unsystematic risk, that is, the prices of the stock do not move in lockstep because they are all in the same or highly-related industries.

Table 2-4
How Many Stocks Make a Diversified Portfolio?

Number of Stocks in Portfolio	Average Standard Deviation of Annual Portfolio Returns	Ratio of Portfolio Standard Deviation of a Single Stock
1	49.24%	100%
10	23.93%	49%
50	20.20%	41%
100	19.69%	40%
300	19.34%	39%
500	19.27%	39%
1000	19.21%	39%

Diversification, while limiting your risks by spreading them over a larger number of securities, also limits the gains you would have received if you had concentrated your investments in a few stocks that turned out to be incredible winners. However, could you stomach investing the bulk of your fortune in a risky stock that may either climb to the moon or go bankrupt? What are the odds that you will identify very early the stock that in 2004 will perform similarly to Microsoft, Dell or Cisco in the 1990s? Probably not great!

Diversifying your portfolio may not make you the next Bill Gates or Warren Buffet (who became rich by focusing their investments), but if you're risk-averse and feel more pain from losing than pleasure from winning, diversification is the way to go.

2.10   Investment Valuation:
Value Equals the Sum of Expected Cash Flows Discounted for Time and Risk

The principal relating to investment valuation states that the value of any investment is equal to the sum of the expected future cash flows of the investment, with the cash flows being discounted to take into account their risk and the time value of money. When we value an asset, two basic sources of uncertainty come to mind—the amount of the expected cash flows, and the discounting rate that we use in calculating the present value of those cash flows.

We address the estimation of expected cash flows associated with projects and ventures, and calculating their discounted cash flow, net present value, and internal rate of return in Chapters 10 and 11. We value cash flows associated with bonds in Chapter 14. We also estimate the expected cash flows associated with stocks in Chapter 15. Estimating cash flow is a complex task but it can be handled once you get the hang of it.

Estimating the discounting rate associated with an asset or investment is another issue. The anxiety level of some of the undergraduate business students that take the introductory finance class at Penn State rises dramatically when we mention the Capital Asset Pricing Model (CAPM). Students think that we'll pepper them with partial derivative equations or invoke the Black-Scholes Option Pricing Model to prove some obscure hypothesis. In reality, CAPM can be described by a short equation that links the expected return on an asset to its risk.

2.10.1 CAPM—What does it do?

The Capital Asset Pricing Model is a simple model that estimates the rate of return an investor should expect to receive on a risky asset. In valuation, its principal purpose is to determine the discount rate to use when valuing an asset. A lot of fancy academic finance theory underlies CAPM, and much of it is beyond the scope of this book. Chapter 12 explains the model, but here are the bare necessities so that you can use it to help you to value an asset.

CAPM states that the expected return of a risky asset, $E(R_i)$, such as a common stock, is equal to the return on the risk-free asset (R_f) plus a risk premium. The stock's risk premium is a function of its price volatility or *Beta* (β_i). That's it! In equation form CAPM looks like this:

$$Expected\ Return\ =\ Risk\text{-}Free\ Rate\ +\ Risk\ Premium$$
$$E(R_i)\ \ \ =\ \ \ R_f\ \ \ +\ \ \ \beta_i * [E(R_m) - R_f]\ \ \ (Eq.2\text{-}5)$$

The risk-free rate (R_f) that we use for valuation is the rate on the long-term (10-year) Treasury bond. The risk premium is a function of two factors: the stock's beta (β_i), and the market risk premium, which is the expected return on the overall stock market (R_m) minus the risk free rate $[E(R_m) - R_f]$.

When we value a risky asset, we assume that investors are risk averse and therefore prefer less risk to more risk (see principle relating to risk preference). Because of risk aversion, investors diversify their holdings and seek the greatest expected return for their chosen level of risk (see principle relating to diversification). And since investors hold diversified portfolios, the measure of risk for any new investment is only its systematic risk as measured by beta.

So what does this mean in real life? It means that investors won't buy risky securities unless they are paid higher returns. How much higher depends on the risk of the stock, as measured by its beta, and the amount of the market risk premium. We represent the simple CAPM risk/return relationship in Exhibit 2-7. If the stock market prices stocks in the manner consistent with the Capital Asset Pricing Model, the expected return on each stock should fall on the diagonal risk/return line shown in Exhibit 2-7.

Exhibit 2-7
Graph of CAPM

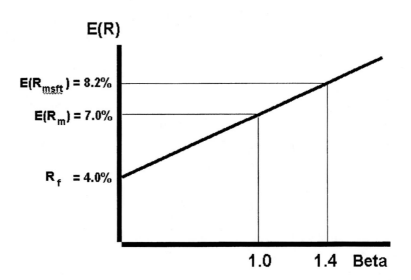

2.10.2 CAPM—a Sample Calculation

If you can estimate an asset's beta and the market's risk premium, you can estimate the expected return for a particular stock. You can find betas for different stocks on Yahoo Finance, Microsoft Investor and numerous other financial websites. We discuss beta and the market risk premium in Chapter 12. As an example, let's look at the expected return for Microsoft. We use a risk-free rate of 4% and an expected return on the stock market of 7%. If we go to the Yahoo Finance website on the Internet and type in the symbol, MSFT for Microsoft, we find a beta estimate of 1.4. When we plug these numbers into the CAPM equation, we get:

$$E(msft) = 4\% + 1.4[\ 7\% - 4\%] = 4\% + 4.2\% = 8.2\%;$$

This means that Microsoft's common stock is expected to generate a return of 8.2% this year.

We use the cost of equity capital calculated by the Capital Asset Pricing Model as an input for our discounted cash flow stock valuation model that we discuss in Chapter 15. CAPM is a simple yet powerful way to estimate the cost of equity, which is usually the most significant component of a company's weighted cost of capital.

Recall that the value of an investment is equal to the expected cash flows of the investment, discounted to the present at a rate that reflects the risk and the timing of the expected cash flows. We believe that CAPM is the best way to estimate the discount rate associated with a risky asset.

2.11   Summary

A trade-off exists between higher expected return on an investment and greater risk. Safe investments have low returns. High returns require investors to take big risks. Most investors do not understand risk, the trade-off between risk and return, or the tendency for stock returns to revert to their average levels, a concept known as *reversion to the mean*. It's important to understand these concepts, and to recognize when a stock's price becomes too high for the operations of the company to support. When that occurs, sell the stock.

The Fama and French study shows that investors can consistently make money by buying stocks with high book value to market value ratios—value stocks, and by selling stocks with low book value to market value ratios—growth stocks.

To a risk-averse investor, the pain of losing a dollar outweighs the pleasure of winning a dollar. Be sure that you understand the risks involved in the asset in which you are investing. If the odds aren't in your favor or the return isn't sufficient to compensate for the risk, take a pass and find an investment with more favorable risk/return characteristics.

Current stock price indicates the amount that the marginal investor, given supply and demand considerations, is willing to pay to acquire a stock. In the short run, price may or may not have anything to do with the true long-term value of a company. Over time, price and value should align. Don't be afraid to sell on the first piece of bad news that doesn't pass your smell test.

Cut all transactions costs to the lowest level possible! Establish tax advantaged retirement accounts and fund them to the maximum that the law and your income allow.

Corporate managers should make investment, financing and dividend decisions in such a way that will create shareholder value, and will maximize the current stock price of the firm.

If you are serious about investing, you should understand how to value stocks and bonds. To do this properly, you need to know the basics regarding the time value of money—the math underlying compounding and discounting. The math is not difficult but does require you to understand the relationship between present and future values, how to use exponents, and how to compound to future value and discount to present value.

If you are to achieve the highest level of return for the amount of risk you can tolerate, diversify our investment holdings over an array of assets classes. The diversification process begins with asset allocation—dividing investment funds among different asset classes. You must decide your desired asset allocation and in what asset classes you want to focus. Your allocation will be a function of your risk/return profile—how much risk you can stomach when it comes to volatility and potential losses in your stock allocation.

Diversification means to spread your wealth among a number of different investments. The goal of diversification is to invest in a group of assets that provides you with the best return possible given a level of risk. Diversification reduces the unsystematic risk of a portfolio. Remember that on average, the negative stock-specific surprises affecting companies in a diversified portfolio will be offset by positive surprises. Most studies suggest that 20 to 25 stocks are sufficient for adequate diversification. It does, however, require that stocks within a portfolio be selected from different industries to reduce the correlation among the assets.

The Capital Asset Pricing Model is a simple model that estimates the rate of return an investor expects to receive on a risky asset. In valuation, its principal purpose is to determine the discount rate to use when valuing a stock. CAPM states that the expected return of a risky asset, $E(R_i)$, such as a common stock, is equal to the return on the risk-free asset (R_f) plus a risk premium. We use the cost of equity capital calculated by the Capital Asset Pricing Model as an input for our discounted cash flow stock valuation model. It is a very simple yet powerful way to estimate the cost of equity, which is usually the most significant component of a company's weighted average cost of capital.

List of Terms
1. Return and Risk
2. Mean reversion
3. Efficient Capital Markets
4. Capital Asset Pricing Model
5. Beta
6. Market risk premium
7. Risk aversion
8. Simple average
9. Compound average
10. Time value of money
11. Present value
12. Future value
13. Compounding
14. Discounting
15. Modern portfolio theory
16. Asset allocation
17. Efficient frontier
18. Systematic risk
19. Unsystematic risk
20. Diversification

Questions

1. If an investor is risk-averse, does that mean he will not take any risk? Explain.
2. What is an efficient market?
3. Explain the risk return trade-off?
4. What are the basic present value and future value equations?
5. What are the factors that affect the time value of money?
6. What are the two kinds of risks? Explain the distinction between them.
7. Define risk premium. How is the CAPM model used to calculate the rate of return on an investment?

Problem Set

1) Ardmore Corporation had following returns on stock over past six years: 4%, 6%, -12%, 3%, 18%, and 5%. Find the simple average return and geometric average return.

2) John has invested $2,000 in a Tech fund in June 2001, the fund had an unsatisfactory performance over the year and dropped 67% by June 2002. How much should the fund increase in next year to break even?

3) Using the following stock performance table for Smith & Co, calculate the simple average return, compound average return, and standard deviation of the return.

4) Johnson Co. stock is selling for $30, and it is expected to be $40 in exactly one year. If you buy 50 shares of this stock today for $1500, there is a transaction fee of $75 to buy these shares. Calculate the return on this stock with and without transaction fee.

5) Solve the following:
   (a) What is the future value of an investment with present value of $600 and invested for 10 years with a compounded annual interest rate of 6%?
   (b) What is the present value of an investment with a future value of $10,000 after 7 years with a compounded annual interest rate of 8%?
   (c) What is the interest rate if an investment with a present value of $7,000 has a future value of $17,500 after 7 years?

6) Assume that the total cost of college will be $50,000 when your child enters school at 18 years. If the rate of return on an investment is 5%, how much should you invest when the child is born to cover the cost of child's education?

7) You have to choose between two different investments: ABC or XYZ, both of which have an initial cost of $10,000. Investment ABC will return $20,000 in seven years and XYZ will return $25,000 in nine years. Which of these investments has the higher return?

Year	Beginning Value	Ending Value
1	$50	$55
2	$55	$52
3	$52	$56
4	$56	$55
5	$55	$52

8) Classify the following as systematic and unsystematic risks.
   (a) Interest rates increase unexpectedly.

(b) The company loses a billion dollar law suit.
(c) The economic growth increased only 1 percent, where as analysts predicted a 3 percent growth.
(d) Corporate tax rates were increased by 2%.
(e) CEO and CFO of the company resign unexpectedly.

9) A stock has a beta of 0.8, the expected return on market is 10%, and the risk-free rate is 5%. What must be the expected return on this stock?

10) If the expected rate of return of the market portfolio is 8%, and the risk free T-bills yield is 4%, what should be the beta of a stock if investors expect a return of 12%?

11) The betas of Central Utility Co. and New Tech Co. are 0.7 and 1.5 respectively. What is the ratio of risk premium for these two stocks?

12) The risk free rate is 5% and the expected return on market portfolio is 11 percent. Is a security with a beta of 1.2 and expected return of 15% overpriced or under-priced?

Assignment #2-1

1) Which of the following best describes a typical investor based on financial theory

    (a) Risk-averse

    (b) Risk neutral

    (c) Risk-seeking

    (d) Risk-indifferent

2) If the intrinsic value of a stock is greater than the stock price and the value/price ratio is greater than 1.0. Which of the following about the stock is true?

    (a) Stock is overvalued

    (b) Stock is undervalued

    (c) Stock is correctly valued

    (d) None of the above

3) The short-term supply and demand analysis of the stock market is the arena for which of the following?

    (a) Fundamental analysis

    (b) Technical analysis

    (c) Both (a) & (b)

    (d) None of the above

4) John bought a stock exactly three years ago for $12. He sold the stock today and had a compounded annual return of 13%. At what price did John sell the stock?

    (a) $17.31

    (b) $15.54

    (c) $20.00

    (d) $14.56

5) Barry Corporation's stock had the following returns over the past seven years: 2%, 8%, -3%, -5%, 20%, 12%, 7%. What is the risk of this stock?

    (a) 9.12%

    (b) 10.01%

(c) 12.12%

(d) 8.71%

6) What is the future value of $1,000 invested for seven years in a money market fund with a constant annual return of 4%?

(a) $1335.92

(b) $1205.90

(c) $1315.93

(d) $1200.95

7) Four years back you invested $10,000 and the value of the investment today is $16,000. What is the return on this investment?

(a) 11.46%

(b) 12.31%

(c) 12.47%

(d) 13.31%

8) Which of the following asset class generally possess high risk compared to others?

(a) Corporate bonds

(b) Small cap

(c) Large value

(d) Large growth

9) If you already own one stock and want to buy another stock, which of the following type of stock should you choose to minimize overall risk?

    (a) Positively correlated

    (b) Negatively correlated

    (c) Uncorrelated

    (d) None of the above

10) If the current risk-free return is 5% and the market return is 12%, what is the beta coefficient of a stock with an expected return of 22%?

    (a) 2.37

    (b) 2.43

    (c) 2.58

    (d) 2.67

Assignment #2-2

1) Stock X has a return of 6% and risk of 5%. Stock Y has a return of 10%. Which of the following might be the risk of stock Y?
(a) 1%
(b) 3%
(c) 5%
(d) 7%

2) If the stock markets are efficient, performing fundamental analysis to identify overvalued and undervalued stocks is useless.
(a) True
(b) False

3) A stock was initially purchased for $20. After five years the stock price is $32. What is the compounded annual return on this stock?
(a) 8.96%
(b) 9.00%
(c) 9.50%
(d) 9.86%

4) David Corporation's stock had the following returns over the past 5 years: 4%, -10 %, 2 %, 30%, and 6%. What is the simple average annual return on this stock?
(a) 8.00%
(b) 5.04%
(c) 6.40%
(d) 9.32%

5) Which of the following bond(s) is exempted from federal income taxes?
(a) Government bonds
(b) Municipal bonds
(c) Corporate bonds
(d) All of the above

6) You will need $10,000 in 5 years to go on a vacation. If you earn a 12% interest on your investments, how much should you invest today in order to reach your savings goal?
(a) $5,674.27
(b) $4,600.38
(c) $5,724.37
(d) $6,220.28

7) If the annual return on your investment is 8%, how long it will take for an investment of $20,000 to become $40,000?
(a) 6 years
(b) 7 years
(c) 8 years
(d) 9 years

8) Which of the following is the standard Wall Street benchmark for asset allocation?
(a) 5% cash, 55% bonds, and 40% common stocks
(b) 10% cash, 10% bonds, and 80% common stocks
(c) 10% cash, 35% bonds, and 55% common stocks
(d) 20% cash, 35% bonds, and 45% common stocks

9) Which of the following type of risk(s) can be avoided by diversification?
(a) Systematic
(b) Unsystematic
(c) Both (a) & (b)
(d) None of the above

10) What is the required return for an asset with beta 1.2, when the risk free and market return are 6% and 12% respectively?
(a) 11.20%
(b) 12.20%
(c) 13.20%
(d) 14.20%

The following provides a brief summary of selected investment personality quizzes. The summaries include the type of quiz (risk, investor personality, etc.), the types of questions asked, and a synopsis of the results.

1. MSN/Money
Style: Risk Tolerance Quiz

      The MSN/ Money quiz is comprised of broad based questions pertaining to financial lifestyle, attitudes toward investments, and current financial position. The quiz looks at two aspects of risk. The first is purely financial and is designed to determine your capacity for risk and your ability to recover from losses. The second focuses on your attitude toward risk and your willingness to face the possibility of losses for the prospect of greater gains. Ideally, your capacity for risk and your attitude toward it should be closely matched. The results then provide advice about portfolio mixes.
http://moneycentral.msn.com/articles/invest/prepare/risktol.asp?special=msnnip

2. American Express Financial Services
Style: Risk Tolerance Quiz

      The American Express quiz asks broad based questions about everyday situations pertaining to money (e.g., questions about saving, income tax returns, and loss aversion). The questionnaire also includes basic investing questions (e.g., portfolio selection, risk versus return, asset allocation). Results of this quiz give the test taker his or her investor type, suggestions about investment strategies, and a graphical representation of ideal portfolios (for a given investor type). The Risk Profile Quiz is intended to provide you with a general indication of your current investment personality. There may be other factors specific to your situation, which are not considered in this quiz. Please keep in mind that your investment personality may change over time. For more information, and an interactive version of this quiz, visit:
http://finance.americanexpress.com/fsc_ss/tools/retirement/riskprofile.asp

3. Banc of America Investment Services Inc.
Style: Investor Personality Quiz

      The Banc of America Services Inc. quiz tests investor's risk levels with investing questions. Questions are about loss aversion, investor time frames, and income levels. There are no general risk questions—all are related to investing. Results provide a specific investor profile and suggest an investing strategy, which is graphically illustrated. For more information and an interactive version of this quiz, visit:
http://www.bankofamerica.com/investments/index.cfm?template=inv_tools_profile.cfm&from=eba

4. Prudential Securities
Style: Investor Personality Quiz

The Prudential Securities quiz is well structured. Question types include attitudes toward money, confidence levels, and investor knowledge. Results place the quiz taker in one of three *personality zones*: cautious, comfort, and action. Advice is provided about investing strategies, including allocation of assets, investor education ideas, and planning ideas. For more information and an interactive version of this quiz, visit: http://www.prufn.com/investments/invest/0,1519,23,00.html

5. Quick and Reilly Investor

Style: Risk Tolerance Quiz

The Quick and Reilly Investor profile is not interactive and is limited in its scope. The questions deal with planning and loss aversion. Results are self-tabulated and provide vague advice about investment strategies. For more information, visit: http://www.quickandreilly.com/out/planning/personality.html

6. Charles Schwab & Co.
Style: Investor Personality Quiz

The Charles Schwab quiz asks questions that deal with attitudes toward risk, investing knowledge, and investor's time frames. The Schwab quiz is simple and short. For more information and an interactive version of this quiz, visit: http://www.schwab.com/SchwabNOW/Exec/plnquiz

7. Sun-Sentinel.com Business

Style: Investor Personality Quiz

The Sun-Sentinel quiz deals with aspects of investor personalities. The questions dealt with attitudes toward risk and investor specific issues like portfolio mixes. Results are fairly narrow with no investing advice. The quiz classifies investors as one of four types:

1. Adventurous (confident/impetuous)
2. Individualist (confident/analytical)
3. Celebrity (impetuous/anxious)
4. Guardians (careful/worried)

For more information and an interactive version of this quiz, visit: http://southflorida.sun-sentinel.com/money/quiz/quiz9.htm

8. iVillage Moneylife

Style: Money Personality

The iVillage Moneylife quiz looks at how people, save, spend, and invest. Questions asked are simple and deal with day-to-day spending activities, investing, financial knowledge, and investors' time frames. Results include a brief summary of the quiz takers specific style of handling money. Web-links are provided to give additional advice about money styles. For more information, and an interactive version of this quiz, visit:

http://quiz.ivillage.com/moneylife/tests/personality.htm

9. Psychonomic Investor Profiler

Style: Investor Personality Quiz

The Psychonomics quiz is by far the most comprehensive quiz on this list. Questions are divided into two sections. The first deals with overall personality questions (e.g., questions about friendliness, commitment, propensity to hoard, etc.). The second section deals with questions about investing, mostly about an investor's attitude toward risk. Psychonomics breaks quiz-takers into six separate categories:

     1. Cautious

     2. Emotional

     3. Technical

     4. Busy

     5. Casual

     6. Informed

The analysis tells the quiz-taker their propensity for risk, and their dominant investment categorization. The results page also provides a link to information based on your specific results. For more information, visit: http://www.psychonomics.com/

To take the interactive version of this quiz, visit:

http://www.psychonomics.com/pages/pp1.html

CHAPTER 3

CORPORATE FINANCE, CREATING SHAREHOLDER VALUE AND CORPORATE GOVERNANCE

This chapter provides an introduction to corporate finance and addresses two basic underlying concepts—creating shareholder value and corporate governance. We begin with a discussion of the position and role of finance in an organization, and cover the responsibilities and duties of the principal finance manager, the Chief Financial Officer (CFO). We then turn to a review of the corporation—the world's predominant business organization. We begin with a discussion of the advantages and disadvantages of the three general forms of business organizations—sole proprietorships, partnerships, and corporations. With respect to the ownership and governance of the corporation, a very important issue is that the creation of shareholder value has become the primary goal of corporate managers. Closely related to this goal are two important issues: the agency problem—the principal/agent conflict, and the stakeholder-stockholder debate.

The learning objectives of the chapter are to:
- Understand the role of finance in business and the economy;
- Appreciate the evolving role of the finance function in business;
- Review the responsibilities of the chief financial officer (CFO) in the new capital markets, and the skill set required of today's CFOs;
- Develop a knowledge of the alternative legal structures for a firm, and their advantages and disadvantages;
- Discuss the principal goal of a publicly-held corporation;
- Define how firms create shareholder value;
- Debate the claims of shareholders versus stakeholders;
- Examine corporate governance and the agency problem;
- Trace the recent changes in corporate governance; and
- Discuss global models of corporate governance.

3.1   Introduction to Corporate Finance

In most firms the individual in charge of the finance function is called the Chief Financial Officer (CFO). Reporting to the CFO (as shown below in Exhibit 3-1) is the Controller, who oversees the organization's accounting function, and the Treasurer, who oversees the investment and management of money functions.

Exhibit 3-1
Corporate Organization Structure
and the Finance Function

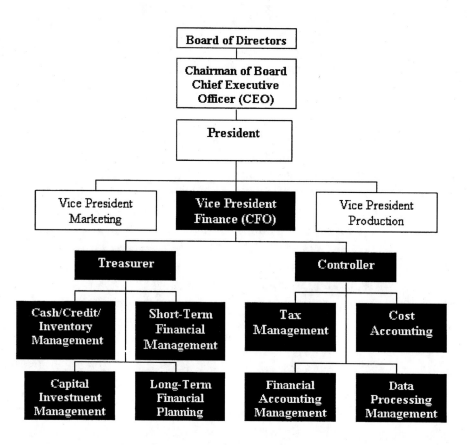

The office of the controller typically is responsible for gathering, auditing, and reporting financial results, managing the financial systems, computing and paying taxes, and producing operating budgets. The primary areas for which the office of the Treasurer is responsible include: long-term investment decisions (*capital budgeting*); capital needs (where and how to raise the funds to finance investments, also known as the *capital structure decision*); and the management of day-to-day financial activities (*working capital management decisions*) including cash and inventory management, credit and collection policy, and paying suppliers.

*The **Controller** is the head accountant of the firm and is responsible for maintaining the company's books and financial statements.*

*The **Treasurer** is in change of managing the company's cash, which includes managing the firm's day-to-day cash inflows and outflows.*

As part of its activities, the finance function also performs the critical role of interacting with the providers of capital for the company. These investors include the providers of debt capital, such as banks and bondholders, as well as the providers of equity capital—the owners and stockholders of the company.

3.2   The Chief Financial Officer as Financial Engineer

The CFO oversees all financing activities of the firm and is the lead financial manager in a company. The traditional role of the CFO included managing the controller and treasury functions. However, with the growing focus of the capital markets over the past two decades on creating shareholder value, the responsibilities and importance of the CFO have expanded greatly.

Additional tasks include playing a key role as a corporate strategist, managing the financing and capitalization of the firm, measuring and managing (through the financial markets) the risk position of the firm, and acting as internal investment banker for growth and acquisition activity. These responsibilities all revolve around the goal of creating shareholder value. The complexity and the importance of performing these tasks relating to value creation have elevated the training and experience requirements as well as the profile of today's CFO.

The CFO deals with the bankers, advisers, and participants in the financial markets to search for strategic opportunities and acquisitions, to fulfill capital needs, and to implement risk management techniques that will increase the value of the firm. In addition, the CFO normally serves as the principal financial spokesperson for the company to the investor community—meeting with Wall Street analysts and making appearances on financial news programs.

SEE BOX ENTITLED CFO'S ON THE HOTSEAT
TO GET AN APPRECIATION FOR THE CRITICAL ROLE PLAYED
BY CFOS TODAY

The role of the finance function has also been evolving over the past two decades. The old and new roles of the finance function are summarized in Exhibit 3-2. Traditionally, the finance department was a stand-alone entity in an organization whose primary purposes were financial planning and control, budgeting and capital allocation, and cash and treasury management. Under this *command and control* environment, the finance function controlled financial information and was not accountable for overall business performance. The finance department was viewed as the *corporate cop* whose primary purpose was overseeing company spending and getting the books closed on a timely basis.

The new model for the finance function is that of a *competitive team*. This new role involves finance personnel acting as business advocates who are assigned to, and very much a part of, individual business units. A major part of this new role is the generating and sharing of key financial information to assist in decision-making. Under this scenario, finance personnel are held accountable for business unit performance. Ford Motor Co. and Merck are among the companies that have led the field in restructuring their finance functions along the competitive team model.

Exhibit 3-2

Evolving Role of the Finance Function

Command and Control	Competitive Team
Corporate Cops	Business Advocates
Financial Planning and Control	Understanding Business Units
Budgeting and Capital Allocation	Achieve Business Unit Targets
Control Financial Information	Share Financial Information
Not Accountable for Performance	Share Accountability for Performance

3.3   The Goal of Financial Management

What is the appropriate goal for the management of a corporation? If you answered profit maximization that would be the most commonly cited answer, but it is not a very precise objective. Do you mean profits for this year? If so, then actions such as deferring maintenance, depleting inventories, and other short-run, cost-cutting measures will increase current profits, but may reduce future profits dramatically.

The goal of maximizing profits may refer to some sort of long run or average profit measure, but the definition of profits is unclear. Do you mean something like accounting net income or earnings per share? As you will see, these numbers may have little to do with what is good or bad for the firm. What do you mean by the long run? As a famous economist once remarked, "In the long run, we're all dead!" More to the point, this goal doesn't tell us the appropriate trade-off between current and future profits.

The financial manager in a corporation should make decisions on behalf of the owners of the firm—its stockholders. Given this priority, we really need to answer a more fundamental question: From the stockholders' point of view, what is the most desirable goal of management? If we assume that stockholders purchase stock in order to receive the greatest financial return, then the answer is obvious: Good decisions increase the value of the stock, and poor decisions decrease it.

Given our observations, it follows that the financial manager acts in the shareholders' best interest by making decisions that increase the value of the company's stock. The appropriate goal for the financial manager in a corporation can thus be stated quite easily: the goal of financial management in a corporation is to maximize the current value per share of the existing stock. This goal avoids the problems that we discussed previously. There is no ambiguity in the criterion, and there are no short-run versus long-run issues. We explicitly mean that our goal is to maximize the current value of the company's stock.

What is the appropriate goal when the firm has no traded stock? Corporations are not the only type of business entity, and the stock in many privately held corporations rarely changes hands, so it's difficult to say what the value per share is at any given time. As long as we are dealing with for-profit businesses, only a slight modification is needed. The total value of the stock in a corporation is simply equal to the value of the owners' equity. Therefore, a more general way of stating our goal is:

Maximize the market value of the existing owners' equity.

With this goal in mind, it doesn't matter whether the business is a proprietorship, a partnership, or a corporation. For each of these entities, good financial decisions increase the market value of the owners' equity and poor financial decisions decrease it. Now, before focusing on creating shareholder value and corporate governance, we review the alterative business organizational forms.

3.4 Strategic Financial Management Decisions

Financial management decisions relate primarily to capital budgeting, capital structure, and working capital management. *Capital budgeting* involves investment in fixed assets, *capital structure* entails choosing to issue either debt or equity instruments to finance investments, and *working capital management* is related to the use and financing of short-term assets and liabilities.

Remember the principle relating to corporate finance and governance that we discussed in Chapter 2—**Corporate Managers Should Make Decisions that Maximize Shareholder Value**. Specifically, we'll look at how those decisions should affect the area of capital budgeting, capital structure and working capital management.

Capital budgeting is the process of planning and managing a firm's long-term investment in projects and ventures. The financial manager tries to identify investment opportunities that are worth more than they cost to acquire or fund, so that the value of the future cash flows generated by an asset exceeds the cost of that asset.

Capital budgeting is the process of planning and managing a firm's long-term investment in projects and ventures

Regardless of the investment, financial managers must be concerned with how much cash (*amount*) they expect to be returned by the investment, when (*timing*) they expect to receive it, and how likely (*risk*) they are to receive it.

Evaluating the amount, timing, and risk of future cash flows is the essence of capital budgeting. In fact, whenever you evaluate a business decision, these factors should be your most important considerations. As we discussed in Chapter 2, the goal of capital budgeting decisions should be to:

Maximize the net present value of the investments that are financed by the firm's capital budget.

Capital structure refers to a firm's specific mixture of long-term debt and equity that it uses to finance its operations and investments. The financial manager has two concerns in this area. First, what is the least expensive source of funds for the firm? Second, how much should the firm borrow?

The capital structure decision involves the mixture of long-term debt and equity to be used to finance the firm's operations and investment

In addition to determining the financing mix, the financial manger has to decide how, when and where to raise the money. The expenses associated with raising long-term capital can be considerable, so the different possibilities must be evaluated carefully. Relating to capital structure, the appropriate goal for the financial manager is to:

Minimize the weighted average cost of capital (WACC) of the company

Working capital management is the third major responsibility of the financial manager. Working capital refers to the firm's short-term assets, such as accounts receivable and inventory, and its short-term liabilities, such as accounts payable that are owed to suppliers and short-term loans.

Working capital management involves the day-to-day managing of the firm's short-term assets and liabilities

Managing the firm's working capital is a day-to-day activity that ensures the firm has sufficient resources to continue its operations and avoids costly financially generated interruptions. Some questions about working capital that must be answered are:

- How much cash and inventory should we keep on hand?
- What credit terms are appropriate for our products and services? And
- How and where will we obtain any needed short-term financing?

A trade-off exists between liquidity and profitability in working capital management. Capital invested in cash on hand, inventories, and accounts receivable do not earn as high a return for the firm as moneys invested in its fixed assets and projects. Because of this trade-off, financial managers try to reduce the costs associated with financing inventories and accounts receivable. Relating to working capital management, the appropriate goal for the financial manager is to:

Minimize the cost of maintaining the net working capital position of the company

3.5   The Legal Forms of Business Entities

The three most common types of companies are: sole proprietorships, partnerships, and corporations. A sole proprietorship is a business owned by an individual, and is the cheapest and most popular business to form and operate. The owner owns 100% of the profits and the losses on this type of company, and has unlimited liability for claims against the business.

*A sole proprietorship **is a business owned by one person***

A *partnership* is a company formed by two or more individuals and can be either a general partnership or a limited partnership. In a general partnership, each partner shares in the profits and losses of the firm. Each partner also has unlimited liability for all of the claims and debts against the partnership. Limited partnerships limit the liability to the amount of cash each partner has contributed to the partnership. However, limited partnerships usually require at least one general partner who manages the business. A partnership usually has a written operating agreement, which specifies the responsibilities of the partners and describes how profits will be shared and losses will be assessed. Most of the major public accounting firms are organized as partnerships.

*A **partnership** is a company formed by two or more individuals.*

A *corporation* is a legal entity that has many of the rights of a person—it can own assets, borrow money, create liabilities, issue stock, and is separate from its owners. Most major firms are corporations, with a corporate charter and operating under a set of bylaws. Bylaws are rules that dictate how the corporation elects directors and operates its business.

*A **corporation** is a distinct legal entity that is owned by one or more entities.*

The owners—the stockholders of the corporation, elect the *directors* of a corporation. The directors represent the stockholders and should run the business with the stockholder's best interests in mind. The directors select the managers of the firm and are responsible for monitoring the activities of management. The stockholders and management are usually separate groups, resulting in a separation of ownership and management.

A corporation has numerous advantages over a partnership and some disadvantages. The main differences between partnerships and corporations are:

- Partnerships are not taxed on their income; the partners pay income tax on their share of the partnership income at the personal level. Corporations are subject to double taxation. First, the corporation pays income taxes on profits. Then, the individuals pay income taxes on dividends received.
- General partners in a partnership are subject to unlimited liability. Corporations have limited liability. The shareholders are not personally liable for the corporation's debts. Shareholders only stand to lose the amount of their investment.
- Transfer of ownership is difficult for a partnership and the partnership's life is usually limited by the life of the partners. Conversely, corporations have an infinite life, and shares of a corporation are very liquid and can be readily exchanged in most cases.

Exhibit 3-3 summarizes the major issues among alternative ownership models.

Exhibit 3-3

Comparison of Major Issues for Alternative Ownership Models

Issues	Sole Proprietorship	Partnership	Corporation
Ease of Formation	Easy	More Difficult	Difficult – Separate Legal Entity
Tax	Profits Taxed as Income	Profits Taxed as Income	Double Taxed – Corp. & Individual
Ease of Transfer	Difficult	More Difficult	Easy
Liability	Liable for Liabilities	Liable for Liabilities	Limited Liability
Ability to Raise Capital	Difficult	Difficult	Relatively Easy

The first corporations in the United States were formed by the railroads in the late 1800s. Building the railroads required a tremendous amount of capital, and the corporation organizational form is well suited for raising capital due to limited liability and the ease of transferring ownership. Since the Federal Constitution did not provide for the chartering of corporations, they are subject to state-by-state chartering. Today over one-half of the corporations that comprise the Standard & Poor's 500 Index are chartered in the state of Delaware. Delaware has tax and organizational laws that are favorable to the chartering of corporations.

3.6 Creating Shareholder Value—The Principal Goal of the Firm

What is the principal goal of a company? This question is the subject of frequent debate between management and stakeholders. Each party argues for the objective that benefits it the most. Should maximizing employees' economic utility and financial wealth be the principal goal of the company? Should it be as profitable as possible? Should the goal be to maximize customer satisfaction? Maximize sales and market share? Make the highest quality products? Have the highest productivity? Maximize the returns to society? Or maximize the salaries of management?

The answers to these questions vary dramatically among the participants in the capital markets. Companies operate under different sets of rules for the various countries and cultures in which they do business. Much of this chapter concentrates on the domestic corporate governance model. In fact, the model of corporate governance in the United States has evolved significantly over the last 25 years. Most companies have adopted this model, and the principal goal of most corporate management teams in the United States is to maximize shareholder value.

Shareholder value is the return that investors receive for their investment in the stock of a company. This return is accomplished through dividend payments, stock buy-backs, and the gains from stock price increases (or losses from stock declines). Creating shareholder value requires management to make business and financial decisions that will lead to a higher share price. In order for companies to create or increase shareholder value, the company must generate free cash flows—excess monies or earnings that are not consumed by the company's normal business operations. Free cash flows are paid to investors in the form of dividends or stock repurchases, or reinvested in additional profitable investments that will maximize the company's return on invested capital.

Shareholder value is the return that investors receive from their Investment in the form of dividends and stock prices increases.

As shown in Exhibit 3-4, creating shareholder value is the principal goal of a firm because it is a single measure that encompasses and reflects all of these other factors—sales, market share, return on equity, profits, growth, and product quality. A firm cannot maximize shareholder value with low quality products, underpaid and demoralized employees, and unhappy customers. If a firm is to maximize shareholder value, the interests of all stakeholders must be satisfied.

Exhibit 3-4

Winning in Business

Creating shareholder value can be viewed from a balance sheet perspective. The asset side of the balance sheet involves management being efficient in allocating capital to investments offering the highest returns while at the same time minimizing the amount of capital needed to meet the company's objective. On the liability side of the balance sheet, management must minimize the cost of capital through the capital structure decision with respect to debt and equity financing, and with the use of financial innovations and strategic risk management. Management should also enhance performance by employing appropriate ownership structures, primarily through acquisitions and divestitures. These approaches are highlighted in Exhibit 3-5.

Exhibit 3-5

Avenues of Shareholder
Value Creation

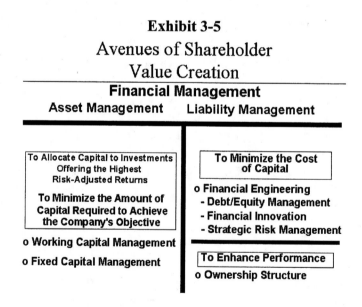

Financial Management

Asset Management	Liability Management
To Allocate Capital to Investments Offering the Highest Risk-Adjusted Returns	To Minimize the Cost of Capital
To Minimize the Amount of Capital Required to Achieve the Company's Objective	o Financial Engineering - Debt/Equity Management - Financial Innovation - Strategic Risk Management
o Working Capital Management	To Enhance Performance
o Fixed Capital Management	o Ownership Structure

Creating shareholder value has become the primary corporate objective in the 2000s. In any recent annual report, it is likely that the mission statement refers to creating value for the company's shareholders. During the 1980s, management attention shifted toward active shareholders who demanded performance for their invested dollars. When companies failed to deliver returns to shareholders, some companies were taken over by corporate raiders; others faced severely depressed stock prices. The financial markets penalized companies that did not focus on creating value and wealth for the owner-shareholders. The focus on creating shareholder value is evident from the mission statements, shown in Exhibit 3-6, from several well-known companies in the world.

The emphasis on creating shareholder value has strengthened over the years as firms that continue to grow stock prices and make dividend payments to shareholders are praised for their stellar management, who are rewarded with healthy bonuses and stock options. Since shareholders possess voting rights within a firm, they have the power to force the resignation of board members and executives that do not act in the best interests of shareholders. Institutional investors like pension and mutual funds have taken the lead in voting for the change of corporate control in numerous corporate governance transactions. Managers of institutional funds are measured based on their investment performance and they hold large positions of companies in their portfolios. Significant ownership means that these institutions control the voting rights which forces management to focus on value creating strategies.

And so who are the best value creators in the U.S.? Each year the *Wall Street Journal* publishes its 'Shareholder Scoreboard' which provides shareholder returns for the largest 1000 companies in the U.S. To determine the best value creator, you must select a time period you want to consider. Exhibit 3-7 provides the best value creators over the ten-year period 1993-2003. In first place is Dell Computer which provided a compounded annual return to stockholders of 57.9%. Many of the other companies in the top-ten list are tech firms who had superior performance during the 1990s but have fallen off since that time.

Also provided in Exhibit 3-7 are the 1-, 3-, 5-, and 10-year returns provide by the 30 companies in the Dow Jones Industrials (DJI). These are among the best-known firms in the U.S., and they are ranked here by their 5-years returns. A review of the results highlights the fact that defining who is best really depends on the time period. Intel, for example, earned a 1-year return of 106.6%, but its 3- and 5- year returns were only 2.5% and 1.8%. And Microsoft earned the highest 10-year return (27.1%) but is performance over the other three time periods was not so good (6.8%, 8.4%, and -4.5%, for 1-, 3-, and 5- years). The most consistent performers were 3M and Caterpillar. They are the only companies in the DJI that earned double-digit returns over the four different time periods.

3.7 Stakeholders vs. Shareholders—Whose Interest Should be Served?

Shareholders are the owners of the common stock of a corporation. The most important control device of shareholders is the right to elect the directors of a corporation, who in turn hire management who carry out the board's directives. Stakeholders are anyone who has a legitimate claim of any nature on a firm and therefore on its economic well-being. Stakeholders include employees, creditors, customers, suppliers, the communities in which the company operates, and stockholders. Since stockholders have invested capital in the firm, they also are stakeholders.

Stakeholders are any entities with legitimate claims on a firm.

Although in some circumstances the interests of the shareholders and stakeholders are aligned, in some situations they are not. This non-alignment leads to a question that has been strongly debated: Whose interest should the corporation serve—shareholders or stakeholders? The traditional view of this topic has corporate directors serving one constituency—shareholders. However, this traditional view has been under attack by many groups. Proponents of the stakeholders' view is that the corporation should be socially responsible and serve the public interest as well as shareholder interests, and that the purpose of a corporation should lie beyond maximizing shareholder value. Some groups even go as far as to say the purpose of a corporation is to create wealth for society.

Exhibit 3-6
Corporate Mission Statements

The Walt Disney Company
Disney's overriding objective is to create shareholder value by continuing to be the world's premier entertainment company from a creative, strategic, and financial standpoint.

The Coca-Cola Company
We exist to create value for our share owners on a long-term basis by building a business that enhances The Coca-Cola Company's trademarks. This also is our ultimate commitment.

As the world's largest beverage company, we refresh that world. We do this by developing superior soft drinks, both carbonated and noncarbonated, and profitable nonalcoholic beverage systems that create value for our Company, our bottling partners, our customers, our share owners and the communities in which we do business.

Amgen
We provide value by focusing on the needs of patients. Amgen creates a work environment that provides opportunities for staff members to reach their full potential. We strive to provide stockholders with superior long-term returns while balancing the needs of patients, staff and stockholders.

Siemens
We generate profitable growth to ensure sustainable success. We leverage our balanced business portfolio, our business excellence and synergies across all segments and regions. This makes us a premium investment for our shareholders.

Our ideas, technologies and activities help create a better world. We are committed to universal values, good corporate citizenship and a healthy environment. Integrity guides our conduct toward our employees, business partners and shareholders.

Papa Johns
Customers
Papa John's will create superior brand loyalty, i.e. "raving fans", through (a) authentic, superior-quality products, (b) legendary customer service and (c) exceptional community service.
Team Members
People are our most important asset. Papa John's will provide clear, consistent, strategic leadership and career opportunities for Team Members who exhibit passion toward their work, (b) uphold our Core Values, (c) take pride of ownership in building the long-term value of the Papa John's brand and (d) have ethical business practices.
Franchisees
We will partner with our franchisees to create continued opportunity for outstanding financial returns to those franchisees who adhere to Papa John's proven Core Values and systems, (b) exhibit passion in running their businesses and (c) take pride of ownership in building the long-term value of the Papa John's brand.
Shareholders
We will produce superior long-term value for our shareholders.

Exhibit 3-7

The Best Value Creators in the U.S.
1993-2003

Source: The Shareholder Scoreboard, Wall Street Journal (March 9, 2004).

Rank	Company	Symbol	10-Year Return
1	Dell	DELL	57.9%
2	Semtech	SMTC	54.7%
3	Veritas Software	VRTS	51.9%
4	W Holding	WHI	50.1%
5	NVR	NVR	47.2%
6	Time Warner	TWX	44.4%
7	Biogen Idec	BIIB	44.0%
8	Emulex	ELX	43.2%
9	Medicis Pharmaceutical	MRX	42.5%
10	Jabil Circuit	JBL	41.1%

Value Creation by the Dow Jones Industrials

Source: The Shareholder Scoreboard, Wall Street Journal (March 9, 2004).

	Company Name	Stock Symbol	1-Year Return	3-Year Return	5-Year Return	10-Year Return
1	3M	MMM	40.6%	14.5%	21.7%	15.4%
2	Citigroup	C	41.6	2.5	17.7	25.0
3	Alcoa	AA	71.0	6.5	17.5	18.1
4	Caterpillar	CAT	86.1	24.1	15.8	16.8
5	United Technologies	UTX	55.4	8.0	13.3	22.0
6	American Express	AXP	37.7	-3.3	8.0	19.9
7	Boeing	BA	30.4	-12.4	6.9	8.6
8	Altria	MO	42.8	13.2	6.3	17.2
9	Wal-Mart Stores	WMT	5.7	0.5	6.0	16.3
10	Johnson & Johnson	JNJ	-2.1	0.9	5.7	18.3
11	Exxon Mobil	XOM	20.6	0.5	4.7	13.3
12	Procter & Gamble	PG	18.5	10.8	3.8	15.5
13	Intel	INTC	106.6	2.5	1.8	23.8
14	General Motors	GM	52.7	6.2	1.8	5.6
15	International Paper	IP	26.6	4.5	1.7	4.9
16	International Business Machines	IBM	20.5	3.6	0.7	21.7
17	DuPont	DD	12.0	1.6	0.1	9.7
18	General Electric	GE	30.7	-11.5	0.0	15.8
19	J.P. Morgan Chase	JPM	60.6	-2.8	-1.6	14.2
20	Home Depot	HD	49.0	-7.5	-2.3	15.5
21	Hewlett-Packard	HPQ	34.5	-8.6	-2.4	12.4
22	Honeywell	HON	43.3	-8.9	-3.6	7.3
23	Coca-Cola	KO	18.1	-4.3	-4.0	10.0
24	Walt Disney	DIS	44.4	-5.9	-4.0	5.9
25	Microsoft	MSFT	6.8	8.4	-4.5	27.1
26	Merck	MRK	-11.2	-17.5	-5.9	13.5
27	McDonald's	MCD	56.8	-8.8	-7.5	6.6
28	SBC Communications	SBC	1.7	-15.1	-10.7	5.6
29	Eastman Kodak	EK	-23.8	-9.3	-15.4	-2.2
30	AT&T	T	-18.8	-3.4	-20.4	-2.6
	DJIA		28.3	1.0	4.5	13.0

The shareholder view of the corporation is that the main goal of management is to increase shareholder value. As noted, the shareholders are the owners of the firm. And one of the primary arguments for increasing shareholder value is that corporate executives should not be allowed to make decisions to use other people's property for their own interest, or even for what they believe to be in the public interest. Furthermore, if managers did serve the stakeholders' interests, accountability would be spread among those many groups.

Although this argument indicates that corporate executives do not have the expertise to decide what is in the best social interest, it is usually in management's best interests to act in a socially responsible manner.[1]

There is one additional argument as to why management must look out for the interests of shareholders over stakeholders. Stakeholders are protected by contracts, whereas stockholders are the recipients of the firm's residual cash flow. Specifically, a firm's suppliers, customers, lenders, employees, and subcontractors all enter into contracts with the corporation in return for their services, products, and/or capital. There is no such contract protection for shareholders. Shareholders get paid after stakeholders, and then only if there is something left over.

Exhibit 3-8 provides an income statement view of the notion that stockholders are the residual claimants of the firm's cash flows. Note that suppliers, employees, lenders, and the government all are taken care of first. Stockholder's receive the 'Profit after Tax,' which is the residual (if any exists) after the other stakeholders have been paid.

Exhibit 3-8
Stockholders as the Residual Claimants:
An Income Statement View

Income Statement		Stakeholder Payments
Revenues	xxxx	
- Cost of Good Sold	xxx	← Suppliers
= Gross Profit	xxx	
-Selling, General & Administrative Expenses	xxx	← Employees
= Operating Profit	xxx	
-Interest Expense	xx	← Lenders
= Profit Before Taxes	xx	
-Taxes	xx	← Government
= Profit After Taxes	xx	

---

[1] For a good discussion regarding why creating shareholder value is the right goal for managers, see Roberto Goizueta's (former CEO of Coca-Cola) letter to shareholders, which is Appendix A of this chapter.

3.8   Corporate Governance

Corporate governance is the interaction between the firm's suppliers of capital and the management of the company. In simple terms, corporate governance is the set of rules and procedures that are employed by investors to insure that managers are acting to increase shareholder value.

> *Corporate governance is the interaction between the firm's suppliers of capital and the management of the company*

Shareholders have a limited say in day-to-day control over the company. But they do have the voting rights designated to owners of a firm to insure that management acts on their behalf. Shareholders can vote for directors who will better represent their interests, vote on initiatives that affect them (stock splits or employee stock option plans), and can accumulate a large amount of the voting rights and threaten a corporate control action if their initiatives are not addressed.

At the heart of corporate governance and the need for interaction between shareholders and management is the fact that shareholders invest capital but do not actively designate the use of the capital for investment. Management does not invest capital (at least not a majority of the capital), but it does use the capital. Management interests and shareholder interests are not always the same. This creates a conflict between management and shareholders. As we discussed in the last chapter, this conflict is known as the agency problem.

3.81   *The Agency Problem*

The principal-agent problem in business refers to the separation of ownership and control of corporate assets that lead to the misalignment of objectives between shareholders and management. Shareholders are the principals (contributors of capital) and management is the agent (authority over the use of capital). If management owns a small percentage of firm equity and makes most of the decisions, it might not be acting in the best interest of shareholders. This leads to *agency costs*.

> The agency problem stems from the Separation
> of the ownership and control of corporate assets.

Agency costs occur when management does not pursue strategies that maximize shareholder value, or shareholders incur costs to monitor and realign management decisions. Agency costs are either opportunity costs of foregone cash flows that could have been paid to shareholders, or are actual expenditures by shareholders to monitor management and make sure it is optimally using contributed capital.

Since most day-to-day decisions occur at the management level without board of director monitoring, management can allocate corporate resources to investments and expenditures that may benefit management more than stockholders. Agency costs are typically considered to be extravagant purchases, such as private jets and ski chalets at Aspen, and other perks that benefit corporate executives but do not provide an adequate return to the owners of the business. The largest agency costs, however, come in the form of large investments, especially in the form of big acquisitions, that do more to serve the interests, status, and power of management than to create shareholder value. Shareholders own the firm and delegate power via the board of directors. The board of directors is supposed to represent shareholder's interests and should constrain management if they waste corporate resources on their own agendas.

Due to the agency problem, the corporate organizational form has control mechanisms. These control features are designed to align the interests of management and shareholders, and are summarized in Exhibit 3-9. These mechanisms are both internal and external to the corporation. The key internal control mechanism is the board of directors. The board, elected by shareholders, has three primary functions:

- Hiring, firing, and rewarding management;
- Reviewing management's performance; and
- Setting overall policy and the strategic direction of the corporation.

Other internal control features are financial statements that are audited by outside public accounting firms, managerial compensation linked to the value of common stock (usually in the form of stock options), and managerial stock ownership interest (managers owning common stock).

External control mechanisms include:
- The managerial labor market—the manager's ability to create shareholder value is reflected in pay for executives;
- The market for corporate control—poorly managed companies are acquired by other companies and existing management is fired; and
- Shareholder activism—large investors become aggressive in corporate governance issues due to poor corporate performance.

Exhibit 3-9

Corporate Control

```
Internal Control Mechanisms
    – Board of Directors
    – Audited Financial Statements
    – Stock Value–Based Compensation
    – Stock Ownership Interest

External Control Mechanisms
    – Managerial Labor Market
    – Market for Corporate Control
    – Shareholder Activism
```

3.82   Corporate Governance in the 1980s: Hostile Takeovers & LBOs

During the 1980s, the solution to the agency problem was the market for corporate control in the form of hostile takeovers. Hostile takeovers occur when one company acquires another company against the wishes and efforts of the management and board of the target company. A company that wants to make a hostile takeover attempt on another company usually uses one of two strategies— a tender offer or a proxy battle.

Hostile takeovers have been around for many decades. But it was not until the 1980s that the multibillion-dollar hostile takeover of high profile public companies came to the markets. Hostile takeovers are usually pursued through a tender offer. When one company (the 'bidder' company) wants to acquire another company (the 'target' company), it usually contacts the management and board of the target to ascertain their interest in being acquired. In a hostile situation, the target company's management will usually reject the proposal. Then the bidder will pursue the transaction through a tender offer. A *tender offer* is when a *bidder company* makes an offer directly to the shareholders of a target company to purchase shares for the purpose of gaining control. The tender offer is made at a price above the current market price. The typical price premium is 20 to 50 percent. The acquiring company will usually stipulate some conditions to the tender offer, such as a minimum and maximum number of shares to be purchased. Individual shareholders can accept the offer by tendering their shares for purchase by the acquiring company, or reject the offer by not tendering. In a typical situation, the management of the target company will then advise their shareholders not to tender, and then lays out a plan of its own to get the stock price up. At this point, the battle for the target company is on.

A tender offer is when an acquiring company makes an offer to purchase shares in a target company for the purpose of gaining control

An LBO is a going-private transaction involving a tender offer for all of a firm's common stock, financed mostly by debt, made by an investment group that usually includes members of the management of the target company. LBOs involving large public companies became quite common in the 1980s as a reaction to the hostile takeover activity. A LBO provided a way for the management of a potential target company to beat a hostile bidder to the punch, allowing management to buy out public shareholders at a stock price premium and continue to run the company.

A leverage but-out (LBO) is a going-private transaction in which a tender offer for all of a firm's common stock, financed mostly by debt, is made by an investment group that usually includes members of the management of the target company

Exhibit 3-10 provides a list of the largest LBOs of the 1980s. The largest acquisition of any kind in the 1980s was the $29 billion LBO of RJR Nabisco by Kolberg Kravis and Roberts. Kolberg Kravis and Roberts, an investment firm that specializes in LBOs, was involved in four of the ten largest LBOs in the 1980s. The targets in the LBO transactions were generally in business that tended to generate a lot of cash (i.e., in businesses that produced cash flow from operations and did not require lots of cash for capital expenditures). This excess cash flow is used in an LBO to repay the large amount of debt that is taken on to make the acquisition.

SEE BOX ENTITLED 'THE INFAMOUS BUYOUT OF RJR NABISCO' FOR A SUMMARY OF ONE OF THE MOST NOTABLE FINANCIAL DEALS

Another method to gain control of a company is a proxy contest. A *proxy contest* occurs when the prospective acquirer solicits voting proxy statements from current shareholders in an attempt to elect its own board of directors. The prospective acquirer will then cast the votes of all proxies solicited for a slate of directors that the acquirer supports. The purpose of a proxy contest is to gain control of the board of directors of the target company. Once control is taken, the new board of directors will replace current management with management that is supported by the acquiring company. The advantage of a proxy fight over a tender offer is that it is a less expensive means of gaining control of a target company since the acquirer does not need to purchase additional shares in order to wage a proxy fight.

A *proxy contest* occurs when the prospective acquirer solicits voting proxy statements from current shareholders in an attempt to gain control of the board of directors.

Exhibit 3-10

Largest LBOs in the 1980's

Rank	Acquirer	Target	Industry	Year	Price ($MM)
1)	Kohlberg Kravis Roberts & Co.	RJR Nabisco Inc.	Food, Tobacco	1989	$29.8
2)	Kohlberg Kravis Roberts & Co.	Beatrice Cos., Inc.	Food, Tobacco	1986	$6.3
3)	Kohlberg Kravis Roberts & Co.	Safeway Stores, Inc.	Supermarkets	1986	$5.3
4)	TF Investments, Inc.	Hospital Corp. of America	Hospitals	1989	$5.0
5)	Thompson, Co.	Southland Corp.	Convenience stores	1987	$4.0
6)	AV Holdings Corp	Borg Warner Corp.	Automotive, chemicals	1987	$4.4
7)	Wings Holdings, Inc.	NWA, Inc.	Airline	1989	$3.8
8)	Kohlberg Kravis Roberts & Co.	Owens-Illinois, Inc.	Glass	1987	$3.7
9)	FH Acquisition Corp.	Fort Howard Corp.	Paper	1988	$3.6
10)	Macy Acquiring Corp.	R.H. Macy & Co., Inc.	Department Stores	1986	$3.6

SOURCE: Mergers & Acquisitions, November/December 1995.

SOURCE: Kaiser, Kevin. Corporate Restructuring: LBOs, MBOs, and Going Private. March 8, 1996, pg. 97.

Both economic and regulatory factors spurred the growth in large takeovers and LBOs in the 1980s. The primary regulatory factors were (1) the Reagan administration's relatively laissez-faire policies on antitrust and securities laws (which allowed mergers that would have challenged in earlier years); (2) the 1982 Supreme Court decision striking down state anti-takeover laws; and (3) the deregulation of many industries, which prompted restructurings and mergers. The primary economic factor was the development of the original-issue high-yield debt instrument. These so-called "junk bonds," pioneered by Michael Milken of the investment firm Drexel Burnham Lambert, provided many hostile bidders and LBO firms with the capital needed to finance multi-billion-dollar deals. Junk bonds are bonds with a high degree of risk (a higher probability of default) that were used by many so-called corporate raiders to finance hostile takeovers.

Many of the hostile takeovers of the 1980s were engineered by individuals who were given the name *corporate raiders*. These raiders included Saul Steinberg, Carl Icahn, Ivan Boesky, T. Boone Pickens, Ronald Perlman, and Sir James Goldsmith. They launched many hostile takeover attempts of poorly performing companies in the 1980s.[2] When they were successful in gaining control of a company, they fired management and hired new managers who focused on maximizing shareholder value. All companies became potential takeover targets. This forced management to cut cost, maximize cash flows, and act in the best interest of shareholders. If they didn't perform for the benefit of stockholders, their companies would be acquired and they would be out of their jobs.

---

[2] Appendix 3-B provides a summary of some of the notable corporate raiders and their most important deals.

In response to the growth of hostile takeovers, companies (along with their attorneys and investment bankers) developed defense mechanisms to protect against unwanted takeovers. These defensive measures have always been controversial because they pose a conflict of interest for management. A top manager's main interest is usually to keep his job, which he often loses after a takeover. But his legal obligation is to get a good price for shareholders, which often means allowing the takeover. Not surprisingly, many managers prefer to try to keep their jobs. Most defense mechanisms involve amending the company's certificate of incorporation to make it more difficult for a raider to gain control of the company. A number of these defensive techniques, which have collectively been termed *shark repellents,* were created in the 1980s and many were given colorful names. Some of these include:[3]

- *Staggered Board.* This involves staggering the election of the board of directors so that one-fourth of the board members are elected each year and serve a four-year term. Hence, no one can get control of the board in one year.
- *The White Knight.* This occurs when the target company finds a friendly merger candidate. This strategy allows a merger to occur in a friendly manner and the current shareholders may also receive greater after-tax market value of securities if the deal is a *tax-free* exchange of stock.
- *The Pac-Man Defense.* Using this strategy, the target company employs a counter-takeover bid for the aggressor. The target company will announce that they are acquiring the aggressor and make the necessary advances to do so.
- *Greenmail.* This occurs when the target company purchases the acquirer's shares at a premium over the market price.
- *Golden Parachutes.* Golden parachutes provide compensation to top-level executives in the event of a change of corporate control.
- *Self-Tender Offer.* The target company agrees to purchase some of the current outstanding shares from its shareholders, usually at a price above what the acquiring company is offering.
- *Poison Pills.* Poison pills are used to make a stock unappealing to others by making a takeover extremely expensive. Poison pills are triggered by an event such as a hostile tender offer or the accumulation of voting stock above a designated threshold (e.g., 10% of outstanding stock) by an unfriendly buyer. When triggered, poison pills provide target shareholders (other than the hostile bidder) with rights to purchase additional shares or to sell shares to the target on very attractive terms. These rights impose severe economic penalties on the hostile acquirer and usually also dilute the voting power of the acquirer's existing stake in the firm.
- *Crown Jewels.* When threatened with a takeover attempt, the target company may sell off some of its most desirable assets, or crown jewels.

---

[3] For a more extensive list and discussion of corporate governance provisions, see Appendix 3-C.

The wave of hostile takeovers in the 1980s resulted not only from the regulatory and economic factors discussed above, but also from the failure of corporate control mechanisms. As noted above, the keystone of control in the corporate organizational form is the board of directors. However, during the 1980s, too many corporate boards were not serving the interests of stockholders, and aligned with management. This misalignment occurred for three reasons:

1. Stock ownership in the United States had become diffused, consisting of many shareholders with small ownership interests. When this occurs, it is too costly for individual shareholders, relative to the value of their holdings, to monitor management and corporate governance issues. It is easier and cheaper to just sell their shares.

2. During the early 1980s, the process for voting for board members was unfair. Management had the advantage of using corporate resources to solicit the proxies of the vast majority of stockholders who voted their share by proxy as opposed to voting at the annual stockholders meeting As a result, managers could nominate and have elected their own chosen board members who were then beholden to management and not stockholders.

3. The ownership of stock by management was at historically low levels, so its interests were not closely aligned with stockholders.

3.83   Corporate Governance in the 1990s

The takeover market in the 1980's centered managerial attention on meeting the requirements of stockholders. As discussed throughout the previous sections, the conflict of interest between management and shareholders had been an ongoing issue in corporate America for many years. However, dramatic restructuring and consolidation in the 1980s forced management to be held accountable for actions, or shareholders would carry out the necessary steps to force accountability.

Corporate governance in the United States changed significantly during the decade of the 1990's. These changes are highlighted in Exhibit 3-9. First, the shareholdings of institutional investors increased. This means that a larger percentage of a company's shares were owned by financial institutions such as commercial and investment banks, pension and mutual funds, and insurance companies. These institutions are sophisticated shareholders who, in pursuit good stock returns, used their large blocks of stock to influence management. This activism by institutional investors rekindled the internal monitoring process by getting the attention of the board of directors. Corporations began to be more closely monitored not only by these institutional investors (and their industry interest group the Council of Institutional Investors), but also by financial news services such as CNBC and Wall Street analysts. The higher institutional stock ownership forced management to place shareholder returns at the top of the corporate agenda.

SEE BOX ENTITLED 'THE ROLE OF INSTITUTIONAL INVESTORS' TO LEARN ABOUT THE ROLE OF INSTITUTIONAL INVESTORS IN CORPORATE GOVERNANCE

A second related factor significantly influencing corporate governance in the 1990s was a change in shareholder communications rules by the Securities and Exchange Commission (SEC). This change, enacted in 1992, relaxed the proxy solicitation rules regarding shareholder communications, which substantially reduced the costs to institutional shareholders of coordinating challenges against underperforming management teams. This effectively gave institutional investors more power and say in corporate governance issues.

The third reason for the corporate governance changes in the 1990s was a change in reporting requirements as mandated by the SEC. This requirement, also imposed in 1992, forced public companies to provide more detailed disclosure of top executive compensation and its relation to firm performance, particularly stock performance.

Exhibit 3-9
Corporate Governance in the 1990s
More Active Governance

The Board Became More Proactive
- CEOs Fired for Poor Performance

Debate over Executive Compensation
- Management Pay Versus Performance
- Issue of Management Stock Ownership

Institutional Investors Became More
  Involved in Corporate Governance Issues
- Proxy Rules are Being Changed (Voting)
- Shareholders Communications Permitted
- The Demise of Managerial Defense
  Mechanisms (e.g., Poison Pills)
- The Move to Shared Governance

The 1990s also saw a noticeable rise in shareholder activism in the United States. This phenomenon led to the startup of various special interest groups that concentrate on investor activism and encourage shareholders to speak out regarding the management of invested capital. The Lens Fund, led by Robert Monks, is a strong advocate of active investing. The Lens Fund searches to purchase stocks in mismanaged firms and then attempts to maximize returns by actively voicing shareholder concern to management and the board. Lens hopes that management will take the necessary steps to increase shareholder value over time and increase its portfolio's investment returns.

In addition to specialty investment funds and other institutions focusing on shareholder activism, there are also special interest groups that encourage individual investor activism. Investors Rights Association of America encourages small investors to voice an opinion in corporate governance issues similar to the large institutions.

Although the monitoring bodies of the 1990s looked very different from the corporate raiders in the 1980s, they served the same purpose. Management was no longer able to waste resources without being severely penalized or fired. As a result, corporations were required to focus on shareholder wealth maximization.

Is good governance good for shareholders? A study by the management consulting firm McKinsey Associates reported that *good governance at the board level adds, on average, 11%* to the value of a firm. This finding indicates that corporate governance, when effectively implemented, creates value for shareholders. This supports the case for actively monitoring investments and in some circumstances seeking out firms in which the stock value can be increased with external monitoring and shareholder activism.

SEE BOX ENTITLED 'HIGHER PRICES FOR GOOD GOVERNANCE' TO FIND OUT IF GOOD GOVERNANCE PAYS OFF FOR STOCKHOLDERS

3.84   Corporate Governance (or the lack thereof) in the Early 2000s

On Wall Street and in corporate America, sometimes the pendulum swings too far. In an effort to create shareholder value, management of some very large firms and their accountants turned to creative accounting and fraud to pump up the stock prices of their companies. As of early 2005, managers for a number of large companies have been indicted for fraudulent activities and a dark cloud has hung over the stock market, which suffered through a three-year bear market.

In the early years of the 21st Century, business news was been bleak. The terrorist attacks of September 11, 2001 crushed the general level of stock prices. Accounting scams at Enron and WorldCom prompted legislative hearings with circus-like atmospheres in Washington. Former CEOs and CFOs, such as 78-year old John Rigas of Adelphia, Enron's CEO Jeff Skilling and CFO Andrew Fastow, Tyco's CEO Dennis Kozlowski and CFO Mark Schwartz, CEO Richard Scrushy of HealthSouth and WorldCom's CEO Bernie Ebbers and CFO Scott Sullivan, were handcuffed and carted off to jail for corporate fraud and mismanagement. In addition, there are insider trading scandals, such as the sale of shares of Imclone by CEO Sam Waskal and superstar stylist Martha Stewart. Taken together, these corporate charades have created drama more compelling than the afternoon soaps.

These individuals and companies were involved in a number of shenanigans with some of the executives headed to the big house. A few examples of the companies and their purported actions include:

- Adelphia is under civil and criminal investigations for hiding more than $3 billion in loans to the Rigas family and for inflating its actual number of customers.
- Enron has admitted to hiding losses and debts in off balance sheet partnerships that were supposedly independent, but actually were not.
- Former CEO Dennis Kozlowski and CFO Marc Swartz of Tyco were found guilty of stealing more than $600 million from Tyco and running a criminal enterprise aimed at defrauding investors.
- In an effort to achieve operating earnings estimates, WorldCom finance personnel regularly categorized short-term operating expenses as long-term capital expenditures. WorldCom transferred more than $9 billion in operating expenses to capital expenditures, resulting in false accounting statements that supported a stock price that defied gravity. Former CEO Bernie Ebbers was implicated and found guilty of corporate fraud.
- Global Crossing and Qwest inflated revenues and profits by entering into sham transactions with other telecom companies in which they swapped fiber optic cable capacity and booked the swaps as revenue.
- Xerox paid a $10 million fine to the SEC and has restated downward more than $6.4 billion in revenue over a five-year period. Many others companies have taken accounting practices beyond the pale.

Many companies have successfully aligned the incentives of management and stockholders. Unfortunately, some companies have corporate performance programs that are poorly designed and may unwittingly encourage corporate management to play loose with the rules. One such company was Computer Associates. In an incredibly stupid and bizarre compensation scheme, CA's three top executives—Charles B. Wang, Sanjay Kumar, and Russell Artzt—were granted 20.25 million shares of Computer Associates to divide among themselves if shares of the stock closed above $53.33 for any 60 trading days during a 13-month period. In May of 1998, the goal was achieved and the shares, which were worth over $1.1 billion at the time, were granted.

Just two months after the grant, CA announced that its profits and sales would fall short of expectations resulting in its shares being pummeled. Pretty good timing by Wang, Kumar, and Artz! The SEC is currently investigating CA to see whether top executives artificially inflated the company's sales and earnings for the sole purpose of receiving the $1.1 billion grant. If ever there were a compensation scheme that encouraged some innovative accounting by top executives, this was it.

The common elements of the current "Crisis in Corporate Governance" include the following:

- *Executive compensation*—with compensation packages dominated by stock options, there is an incentive for short-term price manipulation by management;

- *Board of directors*—the boards have not been independent of the management in many cases, and therefore have not provided effective managerial oversight;

- *Accounting and auditing*—the public accounting firms that audit the books of companies have gotten too close to their clients. Specifically, accounting firms have been negligent in certain instances in providing prudent audit services, especially when they also had lucrative consulting contracts with their clients;

- *Wall Street analysts*—Wall Street firms are paying the price for their biased research. In particular, analysts have been pressured to give positive outlooks for the stocks of companies that employ (or may employ) the analysts' firm for capital raising or merger and acquisition advising services;

- *The Justice Department and the SEC*—Government agencies have to be more proactive in policing corporate financial activities and in punishing those who have broken the law; and

- *Corporate leadership*—Clearly, the ethical behavior of management is in the spotlight in the wake of the many investigations involving fraudulent activities.

The bursting of the technology, telecom, and Internet stock bubble in 2000, the revelations of corporate corruption and misappropriation, and the concern of potential investor outrage at the voting booths spurred Washington to quickly and almost unanimously pass bipartisan legislation. On July 30, 2002, President George W. Bush signed into law the Sarbanes-Oxley Act of 2002. The act strengthens securities and accounting laws and attacks corporate fraud. It creates a board with the responsibility of oversight of the accounting industry and the power to punish accountants for mistakes or wrongdoing. Under the act the company's CEO and CFO are required to certify the contents of the company's quarterly and annual reports. A CEO or CFO who violates the act faces a prison term.

SEE BOX ENTITLED 'SARBANES-OXLEY ACT' TO SEE THE MEASURES PUT IN PLACE BY CONGRESS TO ADDRESS THE CORPORATE GOVERNANCE ISSUES OF THE 2000S

3.85   *Global Models of Corporate Governance*

The discussion in this chapter focuses on corporate governance in the United States. This model of corporate governance involves primarily minority shareholders who elect board members to represent their interests. However this is only one form of corporate capitalism. As highlighted in Exhibit 3-11, there are three general global corporate ownership and governance models. The U.S. model, which is labeled the "Anglo-American" model in Exhibit 3-10, is also predominant in the United Kingdom and Australia. In a relatively few cases, this model also is found in parts of Western Europe and Asia.

This model is known as a "fluid capital" model since it is relatively free of institutional constraints and therefore capital easily flows from individual and institutional investors to those entities that offer the best investment opportunities. But, some argue that in this system investors place too much emphasis on short-term results in valuing shares.

The Japanese and German models are known as "dedicated capital" models. The capital in both cases is called dedicated because the common shares are owned by investors who will not trade or sell the shares. As a result, it is viewed as long-term capital.

In Japan, the predominant business model since World War II has been the *Keiretsu*. A Keiretsu is group of companies, usually formed around a large financial institution, which operates under a common institutional name and shares operational and managerial expertise. They also own each other shares, known as cross-holdings of common stock, and never sell these shares. Since these shares are not sold, the capital is viewed as being dedicated or long-term. These organizations also embrace traditional Japanese business traditions, such as lifetime employment. Mitsibushi and Mitsui are two of the larger Keiretsu in Japan. While the Keiretsu have lost some of their influence in recent years, they are still dominant in Japan.

In Germany, large banks (such as Deutsche Bank) and insurance companies (such as Allianz) have always had a strong influence in corporation finance. A company's *Hausbank* is a financial institution that is the primary supplier of debt and equity capital and that has a large influence on management through the board. The capital is dedicated or long-term since the shares owned by the financial institution are not traded or sold.

The "Rest of the World" model is prevalent in Eastern Europe, Africa, South America, and much of Asia. In this model, a large investor, which could be the government, a family, a financial institution, or some other entity, owns a majority of the outstanding common stock and therefore effectively controls corporate resources, sets corporate goals and objectives, policy, and strategy, and oversees management. Therefore, minority shareholders should be wary since the majority owner may have social, political, and/or economic goals and objectives that do not create shareholder value. For example, in most surveys of global airlines by business travelers, Singapore Airlines is rated as the best airline in the world. However, the company's stock price is the same today as it was ten years ago. The reason is that despite its success in customer satisfaction surveys, the company has made excessive expenditures on new aircraft to keep its fleet age below five years. The company is also the largest employer in Singapore. In short, the problem is that 53% of the company's shares are owned by the Singapore government. And the government is more interested in having an airline that flies a modern fleet and employs lots of its citizens than in the creation of shareholder value.

Exhibit 3-11
Global Corporate Governance Models

Anglo-American Model
- Minority Shareholders with Board
- Governance Issues Led to 1980s Takeovers
- Crisis in 2000s Associated with Conflicts involving Executive
  Compensation, Accounting Firms, Wall Street Analysts, and
  the Board of Directors

Japan-Germany Dedicated Capital Model
- Japan – the *Kierstu* System and Stock Cross Holdings
- Germany – the *Hausbank* System
- Large Equity Owners Provide Oversight
- Equity Owners do not Sell - Hence Very Few Takeovers

Rest of World Majority Owner Model
- Majority Equity Owner (Government, Family, etc.)
  Oversees Management

3.9   Summary

This chapter provides an introduction to corporate finance and covers the principle relating to corporate finance and governance—Corporate Managers Should Make Decisions that Maximize Shareholder Value. Initially we discuss the three alternative business entities—sole proprietorship, partnership, and corporation, including the advantages and disadvantages of each. The main focus of the chapter is on the predominant type of business organization, the corporation. Elements of the corporate organization form are detailed, and the key issue in the corporate organizational form, the agency problem, is discussed. The primary goal of corporate managers—the creation of shareholder value—is presented. At the heart of the agency problem and the goal of the creation of shareholder value is the issue of corporate governance.

The evolution of corporate governance from the hostile takeovers of the 1980s to the shared governance and the role of institutional investors in the 1990s, and the problems associated with corporate fraud and mismanagement in the early 2000s are outlined. Finally, the elements of three alternative global models of corporate governance are detailed and discussed.

List of Terms

1. CFO
2. Controller
3. Treasurer
4. Capital budgeting
5. Capital structure
6. Working capital
7. Shareholder value
8. Corporate governance
9. Sole proprietorship
10. Partnership
11. Corporation
12. Limited/liability
13. Dividends
14. Stock buy-backs
15. Capital gains
16. Free cash flows flow
17. Return on equity
18. Stock options
19. Acquisition
20. Divestiture
21. Agency problem
22. Stock split
23. Corporate raider
24. Hostile takeover
25. Junk bond
26. Voting rights
27. Shark repellant
28. White Knight
29. Pac-man defense
30. Greenmail
31. Golden parachute
32. Self-tender offer
33. Poison pill
34. Crown jewels
35. Proxy solicitation
36. Mutual fund
37. Insider trading
38. Institutional investor
39. Shareholder activism

Questions

1. What are the alternative roles of the CFO?
2. What are the primary activities of a controller versus a treasurer?
3. Discuss the differences between 'Corporate Cops' and 'Business Advocates'?
4. What are the three primary areas of strategic corporate finace?
5. What are the advantages and disadvantages of the alternative legal forms of business?
6. What are the main differences between partnerships and corporations?
7. Why is meant by creating shareholder value and why is it the appropriate business goal?
8. What are the avenues for shareholder value creation?
9. Why may the interests of shareholders and other stakeholders differ? Give some examples.
10. What three reasons does Roberto Goizueta of Coca-Cola give to support the goal of maximizing shareholder value?
11. What does corporate governance mean? Is good corporate governance related to value creation? Why?
12. What role does the board of directors serve?
13. What is the agency problem?
14. What control mechanisms are built into the corporate organization form to protect shareholders?
15. What is different between corporate governance in the 1980s and the 1990s?
16. Who were the corporate raiders and what did they do?
17. How did hostile takeovers in the 1980s work to better align the interests of shareholders and corporate managers?
18. Since the hostile takeovers of the 1980s, what has been the main mechanism of improved corporate governance?
19. Why did dividends decline in popularity in the 1990s? What did corporations do with the retained earnings?
20. How does the United States corporate governance system differ from those around the world (from class)?
21. Who are the institutional investors and what roles do they play in corporate governance?
22. What were the main causes of the corporate malfeasance in the late 1990s and early 2000s?
23. Who is the CIC and what recommendations has it made to insure effective corporate governance?
24. How do companies perform after being placed on CIC's focus list?

Assignment # 3-1

1.   Go to the Harvard Business School's "Corporate Governance, Leadership & Values" under the heading "Board of Directors (Direct link: http://www.corpgov.hbs.edu/directors.html)." Search through the list of articles until you find an article that references a corporate scandal or poor corporate governance. According to the article, what did the board do wrong? What should they have done differently?

2.   Go to the council of institutional investors' website (http://www.cii.org/focuslist.asp) and click on the CII focus list for the most recent year. Which companies are on the S&P 500 list? Click on one of the companies and explain the corrective actions that are being taken by the company.

3.   *Yahoo! Finance* (http://finance.yahoo.com/) provides extensive financial coverage of most publicly traded companies in the United States. Enter the symbol of your focus list company and find the company's chart in *Yahoo!* Compare your company versus the S&P 500. Has the focus list company been underperforming the S&P 500 index? If yes, for how long? Is the company's position improving relative to the S&P 500?

4.   Go to www.hoovers.com and enter the name of a large publicly traded company. Go to that company's "Company Capsule" and scroll through the wealth of information on the right column of the screen. Has this company shown growth in its revenue as well as it net income? How much? Now, click on "Other Key People" in the right column and comment on the pay packages that the company's executives are receiving. If you were a shareholder in this company, would you be satisfied with the pay packages that executives are receiving?

Appendix 3-A
Letter to Shareholders from Roberto Goizueta
The Coca-Cola Company

To Our Shareholders:

At The Coca-Cola Company, our publicly stated mission is to create value over time for the owners of our business. In fact, in our society, that is the mission of any business: to create value for its owners.

Why? The answer can be summed up in three reasons. First, increasing shareowner value over time is the job our economic system demands of us. We live in a democratic capitalist society, and here, people create specific institutions to help meet specific needs. Governments are created to help meet civic needs. Philanthropies are created to help meet social needs. And companies are created to help meet economic needs. Business distributes the lifeblood that flows through our economic system, not only in the form of goods and services, but also in the form of taxes, salaries and philanthropy.

Creating value is a core principle on which our economic system is based; it is the job we owe to those who have entrusted us with their assets. We work for our shareowners. That is—literally—what they have put us in business to do.

Saying that we work for our shareowners may sound simplistic—but we frequently see companies that have forgotten the reason they exist. They may even try in vain to be all things to all people and serve many masters in many different ways. In any event, they miss their primary calling, which is to stick to the business of creating value for their owners.

Furthermore, we must always be mindful of the fact that while a healthy company can have a positive and seemingly infinite impact on others, a sick company is a drag on the social order of things. It cannot sustain jobs, much less widen the opportunities available to its employees. It cannot serve customers. It cannot give to philanthropic causes.

And it cannot contribute anything to society, which is the second reason we work to create value for our shareowners: If we do our jobs, we can contribute to society in very meaningful ways. Our Company has invested millions of dollars in Eastern Europe since the fall of the Berlin Wall, and people there will not soon forget that we came early to meet their desires and needs for jobs and management skills. In the process, they are becoming loyal consumers of our products, while we are building value for our shareowners—which was our job all along.

Certainly, we—as a Company—take it upon ourselves to do good deeds that directly raise the quality of life in the communities in which we do business. But the real and lasting benefits we create don't come because we do good deeds, but because we do good work—work focused on our mission of creating value over time for the people who own the Company. Among those owners, for example, are university endowments, philanthropic foundations and other similar nonprofit organizations. If The Coca-Cola Company is worth more, those foundations have more to give, and so on. There is a beneficial ripple effect throughout society.

Please note that I said creating value "over time," not overnight. Those two words are at the heart of the third reason behind our mission: Focusing on creating value over the long term keeps us from acting shortsighted.

I believe shareowners want to put their money in companies they can count on, day in and day out. If our mission were merely to create value overnight, we could suddenly make hundreds of decisions that would deliver a staggering short-term windfall. But that type of behavior has nothing to do with sustaining value creation over time. To be of unique value to our owners over the long haul, we must also be of unique value to our consumers, our customers, our bottling partners, our fellow employees and all other stakeholders—over the long haul.

Accordingly, that is how the long-term interests of the stakeholders are served—as the long-term interests of the share owners are served. Likewise, unless the long-term interests of the share owners are served, the long-term interests of the stakeholders will not be served. The real possibility for conflict, then, is not between share owners and stakeholders, but between the long-term and the short-term interests of both. Ultimately, everyone benefits when a company takes a long-term view. Ultimately, no one benefits when a company takes a short-term view.

The creation of unique value for all stakeholders, including share owners, over the long haul, presupposes a stable, healthy society. Only in such an environment can a company's profitable growth be sustained. Thus, the exercise of what is commonly referred to as "corporate responsibility" is a supremely rational, logical corollary of a company's essential responsibility to the long-term interests of its share owners. A company will only exercise this essential responsibility effectively if it promotes that social well-being necessary for a healthy business environment. It is as irrational to suppose that a company is primarily a welfare agency as it is to suppose that a company should not be concerned at all about the social welfare. Both views sacrifice the long-term common good to short-term benefits—whether share-owner benefits or stakeholder benefits.

Certainly, harsh competitive situations can sometimes call for harsh medicine. But in the main, our share owners look to us to deliver sustained, long-term value. We do that by building our businesses and growing them profitably.

At The Coca-Cola Company, we have built our business and grown it profitably for more than 110 years, because we have remained disciplined to our mission. Not long ago, we came up with an interesting set of facts: A billion hours ago, human life appeared on Earth. A billion minutes ago, Christianity emerged. A billion seconds ago, the Beatles changed music forever.

A billion Coca-Colas ago was yesterday morning.

The question we ask ourselves now is: What must we do to make a billion Coca-Colas ago be this morning? By asking that question, we discipline ourselves to the long-term view.

Ultimately, the mission of this Atlanta soft-drink salesman—and my 26,000 associates— is not simply to sell an extra case of Coca-Cola. Our mission is to create value over the long haul for the owners of our Company.

That's what our economic system demands of us. That's what allows us to contribute meaningfully to society. That's what keeps us from acting shortsighted. As businessmen and businesswomen, we should never forget that the best way for us to serve all our stakeholders—not just our share owners, but our fellow employees, our business partners and our communities—is by creating value over time for those who have hired us.

That, ultimately, is our job.

Roberto C. Goizueta

Appendix 3-B
Corporate Raiders and Their Deals

Ronald Perelman

Ronald Perelman was also a member of the corporate raider elites of the 1980s. He is most famous for his successful hostile takeover of Revlon Cosmetics in 1985. He ran the company for a few years and was able to turn the company around and make a lot of money for himself and his investors. In addition to Revlon, Perelman made unsuccessful attempts at taking over Gillette and Salomon Brothers investment bank.

Ivan Boesky

Ivan Boesky is the infamous Wall Street arbitrageur of the early 1980s who was near the top of the Michael Milken's insider trading scheme. He is a Russian immigrant, earned a law degree from the Detroit College of Law, and began his Wall Street ventures as an analyst shortly after college. He found this unappealing and moved to the trading side of Wall Street where he quickly made a name for himself. He used to be a <u>notorious risk arbitrageur</u> who placed huge bets (accumulated large positions) in the merger market hoping rumors turned into announced deals or deals turned into hostile bidding wars where stockholders profit tremendously. Over the years, he assembled information contacts at major investment banking firms (including Milken) who would feed him information in exchange for trading profits and other favors. Eventually the ring was dismantled and Boesky spent several years in prison. The insider trading scandal in the mid-1980s is well documented in the book *Den of Thieves* by James Stewart. This book as well as *The Predator's Ball*, which analyzed Drexel and Milken in detail, contributed tremendously to the greedy and dubious image of the late 1980s on Wall Street.

Kohlberg Kravis Roberts

Kohlberg Kravis Roberts (KKR) is the largest leveraged buyout specialty firm on Wall Street. The three partners united back in 1976 right around the beginning of the LBO craze on Wall Street.[4] The firm participated in some of the largest and most famous leveraged buyouts in the 1980's. The companies they

---

[4] A leveraged buyout (LBO) is an acquisition that is mostly financed with borrowed funds. The debt if often secured by a lien on the target company's assets and then paid off with the future cash flows of the target's operations. When successfully engineered, LBO investors are able to take over a firm with a very small equity stake, pay off the debt load, and sell their position in a few years for tremendous profits.

bought out include Storer Communications, Safeway, Beatrice, Owens-Illinois, and Walter Industries. These were just some of the larger names. KKR acted as its own investment adviser on most transactions, using in house analysts to perform the due diligence and research. This allowed the firm to earn profits for advising, a percentage of the operating profits, management fees for portfolio contributors. Because of their prowess and expertise, the partners were able to pick and choose low risk transactions.

After more than ten years in the buyout business, KKR encountered the greatest challenge it had ever faced. RJR Nabisco was a possible buyout target and KKR had approached management about a potential deal. Nothing ever materialized from the early discussion, but within a few months, management and a group of investment bankers announced a management led buyout of the firm at $75 per share. The market price prior to the deal announcement was in the mid-50s. Tobacco stocks have historically traded at a discount to the market for various reasons and RJR Nabisco was no exception. The breakup value of RJR Nabisco was forecasted at $100 a share, so immediately when the bid of $75 was announced, several firms began preparing competing bids. Within a few days, KKR announced a bid of $90 per share for the company well above the management bid. This began one of the most intriguing stories of corporate drama ever documented. The story was so interesting that two *Wall Street Journal* writers took time off from the periodical to document the story in the book, *Barbarians at the Gate*.

After weeks of all night boardroom battles and hostile standoffs, the final deal was signed with KKR instead of the management led group. Management bid $109 per share and KKR bid $108 per share. When valued based on the different financing, the bids were virtually equal. In the end, the board of directors opted for the lower bid from KKR in hopes of better management in the future. The deal was financed with a $15 billion bank loan, $5 billion in junk bonds, and the rest in convertible preferred and common stock. The final price tag was $25.96 billion, representing almost a one hundred percent premium over the market price prior to the transactions. The true winners in the deal were the RJR stockholders and consultants on the deal (lawyers, investment bankers, and accountants). The press visibility hurt the business and RJR Nabisco struggled after the deal. KKR ended up earning only a marginal return when they liquidated their position in the early 1990s.

RJR Nabisco was not being run in the best interest of shareholders prior to the LBO. Management had extravagant lifestyles and excessive spending budgets. The potential to increase cash flows by simply reducing management inefficiency justified the incredible premium paid over the market price prior to the buyout. In the end, this was part of the reason management did not win the bid. If the stock was worth over $100 under one management team, why was the stock trading in the low fifties? The corporate takeovers and LBOs took center stage in the 1980's and built a bad reputation for Wall Street and investment bankers. But these transactions really helped the American corporate structure in the long run.

Management was no longer able to run firms inefficiently and waist shareholder resources. The firms did not belong to management, they belonged to the shareholders. These hostile transactions forced management to be accountable to shareholders and act in the best interest of the owners instead of the executives. The consequences for inefficient management were that some entrepreneur would take over the firm, firing management and restructuring the company in the best interest of shareholders. The junk bond market and the loose credit market made every company in the country a potential target if the deal was right. RJR Nabisco was one of the largest companies in the United States for hundreds of years, yet its management was swept out into the street.

Michael Milken

Although Milken is most remembered for his faults and colossal fall from grace, at one time he ruled Wall Street. Milken was a Wharton School graduate who single handedly built Drexel Burnham into one of the most profitable investment banks in the world. He was able to accomplish such success by building a liquid secondary market for below investment grade debt (junk bonds). Prior to 1975, the junk bond market was little more than an unpopular debt market with slime trading and no new issue activity. Drexel was able to corner the market and control most secondary market trading as it grew into a major source of financing in the economy. Once he established a liquid distribution network, Milken built a primary market for new issue junk bonds to finance smaller corporations and the vast takeover wave. Milken's intelligence and superior trading skills propelled him to the top of Wall Street. Unfortunately he took his trading operations one step too far. He began trading on inside information and executing other illegal securities transactions, all of which would blow up in his face in 1989 when he was indicted on 98 counts of securities fraud and racketeering. He became the ultimate symbol of greed and mistrust in the 1980s and is still remembered as a criminal instead of a financial genius.

The principle investors in the junk bond market were savings and loan firms (S&Ls) and pension funds. Primarily though, Milken built the junk bond market through a network of S&Ls which had large asset pools and were still able to invest in high-yielding investments.

Sources:
1) The *Wall Street Journal* Interactive Edition, July 5, 2000
   "Raiders Return. Hooray!"
   By James A. Glassman
2) *Forbes Magazine*, April 17, 2000
   "Meet the New Michael Milken"
   By Robert Lenzer

Appendix 3-C
Corporate Governance Provisions

Corporate governance provisions have been developed over the years as a means of dealing with the agency problem. Danielson and Karpoff (1998) examined this issue and suggested two reasons why firms employ governance provisions.

    1)   Firms adopt provisions incrementally and in response to specific perceived needs. For example, managers facing a proxy fight might seek a prohibition on the right to act by written consent. This hypothesis suggests that governance structures reflect unique changes in the firms' business conditions and risks of outside takeover.

    2)   Firms acquire restrictive governance provisions without regard to the provisions' specific attributes. This view claims that managers seeking takeover protection adopt many, even sometimes redundant, provisions: "If a little takeover protection is good, more is even better." Therefore, it is also possible that firms mimic each other when adopting provisions and hence, firms use herding behavior, as managers copy their counterparts.

The corporate governance provisions can be classified into four groups:

    (1)   "*External control provisions* are those that directly impede or may be used to impede hostile acquisitions, and which therefore work primarily through their effects on the external market for control."

    (2)   "*Internal control provisions* are those that increase a large shareholder's cost of exercising control or influencing corporate policies, and which therefore directly affect the internal market for control. These provisions do not directly affect a bidder's cost of accumulating a large block of stock."

    (3)   "*State takeover laws*…impose restrictions on both internal and external control mechanisms. For example, poison pill laws provide statutory sanction for poison pills, thereby strengthening the legal position of firms adopting poison pills."

    (4)   *Other miscellaneous provisions* could increase the vulnerability to unsolicited takeover bids, unlike the provisions in the first three categories.

External Control Provisions

    1)   *Poison pills*: Securities that entitle their holders to special rights if the issuing firm becomes the subject of a takeover bid. In a typical case, the poison pill is established by issuing a special dividend in the form of a right to purchase additional shares of the issuing firm's common stock. The rights trade with the common shares until a triggering event such as an unsolicited takeover bid. When such an event occurs, the rights detach and may be exercised at a low price by shareholders other than the bidder.

    2)   *Blank check preferred stock*: Authorized preferred stock for which the board of directors has broad discretion to establish voting, dividend,

conversion, and other rights. Blank check preferred stock can be issued to parties friendly to management to block unwanted hostile bids. A primary use, however, is as a vehicle to implement a poison pill.

3) *Stakeholder clause*: Charter language that permits directors to consider the effects of their decisions on constituencies other than stockholders. For example, directors may, or may be required to, evaluate the impact of a proposed change in control on employees, host communities, suppliers and others. The clause provides a target company's board members with an explicit legal basis to reject takeover bids that are attractive to shareholders.

Internal control provisions

4) *Classified (or staggered) board*: Board in which directors are divided into separate classes and elected to overlapping terms.

5) *Fair price charter amendment*: Requires a large shareholder to pay a price set by formula for all shares acquired in the back end of a two-tier acquisition. Typically, the price to be paid is the highest price the shareholder paid for any shares acquired during the first stage of the acquisition.

6) *Reincorporation to Delaware*: Corporations can change their state of incorporation to strengthen their anti-takeover defenses. Delaware corporate law permits companies to choose whether to classify the board or to make cumulative voting available.

7) *Supermajority vote requirement*: Establishes a level of approval for specified actions that is higher than the minimum set by state law. Such provisions often establish approval levels of 75 or 85% for actions that otherwise would require simple majority approval. These requirements often exceed the level of shareholder participation at a meeting, making action that requires supermajority approval very costly.

8) *Unequal voting rights*: Occurs when common shares do not all have the same voting rights. Under one typical plan called a dual class capitalization, two classes of stock exist, one with voting rights superior to the other. A second type of plan grants long-term stockholders super voting rights.

9) *Shareholder meeting requirements*: Refers to restrictions on either of two mechanisms that otherwise can be used to circumvent the normal corporate decision-making process. The first restriction is on the right to call special shareholder meetings. The second restriction is on the right to act by written consent, which enables shareholders with sufficient votes to take actions that otherwise would have to await a special or annual shareholder meeting. Both restrictions override default provisions in most states' incorporation statutes that permit special meetings or action by written consent.

10) *Firm eliminated cumulative voting or right to alter board size*: Indicates that a firm has eliminated cumulative voting and replaced it with straight voting, or has adopted a charter provision requiring a supermajority vote among directors, shareholders, or both to alter the board size.

State Takeover Laws

11)   *Freeze-out law*: Prohibits a large shareholder from engaging in any business combination with the covered firm for a specified number of years unless approval is obtained from the target firm's directors before the bidder acquires more than a specified fraction of target shares. Even after the mandatory waiting period, most freeze-out laws allow the business combination to proceed only if the transaction satisfies fair price provisions. Thus, the typical freeze-out law is like a fair price law with a forced delay.

12)   *Control share acquisition law*: Requires shareholder approval before a large shareholder may vote shares obtained in a control share acquisition. A control share acquisition refers to an accumulation of shares to above a threshold level, for example, to one-fifth the outstanding shares of a covered corporation.

13)   *Fair price law*: Similar to fair price charter amendments adopted by many firms. These laws regulate the back-end price in a two-tiered takeover bid or other significant business combination involving a large shareholder.

14)   *Cash-out law*: Requires any person who acquires a large stake (20%) in a firm to notify all other shareholders of the acquisition. All other shareholders are then entitled to sell their shares to the acquirer at a price at least as high as the highest price the acquirer paid in the period over which the large shareholder acquired its shares.

15)   *Poison pill law*: Grants firms the right to adopt poison pill takeover defenses. These poison pill laws can be important because the right to use poison pill defenses is presumably more secure when explicitly authorized by statute and is thus less likely to be limited by the courts.

Other miscellaneous provisions

16)   *Anti-greenmail provision*: Greenmail refers to an arrangement in which a company repurchases the stock held by a large shareholder, usually at an above-market price, in exchange for the shareholder's agreement not to launch a contest for control of the company for a specified time period.

17)   *Confidential voting*: Establishes a procedure in which all proxies, ballots, and voting tabulations that identify individual shareholders are kept confidential.

18)   *Cumulative voting*: Permits shareholders to distribute their total votes in any fashion they desire among the nominees to a company's board. Each shareholder's total votes is equal to the number of shares held times the number of directors to be elected. By concentrating votes on selected candidates, minority shareholders can elect a small number of representatives to the board.

19)   *Director/officer liability indemnity*: Such indemnity occurs when the corporation adopts a provision in which it promises to reimburse its directors and/or top officers for legal expenses, damages, and judgments incurred as a result of any lawsuit relating to the directors' and officers' corporate actions. In

virtually all cases, firms that adopt such a provision purchase indemnity insurance to cover risk.

20) *Firm opted out of a state takeover law*: Some state takeover laws contain language that allows affected companies not to be covered by part or all of the law's provisions.

Source: Danielson, Morris G., and Jonathan M. Karpoff, "On the Uses of Corporate Governance Provisions", *Journal of Corporate Finance*, IV (1998), 347-371.

Appendix 3-D
Higher Stock Prices for Good Corporate Governance

A survey by management consulting firm McKinsey & Co. showed that international institutional investors are willing to pay a premium for a company's stock if it had good corporate governance. International investors are prepared to pay as much as 20% more for such stocks. In companies with good corporate governance, most of the directors are outsiders with no ties to management; their compensation is closely tied to the company's performance.

International investors have $3.25 trillion in assets under management. The survey found that 75% of investors consider board practices to be at least as important to them as financial performance when evaluating companies for investment. Some 80% said they would pay more for shares of a well-governed company.

How much more they are willing to pay would depend on the country where the investor is from. The premium for well-governed corporations is as high as 27.1% in Indonesia, 25.7% in Thailand, 24.2% in South Korea and 20.2% in Japan and Taiwan. Outside Asia, the premiums are as follows: 27.6% in Venezuela, 27.2% in Colombia, 18.3% in the United States, and 17.9% in the United Kingdom.

The size of the premiums seems to reflect the state of corporate governance in the respective countries. In Asia and Latin America, where graft is widespread, premiums are higher. In the United States and United Kingdom where corporations disclose all financial information and management is more transparent, premiums are lower. Companies that have good corporate governance are able to deliver higher stockholder value and will find it easier to attract capital for financing growth.

Instances of shareholder activism are rare in regions like Asia and Latin America. Investors refrain from taking legal action because they have no confidence in the legal framework of developing countries. Furthermore, CEOs and other senior executives are seldom fired in Asia even when the companies they manage do not perform well. This is in contrast to the United States where executives do not hold on to their jobs for long if they do not produce results.

Source: The *Wall Street Journal* Interactive, June 19, 2000, "McKinsey Survey Shows Investors Have Desire for Good Governance" By Sara Webb

Appendix 3-D
CFOs on the Hotseat

CFOs have been feeling the heat in the wake of the corporate accounting scandals that have come to light following the high profile bankruptcies of Enron, Adelphia, and WorldCom. The accounting issues range from aggressive revenue recognition to alternative forms of earnings management. CFOs have been under increasing pressure to assure Wall Street and Main Street that their accounting numbers accurately reflect operating performance and follow Generally Accepted Accounting Principles (GAAP). They now must deal with new rules and regulations and face new challenges on the job.

Indeed the CFOs life has become increasingly complex since the bubble days when CFOs took more of a strategic role. Now, financial chiefs must make sure to cross every "t" as investors punish company stocks for something as arbitrary as a rumor. CFOs are working hard to restore confidence in their companies. Carol Tomé, CFO of Home Depot, made sweeping changes immediately after the Enron fiasco was uncovered. Her staff of 1500 now works under much stricter guidelines and her 25 lieutenants must sign off on their numbers.

Other CFOs are also taking a harder line as its back to basics: digging into the nuts and bolts of their company's financials. Audit committees expect CFOs to be tough with finances and say "no" to projects that do not make sense financially. Richard Davidson, CEO of Union Pacific, and his CFO don't necessarily agree on everything, but Davidson says that he needs a CFO that he can "bet my house on."

That sentiment is common across most companies, but with it has come a more grueling job. CFOs are now expected to turn financial reports out at Internet speed. Most companies will have just 75 days after fiscal 2003 ends to publish their annual reports, vs. 90 days before. Next year, they have 60 days. And the pace for quarterly reports is even more punishing: 45 days this year, 40 next and 35 in 2005.

To make matters worse, CFOs are expected to handle bulkier financial statements with surgeon like precision. On the surface, that task seems relatively straightforward, but, at larger companies, thousands of employees from dozens of departments handle different components of a company's financials.

In this difficult investing environment, a small mistake can have dire consequences for a company's share price. Ruth Ann M. Gillis, former CFO of $15 billion electric utility Exelon Corp. "You are making decisions today that perhaps in three months or even three years might become the subject of further scrutiny." She went on to say that "You have investor anger and political pressure and increased regulatory oversight. It has made the job of the CFO many, many more times complicated. As Business Week put it: "As they walk tightropes that rise higher with every new rule and regulation, today's CFOs know that if they slip, they're in for a long, hard fall."

Joseph Weber, "CFOs on the Hotseat," *Business Week*, March 17, 2003.

Appendix 3-E
The Role of Institutional Investors

Institutional investors control a majority of the capital in the financial markets. Institutions own more than half of all outstanding stock, and most daily trading volume comes from institutional investors. Institutional portfolio managers have a fiduciary responsibility to manage client assets. These institutions could be pension funds for the benefit of a corporation, mutual funds for individual investors, or treasury reserves for a major government entity. Nevertheless, institutional portfolio managers are measured by their performance. Traditionally institutional investors did not get involved in corporate governance unless they held a very large position in the company, but this has changed over the last two decades. Today, institutional investors control so much capital that they can have tremendous clout with the management of a corporation.

Institutional ownership has two main effects on the capital markets. The first effect is an increase in shareholder activism in management decision-making. Institutional investors are more likely to monitor corporate performance because they hold much larger stakes in companies as compared with individual investors. Shareholder activism is a regular practice of many large institutional investors. Institutional monitoring and activism in corporate governance influence corporations by reducing the principal-agent problem. Shareholder activism encourages management to maximize value and have a long-term strategic focus. This focus has contributed to the rise in strategic acquisitions and spin-offs of non-core divisions.

The secondary effects of institutional ownership in the capital markets are greater capital mobility and the ease of large accumulations of stock over short periods of time. Institutional investors trade much more than the average individual investor. Increased volume allows easier capital mobility and provides better liquidity in financial markets. Increased liquidity encourages more accurate market valuations and better information flow.

As noted above, institutional investors include pension and mutual funds, commercial and investment banks, and insurance companies. Among those that have been active in pushing for better corporate governance is the California Public Employees' Retirement System (CalPERS). CalPERS is the largest public pension fund in the United States with an asset base of more than $150 billion. More than 1 million people have money invested with CalPERS, so effective portfolio management is important.

Another aggressive pension fund is TIAA-CREF. TIAA-CREF is a financial service organization for colleges, universities, independent schools, and other nonprofit education and research employees nationwide. It is comprised of two separate companies: Teachers Insurance and Annuity Association, and

College Retirement Equities Fund. Combined, TIAA-CREF has about $235 billion of assets under management.

The Council of Institutional Investors (CII) is a group of institutional investors who often act together to bring about good corporate governance. There are five core policies that the CII recommends to maintain effective corporate governance:

1. Directors should be elected annually with confidential voting;
2. At least two-thirds of the corporation's directors should be from outside the corporation to prevent biased opinions;
3. Shareholders should have adequate information regarding director backgrounds and status as independent or associated with the corporation;
4. All members of oversight committees should be independent directors to prevent biased opinions; and
5. A majority vote from common shareholders should be required to pass any major corporate decision.

Each year the CII publishes a list of ten companies that have been performing poorly and have not taken action to turn improve their businesses. If the CII does not see changes being made by the company, presumably institutional investors will become more involved in corporate governance issues or, alternatively, will sell their shares. The box below shows the results of a study that evaluated the stock (left graph) and profit (right graph) performance of companies before and after being added to the focus list. In the graphs, the bar on the left is average for the companies put on the focus list, the center bar is the average performance for their industry, and the right bar is the average performance for the S&P 500. The results clearly show that once these companies are added to the focus list, their profit and stock performance improves relative to their industry and the S&P 500.

Shareholder Activism and Stock Returns

The Council of Institutional Investors Annually Places Poorly Performing Companies on its 'Focus List'

Stock and Profit Performance for Laggard Companies Before and After Being Added to the CII Focus List

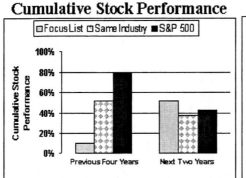

Cumulative Stock Performance

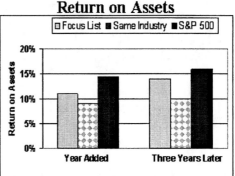

Return on Assets

Source: Qnler, T., Sokobin, J., 1999, "Does coordinated institutional shareholder activism work? An analysis of the Council of Institutional Investors," Ohio State University Working Paper.

Appendix 3-F
The Infamous Buyout of RJR Nabisco

1988-1989

Kohlberg Kravis Roberts & Co. (KKR) is a private equity firm started by Jerry Kohlberg, Henry Kravis and George Roberts, three ex-employees of the investment bank Bear Stearns & Co., in 1976. KKR specializes in private equity transactions, specifically leveraged buyouts (LBOs), and is known for the largest LBO in history. This transaction, for RJR Nabisco, took place towards the end of the 1980's takeover boom and was a whopping $26.4 billion in size.

On October 28, 1988 RJR Nabisco's CEO, Ross Johnson, made a bid for the company at $75 a share. This offer spurred an intense bidding war between Mr. Johnson and his team of investors, First Boston, and KKR. In the end, KKR prevailed and the RJR Nabisco board accepted their bid of $109 per share ($26.4 billion total). Before Ross Johnson's first bid, shares of RJR were trading at a mere $56 a share!

KKR's had many reasons for such a high bid, but a large amount of the premium paid was probably just backed by greed for money and control. At the time, RJR had all the qualities that private equity firms look for when buying out a company. RJR had low business risk, required low capital expenditures relative to revenues, and had a significant low level of debt. KKR also thought that the management of RJR, including Mr. Johnson, was incompetent and were not running the business well. The corporation had eleven corporate jets and four airports, signaling that significant cash and other resources were being tied up in unneeded management luxuries.

The size of this LBO goes down in history and will most likely never be topped because of changes in the high yield and bank debt markets as well as tightened laws and increased government intervention. All in all, the buyout of RJR Nabisco did not turn out as profitable for KKR as they had hoped, but it didn't have any significantly staggering after-effects. The only major downfall was the opportunity cost for KKR. How much higher could their returns have been if the money they invested in RJR Nabisco was invested in another project instead?

Sources:

Christopher, Alistair. "Big Deal: A Look Back At KKR's Buyout Of RJR Nabisco, Still The Largest LBO Ever." Buyouts, June 10, 2002.

Anders, George. "Merchants of Debt: KKR and The Mortgaging of American Businesses." Basic Books, May 1992.

Michel, A., Shaked, I., 1991."RJR Nabisco: A Case Study of A Complex Leveraged Buyout". Financial Analysts Journal, September/October 1991

"Looking Back." BuyOuts, October 20, 2003.

www.kkr.com

Sarbanes-Oxley Act

In response to several major accounting and corporate scandals, George Bush signed the Sarbanes-Oxley Act ("SOX") into law in July 30, 2002. SOX is the most wide sweeping legislation to affect the public accounting industry, corporate governance and financial disclosure since the securities laws promulgated in the early 1930s.

One of the most sweeping changes caused by SOX is the creation of the Public Company Accounting Oversight Board ("PCAOB"). The PCAOB is a board of five full-time members that are appointed and supervised by the SEC. Their duty is to oversee the audits and auditors of public companies, and sanction when necessary for violations of laws. Before SOX, the accounting industry was entirely self-regulated by the accounting firms within the profession. While auditors audited corporate America, there was always a question of "who audited the auditors." The PCAOB provides a solution to this question.

SOX also resulted in large changes in corporate governance to ensure there was greater independence between the board and management. Company loans to officers and directors - which were extremely common before SOX - is no longer permitted. The audit committee of the Board of Directors is now given full responsibility to select and oversee auditors. Previously, management helped make this crucial decision. CEOs and CFOs must now sign the financial statements verifying their accuracy. If the financials that they verify are incorrect they can lose bonuses and be sentenced to jail time.

While many believe SOX has improved legislation significantly, one of the major complaints with the Act has been the costs of compliance. Some people believe SOX may strangle entrepreneurs as they will be bogged down in trying to comply with all of the Acts detailed rules. A study by Financial Executives International estimates compliance of SOX will cost roughly $4.7 million per year for companies with revenues of more than $5 billion.

SOURCES:

http://www.aicpa.org/info/Sarbanes-Oxley2002.asp
http://www.aicpa.org/sarbanes/index.asp
http://www.pwcglobal.com/Extweb/NewCoAtWork.nsf/docid/D0D7F79003C6D
64485256CF30074D66C
http://www.cfodirect.com/cfopublic.nsf?opendatabase&content=http://www.cfodi
rect.com/cfopublic.nsf/vContent/MSRA-5QJQ6C?open
http://www.mlive.com/business/jacitpat/index.ssf?/base/business-
0/1078657621228800.xml

CHAPTER 4

STRATEGIC FINANCIAL MANAGEMENT

Finance involves the management of money. In business, the *financing decision* involves raising funds for the operations of the company by issuing securities such as stocks and bonds or by borrowing from a financial institution. The *investment decision* determines how the firm will use those monies to fund its long-term capital projects and ventures.

This chapter addresses the key strategic issues facing managers in raising and investing money in a business enterprise. These issues include working capital management, capital budgeting, and the capital structure decision—areas that we touched upon in Chapter 3.

The objectives of the chapter include:

- To explain and illustrate short-term investment and financial strategies—working capital management;
- To assess capital budgeting in the context of a firm; and
- To evaluate the role of capital structure and dividend policy in long-term financial strategy.

Exhibit 4-1 provides a balance sheet view of these key areas of financial decision-making.

Exhibit 4-1
Strategic Financial Management

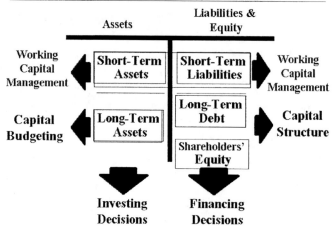

4.1 Working Capital Management

Working capital management is the management of a company's short-term assets and liabilities. Working capital refers to the firm's short-term assets, such as accounts receivables and inventory, and its short-term liabilities, such as accounts payable and bank loans. Managing the firm's working capital is a day-to-day activity that ensures the firm has sufficient resources to continue its operations and avoid costly disruptions. The short-term assets and liabilities of the firm are shown in the upper portion of Exhibit 4-2.

> *Working Capital Management* **is the management of short-term assets and liabilities of the firm.**

A number of questions relating to working capital that the management of the firm must address are:

- How much cash and inventory should we keep on hand?
- What credit terms should we offer to our customers?
- How will we obtain any needed short-term financing?
- If we borrow short-term, how and where should we do it?

Exhibit 4-2

<u>Current Assets</u>	<u>Current Liabilities</u>
Cash/ Securities	**Bank Loans**
Accounts Receivable	Accounts Payable
Inventory	Accrued Expenses
Long-Term Assets	Long-Term Debt
	Preferred Stock
	Common Equity

A company's net working capital is the difference between its current assets and current liabilities:

Net Working Capital = Current Assets – Current Liabilities   (Eq. 4-1)

As stated in Chapter 2 in the principle relating to corporate finance and governance, corporate managers should make decisions that maximize shareholder value. In decisions relating to working capital management, the way to increase the value of the firm is to make decisions that minimize the cost (or maximize the profit) of maintaining the net working capital position of the company.

Working capital management is the operational side of finance. It involves managing the firm's day-to-day financial resources. Working capital management includes: cash management, managing the cash conversion cycle, and managing current assets and liabilities of the firm.

4.1.1 Cash Management

Cash is the most liquid of all assets in a firm, and cash management is an important aspect of working capital management. Although cash is most liquid, firms purchase short-term marketable securities with excess cash and earn a rate of return on its investments. There are three motives for a firm to hold cash or marketable securities:

- *Transaction Motive*—Holding cash or near-cash to make planned payments for items such as materials and wages.
- *Safety Motive*—Holding cash or near-cash to protect the firm from being unable to satisfy unexpected demands for cash.
- *Speculative Motive*—Holding cash or near-cash to be able to quickly take advantage of unexpected opportunities.

Management's goal for cash management is to achieve an optimal balance between cash and marketable securities. If the firm holds too much cash, there will be detrimental effects on its profitability. If it holds too little cash, the firm faces the risk of being unable to pay its bills and continue operations. Efficient management of a company's cash requires analyses of its operating cycle and cash conversion cycle.

4.1.2 The Operating Cycle

From the time a company purchases raw material and provides labor for production to the time it collects payment for its final products is considered its *operating cycle*. The operating cycle has two components: days sales in inventory (DSI) and days sales outstanding (DSO), also known as the average collection period (ACP). Exhibit 4-3 illustrates how DSI and DSO make up an operating cycle.

Exhibit 4-3
The Operating Cycle

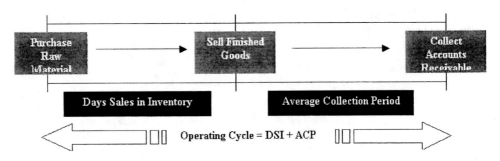

4.1.3   The Cash Conversion Cycle

The *cash conversion cycle* is the length of time between the payment of cash for inventory (or raw materials) and the receipt of cash from accounts. The ability to get credit from suppliers is important to a firm's cash management. Without credit, the firm will have to wait until it receives the cash payment for its products before its original investment is converted back to cash. For example, a company that holds its inventory for 50 days and receives payment in 30 days will have to wait 80 days before it receives its cash back. With credit from suppliers, this wait may be shortened. A company's cash conversion cycle can be calculated as follows:

Cash Conversion Cycle	=	Days Sales in Inventory	+	Days Sales Outstanding	-	Days Payables Outstanding
CCC	=	DSI	+	DSO	-	DPO

Exhibit 4-4 shows how supplier credit reduces a company's cash conversion cycle:

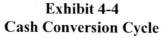

Exhibit 4-4
Cash Conversion Cycle

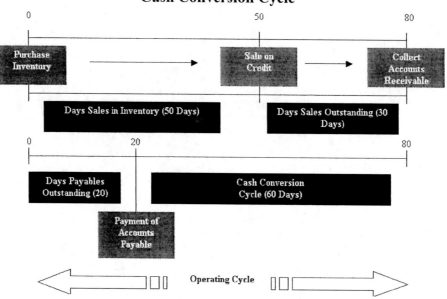

4.1.4 Managing the Cash Conversion Cycle

A company with a *positive cash conversion cycle* effectively finances the purchase of its products for its customers, and the firm requires short-term financing to support its cash conversion cycle. Ideally, firms prefer very short, or even negative, cash conversion cycles. A *negative cash conversion cycle* is good because it means that the company's average payment period is longer than its operating cycle. In general, manufacturing companies have positive cash conversion cycles because they have longer operating cycles. Non-manufacturing firms carry lower inventory and sell their products faster, resulting in shorter operating cycles and negative cash conversion cycles.

To decrease a positive cash conversion cycle, a firm can pursue the following strategies:

- Increase inventory turnover;
- Decrease average collection period by giving customers cash discounts; or
- Increase payment deferral period by as much as possible.

SEE BOX ENTITLED 'HOW DOES YOU FINANCE DEPARTMENT STACK UP?' TO GET A PERSPECTIVE ON KEY MEASURES TO GAUGE INTERNAL FINANCIAL PERFORMANCE

4.1.5 Managing Current Assets

Investment in current assets such as inventory has to be considered carefully because costs are involved in holding these assets. For example, inventory incurs *carrying costs* in the form of warehousing, obsolescence, and insurance costs. Because investment in inventory must be financed, capital costs are incurred as well. These costs rise with increases in current assets. *Shortage costs*, on the other hand, decrease with increases in current assets. For example, if inventory levels fall, the firm runs the risk of losing sales if it is unable to meet demand for its products. Tight credit policies will lower levels of accounts receivable, but this policy may result in a loss of sales.

Exhibit 4-5 illustrates a theoretical approach to the optimal investment in current assets given the existence of carrying and shortage costs. As noted above, carrying costs increase with additional current assets, while shortage costs decrease as current asset holdings increase. The minimum point, which is the lowest total cost of holding current assets, is where carrying costs equal shortage costs. This point, as shown in Exhibit 4-5, indicates the optimal dollar amount of investment in current assets (CA*).

Exhibit 4-5
The Optimal Investment in Current Assets

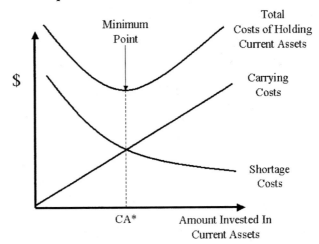

Under a *flexible* short-term financing policy, a firm maintains high levels of inventory and grants liberal credit terms to its customers. This results in a high level of accounts receivable. A *restrictive* short-term financing policy involves holding low levels of inventory and accounts receivable.

Flexible short-term financial policies cost more but should also generate higher future cash flows from additional revenues. For instance, firms with a flexible policy may use liberal credit terms to stimulate sales. Restrictive policies require less investment in current assets, and cost less as a result, but it may reduce the firm's growth prospects.

4.1.6 Managing Current Liabilities

Firms require some form of financing to maintain their ever-changing amounts of current assets. Business cycles change their needs for current assets. As a result, financing requirements change with the changing levels of current assets. Exhibit 4-6 illustrates this challenge in working capital management.

Exhibit 4-6
Financing Working Capital
The Hedged Approach

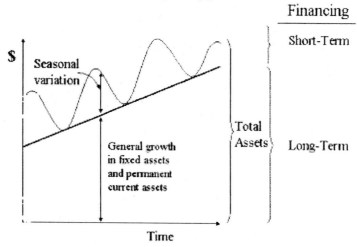

The level of current liabilities depends upon three principal factors:

- *Cash reserves*—a firm with a high level of cash and marketable securities does not require much financing for the other current assets that it holds.
- *Maturity hedging*—this strategy matches the maturities of assets and liabilities. Inventories are financed with short-term loans while fixed assets are paid for with long-term debt.
- *Relative interest rates*—a firm's decision to use either long-term or short-term financing depends on interest rates. Rates are usually lower for short-term loans. The firm decides which term of financing is best for its purposes.

4.1.7 Risk-Return Trade-off in Working Capital Management

The risk-return trade-off in working capital management relates to the firm's liquidity and profitability. A large amount of net working capital can hurt a firm's profitability because current assets such as cash and inventory do not generate as great a return for the firm as investment in fixed assets such as plant and property.

Using current liabilities versus long-term debt to finance current assets also involves a risk-return trade-off. All else equal, the greater a corporation's reliance on current liabilities, the greater its liquidity risk. However, current liabilities cost less and are more flexible than long-term debt for financing fluctuating current assets.

Firms seek to determine the optimal, most profitable level of net working capital. In the economic model of the 1980s, excess working capital was believed to be good for the firm because it ensured that the firm was always liquid. Excess inventory was believed to add value to customers. Under this old model, a current asset to current liability ratio of 2.0 was considered optimal. Suppliers were seen as adversaries and managers negotiated only to get the lowest price.

In the economic model that was introduced during the mid-1990s and is in use in the early 2000s, working capital is considered undesirable for the firm because it hurts profitability. Excess liquidity is a reflection of poor strategic financial management. Managers now try to work hand-in-hand with suppliers and change operating processes to achieve the minimum inventory level possible. In this new business model, timeliness of delivery and quality are almost as important as cost. Instead of the current ratio, advocates of this new model use working capital as a percentage of sales to measure a firm's optimal level of net working capital.

The old and new business models reflect a classic risk-return trade-off. The old model sacrifices profitability for safety while the newer places a greater emphasis on profitability. Ultimately, the financial manager must determine the appropriate amount of working capital. The absolute amount depends in large part on the nature of the business and the level of risk with which management is comfortable.

To illustrate the importance of working capital levels in different industries, Table 4-1 shows the assets and liabilities, expressed as a percentage of total assets, of five well-known companies. These companies are Wal-Mart, Boeing, Consolidated Edison, Hewlett Packard, and EBay. Manufacturing businesses tend to have a relatively long operating cycle, and they usually have larger investments in inventories and receivables. This is exemplified with Boeing and Hewlett Packard. Service companies usually have negligible inventories, and they usually have a smaller investment in current assets. Con Edison, a provider of electricity, and EBay, the online auction site, are examples of a manufacturer and a service company. Retailers such as Wal-Mart usually fall in between these extremes. Whereas Wal-Mart's inventories represent over 25% of total assets, its receivables are relatively small because the company (for the most part) does not extend credit to customers.

Table 4-1
Assets and Liabilities as Percentage of Total Assets
Selected Companies – 2003

	Walmart	Boeing	Con Edison	Hewlett Packard	Ebay
Cash & near cash	2.91	4.46	0.35	15.83	26.9
Marketable sec	NA	NA	NA	0.34	2.17
Acct & notes rec	2.23	9.57	4.06	16.84	3.19
Inventories	26.29	11.81	NA	8.2	NA
Other cur assets	0.77	6.36	4.94	9.81	3.35
Current assets	32.19	32.2	9.35	51.02	35.6
Net fixed assets	54.82	16.75	85.69	9.79	5.29
LT inv't & LT rec	NA	NA	NA	5.64	11.4
Other assets	12.99	51.05	4.96	33.55	47.71
Total assets	100	100	100	100	100
Accounts payable	18.1	8.47	11.94	9.92	1.15
ST borrowings	6.12	3.47	0.08	2.54	0.07
Other ST liab	10.23	25.92	1.89	21.93	8.14
Cur liabilities	34.45	37.85	13.92	34.38	9.36
Long Term Borrowings	20.71	24.05	51.03	8.53	0.33
Other LT liab	1.86	23.4	9.1	5.8	3.27
Total liabilities	57.02	85.3	74.05	48.72	12.97
Preferred equity	0	0	0	0	0
Minority interest	1.44	0	0	0	0.81
Total common equity	41.55	14.7	25.95	51.28	86.23
Shareholder equity	42.98	14.7	25.95	51.28	87.03
Tot liab & equity	100	100	100	100	100

4.2   Capital Budgeting

Capital budgeting is the process of planning and managing a firm's long-term investments. The financial manager tries to identify investment opportunities that are worth more to the firm than they cost to build or acquire. This means that the value of the cash flows generated by an asset is expected to exceed the cost of buying or building and operating that asset. In the capital budgeting decision, financial managers should make decisions that maximize the value of the firm.

***Capital budgeting** is the process of planning and managing long-term investments.*

Regardless of the specific investment under consideration, financial managers must be concerned with how much cash (*return*) they expect to receive, when (*timing*) they expect to receive it, and how likely (*risk*) they are to receive it. Estimating the probable amount, timing, and risk of future cash flows is the essence of capital budgeting. In fact, whenever we value a business decision, these factors are by far the most important considerations. As shown in Exhibit 4-7, capital budgeting usually involves estimating the value of long-term, tangible assets.

Exhibit 4-7
Capital Budgeting

Current Assets	Current Liabilities
Cash/Securities	**Bank Loans**
Accounts Receivable	Accounts Payable
Inventory	Accrued Expenses
Long-Term Assets	Long-Term Debt
	Preferred Stock
	Common Equity

As shown in Exhibit 4-8, capital budgeting decisions are the output of a firm's strategic planning process. Companies must invest capital to pursue their production and marketing strategies. These include such activities as:

- Expanding facilities and infrastructure to support growth,
- Investing in, developing, and introducing new products and services,
- Making acquisitions to fill out market and/or product niches,
- Investing in technology to support customer service, and
- Upgrading aging equipment and facilities.

Exhibit 4-8
The Capital Budgeting Process

4.2.1   The Capital Budgeting Process

The goal of financial managers in the capital budgeting process is to create additional value for stockholders by investing only in projects or ventures that have a *positive net present value*. Financial managers should make capital budgeting decisions that offer the firm the highest risk adjusted return, and that:

> *Maximize the net present value of the investments that are financed by the firm's capital budget.*

Corporate investment normally falls into one of several general categories: replacement, expansion, process improvement, research and development, and environmental. Replacement involves replacing existing assets or increasing their efficiency through capital investment. Expansion adds capacity for existing products, extends product lines, or launches new products. Entering new markets also requires capital investment within this category. Process improvement usually entails investing in technology to improve efficiency or customer service. Research and development investment is essential in certain industries, including those with a heavy exposure to science and those involved with the development and use of technology. Environmental investments are necessary for industries whose business activities may impair the environment. Examples of the types of capital budgeting projects are listed below:

Capital Budget/Expansion/Exploration: Exxon Mobil, with Shell, BP and Phillips Petroleum Co. as partners, has made a capital budgeting decision to spend $16 billion in one of the country's largest, oil exploration projects. It includes building a large natural-gas processing plant and involves natural-gas exploration to feed a petrochemical operation and a string of power and water plants.

R&D Budget: Pfizer, the world's largest privately funded biomedical research operation, has an R&D budget of $7 billion a year. Pfizer has around 120 "new chemical entities," innovative drugs in clinical development.

Expansion: Wal-Mart spent nearly $10 billion in 2002 on its largest expansion program ever. The $10 billion bought Wal-Mart an additional 46 million square feet of retail space, with an addition of 180 to 185 new super centers.

Replacement: Volkswagen North America has invested $1 billion in 2002 in its manufacturing plant in Puebla, Mexico, where the beetle car is built. Half of the money is used in replacing and modernizing the operation, which opened in 1967.

Environmental: The chemical industry is spending more than $4 billion per year on pollution abatement and control. In ten years, total spending is projected to rise to about $11 billion, largely as a result of the 1990 Clean Air Act amendments

A firm's capital expenditure is important because it determines the firm's future profitability. Most capital expenditures are usually long-term in nature and are not easily reversible. For example, building a new plant takes years of planning and construction. Once a project has begun, it is not easily cancelled or reversed. Over the years a number of procedures have been developed to assist management in the analysis of capital budgeting decisions.

SEE BOX ENTITLED 'THE IRIDIUM PROJECT' TO SEE AN EXAMPLE OF A BIG-TIME INVESTMENT THAT WENT BUST'

4.2.2   The Cost of Capital

One of the most important factors to consider when making capital budgeting decisions is the company's *cost of capital*—the cost of obtaining financing for the company's capital expenditures. Firms use their cost of capital as their minimum required rate of return on a venture or project in which they are considering an investment. For example, if a firm's cost of capital is 8%, a new project must earn a return in excess of 8% to be considered as a potential investment (see Exhibit 4-9). The calculation of the cost of capital is discussed later in this chapter.

Exhibit 4-9
Classical Approach to Capital Budgeting
Return on Investment and the Cost of Capital

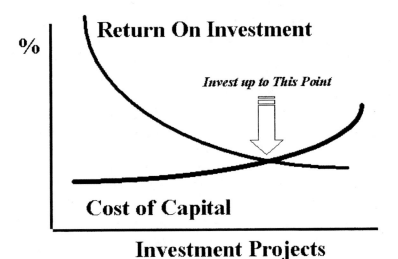

4.2.3   Investment Decision Criteria

- 113 -

When making a capital budgeting decision, firms have an array of methods they can use to value the potential profitability of the investments. These methods are discussed in more detail in Chapter 10 relating to capital budgeting. Common financial approaches to capital budgeting include:

Net Present Value (NPV):

This is the most popular of all investment valuation criteria because it incorporates the idea of a project earning in excess of the firm's cost of capital. In this model, expected cash flows from a project are discounted to the present day. We discuss discounting in greater detail in Chapter 9. The discount rate used in this calculation usually is the cost of capital of the company or a higher rate that is set by the management of the firm. The cost of the investment is then subtracted from this present value of expected future cash flows. If the resulting number is positive, then the project is expected to be profitable and should be undertaken.

The Internal Rate of Return (IRR:

This valuation technique requires that the financial manager find the rate of return that will make the project's net present value equal to zero. In other words, instead of calculating the project's NPV, the manager sets the NPV to zero and works backwards to find the discount rate. Most financial calculators can easily perform this function. The discount rate found with this method of calculation is the project's internal rate of return (IRR). Based on this rule, an investment is acceptable if its IRR exceeds the cost of capital or some higher required rate of return.

The Payback Period Rule:

The payback period is the amount of time required for an investment to generate enough cash flow to recover its initial cost. This is a simpler valuation criterion than net present value because it does not involve discounting cash flows. Based on this rule, an investment is considered acceptable if its calculated payback period is less than a number of years specified by management. This method is flawed because it does not take into consideration the time value of money or the risk associated with an investment. However, it is simple and easy to use.

4.3   Capital Structure

Capital structure refers to the specific mixture of long-term debt and equity the firm uses to finance its operations. The financial manager has two concerns in this area. What are the least expensive sources of funds for the firm? And, how much should the firm borrow?

*Capital Structure **refers to the mix of long-term debt and equity issued by the firm.***

In addition to the capital structure mix, the financial manager decides exactly how and where to raise the money. Expenses associated with raising long-term capital can be considerable, so different possibilities are carefully evaluated. Also, firms borrow money from a variety of lenders in a number of ways. Choosing among lenders and loan types is another decision of the financial manager. The appropriate goal for the financial manager is to create a capital structure that will:

Minimize the weighted average cost of capital (WACC) of the company

There are many financial markets in the investment world in which a firm can obtain financing for its business. These include the equity markets, the bond markets, and the money markets. Each of these markets accommodates the issuance of new securities—the *primary market*, and the trading of existing securities—the *secondary market*.

In this section we address the primary market and the options the firm has when it accesses the primary market to raise capital for business ventures. The first section identifies the basic types of financial instruments and where these are traded. Exhibit 4-10 shows how a firm's capital structure interacts with the economic and institutional environment in delivering shareholder value.

Exhibit 4-10
Capital Structure

Current Assets	Current Liabilities
Cash/Securities	**Bank Loans**
Accounts Receivable	Accounts Payable
Inventory	Accrued Expenses
Long-Term Assets	**Long-Term Debt** **Preferred Stock** **Common Equity**

4.3.1 Common Stock

Common stock represents an ownership stake in a corporation. Common stockholders provide funds to a corporation in exchange for expected future earnings and the assets remaining (the residual cash flow stream) after the payment of expenses, debt, and preferred stockholders. A share of common stock gives its owner the right to vote on matters of corporate governance.

In the United States these governance rights empower the stockholders to vote to elect a board of directors. The board of directors represents the interests of stockholders in important operations of the corporation. These operations include: approval of mergers and acquisitions, selecting public accountants to audit the financial statements of the firm, and approving the issuance of additional capital for the corporation.

Common stock is issued by a corporation and represents ownership of the firm.

The two most important characteristics of common stock are: it has a *residual claim* on assets of the firm; and that the stockholders are subject to *limited liability.*

Owning a *residual claim* means that upon liquidation or bankruptcy stockholders are the last investors to receive payment. Shareholders are paid after all other creditors and investors receive their claim on assets. For firms not in liquidation, shareholders have a claim on the residual cash flows after interest and taxes have been paid, as well as dividends to preferred stockholders. Management can either pay this residual cash to stockholders as a cash dividend, or reinvest it in future growth opportunities of the corporation.

Limited liability means that in the event of failure of the corporation the maximum amount that shareholders can lose is their original investment (the shareholder's stock purchase price). Unlike owners of partnerships, whose creditors can lay claim to their personal assets, the most corporate shareholders can lose is their initial investment. Shareholders are not personally liable for the firm's obligations.

Example of Common Stock:

Coca-Cola Corporation (NYSE stock symbol: KO) is one of the best known companies in the world. The firm currently has 2,475,000,000 shares of common stock outstanding. At a price of $40, the company has a market capitalization of just over $99 billion (2,475,000,000 shares times $40 per share). The book value per share (equity / share outstanding) of KO is less than $5 per share but the power of the Coke brand name and tremendous expected future profits continue to attract investors. A public company such as Coca-Cola can sell additional shares by registering a securities offering with the Securities and Exchange Commission. These offerings will be discussed in greater detail later in the book.

4.3.2   Preferred Stock

Preferred stock is an equity security that has features similar to both debt and equity. Like a bond, preferred stock promises to pay shareholders a periodic dividend payment. However, unlike a bond, preferred dividend payments are not legally binding and the board of directors can withhold dividends during hard times. A typical covenant attached to the issuance of preferred stock is that no dividends may be paid to common stockholders until all dividends to preferred stockholders have been paid.

> **Preferred stock** *is an ownership claim on the firm*
> *that is senior to common stock*

Preferred stock is an equity investment and represents an ownership claim on corporate assets. This claim is senior to that of common stock holders but junior to any outstanding debt. Like common stock, most preferred stock does not have a final repayment date. However, many issues do include some provision for periodic retirement of preferred stock so that the dividend stream of the firm can be limited and eventually retired.

Example of Preferred Stock:

Consolidated Edison (NYSE: ED), better known as ConEd, is the electric utility for New York City. The company has 1,915,319 shares of $5 Series A cumulative preferred stock outstanding. These shares pay an annual dividend to shareholders of $5, and these dividends accumulate over time in the event that the company is unable to pay them. These shares were sold to investors in 1993, and trade on the New York Stock Exchange. As of December 31, 2004, the selling price was $__.

4.3.3 Bonds

A *bond* is a debt, and it is a long-term contractual obligation issued to borrow money. The bond promises to pay interest on the borrowed funds at a specified rate and to pay principal upon maturity. The interest and repayment provisions are defined in a contract called a *bond indenture*. In addition to corporations, the U.S. government, federal agencies, state governments, municipalities, foreign firms, foreign governments, and international agencies also issue bonds to finance projects and other ventures.

> *A* **bond** *is a debt issued by an entity that has interest payments*
> *and the repayment of principal*

A typical bond indenture includes the following provisions:

- The *par value*, or face value, of the bond. This is the amount of money the issuer has agreed to repay upon maturity. The standard par value for bonds is $1000.

- A promise to make periodic interest payments, called *coupon payments*, over the life of the bond. The coupon rate is determined at the time of issue based on securities with comparable credit quality and duration.

- A promise to repay the *principal* amount of the bond in one or more installments throughout the life of the bond. This is usually the par value of the bond, but in some instances bonds are sold at a discount so that the principal value and par values are different.

- The *maturity date* of the bond. The maturity is the end of a bond's life when principal and all interest payments have been fulfilled.

- A *call provision*. This gives the issuer the right, but not the obligation, to pay off the bonds prior to their maturity at a pre-specified call price.

Example of a Bond:

On September 15, 1999, IBM (NYSE: IBM) issued $600,000,000 of senior (priority claim on assets upon liquidation) bonds with a 4.25% annual coupon payment due to mature on September 15, 2009. The bonds have a par value of $1000 and are callable after five years at a price of 105% of par value. As of December 31, 2004, the bonds were selling $_____ for a yield-to-maturity of _____%. The bonds are rated A by Moody's.

4.3.4   Convertible Bonds

Convertible bonds are a financing instrument with features of both stocks and bonds. Convertible bonds pay periodic interest payments and also have an option to exchange convertible bonds for a pre-determined number of shares of common stock. The pre-determined conversion price is set at a premium to the current stock market price so that bondholders will not immediately take advantage of the conversion feature. If the price of the common stock never reaches the conversion premium, upon maturity, the investor receives its principal repayment—the same feature as a traditional corporate bond.

Convertible bonds tend to be sold by small growing companies who need capital. Since they offer investors the upside potential associated with the appreciation of common stock, they have a lower coupon rate than a comparable corporate bond without the conversion feature.

Example of Convertible Bonds:

On June 6, 2001 Baxter International (NYSE: BAX) issued $800 million in convertible bonds. These bonds had an annual coupon rate of 1-1/4% and are due June 6, 2021. The bonds were issued at $1,000 par value and each bond is convertible in 15.34 shares of the BAX common stock at any time prior to maturity. This conversion ratio of 15.34 yields a conversion price of $65.18 per share (1,000/15.34). The bonds are rated A by Moody's.

4.3.5 High Yield Bonds

A *high yield bond* or *junk bond* is any bond that is considered to be below investment grade by the major credit rating agencies. The three major credit rating agencies are Moody's Investor Services, Standard & Poor's, and Fitch. These firms rate most domestic and international publicly traded bonds. Investment-grade bonds are debt securities that have qualified for one of the top four ratings of the credit rating agencies. Bonds that have credit ratings below investment-grade are considered junk bonds.

High yield bonds tend to be one of three types:

- A *fallen angel* which was an investment grade bond that has been subsequently downgraded to a junk rating due to poor financial performance;
- Bonds of a large company that has undergone a significant capital structure change, such as a leveraged buyout (LBO); or
- Bonds of a growing company that needs the capital and cannot achieve an investment grade rating. Growing companies from industries such as telecommunications and gambling ventures were some of the largest issuers of junk bonds in the 1990's.

Example:

*In 1998 Delta Airlines (NYSE: DAL) issued $500 million in 7-year bonds due on December 15, 2005. These high-yield bonds pay an annual coupon rate of 7.625%. The bonds were rated B by Standard & Poor's, which is in the middle of the junk bond range. The bonds initially traded at a premium of 350 basis points (3.5 percentage points) above the yield on Treasuries of similar maturities (the **Spread to Treasuries**). But with the problems of the airline industry, and the bankruptcy of United Airlines and US Airways, the prospects for these bonds have fallen and, as of December 31, 2004, they were trading at $___. This indicates that investors are uncertain about whether Delta will be able to meet their debt obligations.*

4.3.6 Advantages and Disadvantages of Issuing Debt

The biggest advantage to a corporation issuing bonds is that interest on debt is tax deductible as an expense. The United States tax code permits businesses to deduct the interest payments on debt prior to their payment of income taxes. As a result, interest provides a tax shield on income since it reduces pre-tax income and taxes. For most firms, debt financing is less costly on an after-tax basis than equity financing.

The main disadvantage of debt is that it creates a contractual obligation to lenders. When economic times are tough, as in a recession or during an industry decline, interest payments can create a severe burden on organizations. This condition is broadly known as the *cost of financial distress*. Financial distress occurs when the bond defaults. The costs of financial distress include: bankruptcy, lost sales due to a questionable future, and higher costs of future borrowing due to poor credit rating (similar to late credit card payments lowering your personal credit rating).

Credit ratings provide information to investors regarding the probability of default on a bond. Based on a credit rating and likelihood of interest payments, investors establish the required rate of return. Bonds with higher credit ratings usually have lower coupon rates or yields. The table below provides a description of Moody's bond rating categories.

Moody's Bond Rating Categories

Moody's Bond Ratings are intended to characterize the risk of holding a bond. These ratings, or risk assessments, in part determine the interest that an issuer must pay to attract purchasers to the bonds. All information herein was obtained from Moody's Bond Record.

Aaa—Bonds which are rated Aaa are judged to be of the best quality. They carry the smallest degree of investment risk and are generally referred to as "gilt edged." Interest payments are protected by a large or an exceptionally stable margin and principal is secure. While the various protective elements are likely to change, such changes as can be visualized are most unlikely to impair the fundamentally strong position of such issues.

Aa—Bonds which are rated Aa are judged to be of high quality by all standards. Together with the Aaa group they comprise what are generally known as high grade bonds. They are rated lower than the best bonds because margins of protection may not be as large as in Aaa securities or fluctuation of protective elements may be of greater amplitude or there may be other elements present which make the long-term risk appear somewhat larger than the Aaa securities.

A—Bonds which are rated A possess many favorable investment attributes and are considered as upper-medium-grade obligations. Factors giving security to principal and interest are considered adequate, but elements may be present which suggest a susceptibility to impairment some time in the future.

Baa—Bonds which are rated Baa are considered as medium-grade obligations (i.e., they are neither highly protected not poorly secured). Interest payments and principal security appear adequate for the present but certain protective elements may be lacking or may be characteristically unreliable over any great length of time. Such bonds lack outstanding investment characteristics and in fact have speculative characteristics as well.

Ba—Bonds which are rated Ba are judged to have speculative elements; their future cannot be considered as well-assured. Often the protection of interest and principal payments may be very moderate, and thereby not well safeguarded during both good and bad times over the future. Uncertainty of position characterizes bonds in this class.

B—Bonds which are rated B generally lack characteristics of the desirable investment. Assurance of interest and principal payments of maintenance of other terms of the contract over any long period of time may be small.

Caa—Bonds which are rated Caa are of poor standing. Such issues may be in default or there may be present elements of danger with respect to principal or interest.

Ca—Bonds which are rated Ca represent obligations which are speculative in a high degree. Such issues are often in default or have other marked shortcomings.

C—Bonds which are rated C are the lowest rated class of bonds, and issues so rated can be regarded as having extremely poor prospects of ever attaining any real investment standing.

4.3.7 Capital Structure and Maximizing the Value of the Firm

For many years finance theorists have debated the role of a company's capital structure and how it can be used to increase the value of the firm. A firm's *capital structure* relates to the proportion of debt and equity a firm uses to finance its operations and long-term capital projects. Financial managers face the challenge of balancing the benefits and costs of debt financing.

The goal of the financial manager is to implement a capital structure for the firm that will minimize the firm's weighted average cost of capital (WACC) and thereby maximize the value of the firm. In this section we describe the capital structure decision and see how it has evolved.

The Modigliani and Miller Propositions:

At what level should a firm set its debt to value ratio? Two Nobel prize-winning economists, Franco Modigliani and Merton Miller (M&M), in a series of academic journal articles addressed this issue in depth. Their main arguments are that the value of a firm is based on its investment decision—its portfolio of projects and investments and the cash flows that the projects generate. The risk associated with the cash flows is related to the risk on the firm's underlying assets, r_a. The value of the firm is the present value of the cash flows of the firm's assets—its projects and investments. M&M also showed how investors could use their own homemade leverage by borrowing funds to buy stock and increase the risk/reward ratio of owning stock.

Modigliani and Miller showed that the value of two firms with identical assets and operations but with different capital structures are worth the same. They showed that in perfect capital markets—financial markets in which there are no taxes and no transaction costs—the value of the firm depends solely on the firm's investment decision—only on the value of the firm's underlying assets, and the value is independent of the firm's capital structure. M&M named this relationship, M&M Proposition I.

M&M Proposition I: *In perfect capital markets, the value of the firm is independent of its capital structure (debt/value ratio).*

M&M recognized that for a firm with a low debt to value ratio, the cost of a firm's equity capital is higher than its cost of debt. They also recognized that as the debt to value ratio increased, the cost of the firm's debt and equity also increased. Let's assume that the return associated with the underlying assets of Firm A (r_a) is 12%, also equal to the cost of equity in a firm that is 100% financed by equity. Let's also assume that the cost of debt for Firm A at very low financial leverage is 8%. An implication of Proposition I is that the cost of debt capital and equity capital will increase with increasing leverage, such that when Firm A is financed 100% by debt, the cost of debt equals 12%, equivalent to the return on the assets of the firm. This relationship is described in M&M Proposition II and is shown below in Exhibit 4-11.

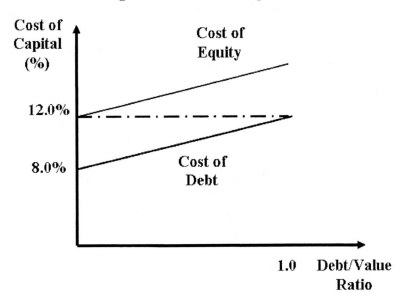

Exhibit 4-11
Modigliani and Miller Proposition II

M&M Proposition II: In perfect capital markets, the cost of equity capital is a linear increasing function of the firm's debt to value ratio.

The M&M Propositions show that a firm's cost of debt and equity are a function of the business risk associated with a firm—the risk associated with the underlying assets of the firm; and the financial risk of the firm—the risk associated with financial leverage—the potential bankruptcy of the firm. For example, the risk and expected returns associated with the assets of an electric utility company, such as Consolidated Edison, should be far lower that the risks and expected returns associated with the assets of a biotechnology firm. As a firm increases its financial leverage and its debt to value ratio approaches 1.0, the firm's financial risk rises and its cost of equity and debt also rises.

M&M Proposition I With Taxes: The value of the firm increases as debt increases because of the interest tax shield.

M&M recognized that the benefit associated with the tax deductibility of debt—a big market imperfection, creates an interest tax shield. *When taxes are included, capital structure definitely matters.* Unfortunately, debt also gives rise to certain risks, such as bankruptcy costs, which risks must be balanced with the benefits of debt financing. Such balancing is described in the section below.

The Static Trade-off Theory:

The main benefit of debt financing is that, since interest payments are tax deductible, debt financing acts as a tax shield and reduces corporate income taxes. In fact, if we consider only the tax deductibility of interest, the cost of capital declines as a firm uses more debt. This would indicate that a firm should use as much debt as possible since adding debt reduces the cost of capital.

However, once we also consider the other primary cost of debt financing—the cost of financial distress—we come to a different conclusion because the cost of financial distress increases as debt financing increases. This also is shown in Exhibit 4-12. From an cost of capital perspective, the costs of financial distress reflect the higher returns required by investors for both debt and equity because of the higher risk brought on by a firm using more debt financing and thereby incurring more fixed financing obligations.

The costs of financial distress come in two forms—direct and indirect. *Direct costs* are the obvious—bankruptcy. When a firm cannot meet its fixed financial obligations, it is usually necessary to declare bankruptcy. Under Chapter 11 bankruptcy, the most typical type of bankruptcy declaration for large companies in the United States, a company's assets are placed under the supervision of a bankruptcy court and the company negotiates with employees, suppliers, creditors, and customers in an attempt to restructure and reorganize its business and financial plans in order to emerge again as a public company.

Bankruptcies have grown in number and size since 2000 with the end of the bubble in Internet, technology, and telecom stocks, the slowdown in the economy, the September 11, 2001 terrorist attacks, and the accounting scandals and litigation associated with economic claims for asbestos and tobacco liabilities. Certainly the number of people put out of work and the billions of dollars lost by investors in such high profile bankruptcies as Enron, World Com, United Airlines, and Adelphia have taught the public much more about bankruptcy.

A company incurs the *indirect costs of financial distress* when it finds that its fixed financing obligations impair business decisions and performance. This normally occurs when a downturn in a company's business—due to a slowdown in sales or an increase in expenses—throws off the company's budgets and financial plans. Since the company must continue to meet its fixed financial obligations, it must cut costs in other areas of the business. This may mean that employees must be let go, capital investment and research and development must be cut, advertising, customer service, and other marketing support areas must be scaled back, and payments to suppliers must be extended.

These actions cause concern among employees, customers, suppliers, and lenders. When word of such actions is spread through the media, the effect is multiplied. Overall, these actions—brought on by the necessity to meet fixed financing obligations—impair the overall value of the business, and increase risk and investor return requirements. Taken together, these are known as indirect costs of financial distress.

Exhibit 4-12
The Static Trade-Off Approach to Capital Structure

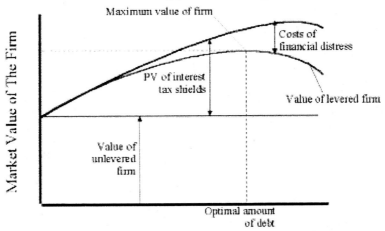

Academicians have described this cost of capital trade-off between the effects of the savings associated with the tax deductibility of interest versus the costs of financial distress as the *Static Trade-off Theory*. This theory prescribes how these two capital cost factors are combined so as to arrive at an optimal capital structure (the optimal mix of debt and equity financing).

The optimal mix of debt and equity is where the overall cost of capital is minimized and the overall value of the firm is maximized. This is shown in Exhibit 4-13. When considered together, Panel A of Exhibit 4-13 demonstrates that the optimal amount of debt for a company (D/A*) is where the incremental savings associated with the tax deductibility of interest are exactly equal to the incremental costs of financial distress. At this mix of debt and equity financing, the overall cost of capital is minimized. Panel B of Exhibit 4-13 then shows that, in terms of financing and the cost of capital, the overall value of the firm is maximized where the cost of capital is minimized.

Exhibit 4-13
The Cost of Capital and Firm Valuation

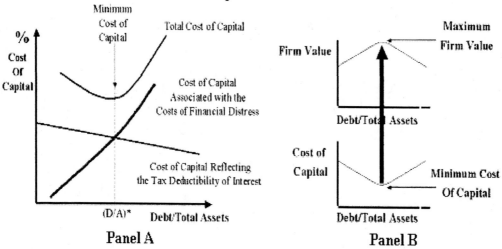

Panel A   **Panel B**

4.3.8 Capital Structures of Major Companies

Exhibit 4-14 shows the capital structure policies for a group of major United States corporations. The companies listed are illustrative of typical financing policies of certain types of companies or industries. Technology firms such as Microsoft and Intel have traditionally used relatively little debt financing. This is also true for drug and biotechnology firms. On the other hand, public utilities, airlines, media, and real estate companies usually employ much more debt financing.

We can abstract from Exhibit 4-14 and arrive at a list of factors that determine how much debt a company uses. These factors include:

- *The tax-shield effect of debt.* Over the years, financial managers have come to realize that the tax deductibility of interest makes the cost of debt financing cheap relative to selling shares of common stock.
- *The relative degree of business risk.* Companies that are in riskier business (e.g., biotechnology, computer software) tend to use less debt financing. Riskier businesses have more volatile sales and earnings and, as a result, are more likely to have difficulty meeting fixed debt obligations and therefore incur financial distress.
- *The nature of a firm's assets.* Firms with tangible assets (such as airlines and hotels) tend to use more debt. On the other hand, companies whose value is more a function of intangible assets such as technology use less debt.
- *Financial slack.* Financial slack is excess cash and unused debt capacity. Financial slack enables the management of a company to move very quickly to take advantage of market opportunities through investments and/or acquisitions. Rapidly growing companies, especially those in high tech businesses, tend to require financial slack.

Exhibit 4-14
Capital Structures Policies of Major Companies

	Debt %	Equity %	# Times Interest Earned	Financial Strength	Sales Growth	Stock Risk 1-Low--5-High
Microsoft	0	100	nmf	A++	12%	4
Intel	3	97	30X	A++	6%	5
Coca-Cola	20	80	21X	A++	6%	2
Merck	22	78	22X	A++	12%	3
WalMart	32	68	10X	A++	12%	3
The Walt Disney Company	35	65	6X	A	5%	4
McDonald's	47	53	7X	A++	5%	3
Consolidated Edison	50	50	4X	A++	2%	1
Hilton Hotels	72	28	2X	C++	2%	4
AMR Corp.	83	17	2X	C	NMF	5
Nextel Communications	86	14	2X	C+	6%	5

Data Source: *Value Line Investment Survey*.

4.3.9 Capital Structure and The Weighted Average Cost of Capital (WACC)

When determining a firm's capital structure, managers try to achieve a financing mix that will minimize the firm's weighted average cost of capital (WACC). By minimizing the WACC, they maximize the firm's value.

To illustrate the calculation of the WACC, let's consider McDonald's. As of 2003, the *Value Line Investment Survey* indicates that McDonald's has $7.5 billion in long-term debt outstanding. The cost of the outstanding long-term debt, which is the interest rate required by investors is 6.0%. At a stock price of $12.50, the market value of McDonald's equity is $37.5 billion.

Let's assume that the cost of equity financing for McDonald's, which represents investors' required return to buy their stock, is 10.0%. Estimating the cost of equity is a topic covered in Chapter 12. Finally, the *Value Line Investment Survey* estimates that the tax rate on McDonald's income is 34%.

The calculation is provided in Exhibit 4-15. There are five steps to calculating the WACC:

Step 1: Compute the market value of debt and equity capital. The total market value of debt and equity capital for McDonald's is $45.0 billion. If McDonald's had preferred stock outstanding, it would also be included in this calculation.

Capital Source	Capitalization Amount
Long-Term Debt	7,500.0
Common Equity	37,500.0
Total	45,000.0

Step 2: *Compute the capitalization ratios.* The capitalization ratios are the proportions of debt and equity capital employed by the firms. Of McDonald's total capital of $45.0 billion, long-term debt represents 0.167 (7,500/45,000) and common equity is 0.833 (37,500/45,000)

Capital Source	Capitalization Ratio
Long-Term Debt	= (7,500/45,000) = 0.167
Common Equity	= (37,500/45,000) = 0.833

Step 3: *Compute the after-tax cost rates.* As previously discussed, interest is tax deductible, which reduces its after-tax cost. In computing the WACC, the cost of debt is calculated on an after-tax basis by multiplying the cost rate times 1 minus the tax rate. For McDonald's, the calculation is 6.0% * (1-.34) = 4.0%. Since the earnings that go to equity holders are already on an after-tax the basis, the equity cost rate, 10% in this case, does not have to be adjusted by the tax rate.

	Tax Adjustment	
After-Tax Debt Cost Rate =	6.0% * (1-.34) =	4.0%
After-Tax Equity Cost Rate =		10.0%

Step 4: *Compute the weighted after-tax cost rates.* The weighted after-tax cost rates are computed as the capitalization ratios times the after-tax cost rates. For McDonald's, these rates are 0.7% (.167 * 4.0%) for debt and 8.3% (.833 * 10.0%) for equity.

Capital Source	Capitalization Ratio		After-Tax Cost Rate		Weighted After-Tax Cost Rate
Long-Term Debt	0.167	X	4.0%	=	0.7%
Common Equity	0.833	X	10.0%	=	8.3%

Step 5: *Sum the weighted after-tax cost rates.* Finally, the WACC is calculated by summing up the individual weighted after-tax cost rates.

Capital Source	Weighted After-Tax Cost Rate
Long-Term Debt	0.7%
Common Equity	8.3%
WACC	9.0%

Exhibit 4-15
McDonald's Weighted Average Cost of Capital

Capital Source	Capitalization Amount	Capitalization Ratio	After-Tax Cost Rate	Weighted After-Tax Cost Rate
Long-Term Debt	7,500.0	0.167	4.0%	0.7%
Common Equity	37,500.0	0.833	10.0%	8.3%
Total	45,000.0			9.0%
After-Tax Debt Cost Rate =	.06*(1-.34) =	4.0%		
After-Tax Equity Cost Rate =		10.0%		

4.3.10 The Dividend Decision and its Relation to Capital Budgeting and Capital Structure

Dividends are cash distributions that are paid by companies to stockholders. As such, dividends represent a return of capital to shareholders. When a company generates excess cash from operations, managers must decide whether to:

- invest it in capital projects or to make acquisitions;
- use the cash to restructure the firm's capital structure (buy back stock or debt, pay off loans, etc.);
- retain it for a rainy day; or
- pay dividends to stockholders.

From a financial perspective, dividend policy is integrated strategically with both capital budgeting decisions and capital structure policy.

The return that investors expect to receive from owning stock comes in two forms: the cash dividend (if one is paid), and an expected increase in share price over time. With respect to the dividend, one of the more persistent findings is that stock prices tend to increase (decrease) when dividend increases (decreases) are announced by firms. This observation is illustrated in Exhibit 4-16, which shows the abnormal stock performance (adjusted for the market return and risk, in percent return) for the days (-5 to +10, where day 0 is the announcement day) around announcements of increases and decreases in dividends. For dividend increases, the cumulative abnormal performance around the announcement date is about +3.0 percent and for dividend decreases, the cumulative return is approximately –7.0 percent.

Exhibit 4-16
Stock Prices and Dividend Changes

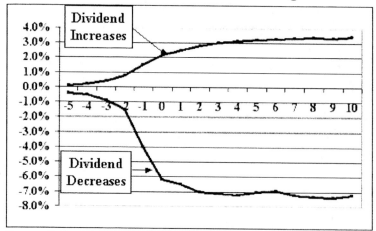

Source: J. Randall Woolridge, Dividend Changes and Stock Returns"

At first glance, this seems to indicate that investors find value in the dividend itself and boost the shares in reaction to a dividend increase, or penalize the shares in response to a dividend cut. It is important to note that on the day the dividend is effectively paid (known as the ex-dividend date), the stock price falls by the amount of the dividend. Therefore the price change at the announcement is not due to the dividend itself, but in the information that the dividend change provides to investors. Specifically, managers will only increase dividends when they expect good performance (i.e., higher earnings) in the future, and they will only cut dividends when they expect bad performance. Hence, investors revalue shares higher in response to the positive information associated with announcements of dividend increases, and lower in response to the negative information related to announcements of dividend decreases. This concept is known as the *information content of dividends*.

Young growing firms have a tremendous need for cash to grow and normally do not pay dividends to shareholders. But at some point, most companies elect to begin paying dividends to stockholders. A good recent example is Microsoft, which did not pay a dividend for its first 20 years of existence. But in the first quarter of 2003, with growth slowing and investors calling on the company to pay out some of its $40 billion in cash, the board declared its first cash dividend. Unless dividend payments must be interrupted by poor business conditions, companies usually prefer to pay a quarterly dividend with annual increases in the amount paid out. In addition, due to very negative market reactions, companies are very reluctant to reduce dividends.

Dividends tend to be much more stable than earnings over time. This is highlighted in Exhibit 4-17, which shows the earnings and dividends (left scale) and the dividend payout ratio (right scale) for the S&P 500 since 1960. The dividend payout ratio is calculated as dividends/earnings, and represents the percentage of annual earnings that are paid out to stockholders as dividends. In addition to demonstrating the greater stability of dividends, Exhibit 4-17 illustrates that dividend payout ratios have declined from the 50-70 percent range to the 30-40 percent range over the years.

One reason for the decline in the dividend payout ratio is the large increase in stock repurchases. In a stock repurchase, a firm buys its own shares in the marketplace with cash. In this way a stock repurchase acts as an alternative to a dividend for distributing cash to stockholders. While a stock repurchase program can be implemented in different ways, the net effect is to reduce the number of shares outstanding as well as shareholders' equity on the balance sheet. Stock repurchases have certain advantages over dividends as a means to distribute cash to shareholders. In particular, given the reluctance to cut or reduce dividends, a stock repurchase may be preferable to a dividend increase since a stock repurchase is normally viewed as one-time event.

SEE BOX ENTITLED 'MICROSOFT PAYS A DIVIDEND' TO SEE HOW THE SOFTWARE GIANT WAS COMPELLED TO PAY A CASH DIVIDEND

Exhibit 4-17
Earnings, Dividends, and Dividend Payout Ratios
For S&P 500 Stocks

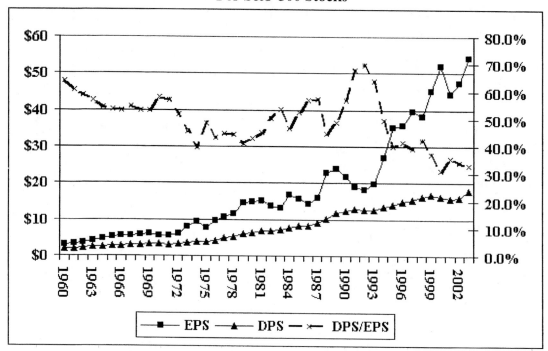

Exhibit 4-18 provides information on the dividend policies of some major, well-known companies in the United States. The dividend yield is the annual dividend divided by the stock price. This indicates the annual investment return from the dividend given the current stock price. Note that the dividend yields range from a low of 0.6% for Microsoft to a high of 5.9% for Consolidated Edison. Generally speaking, the higher the expected dividend growth rate (the far right hand column), the lower the dividend yield. The dividend payout ratios are also provided in Exhibit 4-16, and again Microsoft is the lowest (8.4%) and Consolidated Edison is the highest (76.1%).

Exhibit 4-18 does provide several insights into dividend policy. First, companies that do not pay dividends need cash for other reasons, such as to finance investment growth or to bolster sagging operations (AMR and Nextel). The second observation, which is related to the first, is that the dividend payout ratio is generally inversely related to a firm's investment opportunities. Companies with lots of good investment and growth opportunities (such as technology and growing companies) tend to pay out a small percentage of earnings, while companies with limited investment and growth opportunities (such as public utilities like Consolidated Edison) tend to pay out a high percentage of earnings.

Exhibit 4-18
Dividend Policies of Major Corporations

	Stock Price	2003 Dividend	Dividend Yield	2003 Earnings	Dividend Payout Ratio	Projected Dividend Growth
Microsoft	$ 25	$ 0.08	0.3%	$ 0.95	8.4%	25%
Intel	$ 16	$ 0.10	0.6%	$ 0.60	16.7%	10%
Coca-Cola	$ 40	$ 0.84	2.1%	$ 1.92	43.8%	8%
Merck	$ 60	$ 1.46	2.4%	$ 3.45	42.3%	8%
WalMart	$ 48	$ 0.32	0.7%	$ 2.05	15.6%	12%
The Walt Disney Company	$ 16	$ 0.21	1.3%	$ 0.70	30.0%	0%
McDonald's	$ 13	$ 0.26	2.0%	$ 1.45	17.9%	5%
Consolidated Edison	$ 40	$ 2.36	5.9%	$ 3.10	76.1%	1%
Hilton Hotels	$ 12	$ 0.08	0.7%	$ 0.45	17.8%	0%
AMR Corp.	$ 2	$ -	NMF	$ (7.50)	0%	Nil
Nextel Communications	$ 12	$ -	NMF	$ 0.70	0%	Nil

Data Source: *Value Line Investment Survey*.

To sum up dividend policy, three important issues need to be emphasized:

- A firm's dividend policy is primarily a function of its investment and growth opportunities;
- Announcements of dividend changes are usually accompanied with like changes in stock prices; and
- Since the stock price falls by the amount of the payment on the ex-dividend date, the stock price change at the announcement is not due to the dividend itself, but to the information conveyed by the announcement.

4.4   Summary

This chapter covers strategic financial management, including: working capital management, capital budgeting, and the capital structure decision.

Working capital management revolves around the firm's short-term investment and financial strategy. This primarily relates to the levels of inventories, receivables, and payables, as well as managing the firm's short-term cash and borrowing positions.

Capital budgeting includes decisions relating to investing in property, plant, and equipment (PP&E)and long-term assets—capital expenditures. These assets should be expected to produce positive net present values, or the firm should not invest in them.

Finally, the area of capital structure involves long-term financing decisions. The critical issue is if debt or equity financing should be employed, and in what amounts. This decision directly affects a firm's weighted average cost of capital. In addition, dividend policy, which is integrated strategically with both capital budgeting decisions and capital structure policy, is discussed.

List of Terms

1. Working capital management
2. Capital budgeting
3. Capital structure
4. Short term asset
5. Short term liability
6. Cash management
7. Net working capital
8. Transaction motive
9. Safety motive
10. Speculative motive
11. Marketable securities
12. Operating cycle
13. Cash conversion cycle
14. Days sales in inventory
15. Average collection period
16. Days payables outstanding
17. Carrying costs
18. Shortage costs
19. Cash reserves
20. Maturity hedging
21. Net present value
22. Payback rule
23. Current ratio
24. Cost of capital
25. Discounted payback rule
26. Average Accounting return
27. Internal rate of return
28. Common stock
29. Long term debt
30. Money markets
31. Primary market
32. Secondary market
33. Limited liability
34. Residual claim
35. Preferred stock
36. Bond
37. Basis points
38. Par value
39. Face value
40. Coupon payment
41. Call provision
42. Convertible bond
43. Fallen angel
44. Junk bond
45. High yield bond
46. Static Trade-off Theory
47. Financial leverage
48. Weighted average cost of capital
49. Dividend
50. Dividend yield

Questions

1. What are the two balance sheet categories involved in working capital management?
2. How do you calculate net working capital?
3. List and describe the three motives for a firm to hold cash and marketable securities.
4. Define operating cycle.
5. Define cash conversion cycle. What is the formula for calculating a firm's cash conversion cycle?
6. Should the ideal cash conversion cycle be positive or negative? Why?
7. List three ways a firm can reduce its cash conversion cycle.
8. How do carrying costs and shortage costs change as inventory increases?
9. What is the relationship between carrying costs and shortage costs? What is the optimal level of inventory for a firm looking to minimize its total costs of holding current assets?
10. What are the three main factors of consideration when determining a firm's level of current liabilities?
11. Describe the risk-return trade-off in working capital management.
12. What are the differences between the old and new paradigms of working capital management?
13. Refer to table 4-1. In terms of capital structure, which companies are the most highly leveraged (as a percentage of total assets)? Does this coincide with fixed assets? Why?
14. What is the difference between working capital management and capital budgeting?
15. What are the two general categories of capital expenditure?
16. Do capital expenditures have an effect on short term profitability? On long-term profitability?
17. What role, if any, does the cost of capital play in a capital expenditure decision?
18. List three investment evaluation rules used in the capital budgeting process.
19. Why is net present value the most widely method used in capital budgeting decisions?
20. What is capital structure? What effect can it have on a firm's cost of capital?
21. What are the two most important characteristics of common stock?
22. What are the differences between preferred and common stock?
23. What are residual cash flows?
24. Explain why some companies have a higher debt rating than others. Name one rating that Moodys would give to a company that is not investment grade.
25. Which is the most and least senior, a company's common stock, preferred stock, or long term bonds? In a healthy company, which is the lowest risk?
26. What are the advantage(s) and disadvantage(s) of using bonds to finance a company?
27. Why are convertible bonds considered hybrids of stocks and bonds?
28. When might a company consider issuing convertible bonds over a standard zero coupon bond?
29. When an investment grade bond becomes a fallen angel, what kind of a bond is it?
30. What is the Static Trade-off Theory?
31. What are the direct and indirect costs of financial distress?
32. Name and briefly describe the four factors that a firm considers when it is deciding how much debt to use.
33. The formula for computing a company's weighted average cost of capital is

$$\text{WACC} = R_d(1-T_c)\, \frac{D}{V} + R_e\, \frac{E}{V}$$

Where:

R_d The pre-tax cost of debt, based on the current yield on traded company debt instruments or estimated, taking account of company gearing, size, industry risk, etc.

T_c The marginal corporate tax rate

D, E   D and E are the market values of the business' debt and equity respectively
& V   and V is the sum of D and E. Therefore, D/V and E/V represent the relative weightings of debt and equity employed in the business' operations.

R_e The cost of equity capital

Suppose that a company has 6 million shares outstanding and is trading at $10 per share. The company has $100 million of outstanding debt at a 10% interest rate (assume that 10% is also the current market cost of debt). The expected return on equity is 20%. The company has a marginal corporate tax rate of 40%. What is the company's WACC?

34.   What are the four standard choices facing managers when dealing with excess cash?

35.   Why do dividends affect a company's stock price both at the time of announcement and when they are actually paid out?

36.   Why do some companies choose to distribute excess cash by buying back stock rather than announcing a dividend?

37.   What effects does financial leverage have on earnings per share and return on equity?

Assignment #4-1

1.   The Cash Conversion Cycle:

-          Get the financial statements for WalMart from an online information source (e.g., www.Zacks.com). Fill in the following table for the most recent two years.
-

Revenue		
Cost of revenues		
Inventory		
Total receivables, Net		
Accounts payable		

-
-          With the data you have just obtained, calculate the following:
-

Days sales outstanding		
Days sales in inventory		
Days payables outstanding		

-
-          Determine the company's cash conversion cycle for the two years.
-          Is the cash conversion cycle from year to year positive or negative?
-          Is the change good or bad?
-          What can be done to improve Wal-Mart's cash conversion cycle?
-

Problem Set 1

Company One

Balance Sheet
(in millions)

	2003
Assets	
Cash	60
Accounts Receivable	24
Inventories	7
Current Assets	91
Net Fixed Assets	35
Total Assets	**126**

Liabilities & SH Equity	
Accounts Payable	15
Notes Payable	11
Accrued taxes	20
Current Liabilities	46
Long term debt	33
Common Stock	40
Retained Earnings	7.25
Total Stockholders equity	47.25
Total Liabilities & SH Equity	**126**

Company One

Income Statement
(in millions)

	2003
Net Sales	125
Cost of Goods Sold	(45)
Gross Profit	80
SGA expenses	(12)
Interest expense	(8)
Earnings before taxes	60
Income taxes	(15)
Earnings after taxes	**45**

Cost of debt	8%
Cost of equity	10%
Value of common stock	$300 million

Questions:

2. What is the company's total debt for 2003?
3. What is the company's tax rate?
4. Calculate the company's weighted average cost of capital.

Problem Set 2

Company Two

Balance Sheet

	2003
Assets	
Cash	10,360
Accounts Receivable	35,300
Inventories	60,400
Office/Store supplies	1,696
Current Assets	107,756
Fixed Assets (land, equip)	29,060
Intangible Assets	500
Total Assets	**137,316**

Liabilities & SH Equity	
Notes Payable	15,000
Accounts Payable	25,683
Salaries Payable	2,000
Total Current Liabilities	42,683
Long term Liabilities	17800
Total Liabilities	60,483
Common Stock	50,000
Additional paid in capital	5,000
Retained Earnings	21,833
Total Stockholders equity	76,833
Total Liabilities & SH Equity	**137,316**

Company Two

Income Statement

	2003
Net Sales	289,656
Cost of Goods Sold	(181,260)
Gross Margin	108,396
Selling Expenses	(54,780)
Gen & Admin Expenses	(34,504)
Income from Operations	19,112
Interest income	1,400
Interest expense	(2,631)
Excess of other	(1,231)
Income before income tax	17,881
Income taxes	(3,381)
Net Income	**14,500**

Questions

1. Calculate the company's days sales outstanding or average collection period.
2. Calculate inventory turnover.
3. Determine days sales in inventory.
4. What is the company's days payables outstanding?
5. Calculate the company's cash conversion cycle.
6. Is it a good number? Why?
7. How can it be improved?

The Iridium Project

The concept for the Iridium system was proposed by Motorola engineers in 1987. They envision a constellation of low orbiting satellites that will enable users of Iridium phones to make phone calls anywhere, anytime. Making this vision become reality, however, required 10 years of research and development. In 1991, Motorola incorporates Iridium as a separate company to develop and deploy the network.

In 1992, Iridium signed a US$3.37 billion contract with Motorola for system development, construction, and delivery. Motorola became the prime contractor supplying satellites, gateways, and communication products for the Iridium system. A year later, Iridium completed its first round of financing, securing US$800 million in equity. In 1994, the company successfully secured yet a second round of equity financing, bringing the total raised capital to US$1.6 billion.

The first Iridium satellite flight bus subsystem was delivered by Lockheed Martin to Motorola Satellite Communication facilities in Chandler, Arizona in 1995. In 1996, US$315 million in additional investor funding was secured, bringing the total project support to US$1.9 billion. The company then selected Chase and BZW banks as arrangers of senior credit facilities, and to help complete a US$750 million bank credit facility. In addition to debt financing, Iridium offered a total of US$240 million in stock through an initial public offering - Iridium World Communications Ltd. (NASDAQ: IRID) was established. In 1998, an additional US$350 million in high yield bonds is secured.

Since the establishment of Iridium, Motorola has not been able to get the company to make a single cent of profit. On top of that, analysts forecast that the company will never make a profit. Today, time is running out for Iridium Systems LLC. Iridium filed for Chapter 11 protection in August 1999, after amassing US$3 billion in debt and only getting about 55,000 subscribers. The company's system never lived up to promises of global anywhere wireless phones and paging. Its large, clumsy phones that cost US$3,500 each never really appealed to consumers and debts mounted.

New York merchant bank Castle Harlan Inc., together with other potential suitors, withdrew its $50 million bid to acquire assets of the company, expressing doubt that Iridium could generate revenue. In a statement, Castle Harlan said "...our due diligence and marketing studies were unable to confirm that Iridium would be able to generate even low levels of revenue with a high degree of certainty." Motorola plans to deactivate the system if it does present a viable proposal. Motorola has been maintaining Iridium satellites at a cost of millions a month, offering limited phone services.

On July 31st, 2000, Motorola cleared the last hurdle to allow it to pull down satellites orbiting the earth for the bankrupt Iridium. Following a hearing in the US bankruptcy court in New York, the company said Iridium had withdrawn its motion seeking to prevent Motorola from bringing down the satellites. However, last night Motorola would keep the satellites running until August 9 to allow for any possible last-minute rescue bids. Barring a death's-door white knight suitor to buy Iridium, Motorola is likely to begin lowering the US$ 5 billion venture's satellites out of orbit in two weeks to let them burn up in the earth's atmosphere.

What went wrong? How could a company as savvy as Motorola Inc. have made such a bad capital investment?

First of all, there was no sustainable need for the service and the cost was too prohibitive. Satellites are not fibre-optics. They start to fall out of the sky the minute they are launched, especially if they are on low-Earth orbit. So while fibre-optics will stay in the ground for 20 years, a US$9 billion investment in satellites is going to last just six years -- at US$1.5 billion per year. If the company had only 100,000 subscribers, their cost will be US$15,000 per year, per subscriber. Even if there were one million subscribers, the cost per subscriber would be US$1,500 per year. Assuming that a customer uses his/her phone for just 25 days per year when they were not within cellular serving areas, the cost comes out to US$60 per day -- and that's what it costs, not what the company would charge.

Motorola's experience with Iridium is a perfect example of why financial managers should carefully analyze the expected cash flows from a proposed capital investment before accepting the investment. Motorola's misjudgment of the wireless phone market and the cash flows it expects to generate from Iridium resulted in a multi-billion failure.

Sources:

Securities Data Publishing, Mergers and Acquisitions Report, August 2000, "Iridium Is in Peril After Buyer Flees"
By Ricado Roberts

Financial Times (London), August 1, 2000, "Motorola Set to Bring Down Bankrupt Iridium's Satellites"
By Christopher Bowe

Canadian Business and Current Affairs, May 5, 2000, "Iridium's Untimely Demise: A Classic Case of Misreading the Market"
By Anderson, Howard

Information on company history from Iridium corporate website: http://www.iridium.com

Microsoft Decides to Pay a Cash Dividend

On January 16, 2003, the Board of Directors of Microsoft declared the company's first cash dividend of eight cents per share, payable March 7. Microsoft Chief Financial Officer John Connors said Microsoft's board has regularly considered paying a dividend but decided to go ahead for two reasons: Microsoft's continuing "financial strength" and the resolution of some outstanding legal issues.

Historically, stock dividends have been heresy to technology firms like Microsoft. Technology companies need capital to finance growth and to make the investments required to remain competitive. Paying dividends to stockholders was viewed as a poor use of capital, and an indication that a firm had become old and stodgy, instead of nimble and fast-growing. Microsoft Chief Executive Steve Ballmer "historically has said no way" to the idea of a dividend, and the company has opted to reinvest its cash back into its business, make strategic investment in other companies, and buy back its own stock to offset the share dilution caused by its huge employee stock-option program. In its last fiscal year, Microsoft spent just over $6 billion on stock buybacks.

In declaring its first dividend, Microsoft is seen as bowing to mounting pressure to return some of its huge cash hoard to investors. With more than $43B in cash, Microsoft has more cash on its balance sheet than any other U.S. corporation. And Microsoft is a "cash machine" that is "maturing," says Steve Milunovich, Merrill Lynch's top technology strategist. Money at Microsoft builds up so fast because profit from the company's core, Windows and Office products far surpasses the costs needed to create and manufacture new versions of the software. These days, Microsoft is more or less "stamping out software CDs at two cents a disc," Mr. Milunovich says. The interest and dividends earned on Microsoft's cash pile now represent about 19% of operating income. Richard Sherlund, the Goldman software analyst, estimates that Microsoft generates about $1 billion in free cash flow a month. As such, most analysts believe that it was time for tech firms like Microsoft to consider dividends. After all, a few Silicon Valley companies have paid dividends for years: Hewlett-Packard Co. began issuing payouts in the 1960s and Intel Corp. began paying them in 1992.

But the Microsoft dividend has been called "token" by some analysts. With Microsoft's 5.44 million shares outstanding, the initial payout should be about $850 million. Yet the dividend's yield works out to only 0.29%, far below the 1.71% average yield on the companies in the S&P 500 stock index. John Conners, the CFO, said the dividend will allow more institutional investors, especially fund managers who can only invest in stocks that pay dividends, to buy Microsoft shares.

The new dividend will provide a boost in income for the top Microsoft executives. Chairman Bill Gates, who holds 621.7 million shares of Microsoft (11.6% of the company), will get an annual dividend check of $99.48 million. CEO Steve Ballmer, who holds 235.5 million shares, will get dividends of $37.68 million.

Some analysts maintain that paying a dividend could be an efficient use of excess capital. There are few investments Microsoft can make that will match the huge profit margins of its core desktop-software business, which generated all the cash in the first place. "It's hard to replicate 90% gross margins," says Tom Rath, a portfolio manager and analyst at Safeco Asset Management in Seattle. "That's why returning the money to shareholders makes sense." Furthermore, there are questions about the ability of the company to effectively invest the cash. The company likely doesn't have the management breadth to oversee many more new businesses, now that it is already in everything from video games to television. And the recent track record with big investments isn't so great, either. This is evidenced by the huge charges to earnings to write down the value of poorly performing investments in telecommunications, cable and Internet stocks, in the recent past.

The bottom line is this: "Does Microsoft really need $43 billion in cash, especially when that figure grows by $1B per month?" The answer is 'No,' and that's why the dividend made sense.

Rebecca Buckman, "Awash in Cash, Declares Its First Dividend," *Wall Street Journal*. (Jan 17, 2003) p. A.1

Rebecca Buckman, "A Cash-Rich Microsoft Faces Shareholder Call for Dividend," *Wall Street Journal*. (Jan 2, 2002) p. A.1

How does Your Finance Department Stack Up?

There are several different ways to assess a finance department. But how can one finance department be measured against the other. CFO.com has the answer with ten metrics that they use to identify a poor finance department.

1. Slow Closes

A properly skilled staff should turn out a complete financial statement within ten days of the quarter's end. Why should a leisurely close be cause for alarm? It may mean that policies need tweaking to make the unit more efficient.

2. Outrageous Audit Fees

There are two perspectives on this issue. One, audit fees can skyrocket as a growing company becomes more complex, and two, high fees, including those for non-audit services, can be traced to an underperforming finance department that requires an abnormal amount of "cleanup." CFO's should keep tabs on problems like slow shipments, bloated inventories and out of control receivables. All of these things can be very costly for an auditor to catch and correct.

3. High DSO

Days sales outstanding is the average time that it takes a company to collect payments from its customers. When DSO begins to creep up, a lapse in the accounts receivables process is usually to blame. DSO's will fluctuate, but, when the number moves upward month after month, there is cause for alarm.

4. Multiple Payments

Sometimes a company will pay a supplier more than once for the same order. In an outwardly amusing way, this is good for credit, but bad for cash flow. The problem usually does not lie with the accounts-payables system. Instead, it often originates in operations. Increasingly complex procurement systems have added another layer of difficulty to the payment process. Even if it is an operations problem, the buck stops with the finance department!

5. Earnings Restatements

According to the U.S. General Accounting Office, during the past five years 10 percent of all publicly traded companies restated their earnings because of accounting irregularities. About 250 companies, the GAO estimates, will restate by the end of this year, far more than the 92 companies that restated in 1997. A restatement usually does not mean fraud, it is usually the result of common accounting errors and oversights.

Most errors are caught internally, but when the errors slip through the cracks, the accounting and financial functions are having problems with their accounting judgments.

6. Manual Entries

Most Fortune 500 companies use spreadsheets to enter data rather than a firm wide accounting system that is linked together. These stand-alone spreadsheets "violate the audit trail." More opportunities exist for mistakes or wrongdoing. In addition, the widespread use of spreadsheets renders a firm's financial-database history useless.

7. Lack of Transparency

Internally, the department must respond to questions with timely and logical answers. Externally, the finance department should meet all disclosure requirements and meet them quickly. Otherwise red flags could be raised about the quality of the numbers contained in the financial statements.

8. Dubious Structure

The internal audit team should not be reporting to the CFO because of conflict of interest issues. Another crack in the structural foundation is improper division of duties. For example, internal audit rules usually require that the employee that receives checks doesn't post them, and that the employee who prepares checks doesn't sign them.

9. Overly Cozy With Sales

This can create a clear revenue recognition problem. The finance department is responsible for educating the sales force about when to book revenue. The consequences of aggressive revenue recognition can be dire and ultimately land a company in bankruptcy.

10. Staff Turnover

Where there's churn, there's trouble. When employees leave a finance department, it is frequently because of poor structure, which indicates that a finance department is not working at maximum efficiency.

Maria Leone, "Your Finance Department Is Second-Rate," *CFO Magazine*, February 2003

CHAPTER 5

FINANCIAL STATEMENTS, ANALYSIS, AND FINANCIAL ETHICS

This chapter gives an overview of financial accounting and the three fundamental financial statements—the balance sheet, the income statement, and the statement of cash flows. It covers the purpose and uses of accounting and financial statements, as well as a detailed description of the different items found in financial statements, generally accepted accounting principles (GAAP), and the role of the SEC. The financial statements of Target Corporation are used for illustrative purposes.

The objectives of the chapter include:

- To give an overview of financial accounting and financial statements;
- To provide an understanding of basic accounting conventions and how they affect financial statements;
- To explain the three basic financial statements and how they are interrelated;
- To give framework for performing a financial statement analysis to gauge the health and performance of a business;
- To review the financial statements of Target Corporation and an understanding of how to compute financial ratios and what they mean; and
- To provide a discussion of aggressive accounting practices and their effects on valuation.

5.1   Financial Accounting

Financial accounting is the language of numbers and it is used by a company to communicate its financial performance to the public. Investors, creditors, and other parties that are interested in a company analyze public accounting information to make investment and credit decisions. Accounting is used throughout the world as the universal measurement of business performance.

***Financial accounting** conveys the financial performance of a company to investors, creditors and the public*

Accounting information is used internally by a firm's management and by the board of directors to establish performance goals and to monitor business units. Current and prospective investors and creditors also use accounting information to assess the performance and future prospects of a firm. In the United States, accounting standards have been developed so that transactions are recorded in a similar manner for all public businesses—in accordance with generally acceptable accounting principles (GAAP). These standards establish comparability and universality of financial reporting.

Example of Financial Statement Comparability:

Boeing and McDonald's make totally different products for a diverse customer base. However, they both prepare periodic financial statements and can be compared based on a number of different accounting measures and ratios. The financial statements that each submits are set up in the same way and report the same measurements (revenues, net income, cash, retained earnings, etc).

The objective of financial statements is to convey the economic impact of completed transactions and other events on the financial health of an organization. Four accounting statements provide readers with information that may be used to measure the value and performance of a firm.

1. The *balance sheet* reports the financial position of a company at a specific point in time. It distinguishes the amount of assets, liabilities, and equity on the date of the financial statement.
2. The *income statement* reports the revenues, expenses, and net income (or loss) for the company over a specific period of time.
3. The *statement of cash flows* reports the sources (inflows) and uses (outflows) of cash for the firm over a specific period of time.
4. The *statement of retained earnings* reports the changes in a company's accumulated earnings for the period.

All publicly traded companies are required to prepare periodic financial statements so that information is disclosed regularly to investors. Financial statements are examined and *audited* by independent organizations (usually one of the big public accounting firms) to lend credibility to the information that is disclosed.

5.1.1   The World According to GAAP

Generally accepted accounting principles (GAAP) are broad guidelines, conventions, rules, and procedures of accounting that are gathered from various financial accounting standards and authoritative organizations (The SEC, Accounting Principles Board, etc.). Accounting standards are intended to make accounting information provided in financial statements relevant to the types of decisions users must make. The goal of GAAP is to make accounting information relevant, reliable, comparable, and consistent over multiple periods of time and across different industries.

5.1.2   Financial Reporting Requirements of Publicly Traded Companies

In an attempt to standardize information disclosure to investors, the Securities Exchange Commission requires that all publicly traded companies file periodic financial reports covering accounting measurements and various aspects of the company's business. The SEC also requires companies to submit many different reports, including registration of public offerings, reports relating to proxy issues, and quarterly and annual financial statements.

For investors, financial statements are by far the most popular SEC filings. The SEC requires firms to submit two major types of financial reports, a 10-K and a 10-Q. The 10-K is the report that is required to be filed **annually**, and includes all of the financial information about the firm, a discussion by the management of the company, and a summary of operations.

The 10-Q report is a report that is filed **quarterly**, which contains much of the same type of information disclosed in the annual report. Quarterly reports are abbreviated as compared to annual reports, but serve the purpose of reporting interim data to investors and creditors between annual reports. Companies are required to distribute an annual report to investors but are not required to distribute quarterly reports or quarterly financial statements to investors.

5.2 The Annual Report

The Annual Report is the fundamental document of communication between management of a corporation and its shareholders. The 10-K form must be filed with the SEC within 90 days of a company's fiscal year-end. Most annual reports are broken down into three sections:

- *The Letter to Shareholders*—Gives a broad overview of the company's business and financial performance.
- *The Business Review*—Summarizes the company's recent developments, trends, and business objectives.

- *The Financial Review*—Presents a company's business performance in financial terms, and includes audited financial statements, management discussion and analysis, and supplementary information.

When a company files its 10-K with the SEC, the reporting requirements are much more specific. The SEC requires all forms to be standardized and includes all of the *Components of an Annual Report*. All documents filed electronically with the SEC are available online through the *EDGAR database* at www.sec.gov.

Definitions Relating to Annual Reports:

Assets are economic resources owned by a firm that are measurable and are likely to produce future economic benefits. Assets include all goods and property owned, and uncollected amounts due to the company. Assets are separated into *current* and *long-term* classifications based on their intended use and expected useful life and are grouped in this manner on the balance sheet. For example, cash is always a current asset and is usually the first amount reported on a balance sheet. However, investments may be classified as short-term—if they are expected to be sold during the year, or long-term—if they are expected to be held for longer than one year.

Liabilities are probable future economic obligations of a firm. Liabilities include all debts of the firm and amounts payable by the firm to employees, suppliers, and creditors. Liabilities also are categorized as either current or long-term based on when payment is expected to be made on the liability.

Equity is a measure of ownership or the residual interest in the assets of a business entity. Equity is equal to assets minus liabilities.

Cash accounting records all cash payments and receipts for a specific time period at the time when cash actually flows into and out of the firm. This type of accounting is often used by small businesses to monitor cash flows. Cash accounting is not GAAP compliant in that it does not accurately represent the total economic changes of a firm during an accounting period.

Accrual accounting requires that an event that alters the economic status of a firm, as represented by its financial statements, be recorded in the period in which the event occurred rather than when the physical cash changes hands. Accrual accounting is what all public companies submitting financial statements adhere to and is the only acceptable accounting method under GAAP.

Example of Accrual versus Cash Accounting:

Suppose that you are examining the books of a small grocery store to compare the difference between cash and accrual accounting. The store has five full-time employees who are paid on every other Friday. The last day of the annual fiscal year is the Wednesday before payday for the grocery store. The store has accumulated salary expenses of $4800 for the week and a half that has not yet been paid. If the grocery store operates under a cash accounting basis, the $4800 of wages will not be recorded until next year. This understates expenses for the preceding year and will overstate expenses for the forthcoming year. Under the accrual accounting method, the $4800 would be recognized in the appropriate period when the wages were earned regardless of when the physical cash changes hands.

5.3 The Makeup of Financial Statements

5.3.1 The Balance Sheet

The *balance sheet* represents the financial picture of a company as it stood at a particular time, usually the last day of the fiscal year of the company. The balance sheet is divided into two areas: the top or left side lists all of the company's assets; the bottom or the right side lists all liabilities of the company and its shareholder's equity. The balance sheet identity is:

$$\textbf{\textit{Assets} = \textit{Liabilities} + \textit{Equity}} \qquad \textbf{\textit{(Eq. 5-1)}}$$

Definitions Relating to the Balance Sheet:

Current assets include cash and other assets that are expected to be realized in cash or be sold or consumed during the normal operating cycle of the business or within one year from the balance sheet date, whichever is longer. Current assets are considered working capital assets because they are liquid (meaning they can and will be converted into cash or consumed in the business in the near future). Examples of current assets include: cash, short-term investments, inventory, accounts receivable, and prepaid expenses (only the portion that will be realized within the normal operating cycle).

Long-term assets are assets that are not expected to be completely used up in a single operating cycle and assets that management plans to retain for more than one year from the balance sheet date. Examples of long-term assets include: long-term investments, property, plant and equipment (PP&E), intangible assets, goodwill, other assets, and deferred charges.

Current liabilities are obligations of a firm that are expected to be liquidated using current assets or refinanced by other short-term liabilities within one year of the balance sheet date or within the normal operating cycle of the firm. Examples of current liabilities include: accounts payable, short-term payables, current maturity of long-term debt, unearned revenue, accrued expenses, and current portion of deferred income taxes.

Long-term liabilities are obligations that do not require the use of current assets for payment during the next operating cycle or within the next reporting year. All liabilities that are not classified as current liabilities are reported as long-term liabilities. Examples of long-term liabilities include: long-term debt, lease agreements, warranty obligations, and other liabilities and commitments.

Equity is the owners' residual interest in the firm and is equal to assets minus liabilities. Examples of measures for equity include: common stock, paid in capital in excess of par, other classes of stock, treasury stock, and retained earnings.

Off-balance sheet activities are accounts and financial instruments that are not recorded on the balance sheet. GAAP accounting at this time does not require firms to disclose the realizable value of derivative contracts that the firm has entered. Effectively, companies are able to hide some of the more risky transactions from investors. Besides derivative contracts, other financing transactions are not required to appear on financial statements. Off-balance sheet financing includes joint ventures, R&D partnerships, and capital equipment leases. None of these items are required to appear on the balance sheet of the firms but all can generate royalties and expenses to participating companies. Examples of off balance sheet activities include: options, futures, forward contracts, swaps, and similar derivative instruments, joint ventures, R&D partnerships, and equipment leasing.

Target Corporation

Using the figures for 1/31/2005, answer the following questions:

1. What are the three primary assets for TGT?
2. Did inventories grow or decline over the past year? Why?
3. What might be included in Other current assets
4. What is Net Property & Equipment "net" of?
5. What is the largest current liability? What does this represent?
6. Does Target use more debt or equity financing?
7. Total Shareholders' equity increased in 2005. Why?

Exhibit 5-1
Target Corporation
Annual Balance Sheet

(in millions of USD)	As of January 31,		
	2003	2004	2005
Assets			
Cash & Cash Equivalents	758	716	2,245
Accounts & Notes Receivable	5,565	5,776	5,069
Inventories	4,760	5,343	5,384
Other Current Assets	852	1,093	1,224
Total Current Assets	11,935	12,928	13,922
Fixed Assets, Net	15,307	16,969	17,066
Other assets	1,361	1,495	1,305
Total Assets	28,603	31,392	32,293
Liabilities			
Accounts Payable	6,548	7,448	7,716
Short-Term Debt	975	866	504
Total Current Liabilities	7,523	8,314	8,220
Long-Term Debt	10,186	10,217	9,034
Other Long-Term Liabilities	1,451	1,796	2,010
Total Liabilities	19,160	20,327	19,264
Stockholders' Equity			
Common Stock	76	76	74
Capital Surplus	1,260	1,344	1,807
Retained Earnings	8,107	9,645	11,148
Total Stockholders' Equity	9,443	11,065	13,029
Total Liabilities + Equity	28,603	31,392	32,293

5.3.2 The Income Statement

The *income statement* presents all revenues, gains, expenses, and losses recognized by a firm for a specific time period, usually one year. The income statement links a company's beginning and ending balance sheets for a given accounting period. It also explains changes in shareholder equity resulting from business operations during a period.

The *Revenue Principle* requires the recognition of revenues in accordance with accrual basis accounting principles. Revenues are defined as cash or other asset inflows, settlements of liabilities, or a combination of the two. Completed transactions for sales of goods and services on credit are therefore recognized in the period in which the service occurs and not when the actual cash changes hands.

The *Matching Principle* is the elementary accounting concept that states all expenses incurred in earning the revenue recognized during an accounting period should be recognized during the same period.

Definitions Relating to the Income Statement:

Revenues [Sales] represent inflows of assets or settlements of liabilities during a particular accounting period.

Expenses represent outflows of assets or incurrence of liabilities during a particular accounting period.

Cost of goods sold measures the direct cost of goods sold or the cost of services provided in generating the recorded revenues for the period.

Gross margin is the difference between revenues and cost of goods sold during a particular accounting period.

Selling expenses are expenses incurred by the company in its efforts of generating revenue. It includes marketing costs, costs of delivering goods, and overhead associated with the selling process.

General & administrative expenses are expenses related to personnel, accounting, and finance activities, the operating costs of organization overhead, and associated items.

Other operating expenses are the general classification for all other expenses incurred during normal business operations that are not included in the above classifications. Examples of other expenses include research and development, depreciation, and amortization.

Non-operating section includes income and expense items that are routine but not components of a company's normal ongoing business operations. Examples include interest income and expense, dividend income, and other non-operations revenues and expenses.

Income tax expense represents the portion of federal and state taxes applicable to the income recognized during the reported accounting period.

Net income is the bottom line of operations for the reported accounting period. It represents the excess of revenues over all related expenses. Although earnings calculations are fairly standardized, management may make choices regarding accounting measurements that can affect the quality of reported earnings. Generally, earnings are considered higher quality when management chooses accounting measurements that delay the recognition of revenues, but does not delay the recognition of expenses.

Earning per share is the computation of net income after taxes divided by the amount of shares of outstanding common stock. EPS helps investors make relative profit performance comparisons among companies of different size and with different numbers of shares outstanding.

Earnings per share dilution reflects the potential dilution that could occur if option, securities or other contracts that require the company to issue additional common stock were exercised or converted into common shares that would then participate in the earnings of the firm. This calculation is adjusted to take into effect the dilution associated with convertible securities, warrants, and stock options.

Target Corporation

The income statement of TGT is provided in Exhibit 5-2. Use the figures for 1/31/2005 to answer the following questions:

1. What's growing faster for Target – sales or cost of goods?
2. What is Target's gross profit margin as of 1/31/2005? Did it increase or decrease from the previous year?
3. Have S&A and D&A expenses increased or decreased in recent years? What might explain this?
4. Between 1/31/2004 and 1/31/2005, which grew faster—sales or net income? Why?
5. Between 1/31/2004 and 1/31/2005, which grew faster—net income or diluted net EPS? Why?

Exhibit 5-2
Target Corporation
Income Statement

(in millions of USD)	2003	2004	2005
Sales	43,917	48,163	46,839
Cost of Goods Sold	29,260	31,790	31,445
Gross Profit	**14,657**	**16,373**	**15,394**
SG&A	10,181	11,534	10,534
Other Operating Expenses	1,212	1,320	1,259
Earning Before Interest & Taxes	**3,264**	**3,519**	**3,601**
Interest Expense	588	559	570
Earning Before Taxes	**2,676**	**2,960**	**3,031**
Income Tax Expense	1,022	1,119	1,146
Income from Continuing Operations	**1,654**	**1,841**	**1,885**
Gain from Sale of Discontinued Operations	-	-	1,313
Net Income	**1,654**	**1,841**	**3,198**
Earnings Per Share Figures			
Weighted Average Shares- Basic	908.00	911.00	903.80
Weighted Average Shares- Diluted	914.30	919.20	912.10
Basic EPS (Continuing Operations)	1.82	2.02	2.09
Diluted EPS (Continuing Operations)	1.81	2.00	2.07
Stock Price (end of fiscal yr.)	28.21	37.90	50.77

5.3.3   The Statement of Cash Flows

The *Statement of Cash Flows* provides information on the changes in the cash position of a company over the specific accounting period. The statement of cash flows serves as a bridge between accrual accounting and cash accounting by breaking down the inflows and disbursements of every cash transaction so investors know exactly the sources and uses of every dollar in the organization.

Most stock valuation models that are used by Wall Street stock analysts deal with cash flows as opposed to net income (accounting earnings), and the statement of cash flows is extremely important to financial analysts. The statement of cash flows is used to assess a firm's ability to meet current and long-term obligations, to gauge the need for external financing, to value the company's stock, to assess the company's bankruptcy risk, and to show the ability of the firm to generate operating cash flows (as opposed to generating accounting profits).

The statement requires firms to allocate the transactions affecting cash and cash equivalents into one of three categories: operating, investing, and financing activities. The statement of cash flows separates a company's cash account into the following classifications of sources and uses:

Definitions Relating to the Statement of Cash Flows:

<u>*Operating activities*</u> relate to the normal ongoing business of the company required to generate cash from operations. This includes sales, collection of accounts receivables, and cash payments to suppliers, taxes, and interest transactions. Interest payments are classified as operating cash flows even though the principal borrowing and repayment are classified as financing activities. When all operating activities have been reconciled with net income, the bottom line is cash flows from operations. This number assesses the cash flow generation ability of normal operations of the company. Examples of operating activities include: payments from customers, payments to suppliers, interest, dividends received, income taxes, unearned revenues, settlements of lawsuits, and any other cash transaction related to the income-producing activities of a company.

Investing activities relate primarily to the changes in the company's non-current assets. This includes cash flows associated with investing in and disposing of plant assets, certain securities, making and collecting loans, and other activities. The fundamental distinction between operating cash flows and investing cash flows is the anticipated benefits from each. Operating cash flows are expected to result in immediate benefits and revenue generation while investing cash flows are expected to yield benefits over multiple time periods. Examples of investing activities include: cash purchases and sales of plant and long-term assets, securities not classified as cash equivalents (securities available for sale), real estate, loans made to other parties, and the repayment of loan proceeds.

Financing activities relate to changes in borrowing and owners' equity. Payment of dividends is also classified as a financing activity. Both short and long-term borrowings appear as financing activities even though short-term borrowing is considered working capital. Examples of financing activities include: proceeds and payments from stock issuance, bond issuance and redemption, loans from financial institutions, capital leases, and dividend payments to shareholders.

The statement of cash flows is very useful in telling us if a company is doing well or poorly. We begin by looking at the cash flows from investment activities to see if the company is using cash or generating it from its investments. While we expect a positive cash flow from operating activities, we also expect a healthy company to invest continually in additional plant, equipment, and other fixed assets to replace those that have depreciated. We expect cash flows from investing activities to be generally negative. Watch out for companies that have high positive cash flows from investing activities. They might be shrinking instead of expanding because they are selling off portions of their businesses.

Target Corporation

Using the figures for 1/31/2005, answer the following questions:

1. What are the two largest sources and uses of cash from operating activities? Explain what each represents.
2. Are investing activities a source or use of cash for TGT?
3. Did the cash flow from operating activities cover the cash flow from investing activities? What does this mean?
4. Were cash flows from financing activities a source or use of cash for TGT?
5. Explain the change in TGT's cash balance between 2004 and 2005 using the statement of cash flow.

Exhibit 5-3
Target Corporation
Statement of Cash Flows

(in millions of USD)	2003	2004	2005
Operating Activities			
Net Income (from continuing operation	1,654	1,841	3,198
Depreciation and Amortization	1,212	1,320	1,259
Adjustment to Net Income	934	846	(437)
Changes in A/R	(2,194)	(744)	(209)
Changes in Inventories	(311)	(583)	(853)
Changes in Curr. Liabilities	424	912	1,064
Change in Other Op. Activities	(129)	(432)	(827)
Cash Flow from Operations	1,590	3,160	3,195
Investing Activities			
Capital Expenditures for PPE	(3,221)	(3,004)	(3,068)
Other Investing Activities	32	85	4,247
Cash Flow from Investing	(3,189)	(2,919)	1,179
Financing Activities			
Dividends	(218)	(237)	(272)
Sale (Purchase) of Stock	(14)	0	(1,144)
Net Borrowings	2,082	(72)	(1,477)
Other Financing Activities	8	26	56
Cash Flow from Financing	1,858	(283)	(2,837)
Beginning Cash Balance	499	758	716
Net Change in Cash	259	(42)	1,537
Exchanges Rate Adjustment			(8)
Ending Cash Balance	758	716	2,245

5.3.4 The Relationships Among Financial Statements

To understand financial accounting, it is essential to know the relationships among the three primary financial statements. These relationships are summarized in Exhibit 5-4.

You can follow the arrows to see how a transaction affects the income statement, balance sheet, and statement of cash flows. For example, a sale on credit is recorded on the income statement, and that amount goes to the balance sheet as an account receivable, and the same amount goes to the statement of cash flow as a use of cash (because while a sale has been recorded, no cash has been received). At the same time, the direct costs (purchases, direct expenses, etc.) of producing the product or service are recorded as a cost of goods sold, with the same amount coming out of inventories (specifically, finished goods inventory) on the balance sheet and inventory requirements on the statement of cash flow.

Exhibit 5-4
The Relationship Between Financial Statements

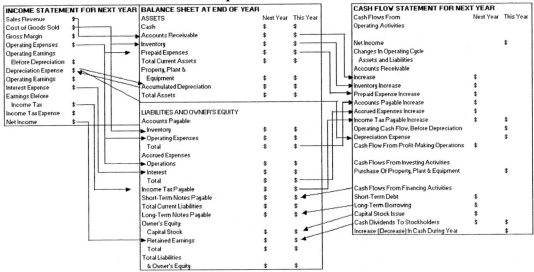

Source: John A. Tracey, *How to Read a Financial Report* (1999).

5.4   Common Size Financial Statements

Common size financial statements are regularly used to analyze a company's year-to-year financial performance or to make comparisons between two different companies. In a common size statement, balance sheet and income statement items are computed as percentages. In a common size balance sheet, all items are computed as a percent of total assets. In a common size income statement, all items are expressed as a percent of sales.

Target Corporation

The common size balance sheet and income statement for TGT are provided in Exhibits 5-5 and 5-6 for the year ending 1/31/2054. Use these figures to answer the following questions:

1. What percent of total assets is made of current assets?
2. Which asset item increased the most as a percent of total assets in 2004?
3. As indicated by the percent of total assets, has TGT made any significant changes in its financing (debt and equity) of total assets in the last three years?
4. Provide the 2004 figure as well as an explanation of the percent of sales represented by net income.
5. The operating margin is operating profit as a percent of sales. Provide an explanation of its meaning and its trend over the past three years.

Exhibit 5-5
Target Corporation
Common Size Balance Sheet

(in millions of USD)	As of January 31,		
	2003	2004	2005
Assets			
Cash & Cash Equivalents	2.7%	2.3%	7.0%
Accounts & Notes Receivable	19.5%	18.4%	15.7%
Inventories	16.6%	17.0%	16.7%
Other Current Assets	3.0%	3.5%	3.8%
Total Current Assets	41.7%	41.2%	43.1%
Fixed Assets, Net	53.5%	54.1%	52.8%
Other assets	4.8%	4.8%	4.0%
Total Assets	100.0%	100.0%	100.0%
Liabilities			
Accounts Payable	22.9%	23.7%	23.9%
Short-Term Debt	3.4%	2.8%	1.6%
Total Current Liabilities	26.3%	26.5%	25.5%
Long-Term Debt	35.6%	32.5%	28.0%
Other Long-Term Liabilities	5.1%	5.7%	6.2%
Total Liabilities	67.0%	64.8%	59.7%
Stockholders' Equity			
Common Stock	0.3%	0.2%	0.2%
Capital Surplus	4.4%	4.3%	5.6%
Retained Earnings	28.3%	30.7%	34.5%
Total Stockholders' Equity	33.0%	35.2%	40.3%
Total Liabilities + Equity	100.0%	100.0%	100.0%

Exhibit 5-6
Target Corporation
Common Size Income Statement

(in millions of USD)	2003	2004	2005
Sales	100.0%	100.0%	100.0%
Cost of Goods Sold	66.6%	66.0%	67.1%
Gross Profit	33.4%	34.0%	32.9%
SG&A	23.2%	23.9%	22.5%
Other Operating Expenses	2.8%	2.7%	2.7%
Earning Before Interest & Taxes	7.4%	7.3%	7.7%
Interest Expense	1.3%	1.2%	1.2%
Earning Before Taxes	6.1%	6.1%	6.5%
Income Tax Expense	2.3%	2.3%	2.4%
Income from Continuing Operations	3.8%	3.8%	4.0%
Gain from Sale of Discontinued Operations	0.0%	0.0%	2.8%
Net Income	3.8%	3.8%	6.8%

5.5   Global Accounting

The generally accepted accounting principles that are used in the capital markets in the United States are the most comprehensive in the world. They attempt to accurately disclose as much material information about a company as possible while limiting individual interpretation. GAAP financial reports are the foundation for the financial markets and the cornerstone of valuing companies.

Unfortunately, not all countries use GAAP. In today's global financial markets, institutional investors (mainly mutual funds) regularly value and invest in stocks of foreign companies and compare them to domestic investments. Most foreign accounting standards are less conservative than GAAP, making comparability very difficult. In the 1970's, international accounting standards were developed to establish uniformity in international financial reporting. However, not all countries conform to these standards. As demand increases for international investments, accounting standards are becoming a major issue. When a foreign company wants to list its shares in the United States, the SEC requires that the company report financial statements using GAAP.

5.6　Financial Statement Analysis

This section introduces the use of fundamental financial ratios to access and monitor corporate performance based on accounting information. The ratios are all applied to a case study of the Target Corporation. Accounting ratios are normally tracked over time to detect trends and to compare them to industry averages.

5.6.1　Liquidity Ratios

Liquidity ratios are used to indicate the ability of a company to pay its bills on time.

Current Ratio:

The current ratio measures a company's working capital to assess if there are adequate short-term assets to meet short-term liability claims. A current ratio of 1.1 to 1 is considered adequate for working capital management. This means that the company has $1.10 of current assets for every $1 of short-term liabilities.

For 2004, TGT's current ratio was:

$$\frac{\text{Current Assets}}{\text{Current Liabilities}} \qquad \frac{12{,}928}{8{,}314} \qquad = \qquad 1.55$$

Target's 2004 current ratio is 1.55, implying that TGT has $1.55 of current assets for every $1 of current liabilities. Compute TGT's 2005 current ratio. Did it improve or not? The industry average current ratio is 1.23.

$$\frac{\text{Current Assets}}{\text{Current Liabilities}} \qquad\qquad =$$

Quick Ratio:

The quick ratio is a modified version of the current ratio with inventories removed from current assets. This is a more refined measure of liquidity in that inventories are the least liquid of a firm's current assets. For 2004, TGT's quick ratio was:

$$\frac{\text{Current Assets-Inventory}}{\text{Current Liabilities}} \qquad \frac{(12{,}928-5{,}343)}{8{,}314} \qquad = \qquad 0.91$$

The industry average quick ratio is 0.38. TGT's quick ratio is 0.91. The larger the quick ratio, the more liquid the position of the company. Target has adequate liquidity compared to industry averages. Compute TGT's 2005 quick ratio. Did it improve or not?

$$\frac{\text{Current Assets-Inventory}}{\text{Current Liabilities}}$$

5.6.2 Activity/Efficiency Measures

The ratios in this section are used to assess the effectiveness with which a firm is managing assets and liabilities to generate sales. An efficient firm is one that uses its assets to generate the most sales while meeting liabilities in a manner that maximizes cash flow management.

Asset Turnover:

Asset turnover measures how many dollars of sales a firm is able to generate for each dollar of assets. Greater asset turnover implies more productive uses of assets to generate sales revenue. This number varies dramatically across industries and is based on levels of capital intensity. For example, Intel spends billions of dollars to build large semiconductor manufacturing plants that will generate revenues, while software companies might have an office and a few computer workstations to generate their revenues. TGT's 2004 total asset turnover was:

$$\frac{\text{Sales}}{\text{Total Assets}} \qquad \frac{48,163}{31,392} \qquad 1.53$$

TGT's asset turnover ratio is 1.53. Compute TGT's 2005 total asset turnover. The industry average asset turnover is 2.26. Is Target's asset turnover better or worse?

$$\frac{\text{Sales}}{\text{Total Assets}}$$

Inventory Turnover:

Inventory turnover measures how well a firm manages its inventories. The inventory turnover ratio specifies how many times inventory is bought, processed, and sold during a year. TGT's 2004 inventory turnover ratio was:

$$\frac{\text{Cost of Goods \& Services Sold}}{\text{Inventory}} \qquad \frac{31,790}{5,343} \qquad = \qquad 5.95$$

Compute TGT's 2005 inventory turnover. The industry average is 6.53. Is Target's better or worse?

$$\frac{\text{Cost of Goods \& Services Sold}}{\text{Inventory}}$$

Days Sales in Inventory(DSI):

Days sales in inventory (DSI) uses inventory turnover to determine how many days of operating activity are supported by the level of inventory. This is an extremely specific industry measure. TGT's 2004 days inventory measure was:

$$\frac{365 \text{ Days}}{\text{Inventory Turnover}} \qquad \frac{365}{5.95} \qquad 61.34 \text{ Days}$$

Compute TGT's 2005 days inventory. Did it increase or decrease over the past year?

$$\frac{365 \text{ Days}}{\text{Inventory Turnover}}$$

Receivables Turnover:

Receivables turnover is a ratio that measures working capital management efficiency. Receivables turnover reflects the number of times the firm collects its accounts receivables per year. TGT's 2004 receivables turnover was:

$$\frac{\text{Sales}}{\text{Accounts Receivable}} \qquad \frac{48,163}{5,776} \qquad = \qquad 8.34$$

Increasing the number of times A/R are collected improves cash flow management since sales dollars are collected more quickly and are able to be reinvested or used to pay bills.

Compute TGT's 2005 receivables turnover. Did it improve?

$$\frac{\text{Sales}}{\text{Accounts Receivable}}$$

Days Sales Outstanding (DSO) or Average Collection Period:

The days sales outstanding (DSO) or average collection period is the number of days sales that are outstanding. This is used as a proxy for how long credit sales are outstanding before they are collected. Credit terms vary depending on amount of credit sales and the credit quality of buyers. Usually, average collection periods are between 30 and 45 days. TGT's 2004 average collection period was:

$$\frac{365 \text{ Days}}{\text{Receivables Turnover}} \qquad \frac{365}{7.27} \qquad 43.77 \text{ Days}$$

Compute TGT's 2005 average collection period. Did it improve?

$$\frac{365 \text{ Days}}{\text{Receivables Turnover}}$$

Payables Turnover:

Payables turnover reflects the number of times that purchases are turned over per year. It represents how many times a company pays its bills in a year. Again, in TGT's case, this would include the cost of services sold as well. TGT's 2004 payables turnover was:

$$\frac{\text{Cost of Goods \& Services Sold}}{\text{Accounts Payable}} \qquad \frac{31{,}790}{7{,}448} \qquad 4.27$$

Compute TGT's 2005 payables turnover. Did it improve?

$$\frac{\text{Cost of Goods \& Services Sold}}{\text{Accounts Payable}}$$

Days Payable Outstanding (DPO):

Days payable outstanding (DPO) reflects the average number of days purchases that are supported by accounts payable. Whenever possible, a company wants to have its credit terms with suppliers extended longer that its credit terms with customers to maximize its cash on hand. TGT's 2004 average payables period was:

$$\frac{365 \text{ Days}}{\text{Payables Turnover}} \qquad \frac{365}{4.27} \qquad = \qquad 85.51 \text{ Days}$$

TGT's average days payable of 85.51 days reflects the credit terms that Target negotiates with its suppliers.

Compute TGT's 2005 average payables period. Did it increase or decrease?

$$\frac{365 \text{ Days}}{\text{Payables Turnover}}$$

5.6.3   Leverage Ratios

Leverage ratios indicate the extent to which a firm has financed its assets with non-owner sources of capital (debt financing). There are several potential benefits to debt financing:

- First, the interest rate on debt is typically lower than the expected return on equity because it is more secure and the firm promises predetermined payment terms to bondholders.
- Second, interest expense on debt is tax deductible (in most countries, including the United States) whereas dividends to shareholders are not tax deductible.
- Third, debt poses constraints on management that minimizes the wasting of cash flows on non-value producing projects (defined as the agency problem).

Too much reliance on debt financing is potentially costly to the shareholders of the firm. Interest and principal payments are binding on the firm and may constrain its operations, especially during weaker economic periods. The optimal debt and equity mixture varies across industries, and different firms prefer different capital structures. These ratios are used to determine, relative to other firms and industries, how much debt financing should be used and the likelihood that the firm will be able to service the debt.

Total Debt Ratio:

The total debt ratio indicates what percentage of assets is financed by sources of capital other than owner's equity. TGT's 2004 figure was:

$$\frac{\text{Total Assets} - \text{Shareholders Equity}}{\text{Total Assets}} \qquad \frac{(31,392-11,065)}{31,392} \qquad 64.75\%$$

Compute TGT's 2005 total debt ratio. Is TGT using more or less debt financing?

$$\frac{\text{Total Assets–Shareholders Equity}}{\text{Total Assets}}$$

Debt-to-Equity Ratio:

The *debt-equity ratio* is one of the most popular ratios in financial analysis. It indicates how many dollars of long-term debt financing the firm is using for each dollar invested by shareholders. TGT's 2004 figure was:

$$\frac{\text{Long-Term Debt}}{\text{Equity}} \qquad \frac{10{,}217}{11{,}065} \qquad 92.33\%$$

Compute TGT's 2005 total debt ratio. Did it increase or decrease over the past year? The industry average is 53% Does TGT use more or less debt financing than the industry?

$$\frac{\text{Long-Term Debt}}{\text{Equity}}$$

Financial Leverage(Equity Multiplie):

Financial leverage indicates how many dollars of assets the firm is able to deploy for each dollar invested by shareholders. If a firm levers some of its equity, it is able to have access to an asset base larger than its equity base. A firm can leverage its equity through borrowing or through the creation of other liabilities, such as accounts payable and accrued liabilities. Financial leverage, however, increases a firm's risk because the more debt a firm assumes, the less flexible the firm will be in bad times. TGT's 2004 equity multiplier was:

$$\frac{\text{Total Assets}}{\text{Equity}} \qquad \frac{31{,}392}{11{,}065} \qquad 2.83$$

Compute TGT's 2005 equity multiplier. Is TGT more heavily levered than in 2004?

$$\frac{\text{Total Assets}}{\text{Equity}}$$

Interest Coverage [times interest earned]:

Interest coverage is a popular debt covenant because it represents exactly how many dollars of income are earned relative to the interest expense. A *debt covenant* is a provision in a loan agreement that requires the firm to maintain a minimum financial ratio. If the interest coverage provision is violated by the firm, the loan can be accelerated. Interest coverage ratios of at least 2.0 of earnings before interest and taxes (EBIT) are often written into loan contracts. Interest coverage of only 1.0 implies that a firm is making only enough money to be able to service interest requirements with earnings. TGT's 2004 figure was:

$$\frac{\text{EBIT}}{\text{Interest Expense}} \qquad \frac{3,519}{559} \qquad 6.29$$

The industry average interest coverage ratio is 13 times. Compute TGT's 2005 interest coverage. Is Target's coverage better or worse than the industry?

$$\frac{\text{EBIT}}{\text{Interest Expense}}$$

5.6.4 Profitability Measures

Profitability ratios serve as an overall measurement of firm performance and the effectiveness of the firm's management. By relating income to different accounts, it is possible to assess the value added by management. Profitability ratios vary drastically across industries and are related to firm strategies and performance.

Profit Margin [Return on Sales]:

Profit margin is equal to net income divided by total sales. It measures the dollars of income generated for each dollar of sales. TGT's 2004 figure was:

$$\frac{\text{Net Income}}{\text{Sales}} \qquad \frac{1,841}{48,163} \qquad = \qquad 3.82\%$$

The industry's average profit margin is 3.69%. Compute TGT's 2005 profit margin. For all profit measures, you should use the 2005 net income from continuing operations (1,885), and exclude the gain from the sale of discontinued operations. Using this figure, is TGT's profit margin better or worse than the industry average?

$$\frac{\text{Net Income}}{\text{Sales}} \qquad =$$

Gross Margin:

Gross margin is equal to gross profit or income (sales minus cost of goods sold) divided by total sales. It measures the margin on sales after accounting for direct costs (labor and supplies) of producing the product or service being sold. TGT's 2004 gross margin was:

$$\frac{\text{Gross Profit}}{\text{Sales}} \qquad \frac{16{,}373}{48{,}163} \qquad = \qquad 34.00\%$$

The industry's average operating margin is 32.80%. Compute TGT's 2005 gross margin Is it better or worse than the industry average?

$$\frac{\text{Gross Profit}}{\text{Sales}} \qquad =$$

Operating Margin:

Operating margin is equal to operating income (earnings before interest and taxes) divided by total sales. It measures the margin on sales after accounting for all business expenses (but not interest and taxes). TGT's 2004 operating margin was:

$$\frac{\text{EBIT}}{\text{Sales}} \qquad \frac{3{,}519}{48{,}163} \qquad = \qquad 7.31\%$$

The industry's average operating margin is 6.69%. Compute TGT's 2005 operating margin Is TGT's operating margin better or worse than the industry average?

$$\frac{\text{EBIT}}{\text{Sales}} \qquad =$$

Return on Assets:

Return on assets is calculated by dividing net income by total assets. It measures dollars of income for every dollar of assets invested. It is a basic measure of efficiency used to allocate and manage resources. This measure is highly sensitive to the capital intensity of an industry. TGT's 2004 figure was:

$$\frac{\text{Net Income}}{\text{Total Assets}} \qquad \frac{1,841}{31,392} \qquad 5.86\%$$

The industry average ROA is 8.07%. TGT's 2005 return on assets. Is Target's return on assets better or worse than the industry average?

$$\frac{\text{Net Income}}{\text{Total Assets}}$$

Return on Equity:

Return on equity is the most popular benchmark of financial performance for investors and management. ROE measures the efficiency with which a firm utilizes shareholder's invested dollars. TGT's 2004 return on equity was:

$$\frac{\text{Net Income}}{\text{Shareholder's Equity}} \qquad \frac{1,841}{11,065} \qquad 16.64\%$$

The industry average return on equity is 17.40% Compute TGT's 2005 return on equity. Is it better or worse than the industry average?

$$\frac{\text{Net Income}}{\text{Shareholder's Equity}} \qquad =$$

5.6.5 Valuation Ratios

Valuation ratios are used to compare accounting numbers to the current market price.

Price-Earnings Ratio:

The *P/E ratio* measures the relationship between earning per share and the market price of common stock. Generally speaking, a stock with a high P/E multiple relative to other companies in the same industry implies that investors have confidence in the company's ability to generate higher future profits. Earnings per share (EPS) are computed as net income available for common stock divided by the diluted number of shares outstanding. With 2004 net income of $1,841M, and weighted average diluted shares outstanding of 919.2M, Target's EPS for 2004 was $2.00.

Target's year-end stock price for 2004 was $37.90 and so its P/E ratio was:

$$\frac{\text{Stock Price per Share}}{\text{Earnings Per Share}} \qquad \frac{37.90}{2.00} \qquad 18.92$$

Using a 2005 stock price of $50.77 per share and 2005 earnings per share of 2.07 (1,885//912.1), compute TGT's price-earnings ratio. Did it increase or decrease? Why?

$$\frac{\text{Stock Price per Share}}{\text{Earnings per Share}}$$

5.6.6 *Strategic Profit Model (SPM):*

As mentioned earlier, return on equity is normally viewed as the most important accounting measure of a firm's performance. One common way of evaluating performance is to break down ROE into three components. Popularly known as the DuPont formula, these components are the profit margin, asset turnover, and financial leverage (See Box). Profit margins measure the profitability of sales. Asset turnover measures how efficient the firm is in utilizing its assets to generate sales dollars. Financial leverage reflects how performance is magnified by debt. These three ratios are combined to monitor the changes in ROE. It is sometimes also called the strategic profit model (SPM).

Profit Margin		*Asset Turnover*		*Return on Assets*		*Financial Leverage*	*Return on Equity*
$\frac{\text{Net Income}}{\text{Sales}}$	X	$\frac{\text{Sales}}{\text{Assets}}$	=	$\frac{\text{Net Income}}{\text{Assets}}$	X	$\frac{\text{Assets}}{\text{Equity}}$ =	$\frac{\text{Net Income}}{\text{Equity}}$

Target's SPM analysis for 2004 was:

3.82%	X	1.53	=	5.86%	X	2.84	=	16.5%

Compute TGT's SPM for 2005 and analyze the changes that occurred between 2004 and 2005. Did TGT's performance get bettwe or worse? What factor (s) led to the change in TGT's ROE between 2004 and 2005?

Target's SPM analysis for 2005:

Profit Margin	Asset Turnover	Return On Assets	Financial Leverage	Return On Equity

- 173 -

5.7   Financial Ethics and Aggressive Accounting

The Enron debacle, followed by WorldCom, Adelphia, Global Crossing, HealthSouth, and others, has focused the investment community and regulators on financial ethics and aggressive accounting. Even with all of the accounting standards and principles, there is still a lot of discretion regarding how and when companies recognize certain accounting items.

Conservative accounting delays revenue recognition and does not delay recognizing expenses. This practice assures investors that, if there is a mistake, the company is underreporting financial results. However, the importance of accounting numbers and their effect on the price of a company's stock leads some companies to use aggressive accounting practices to meet and exceed financial market expectations. Howard Schilit, in his book *Financial Shenanigans*, highlights seven areas where managers can "cook the books." These seven shenanigans are reviewed below.

5.7.1   Recording Revenue Too Soon

In order to boost current period revenue, some companies accelerate the recognition of revenue. Companies usually do not recognize revenue until goods are physically shipped, but some companies ship goods before sales are finalized so they can recognize the revenue. This is not a common practice for most firms, but some companies try to squeeze additional sales into the last week of the accounting period to meet revenue and profit expectations.

5.7.2   Recording False Revenues

It is possible to record income even when income does not exist. Companies that are desperate to meet revenue and earnings projections record questionable revenues. Refunds from suppliers should be a credit to the cost of goods sold account, but some companies recognize them as revenue to make sales appear higher. Additionally, revenue can be recognized when similar assets are exchanged.

For example, in 1998 Cendant Corp. was discovered to have recorded false revenues and to have used other shenanigans, and was forced to restate financial reports for 1997. Among the games that the telecom companies played in the late 1990s was to swap fiber-optic cable capacity and record revenues from the swap, even though no money ever changed hands.

5.7.3   Boosting Income with One-time Gains

Some companies have undervalued assets or investments that are recorded at book value but actually have a market value that is much higher. These assets can be strategically sold in periods of weaker operating results, and gain associated with the sale can give the appearance of a healthy financial operation. Another example of a one-time gain appearing to boost ongoing income is if a company fails to separate unusual and nonrecurring gains or losses from recurring income.

5.7.4 Shifting Expenses to a Later Period

You may have received a free disk from America Online with free hours of online service. This was an aggressive marketing campaign to boost AOL's subscriber base. For years AOL has included free disks in magazines, newspapers, and even with textbook purchases.

Conservative accounting practices would have recognized all the marketing expenses of these disks during the period when distributed. AOL deferred the costs of the marketing expense and amortized these costs over twelve to eighteen months. This allowed AOL to defer expenses to later periods and report higher current income. Many investors complained about this practice and in the second quarter of 1996, AOL changed their aggressive accounting methods to recognize all of the deferred charges in the current period. The one-time charge associated with this change amounted to $385 million and was reported as a part of continuing operations. AOL reported a net loss for the first six months of 1996 of $509 million.

5.7.5 Failing to Record or Disclose All Liabilities

To enhance a company's financial position, it is possible to overlook certain liabilities and even record some expenses as revenue. This practice enhances the book value of the firm and improves profits. Accrued expenses or contingent liabilities are a good example of items that might not be recognized during the proper accounting period. If these are overlooked, expenses and liabilities are understated and net income will be overstated. There are also some financial transactions used to keep debt off the books. Enron specialized in this type of financial deception by transferring debts and liabilities to off-balance sheet subsidiaries.

5.7.6 Shifting Current Income to Later Periods

This practice creates future reserves so that when times are bad in the future, the company is able to tap those reserves and bring them into income, thus maintaining the appearance of ongoing profitable operations. Many financial companies have been accused of this type of accounting. This is a type of conservative accounting in that it understates the profitability of a company in the short-term. But when it is used in its extreme for revenues that should be recognized in the current period, it becomes a revenue-smoothing device. Waste Management was caught delaying depreciation expenses so as to boost current income, along with some other aggressive accounting practices.

5.7.7   Shifting Future Income to the Current Period

If a company signs a long-term contract that will last more than one period, in accordance with the revenue principle, revenue is recognized when it is earned throughout the contract. The contract costs are supposed to be recognized as costs incurred and the services under the contract are provided or completed. However, if a company receives payment for the contract up-front, it could recognize all revenues in the current period as opposed to recording the unearned revenue on the balance sheet. The recording of the total contract as current income boosts current profits and sacrifices future income when it is actually earned.

5.7.8   Aggressive Accounting Summary

Companies that are required to restate financial results due to fraudulent accounting practices usually see their stock prices tumble in the markets. These practices are normally discovered in SEC investigations. Usually the SEC finds that managers of companies involved in fraudulent accounting are trying to meet or exceed the expectations of Wall Street—the primary reason behind most of these investigations.

5.8   Summary

This chapter provides an overview of financial accounting and the three fundamental financial statements of the firm: the balance sheet, the income statement, and the statement of cash flows. The roles of the SEC and generally accepted accounting principles (GAAP) are detailed. In addition, the relationships between financial statements are laid out, and elements of aggressive accounting practices presented.

This chapter also covers financial statement analysis using financial ratios. These ratios include measures of liquidity, activity or efficiency, leverage, profitability, and market valuation. Such an analysis is routinely performed to evaluate corporate financial performance both internally by management and externally by banks, security firms, and other creditors and underwriters. A ratio analysis is performed on the Target Corporation. The concept of the strategic profit model is introduced as a way to integrate financial analysis.

List of Terms

1. Financial accounting
2. Balance sheet
3. Income statement
4. Statement of cash flows
5. Statement of retained earnings
6. GAAP
7. Assets
8. Liabilities
9. Equity
10. Revenue
11. Expenses
12. Net Income (loss)
13. Auditing
14. 10 – K
15. 10 – Q
16. Cash accounting
17. Accrual
18. Current assets
19. Inventory
20. Accounts receivable
21. Current liabilities
22. Long-term assets
23. Goodwill
24. Long-term liabilities
25. Off-Balance Sheet Activities
26. Cost of goods sold
27. Gross margin
28. Selling expenses
29. General and administrative expenses
30. Operating margin
31. Income tax expenses
32. Earnings per share
33. EPS dilution
34. Operating activities
35. Investing activities
36. Financing activities
37. Common size statement
38. Liquidity ratios
39. Current ratio
40. Quick ratio / Acid-test ratio
41. Activity/efficiency ratios
42. Asset turnover
43. Inventory turnover
44. Days sales in inventory

45. Receivables turnover
46. Payables turnover
47. Days sales outstanding - average collection period
48. Days payable outstanding
49. Leverage ratios
50. Total debt ratio
51. Debt-to-equity ratio
52. Equity multiplier (Financial leverage)
53. Times interest earned (Interest coverage)
54. Profit margin (Return on sales)
55. Return on assets
56. Return on equity
57. Price-earnings ratio
58. Market capitalization
59. Strategic profit model

Questions

1. What are the various uses of accounting information?
2. List the four accounting statements you would find in a financial report.
3. What is GAAP? What purpose does it serve?
4. What is the objective of the financial statements?
5. What are the 10-Ks and 10-Qs? What is reported in them?
6. How would you distinguish between current and long-term assets and liabilities?
7. How is accrual accounting different from cash accounting?
8. Explain the concept of the revenue principal?
9. What are off-balance sheet activities? Name three examples.
10. What is the matching principle?
11. What is the difference between gross income and net income?
12. What happens in EPS dilution?
13. Why is the statement of cash flows important? Why don't financial analysts just look at the income statement?
14. What are the three main categories of cash flows in a statement of cash flows?
15. What is a common size statement? Why do we use common size statements?
16. What does the current ratio measure? What level is considered adequate for working capital management?
17. How is the quick ratio different from the current ratio?
18. How is asset turnover a measure of management effectiveness?
19. Why would a company want to collapse its receivables turnover as much as possible?
20. Why does a company try to have its credit terms with suppliers extended longer than its credit terms with customers?
21. What does inventory turnover and days inventory tell us?
22. Why would a company aim for receivables turnover that is at least equal to its payables turnover, if not higher?
23. What do leverage ratios in general measure?
24. Is it desirable to have a high interest coverage ratio?
25. What are the three components of the Strategic Profit Model?
26. How does giving a high equity multiplier help increase a company's return on equity? Explain using the Strategic Profit Model.
27. What is market capitalization? Why is it an important measure?
28. Why is the price-earning ratio not a good metric for valuing a company?

Assignment #5-1

1. Ratio Analysis: Wal-Mart vs. Target

    -   Go to Market Guide's website at www.marketguide.com.
    -   In the top left corner, enter Target stock symbol (TGT) and click "Go."
    -   On the next page, click on "Ratios" in the left column.
    -   Next, you will see a list of ratios for Target, the industry, sector and market.
    -   Using the numbers for the company itself, fill in the following table:

Ratio	Target	Wal-Mart
P/E (TTM[5])		
Quick Ratio (MRQ[6])		
Current Ratio (MRQ)		
Net Profit Margin (TTM)		
ROA (TTM)		
ROE (TTM)		
Inventory Turnover (TTM)		
Asset Turnover		

-   Repeat the above steps to fill in the numbers for Wal-Mart as well.
-   Compute a strategic Profit Model for each company.
-   Based on the numbers you have found, which company looks more favorable to you?
-   In what areas is the company you have chosen superior/inferior to the other? Why?
-

2. Go to the EDGAR website
    (http://www.sec.gov/edgar/searchedgar/companysearch.html) and in the "company name" box, enter "Kraft Food." Find Kraft's most recent 10-K and click on it. Find Kraft's consolidated financial statements. For Kraft, compute the following ratios:

Measure	Formula	Value
Profit Margin	(Net income) / Sales	
Return on equity	(Net income) / (Shareholder equity)	
Current Ratio	(Current Assets) / (Current Liabilities)	
Total debt ratio	(Total Debt) / (Total Assets)	
Interest coverage	EBIT / (Interest Expense)	

---

[5] TTM: Trailing Twelve Months
[6] MRQ: Most Recent Quarter

Problem Sets
Company ABC

Balance Sheet

(in thousands)

	2003
Assets	
Cash	561
Accounts Receivable	1,963
Inventories	2,031
Prepaid Expenses	50
Accum. Tax Prepaymnts	47
Current Assets	4,652
Fixed Assets (land, equip)	3,000
Less: Accum.	-555
Net Fixed Assets	2,445
Total Assets	**7,097**

Liabilities & SH Equity	
Bank loans & notes	250
Accounts Payable	1,862
Accrued taxes	20
Other accrued liabilities	285
Current Liabilities	2,417
Long term debt	500
Common Stock	1,500
Additional paid in capital	1,400
Retained Earnings	1,280
Total Stockholders	4,180
Total Liabilities & SH	**7,097**

Company ABC

Income Statement

(in thousands)

	2003
Net Sales	11,863
Cost of Goods Sold	(8,537)
Gross Profit	3,326
SGA expenses	(2,276)
Interest expense	(73)
Earnings before taxes	977
Income taxes	(390)
Earnings after taxes	587

Problems:

1. What is the current and quick ratio for Company ABC?

2. Using those ratios, explain if Company ABC is capable of meeting its financial needs for day-to-day operations.

3. Determine Inventory Turnover, Net Profit Margin and Gross Profit Margin for Company ABC.

4. What is the company's Days Inventory? What would happen to days inventory if inventory turnover decreased? Why?

Company XYZ

Balance Sheet
(in thousands)

	2003
Assets	
Cash	178
Accounts Receivable	678
Inventories	1,329
Prepaid Expenses	21
Accum. Tax Prepaymnts	35
Current Assets	2,241
Fixed Assets (land, equip)	1596
Less: Accum. Depreciation	(857)
Net Fixed Assets	739
Investments, long term	65
Other assets, long term	205
Total Assets	**3,250**
Liabilities & SH Equity	
Bank loans & notes	448
Accounts Payable	148
Accrued taxes	36
Other accrued liabilities	191
Current Liabilities	823
Long term debt	631
Common Stock	421
Additional paid in capital	361
Retained Earnings	1,014
Total Stockholders	1,796
Total Liabilities & SH	**3,250**

Company XYZ

Income Statement
(in thousands)

	2003
Net Sales	3,992
Cost of Goods Sold	(2,680)
Gross Profit	1,312
SGA expenses	(912)
Interest expense	(85)
Earnings before taxes	315
Income taxes	(114)
Earnings after taxes	201

Problems:

1. What is the company's asset turnover and ne profit margin?

2. Using the above two ratios, calculate the company's return on assets.

3. Determine the company's financial leverage.

4. Calculate the company's return on equity bas on its ROA and financial leverage.

5. How else could you have calculated the ROE Show your work.

Company X

Balance Sheet

(in thousands)

	2003
Assets	
Cash	19
Marketable Securities	56
Accounts Receivable	293
Inventories	253
Current Assets	621
Fixed Assets (land, equip)	1,036
Less: Accum. Depreciation	(337)
Net Fixed Assets	699
Total Assets	**1,320**

Liabilities & SH Equity	
Accounts Payable	149
Notes Payable	50
Accrued Expenses	122
Current Liabilities	321
Long term debt	220
Deferred Income Taxes	140
Total Liabilities	681
Common Stock	100
Paid-in Surplus	288
Retained Earnings	251
Total Stockholders equity	639
Total Liabilities & SH Equity	**1,320**

Company X

Income Statement

(in thousands)

	2003
Net Sales	1479
Cost of Goods Sold	(1062)
Gross Profit	417
SGA expenses	(141)
Marketing expense	(50)
Depreciation expense	(10)
EBIT	216
Interest expense	(26)
Earnings before taxes	190
Income taxes	(76)
Earnings after taxes	114

Problems:

1. Calculate the company's receivables turno

2. Calculate its payables turnover.

3. Determine the company's average collectio period.

4. Calculate its average days payable.

5. Which is higher, the company's average collection period or days payables? What doe tell you about the company's working capital management?

Company ONE

Balance Sheet

	2003
Assets	
Cash	2507
Accounts Receivable	70360
Inventories	77,380
Other Current Assets	6316
Current Assets	156563
Net Fixed Assets	79187
Other long-term assets	4695
Total Assets	**240445**

Liabilities & SH Equity	
Accounts Payable	35,661
Notes Payable	20,501
Other Current Liabilities	11,054
Current Liabilities	67,216
Long term debt	888
Total Liabilities	68,104
Common Stock	12650
Additional paid-in capital	37950
Retained Earnings	121741
Total Stockholders equity	172341
Total Liabilities & SH Equity	**240,445**

Company ONE

Income Statement
(in thousands)

	2003
Net Sales	323780
Cost of Goods Sold	(148127)
Gross Profit	175,653
SGA expenses	(131809)
Depreciation	(7700)
Interest expense	(1711)
Earnings before taxes	34,433
Income taxes	(12740)
Earnings after taxes	**21,693**

Problems:

1. What is the current ratio for Company ONE

2. Calculate the quick ratio for this company.

3. Which ratio is a better measure of the company's ability to pay its short-term creditor (e.g. suppliers)? Why?

4. Determine the company's asset turnover. W does this number represent?

5. Calculate ROA and ROE for the company. Which ratio is a better measure of the compar ability to create shareholder value? Why?

The DuPont Model – Simple and Effective

In 1919, a finance executive at E.I. du Pont de Nemours and Co., of Wilmington, Delaware, developed the DuPont model for measuring a company's financial performance. The DuPont system helps companies visualize the critical components in return on assets (ROA) and return on investments (ROI). Entries that make up pre-tax ROI include cost of goods sold (COGS), selling expenses, administrative expenses, inventories, accounts receivable, and cash. At different stages, these items are added, subtracted, divided or multiplied until return on equity (ROE) is obtained.

THE DUPONT IDENTITY

Profit Margin	*	Asset Turnover	=	Return on Assets	*	Financial Leverage	=	Return on Equity

The DuPont model has proven itself to be very effective. It is a good tool for employees to understand how their actions have an impact on the company's overall performance. Caterpillar Inc., has seen its ROA reach double digits since adopting the DuPont system in its financial management. The company has also produced record earnings for 13 of the past 15 quarters. The DuPont system has helped the company achieve greater accountability for different parts of its business.

Nucor Corp., a producer of steel and steel products, has also used ROA within the DuPont system to help improve its corporate performance. The company prefers this system to other financial metrics for its simplicity. This characteristic allows all of Nucor's employees to understand the model.

Proponents of other financial metrics like EVA (economic value added) argue that the ratio-based DuPont has its flaws too. For example, the guesswork inherent in GAAP (Generally Accepted Accounting Principles) is carried over to DuPont. The guesswork involved leaves room for managers to manipulate results or make shortsighted decisions.

Ratio measures in DuPont also create a conflict of interests between management and shareholders. EVA, on the other hand, calculates returns that exceed a company's cost of capital – a formula that help decision-making in creating shareholder value.

Critics also say that the DuPont model only allows a company to determine how it has performed but has no way of predicting future results. It also does not include intangible assets in its calculations.

In the DuPont system, however, simplicity has priority over methodology. A mid-level manager for example, does not know what the cost of capital is for his company if he has to use EVA. When using the DuPont model, this piece of information is not necessary. He is simply given a hurdle rate that he has to achieve. Furthermore, it is also possible to combine return on investments with measures that do incorporate growth prospects. Securities analysts also like the DuPont model because it is much easier to use and accurate at the same time.

Source: CFO Magazine, Jan 1998
  " 'Tis The Gift To Be Simple"
  By Robin Blumenthal

CHAPTER 6

THE FINANCIAL LIFE CYCLE OF THE FIRM: FROM RAISING CAPITAL TO ACQUISITIONS, MERGERS AND SPINOFFS

This chapter covers the financial life cycle of a firm—from its early stages of capital formation using owner funds and bank financing, to venture capital and initial public offerings. We follow the financial evolution of a firm from a start-up business, to IPO, through mergers and acquisitions, to divestitures.

The chapter includes: a description of the role of the Securities and Exchange Commission (SEC) in regulating the financial markets in the United States; the types of financial instruments employed by companies to raise capital; the capital raising process for initial public offerings and secondary offerings; mergers, takeovers and acquisitions; and spinoffs and equity carve-outs.

The learning objectives for the chapter include an understanding of:

- The role of the SEC in the financial markets;
- The stages of the financial lifecycle of the firm;
- The venture capital market and its role in financing new opportunities;
- How securities are sold to the public;
- The role of investment banks in the capital raising process;
- Initial public offerings and secondary offerings; and
- Mergers, acquisitions, and spinoffs.

6.1 Regulating the Financial Markets: The Securities and Exchange Commission

The principal regulator of all primary and secondary market activity in the United States is the Securities and Exchange Commission (SEC). Following the stock market crash of 1929 and the Great Depression of the early 1930s, a wave of financial regulation was implemented to curb market speculation and fraud, and to strengthen investor confidence.

The *Securities Exchange Act of 1934* created the SEC. The SEC is responsible for licensing securities professionals, collecting public disclosure information (e.g., quarterly and annual reports), and enforcing the various securities laws in the United States. This section will review the SEC's activity in the primary and secondary markets and introduce some of the information resources available from the SEC on the Internet.

The SEC's primary objective is to provide investors with complete disclosure of all material information concerning publicly traded securities. Its goal is to create a level playing field for investors and minimize the information asymmetries that existed in the early 1900s.

Prior to the creation of the SEC, Congress initially passed *The Securities Act of 1933*. The Securities Act of 1933 is designed to regulate the primary securities markets by providing investors with the necessary information to make informed decisions regarding an issue of new securities. A lot of technicalities are involved, and numerous lawyers are employed in issuing a new security—a stock or bond issue, from the preparation of a registration statement and the filing with the SEC, to the distribution of a preliminary prospectus, to the sale of the securities to investors either directly or through a group of investment banks.

The Securities Exchange Act of 1934 also implemented regulation pertaining to the sale and trading of securities in the secondary markets—after the initial issuance of securities. This act regulates the activities of the various stock and bond exchanges in the United States and all of the financial institutions and finance professionals that participate in this market.

With the growth of computer technology and the Internet, the SEC has opened a database that allows access to all public information electronically filed with the SEC, at its web address: www.sec.gov/. The EDGAR database is the SEC electronic public document access system; it may be accessed directly through the website.

Exhibit 6-1
The Financial Life Cycle of the Firm

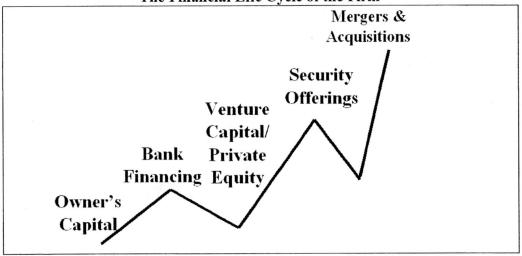

6.2   Early Stages of the Financial Life Cycle of the Firm

All businesses are started using capital provided by the owners of the firm. Owners' capital includes capital provided by the founders and their families and friends. In this sense, owners' capital refers to the actual cash put into the business and does not include the sweat equity that the owner-entrepreneurs put into their business to make it a success.

6.2.1 Bank Financing

Bank financing is usually the first stage of outside capital that a business uses to finance its growth. Banks are often very conservative lenders and usually only loan money to stable, profitable companies and individuals to help finance shorter-term business operations and expansion. Bank loans are usually for a specified time frame, often one year or less.

Typically, the borrower pays a fixed amount per month, which includes a portion of the principal plus interest. The percentage rate on the loan is high enough to cover the bank's cost of funds, its operating expenses, a reasonable profit margin, and a margin of safety to take care of default risks on the underlying loan.

Bank financing can be a good source of capital:

• To finance a specific large purchase or business opportunity that will increase current profitable activities;

• When cash flow is strong, and it is clear that firm's income from operations will cover the debt service payments to the bank; and

• When the firm has sufficient collateral to cover the value of the loan in case of default.

6.2.2 Private Equity/Venture Capital[7]

Private equity/ venture capital is a phase of the financial life cycle that many companies go through as they grow and mature in today's capital markets. At this early stage in the firm's operating history, investing in the company is a high-risk investment. Venture capital investors require a higher rate of return relative to returns associated with larger, more proven companies that have shares traded in capital markets. The trade-off associated with the potentially higher returns of private equity are the higher risks associated with the investment.

To reduce the risks of venture capital, financing is often provided in stages, with each stage of financing providing just enough money to reach the next stage. The ultimate goal of the financing plan and the venture capitalist is to hold a large stake of the equity in the firm prior to the firm selling shares to the public, and cashing in on that stake when the firm goes public through an initial public offering.

Stages of Venture Capital Financing:

Seed financing is the first money provided by venture capitalists and involves an initial investment of up to several million dollars. Seed financing may be made when a company is composed of just a few people and a good idea. At this point in time, the company usually does not even have a tangible product or any revenues. A business plan is developed by entrepreneurs and is shown to one or more providers of private equity. One or more private investors or groups of investors may decide to provide this start-up financing in return for a certain percentage of ownership in the company. Financing is determined based on the business plan and the management experience.

First round funding involves investment by venture capitalists of up to several million dollars or more in private companies that have tangible products that are nearly developed and will soon be marketed. At this point the company may still have little or no revenue and a limited operating history. Often, the private equity investors and venture capitalists that provided the seed financing will also participate in first round funding. This stage provides capital to launch the production and sale of the product.

Intermediate funding—At this stage, the product seems to be gaining acceptance in the marketplace and the firm is generating revenue and has compiled an operating history, although it may not yet be making a profit. Funds are now needed to finance inventories, production processes, shipping, and accounts receivables. Private investments ranging from $1 million to $20 million

---

[7] Information on venture capital was obtained from the *Harvard Business Review*, Nov/Dec 1998, "How Venture Capital Works", by Bob Zider.

are often funded during this stage by institutional investors, such as insurance companies and pension funds, and venture capital pools seeking more aggressive investments. The firm is established to the point that it may search for later stage funding or proceed with a public offering.

Later stage funding—At this point, the company has matured and needs additional funding for growth and product expansion. The firm may be capable of an initial public offering at any time and may be waiting for a hot IPO market—*a market conducive to IPO issuance—before offering its shares to the public. Funding for this stage again can range between several million and $20 million.*

Venture Capital's Niche—Filling a Void:

Venture capital is one of the many sources of capital that entrepreneurs can seek. Contrary to popular perception, only a small proportion of the billions invested by venture capitalists are for basic innovation. Venture capitalists invested more than $10 billion in 1997—and only 6% of it went to start-ups. The majority of venture capitalists' investments went to follow-on funding. The government or large corporations usually provide funding for the initial stages of innovations. Although venture capital funds are small compared to other sources of funding, they have grown in size over the years. In 1980, the average venture capital fund was $20 million. Today, that amount is more than ten times larger.

Because of the structure and rules of the capital markets in the United States, venture capital plays a special role in providing funding for entrepreneurs. Usury laws limit the interest rates that banks and some other financial institutions can charge borrowers. The higher risks inherent in start-up financing usually justify higher rates of return than banks are permitted to charge under the usury laws. Furthermore, most start-ups do not have hard assets they can use as collaterals for bank loans. Regulations and operating practices meant to protect the public investors from losing money due to the bankruptcy of savings institutions prevent commercial banks and savings institutions from participating in high-risk ventures.

Venture Capital Funds—Sufficient Returns at Acceptable Risk:

Venture capital funds, in order to attract investors to fill the void of financing for start-ups, require high expected returns, and must earn superior returns on very risky businesses. Investors in venture capital funds are usually large institutions that can afford to risk a small portion of their portfolios to earn returns well above the market average. They typically expect a 25% to 35% return over the life of their investments in venture capital funds.

To meet the demanding return requirements of their investors, venture capital funds must carefully structure their deals and manage their investments. The myth that venture capital funds look for good ideas first is far from true.

Managers of these funds look for good industries before looking for good ideas within those industries. This strategy follows the logic that if a business is in an industry experiencing high growth, it will only require a sound execution plan to succeed. In this way, the venture fund cuts down its risk exposure.

Another way that venture capitalists reduce their risk is to structure the deals in a manner that will offer them a certain degree of security. In a typical private equity transaction, the venture fund will invest in a company and will have various protective clauses in a written operating agreement to safeguard its investment. These clauses may include (but are not limited to) the following:

- The venture capitalists receive liquidation preference. In the event that the company has to be liquidated, the venture capitalists will receive their money before any other parties get a share of the proceeds.
- The venture capitalists may have blocking rights or disproportional voting rights over key decisions, including the sale of the company or the timing of its IPO.
- The venture capitalists may also be protected against equity dilution if the company seeks subsequent rounds of financing. Should more financing be obtained, the venture capitalist firms will be allowed to purchase enough shares to maintain their initial percentage ownership of the company.
- The venture capitalists may be permitted to invest additional money in the business at a predetermined price. This clause will allow the venture capitalists, in the event that the company is performing very well, to increase their stake in a successful venture at a price below the market value of the stock.

Venture capitalists also reduce their risk exposure when they invest in a company along with other venture capitalists. In a deal, a lead venture capital investor typically represents the interests of all of the venture firms that are involved in the transaction. In this way, each venture capital fund is able to diversify and spread its money among a number of deals. This arrangement reduces the workload of individual venture capitalists because other VC investors are involved in assessing the risk, managing the deal, and protecting the interests of all of the VCs.

In the United States capital markets, the probability of good plans and good management succeeding and hitting a grand slam with a twenty-fold return on investment is a long shot. However, given a portfolio diversification approach of many venture capitalists, only 10% to 20% of their investments have to be real winners for them to achieve the desired 25% to 35% return on their investment. A sample distribution of returns for $1000 allocated to a portfolio of venture capital investments might look like Exhibit 6-2:

Exhibit 6-2
Probable Return Distribution from Venture Capital Investments

	Bad	Alive	Okay	Good	Great	Total
$ Invested	200	400	200	100	100	1,000
Payout (Yr 5)	0	1X	5X	10X	20X	
Gross Return	0	400	1,000	1,000	2,000	4,400
Net Return	(200)	0	800	900	1,900	**3,400**

Attractive Returns for the VC:

As a reward for the risks it undertakes in start-up transactions, a venture capital fund can expect a five to ten-fold increase in its initial investment over a five-year period. Funds are structured to guarantee the partners of the venture capital firm a comfortable return. VC firms receive a flat 2% to 3% fee of assets under management, regardless of the venture capital fund's performance, plus a percentage of the appreciation of the portfolio. The limited investors in the fund usually receive 80% of the capital gains while the venture capitalists get the remaining 20% of the gains. Exhibit 6-3 shows the typical payout structure for a venture capital firm managing a $20 million investment:

Exhibit 6-3
Typical Payout Structure for a VC Firm

Annual IRR of Fund Over Five Years					
0%	10%	20%	30%	40%	50%
Average Annual Compensation (in $millions) for Managing $20 million					
0.2	0.6	1.4	2.4	3.8	5.4

The partners and employees of the venture capital funds must identify their investments, structure the financing while protecting their interests, monitor their existing deals, allocate additional capital to the most successful deals, consult with the company, and assist with exit options such as providing entrees to financial institutions and investment banks for initial public offerings. Exhibit 6-4 summarizes how venture capitalists work.

Exhibit 6-4

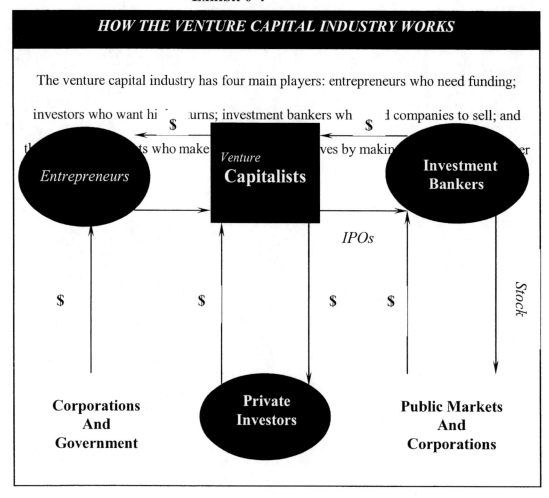

To gain a better understanding of the venture capital process, see the box entitled, *CacheFlow: The Life Cycle of a Venture Capital Deal,* at the end of this chapter.

Several questions that you might have relating to venture capital and its role in the financial life cycle of the firm include:

• What industries have been the leading recipients of venture capital dollars in recent years? Technology and biotechnology companies have dominated the venture capital markets for the past ten years, accounting for almost 50% of all venture capital financing.

• Why is traditional debt financing and bank borrowing often not available to small start-up businesses? Due to the short operating history and lack of assets to back traditional debt financings and borrowings, there are significant risks involved in lending funds to the firm. Due to usury laws, banks are unable to loan firms money and charge an interest rate sufficient for the risks involved. Therefore, many start-up firms seek venture capital to finance early growth and development.

• Who are venture capital *angels* and during what stage of financing do they mostly contribute? Angels provide the vast majority of start-up financing to get small businesses off of the ground. The financing decision is usually based on only a business plan or a product prototype.

• Why do venture capital backed IPOs outperform non-venture backed IPOs? Some reasons why venture capital backed IPOs outperform non-venture backed IPOs include: stringent management controls implemented by venture capital firms, the additional capital availability, and the reputation of the venture capital firms that have invested in the start-up.

6.2.3 *Equity Loans and Mezzanine Financing*

Equity loans and mezzanine financing are high-risk hybrid types of financing that include aspects of both debt and equity investments. Often debt investments are combined with equity options offering an ownership position along with the loan. This is an interim stage transaction that tides the firm over while it prepares for an IPO. If the market for IPOs is suffering from a case of indigestion, or due to a general bear market—such as the stock market has experienced during the period 2000 to 2002, it may be beneficial for the company to postpone an IPO. The company still needs to finance its operations and venture capitalists often may organize a final round of private equity or mezzanine debt.

Private equity will be sold generally to financial institutions at a return that is significantly lower than the 25% to 35% expected by venture capital, but well above the 8-12% return expected on a normal risk stock. Mezzanine debt financing is a bridge between later stage equity financing and the initial public offering. Usually bonds are issued that have a relatively high interest rate and a five to ten year maturity, but there is an expectation that the bonds will be retired with the proceeds of the initial public offering of the firm, which usually is expected within the following eighteen months.

An initial public offering is the exit stage of financing when a firm goes from private ownership to public ownership. At this point, the venture capitalists and private equity investors can begin to sell a portion of their ownership position in the company. As a condition of the IPO, there may be some amount and time restrictions placed upon the sale of stock by insiders. We discuss initial public offerings later in this chapter.

6.3   Security Offerings

6.3.1 *The New Issuance Process and the Role of Investment Banks*

The offerings of *newly issued securities* to investors are made in what is called the *primary securities market*. The primary securities market involves the distribution to investors of newly issued debt securities by central banks, governments, and corporations, and equity securities of corporations.

***The primary securities market involves the sale of newly issued
stocks and bonds to investors.***

The issuance of securities and the eventual sale of those securities to the public is a highly regulated process that is overseen by the SEC. The new issuance process consists of a number of steps. For the issuance of equity securities by a corporation, those steps are as follows:

- The board of directors of the corporation approves the securities offering.

- The investment banks that are acting as underwriters and their lawyers, and the lawyers for the issuing corporation, prepare a registration statement. They also perform due diligence and evaluate the firm, its facilities, management, products, financial statements, and other factors in preparing the prospectus—the offering document describing the financing.

- The finance professionals prepare a preliminary prospectus, also known as a *red herring* (because sections of the preliminary prospectus are printed with red letters), and file it with the SEC and distribute it to potential investors.

- If the transaction is an initial public offering of stock, the issuing firm and its investment bankers conduct a road show and describe the offering to institutional investors.

- After the initial registration with the SEC, the registration statement becomes effective on the 20th day after its filing. The SEC only makes sure that its rules and regulations are followed in the offering—it does not review the registration statement for valuation of the security nor does it determine whether the transaction is a good or bad deal economically for investors.

- The 20-day registration period is known as the Quiet Period. The company cannot comment publicly on the transaction while the offering is in the registration process at the SEC.

- Based on information in the Red Herring, the underwriters will poll prospective investors to estimate the level of interest in the offering.

- The underwriters may form an investment banking syndicate, which will take responsibility for buying the securities and remarketing them to the ultimate investors.

- On the date the registration statement becomes effective, the underwriters and the issuer negotiate a price on the security and the securities are offered to investors. A Tombstone Advertisement—a sample tombstone advertisement for the IPO of Flower Industries is shown in Exhibit 5-5—is often placed in financial newspapers to describe the final details of the offering and to list the investment banks that participated in the underwriting syndicate. The lead investment bankers of the Flower Industries, Inc. offering are Morgan Stanley Dean Witter and SBC Warburg Dillon Read.

- The issue is sold in market, securities are delivered to the investors, and the net proceeds of the issue are received by the issuer of the securities.

Exhibit 6-5
Tombstone Advertisement

An investment bank is a financial intermediary in the marketplace that works with issuers to distribute new securities and link investors and issuers. During the securities issuance process, an investment bank performs one or more of the following three functions:

- It advises the issuer on the terms, price, and timing of the offering;
- It purchases the securities from the issuer at a fixed price; and
- It distributes and sells the issue to the public.

The function of buying the securities from the issuer is called *underwriting*. When an investment bank buys the securities from the issuer, it accepts the risk of selling the securities to investors and is referred to as an underwriter.

> ***Underwriting*** *is when an investment bank purchases newly issued securities from a company and guarantees a fixed price.*

The typical underwriting transaction involves the potential risk of a significant loss. A single investment bank underwriting a transaction alone may be exposed to the danger of losing a substantial portion of its capital. To share the risk, the lead investment bank forms a group or syndicate of other investment banking firms to underwrite the issue. The gross spread, or profits or losses on the transaction, is then divided between the lead underwriter and the rest of the syndicate.

In addition to underwriting securities in the primary market, investment banks advise corporations on mergers and acquisitions, optimal capital structures, and investment strategies. Investment banks attempt to act in the best interests of both investors and issuers in the primary markets.

Investment banks specialize in underwriting securities and their expertise on pricing and information relating to valuation is extensive. Prior to underwriting a sophisticated transaction such as an IPO, investment banks perform extensive research on a financing. This research process in known as due diligence and is a valuable service that investment banks provide during the underwriting process. Following an IPO, the investment bank that is the lead underwriter in the transaction usually provides research and trading support for the company's stock in the secondary market.

To better understand the security issuance process, see the box entitled Anatomy of a Deal: The Microsoft IPO at the end of this chapter.

6.3.2 *Initial Public Offerings*

Companies sell initial public offerings of common stock for a number of reasons. The most common are: the need by the firm for additional capital; the desire to provide liquidity to the private investors in the company; and to provide better access for the firm to the capital markets.

An IPO creates advantages for the firm, such as liquidity for its investors, capital to the firm for expansion, and the possibility of an employee stock ownership plan. IPOs also have some disadvantages, namely they are expensive, organizations are forced to provide complete disclosure of their operations, inside investors lose control over the finances of the company, boards of directors must be appointed and paid, and outside auditors must be hired and paid. Going public is a costly process for a company.

Short-Run Performance of IPOs:

IPOs usually perform well on their first day of trading. The average first day return for an IPOs that were offered in the United States markets over the past forty years has been in excess of 15%. The first day performance of Internet IPOs in the late 1990s was extraordinary—V.A. Linux Systems soared 733% on the day it was issued. FreeMarkets, webMethods, Akamai, and CacheFlow all had first-day closing prices of over 400% higher than their IPO offering price. CEOs of Internet companies didn't worry about revenues, products, or employees. As long as they had a catchy business model and the endorsement of Merrill Lynch analyst Henry Blodget, or Salomon Smith Barney's Mary Meeker, they would become billionaires the minute the IPO was priced.

The extraordinary performance of Internet IPOs were just that—*extraordinary* and unsustainable! Many of the stocks of the most successful IPOs, based on one-day closing price performance, crashed and burned, often resulting in the bankruptcy of the company.

The abnormal one-day return for IPOs is commonly known as the underpricing effect. Generally, the offering price that is set by the underwriters for IPOs is *below* the level where supply meets short-term demand. The result is an excess demand for the issue and a sharp increase in price during the first day of trading. This type of abnormal first day return has been found in numerous countries around the world in which there are IPOs. Extensive research confirms these abnormally high returns.

Three possible reasons why IPOs are underpriced include:

- It makes it easier and less risky for the underwriters to sell the IPO;
- Because the shares have never traded before in the marketplace, investors demand a higher short-term rate of return to compensate for higher risk; and
- If the offering increases in price and performs well in the aftermarket, there is a lower likelihood of shareholder lawsuits.

Long-Run Performance of IPOs:

Although IPOs are believed to be underpriced at the time of the offering and can generate strong short-term returns, the long-run performance of new issues has been abysmal. Academic research documents some of the problems with IPOs over the long run. The long-term performance of IPOs has been an issue in finance for some time. A study performed by Tim Loughran and Jay Ritter (see box at the end of the chapter) sampled almost 5000 IPOs during the period from 1970 to 1990. The study paired the performance of IPOs with matching firms with similar market capitalization. The authors found that the average five-year returns of IPOs totaled 15.7%, compared to 66.4% for the matching firms. Research indicates that this weak long-term stock returns for IPO firms reflect a decline in their growth and operating performance (see box at the end of the chapter).

On August 8, 1995, Netscape Communications went public in a $140 million IPO. The demand for Netscape's shares was overwhelming. Netscape *developed the first Internet browser, and people loved its product and wanted to buy its shares. Netscape's IPO was one of the most phenomenal in US capital markets history as its share price traded at nearly three times the offer price ($28) on the first day of trading and volume was triple the number of shares available for trading. Netscape was the first of the Internet IPOs. The ones that followed during the bubble days of the late 1990s were even more outrageous. For a good example, see the box entitled* IPO Hall of Fame: the WebMethods IPO *at the end of this chapter.*

Privatization:

Privatizations are a unique form of an initial public offering. Privatization is when a government owned entity is sold to investors in the market. Just like any other IPO, the government hires an investment bank to complete the underwriting and provide advice regarding the transaction. Some examples of major government privatization ventures include Deutsche Telekom, Telebras, and Federal National Mortgage Association (Fannie Mae).

6.3.3 Seasoned Equity Offerings

A seasoned equity offering, or secondary offering, is an issuance process that is similar to an initial public offering. A corporation issues new securities that are sold to investors in the primary market, and the issuer receives cash for the new securities. However, unlike an IPO, a seasoned offering means that the stock of the firm already trades in the market, and investors know the value of the company's stock. The analysis necessary to establish a fair price, which is associated with an IPO, is avoided in a seasoned equity offering. Since there is already an active secondary market for the security, most often the road show can be shortened or eliminated.

Several questions that you might have relating to terms that you may have heard that are associated with security offerings, initial public offerings, and the role of investment banks include:

• What is a *green shoe option*? A green shoe option is the over-allotment option granted to investment banks, which allows the investment bank to sell up to an additional 15% of the offering to investors when the demand for a deal exceeds the planned offering size.
• What is the difference between a *best efforts* offering and a *firm commitment* underwriting? A firm commitment is when the investment bank purchases all shares of the offering from the issuer at an agreed upon price and takes responsibility for reselling the shares to the public. Under a best efforts transaction, the investment bank does not commit to purchase the shares from the issuer—it just agrees to attempt its *best efforts* to sell the shares to the public.
• What is included in the *prospectus* for a security offering? A prospectus includes the firm's comprehensive financial background, information on the

management team, the firm's primary competitors, and the firm's long-run growth strategy.

• When is the best time to go public? Determining the timing of an IPO can be critical to its success in the aftermarket and reduce the potential losses to the underwriting syndicate. Usually, the best time for an IPO is when the new issue market is *hot* and demand for new issues is overwhelming, such as during the period from 1995 to 1999. When the IPO market is poor, such as during the period from 2000 to 2003, even the best offerings are not well received by investors.

6.4 The Consolidation of Companies—Mergers, Takeovers, and Acquisitions

As shown in Exhibit 6-6, there was a virtual merger and acquisition wave during the 1990s. The year 1998 was a year of the colossal deals: Exxon-Mobil, Bell Atlantic-GTE, Travelers-Citicorp, and Daimler-Chrysler, to name a few. In 1999, $1.43 trillion worth of mergers and acquisitions in the United States reshaped industries nationwide—a 19.5% increase over 1998, according to the financial website, MergerStat.

Consolidations have dramatically changed the competitive landscape in many industries, particularly in telecommunications, electric utilities, banking and financial services, pharmaceuticals, and the media. The deal-making wave has declined dramatically since the year 2000 as merger and acquisition activity tends to closely follow the stock market.

Exhibit 6-6
Merger and Acquisition Activity

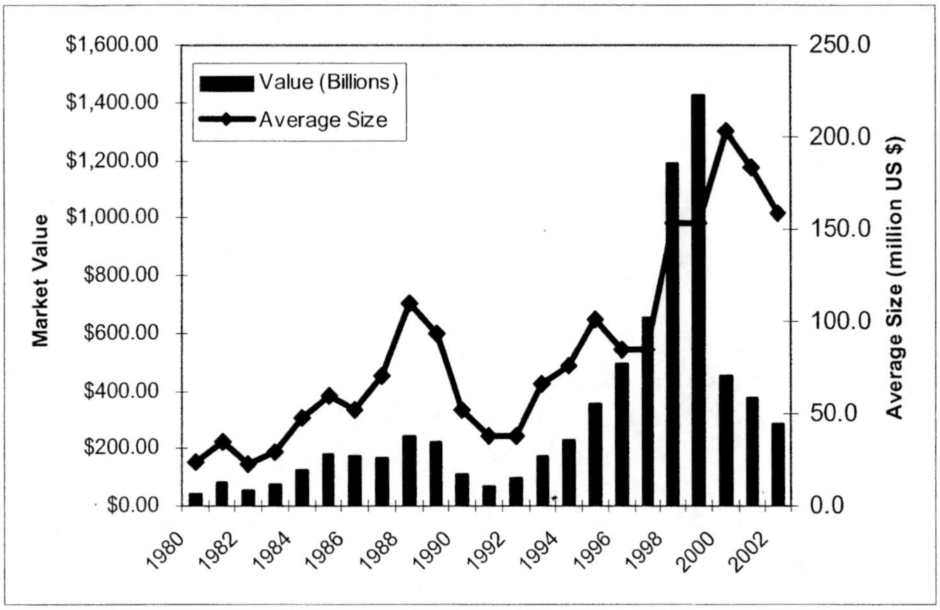

6.4.1 Merger and Acquisition Basics

A merger is when two or more firms agree to combine the separate companies into a single entity. The surviving entity is called the *acquirer*. The firm merged into the acquiring firm is called the *target*. An example is Bell Atlantic's merger with NYNEX. Bell Atlantic as the acquirer offered to buy NYNEX, the target, for $21 billion and NYNEX agreed to be purchased.

> A **merger** is when two or more firms combine, with one firm acquiring the other, to form a single surviving firm.

Another form of corporate merging is a consolidation. A consolidation is when the two separate firms combine and form a new entity separate from the previous two firms. An example of consolidation is the recent joining of Ciba-Geigy and Sandoz forming the new entity Novartis.

> A **consolidation** is when two or more firms combine and form a new firm separate from the previous firms.

Although many companies throughout the world are merging, there are other ways for firms to join forces without formally merging together. One way for two companies to cooperate without merging is a *strategic alliance*. A merger combines all of the assets of the firms involved, where an alliance can range from as little as a marketing agreement to as much as the joint ownership of operations.

In between a strategic alliance and a formal merger is a third type of cooperation, called a joint venture. A *joint venture* is when two firms combine parts of their individual operations to achieve a common goal. Joint ventures usually include the sharing of research, or cooperative research and development, sharing distribution channels, and production efficiencies. A joint venture is a small-scale merger in that the companies work together to achieve a common goal. A joint venture can also be a good alternative when the board of directors would not approve a formal merger.

6.4.2 Takeovers

Unlike the traditional friendly merger in which the target firm's board of directors approves the merger and the transaction is completed on terms that are mutually agreed upon by both firms, a takeover usually is a hostile transaction. In a takeover, another firm attempts to gain control over the target firm against the wishes of management or the board of directors.

> A hostile takeover is when an attempt to acquire a company is resisted by the target.

In a takeover the management personnel of the target firm, who believe they soon may be out of a job, opposes the transaction. Remember that management does not own the firm—the shareholders do. If the acquiring firm is able to purchase all, or at least a majority, of the shares from shareholders, it may be able to acquire the company, even if the management opposes it.

When an attempt to acquire a company is resisted by the target company, it is referred to as a hostile takeover. The actual number of takeovers is small compared to traditional mergers, however they receive a large amount of media attention and the participating parties often attract negative press. For this reason, attempted takeovers are highly visible transactions.

6.4.3   Tender Offers

In the previous section, we mentioned that management often may reject a merger proposal. When the target's management rejects a takeover offer, the bidding firm can attempt to acquire a controlling interest of the company's stock and force management to accept the offer.

The acquiring firm may offer to buy shares directly from the shareholders regardless of management's position. This is referred to as a *tender offer*. In a tender offer, the acquiring company offers to buy a portion of the outstanding shares of the firm at a premium to the current market price. It is usually necessary to acquire more than 50% of the outstanding voting shares, and this amount can vary based on state regulations and the company's charter.

A cash tender offer is often the quickest means of gaining control of a target firm. In the market for corporate control, speed is of the essence. If a takeover transaction is long and drawn out, competing bidders may marshal their resources to prepare and present a deal that may be more favorable to the target and include the current management of the target. This may also increase the premium that the acquiring firm pays for the target. The acquirer also may lose a bidding war. In a cash tender offer, no terms need to be negotiated and no securities need to be registered so the transaction can be completed quickly and efficiently.

Tender offers are extremely flexible when compared to other acquisition methods. The acquiring firm can offer to tender for as little as 20% to 40% of the outstanding shares, and still be successful. Once a block of shares this size is accumulated, management resistance to the bidding firm, now a substantial owner, declines. Then, the acquiring firm can negotiate with management and complete a friendly acquisition.

One example of an unsuccessful, yet highly visible, hostile takeover was the Bank of New York's bid for Mellon Bank. On April 22, 1998, Bank of New York offered $84 a share, amounting to $24 billion for the Pittsburgh-based commercial bank. Mellon was known for its high margin fee income and strong growth strategy, which had been pursued by many other banks seeking an alliance for the past few years. Mellon's management had decided that it wanted to remain independent and had rejected all previous offers.

After two years of friendly talks between the parties resulted in nothing, Bank of New York elected to circumvent management and bring the proposal directly to the shareholders. However, the strong opposition by the board and management would have made a combination very difficult to complete. Within a month, Bank of New York dropped the offer due to a lack of cooperation by Mellon's board of directors and management.

6.4.4 Proxy Contests

A proxy contest is when a group of outsiders try to gain control of a corporation by persuading existing shareholders to oust the current board of directors and elect a new board. The new directors, who are often large shareholders, will be sympathetic to the group that led the proxy fight and will proceed with whatever strategy that will maximize shareholder value. Proxy contests have been used in the past to change management teams, to change management strategy, and also to gain approval for a merger.

A proxy contest is a time-consuming and expensive process, particularly as corporations adjust their defensive tactics to better fight proxy contests. One way that corporations have been able to avoid proxy contests is to stagger the election of directors. This forces proxy contests to extend over multiple-year periods until the shareholders can elect an adequate number of directors to control the firm.

6.4.5 Payment for Transactions

Cash is the most favored currency in merger transactions with little doubt of its ultimate value. "Cash is king" was a popular slogan in the mid-1980s referring to the importance of cash bids relative to stock bids. The price of a company's stock fluctuates minute to minute, so the long-term value of a stock transaction can be much lower than its initial value at the time of a takeover offer. The only down side to a cash transaction is that it triggers a taxable event for shareholders. The shareholders of the target firm effectively sell their shares in exchange for cash and have to recognize capital gains (or losses) on the transaction.

Stock is being used more frequently in takeover transactions and was used much more than cash in the corporate control transactions of the 1990s. Stock was a more acceptable currency because of increasing equity valuations and the broad acceptance of stock during the high-tech run up of the late 1990's. Stock is easy to obtain, firms simply issue additional shares (approved by the board) and are then able to use this as their currency for acquisitions. Since target shareholders exchange shares of the target for shares of the acquiring firm, this type of transaction does not trigger a taxable event.

Stock transactions also have favorable implications for the earnings of the acquiring company. GAAP allows the acquirer to account for the transaction as a *pooling of interests* so the firm does not have to account for any goodwill. Goodwill is the price paid for a firm in excess of the book value of equity. This is a non-cash expense that reduces net income for years to come. To avoid the recognition of goodwill, companies finance acquisitions with stock and avoid the long-term expense.

6.4.6   Classes of Acquisitions

Horizontal—a horizontal merger is a merger between two firms in the same line of business and at the same level of production. For example, the bank merger between First Interstate Bank and Wells Fargo in 1996 was a horizontal merger. Both firms compete in the same markets and offer the same products. Horizontal mergers usually exploit the cost advantages of economies of scale.

Vertical—a vertical merger is a merger within the same industry, but at different levels of production. An example of a vertical merger is when a firm buys one of its suppliers or distributors. Auto manufactures were famous for being vertically integrated. However, in the last fifteen years, it has become apparent that specialization is more profitable than vertical integration. Many firms choose now to outsource the different levels of the supply chain and focus on their competitive advantage. The number of vertical mergers is small compared to horizontal mergers.

Conglomerate—a conglomerate is the merger of two companies that have unrelated lines of business. For example, GE is the world's largest and most profitable conglomerate, but their lines of business vary from jet engines to financial services. These firms are difficult to manage effectively due to their divergent lines of business. There was a burst of conglomerate mergers in the 1960s as firms attempted to reduce the risks of cyclical businesses. The long-run performance of these firms lags the performance of firms that focus on a specific line of business. During the economy of the late 1990s and early 2000s there have been very few conglomerate mergers. Much of the activity in the market for corporate control during the last 20 years has actually been the breaking up of old conglomerates.

6.4.7   Leveraged Buyouts

A leveraged buyout is an acquisition of a firm or a division of a firm that is financed principally with borrowed funds. The large amount of debt needed to finance the transaction is secured by a lien on the target firm's assets. Leveraged buyouts (LBO) are usually for companies that have stable and predictable operating cash flows. Due to the tremendous debt load, cash flows must be adequate to cover the payment of interest on the debt. LBOs tend to be most successful for firms and companies in stable and mature industries where cash flows are steady and predictable over the long-term.

The largest and most noteworthy LBO was the 1988 leveraged acquisition of RJR Nabisco by Kohlberg Kravis Roberts (KKR) for almost $26 billion. The deal symbolized the culmination of merger activity of the 1980s. The deal was in the spotlight as press releases filtered to the major periodicals exposing all of the details to the world. The book *Barbarians at The Gate* detailed every aspect of the deal and exposed the competing personalities and egos that dominated corporate America in the 1980s.

6.4.8   Takeover Defenses

A *poison pill* is a takeover defense in which a target firm issues rights to its shareholders that entitle existing shareholders to purchase additional shares at a substantial discount to the current market price. Poison pills often are used when an individual bidder acquires a large percentage of stock and is threatening to takeover a company. A poison pill allows the firms to sell shares to all shareholders except the corporate raider. This makes a takeover so expensive, if implemented, that since their emergence in the early 1980s no firm has ever had to exercise a poison pill to ward off a takeover.

Staggered election of board members dramatically reduces the possibility of a proxy contest because of the time required for an acquiring firm to gain a majority of board seats. Under this defense, usually one-third of the directors are elected each year so a proxy contest would take at least two elections to gain control of a board of directors. This is an eternity in the merger market.

Asset sales by a firm, including its prized assets, called crown jewels, makes an acquirer much less interested in buying the firm. When a firm sells its crown jewels and the acquirer aborts the transaction, the target firm is left without its prized possession.

Pac-Man Defense is when a potential acquirer bids for the target firm, and the target firm makes a counter bid for the acquirer.

Litigation is the easiest way to delay a merger by immediately filing a lawsuit against the bidding firm. Even if the lawsuit is unsuccessful, it delays completion of the transaction and gives the target additional time to look at other alternatives. The most common lawsuits that are filed relate to antitrust grounds, state takeover statutes, and securities law violations.

Greenmail is the term for a targeted share repurchase program. This practice originated during the 1980s. A corporate raider would accumulate a large block of shares (between 5% and 10%) and threaten to take over a company. The raider continues to accumulate shares and issues an ultimatum to management. The raider would negotiate to sell all its shares back to the firm at a premium to the current market price in exchange for dropping the takeover transaction. This became an extremely unpopular practice with non-participating shareholders because they were the ones that lost money in the transactions.

The *White Knight* defense is a friendly alternative to a hostile bid. When a firm is the target of a hostile bid, it can put itself on the market and seek a friendly suitor who will be sympathetic to the desires of management. An example of the use of a white knight defense was Warren Buffett's role in a raid on Salomon Brothers, an independent investment bank, in the 1990s. When Ronald Perelman hinted that he would purchase a 14% stake in the company, the CEO (John Gutfreund) sought a friendly suitor who would let the firm continue operating and not fire current management. The firm was facing hard times but insisted they could pull through. Buffett invested $700 million in convertible preferred stock. Salomon used the proceeds to buy out Perelman and the block of shares he was seeking, and retained its independence until it sold itself to Citigroup.

6.5   Focus and Disposition of Companies—Spinoffs and Equity Carve-Outs

Alongside the merger wave of the 1990's, companies have become more focused on core operations and have been disposing of subsidiaries and business lines that are not strategic to the growth and operation of the company—a de facto demerger wave. Dispositions involve the divestiture of one or more business units, usually through a spinoff or equity carve out or both.

Spinoffs involve the divestiture of a business division through a distribution of the common stock of the subsidiary to the shareholders of the parent company in the form of a stock dividend. In most cases, the spinoff is structured to be a tax-free distribution of shares from the parent company to its shareholders. Notable spinoffs include Quaker Oats-Fisher Price Toys, Adolph Coors-ACX Technologies, General Motors-EDS, Pacific Telesis-Air Touch, Union Carbide-Praxair.

In an *equity carve out*, a parent sells equity in the form of an initial public offering in a subsidiary of the company. In most cases, the parent retains a majority equity stake in the subsidiary. Equity carve outs also have grown significantly and have included AT&T-AT&T Capital, Textron-Paul Revere, and Thermal Electron and its many carve outs, including Thermolase, Thermo Instrument, and Thermo Fibertek, among others. Finally, there have been numerous equity carve out/spinoff combinations. These types of divestitures, often called spinouts or two-stage spinoffs, involve an equity carve out in a subsidiary, followed by a spinoff of the parent's remaining equity interest. Notable two-stage spinoffs include AT&T-Lucent Technologies, Sears Roebuck-Allstate Insurance and Pacific Telesis-Air Touch.

Motivations for spinoffs and equity carve outs vary. Sometimes there may be a perceived undervaluation of a combination of businesses by the stock market. This undervaluation may be due to a lack of synergy between the parent and subsidiary or between business units; to a poor understanding by the market of the combined entity; or to the excessive operating volatility of one of the entities. Sometimes separating a subsidiary from other business units is useful for strategic, human resource, or financing reasons. Generally, if alternative units require divergent strategies for success, if they require different managerial talents (entrepreneurial versus tight controls), or if they have dissimilar capital and financing requirements, a separation may be beneficial. Finally, a divestiture through a spinoff or equity carve out can eliminate inefficient cross-subsidies and lead to a more focussed organization in which operating performance and compensation are more closely matched.

6.6   Summary

This chapter discusses the financial life cycle of a firm. The stages identified are owner capital, bank financing, venture capital/private equity, initial and secondary public offerings, and mergers, acquisitions, and spinoffs. We follow the financial evolution of a firm from a start-up business, to IPO, to mergers and acquisitions, to divestitures. It includes a description of the role of the Securities and Exchange Commission (SEC) in regulating the financial markets in the United States, the types of financial instruments employed by companies to raise capital, the capital raising process, initial public and secondary offerings, and mergers, takeovers, acquisitions, and spinoffs and equity carve outs.

List of Terms

1. Initial public offering
2. Secondary offering
3. Prospectus
4. Owner's capital
5. Bank financing
6. Private equity
7. Venture capital
8. Angel
9. Seed funding
10. First round funding
11. Intermediate funding
12. Later stage funding
13. Equity loan
14. Mezzanine funding
15. Start-up financing
16. Underwriting
17. Road show
18. Quiet period
19. Red herring
20. Tombstone advertisement
21. Green shoe option
22. Best-effort
23. Firm commitment
24. Privatization
25. Direct public offering
26. Seasoned equity offering
27. Merger
28. Strategic alliance
29. Joint venture
30. Tender offers
31. Takeovers
32. Goodwill
33. Proxy contests
34. Leverage buyouts
35. Horizontal merger
36. Vertical merger
37. Conglomerate merger
38. Poison pill
39. Staggered election
40. Crown jewel
41. Pac-man defense
42. Greenmail
43. White knight
44. Spinoff - Carve out

Questions

1. What is the difference between primary and secondary markets for securities?
2. What is the primary objective of the Securities Exchange Commission?
3. What are the six stages of the financing life cycle of a typical company?
4. What are the advantage(s) and disadvantage(s) of initial public offerings?
5. What are the primary functions of an investment bank in an equity offering?
6. What are the 10 steps to launching an IPO?
7. What do green show options allow investment banks to do with an IPO?
8. What is the difference between a best-effort and firm commitment offering?
9. How is a direct public offering different from an IPO?
10. What is a seasoned equity offering?
11. How are strategic alliances and joint ventures different?
12. What is a proxy contest? How does it allow a company to takeover another?
13. What are leverage buyouts?
14. What are the various classes of acquisitions?
15. List the seven takeover defenses.
16. How are spinoffs and carve-outs different?

CacheFlow—The Life Cycle of a Venture Capital Deal
ONE Birth of CacheFlow, Inc., March 13, 1996

CacheFlow was born when founder Michael Malcolm had an idea to enable web surfers to gain faster access to their favorite websites. The key was to provide local storage, or "caching", of frequently used Internet data via an appliance added to customers' computer networks. Malcolm and his partner, Jim Pruskowski, managed to raise $1 million from angel investors to get their business started up. Although the new company had enough cash to survive, venture capitalists were after the two founders because they wanted a piece of the business, which they thought had the potential for incredible returns.

TWO First financing from venture capital firm, October 1996

Benchmark was the first VC firm to offer CacheFlow capital financing. The firm bought 3.2 million Series A preferred shares at 87.5 cents each – a total of investment of $2.8 million. That gave Benchmark a 25% stake in CacheFlow. The founders, angels, and employees own the rest of the company. The money raised from Benchmark was to be used in hiring more managers to develop the product.

January 1997

Malcolm invited Stuart Phillips, a senior executive at Cisco, to join the board as an outside director. Six months later, Phillips left Cisco to join US Venture Partners, another VC firm.

June 1997

Pruskowski stepped down as president and CEO for personal reasons but kept his 58,572 Series A shares. Malcolm became the interim CEO.

August 1997

The company started to get feedback from users trying out its prototype. Still no revenues.

THREE Testing of product, November 1997

After testing its product, CacheFlow seeks financing to market it. Phillips asked his firm to invest in the company.

December, 1997

CacheFlow still does not have a single cent in revenues. US Venture Partners invested $6 million to get a 17% share of the company. Benchmark put in another $1.8 million to maintain its 25% share. The company is now worth 158% more compared to 14 months ago.

May 1998

In the following three months, CacheFlow recorded revenues of $809,000. Clients included large corporations such as Xerox, Delta Airlines, and Goldman Sachs.

June 1998

In pursuit of huge fees, investment bankers start to knock on the company's doors, persuading them to do an IPO.

March 1999

Veteran tech executive Brian NeSmith is hired. NeSmith talked VC firms into further financing for the company. Technology Crossover put in $8.7 million for a 7% stake while Benchmark and US Venture Partners invested another $5.5 million in total. Stock option grants given to company executives diluted the VC firms' share of the company. Benchmark now had an 18% share while US Venture Partners owned 12% of the firm.

FOUR Board interviews bankers, July 1999

CacheFlow started talking to investment bankers about launching an IPO to raise more funds for the company.

August 1999

Goldman Sachs is eliminated from CacheFlow's list of potential investment bankers for its IPO because it advised one of the company's competitors, Inktomi, in a separate deal. In September, Morgan Stanley Dean Witter was picked as the lead underwriter while Credit Suisse First Boston was co-lead and Dain Rauscher was co-manager.

September 1999

CacheFlow files a registration with the Securities Exchange Commission for the sale of 5 million shares or 15.6% or the company's stock. The company also reported revenues of $2.2 million and a net loss of $6 million. CacheFlow had 120 employees then.

FIVE CacheFlow goes public, November 1999

Underwriters wanted to price the IPO at $13 a share. That month, Marc Andreesen, co-founder of Netscape, joined the board. The firm was getting more publicity and the underwriters increased their price to $20 a share. Finally, the IPO was launched at $24 a share. It closed at $126.375 on the first day of trading. That gave the original Series A shareholders a 14,342% gain!

February 2000

CacheFlow's stocks trades at $112.875, up 370.3% frm its IPO price. Benchmark's original $8 million investment is now worth $536.9 million. US Venture Partners' $8.1 million share is worth $351 million. Meanwhile, Malcolm, the founder of the firm, has become $575.7 million richer!

Source: The Wall Street Journal, February 22, 2000, "CacheFlow: The Life Cycle of a Venture-Capital Deal"

Anatomy of a Deal—The Microsoft IPO

Microsoft generates large amounts of internal cash flows, more than adequate to finance the company's operations. So why did the company conduct an initial public offering? The answer: Microsoft needed to provide liquidity to employees and investors who had equity stakes in the organization. For years, the firm had been issuing shares to compensate employees and early venture capital investors. To provide liquidity for his employees and investors, CEO BillGates decided in 1985 to take Microsoft public.

The first step in a public offering is to select an investment bank to manage the offer. By this time Microsoft was a well-established software company with a lock on the IBM PC operating system (MS DOS). Many investment banks had been soliciting Microsoft for years, anticipating an IPO. Microsoft executives agreed that they would hire a premiere Wall Street investment bank as the lead underwriter. In addition, they considered hiring a smaller bank specializing in technology financing to co-manage the deal.

Microsoft contacted eight investment banks and explained that it was planning an IPO. Each firm would have a chance to present a proposal on how they would structure the deal. Microsoft appointed its chief financial officer, Frank Gaudette, to rank the banks based on 19 different categories, and he alone would decide who would lead the deal. All of the banks solicited were capable of managing the deal; the winner would be the firm that was most compatible with Microsoft's management.

Two weeks after the presentations, Gaudette contacted the San Francisco office of Goldman Sachs, who had been soliciting Microsoft for over two years. Gaudette said, "I like you guys," and set a dinner the following week to discuss the details.

At the meeting (December 11, 1985), Goldman representatives discussed their ambitions to make the offering the most visible IPO of the year and told how great a job they would do. Now Microsoft had to select, based on the remaining candidates, who would co-manage the underwriting. This is where one of the smaller technology boutiques would participate. Microsoft selected Alex Brown because it was the first firm to contact it regarding an IPO. Three days later, the board of directors approved the selection of Goldman Sachs and Alex Brown. The deal was underway.

The deal formally kicked into gear December 17, 1985, when all participants involved were officially gathered together. This group included all the investment bankers, accountants, lawyers, and Microsoft's management. The 27-point agenda covered every phase of the deal. Microsoft planned to raise about $30 million by selling two million shares priced roughly at $15 per share. Current shareholders wishing to sell shares would comprise about 600,000 shares or about $10 million. The underwriters would be granted a green shoe option to sell an additional 300,000. The IPO would distribute roughly 12% of the companies stock in the public's hands. This would be enough to satisfy the goal of creating a liquid market for the employees and investors.

The most tedious part of the IPO was writing the prospectus. According to the Securities Act of 1933, Microsoft's stock could be sold only based on the information included in the prospectus. Although the prospectus provides useful information about the upcoming offering, it is more of a legal liability than a marketing tool. If the market price of the issue drops promptly following the offering, investors will comb the text for any sign of misrepresentation and sue the company. Therefore, the prospectus needs to be a bulletproof document. Work on the prospectus was ongoing with weekly meetings to review the progress.

On January 1986 the underwriter's security analysts began the formal due diligence. They examined every aspect of the company looking for potential obstacles and problems. The process took more than ten hours in which Gates and other top executives explained the potential risks of the software industry.

By late January, the only item left undetermined was the price range for the offering. Because of a strong market for software companies, the underwriters suggested a range between $17-$20 a share. Microsoft did not need the capital, they just wanted the shares sold quickly and easily. Gates insisted on a lower range, between $16 and $19. This was unusual, most companies want to maximize IPO proceeds, but money was not the issue in Microsoft's case.

On February 1 the lawyers approved the final draft of the prospectus. Two days later the Microsoft registered the offering with the SEC and the underwriters sent out 38,000 copies to potential investors worldwide.

The next step was the road show. This is the major marketing campaign designed to create demand for the offering. On February 18, the road show debuted in Phoenix, Arizona. Over the next ten days, they visited eight cities including London and Edinburgh. The demand following the road show was so strong that the underwriters decided they had to raise the offer price.

The SEC called on March 4 to review some necessary changes in the formal prospectus. The final prospectus was completed on March 7 and the deal was formally approved.

The 'book' on Microsoft [*the list of institutional investors expressing interest in the offering*] was one of the strongest in Goldman's history. The parties agreed to raise the offer price to between $20-$21 anticipating market demand at about $25 a share. Microsoft would go public the next week.

Monday, March 10, the Dow Jones Industrial Average was flat. But on Tuesday, the market was up 43 points in the morning (about 2%). Based on this information, the final offer price of $21 was agreed upon. Oracle Systems had gone public Tuesday morning at $15 and opened at $19.25. The investment banks were confident that the market was right for the offering and there would be no problems selling all the shares.

The only remaining issue was to determine the underwriting spread—*the difference between the issue price and the proceeds to Microsoft*. After considerable debate, they agreed on a $1.31 per share spread. This amounted to a little over four million dollars distributed proportionally to the syndicate banks.

At 9:35 AM on March 13, 1986, Microsoft's stock began trading on the NASDAQ at $25.75. Within minutes, Goldman Sachs and Alex Brown exercised their green shoe option and sold an additional 300,000 shares. By the end of the first day of trading, more than 2.5 million shares had changed hands representing all of the shares outstanding. Microsoft closed at $27.75 a share. The deal was a huge success.

On a final note, Bill Gates was a 45% owner in Microsoft when the firm went public in 1986. After the first day of trading, the market value of Gates' holdings was worth more than $350,000,000. Gates has sold some of his shares since the IPO. He now owns only 22.6% of the company. That smaller position is worth $46,000,000,000 ($46 billion) making Gates the richest individual in the world. When you un-adjust Microsoft shares for the seven stock splits since the IPO, it would be trading at $6142 per share based on the $21 a share offer. Not a bad deal for the college dropout.

Sources:
Uttal, Bro. *Inside the Deal that made Bill Gates $350,000,000. Fortune.* July 21, 1986.

The New Issues Puzzle
Tim Loughran and Jay Ritter

This analysis focuses on the long-run equity returns of new issues between 1970 and 1990. The authors look at both IPOs and seasoned equity offerings. We are only concerned with the IPO data, but the results were similar for both initial and seasoned offerings. It has been widely documented that IPOs underperform matching firms over 3 and 5-year periods following the offering. Ritter researched this hypothesis in 1991 and confirmed these results. This analysis updates his past findings based on a larger sample for firms.

The relative benchmarks for the IPOs were matching firms with the same market capitalization that did not issue stock during the five-year period following the IPO. The first graph looks at the average annual returns for all firms in the analysis. Throughout the first four years following an IPO, firms obviously underperform their benchmarks. There is only a slight underperformance in the fifth year. However this again confirms that in every year following an IPO, the IPO returns will lag the average matching firm. This raises the question of why investors buy and hold the new issues when it is well documented that they underperform the market.

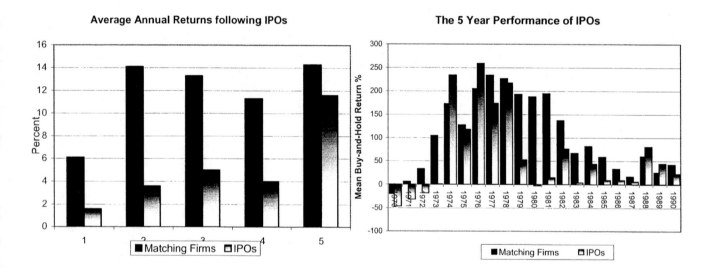

The graph on the right compares the 5-year cumulative returns of IPO and non-IPO firms. During the early 1970's when the market was very weak, IPOs showed negative returns greater than the matching firms. In the early 1980's the results are even more compelling. The authors sampled nearly 5000 IPOs between 1970-1990. During that 20-year period, IPOs outperformed the non-IPOs in only four of the twenty years. The average five-year returns for IPOs were 15.7% compared to 66.4% for the matching firms.

So why do investors still buy IPOs and hold them in their portfolios. The authors concluded that most firms go public when they are able to take advantage of market overvaluations. There is no evidence to why people still invest in new issues based on the widely documented underperformance. One possibility suggested by the authors is that investors are betting on longshots. Out of all the IPOs, a select few will greatly outperform the market. Investors seem to be too optimistic about the probability of investing in a star. The market is looking to find the next Microsoft and hence place too much faith in new issue investments. The long-term results of this strategy are not very favorable for investors.

Source:
Loughran, Tim., Ritter, Jay. *The New Issues Puzzle*. <u>Journal of Finance</u>. March 1995.

The Post Issue Operating Performance of IPO Firms
Bharat Jain and Omesh Kini

This study examined the operating performance of IPOs comparing pre-IPO and post-IPO results. The analysis indicates a significant decline in operating performance following the IPO. Although these firms experienced declines in operating performance, both sales and capital expenditures increases considerably following the IPO. The results indicate that investors value IPOs based on the expectations that current earnings growth will be sustained following the IPO. This performance level is not maintained and hence the long-run underperformance of IPO stock return.

The graphs below illustrate the findings of this study. Operating return on assets is defined as operating income (before depreciation and taxes) divided by total assets. Operating cash flows / total assets is defined as operating income less capital

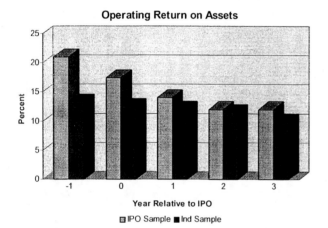

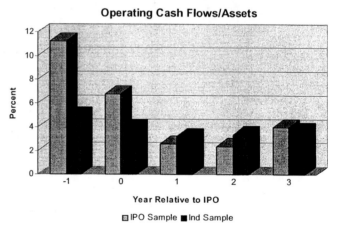

expenditure divided by total assets.

The data reported in the graphs above indicate that the operating performance measures of IPO firms decline relative to their pre-IPO levels (Year -1). The authors note three reasons for the decline in operating performance. First, the IPO reduces manager ownership in the firm and creates potential agency problems. Using the proceeds of the IPO in non-value maximizing projects results in a decline in operating performance (basically management waists the proceeds of the IPO). Second, managers could manipulate accounting numbers prior to going public. This would overstate pre-IPO performance and understate post-IPO performance. This is almost impossible to prove but is a possibility. Finally, management times the IPO with periods of unusually good performance levels. This is the most compelling argument. Unfortunately the strong growth levels will not be sustained into the future. The operating performance will eventually return to the industry averages as the data displays.

These results indicate that IPO firms are unable to sustain their pre-issue performance levels. IPO firms do display high post-issue growth in sales and capital expenditures, but measures of performance decline. This is consisted with the results of Loughran and Ritter (1995) analyzing the long-run underperformance of IPO stock returns. It appears that IPO firms are priced with the expectations that profit margins will continue to grow beyond pre-IPO levels, while in reality they decline over time.

Source:
Jain, Bharat., Kini, Omesh. *The Post-Issue Operating Performance of IPO Firms.* Journal of Finance. December 1994.

IPO Hall of Fame: webMethods, Inc.

In November 1999, webMethods, Inc. announced that it has filed a registration statement with the Securities and Exchange Commission for an initial public offering of the company's common stock. webMethods, Inc. is a leading provider of infrastructure software and services that allow companies to achieve business-to-business integration, or B2Bi. B2Bi software is a category of software that enables companies to work more closely with their customers, suppliers and other business partners through the real-time exchange of information and transactions. The company's software solution, webMethods B2B(TM), permits its customers to rapidly and cost effectively deploy real-time business-to-business e-commerce applications over the Internet by integrating their existing enterprise applications with those of their customers, suppliers and other business partners.

Morgan Stanley Dean Witter was acting as lead manager of the offering. Merrill Lynch & Co., Dain Rauscher Wessels, and Friedman Billings Ramsey were acting as co-managers.

Before its IPO, webMethods did not get a lot of press because its product is invisible: The software enables companies to share data, whether or not they use compatible software. But the Fairfax, Virginia-based company has become a major player in B2B electronic marketplaces because it enables companies to integrate their back-office systems with the marketplaces without manually re-entering online transaction data. That saves millions of dollars and provides a significant part of the efficiencies that have spurred Internet marketplaces. webMethods commenced operations in June 1996 and shipped its first product in June 1998 therefore its limited operating history is a huge risk factor when looking at webMethods as an investment. The company isn't unlike other Internet investments; it carries a significant amount of added risk.

In January 2000, webMethods and their lead underwriter, Morgan Stanley, decided to set the price of their IPO at $11-$13 a share. 4.1 million shares will be sold in the offering. webMethod's original filing in November 1999 did not contain such details as how many shares were in the offering or their projected price range. If the shares were to be priced at $12 each, the company predicted it would make about $44.6 million after expenses. It plans to use the proceeds for working capital and general corporate purposes, including research and development. The company may also use the net proceeds for sales and marketing.

The underwriting group led by Morgan Stanley had an option to buy 615,000 more shares if there is heavy demand for the 4.1 million shares. After filing with the SEC, the company went on to apply to trade the stock on Nasdaq under the symbol "WEBM".

On February 10th, 2000, webMethods announced that it will nearly triple its projected price range for its initial public offering to $28-$30 per share from the $11-$13 a share range set in January. The company did not say in the amended prospectus filed with the Securities and Exchange Commission what it would likely net from the 4.1 million shares of common stock sold in the new price range. After the offering there would be about 31.2 million shares of common stock outstanding in the company, putting its initial market capitalization at about $904.8 million based on a $29 per share initial price, the midpoint of the new range. The stock was set to begin trade in February 2000.

Just before the webMethod's IPO went on the market, the company surprised Wall Street when it announced it final IPO price of $35, easily beating all versions of estimated pricing. This will bring the offering proceeds to a total of $144 million. With a slew of high profile clients, a rapidly emerging market, a stellar underwriting team and most of all an impressive list of inside owners, webMethods was set to become one of the best all-time first day performances. Adding to the company's growing credibility was its strategic alliance with SAP AG. Among its other customers are many of the top emerging business-to-business e-marketplaces such as mySap.com, Ariba.com and Dell Direct.

Finally, adding to the credentials of webMethods are its all-star lineup of venture capital holders that include The Mayfield Fund, FBR Technology, Venture Partners, Goldman Sachs Group and Dell USA, the investment engine of Dell Computer. Collectively, the group maintains a post-offering stake of roughly 44%.

Living up to investors' expectations, webMethods became the biggest first-day gainer in the first quarter of 2000. Its shares rose 508% on its first day - from $35 to $212 5/8. For the entire first quarter, it was up 590 percent. Without a shadow of a doubt, the best deal by aftermarket performance for the month of February 2000 was webMethods. By the end of the month, the stock had racked up a monstrous gain of 780.18% and was nearly 60% above its $195 opening price.

Facts of the Deal[8]

Company	webMethods, Inc.	Stock Symbol	WEBM
Lead Underwriter	Morgan Stanley Dean Witter	Final IPO Price	$35
Co-Managers	Merrill Lynch & Co.	Final Offering Amount	$165,025,000
	Dain Rauscher Wessels	Est. Offering Expenses	$1,250,000
	Friedman Billings Ramsey	Number of Shares Offered	4,100,000
Filing Date	11/19/99	Green Shoe Option	615,000
Pricing Date	02/10/00	Total Shares Outstanding	30,118,932
First Trading Day	02/11/00	Percent Floated	15.65%
Quiet Period Exit	03/07/00	Market Cap at IPO	$1,054,162,620

---

[8] Data from http://www.ipo.com

CHAPTER 7

OVERVIEW OF THE FINANCIAL MARKETS

In this chapter we examine the financial markets—the stock and bond markets where securities are purchased and sold, and the foreign exchange and derivatives markets. We discuss the role of the primary and secondary securities market, the money and capital markets, the major stock exchanges, the over-the-counter market, and the manner in which trades take place in the markets, as well as different ways to measure the performance of the markets.

The learning objectives for the readers of this chapter are to develop an understanding of:

- The nature and role of the primary and secondary securities market;
- The difference between the capital and the money markets;
- The major financial exchanges, their classification, and the type of issues traded on these exchanges;
- The roles of the specialist and the market-maker;
- The types of buy and sell orders that can be placed in financial markets;
- The major financial markets performance indices, how they are calculated and what they measure; and
- The services and costs of full service, discount, and electronic brokerage firms.

7.1   Introduction to Financial Markets

Financial markets exist so that excess monies from investors can be transferred cheaply and efficiently to businesses, governments, individuals and other entities that have profitable investment opportunities and a shortage of funds. In return for the use of these monies, the user of the funds sells an investor a *security*—a claim against the assets or cash flows of the entity. The markets in which the issuers of securities receive the funds directly from the initial sale of securities are called primary markets.

Another function of financial markets is to provide *liquidity*—the ease with which an owner of a security can sell an investment to another investor or trade it in the securities markets. Securities markets provide a marketplace where buyers and sellers of securities can complete transactions quickly and efficiently, and save investors from a costly search for potential buyers and sellers of the stock or bond. Securities markets also provide investors, issuers and other economic participants information about the current market value of their securities. The markets in which the current owners of securities receive the funds from the buyers of securities are called secondary markets.

If the security is an equity claim, such as a common stock, the investor of funds receives ownership rights in the firm in an amount that represents the percentage of the firm's stock that he owns. The stockholder also has the right to any dividends if declared by the firm and to the residual value of the firm after all business expenses and creditors are satisfied. The stockholder also has certain voting rights and participates in electing the firm's board of directors. If the security is a debt—a bond or debenture, the bondholder receives periodic payments of interest at a specified interest rate, and the repayment of principal on a predetermined date.

7.1.1 How Financial Markets Work

During the decade of the 1990's, the stock markets in the United States performed spectacularly. Fueled by the birth and growth of the Internet and the significant reduction of transactions costs, the Dow Jones Industrial Average rose from a level of 2,753 at the end of 1989 to 11,453 at the end of the Millennium. Likewise, the S&P 500 moved from 353 points to 1,469, and the NASDAQ Index rocketed from 454 to 4,069—a nine-fold increase.

All good things must come to an end. The Internet bubble burst and markets retreated severely in 2000, 2001 and 2002—the NASDAQ plummeting a total of 75%, the S&P 500 down 40%, and the DJIA dropping 27%. In 2003, stock markets around the world rallied by an average increase of from 25% to 55%. And in 2004, the DJIA increased by 3%, the S&P 500 jumped 9%, and the NASDAQ Index increased by 8.6%. Investors familiar with the stock markets know that stock returns and prices can fluctuate substantially.

Exhibit 7-1
20-year History of DJIA, S&P 500, and NASDAQ Indices

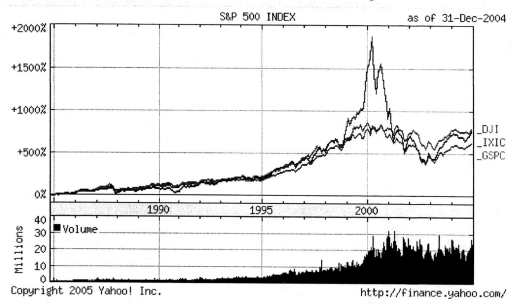

Each business day millions of investors around the world trade stocks and bonds in the financial markets and stock and bond prices go up or down—often it seems for no specific reason. Perhaps you've wondered, what the principal factors are that propel these daily stock prices fluctuations.

The economics underlying the movements of the stock and bond markets are a mystery to most people. At the end of trading each day, analysts on CNBC and other financial news networks attribute price movements to any number of factors: government reports on consumer or wholesale prices: changes in interest rates; the increasingly bullish or bearish sentiment of investors; statements by Federal Reserve Chairman, Alan Greenspan; or company earnings reports exceeding or falling short of expectations. Below, we briefly examine some of those reasons.

Supply & Demand:

Like all competitive markets, the fundamental determinants of the price of a security in the secondary market are the supply and demand functions for that particular security. The market-clearing price for a security is the price at which the current supply of the security that is owned by potential sellers equals the

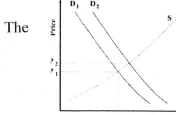

demand for the security among potential buyers. The current price of a security is where the supply equals the demand.

The current price of an asset, such as a stock, indicates the amount that the marginal investor, given supply and demand conditions, is willing to pay to acquire as little as 100 shares of a stock. In the short-run, this market-clearing price may have nothing to do with the true long-term value of a stock. The current price may be heavily influenced by a very temporary and extreme supply and demand imbalance.

In Chapter 2, we discuss the price movement of the stock of EntreMed (ENMD), a biotechnology company in which the price of its shares between its close on a Friday and its opening on a Monday increased six-fold due to a favorable news article in *The New York Times*. The following factors contribute to investment demand for a fixed supply of shares of a stock.

Movements in Interest Rates and Economic Events:

New information about economic variables often has major impact on the bond and stock market as a whole. Variables such as inflation, interest rates, foreign exchange rates, and unemployment reports often act to drive movement in the bond, stock, mortgage, currency and derivative securities markets. For reasons that we describe in later chapters, asset prices react significantly to changes in interest rates or the rate of inflation. When interest rates or the rate of inflation goes up, stock and bond prices go down. When interest rates or the rate of inflation goes down, stock and bond prices generally go up.

Company Financial Performance:

Investor demand for the stock of a particular company is usually affected by events that impact how a firm performs in the market, and the effect of measuring the performance through a fundamental financial analysis of a company. Fundamental analysis looks at the expected future revenues, cash flows, and earnings of a company to determine what the appropriate value of the stock should be.

New information is continuously revealed to the market. The result is a constant changing of the prospects of a company. For example, the announcement of a lawsuit alleging patent infringement indicates a possibility of future problems. The lawsuit may reduce the valuation and lower investor demand for the stock. Conversely, positive news relating to a company that results in expectations of increased expected revenues and earnings should increase the price of the company's stock.

Industry Performance:

The expected performance of an industry often affects all of the individual companies comprising that industry. For example, Internet stocks reacted dramatically to industry performance expectations. During the 1990s, if a report was issued that the Internet is expected to grow at a higher annual rate than the market had expected previously, the majority of the stocks of companies in the Internet industry adjusted positively to the new information contained in that report. Alternatively, if an industry leader reported poor earnings or losses that were greater than anticipated, the stocks of other companies in that industry would fall. Investors were concerned that the factors that lowered the earnings of the industry leader will come to bear on the stock prices of the other companies in the industry.

National and World News Events:

Major news stories influence investor demand. The possibility of war in the Middle East or an international recession resulting from the devaluation of an Asian currency can dramatically influence people's attitude toward risk and investing. Negative news, such as the news relating to the terrorist attacks of September 11, 2001, causes the price of risky assets such as common stock to drop precipitously. The same negative news also causes the price of risk-free assets such as U.S. Treasury Bonds to increase substantially. This type of market reaction due to a reevaluation of risk in the market—fleeing risky securities such as stock, and redeploying funds into less risky U.S. Treasuries, is called a *flight to quality.*

7.1.2 Regulation of the Financial Markets in the United States

The principal regulator of all primary and secondary market activity in the United States is the Securities and Exchange Commission (SEC). Following the stock market crash of 1929 and the Great Depression of the early 1930s, a wave of financial regulation was implemented to curb market speculation and fraud, and to strengthen investor confidence.

The *Securities Exchange Act of 1934* created the SEC. The SEC is responsible for licensing securities professionals, collecting public disclosure information (e.g., quarterly and annual reports), and enforcing the various securities laws in the United States. This section reviews the SEC's activity in the primary and secondary markets and introduces some of the information resources available from the SEC on the Internet.

The SEC's primary objective is to provide investors with complete disclosure of all material information concerning publicly traded securities. Its goal is to create a level playing field for investors and minimize the information asymmetries that existed in the early 1900s.

Prior to the creation of the SEC, Congress initially passed *The Securities Act of 1933*. The Securities Act of 1933 is designed to regulate the primary securities markets by providing investors with the necessary information to make informed decisions regarding an issue of new securities. A lot of technicalities are involved, and numerous lawyers are employed in issuing a new security—a stock or bond issue, from the preparation of a registration statement and the filing with the SEC, to the distribution of a preliminary prospectus, to the sale of the securities to investors either directly or through a group of investment banks.

The Securities Exchange Act of 1934 also implemented regulation pertaining to the sale and trading of securities in the secondary markets—after the initial issuance of securities. This act regulates the activities of the various stock and bond exchanges in the United States and all of the financial institutions and finance professionals that participate in this market.

With the growth of computer technology and the Internet, the SEC has opened a database that allows immediate access to all public information electronically filed with the SEC, at its web address: www.sec.gov/. The EDGAR database is the SEC electronic public document access system; it may be accessed directly through the SEC's website.

7.1.3   Primary Versus Secondary Securities Markets

The *primary securities markets* are the markets in which *newly issued securities* are sold to investors. The primary securities market for bonds involves the distribution to investors of newly issued debt securities by corporations, central banks, governments, and agencies. The primary securities market for stock includes the first time issuance of common stock for companies, called *initial public offerings (IPOs)*, the sale of issues of preferred stock, and the sale of additional common equity securities of corporations.

The primary securities markets involve the sale of newly issued stocks and bonds to investors.

The issuance of securities in the primary markets and the eventual sale of those securities to the public is a highly regulated process that is overseen by the SEC. The new issuance process consists of a number of steps, which we describe in Chapter 6.

An investment bank is a financial intermediary in the marketplace that works with issuers to distribute new securities in the primary markets and link investors and issuers. During the securities issuance process, an investment bank performs one or more of the following three functions:

- It advises the issuer on the terms, price, and timing of the offering;
- It purchases the securities from the issuer at a fixed price; and
- It distributes and sells the issue to the public.

The function of buying the securities from the issuer is called *underwriting*. When an investment bank buys the securities from the issuer, it accepts the risk of reselling the securities to investors, and the investment bank is referred to as an underwriter. In addition to underwriting securities in the primary market, investment banks advise corporations on mergers and acquisitions, optimal capital structures, and investment strategies. Investment banks attempt to act in the best interests of both investors and issuers in the primary markets.

Secondary securities markets are where financial assets that previously were issued in the primary markets are traded among investors. The key distinction between a primary market and a secondary market is that the issuer of the security does not receive funds from the buyer in a trade in the secondary market. Instead, the security changes hands, and funds flow from the buyer of the security to the seller—the previous owner of the security.

Secondary securities markets are markets where the funds flow from the buyer of a security to the seller—not to the issuer of the security.

Liquidity is the ability to cheaply, quickly and efficiently turn an asset into cash. The secondary market provides investors with liquidity for securities. The periodic trading of a financial asset discloses information about the asset's value. Furthermore, secondary markets bring together many interested parties and reduce the search costs of buying and selling securities. This reduces transaction costs and the time required to trade financial assets. By keeping search and transaction costs low, the secondary market facilitates trading and investing in financial assets.

Trading induces additional trading. If no one trades, there is no liquidity in the market, there is no price discovery, and higher search costs. However, as long as investors are willing to participate in a secondary market, the market will facilitate trading.

To minimize search costs and to gather investors, it is helpful to have a physical central trading location. For stocks and bonds, this location is called an *exchange*. If goods and services are traded, this location is called a trading post. Nothing is made or issued at the exchange or trading post—only traded.

Stock exchanges are formal organizations, approved and regulated by the Securities and Exchange Commission (SEC). The only individuals that are able to trade on the exchange floor are *official members* of the exchange. Stocks that are traded on a given exchange are said to be *listed issues*.

> *Stock exchanges are organizations where stocks are traded*
> *by the members of the exchange.*

To become a member of an exchange, securities firms and individuals must buy a seat on the exchange. The number of seats on an exchange is limited—there are 1,366 seats on the New York Stock Exchange. The cost of the seat is determined by supply and demand. The highest price paid for a seat on the NYSE was $2 million in March 1998. Purchasing a seat gives its owner the right to be on the floor of the NYSE.

7.1.4 Money Markets Versus Capital Markets

In *money markets,* debt securities with original maturities of one year or less are traded. Money markets serve to transfer funds from market participants with short-term excess funds to governments, corporations, and agencies that have short-term needs for funds. Investors usually purchase money market instruments as a temporary investment to park excess cash prior to its use for longer-term investments in a business or a capital asset.

Securities such as Treasury bills, federal funds, commercial paper, certificates of deposit, repurchase agreements, banker's acceptances and other short-term instruments are traded in the money market. Investors purchase low-risk, liquid money market securities with short-term excess monies. Characteristics of money market instruments are:

- They are sold in large denominations (usually $1 million and larger);
- They have a low default risk; and
- They have an original maturity of one year or less.

Interest rates on money market securities generally are lower than interest rates on assets that are traded in the capital markets, such as long-term bonds or the expected returns associated with common stock. Exhibit 6-4 below shows the interest rates on money market securities on December 30, 2004, as taken from the Federal Reserve's web site. Short-term interest rates over the two years prior to this date have been very low on a relative basis. The Federal Reserve has raised the Federal Funds rate by ¼% on four occasions during the past year. Absent the quote for the prime rate and the discount rate, the actual interest rates or re-offering yields for the instruments in Exhibit 7-4 range from 2.77% for 1-year constant maturity Treasuries to 1.71% for four-week Treasury Bills.

Exhibit 7-4
Federal Reserve Web Site, Interest Rates of 1/1/2005

```
H.15 DAILY UPDATE: WEB RELEASE ONLY          For immediate release
SELECTED INTEREST RATES                         December 30, 2004


Yields in percent per annum
```

Instruments	2004 Dec 27	2004 Dec 28	2004 Dec 29	2004 Dec 30
Federal funds (effective) 1 2 3	2.24	2.24	2.23	
Commercial paper 3 4 5				
Nonfinancial				
1-month	2.29			
2-month				
3-month				
Financial				
1-month	2.27	2.32	2.30	
2-month	2.37	2.38	2.35	
3-month	2.44	2.41	2.41	
CDs (secondary market) 3 6				
1-month	2.36	2.36	2.37	
3-month	2.50	2.50	2.50	
6-month	2.72	2.73	2.73	
Eurodollar deposits (London) 3 7				
1-month	2.35	2.35	2.35	
3-month	2.47	2.47	2.48	
6-month	2.70	2.70	2.70	
Bank prime loan 2 3 8	5.25	5.25	5.25	
Discount window primary credit 2 9	3.25	3.25	3.25	
U.S. government securities				
Treasury bills (secondary market) 3 4				
4-week	1.82	1.84	1.71	
3-month	2.24	2.22	2.19	
6-month	2.56	2.55	2.53	
Treasury constant maturities				
Nominal 10				
1-month	1.90	1.88	1.76	
3-month	2.26	2.25	2.22	
6-month	2.63	2.62	2.60	
1-year	2.78	2.77	2.77	

In *capital markets*, investors buy and sell debt securities with an original maturity longer than one year, common and preferred stock, and mortgages and mortgage-backed securities. Corporations, governments, municipal entities and agencies issue the long-term securities that are traded in the capital markets. The principal purchasers of these long-term securities are financial institutions and individual investors.

The price fluctuations of long-term securities can be quite substantial. Academic studies have shown that the average price fluctuation of the shares of common stock in the United States is almost 50% per year. Price fluctuations of long-term bonds, which also can be significant, generally are dependent in changes in interest rates. Investors, who wish to test their stock picking skills or try to earn returns in excess of those available in the money market, may relish the challenges of investing in the capital markets.

7.1.5   Foreign Exchange Markets

Each year, the world seems to grow smaller. With the Internet and news and media organizations providing instantaneous access to information from even the most remote places on earth, events that affect businesses and governments in one country has immediate and ripple effects throughout the world. Today, many U.S. corporations act on a global basis: buying raw materials for a product from different South American countries; producing components of the product in the Far East; assembling the product in Mexico; and selling the product in France or Germany or Great Britain. Many foreign corporations act in a similar manner.

It is important for financial managers of corporations to understand the foreign capital markets and to know how the foreign exchange markets operate. Many of the raw materials that a corporation buys are denominated in foreign currency. Additionally, the company may have production and assembly plants with a significant amount of employees paid in local currencies that are based in other countries. Movements in the value of foreign currency can greatly increase or decrease a corporation's revenues and profits.

Foreign exchange rates are the rates at which the currency of one country can be traded for the currency of another country. For example, on December 31, 2004, the foreign exchange rates for Euros, British Pounds, and Japanese Yen to U.S. dollars were:

1 Euro = $1.3556 U.S. Dollar
1 British Pound = $1.919 U.S. Dollar
102.54 Japanese Yen = $1 U.S. Dollar

The exchange rates listed above as well as others are shown in Exhibit 7-5, and are called *spot exchange rates*. The spot exchange rate is the rate of exchange for the immediate delivery of currencies. Spot rates are the currency rates that are of most importance to the international traveler or tourist. Spot rates affect the real out of pocket cost for an American visitor in Europe for a glass of wine at Café Deux Magots in Paris, or a plate of Manchego cheese at La Trucha in Madrid.

Exhibit 7-5
Spot Exchange Rates-December 31, 2004

Major Currency Cross Rates

Currency Last Trade		U.S. $ N/A	Yen 4:47pm ET	Euro 4:49pm ET	Can $ 4:43pm ET	U.K. £ 4:49pm ET	AU $ 4:49pm ET	Swiss Franc 4:47pm ET
1 U.S. $	=	1	102.5400	0.7377	1.2006	0.5210	1.2789	1.1392
1 Yen	=	0.009752	1	0.007194	0.011709	0.005081	0.012473	0.011110
1 Euro	=	1.3556	139.0032	1	1.6275	0.7062	1.7337	1.5443
1 Can $	=	0.8329	85.4073	0.6144	1	0.4339	1.0652	0.9489
1 U.K. £	=	1.9195	196.8255	1.4160	2.3046	1	2.4549	2.1867
1 AU $	=	0.7819	80.1760	0.5768	0.9387	0.4073	1	0.8907
1 Swiss Franc	=	0.8778	90.0105	0.6475	1.0539	0.4573	1.1227	1

Source: Yahoo Finance Web Page-December 31, 2004

Other categories of foreign exchange rates are *forward exchange rates*. Forward rates are rates for the exchange of currencies at certain dates in the future, and can be higher than, lower than, or equal to current spot exchange rates. Forward exchange rates are used extensively by corporations and financial institutions to hedge the risk of a change in the spot exchange rates. Forward markets allow corporations to lock in exchange rates to pay for the delivery of goods or services in the future, or to receive funds for the sale of products to foreign purchasers to be delivered in the future. Forward foreign exchange rates can be used to reduce the currency risks associated with doing business in a foreign country.

The levels of spot and forward foreign exchange rates can fluctuate quite substantially, and are dependent upon many variables, including the fiscal and monetary policies of a country. Usually, a country that manages its fiscal and monetary policies on a conservative basis, meaning that it runs domestic budget and foreign trade surpluses, and does not set artificially low interest rates, has a strong currency. This means that the exchange rate of the domestic currency will generally increase.

For example, during the late 1990's the United States was in a rare situation of generating budget surpluses, and in October 2000, the dollar increased in value to a level of $0.83 dollars = 1 Euro. At the end of 2004, due to increased spending associated with wars in Afghanistan and Iraq, the United States was running record budget deficits and trade deficits, and had relatively low interest rates. One Euro has appreciated to $1.355 dollars—a tremendous gain of over 60% against the dollar since 2000. This makes that plate of Manchego cheese and glass of rioja wine much more expensive in U.S. dollars for American tourists in Europe. International travelers want a strong domestic currency so their money can buy more foreign goods and services.

Conversely, corporations and businesses that produce goods and services domestically and export products generally prefer a weak currency. A weak dollar permits firms to take advantage of a depreciating exchange rate to ship more products and convert that lower exchange rate into a greater amount of dollars. A weak exchange rate also encourages investors to purchase investments that are denominated in the foreign currency. As the domestic currency depreciates, the value of the foreign investment appreciates in domestic terms.

7.1.6 Derivatives Securities Markets

A *derivative security* is a security in which the value and payoff of the derivative is based upon the value of another security. For instance, a stock option is a derivative security because the value of the option is based, among other things, upon the value of the underlying stock. And as the value of the underlying security changes, the value of the derivative security also changes.

> *A derivative security is a security in which the value of the derivative is based upon the value of another security.*

Derivative securities consist of forwards, futures, swaps and options contracts and of more complex equity and debt securities that are embedded with these types of contracts. The markets in which derivatives trade are called derivative securities markets. Derivative securities and contracts are traded on organized commodities and stock exchanges, such as the Chicago Board of Trade and the American Stock Exchange.

Certain characteristics of derivative securities make them desirable as assets that can be easily structured and traded in the financial markets to manage and transfer risk. Investors who use these instruments to reduce risk are called *hedgers*. Investors who use these instruments to increase risk are called *speculators*. We describe derivative securities and the markets in which they trade in Chapter 16.

7.2   Organization of the Financial Markets

There are seven major organized stock exchanges in the United States. The two largest national stock exchanges are the New York Stock Exchange (NYSE) and the American Stock Exchange (AMEX). The NYSE is the largest stock exchange in the United States. Exhibit 7-6 below breaks down the share and dollar volume of annual trading activity.

Exhibit 7-6
2002 Trading Volume by Market

Trading Volume (2002)[1]		
	Share Volume (billions)	Dollar Volume ($ billions)
New York Stock Exchange	363.1	8,900
American Stock Exchange	7.3	208
NASDAQ	433.7	7,200

7.2.1   New York Stock Exchange

The history of the New York Stock Exchange is deeply rooted in that of the United States and the evolution of the economy. The NYSE began operations on May 17, 1792, when 24 individuals gathered under a buttonwood tree and declared the membership requirements and designated participation in the exchange. Over the last 200 years, the NYSE has become the center of the financial world where the market capitalization (the market value of all of the outstanding shares) of the listed companies is greater than the gross domestic product of every other industrialized nation in the world.

The New York Stock Exchange is the largest stock exchange in the world with a market capitalization in excess of $10 trillion dollars. The NYSE is an auction market where the price of securities is determined by the open bids and offers made by exchange members, on their own behalf or on the behalf of their clients. Each listed security is traded at only one location called a *trading post*, on the floor of the NYSE and all trading is monitored and facilitated by the specialist assigned to the particular issue.

> *A trading post is the location on the floor of a stock exchange where a particular security is traded.*

The NYSE is the most liquid stock exchange in the world. The average daily trading volume has grown from 50 million shares per day in 1980 to over 1 billion shares per day in 2004. There are more than 200 billion shares on the NYSE issued by more than 3,000 companies. To be listed on the NYSE, companies must meet the exchange's listing requirements, which include a minimum number of shareholders, a minimum market capitalization of $100 million, a certain trading volume, and minimum annual earnings of $2.5 million.

The Role of the Specialist:

Specialists are members of the exchange who are selected to specialize in the buying and selling of shares of one or more specific stocks. Specialists are individuals and firms who are willing to buy or sell the securities that they represent whenever anyone is interested in trading in the issue. Specialists are expected to stabilize the stock price whenever possible by buying and selling stock out of their own inventory account. To be a specialist on the NYSE, a minimum trading capital requirement of $1 million is required. Exhibit 7-7 lists some of the largest specialists on the NYSE.

Exhibit 7-7
NYSE Specialist Firms

Firm/Ownership	Total Common Stocks	Share by Dollar Value of Specialist Trades	No. of DJIA Stocks	Big Name Stocks
LeBranche & Co. (Publicly traded)	582	26.9%	9	3M; AT&T; Berkshire Hathaway; Delta Airlines
Spear, Leeds, & Kellogg Specialists (unit of Goldman Sachs)	573	23.4%	3	Allianz AG; Fannie Mae; FedEx; IBM; MetLife
Fleet Specialists (unit of FleetBoston Financial)	435	20.3%	9	Coca-Cola; Home Depot; GE; GM; McDonald's; Sprint
Van Der Moolen Specialists (publicly traded)	376	10.8%	3	Apache; Cendant; Disney; Harley-Davidson; IDT
Bear Wagner Specialists (minority partner: Bear Stearns)	340	15.2%	4	Proctor & Gamble; Citigroup; Deutsche Telekom; Merrill Lynch
Performance Specialist Group (privately held)	139	1.2%	0	CEC Entertainment; Illinois Tool Works; Sony (ADRs); Pep Boys
Susquehanna Specialists (privately held)	122	2.2%	0	Borders Group; IHOP; OfficeMax; Reebok

Specialists can act as either *brokers* or *dealers* on the exchange. When acting as a broker the specialist acts as an agent for another member, and the specialist executes transactions for other floor brokers in exchange for a commission. When acting as a dealer the specialist acts on his own behalf, and the specialist will buy and sell out of his own account, assuming the risks associated with owning or selling the stock.

When new information has a substantial impact on the price of a particular stock, the stock may become temporarily illiquid. Investors are not sure at what price the stock should be trading. When the market is illiquid or trading is sporadic, the specialist is required to intervene as much as possible to minimize the temporary imbalances between market supply and demand. For this reason, the specialist often takes what is known as a *contrarian position*—when the market is selling, the specialist will begin buying, and vice versa.

Exhibit 7-8
The Anatomy of a Trade

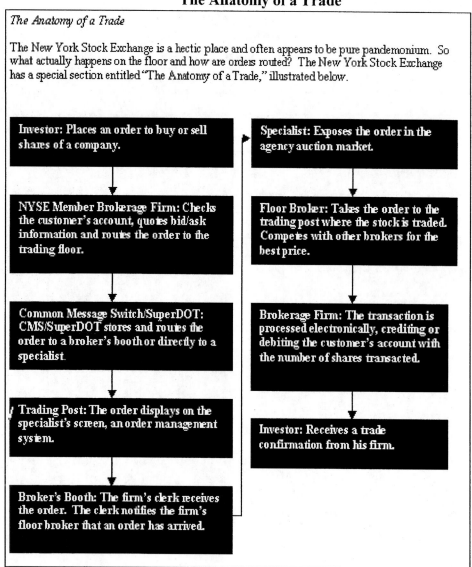

The Anatomy of a Trade

The New York Stock Exchange is a hectic place and often appears to be pure pandemonium. So what actually happens on the floor and how are orders routed? The New York Stock Exchange has a special section entitled "The Anatomy of a Trade," illustrated below.

Investor: Places an order to buy or sell shares of a company.

NYSE Member Brokerage Firm: Checks the customer's account, quotes bid/ask information and routes the order to the trading floor.

Common Message Switch/SuperDOT: CMS/SuperDOT stores and routes the order to a broker's booth or directly to a specialist.

Trading Post: The order displays on the specialist's screen, an order management system.

Broker's Booth: The firm's clerk receives the order. The clerk notifies the firm's floor broker that an order has arrived.

Specialist: Exposes the order in the agency auction market.

Floor Broker: Takes the order to the trading post where the stock is traded. Competes with other brokers for the best price.

Brokerage Firm: The transaction is processed electronically, crediting or debiting the customer's account with the number of shares transacted.

Investor: Receives a trade confirmation from his firm.

Other NYSE Members:

There are several different types of memberships in the New York Stock Exchange. Each category of membership serves a different function on the trading floor. The largest single membership group consists of floor brokers. There are two types of floor brokers: commission brokers and independent floor brokers. Stock brokerage firms that are members of the NYSE employ commission brokers. Darting from booth to trading post, commission brokers buy and sell securities for the general public—the clients of the firm. In return for their efforts, they earn salaries and commissions.

Independent floor brokers are brokers who work for themselves. They handle orders for brokerage houses that do not have full-time brokers or whose brokers are off the floor or too busy to handle a specific order. Independent floor brokers are often referred to as *$2 brokers*—a term coined back in the days when they received $2 for every 100 shares they traded.

Trading Systems—Super DOT and Intermarket:

The *Super DOT System* is an electronic order routing system designed to send smaller orders, usually less than 1200 shares, from member firms directly to the specialist's post instead of being transmitted through a floor broker. In reality, the order goes from the computer system of the member firm to the computer system of the specialist in the stock in a nanosecond. This direct placement lessens the execution time. The orders are then matched by the system with orders of similar size and price without the physical negotiation of the specialist. This reduces the dependence on the specialist for small order execution. While the specialist monitors the trading through the Super Dot system, the specialist is not directly involved with the transactions.

The Intermarket Trading System (ITS) is an electronic communications network implemented in 1978. Its purpose is to link the NYSE with all of the regional exchanges so that investors are able to get the best price possible when they trade.

Types of Orders:

A *market order* is an order, either to buy or sell, which is to be executed at the best possible market price when it reaches the floor of the exchange. Most individual investors use market orders when trading because the orders are executed immediately, and the size of the trades of most individuals is not large enough to significantly affect the stock's price in the market. The main concern with market orders is that the price of the stock could move adversely to the investor between the time when the order was entered and the time it is executed.

A *limit order* is a trade that occurs at a pre-specified price or better. Limit orders avoid the problem of paying more or receiving less than the investor expected on a market order. Buy limit orders are only executed when the market price reaches or falls below the fixed limit price that was designated by the buyer. A sell order is only executed when the stock price reaches or exceeds the price that was designated by the seller. A key difference between market orders and limit orders is that the stock price may never reach the designated level to trigger the limit order, and the trade will not be executed.

7.2.2 The American Stock Exchange

The American Stock Exchange (AMEX) is the other national stock exchange that serves the capital markets of the United States. While it has not been able to attract the larger companies, such as those that are traded on the NYSE or the popular technology firms that trade in the NASDAQ over the counter market, the AMEX has carved its own niche in the capital markets. That niche is in the listing of stocks of mid-cap companies, and the trading of stock-based derivative securities. Although most large cap firms list on the NYSE, many medium sized companies list on the AMEX. In addition to mid-cap stocks, derivative trading is growing rapidly on the AMEX.

The most actively traded issue on the AMEX is a derivative security called the *Standard & Poor's 500 Depository Receipts (Spiders)*. This derivative security corresponds to a $1/10^{th}$ amount in the performance of the S&P 500 index. We describe the S&P 500 Index later in this chapter. Purchasing Spiders is an inexpensive way for investors to buy the performance of the S&P 500 Index without purchasing all of the stocks in the index, or an index fund. The AMEX also has a similar derivative instrument, which is designed to represent the performance of the thirty firms in the Dow Jones Industrial Average. The trading of new financial instruments and mid-cap companies differentiates the AMEX from the NYSE.

Similar to the NYSE, the AMEX is also an auction market with one specialist appointed to trade each issue. There are 900 different companies listed on the AMEX and thousands of different options and derivative securities. The market structure of the AMEX is very similar to the structure of the NYSE. The trading floor is divided into three different areas, and within each area members trade a different type of financial instrument. One trading area is for equities, one area is for derivatives, and one is for bonds.

7.2.3 The Over-The-Counter Markets and the NASDAQ

The over-the-counter (OTC) market differs from the NYSE and AMEX in that there is no physical trading floor and no specialists. All trading takes place between brokers and dealers of securities over telephones and computer networks. The National Association of Securities Dealers (NASD) oversees all trading and regulation in the OTC market under the supervision of the SEC. The National Association of Securities Dealers Automated Quotation system, known as NASDAQ, is an electronic quotation system that provides market participants with price quotations for securities that are traded in the OTC market.

The NASDAQ is not a stock exchange like the NYSE and the AMEX, both of which have a physical location where trading takes place. NASDAQ is an automated quotation system connecting securities firms electronically through an extensive telecommunications and computer network. The computer network is used to provide quotes, route orders, and report trading activity to all participants.

Over 600 securities dealers trading almost 15,000 different over-the-counter issues are on the NASDAQ system. The requirements to become dealers, also called market makers, are: a minimum capital requirement, an electronic interface standard to quote prices and report transactions, and the willingness to make a continuous two-sided market (both buying and selling). If market makers do not continuously post bids and offers for securities, the NASD may penalize them.

The NASDAQ is not an auction market like the NYSE. Instead market makers compete against each other by posting quotes, and bid and ask prices, which attract order flows. Market demand for a specific security determines how many dealers will participate as market makers in each security. Some high volume issues, such as the stock of Intel and Microsoft, have in excess of 60 dealers quoting prices. Smaller issues with less active stock might have only one or two dealers making a market in the security.

The Bid-Ask Spread in the OTC Market:

Prices for securities that are traded in the OTC markets are quoted in a manner that is different from the price quotes on the NYSE and AMEX. Instead of a common market price determined by the auction process on the NYSE or AMEX, OTC prices depend on whether you are buying or selling the security. These prices are referred to as the *bid*—the price a dealer is willing to pay to purchase a security; and the *ask*—the price a dealer is willing to receive to sell a security.

> *Bid—the price a dealer is willing to pay to purchase a security.*
> *Ask—the price a dealer is willing to accept to sell a security.*

The difference between the two prices is called the bid-ask spread. The bid-ask spread is the commission that dealers receive on a transaction if they buy at the lower bid price and sell at the higher ask price.

Bid-Ask Spread Example:

If Merrill Lynch makes a market in Dell Computers (meaning it is a dealer of Dell stock), the dealer will always have two different prices at which it is willing to trade. Assume the market trading range for Dell is between $40 and $41 a share. The dealer may quote a bid price of $40 a share, at which it is willing to purchase Dell stock.

The dealer also posts an asking price of $40.25 at which it is willing to sell shares of Dell. The dealer earns a bid-ask spread of $.25 for every share of Dell that the dealer trades at this bid-ask level. The stocks that are heavily traded have smaller bid-ask spreads (now as low as $.01) but stocks with little trading volume can have spreads of a dollar or more per share.

Bidding Collusion on NASDAQ:

In 1994 an academic research study presented evidence that NASDAQ dealers may have been colluding to raise bid-ask spreads on the most active issues. This evidence was supported by the lack of odd-eighth quotes by dealers. For example, dealers would quote a stock price of $25-¼ bid, $25-½ offered, but not $25-3/8 bid, $25-½ offered—dealers were not posting bid and ask prices at 1/8, 3/8, 5/8, and 7/8. The study created considerable negative press for the NASDAQ, and led to a number of lawsuits that required dealer firms to pay out over $100 million to investors.

The Merger between the NASDAQ and the AMEX:

In 1998 NASDAQ and AMEX merged, effectively linking together two different markets—a specialist auction market and a dealer bid-ask market. The presumed benefits are that the merger will provide the resources to upgrade the technologies on the AMEX and allows the markets to increase order execution efficiency while reducing costs. The merger will also strengthen the AMEX's options trading abilities and will allow it to compete for derivative securities business more effectively against the Chicago Board Options Exchange.

The OTC Market and Securities Other than Stock:

The trading of debt securities and derivative securities also takes place in the over-the-counter market and is done primarily by brokers who are arranging purchases for their clients, or dealers who are buying and selling for their own accounts. The size of the daily trading of debt securities in the OTC market, which securities encompass corporate bonds, municipal bonds, and government and agency debt, is larger and more profitable for financial institutions than the trading of stock. Large investment and commercial banks dominate the trading activity in these markets.

7.2.4   The Regional Stock Exchanges

In addition to the two national exchanges and the NASDAQ market, five regional exchanges trade stocks in the United States. These exchanges are: Philadelphia Stock Exchange, Chicago Stock Exchange, Pacific Stock Exchange, Boston Stock Exchange, and Cincinnati Stock Exchange.

Regional exchanges perform several functions in the secondary market. First, regional exchanges list local companies that do not meet the formal listing requirements for one of the national stock exchanges. Second, most of the actively traded issues on the major exchanges are dually listed on the regional exchanges. This allows local brokerage firms to purchase a membership on the regional exchange and trade shares of most NYSE companies without having to purchase a seat on the NYSE or trade through a member firm and forfeit some of the commission.

The trading volume on the regional exchanges is substantially lower than the volume on the NYSE. This could make the regional exchange dual listings less liquid, but because of the Intermarket Trading System, the regional exchanges receive the same quote information that is available on the floor of the NYSE.

7.2.5 *International Stock Exchanges*

The capital markets of countries around the world have been active in developing and broadening the role of the stock and bond markets. In the Far East, the Tokyo Stock Exchange dominates trading activity, much the same as the New York Stock Exchange does in the United States. It lists about 1700 companies with a total value of several trillion dollars. Active exchanges in the Far East are in Hong Kong—the Hang Seng, Taiwan, Shanghai, and South Korea—KOSPI.

In Europe, the London Stock Exchange is the principal exchange, and serves Great Britain and Ireland. More than 2600 companies are listed with a market value of almost a trillion dollars. Active stock markets exist in Germany—DAX, Paris—CAC, Italy—Milan BITtel, Spain—IBEX, Belgium, and Sweden—SX.

In the Americas, besides the exchanges that we described in the United States, major stock exchanges in various countries are as follows: Argentina—Merval, Brazil—Sao Paulo Bovespa, Canada—Toronto, Chile—Santiago IPSA, and Mexico—I.P.C. Most developed countries have a stock exchange and new exchanges are being established around the world with the development of newly emerging economies.

7.2.6 *Electronic Communications Networks (ECNs) and After-Hours Trading*

Technology has dramatically changed the markets. One of the biggest developments in the secondary markets has been electronic communication networks (ECNs). These computer-based order-matching systems, which include Instinet, Island, Archipelago, and Redibook, match bids and offers on a network, thereby giving buyers and sellers the best prices possible. The oldest ECN,

Instinet, was developed in 1969 and for years functioned primarily as an after-hours market for institutions. Today, there are nine ECNs linked to the NASDAQ system, and they control about 30% of the daily volume of trading. (See discussion at the end of this chapter.)

7.3   Measuring the Performance of the Financial Markets

Financial assets have been traded in the United States for over two hundred years. More than ten thousand different securities trade every day on the different exchanges around the United States. Perhaps ten times this amount of securities trades daily on a worldwide basis. So how does the average investor monitor all of these different securities across different exchanges throughout the world?

Investors depend on financial indices to measure everything from the price of commodities to the overnight performance of stocks that are traded on the Hong Kong stock exchange. In every major newspaper publication there is some reference to a financial index. In the United States, the most often cited indices are the Dow Jones Industrial Average, the Standard & Poor's 500 Index, and the NASDAQ Composite Index. What do these indices actually measure and how are they calculated?

Most major indices are classified as either a price-weighted index or a market-weighted index. We calculate a price-weighted index by adding all of the prices of the stocks in the index and divide that sum by a *divisor*. The Dow Jones Industrial Average (DJIA) is the world's most popular price-weighted index. First calculated in 1896, the index computed an average price of 12 industrial stocks.

The DJIA has been calculated for over one hundred years and stocks in the DJIA have changed over time. Currently, there are 30 stocks (see Exhibit 7-11) in the DJIA. The divisor has changed over time and has been adjusted for stock splits. The divisor for the DJIA as of January 29, 2004 was 0.13500289. In a price-weighted index, the index weighting of each firm is dependent on the price per share of its stock rather than the market value of the firm. Another widely used price-weighted index is the Nikkei average of 225 large Japanese stocks.

Most other major stock indices are calculated using a market value weighting method. With a market value index, the percentage weight of each firm is dependent on the relative market value of the firm's stock divided by the market value of the stocks of all of the firms in the index. The weighting of companies by their total stock market value allows the index to change in a manner that is directly proportional to the change in the stock market values of the companies that comprise the index. A market value-weighted index gives a more accurate measurement of the actual performance of the market since firms with a higher market value represent more of the invested dollars in the market. The most famous market value-weighted index is the Standard & Poor's 500. Other market-value-weighted indexes include the NASDAQ Composite, Russell 2000, Wilshire 5000, and the Morgan Stanley EAFE.

As an example of market value weighting, assume that the value of all of the stocks in the JRW Index is $10 trillion (a very big number) and the stock market value of one of its components, Big Firm, is $500 billion. Big Firm's stock represents a 5% share ($500 billion/$10,000 billion = 5%) of the JRW Index. Assume that another firm, Little Firm, is also in the index and the total market value of the stock of Little Firm is $100 million. Little Firm's stock represents a 0.001% share ($100 million/ $10,000,000 million = .001%) of the JRW Index. A one percent price movement in the stock of Big Firm will move the JRW Index much more—five thousand times more—than a similar percentage price movement in the stock of Little Firm.

7.3.1 Dow Jones Industrial Average

The DJIA is a price-weighted average of thirty stocks out of over ten thousand stocks in the United States equity markets. Although these firms represent a large portion of the market capitalization of U.S. firms, the DJIA is a small sample. All but two of the firms, Microsoft and Intel, are traded on the NYSE. The index is designed to include the largest industrial firms in the U.S. that have a history of success and growth. The stocks are reviewed periodically by the editors of *The Wall Street Journal,* and stodgy stocks that have not done well may be replaced with new up-and-coming stocks. In 1999, four companies in the DJIA—Sears, Goodyear, Chevron and Union Carbide—were jettisoned and Home Depot, Intel, Microsoft, and SBC Communication were added.

Exhibit 7-10
Chart of DJIA 1929-2004

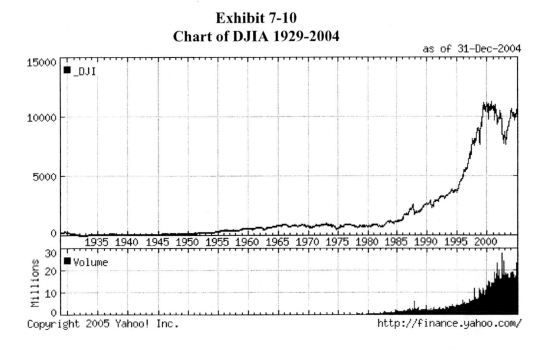

- 243 -

Dow Jones calculates two additional price-weighted indices: a transportation index and a utility index, the stocks of which are not represented in the DJIA. Although it represents the performance of a small number of stocks, the DJIA correlates very closely with the S&P 500 and is a more famous measure of stock market performance.

Dow Jones Industrial Average Computation:

Exhibit 7-11 below shows the thirty stocks in the DJIA and their respective closing prices on December 31, 2004. The market capitalization for these thirty stocks at that time was $3.792 trillion. The manner in which the DJIA is computed is to add the prices of the 30 component stocks—in this case they total 1,459.26. The total is then divided by the divisor. The divisor on December 31st was 0.13532775 and is listed daily in the Markets Lineup page in Section C of *The Wall Street Journal*. The divisor changes often to take into account stock splits and listing changes. Dividing the total of 1,459.26 by the divisor is equal to:

1,459.26 / 0.13532775 = 10,783

Exhibit 7-11
Computation of DJIA on December 31, 2004

DJIA on 12/31/2004 = 10,783   Divisor = 0.13532775

Company	Symbol	Closing Price	Company	Symbol	Closing Price
Alcoa	AA	31.42	IBM	IBM	98.58
American Express	AXP	56.37	Intel	INTC	23.39
AmerIntGrp	AIG	65.67	Verizon	VZ	40.51
Boeing	BA	51.77	J.P. MorganChase	JPM	39.01
Caterpillar	CAT	97.51	Johnson & Johnson	JNJ	63.42
Citigroup	C	48.18	McDonalds	MCD	32.06
Coca Cola	KO	41.64	Merck	MRK	32.14
DuPont	DD	49.05	Microsoft	MSFT	26.72
Pfizer	PFE	26.89	MMM	MMM	82.07
Exxon Mobil	XOM	51.26	Altria Group	MO	61.10
General Electric	GE	36.50	Proctor & Gamble	PG	55.08
General Motors	GM	40.06	SBC Communications	SBC	25.77
Home Depot	HD	42.74	United Technologies	UTX	103.35
Honeywell	HON	35.41	Wal-Mart	WMT	52.82
Hewlett-Packard	HPQ	20.97	Walt Disney Co.	DIS	27.80
			Total of 30 DJIA Stock Prices		1,459.26
			Total Prices / Divisor		10,783

At $103.35, the stock of United Technologies has the highest share price of the thirty stocks in the DJIA. The stock of Microsoft, at $26.72, has a relatively low share price. Since the DJIA is price weighted and the $103.35 per share price of United Technologies is almost four times the $26.72 price of Microsoft, a 1% (equal to $1.03) move in United Technologies will affect the movement of the DJIA average about four times as much as a 1% move (equal to $0.27) in Microsoft. The total market capitalization of United Technologies on December 31, 2004 was $52.7 billion, while that of Microsoft was $291 billion. In market-value weighted indices such as the S&P 500, the price movement of Microsoft would have more than five time the effect of the same percentage price movement of United Technologies.

7.3.2   The Standard & Poor's 500 Index

The Standard & Poor's 500 Index is a market value-weighted index that represents $8.6 trillion of stock market capitalization. As such, its performance gives a better representation of the performance of the entire stock market than the performance of the DJIA. The S&P 500 Index incorporates 500 different stocks from all sectors that are listed on the three major U.S. stock markets— NYSE, AMEX, and NASDAQ.

Exhibit 7-12
Chart of S&P 500 1982-2004

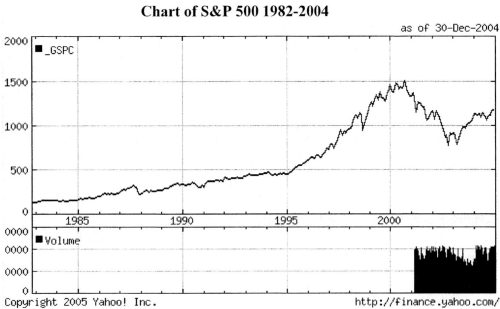

Of the 500 companies included in the index, 460 of the companies are listed on the NYSE. The S&P 500 excludes many of the smaller firms listed on the AMEX or traded in the NASDAQ over-the-counter market. The S&P 500 Index does represent most of the dollars invested in public stocks in the United States. Three of the larger companies in the S&P 500 Index are Microsoft, GE, and IBM. The market weightings of each firm changes on a daily basis as the market values of the individual firms vary constantly.

The NASDAQ stock market performed spectacularly during the late 1990s as it became the preferred market of the entrepreneurs that controlled the listing of high-tech companies. Intel, Microsoft, Cisco Systems, Dell Computers, and many others are some of the companies, which have stocks that trade on the NASDAQ system. The performance of the stocks of these companies and others carried the NASDAQ to a level of over 5,200 points in March of 2000, before plummeting over 75% in the stock market crash of the early 2000s to less than 1,200 in October 2002.

The NASDAQ competes directly and fiercely with the NYSE for domestic and international company listings. The NASDAQ Composite Index measures a market value-weighted average of the stocks of more than 5000 domestic and international companies that are listed on the NASDAQ. The Composite Index was introduced on February 5, 1971, and at that time it had a base value of 100.0.

Exhibit 7-13
Chart of NASDAQ 1985-2004

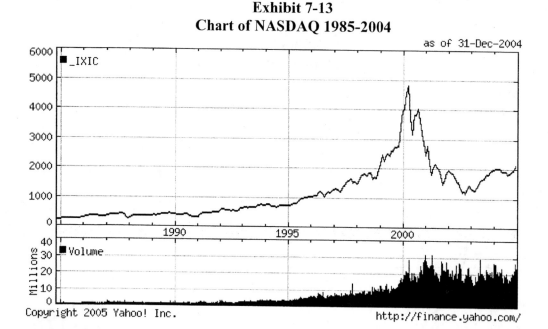

The strong stock market performance of the high-tech sector has increased the popularity of the NASDAQ Composite and it is quoted in most major news publications alongside the S&P 500 and the DJIA. The largest companies in the NASDAQ Index are Microsoft, Cisco Systems, and Intel. Due to the tremendous returns over the past twenty years for each of these three issues, their shares are major influences on the direction of the NASDAQ Composite Index.

7.3.4   Other Stock Indices

Russell 2000 Index:

The Russell 2000 Index is a widely accepted index that measures the performance of small cap stocks. The Frank Russell Company calculates many different indices designed to measure certain sectors of markets worldwide. Based on the three thousand largest capitalized companies in the United States, the Russell 2000 measures the performance of the smallest two thousand firms. The Russell 2000 is a market value-weighted index. The average firm in the Russell 2000 Index has a market capitalization of less than $200 million.

Wilshire 5000 Index:

The Wilshire 5000 Index tracks the performance of all United States stocks. Originally it was comprised of 5,000 different stocks, but today more than 7,000 stocks make up the index. The market value-weighted index was introduced in 1974 to track the entire United States equities markets.

Morgan Stanley EAFE Index and Other International Stock Indices:

The Morgan Stanley Capital International Europe Australia and Far East index has become the broadly accepted benchmark to track the performance of international equities. The index is a market value-weighted index tracking the performance of $ 17 trillion of securities that are traded on various international exchanges. Morgan Stanley also computes other international indices including a world Index

Dow Jones also has a world index that contains more than 2,000 companies from over 100 industry groups that are traded in more than 30 countries. The countries are divided into three regions: the Americas, Europe, and Asia Pacific. The performance of stocks in each of the countries, the average performance of the regions, and the performance of the Dow Jones World Stock Index are shown in both local currencies and dollars. The Dow Jones Global Indexes are published every day in *The Wall Street Journal*, and gives a good summary of how stock markets around the world have performed.

Bond Market Indices:

Four investment firms, Lehman Brothers, Merrill lynch, Ryan Treasury, and Salomon Smith Barney, have created and compute United States investment grade bond indices. Investment grade means that the bonds are rated Baa or higher by Moodys Investor's Services, or BBB or higher by Standard & Poor's Corporation. Indices are provided for U.S. Treasury securities, U.S. corporate debt issues, tax-exempt municipal bonds, mortgage-backed debt securities, high yield bond indices, and global government bond issues. Bond market data and the performance of bond market indices is available in the Bond Market Data Bank section of *The Wall Street Journal*.

7.4   Stock Brokerage Firms

Stock brokerage firms are firms that act to buy and sell stocks, bonds, and other securities for or on behalf of clients of the firm. Broadly, stock market firms can be classified as full service brokerage firms such as Merrill Lynch and Smith Barney, discount stock brokerage firms such as Charles Schwab, and online stock brokerage firms such as E-Trade or Ameritrade. Below, we discuss the different types of services that each of these firms offer to investors and the difference in costs and services.

7.4.1   Full Service Brokerage Firms

A full service brokerage firm provides a broad array of financial services to investors. Those services include complete financial analysis, investment planning, and retirement planning. Full service brokers, such as Merrill Lynch and Paine Webber, are members of all major exchanges and usually make markets in most NADAQ issues.

Investors have access to many different financial instruments including common stock, bonds (corporate, government, municipal, and international), derivative products (options, futures, and other products), commodities, foreign currency, and just about any other publicly traded investment product. To accompany the full array of investment products, most full service brokers provide their own research and forecasts of economic, industry, and company conditions. This gives investors who are clients of the firm immediate access to information and recommendations.

Some investors allow their brokers to make all trading decisions, independent of the client's input. This arrangement is called a *discretionary account*, and only should be used when the client has complete trust in his broker.

7.4.2   Discount Brokerage Firms

Unlike full service brokers, the fees of which can be substantial, discount brokers offer basic investment services with no frills attached. Discount brokers provide fewer services to investors and have lower overhead expenses and therefore are able to charge lower commissions. Research may be limited or nonexistent and product availability may also be limited to stocks and mutual funds.

Although discount brokerage firms are offering some additional services in an attempt to compete with the full service firms, their main appeal has always been through the charging of lower commissions. Discount brokers attract investors who pick their own stocks and manage their own portfolios. These investors prefer the lower cost commissions.

7.4.3 Online Brokers and E-Trading

The growth of the Internet and services such as America Online spurred a new type of brokerage service. Electronic trading allows investors to trade stocks, bonds, and other securities through accounts that they have established with stock brokerage firms that have online services.

The pure electronic stock trading firms include Etrade, Ameritrade, and Datek, among others. Trades are placed via the telephone or the Internet without ever speaking to an individual. The fewer people that are involved in a transaction, the lower the commission rates. Electronic trading offers commission rates comparable to and even lower than the rates associated with deep discount brokerage firms. This niche grew dramatically during the Internet bubble of the late 1990s, as full service, discount, and start-up brokerage firms established online trading capabilities.

Some of the basic services that full service brokers offer are also available from electronic trading firms at a fraction of the cost. Despite the popularity of online brokers, their high costs of customer acquisition and low profitability have resulted in a decline in market valuation of these companies.

7.4.4 Brokerage Related Definitions

Round lot trades are trades executed in multiples of 100 shares.

Odd lot trades are trades that are for less than 100 shares. For example, if you received 5 shares of Disney from a relative for a birthday present and you sold them through a stockbroker, that sale would have been an odd lot sale.

Payment for order flow is a rebate paid to brokerage firms for directing trades to particular market markers.

Block trades are defined as trades of 10,000 shares or more of a given stock, or trades of shares with market value of $200,000 or more. In 1961, there were about nine block trades per day, which accounted for about 3% of the daily trading volume. In recent years there are often in excess of 3,000 block trades per day, accounting for approximately half of the daily volume.

Program trading is a computer-assisted strategy of buying and or selling a large number of securities simultaneously. Program trading is also called basket trading because the transaction usually consists of a coordinate number of trades in different securities. Since a large amount of capital is required to coordinate and execute the underlying trades, institutional investors are the principal market participants who use program trading.

An example of a program trade is if a pension fund wanted to invest $50,000,000 directly into the stocks that comprise the S&P 500 Index, and not through a mutual fund. A full service brokerage firm would design a computer trading program that would buy shares in the appropriate weightings of all 500 stocks in the S&P 500 at the same time. This coordination gives an institutional investor immediate execution instead of waiting for 500 separate orders to be filled.

With program trading, the transaction can be completed in a matter of minutes instead of taking a few hours with individual executions. Program trading is also used to rebalance portfolios while limiting market fluctuations during the time the trade is being executed.

7.5   Summary

In this chapter we examined the financial markets—the stock and bond markets where securities are purchased and sold, and the foreign exchange and derivatives markets. We discussed the role of the primary and secondary securities market, the money and capital markets, the major stock exchanges, the over-the-counter market, and the manner in which trades take place in the markets, as well as different ways to measure the performance of the markets.

Our learning objectives for the chapter included an understanding of: the nature and role of the primary and secondary securities market; the difference between the capital and the money markets; the major financial exchanges, their classification, and the type of issues traded on these exchanges; the roles of the specialist and the market-maker; the types of buy and sell orders that can be placed; the major financial markets performance indices, how they are calculated and what they measure; and the services and costs of full service, discount, and electronic brokerage firms.

List of Terms

1. Secondary securities market
2. Liquidity
3. Securities and exchange commission
4. Over-the-counter market
5. Specialist
6. Market maker
7. Financial indexes
8. Trading posts
9. Super DOT
10. Intermarket Trading System
11. Listed issues
12. Dealer
13. Broker
14. Contrarian
15. Limit order
16. Market order
17. Spiders
18. Financial indices
19. Price-weighted index
20. Market-weighted index
21. Small-cap
22. Large-cap
23. Bid-ask spreads
24. ECNs
25. Bidding collusion
26. Price-weighted index
27. Market value-weighted index
28. Discretionary account
29. Full service broker
30. Discount broker
31. Round lot trades
32. Odd lot trades
33. Block trade
34. Program trading
35. Basket trading
36. Payment for order flow
37. Decimalization
38. Minimum trading increment
39. Dual-exchange

Questions

1. What roles does a stock exchange play in the trading of securities in the secondary market? Why is it helpful to have a central trading location?

2. Why does the trading of a security disclose information about the asset's value?

3. Who is allowed to trade on the floor of the New York Stock Exchange?

4. Which are the two largest stock exchanges in the United States?

5. What is the role of a specialist? Why are they important?

6. Is a specialist a dealer or broker?

7. What are the two categories of floor brokers?

8. How is a limit order different from a market order?

9. Why would an investor elect to buy a derivative rather than the underlying asset?

10. How does the NASDAQ differ from the New York Stock Exchange?

11. Explain why collusion in trading is a bad thing. Why is it illegal?

12. What functions do regional exchanges play?

13. List five factors that contribute to the fluctuation in stock prices.

14. If a large investor wants to sell a large number of shares in a particular company (greater than 100,000), what happens to price and why?

15. What is the difference between a price-weighted index and a market value-weighted index?

16. The Dow Jones Industrial Average is comprised of 30 large companies while the S&P 500 has 500 companies in it. Is the Dow a bad measure of total market performance?

17. Why is it cheaper to trade through a discount broker as opposed to a full service broker?

18. What is electronic trading? What are the advantages and disadvantages of electronic trading? Why did it grow dramatically during the stock market bubble of the 1990s?

19. What is program or basket trading?

20. Why is it necessary for large institutional investors to use program trading?

21. How will the decimalization of stock prices benefit investors?

Assignment #7-1:

1.   The New York Stock Exchange:

-   Visit the NYSE's website at www.nyse.com
-   On the main menu, click on "The Trading Floor."
-   On the next page, click on "The Floor Community."
-   Read the section on "Trading Floor FAQs" and answer the following questions:
-   How many trading posts are there on the floor?
-   What kinds of data do the computer monitors at each trading post display to the brokers?
-   How many trading booths are there?
-   What are the two ways an order can be transmitted to the floor brokers?

2.   NASDAQ:

-   Go to NASDAQ's website at www.nasdaq.com.
-   On the menu bar at the top of the page, click on "About Us."
-   Next, scroll down and click on "The Nasdaq Difference." You will see another menu appear under that heading after clicking on it.
-   Click on "ECNs", read that section and answer the following questions:
-   What are ECNs?
-   How is an order transmitted through an ECN handled differently as orders that go through the NYSE?
-   How do investors benefit from this method of handling orders?

3.   Dow Jones Indexes

-   Go to The Dow Jones Indexes Webpage at http://www.djindexes.com/jsp/industrialAverages.jsp
-   Click on "The performance of the Dow Jones Industrial Average after major world events"
-   Observe the last five most recent events. Were they positive or negative? How was the Dow affected that day? One year later?
-   Go back to the original page and click on "Components" under the Dow Jones Industrial Average under Investable Indexes.
-   Click on "Get Report" and scroll down to the companies. Which company has the highest weighting and which has the lowest weighting?
-   Calculate the effect on the value of the Dow when JPMorgan Chase appreciates by $1.

Increasingly, low-cost, sophisticated technology is changing the way business is done on Wall Street. The easy money from overseeing transactions in securities markets is getting a lot harder to come by. Take the underwriting business for example. When Net2Phone Inc. was looking for someone to underwrite its IPO, all the investment banks wanted to charge a 7% fee. The Antitrust Division of the U.S. Department of Justice is investigating this standard fee. However, the Internet will be the real catalyst in changing the industry. Today, Web-based auctions of IPOs cost about 10% less than a traditional underwriting.

Secondary markets for securities are also made more efficient with technology. Both transaction cost and cost of capital can be lowered with the use of electronic communication networks (ECNs). These computer-based order-matching systems match bids and offers on a network. They give buyers and sellers the best prices possible. The oldest network, Instinet, has been around since 1969 and once functioned primarily as an after-hours market for institutions. Today, there are nine ECNs linked to the NASDAQ system. On these ECNs, a trade can be executed in less than a second and for an average of 7.5 cents per 100 shares. This is possible because ECNs run on powerful supercomputers. The Optimark, for example, is a trading system that runs on IBM supercomputers capable of assembling orders and conducting an auction that matches buyers and sellers every 90 seconds. It also allows investors to rank the desirability of different trading outcomes. The speed and low cost has attracted more than 140 broker-dealers to notify the SEC of their intention to form their own ECNs.

ECNs are important because they provide the competition that help lower costs. In 1995, studies on bid-ask spreads on NASDAQ suggested that dealers were colluding to fix wide spreads in and attempt to make more money from investors. NASD dealers had to pay $1 billion to settle a class-action suit. Subsequently, the SEC imposed new order-handling rules that force dealers to display customer limit orders that are as good or better than the dealer's own quote. ECNs have helped enforce this new rule by posting the size and price of customer orders on their networks. Since the new rule was imposed, bid-ask spreads have fallen by more than 30%.

More recently, in a new NASDAQ Stock Market initiative, investors will be able to trade NYSE-listed stocks on NASDAQ through three electronic trading systems. These three systems (Brut ECN LLC, MarketXT Inc., and Bloomberg Tradebook) will be joining the Intermarket Trading System. The Intermarket includes the Big Board, regional stock exchanges and members of the National Association of Securities Dealers (NASD). Prices of stocks will appear in the Consolidated Quotation System, the distributor of up-to-date stock prices to information vendors worldwide.

The NYSE is also under pressure to bring about competition in its market. There exists today an Intermarket Trading System (ITS) that links the NYSE with exchanges in Boston, Chicago, Philadelphia, Cincinnati, and San Francisco. However, the ITS is underdeveloped and does not live up to its full potential. It not only does not create a national market ideal but instead has become a means for the NYSE to keep out competition and favor exchange members.

With the NYSE floor handling 82.5% of all listed stock trading, specialists can share the information they have with anyone they want. One broker, John D'Alessio, filed a $22 million lawsuit against the NYSE for turning a blind eye to traders' illegal activities. Specialist firms have enjoyed consistently high profits even in bear markets because of the lack of regulation and competition within the NYSE.

The NYSE is also under pressure to scrap its anti-competitive rules. Rule 390, for instance, prevents stocks listed before 1979 from being traded outside the ITS. Some of these stocks are companies in the Dow Jones Industrial Average and are among the most liquid stocks in the world. The exchange is also planning to convert to decimal pricing to further reduce bid/ask spreads. There is also talk on setting up an ECN for the NYSE.

Today, exchanges are not just threatened by ECNs on Wall Street but also by those from overseas. Both the Frankfurt-based Eurex and London-based LIFFE exchange have terminals in the United States. Electronic futures trading firms such as Marquette Partners have late night shifts to trade all kinds of new financial products on Eurex and other overseas markets. To counter the threat, the Chicago Board of Trade and the Chicago Mercantile Exchange have set up their own electronic trading systems. Nonetheless, they are far behind the European bourses. The Eurex, for one, has overtaken the CBOT as the largest futures exchange in the world.

Options exchanges are facing the same competitive threat. The International Securities Exchange (ISE), founded by the former head of E*Trade, Bill Porter, opened in March of 2000 and help keep American options exchanges competitive. It picks the best option contracts from the four main exchanges in the United States and offers them on an electronic platform. Goldman Sachs and the Chicago Stock Exchange are also planning to launch another similar electronic exchange.

New technology and the SEC order-handling rule have made U.S. equity markets more efficient. Surveys have shown that total trading costs have fallen in

1998 by 25% at the NYSE and 23% at NASDAQ. This translates to $1.8 billion in savings for investors. However, there are still issues that bother skeptics. One of these is the problem of market fragmentation. With the increasing number of independent trading venues like the numerous ECNs we have, it is harder for brokers to provide customers with the best possible execution price. The market needs consolidation and the question is whether to use regulation or competition to get there. Chairman of the SEC, Arthur Levitt, favored the latter because it would allow exchanges to implement new trading structures without having to go through the time consuming process of lobbying in Washington.

Another issue facing the industry is the lack of liquidity ECNs might cause for some stocks. Traditionally, market makers ensure that liquidity exists but with ECNs, the middleman is taken out, and for stocks that do not enjoy high trading volume, this liquidity is lost. The solution to this problem is also to consolidate ECNs so that more buyers and sellers are brought together at one location. Without consolidation, investors may even end up paying more for their trades. ECNs have been known to pay online brokerages for a share of their orders. Although ECNs bode well for the future of securities trading, there is still a lot to be done in order to exploit the full potential of their technology and efficiency.

CHAPTER 8

THE FINANCIAL SYSTEM, INTERMEDIATION, AND FINANCIAL INSTITUTIONS

This chapter provides an overview of financial intermediation and financial institutions. Financial institutions dominate the financial system in economies around the world. This chapter explores the different types of financial institutions and why they are such an integral part of the global economy.

In this chapter we examine:

- The functions of the financial system and the need for financial intermediaries in this system;
- The different forms of financial intermediation and how these are exploited by financial institutions; and
- The different types of financial institutions and their roles in the economy.

8.1   The Role of Financial Institutions

Financial institutions (*FIs*) provide important services to the economy of the United States and the world. You probably rely on financial institutions much more than you realize:

- When you use your credit card to purchase books at the Student Book Store;
- When you send a check to the Bryce Jordan Center to order tickets for the Bon Jovi concert;
- When you cash in on a hot tip from a classmate and buy 100 shares of C-Cor online through your broker; and
- When you run low on funds and you tap the ATM machine at the HUB.

In Chapter 7 we discussed the primary markets in which governments, agencies and municipal entities issue debt securities and corporations issue stocks and bonds to investors and receive the proceeds from the issuance of securities. The process, in which issuers receive funds directly from the purchasers of stocks and bonds in the markets, is called *direct finance*. We also discussed the secondary markets in which stocks and bonds are traded after their initial issuance.

In this chapter we describe *indirect finance*—the process of funds moving from investors through financial intermediaries to borrowers. Financial institutions and financial markets exist so that excess monies from investors can be transferred cheaply and efficiently to businesses, governments, individuals and other entities that have profitable investment opportunities and a shortage of funds. A financial intermediary borrows funds from savers/investors by issuing a claim—a deposit, or a contract such as an insurance policy or pension obligation—and uses those funds to make loans or to purchase higher yielding securities. This process is called *financial intermediation*. We examine the process of financial intermediation in the next section.

8.2   Financial Intermediation

Financial institutions, such as commercial, investment and savings banks, life, property and health insurance companies, pension funds and mutual funds, act as middlemen in the capital markets. They perform numerous functions for their clients, but in general, financial institutions link lenders and borrowers in the economy through a process known as financial intermediation.

> ***Financial intermediation*** *involves the creation and sale of*
> *secondary securities by financial institutions, and using*
> *those proceeds to purchase primary securities.*

Secondary securities include: savings and checking accounts, annuities, insurance policies and pension plans, and mutual funds. Secondary securities are designed to fulfill one or more needs of the clients of the financial institution—the individuals, households, corporations, retirees, and entrepreneurs—that deposit moneys with and borrow funds from the financial institutions.

The financial institutions sell these secondary securities or services to their clients and use the funds provided by their clients to purchase what are know as *primary securities*—stocks, bonds, loans, mortgages, and other financial assets. The interest, dividends, principal, and gains from the primary securities, along with the other assets of the FI, pay the cash flows associated with the secondary securities—the monthly pension checks, or the claims under a casualty policy, or the life insurance payment—whatever products the FI has created and the payments under which they honor.

Exhibit 8-1 illustrates the relationship between institutions and markets. The diagram is widely known as the flow of funds framework. Private placement is included and funds can be demanded and supplied by either foreign or domestic entities.

Exhibit 8-1
The Flow of Funds

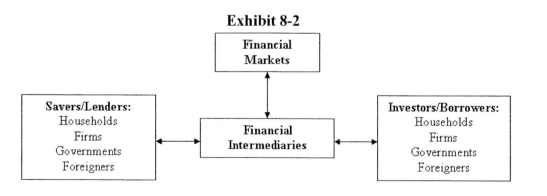

Source: Gitman, *Principles of Managerial Finance*, Third Edition

The activities underlying most financial institutions are based upon buying and selling claims to different streams of money—secondary securities such as a pension fund, annuity or savings accounts, versus primary securities such as corporate bonds or car loans. There is a cost or yield associated with these secondary securities. Let's assume that yield on average is 5%. Let's also assume that the average yield on the primary securities that the FI purchases is 10%. The difference in yield between the primary securities (10%) that the financial institution owns and the secondary securities and services that it sells (5%) is the *gross spread* that the financial institution earns on its activities. From that gross spread the financial institution pays its costs of operations, covers the defaults on the primary securities that it has purchased (car and credit card loans, mortgage defaults, WorldCom bonds, etc.), and generates a profit for its owners and shareholders.

This linkage of the financial markets and institutions with their clients is shown below in Exhibit 8-2.

Exhibit 8-2

Financial Markets

Savers/Lenders:
Households
Firms
Governments
Foreigners

Financial Intermediaries

Investors/Borrowers:
Households
Firms
Governments
Foreigners

Financial intermediaries perform the following functions:

- They act as middlemen to transfer the assets of one group of clients (savers—such as retirees in the form of savings certificates) into the liabilities of another group of clients (borrowers—such as students in the form of education loans);
- They act as issuers of secondary securities when they transform the financial assets of one group (the money from depositors) into the liabilities (the checking and savings accounts) of the financial institution;
- They create primary securities for their customers (mortgage loans, credit card loans, car loans, insurance policies) and may sell those financial assets to other market participants in the primary market;
- They may provide investment advice and services, and portfolio management services for a fee to clients.

8.2.1 Types of Financial Intermediation

Let's assume that you deposit money in the checking account of a commercial bank. Your money is available to you upon demand. The bank may use your money to make a three-year car loan or a thirty-year home mortgage loan to one of your neighbors. There is a possibility that your neighbor may default on his loan. That car or mortgage loan does not have a high degree of liquidity.

You can withdraw funds from your checking account at any time and the bank accepts the risk that you will draw down your checking account before your neighbor fully amortizes his loan. Your bank recognizes that they have assumed the risk of default on the underlying car loan and that a maturity mismatch exists between the term of its car loan and the probable life of your checking deposits. Financial intermediation encompasses a financial institution to accept a number of risks. A financial institution performs the following functions when it acts as a financial intermediary.

Maturity Intermediation:

Maturity intermediation is the process that an FI performs when it issues short-term liabilities and uses the proceeds from those liabilities to originate longer-term loans and purchase long-term assets. Maturity intermediation allows a financial institution to create a car or mortgage loan for the length of time that a borrower desires, while the depositor owns a checking account with complete liquidity that satisfies his investment desires. Commercial and savings banks, credit unions and other depository institutions perform this function regularly when they issue long-term loans and mortgages that are financed mostly by short-term deposits and savings accounts.

Maturity intermediation plays two significant roles in the economy. First, it provides investors with additional choices relating to possible investments. Borrowers can finance purchases with a long-term amortization that satisfies their needs, while depositors and lenders are able to invest for a short period, or as long as they desire. Second, because investors are risk-averse and are naturally reluctant to commit funds for long time periods, it forces long-term borrowers to pay a higher interest rate than short-term borrowers.

Liquidity Intermediation:

Liquidity is the ability to readily convert a financial asset into cash. Checking accounts are highly liquid assets, whereas loans to businesses are not. By taking funds that are maintained in the checking accounts of individuals and households and making longer-term commercial loans to businesses, financial institutions provide liquidity intermediation. Financial institutions offer individuals what they want—liquid financial assets, and use the funds provided by those assets to give business what they want—longer-term loans.

Diversification Intermediation and Default Risk:

A basic principle of finance is that diversification reduces risk to investors. Diversification means to invest in a number of different asset groups and in many different investments. Diversification is sometimes difficult to achieve for individual investors with limited amounts of money and investment opportunities. However, when a financial intermediary pools the funds of many investors, the financial intermediary may be able to take advantage of economies of scale and specialized expertise in analyzing default risk. Due to these economies of scale, the financial intermediary is able to hold a diversified portfolio of loans or assets, and it allows the investors or depositors in the FI to share in the diversification benefits.

As an example, a commercial bank in Texas lends primarily to companies in the oil industry. This concentration of lending exposes the bank to the price of oil because as oil falls, the default risk of all of its loans increases. If the bank is able to diversify across regions and industries, the bank could loan funds to someone who benefits from lower oil prices, such as firms in the auto industry, and hedge some of the risk exposure. Therefore, if the bank diversified its loans between Texas and Michigan and between oil and autos, the bank lowers the risk of the loan portfolio relative to changes in oil prices. Lower risk allows investors to accept lower returns on invested assets and allows lower rates on loans.

Intermediation and Economies of Scale in Information and Costs:

In addition to maturity, liquidity, and diversification intermediation, financial intermediaries also are able to take advantage of economies of scale in search, information, and transactions costs. Search costs to find investors and investment alternatives are time-consuming and considerable. Financial intermediaries are able to pool investment assets and provide the necessary information at a considerably lower cost than what would be available to an individual investor.

For example, consider an individual interested in selling 100 shares of Disney. She could place an advertisement in the paper offering to sell the shares at a given price or ask friends and family of their interest. Since she does not own a membership in the NYSE, she is not able to sell her shares directly on the exchange. However, if she uses a financial institution such as her stockbroker to sell her shares, the trade would be performed immediately and she would receive the best available price. When she sells an actively traded stock, her search costs would be negligible.

8.2.2   Financial Institutions and Financial Intermediation

In recent years financial institutions have been consolidating and growing larger and more diverse in the capital markets of the United States. Mergers among commercial and investment banks and insurance companies, such as Citigroup, which is composed of Citibank commercial bank, Salomon Smith Barney investment bank, Traveler's Insurance Company, and many other subsidiaries, allow financial institutions to perform in all categories of financial intermediation.

Generally, there are three categories of financial intermediaries:

- *Depository intermediaries*, such as commercial banks, savings and loan associations, savings banks, and credit unions, which take your deposits and issue you highly-liquid secondary securities, such as checking and savings accounts. They use your money to make business, mortgage, and car loans and invest it in other illiquid primary securities and loans.
- *Contractual intermediaries*, such as pension funds, life insurance companies, and property and casualty insurance companies. The common element for contractual intermediaries is that their client base pays for a contractually determined source of funds that are stable and predictable, such as life and car insurance premiums or pension funding payments from corporations and individuals.
- *Investment intermediaries*, such mutual funds, investment companies and finance companies. The common element for investment intermediaries is that the investment intermediary pools the resources of many small investors by selling them shares and then uses the proceeds to buy securities. Clients get the benefit of lower costs and diversified portfolios and pay a management fee and for the services performed by the financial institution.

8.3   Depository Financial Intermediaries

Many types of financial institutions and intermediaries exist throughout the world, and they transfer trillions of dollars from entities with excess funds to borrowers and corporations that have profitable investment opportunities. In the U.S. and all of the other countries in the world, indirect finance, which involves financial intermediation, raises much more funds for corporations than direct finance. The most important type of financial intermediaries in the United States is depository financial institutions. Exhibit 8-3 shows the twenty largest depository institutions in terms of deposits in the United States, as ranked by the *American Banker*, at the beginning of 2004.

Exhibit 8-3
Twenty Largest US Depository Institutions

Rank	Name	Headquarters	Deposits (billions)	Assets (billions)
1	Bank of America (& Fleet)	Charlotte, NC	$612	$937
2	Citicorp	New York, NY	$474	$1,264
3	JP Morgan Chase	New York, NY	$326	$771
4	Wells Fargo	San Francisco, CA	$248	$388
5	Wachovia	Charlotte, NC	$224	$401
6	Bank One	Columbus, OH	$164	$327
7	Washington Mutual	Seattle, WA	$120	$235
8	U.S. Bancorp	Minneapolis, MN	$119	$189
9	SunTrust Bank	Atlanta, GA	$81.2	$125
10	HSBC Holding	London	$64.5	$93.0
11	National City	Cleveland, OH	$63.9	$114
12	BB&T Corporation	Winston-Salem, NC	59.3	$90.5
13	Royal Bank of Scotland	Edinburgh	$57.9	$77.7
14	Fifth Third Bancorp	Cincinnati, OH	57.1	$91.1
15	ABN Amro (LaSalle Bank)	Amsterdam	$57.0	$107
16	Bank of New York	New York, NY	$56.4	$92.4
17	KeyCorp	Cleveland, OH	$50.9	$84.1
18	State Street Corp.	Boston, MA	$47.5	$87.5
19	Golden West (World Savings)	Oakland, CA	$46.8	$82.0
20	PNC Bank	Pittsburgh, PA	$45.3	$68.2

Source: American Banker Magazine

Commercial banks are the largest and most important type of financial institutions in the United States. Savings and loan associations, savings banks, and credit unions are other depository financial institutions that compete with commercial banks.

8.3.1 Commercial Banks

General:

The approximately 8,000 commercial banks in the United States make up the nations most important type of financial intermediary. Commercial banks are depository intermediaries, and they have a principal role in the payments system and are crucial to the flow of money in the economy of the United States. They provide consumers with checking and savings accounts and make loans to businesses, consumers, governments and agencies totaling over $6 trillion in loans annually.

The history of commercial banking in the United States is checkered with bank failures and controversy. In the early 19th century Americans had a great distaste for centralized power and moneyed interests and there was concern about centralized banking. Prior to 1863, all of the banks in the United States were state chartered and regulated by the banking commission in the state in which it was chartered. The National Banking Act of 1863 created national banks, which were federally chartered and supervised by a department of the US Treasury—the Office of the Comptroller of the Currency. Today, state chartered and federally chartered banks both operate in the U.S. creating a dual banking system.

Bank Assets and Liabilities and Income:

Commercial banks are highly-levered companies with deposits and borrowings comprising 92% of their balance sheets and equity of only 8%. Banks sell liabilities, such as checking accounts—which make up approximately 10% of their liabilities, time deposits and savings deposits—almost 60% of their liabilities, borrowings—23%, and bank capital of 8%.

For assets, banks prefer to make short-term business related loans with variable rates of interest. Business, real estate and other types of loans make up about 72% of the banks uses of funds, securities—22%, reserves and cash only 1%, and physical property—5%. The balance sheet equation for a bank is similar to other corporate entities:

$$Total\ Assets = Total\ Liabilities + Capital \qquad (Eq.8\text{-}1)$$

Commercial banks make money by borrowing at a low rate (interest rate paid on deposits) and lending at a higher rate (interest rate earned on loans). This is the principal revenue source for commercial banks.

In addition to the spread between borrowing and lending rates, banks generate revenues from fees charged on transaction processing, credit applications, and business lending services. Commercial banks provide numerous products and services in the financial system to link lenders and borrowers. These services can be broken down into the following categories: personal banking, institutional banking, and global banking.

Types of Banking Services:

Personal Banking Services: Commercial banks provide personal banking services to individual lenders and borrowers. These services include: accepting deposits and paying interest on deposits, checking accounts, credit card financing, mortgage loans, car loans, personal loans, school loans, and installment loans. A commercial bank also acts as the clearinghouse for transactions under which consumers purchase goods with non-cash instruments (credit cards, checks, and debit cards). All of these services are targeted at individual consumers, who need banking intermediation to save, borrow, and exchange money.

Institutional Banking Services: Institutional banking is when a bank lends and borrows with other financial corporations, non-financial corporations, and government agencies. Most of these services are concentrated in loans and cash flow management of deposits. In addition, banks finance commercial real estate, arrange leases, and factor accounts receivables. Since institutional customers handle large amounts of cash, the relative sizes of institutional accounts are huge. For example, Microsoft reported $47.8 billion in cash and equivalents on its June 30, 2002 annual report. This cash was not held in the vault in Redmond, Washington. Instead, Microsoft immediately deposits cash with financial institutions so the company is able to earn interest on every single dollar for as long as it is in the company's possession. Thousands of businesses worldwide depend on institutional banking services.

Global Banking Services: In addition to traditional banking, some firms need additional services beyond the normal scope of institutional banking. Many companies sell products internationally and not all of the trading partners deal in United States dollars. Therefore, companies with international distribution need to hold and exchange foreign currencies to trade in the international marketplace. Commercial banks dominate foreign currency transactions. Companies, governments, or individuals that want to exchange different currencies contact commercial banks because they have the scale and network to exchange significant amounts immediately.

8.3.2   *Savings and Loan Associations*

In the early 1800's commercial banks principal assets were short-term loans to businesses and no institutions serviced the needs of individuals. In 1816 Congress, in its desire to encourage home ownership, passed regulations that allowed for mutual saving banks and savings and loan associations that were to principally make home mortgage loans to families. Like banks these financial institutions take deposits and make loans, but their focus is more on home mortgage loans and personal loans, and less on business loans.

The business of savings and loan associations was to accept savings accounts from small depositors and use those moneys to fund long-term mortgage loans. S&L's thrived until the early part of the 20th century with more than 10,000 in operation in the mid-1920's but many thousands fell victim to the depression of the early 1930's.

S&L's also had a rough time during the late 1970's and early 1980's. In 1979 inflation rates of over 13% drove the interest rates on short-term government bonds rose to 15%, and the long-term mortgage loans owned by S&L's plummeted in value. Further, S&L's were restricted by a cap of 5.5% on interest rates that it could pay on savings accounts. Through mismanagement at many savings and loan associations and poor regulation by the Federal Home Loan Bank Board and the Federal Savings and Loan Insurance Fund, many savings and loans failed.

As of 2001, there were about 1,500 savings and loan associations located in the U.S. and their number and market share of deposits are shrinking. Over 1.2 trillion of total assets are on the books of savings and loan associations in 2001. S&Ls are more highly levered than commercial banks and their dominant assets are local single-family mortgages.

8.3.3 Mutual Savings Banks

Mutual savings banks mean that the depositors or the bank are also the owners of the bank. No stock is issued by a mutual savings bank—the depositors own a percentage of the bank in proportion to the amount of funds they have in the bank. The function of mutual savings bank are similar to S&L's and are found primarily in the northeastern United States. However, because of the mutual ownership structure, mutual savings banks were more conservative with their funds and they suffered far fewer failures than the savings and loan industry.

The asset base of a savings bank includes mortgages, private placements and corporate loans and it is more diverse than the asset base of a savings and loans. There are approximately 800 mutual savings banks in the United States and most of them are state chartered. Mutual savings banks can insure deposits with the FDIC or with the state agencies through which they are chartered

8.3.4 Credit Unions

About 10,000 credit unions are located in the United States. A credit union is a financial institution that services the banking needs of its members and is similar to a specialized S&L. The members of a credit union have a common bond. For example, The Pennsylvania State University has a credit union for its employees. Credit unions sell credit shares, similar to a savings account, and invest monies in mortgages that are made primarily to members of the credit union.

Like mutual savings banks, credit unions are organized as mutual organizations and are owned by their depositors. Customers receive shares when deposits are made and earn dividends on their funds. Credit unions only allow members of a particular organization, occupation, employer, or geographic area. Credit unions are non-profit organizations and are exempt from federal income taxation.

The principal assets owned by credit unions are loans to member. New and used automobile loans make up almost 40% of credit union assets. First mortgage loans and other real estate loans make up an additional 40%, while unsecured and credit card loans make up 14%. Most loans are relatively small with an average size of approximately $4,000.

Since credit unions were first established in 1910, the number of credit union members has increased steadily. Many credit unions get the help of the employer, which may provide fee office space and other amenities to support its credit union. The tax-exempt status of credit unions effectively allows credit unions to have lower loan rates and pay dividend rates on shares.

8.4   Contractual Financial Intermediaries

8.4.1   Pension Funds

Pension funds are the most important contractual financial intermediary. Pension funds account for 18% of intermediated assets in the United States, and the market share of pension funds is growing as life expectancy increases. As employers and employees contribute money to pension funds, those moneys are invested and grow on a tax-free basis, until retirement when they begin to receive payments under the pension program—so the worker does not pay taxes on the funds until the funds are received.

Corporate employers, workers' unions, and state and local municipal entities act as pension *fund sponsors*. The largest pension fund programs in the United States are sponsored by entities that represent the California Employees (CALPERS) and the New York State & Local Employees, each with over $100 billion in assets at the end of 2004. The largest pension fund programs that are sponsored by corporations are General Motors with over $80 billion and General Electric with almost $70 billion in assets at the end of 2004.

Pension funds sell a contractually assured stream of retirement benefits called *pension plans*. Retirees have options on the type of payment streams that they can receive. The two types of pension plans that are used most frequently are the *defined benefit plan* and the *defined contribution plan*. Under the defined benefit plan, the sponsor of the plan agrees to pay a predetermined amount of money, usually on a monthly basis, to the pensioner or his or her beneficiary. So the sponsor guarantees a certain amount upon retirement, and is responsible for the payment of a stream of retirement payments—essentially guarantying the performance of the investments associated with the pension fund. Under the defined contribution plan, the fund sponsor makes a periodic contribution into the employee's account of the pension fund. The sponsor does not guaranty the performance of the investments in the fund or the stream of payments the worker will receive at retirement.

Pension funds invest in domestic and foreign equities and bonds, and in alternative investments such as hedge funds. Because of the predictability of their payment streams, the focus of pension funds is on long-term investment performance and the liquidity of their assets is not a major concern.

8.4.2   *Life and Property and Casualty Insurance Companies*

Insurance companies are contractual intermediaries that pool risk and spread the costs of insurance over as many individuals or entities as possible to minimize the effect of losses suffered by any individual event or occurrence. Insurance companies charge a premium, such as car and life insurance payments, for the assumption of risk. The amount of the insurance premium payment is usually based on actuarial probabilities of an adverse event that triggers a claim occurring. The premiums that are received by the insurance company are then invested until such time that they are needed to pay claims under the insurance policy.

As long as the group of entities that is insured is large enough that the events that occur which results in payments under the policies approximate historical averages, insurance companies are profitable and individuals obtain adequate coverage for a reasonable premium. However, overexposure to certain industries or geographic regions and catastrophic events can require insurance companies to pay significant claims all at one time. The terrorist events of September 11, 2001, triggered massive and unanticipated claims under property and casualty policies and life and health insurance policies. Major hurricanes in Florida are also known for causing problems for poorly diversified insurance companies.

The primary revenues sources for insurance companies are insurance premiums and the income from investments that insurance companies earn by investing this premium income. The primary expense category is insurance claims and benefits. Most insurance companies specialize in a particular type of insurance like life, health, property and casualty, such as car insurance, and special risks, such as disability insurance.

Life insurance companies sell protection against premature death and also sell a special type of retirement benefit known as single premium deferred annuities. The principal liabilities of life insurance companies are reserves for the payments of death benefits, and the contractually assured retirement streams. These payments are fairly predictable according to actuarial tables as long as there are a large number of insured entities so that they can conform to probability distributions associated with the law of large numbers. The principal assets of life insurance companies are corporate bonds, equities, and mortgages. Life insurance companies are taxed at very low rates and their market share of intermediated assets in the United States is about 10%.

Property and casualty insurance companies sell protection on property and health through auto, fire, health, and other types of insurance. The principal liabilities of property, casualty and health insurers are reserves for policy payments. The payments under these policies often are caused by a catastrophic event, such as hurricanes, earthquakes, and other disasters, and are much less predictable than the payment streams for life insurance companies. Property and casualty companies are taxed at corporate tax rates of up to 34% and they buy tax-advantaged investment such as municipal bonds, along with equities and corporate bonds, and their market share of intermediated assets in the United States is about 3%.

The largest insurance companies by stock market capitalization in the United States as of 2003 are listed in Exhibit 8-4. Is your insurance company on the list?

Exhibit 8-4
Largest Insurance Companies in the United States
(by Market Equity $Bn)

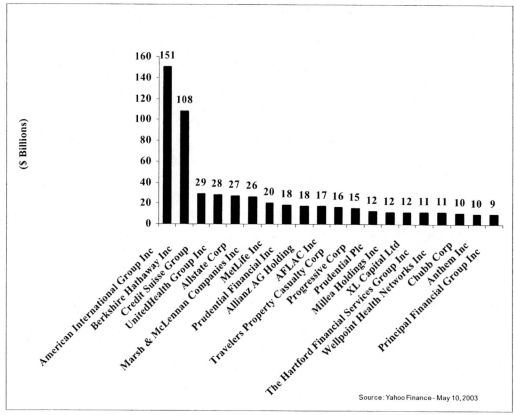

Source: Yahoo Finance - May 10, 2003

8.5   Investment Intermediaries

8.5.1   Mutual Funds and Investment Companies

A mutual fund is a pool of money managed and invested by professional managers. Mutual funds raise money by selling shares in the fund to investors, and then take this money to buy securities. Most mutual funds have redemption features known as *open-end*, which means they are continuously willing to sell or buy back shares at their net asset value per share (total value of investment holdings divided by number of mutual fund shares outstanding). *Closed-end* funds, which represent a small percentage of mutual funds, operate like a normal corporation in that they sell a fixed number of shares and then invest the proceeds.

There are three general types of mutual funds as defined by their investment objective—money market funds, bond funds, and stock funds. Money market funds invest in short-term, highly marketable securities like U.S. Treasury Bill. Bond funds invest in bonds issued by the U.S. Treasury, corporations, or other economic entities. Stocks funds invest in the common stock issued by corporations. There are many, many different types of funds within these three general categories. For example, the types of stock funds include value funds, growth funds, small- and large-capitalization funds, global funds, and sector funds (health care, energy, financial, etc.).

Stock funds or equity funds involve more risk than money market or bond funds, but they also can offer the highest returns. A stock fund's value can rise and fall quickly over the short term. Historically, stocks have performed better over the long-term than other types of investments.

The risk associated with bond funds generally falls in between the risks associated with stock and money market funds. However, because of the wide range of risks of bonds, bond funds can be structured to assume a high degree of credit risk, such as a fund that invests primarily in high-yield junk bonds or in bonds with low credit risk, such as in Treasury and agency bonds. Investors in high-yield bond funds expect a return that is considerably greater than the return associated with a bond fund that invests only in Treasury bonds. This expectation reflects the basic trade-off between risk and expected returns.

Money market funds invest in high quality debt securities that have a short maturity and lower risk when compared with the assets of other mutual funds. By regulation, they are limited to invest in certain high-quality, short-term investments. Money market funds try to keep their net asset value at a stable $1.00 per share. Losses for investors in money market funds are rare, but they are possible.

Financial research shows that a diversified portfolio of securities offers greater returns with lower risk than a portfolio with investments that are concentrated in a few stocks or industries. Mutual funds offer investors an easy way to diversity their investment holdings. In addition, mutual funds offer investors professional management (which comes with the economies of scale afforded through the fund) and liquidity. All this comes with a cost however. The average annual fee is about .75% for a bond fund and 1.50% for a stock fund.

Stock mutual funds grew tremendously during the bull market of the 1990s. Today, there are more than 6,000 different equity mutual funds in the United States. The largest stock mutual funds, as of 2003, are listed in Exhibit 7-5. It should be noted however that the largest mutual fund is no longer a stock fund. Due to the declining stock market since the year 2000, declining stock prices and investor withdrawals have reduced the size of the two largest stock funds—Vanguard's 500 Index Trust and Fidelity's Magellan by almost 50%. Today, with almost $70B in funds, the PIMCO Total Return Fund – which invests exclusively in bonds, is the largest mutual fund.

Exhibit 8-5
The Largest Equity Mutual Funds

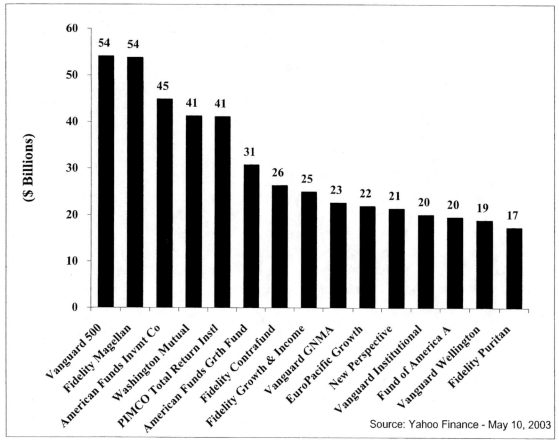

Source: Yahoo Finance - May 10, 2003

8.5.2 Finance Companies

Finance companies came into existence in the early part of the 20th century and are used principally to finance loans to individuals and businesses that purchase products manufactured by an entity with a relationship to the finance company. For example, one of the largest finance companies in the United States is the General Motors Acceptance Corporation (GMAC). An important part of GMAC's activities is to finance the purchases of General Motor's automobiles. Until 2003, Sears Roebuck had a finance company—the Sears, Roebuck Acceptance Corporation, that financed the consumer purchases of products sold at Sears & Roebuck.

Finance companies are financial institutions that have very little regulation in comparison to depository financial intermediaries, such as banks and savings and loan associations. Finance companies typically make loans to investors whose credit ratings are less than stellar. Consequently, the loans are of much higher risk. Because of this higher risk, finance companies generally charge a much higher interest rate than the rates on typical bank loans. Historically, finance company loans have a much higher chance of default. The levels of interest rates that finance companies can charge is based on usury rates permitted by the various states. Such rates often depend on the type, size and maturity of a particular loan.

Finance companies act as intermediaries by borrowing short-term, variable-rate funds in the commercial paper market and they use the proceeds to make long-term fixed-rate loans to borrowers. They accept the risk associated with default of their borrowers and the liquidity risk of constantly rolling over their liabilities, and owning very illiquid assets funded from those liabilities. Business loans make up 50% of the assets of finance companies with consumer loans at 33% and real estate loans at 17%. At the end of 2001, finance companies had over $1.3 trillion in total assets.

8.6   Transactional Financial Institutions

8.6.1   Investment Banks

Investment banking is the set of activities that financial institutions, usually stock brokerage firms and commercial banks, conduct in the capital markets that help the origination and the sale of securities to investors. Investment banks are transactional intermediaries that raise capital for corporations and governments through the public and private financial markets by linking investors and borrowers. Investment banking is transaction-oriented and involves only a very short-term holding of assets that are issued by its clients, prior to the sale of those assets to the ultimate investors. Investment banks make funds through the underwriting fees that they charge to the issuers of securities. In contrast, commercial banks lend their own funds to clients and they make asset/liability and risk mismatches to earn a profit between their cost of funds and the yield on their investments.

Instead of accepting deposits and loaning those deposits to clients directly, investment banks link investors to issuers through the sale of primary securities. Investment banks also provide strategic and financial advice to clients, lend and invest the firm's own capital, provide research for securities and markets, trade securities for clients and for their own account, and manage investment portfolios.

"The investment banker was a breed apart, a member of a master race of deal makers. He possessed vast, almost unimaginable talent and ambition. If he had a dog, it snarled. He had two little red sports cars yet wanted four. To get them, he was, for a man in a suit, surprisingly willing to cause trouble."
                                        Michael Lewis Liar's Poker

Investment banks perform a variety of different services for investors and issuers. Those services include:

- *Advising the issuer of securities and originating the financing.* An investment bank is very close to investors and market sentiment and can give the issuer insights on the state of the capital markets and features that investors prefer and will pay for in the structuring of a debt or equity offering.
- *Underwriting the financing.* Underwriting is the process of guaranteeing a price or yield on a security to an issuer. An investment bank often forms an underwriting syndicate consisting of a number of investment banks that will share the profits and the risks in the transaction. Once the securities are underwritten, the investment banks that underwrite the transaction bear the risk of loss in the sale of those securities to investors.
- *Distributing the financing to the ultimate investor.* The investment banks that are underwriting the transaction canvass potential investors and offer the transaction for sale to the general market.

Most investment banks have three divisions: a corporate finance and investment banking division, a sales and trading division, and a research department. The corporate finance and investment banking division handles security underwriting, mergers and acquisitions, and restructuring. Sales and trading interacts with clients and the financial markets to market and trade securities. Salespeople are assigned to clients and cover clients and contact traders to execute transactions, either on an agency or principal basis, on behalf of the client.

When an investment bank acts as an agent, it simply is a middleman between the buyer of a security and the seller. When it acts as a principal, it buys and sells securities directly for the benefit of the firm, and it makes or loses money based upon the prices that it buys and sells. As principals, investment banks execute trades and hold inventory of certain securities attempting to make a profit.

Bulge bracket investment banks are the banks that control the majority of transactions in the financial markets. Being in this category is based on a combination of size, reputation, presence in specific areas, and distribution network. These firms serve mainly Fortune 100 clients, and international governments, and participate in the world's largest deals. The bulge bracket consists of the five or six largest multinational investment banks that control most of the major headline deals. Depending on mergers and SEC investigation, bulge bracket is not set in stone, and firms rotate based on deals and order flow. The bulge bracket firms currently are: Goldman Sachs & Co., Merrill Lynch, Morgan Stanley Dean Witter, Credit Suisse First Boston, Salomon Smith Barney, and Lehman Brothers (see Exhibit 8-6).

Exhibit 8-6
Market Share of Top Underwriters

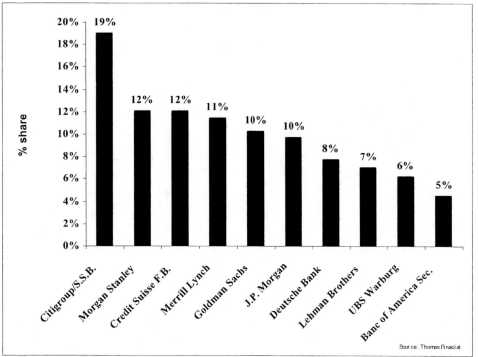

Source: Thomas Finacial

8.6.2   Stock Brokerage Firms

Stock brokerage firms are firms that act to buy and sell stocks, bonds, and other securities for or on behalf of clients of the firm. Broadly, stock market firms can be classified as full service brokerage firms such as Merrill Lynch and Smith Barney, discount stock brokerage firms such as Charles Schwab, and online stock brokerage firms such as E-Trade or Ameritrade.

A full service brokerage firm provides a broad array of financial services to investors. Those services include complete financial analysis, investment planning, and retirement planning. Full service brokers, such as Merrill Lynch and Paine Webber, are members of all major exchanges and usually make markets in most NADAQ issues.

Investors have access to many different financial instruments including common stock, bonds (corporate, government, municipal, and international), derivative products (options, futures, and other products), commodities, foreign currency, and just about any other publicly traded investment product. To accompany the full array of investment products, most full service brokers provide their own research and forecasts of economic, industry, and company conditions. This gives investors who are clients of the firm immediate access to information and recommendations.

Unlike full service brokers, the fees of which can be substantial, discount brokers offer basic investment services with no frills attached. Discount brokers provide fewer services to investors and have lower overhead expenses and therefore are able to charge lower commissions. Research may be limited or nonexistent and product availability may also be limited to stocks and mutual funds.

The growth of the Internet spurred a new type of brokerage service. Electronic trading allows investors to trade stocks, bonds, and other securities through accounts that they have established with stock brokerage firms that have online services. The pure electronic stock trading firms include Etrade, Ameritrade, and Datek, among others. Trades are placed via the telephone or the Internet without ever speaking to an individual. The fewer people that are involved in a transaction, the lower the commission rates. Electronic trading offers commission rates comparable to and even lower than the rates associated with deep discount brokerage firms.

8.7   The Regulation of Financial Institutions

Financial institutions in the United States come under the control of numerous federal and state agencies. For depository financial intermediaries, besides the Federal Reserve Board, the Federal Deposit Insurance Corporation (FDIC) and the Controller of the Currency exert various powers. For contractual intermediaries, each state has an insurance commission that effects the operations of insurance companies within each state. For transactional intermediaries, the Securities and Exchange Commission, along with the National Association of Security Dealers (NASD), have primarily responsibility to make sure that transactions follow the letter of the securities laws.

8.7.1   The Federal Reserve System

While not formally considered a financial institution, the Federal Reserve System, under the Federal Reserve Board of Governors, is the federal agency overseeing domestic monetary policy. It is an extremely important element of the financial system and is the most important central bank in the world.

The twelve Federal Reserve Banks are spread across the United States and are each responsible for servicing a geographic segment of the country. The Federal Reserve Banks are responsible for:

- Issuing new currency and withdrawing damaged currency from circulation;
- Clearing checks and administering the payments system in the United States;

- Approving and making discount loans to the commercial banks in their districts;
- Examining bank holding companies and state-chartered member banks;
- Collecting information and data relating to local economic and business conditions and acting to represent the business interests of their district in the Federal Reserve System.

All national banks, which are banks chartered by the Office of the Comptroller of the Currency, are required to be members of the Federal Reserve System. Banks chartered by state banking and regulatory agencies can be members of the Federal Reserve System, but are not required to join. All depository institutions that do business in the United States are required to keep deposits at the Federal Reserve in the form of reserves. The size of reserves depends on the size and type of deposits that are held by a depository intermediary. The reserves of commercial banks that are kept on deposit at the Federal Reserve do not earn interest.

For the last fifteen years the *Fed* has concentrated its efforts on low inflation, low unemployment, and stable economic growth. During the late 1970s and early 1980s while under the stewardship of Paul Voelcker, the Chairman of the Board of Governors, the Fed concentrated on fighting rampant double-digit inflation in the economy. To overcome inflation, the Fed focused on a goal of a steady money supply and allowed interest rates to fluctuate wildly, based on a fixed money supply. The prime rate rose to 21% and the yield on long-term United States Government debt exceeded 15% during the early 1980s.

Today, under the leadership of Alan Greenspan, the Fed monitors the money supply and interest rates in an attempt to keep the economy out of a recession and to minimize inflation and interest rate volatility, which appears to be a key component to long-term economic growth. Exhibit 8-7 illustrates the branch of the Fed that controls monetary policy, the Federal Open Market Committee.

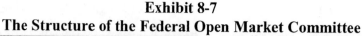

Exhibit 8-7
The Structure of the Federal Open Market Committee

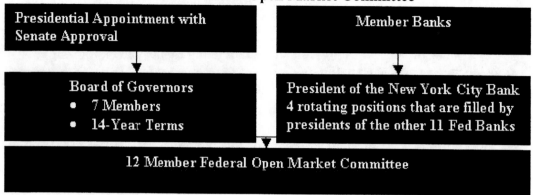

Presidential Appointment with Senate Approval	Member Banks
Board of Governors • 7 Members • 14-Year Terms	President of the New York City Bank 4 rotating positions that are filled by presidents of the other 11 Fed Banks
12 Member Federal Open Market Committee	

The Federal Open Market Committee (FOMC) meets eight times a year and makes decisions relating to the level of the money supply and short-term interest rates. The FOMC has several tools in its arsenal in conducting monetary policy. The most important tool is that it is responsible for conducting open market operations. Open market operations means that the Fed is: either buying securities in the market and adding to the money supply, thereby reducing interest rates; or, selling securities in the market and reducing the money supply, and increasing short-term interest rates. Other monetary tools relate to the setting of reserve requirements, and the determination of the discount rate associated with loans made by the Federal Reserve to commercial banks.

8.7.2   The FDIC

Born as a result of over 9000 bank failures during the Great Depression, the Federal Deposit Insurance Corporation was created by the Glass Steagall Act of 1933. The FDIC provided insurance against bank failures, and required that all national banks and members of the Federal Reserve System purchase federal insurance on their deposits. Non-member banks of the Federal Reserve were permitted to purchase FDIC insurance, and most purchased the insurance.

The deposit insurance of the FDIC is a guarantee under which depositors of a bank are paid off on the first $100,000 that it has on deposit in a bank that fails. If a bank fails, the FDIC can use one of two methods to pay off the depositors in a bank. The *payoff method* involves the FDIC paying the depositors up to $100,000 on their accounts For funds over that amount, the FDIC and the depositors join the other creditors of the bank and are paid their proportionate share of the carcass upon the recovery of all of the assets upon liquidation. The *purchase and assumption method* involves the FDIC finding a willing merger partner who takes over all of the banks deposits and no depositor suffers a loss.

The FDIC is responsible, along with the state banking commission in which a bank is located, for regulating almost 6000 state-chartered banks that have FDIC insurance.

8.7.3   The Securities and Exchange Commission

The principal regulator of all primary and secondary financial market activity in the United States is the Securities and Exchange Commission (SEC). Following the stock market crash of 1929 and the Great Depression of the early 1930s, a wave of financial regulation was implemented to curb market speculation and fraud, and to strengthen investor confidence.

The *Securities Exchange Act of 1934* created the SEC. The SEC is responsible for licensing securities professionals, collecting public disclosure information, and enforcing the various securities laws in the United States. The SEC's primary objective is to provide investors with complete disclosure of all material information concerning publicly traded securities. Its goal is to create a level playing field for investors and minimize the information asymmetries that existed in the early 1900s.

The Securities Exchange Act of 1934 also implemented regulation pertaining to the sale and trading of securities in the secondary markets—after the initial issuance of securities. This act regulates the activities of the various stock and bond exchanges in the United States and all of the financial institutions and finance professionals that participate in this market.

Prior to the creation of the SEC, Congress initially passed *The Securities Act of 1933*. The Securities Act of 1933 is designed to regulate the primary securities markets by providing investors with the necessary information to make informed decisions regarding an issue of new securities.

8.7.4   State Banking, Insurance, and Securities Regulation

The purpose of government regulation of financial institutions is to protect clients, depositors, or claim holders from losses due to improper management or the insolvency of the financial institution. In an effort to protect their constituents from fraud and improper practices, most states have insurance, banking and security regulators and commissions that are responsible for overseeing the financial companies that operate in the particular state. These regulators often act in concert with their federal counterparts to investigate and prosecute any unfair or improper activities.

State banking regulators work closely with the FDIC to examine state chartered banks that also have purchased FDIC insurance. State banking regulators are solely responsible for examining and regulating approximately 500 state-chartered banks that have not purchased FDIC insurance.

The McCarran-Ferguson Act of 1945 exempts insurance companies from federal regulation so state regulators perform most of the regulation of insurance companies. Insurance companies must follow the regulations of each of the states in which it does business. For insurance companies, the State of New York is the most stringent state as far as regulations are concerned, and it is a very large market for insurance products. If an insurance company does business in the State of New York and abides by New York's insurance regulations, it usually qualifies to do business in the other states. To insure that agents and brokers have the proper training and knowledge about the products that they are selling, insurance agents and brokers must be properly licensed by the insurance regulator in the state that they are doing business.

State securities regulators are also very actively involved in examining and regulating activities of the financial institutions that operate or are domiciled in their particular state. Often, a state securities regulator discovers illegal activities of a financial institution and will institute civil or criminal proceedings. Recent examples of this type of activity occurred with actions initiated by the State of New York for bogus research provided by New York based investment banks; and by the Commonwealth of Massachusetts against the management companies of certain mutual funds for allowing market timing and improper late trading by hedge funds. The SEC and state securities regulators often will work together in administering and prosecuting financial institutions that have violated federal and state securities laws.

8.8   Recent Developments Relating to Financial Institutions

8.8.1   Repealing The Glass Steagall Act—The Financial Services Modernization Act of 1999

Following the stock market crash of 1929 and the Great Depression, extensive financial market regulation was passed to curb mistrust and criminal practices in the financial markets. One of most important regulations passed during the 1930s was the Glass-Steagall Act in 1933. Glass-Steagall forced the separation of traditional commercial banking and investment banking activities. This prohibited commercial banks from underwriting securities, and created the separation of commercial and investment banks. In recent years innovation by financial services firms and financial services deregulation has watered down the importance of the Glass-Steagall Act, but this legislation had a major impact on the development of the financial services industry in the United States.

In 1999, Congress passed The Financial Services Modernization Act. The principal effect of this act is to eliminate most of the remaining Depression-era firewalls between banks, securities firms, and insurance companies that the Glass-Steagall Act had imposed. The cross-ownership of banks, securities firms, and insurance companies is now possible, as is the conduct of commercial banking, merchant banking, investment management, securities underwriting, and insurance within a single financial institution, using a holding company structure. This liberalization of United States banking and financial services regulation applies both to domestic institutions and foreign institutions conducting business in the United States.

8.8.2 Online Banking and Investing

Internet banks such as NetBank offer normal banking services and can pay a higher interest rate on deposits than traditional branch banks. Internet banks have smaller fixed overhead costs and lower transaction costs so their interest rate spreads do not need to be as large as traditional banks, which have the costs of property and equipment and larger personnel costs. Internet banks use the newest and best encryption software and firewall hardware to restrict unwanted access and external tampering with records. Many Internet banks claim that e-banking is safer than traditional systems using the telephone or snail mail to process credit card information.

Firms that offer traditional stock and securities brokerage have been dealt a serious competitive challenge by the online trading firms like E*Trade. Like online banks, online brokerage firms have much lower cost structures and can offer stock trades for as little as $5 per trade. This compares to trades that could cost you several hundred dollars at a full service investment firm. We discuss online stock trading in Chapter 6 relating to the securities markets.

8.8.3 Online One-Stop Financial Services

The recent passage of the Financial Services Modernization Act has allowed banks, insurance companies, and securities firms to offer customers a wide array of financial products at one location, from one financial services firm. The deregulation of the financial markets, together with the conveniences the Internet provides, has made it possible for consumers to manage all their finances on one single website. To serve these consumers, banks are integrating brokerage and banking services on one website. Wells Fargo & Co. has a website where customers can pay bills, transfer funds, and apply for loans. It is also connected with Wells Trade, the company's e-brokerage arm.

Traditional banks face a number of challenges in trying to please their clients. Exhibit 8-8 shows the distribution channel for an integrated financial services firm.

Exhibit 8-8
Distribution Channel for Integrated Financial Services Firm

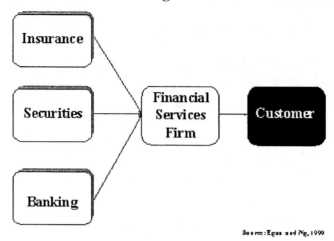

Source: Egan and Ng, 1999

As federally insured depositories, banks are tied down by unique privacy and legal concerns. There are limitations on sharing information between banking and brokerage units. These limitations force institutions to erect costly technical and organizational firewalls, making it difficult to cross sell different financial services. Separating the banking and brokerage units also means that the brokerage unit has to pay fair market prices for services it receives from the parent bank. Federal law does not allow for discounts or freebies between the parent company and the subsidiary.

Banks are also playing catch-up with non-bank firms in the e-brokerage industry like E*Trade and Schwab. According to the Federal Deposit Insurance Corp., bank deposits make up only 30% of household assets, compared to 38% eight years ago. More and more households are putting their money in stocks, bonds and mutual funds rather than in bank deposits. This trend is one of the reasons why banks are rushing to get into the e-brokerage business.

The online market for one-stop financial centers is significant. Banks will benefit from this trend when they recapture money that has been flowing out of banks to online brokerage firms. There is also a large cost savings for banks in this market. It costs a bank $1.07 each time one of its customers carries out a transaction at a teller window. This cost is cut reduced to $0.27 per transaction on an ATM. It is further reduced to just 1 cent for an Internet transaction.

8.8.4 Risk Management

Financial institutions are exposed to significant risks in their daily business activities. These risks include credit and default risk, interest rate risk, currency and exchange rate risk, commodity price risk, and stock market risks. Commercial banks, for example, assume an enormous amount of credit risk from borrowers. To minimize the risks of loan default, rising interest rates, and a run on bank capital, banks use various strategies and financial instruments to limit risk exposure.

Most risk management falls into one of the following categories: credit risk management, interest rate risk management, foreign exchange risk management, liquidity management, and the attempt to reduce potential loss producing events. When these potential risks are addressed and hedged prior to occurrence, commercial bank risk exposure declines. However, risk reduction involves a cost. We discuss the costs of hedging credit, foreign exchange, interest rates, and liquidity in Chapter 16.

8.8.5 *Consolidation*

Mergers and acquisitions have become the way to grow in the financial services business over the past decade. Mergers have been occurring for different reasons. Consider the two following examples:

Citigroup:

Traveler's Corporation was a diversified financial services company that included everything from insurance, annuities, credit cards, retail brokerage, and a terrific investment banking presence through the Salomon Smith Barney subsidiary. Citigroup hopes to leverage the Traveler's products and distribute them through the huge customer base of Citicorp. The retail customers of Citicorp were the target market for the retail investment and financial products of a securities firm while their institutional clients were the investment banking targets of the new Citigroup. A one-stop financial supermarket is the ultimate goal of this merger. Cross selling of products is the long-term source of expected top-line growth and the primary motivation for the merger.

BankAmerica-Nations Bank:

The BankAmerica-Nations Bank merger was not a top-line growth merger, but it was a cost cutting synergy driven merger. The merger consolidated two super regional commercial banks and formed the first major commercial bank with national scope. The combined firm was the largest depository institution in the country, banking in more than 22 states. The primary reasons for this merger were to expand the geographical reach of the company, and to diversify the asset and funding base while simultaneously driving down transaction costs.

8.9   Summary

This chapter covers financial intermediation and financial institutions. Financial institutions dominate the financial system in the United States and around the world. This chapter explains the forms of financial intermediation that are exploited by financial institutions. In addition, the different types of financial institutions are discussed and recent developments in financial institutions are covered.

In this chapter we explained:

- The functions of the financial system and the need for financial intermediaries in this system;
- The different forms of financial intermediation and how these are exploited by financial institutions; and
- The different types of financial institutions and their role in the economy.

List of Terms

1. Financial intermediation
2. Financial institution
3. Financial markets
4. Primary/secondary
5. Gross spread
6. Portfolio management
7. Maturity intermediation
8. Liquidity intermediation
9. Diversification
10. Default risk
11. Economies of scale
12. Monetary policy
13. Market capitalization
14. Investment bank
15. Government agencies
16. Commercial bank
17. Clearing house
18. Institutional banking
19. Global banking
20. Pension plans/fund
21. Defined benefit plan
22. Defined contribution plan
23. Annuity
24. Investment bank
25. Primary security
26. Secondary security
27. Bulge bracket
28. Underwriting
29. Mergers and acquisitions
30. Initial public offer
31. High-yield debt
32. Mutual fund
33. Open-end/close-end fund
34. Net asset value
35. Equity fund
36. Bond fund
37. Money market fund
38. Fannie Mae
39. Federal Reserve
40. Monetary policy
41. FDIC
42. Glass-Steagall Act
43. The Financial Services
Modernization Act of 1999

44. Holding company
45. Default risk

Questions

1. What are the roles of financial institutions?
2. Generally speaking, where do financial intermediaries generate most of their revenue?
3. Briefly explain the services provided by commercial banks.
4. Why wouldn't a wealthy individual choose to bypass a bank, and loan funds directly to a borrower?
5. What are the two primary roles that financial intermediation plays in the economy?
6. Why is diversification important for individual investors and commercial banks? Is there a correlation between default risk and diversification for commercial banks?
7. What are the three categories of financial intermediaries? Give an example of each (e.g., Merrill Lynch rather than Investment Bank).
8. What is the nation's most important category of financial institutions?
9. What are the differences between private, institutional, and global banking?
10. Why are pension funds growing? Given the current environment, would you expect them to be over funded, or under funded?
11. Describe the different types of insurance companies that exist. Which would you expect to have the most stable revenues, the least stable?
12. What does an investment bank do? Generally speaking, which sector(s) of the economy does an investment bank cater to?
13. What are the three divisions in a typical investment bank? What are their respective functions?
14. What are the advantages of investing in a mutual fund?
15. Why would an investor choose to invest in a mutual fund rather than buy a similar basket of securities?
16. If a mutual fund has appreciated to a total value of $1000 from $800 and there are 100 shares outstanding, what is this fund's current net asset value?
17. Briefly describe an open-ended and closed-ended mutual fund.
18. Fundamentally speaking, why do investors expect a stock mutual fund to have a return that is greater than that of a money market fund?
19. What type of risks are financial institutions exposed to?
20. What are the ramifications of the Glass-Steagall Act?
21. Why has there been a marked increase in mergers between commercial and investment banks in the last four years?
22. Why are holding companies popular in banking?
23. How do the Traveler's-Citicorp merger and the BankAmerica-Nations Bank mergers differ?

Assignment #8-1:

1. Morningstar is an authority on analysis and review of mutual funds. Go to the website http://screen.morningstar.com/Movers/FdMovDef.html?fsection=gainers. This is the Morningstar "Fund Movers" webpage. Click on the first entry and evaluate the fund's performance versus the S&P 500. Based on the information presented, would this fund be an acceptable investment for you?

2.

3. The Federal Deposit Insurance Corporation (FDIC) was designed to originally restore and ultimately to maintain order in the United States banking system. Go to the FDIC's statistical resource page (http://www.fdic.gov/bank/statistical/statistics/sectiona.html) and comment on the trends of FDIC insured banks since the 1930s. Do you think that the FDIC has played a significant role in the growth of commercial banking in the United States? To have a well-formed answer, navigate the FDIC homepage (www.fdic.gov) and look under "history." Do you think that the banking industry would be different without the formation of the FDIC?

CHAPTER 9

THE TIME VALUE OF MONEY: COMPOUNDING AND DISCOUNTING

In this chapter we discuss how an investment grows over time through compounding, and how to value a project or investment through the process of discounting its expected future cash flows. These are important concepts in finance for you to understand. As an individual investor or a corporate financial manager, the mathematical mechanics of compounding and discounting will help you to know:

- How much money you need to save today to fund your retirement in forty years;
- How much money you should save annually to pay for your children's college tuition payments that begin in fifteen years;
- If your firm invests in a venture or a project today, that the payments from that product in the future are more than sufficient to justify its cost; and
- If the amount that a company is budgeting and investing today is sufficient to fund employees' future retirement benefits to fulfill the firm's payment obligations in the future.

When we invest, we use today's dollars to purchase financial assets that we hope will produce the greater cash flows of tomorrow. In fact, any investment involves spending money today and receiving cash payments in the future. To assess if an investment is good or bad, you must be able to compare the value of money that you invest today with the value of the money that the investment is expected to generate in the future.

As we discussed when we examined the ten principles of finance in Chapter 2, the key to understanding the time value of money is to recognize that **Time and the Value of Money are Inversely Related**. The farther out in the future that you expect a payment, the less it is worth today in present value terms. If you are serious about investing, it is essential that you understand how to properly value stocks and bonds. This requires that you know the math underlying compounding and discounting. The math is not difficult but does require you to understand the relationship between present and future values, how to use exponents, and how to compound to future value and discount to present value.

The discounting of expected cash flow is based upon two fundamental concepts that underlie finance theory. The first concept is that of *positive interest rates* and may be characterized by the saying, "A dollar invested today is worth more than a dollar promised tomorrow." The second concept relates to *risk aversion*, and can be captured by the phrase, "A safe dollar is worth more than a risky one."

Your objectives for this chapter are to understand how to:
- Calculate the future value of a one-time investment;
- Calculate the future value of an investment with multiple payments;
- Calculate the present value today of money to be received in the future;
- Find the payments on a loan and the rate of return on an investment.

9.1   Compounding and Future Value

A key to valuing any investment is to understand the concepts of compounding and discounting. *Compounding* is the process of going from today's value, or present value (*PV*), to some expected but unknown future value (*FV*). Compounding also means to multiply, over a number of time periods, by a number greater than 1.0. You'll see what we mean by this statement in a minute.

> **Compounding** is the process of going from a value today to an expected but unknown value in the future.

Future value is the amount of money that an investment will grow to at some future date by earning interest at a certain rate. Let's look at an example to see how compounding and future value works.

> **Future value** is the amount an investment is expected to grow to at some future date.

9.1.1   How a Single Period (one-time) Investment Grows

Suppose Jane invests $1000 with her local bank at an interest rate of 8% per year, compounded annually. How much will it grow to over the period of five years? Table 9-1 below shows how Jane's bank account is expected to grow over time, compounding by 8% per year over the five-year period. The future value of the account, compounded at a rate of 8%, is $1,469.

Table 9-1
Jane's Bank Account
Compounding and Future Value Schedule

Year	Beginning Bank Account	Interest Payment	Ending Balance
1	$1000	$80	$1080
2	$1080	$86	$1166
3	$1166	$93	$1260
4	$1260	$101	$1360
5	$1360	$109	$1469
Total Compound Interest		$469	

The equation for calculating the annual interest payment is simply:

Beginning Balance * Interest Rate = Annual Interest Payment (Eq.9-1)

So for Jane's bank account, with a beginning balance of $1000 and an annual interest rate of 8%, the interest payment for year 1 is $80 and the ending balance is:

_$1000 * 8% = $80_

Ending Balance = Beginning Balance + Interest Payment
_$1080 = $1000 + $80_

Jane's beginning bank account balance of $1000 has grown by the factor of $(1.0 + .08) = (1.08)$ and results in a balance at the end of year one of $1080. For any interest rate-r, the value of an investment at the end of a year that earns an annual return of r, is equal to:

Ending Balance = Beginning Balance * (1.0 + r)   (Eq.9-2)
_$1080 = $1000 * (1.08)_

What happens to Jane's account in year 2? If she is earning compound interest, her beginning year 2 balance of $1080 will again earn interest at the rate of 8% and will grow as follows:

Interest in Year 2 = $1080 * (.08) = $86.40

Ending Balance (Year 2) = Beginning Balance + Interest Payment
_$1166.40 = $1080 + $86.40_

So Jane's investment increases each year by a factor of 1.08—from $1000 to $1080 to $1166.40. In this example, when we compound we multiply the beginning bank account value of $1000 by 1.08 over five annual periods:

_$1000 * (1.08) * (1.08) * (1.08) * (1.08) * (1.08) = $1469_

Compound interest _is when an investment earns interest on both the original principal and the accumulated interest._

When we compound, if r or i is the compounding rate (also called a _growth rate, interest rate_ or _yield_), n is the number of years, _PV_ is the present value of a single payment investment, then the future value (_FV_) of the single payment investment is:

Future Value of a Single Payment Equation

$$FV = PV * (1.0 + r)\wedge n \qquad (Eq.9\text{-}3)$$

In math terms this equation means that if you compound a number or present value, *PV,* at a rate *(1.0 + r)* for *n* periods, the future value is equal to the present value times (1.0 plus the compounding rate), raised to the *n*th power. Jane's Bank Account example looks like this:

$$\$1469 = \$1000 * (1.0 + .08)\wedge 5$$

When you calculate compound interest and future values, the *future value factor* is the number by which you multiply the present value of an investment to arrive at the future value of an investment. In the example above it is equal to:

$$\textbf{\textit{Future Value Factor}} = \textbf{\textit{(1.0 + r)}}\wedge \textbf{\textit{n}} \qquad \textbf{\textit{(Eq.9\text{-}4)}}$$
Future Value Factor = (1.0 + .08)^5 = 1.469

Jane's account balance grows each year as interest is added so that the interest earned on the account balance also grows. Jane is earning interest on interest. When interest is earned on interest, it is known as *compound interest.*

Conversely, *simple interest* involves earning interest only on the original deposit in the account. If the bank paid simple interest on Jane's account, Jane would only earn 8% on the original $1000 balance or $80 per year. Over a five-year period, Jane's balance would earn $80 per year times 5 periods for a total of $400 in interest, significantly lower than the $469 that she will earn on a compound basis.

> **Simple interest** *is when an investment pays interest*
> *only on the original principal.*

The Rule of 72 is a simple and inexact rule of thumb that people who are familiar with compounding use as a quick and easy way to estimate the yield on a single (one-time) investment. The Rule of 72 tells us how long it takes money to double in value for a given compound interest rate, or what compound interest rate is required for an investment to double over a given period of time. When using the Rule of 72, you divide the number 72 by the interest rate to get the number of years in which the investment will double. Or you can divide 72 by the number of years to find what interest rate is required to double your money in that period of time.

For example, if the compound interest rate is 8% on Jane's bank account, how long will it take her $1000 deposit to double?

- The inexact rule of 72 says it should take (72/8) = 9 years to double your money at 8%.
- When we check this answer by using the future value factor discussed above, we calculate that 8% compounded over nine periods is just south of 2—equal to: $(1.08)\wedge 9 = 1.9990$. The Rule of 72's estimate of 9 years is close but not exact. It

takes slightly more than 9 years to double our money based upon a compound annual interest rate of 8%.

What interest rate does George need to earn on his investment in order to double his $5000 savings in 6 years?

The rule of 72 says it should take a return of (72/6) = 12% for George to double his money in 6 years.

9.1.2   How a Multiple Period Investment Grows

So far we only have considered calculating the future value of an investment associated with a one-time, lump-sum payment. Often people, such as parents who are investing annually to provide moneys to send their children to college, or who are investing for retirement, make periodic payments into an investment program and may invest a few thousand dollars each year. Let's examine the case in which Mary intends to save $1000 per year for each of the next five years. How much money will Mary accumulate if the return on her investment is 8% compounded annually?

If Mary deposits $1000 at the end of year 1, and $1000 at the end of years 2, 3, 4 and 5, what is the future value at the end of year 5? Equation-wise, Mary's investment program looks like this:

$$FV = (1000*1.08^4) + (1000*1.08^3) + (1000*1.08^2) + (1000*1.08^1) + (1000*1.08^0)$$

And if we factor out the $1000 from each term inside the parentheses, we arrive at:

$$FV = \$1000 * (1.08^4 + 1.08^3 + 1.08^2 + 1.08^1 + 1.08^0)$$
$$FV = \$1000 * (1.3605 + 1.2597 + 1.1664 + 1.08 + 1.0)$$
$$FV = \$1000 * 5.8666 = \$5,866.66$$

A *future value annuity factor* is the amount produced by investing $1 per period for a specified number of periods. In Mary's example, the future value annuity factor is 5.8666. The $5,866.66 produced in Mary's case is the future value of the annuity for an investment of $1,000 per year at the end of each year for a 5-year period at 8%.

9.1.3   Changing the Compounding Period

Financial institutions may advertise that their savings or investment accounts have interest earnings that are compounded more often than annually. Interest may be compounded semi-annually, quarterly, monthly, or even on a daily basis. The compounding period is the period of time over which the bank calculates the amount of interest your account has earned. The interest earnings are added to your balance at the end of that period and you then earn interest on this additional interest.

Let's suppose that a bank is advertising a 10% annual interest rate on a savings account, compounded on a semi-annual basis. This rate sounds to you like a good deal and you deposit $1000 into a savings account at the bank. Semi-annual compounding means that the bank is offering 5% interest paid per each half-year on your deposit. After the first half-year the bank credits your account with $50 in interest. For the second half of the year, you earn interest at the rate of 5% on the $1050, so you earn interest on the $1000 principal plus compound interest on the $50 of interest paid by the bank for the first six months, for a total of:

$$\$1,050 * 5\% = \$52.50$$

The easy way to think of semi-annual compound interest is that the period is six months and the interest rate is ½ of the annual percentage rate—in this case, 5% per period. Every period, your money grows by a factor of 1.05. Therefore, in one year your initial one-time $1000 deposit would grow to:

$$\$1000 * 1.05^2 = \$1102.50$$

The amount that your savings account receives from earning 10% per year with semi-annual compounding is larger than amount that your savings account would receive based on 10% per year with annual compounding. Due to semi-annual compounding, you effectively earned interest at an annual compounding rate of 10.25%, since $1000 grew to $1102.50; and the 10.25% is called the effective annual interest rate (*EAR*).

Effective Annual Rate (EAR) *is the interest rate that is annualized by using the compound interest earned on an investment.*

If The First National Bank of Lemont advertises that it is paying 8% annual percentage rate compounded quarterly, what is the effective annual rate?

Good question. An 8% annual percentage rate compounded quarterly is equivalent to 2% per period with four periods in the year. The EAR calculation would look like this:

$$EAR \; (quarterly \; @8\%) = 1.02^4 = 1.0824$$

So the EAR in this example is <u>8.24%</u>.

How about monthly compounding? Suppose the Memorial Day Bank of Boalsburg advertises 12% annual interest compounded monthly. What is the effective annual rate? We rigged this example to be the equivalent of 1% per period with 12 monthly periods. The EAR is as follows:

$$EAR \; (monthly \; @12\%) = 1.01^{12} = 1.1268$$

In this example, the EAR is 12.68%.

With shorter compounding periods and the same annual percentage rate, all else equal, the effective annual rate increases. In fact, as the compounding frequency increases from an annual period (*p*) to quarterly to daily, the EAR approaches a limit associated with continuous compounding. Table 9-2 show the EARs for different compounding periods and an interest rate of 12%.

Table 9-2
EARs for an Interest Rate of 12%

Compounding Period	*p*	EAR
Annual	1	12.0000%
Semi-Annual	2	12.3600%
Quarterly	4	12.5509%
Monthly	12	12.6825%
Weekly	52	12.7341%
Daily	365	12.7475%

9.1.4 Future Value Annuity Tables

Table 9-3 lists the future value of a single payment, based on interest rates of between 1% per period and 12% per period, with the periods ranging from 1 to 50. It is assumed that $1 is invested today at time 0, and no further investments are made in the future.

Table 9-3
Future Value of a Single Payment
(Future Value of $1 invested at time zero, and no further investment)

Rate=r Period=n	1%	2%	3%	4%	6%	8%	10%	12%
1	1.0100	1.0200	1.0300	1.0400	1.0600	1.0800	1.1000	1.1200
2	1.0201	1.0404	1.0609	1.0816	1.1236	1.1664	1.2100	1.2544
3	1.0303	1.0612	1.0927	1.1249	1.1910	1.2597	1.3310	1.4049
4	1.0406	1.0824	1.1255	1.1699	1.2625	1.3605	1.4641	1.5735
5	1.0510	1.1041	1.1593	1.2167	1.3382	1.4693	1.6105	1.7623
6	1.0615	1.1262	1.1941	1.2653	1.4185	1.5869	1.7716	1.9738
7	1.0721	1.1487	1.2299	1.3159	1.5036	1.7138	1.9487	2.2107
8	1.0829	1.1717	1.2668	1.3686	1.5938	1.8509	2.1436	2.4760
9	1.0937	1.1951	1.3048	1.4233	1.6895	1.9990	2.3579	2.7731
10	1.1046	1.2190	1.3439	1.4802	1.7908	2.1589	2.5937	3.1058
11	1.1157	1.2434	1.3842	1.5395	1.8983	2.3316	2.8531	3.4785
12	1.1268	1.2682	1.4258	1.6010	2.0122	2.5182	3.1384	3.8960
13	1.1381	1.2936	1.4685	1.6651	2.1329	2.7196	3.4523	4.3635
14	1.1495	1.3195	1.5126	1.7317	2.2609	2.9372	3.7975	4.8871
15	1.1610	1.3459	1.5580	1.8009	2.3966	3.1722	4.1772	5.4736
20	1.2202	1.4859	1.8061	2.1911	3.2071	4.6610	6.7275	9.6463
25	1.2824	1.6406	2.0938	2.6658	4.2919	6.8485	10.8347	17.0001
30	1.3478	1.8114	2.4273	3.2434	5.7435	10.0627	17.4494	29.9599
35	1.4166	1.9999	2.8139	3.9461	7.6861	14.7853	28.1024	52.7996
40	1.4889	2.2080	3.2620	4.8010	10.2857	21.7245	45.2593	93.0510
45	1.5648	2.4379	3.7816	5.8412	13.7646	31.9204	72.8905	163.9876
50	1.6446	2.6916	4.3839	7.1067	18.4202	46.9016	117.3909	289.0022

Future Value of Single Payment Examples:

Future Value of a Single Payment: Let's use Table 9-3 to calculate the future value of a single payment. Suppose George invests $250 in a bank at an interest rate of 8% compounded annually. How much will be in George's account, assuming that he allows it to compound for 10 years?

Our equation for this example looks like this:

$$FV = PV * (1.0 + r)^n$$

If PV = $250, and r = 8%, n = 10, we find the factor for r = 8%, n = 10 years in Future Value of Single Payment Table 9-3 to be 2.1589. The equation then becomes:

$$FV = \$250 * 2.1589 = \$539.73$$

What happens if a compounding rate *r* or a period *n* is not shown in the future value table? How should you handle that situation? You can easily solve this type of equation with a financial calculator (see discussion later in this section). If you don't have a financial calculator, the answer is *extrapolation* or *estimation*. Below is an example of extrapolation.

Suppose Ali is saving her money to take a trip to Europe after she graduates from college in four years. Her bank is offering to pay 9% compounded annually for a 4-year savings certificate. If Ali has $1000 to invest today, how much will it grow to in 4 years?

In Table 9-3, the factor corresponding to n = 4, r = 8%, is 1.3605, and the factor for n = 4, r = 10%, is 1.4641. The factor for n = 4, r = 9% would be midway between these two factors and a simple averaging procedure will give us the approximate answer. In this case the average is equal to: (1.3605 + 1.4641)/2 = 1.4123. Ali's $1000 would only grow to:

$$\$1000 * 1.4123 = \underline{\pmb{\$1412.30}}$$

At today's prices, Ali will need to take the budget backpacking tour of Europe and plan to sleep on park benches and drink very inexpensive local wines.

Calculate the Rate of Return r on a Single Payment: Suppose Ainsley made a one-time investment of $1,000 in 1990 in a growth stock mutual fund. Ten years later in 2000 at the height of the stock market, its value had grown to $3,105.80—over three times her original investment. What is the average rate of return that she earned over this period?

Our equation for this example looks like this:

$$FV = PV * (1.0 + r)^{\wedge}n$$

If FV = $3,105.80, PV = $1000, and n = 10, we know everything but r. Let's solve for the future value factor and then find what interest rate in Table 9-3 corresponds to that factor when n = 10. The future value equation then becomes:

$$\$3,105.80 = \$1,000 * (1.0 + r)^{\wedge}10$$

Divide both sides of the equation by $1,000

$$\$3,105.80/\$1,000 = (1.0 + r)^{\wedge}10$$
$$3.1058 = (1.0 + r)^{\wedge}10$$

When we examine Table 8-3 along the row where n = 10, we find that the factor 3.0158 corresponds to the row where $\underline{\pmb{r = 12\%.}}$

Find the Number of Periods n for a Single Payment: Claire wants to purchase a car but she does not want to go into debt. Her bank is paying interest at the rate of 10% compounded annually and Claire has saved $2,000 from her babysitting job. She figures that she'll buy a cheap car for about $4,287.20 (conveniently priced to coincide with a future value factor from Table 9-3) for the sole purpose of getting her from point a to point b. How long will it take for Claire's $2,000 savings to compound to $4,287.20 at a rate of 10%?

If FV = $4,287.20, PV = $2,000, and r = 10%, we know everything but n. Let's solve for the future value factor and then find what period n in Table 9-3 corresponds to that factor when r = 10%. The equation then becomes:

$$\$4,287.20 = \$2,000 * (1.0 + .1)^n$$

Divide both sides of the equation by $2,000

$$\$4,287.20/\$2,000 = (1.1)^n$$
$$2.1436 = (1.1)^n$$

When we examine Table 9-3 along the column where r = 10%, we find that the factor 2.1436 corresponds to the column where **n = 8**.

Future Value of Multiple Payments Examples:

Table 9-4 lists the *future value of multiple payments*, based on interest rates of between 1% per period and 12% per period, with the periods ranging from 1 to 25. We assume that the first dollar is invested at the end of the first period at time = 1, and $1 is invested at the end of each subsequent period.

Table 9-4
Future Value of Multiple Payments
(Future Value of $1 invested at n =1, and at end of each subsequent period)

Rate=r Period=n	1%	2%	3%	4%	6%	8%	10%	12%
1	1.0000	1.0000	1.0000	1.0000	1.0000	1.0000	1.0000	1.0000
2	2.0100	2.0200	2.0300	2.0400	2.0600	2.0800	2.1000	2.1200
3	3.0301	3.0604	3.0909	3.1216	3.1836	3.2464	3.3100	3.3744
4	4.0604	4.1216	4.1836	4.2465	4.3746	4.5061	4.6410	4.7793
5	5.1010	5.2040	5.3091	5.4163	5.6371	5.8666	6.1051	6.3528
6	6.1520	6.3081	6.4684	6.6330	6.9753	7.3359	7.7156	8.1152
7	7.2135	7.4343	7.6625	7.8983	8.3938	8.9228	9.4872	10.0890
8	8.2857	8.5830	8.8923	9.2142	9.8975	10.6366	11.4359	12.2997
9	9.3685	9.7546	10.1591	10.5828	11.4913	12.4876	13.5795	14.7757
10	10.4622	10.9497	11.4639	12.0061	13.1808	14.4866	15.9374	17.5487
11	11.5668	12.1687	12.8078	13.4864	14.9716	16.6455	18.5312	20.6546
12	12.6825	13.4121	14.1920	15.0258	16.8699	18.9771	21.3843	24.1331
13	13.8093	14.6803	15.6178	16.6268	18.8821	21.4953	24.5227	28.0291
14	14.9474	15.9739	17.0863	18.2919	21.0151	24.2149	27.9750	32.3926
15	16.0969	17.2934	18.5989	20.0236	23.2760	27.1521	31.7725	37.2797
16	17.2579	18.6393	20.1569	21.8245	25.6725	30.3243	35.9497	42.7533
17	18.4304	20.0121	21.7616	23.6975	28.2129	33.7502	40.5447	48.8837
18	19.6147	21.4123	23.4144	25.6454	30.9057	37.4502	45.5992	55.7497
19	20.8109	22.8406	25.1169	27.6712	33.7600	41.4463	51.1591	63.4397
20	22.0190	24.2974	26.8704	29.7781	36.7856	45.7620	57.2750	72.0524
21	23.2392	25.7833	28.6765	31.9692	39.9927	50.4229	64.0025	81.6987
22	24.4716	27.2990	30.5368	34.2480	43.3923	55.4568	71.4027	92.5026
23	25.7163	28.8450	32.4529	36.6179	46.9958	60.8933	79.5430	104.6029
24	26.9735	30.4219	34.4265	39.0826	50.8156	66.7648	88.4973	118.1552
25	28.2432	32.0303	36.4593	41.6459	54.8645	73.1059	98.3471	133.3339

Future Value of Multiple Payments: Let's use Table 9-4 to calculate the future value of multiple payments. Suppose George decides to invest $250 *per year* in a bank at an interest rate of 8% compounded annually. How much will be in George's account assuming that he makes annual payments and allows them to compound for 10 years?

Our equation for this example looks like this:

Future Value Multiple Payments Equation
$$FV = PMT * FV\ Factor(r,n) \qquad (Eq. 9\text{-}5)$$

If r = 8% and n = 10, we find that the Future Value Factor (r = 8%, n = 10 years) in the Future Value of Multiple Payments Table 9-4 to be 14.4866. If PMT = $250, the equation then becomes:

$$FV = \$250 * 14.4866 = \underline{\boldsymbol{\$3,621.65}}$$

What happens if a compounding rate r or a period n is not shown in the future value of multiple payments table? How should you handle that situation? You guessed it—extrapolation or estimation!

Let's again examine Ali's savings account and assume that her bank pays 9% compounded annually and that Ali invests $1000 per year over the next 4 years. How much will these payments grow to at the end of 4 years?

In Table 9-4 the future factor corresponding to n = 4, r = 8%, is 4.5061, and the factor for n = 4, r = 10%, is 4.6410. The factor for n = 4, r = 9% would be approximately midway between these two factors and a simple averaging procedure will give us an estimate of the factor. In this case the average is equal to: (4.5061 + 4.6410) / 2 = 4.5735. Ali's $1000 per year would now grow to:

$$\$1000 * 4.5735 = \underline{\mathbf{\$4,573.50}}$$

Ali can now afford to take the luxury tour of Europe. She can afford to visit Paris, Rome, London, and Madrid, stay in comfortable hotels, eat three decent meals a day, visit a couple of dance clubs, go to a show at the Moulin Rouge, and attend a bullfight in Madrid.

Calculate the Rate of Return r on Multiple Payments: Suppose Ainsley made annual investments of $1,000 beginning in 1990 in a growth stock mutual fund and ten years later in 2000 at the height of the stock market, its value had grown to $17,548.70. What is the average rate of return that Ainsley earned over this period?

Our equation for this example is:

$$FV = PMT * FV\ Factor\ (r,n)$$

If FV = $17,548.70, PMT = $1,000, PV = 0, and n = 10, we know everything but r. Let's solve for the future value factor and then find the interest rate in the Future Value of Multiple Payments Table 9-4 that corresponds to that factor when n = 10. The equation then becomes:

$$\$17,548.70 = \$1,000 * (1.0 + r)^{10}$$

Divide both sides of the equation by $1,000

$$\$17,548.70/\$1,000 = (1.0 + r)^{10}$$
$$17.5487 = (1.0 + r)^{10}$$

When we examine Table 8-4 along the row where n = 10, we find that the factor 17.5487 corresponds to the row where $\underline{\mathbf{r = 12\%}}$.

Find the Number of Periods n of Multiple Payments: Claire wants to purchase a car but she does not want to go into debt. Her bank is paying interest at the rate of 10% compounded annually and Claire intends to save $2,000 per year from her babysitting job. She figures that she'll buy a pretty decent car for about $22,871.80 (conveniently priced to coincide with a future value factor from Table 8-4). She may even be able to buy a convertible. How long will it take for Claire's $2,000 per year savings to compound to $22,871.80 at a rate of 10%.

If FV = $22,871.80, PMT = $2,000, PV = 0, and r = 10%, we know everything but n. Let's solve for the future value factor and then find that value in the r = 10% column in Future Value of Multiple Payments Table 9-4. The equation then becomes:

$$\$22,871.80 = \$2,000 * FV\ Factor\ (10\%, n)$$

Divide both sides of the equation by $2,000

$$\$22,871.80/\$2,000 = FV\ Factor\ (10\%, n)$$
$$11.4359 = FV\ Factor\ (10\%, n)$$

When we examine Table 9-4 along the column where r = 10%, we find that the factor 11.4359 corresponds to the column where **n = 8**, so Claire will need to save $2,000 per year for 8 years to have those payments compound to $22,871.80.

9.1.5 Calculating Future Values Using a Financial Calculator

There are a number of different ways to calculate future value and rates of return. We can multiply the present value by (1 + interest rate) times the number of periods, n, as we did in Section 9.1.1. We can look up the future value in a future value table as we did in Section 9.1.4. Or we can use a financial calculator to come up with the most precise answer possible, and not worry about the extrapolation and estimation concerns associated with future value tables and future value factors.

Financial calculators are preprogrammed to calculate present values, future values, rates of return, payment factors, and many other financial functions. Some calculators are even preprogrammed to value options through the use of the Black-Scholes option pricing model and other complex equations.

When you use a financial calculator or a computer, remember the phrase, "Garbage in! Garbage out!" If you don't input the correct numbers into the calculator, you'll get the wrong result. You also must be careful to clear the calculator and the financial function registers after a calculation. Otherwise, an old input that is incorrect for the current calculation may be injected into the equation and result in a garbage solution.

You also will want to critically examine the answer that the financial calculator spits out, and decide if the answer is reasonable given the problem. Take the example of Ali's trip to Europe described in the section above. If Ali is depositing a $1000 per year at a compounding rate of 7% over a 4-year period, and if the calculator comes up with an answer of $85,327, common sense should tell you that the $85,327 might seem excessive considering that she only deposited a total of $4,000 and only earned interest for 4 years. **Think through the problem and make sure that your answer seems reasonable.**

If you have a financial calculator, take it out now and let's practice on some examples. The five most important financial function keys that we will use are labeled, *n—number of periods, r or i—interest rate or yield, PV—present value, PMT—payment, and FV—future value.* When you know four of these inputs, the financial calculator will solve the equation for the fifth input. It is a good idea to input each of the four known inputs, even if that input is zero.

Compounding and Future Value Examples:

Future Value of a Single Payment: Nancy is 35 years old and she wants to invest a lump sum of $5000 today in an account with a bank that promises to pay her 5% per year for 30 years. What will be the future value of the $5000 compounded over 30 years at 5%?

Clear your calculator! Inputs are: n = 30, i = 5, PMT = 0, PV = -$5000—the cash outflow deposited by Nancy with her bank, **solve for FV**, which is equal to **$21,609.71**.

Future Value of Multiple Payments: Bill is 25 years old and wants to save $2,000 per year for the next 40 years to pay for his retirement. He believes that he can put his retirement money in a mutual fund that will earn an average of 7% per year. If Bill does earn that 7% compounded annually, how much will he have accumulated when he retires in 40 years?

Inputs are: n = 40, i = 7, PV = 0, PMT = -$2000—per year cash outflow, **solve for FV**, which is equal to **$399,270.22**.

Calculate the Rate of Return on a Single Payment Investment: Suppose Maureen made a one-time investment of $2,000 in 1980 in an S&P 500 Index mutual fund, and twenty-three years later in 2003, its value had grown to $28,000—fourteen times her original investment. What is the average rate of return that she earned over this period?

Inputs are: n = 23, PMT = 0, PV = -$2,000, FV = $28,000, **solve for i**, which is equal to **12.15836%**.

Calculate the Rate of Return on Multiple Payments: John began making payments of $1,000 per year to a bank account that grew to $30,000 over a twenty-year period. What was the average rate of return that John earned in his account?

Inputs are: n = 20, PMT = -$1000, PV = 0, FV = $30,000, **solve for i**, which is equal to **4.07151%**.

Calculate the Annual Payment Required: Larry is 30 years old and wants to save a total of a million dollars so that he can retire in style in 35 years. If he believes that he can earn an average of 8% per year on his investments, what is the payment per year that he should contribute to his retirement account so that he has a million dollars when he is 65?

Inputs are: n = 35, PV = 0, FV = $1,000,000, i = 8%, **solve for PMT**, which is equal to **-$5,803.26**—a yearly cash outflow.

Calculate the Amount of Years Needed with Annual Payments: Eric is 35 and he can afford to contribute $10,000 per year to his retirement account. He believes that he can earn an average return of 7% in the account. How long will it take for his account to reach $1,000,000 so that Eric can retire as a millionaire?

Inputs are: PV = 0, PMT = -$10,000, FV = $1,000,000, i = 7%, **solve for n**, which is equal to **31 years**.

9.1.6 *Compounding and The Effect of Taxes*

Unfortunately, calculating values relating to compounding becomes more difficult and complex once the effects of taxes are introduced into finance and investing. Individual investors in the United States almost always pay taxes on the interest and dividends that they earn on their investments. The tax brackets of investors varies greatly and depend upon how much taxable income the investor earns per year. The maximum marginal tax bracket payment for individuals at the time of this writing was approximately 39%, and is scheduled to decline to 35% by the year 2006.

Let's assume that Tom makes a one-time deposit of $100 in an account with an annual interest rate of 10%, giving him an annual interest payment of $10 per year. Let's also assume that Tom is in the 30% marginal tax bracket. This means that for every additional dollar that Tom earns, he must pay 30 cents to the U.S. Government in Federal income taxes. Since Tom keeps only $7 of the $10 in interest, his *after-tax rate of return* is 7%. In general, if an investor pays taxes at a tax rate of *t*%, the investor's after-tax rate of return is equal to the pre-tax rate of return, r, multiplied by (1 – t).

Calculation of After-Tax Rate of Return
After-Tax Rate of Return = r * (1 – t)   *(Eq. 9-6)*

Suppose that Kayla is in the 25% tax bracket and she makes a one-time investment of $1,000 in a savings account that pays her 8% per year compounded annually. If she uses a portion of her interest earnings to pay her taxes, how much money will she have in her account at the end of five years?

Inputs are: n = 5, PV = -$1,000, PMT = 0, after-tax interest = 8% * (1 - .25) = 6%, **solve for FV**, which is equal to **$1,338.22**.

Jeremy is in the 33-1/3% tax bracket and he intends to invest $2,000 per year for 30 years and then retire. He believes that he can earn an average of 12% pre-tax per year by aggressively trading stocks. If he averages that return and sticks to his investment plan, how much money will he have when he retires.

Inputs are: n = 30, PV = 0, PMT = -$2,000, after-tax interest = (1 - .33-1/3) * 12% = 8%, **solve for FV**, which is equal to **$226,566.42**.

The effect of taxes is quite negative to compounding, future values, and investment results. Tax payments greatly decrease the after-tax return on your investments, if those investments are held in a taxable account. Luckily, the United States tax code has created a number of ways that investors can save for retirement and either avoid or defer the taxes that investors pay on their investments. Investors can establish tax-advantaged accounts to accumulate retirement assets. Three types of accounts that are available at the time of this writing are individual retirement accounts (IRAs), Roth IRAs, and 401(k) retirement accounts.

An investor's annual contribution to an IRA is tax deductible if the investor's taxable income does not exceed a certain level. The current maximum tax-deductible contribution to an IRA is $2,000 (which is scheduled to increase to $5,000 over time). Tax on the income received on the IRA is deferred until money is withdrawn. Such moneys are then taxed as current income.

Contributions to a Roth IRA are not tax deductible, but the Roth IRA allows dividends, interest, and capital gains on investments in the account to compound on a tax-exempt basis. If the investor is at least 59½ and has invested for at least 5 years, he may withdraw money on a tax-free basis. This is similar to the treatment of interest on a municipal bond, which interest is generally exempt from federal income taxes and often exempt from state income taxes as well.

Many employers establish 401(k) plans for their employees, allowing them to make tax-deferred investments to a retirement account. Employers often match contributions made by the employee. As with IRAs, taxes on 401(k) plans are deferred until the money is withdrawn and is then taxed as ordinary income. Self-employed professionals may have substantial pension programs that permit taxes to be deferred until distributions are made to the pensioners.

Taxes are complex. Investors should take full advantage of the tax laws and establish tax-advantaged accounts for retirement. Investors should fund tax-advantaged accounts to the maximum that the law and the investor's income will permit. Given a choice of tax-class, an investor should hold tax-advantaged assets such as municipal bonds or stocks that earn tax-sheltered income in fully taxable accounts, and use tax-advantaged accounts, such as IRA's and Roth IRA's, to trade stocks or to own assets that have substantial dividend or interest payments.

9.2   Present Value and Discounting

Problems relating to present value are concerned with how much money needs to be invested now at a certain interest rate or rate of return to receive specific amounts at a pre-determined time in the future. Examples of present value problems are:

- Pat is 30 years old and wants to retire with $1,000,000 at the age of 62. How much must he invest today if he is expected a return on investment of 9% per year?
- Honda is building a $3 billion factory in the United States and, based on a detailed sale and profit forecast, management wants to know if the company will make money on this investment, resulting in an increase in the value of the company's stock.
- George wants to buy a BMW for $50,000 and needs to know his monthly payments to determine if he can afford the car and still go to the Lion's Den every Friday and Saturday evening.
- Georgette's been stung in the stock market and wants to purchase bonds. Calculating the return on a bond and its current value is a present value problem.
- Randy is considering the purchase of shares of Cisco at the current price of $14.55 a share. He wants to know if Cisco is overvalued or undervalued at this price. If it is overvalued he should not buy it now. If it is undervalued, he may want to pounce on it. Stock valuation is a present value problem.

The math underlying discounting and the calculation of present value (*PV*) is the exact flip side to the process of compounding and future value. Present value is the mirror image of future value and discounting is the opposite of compounding. *Discounting* is the process of going from an expected future value to a present value. Discounting also means to multiply an amount by a number less than 1.0, over a number of time periods. Present value is what an investment is worth today, if an expected future value is discounted for a certain period of time at a certain rate—the *discount rate*. Let's look at an example to see how discounting and present value works.

> *Present value* is the current value of future expected cash flows
> discounted at the appropriate discount rate.

> *Discount rate* is the rate used to calculate the present value
> of a future cash payment.

9.2.1   Discounting a Single Cash Flow

We have seen from our discussion of future value in Table 9-1, that Jane's $1,000 invested at 8% grows to $1,080 at the end of year 1. Present value calculates the amount that Jane would have to invest today at 8% to receive $1080 at the end of one year. In equation form, the present value of Jane's $1,080 investment looks like this:

$$PV * (1.08) = \$1,080$$

Divide both sides of the equation by (1.08) and the answer is:

$$PV = \$1,080 / (1.08) = \$1,000$$

More generally, the present value equation for discounting a one-time cash flow for one period is equal to:

Present Value Equation-Single Cash Flow, One Period
$$PV = FV / (1.0 + r) \qquad (Eq.\ 9\text{-}7)$$

And the equation for finding the present value for a one period discount factor for a one-time cash flow is:

Discount Factor Equation-One Payment, One Period
$$Discount\ Factor = 1 / (1 + r) \qquad (Eq.\ 9\text{-}8)$$

Let's take a look at an example for discounting a one-time cash flow over multiple periods. Today's your birthday and Aunt Gertie promises you a one-time present of $100 to be given to you at some time in the next five years. What is the present value of a promise of $100? This is a tough one. There's a slight chance that Aunt Gertie may forget the promise or may die before she pays you, so some risk is involved. We talk more about risk and its effect on the discounting rate in Chapter 13. You're also not sure exactly when that $100 is going to flow to you. Due to the uncertainty of both risk and timing, this sounds like a problem for a present value table. In Table 9-5 we lay out the possibilities, with the number of years, n, ranging from 0 to 5, and the discounting rates ranging from 6% to 8% to 10%.

Table 9-5
Aunt Gertie's $100 Gift
Present Value Factors

Year (n)	r = 6%	r = 8%	r=10%
0	1.0000	1.0000	1.0000
1	0.9434	0.9259	0.9091
2	0.8890	0.8573	0.8264
3	0.8396	0.7938	0.7513
4	0.7921	0.7350	0.6830
5	0.7473	0.6806	0.6209

The numbers listed in Table 9-5 are known as *discount factors*. These factors give the present value of a dollar that you expect to receive at some time, *n*, in the future, discounted at a rate, *r*. We include a more complete list of discount factors in Table 9-6 below.

As you can see in Table 9-5, as *n* increases and the payment is expected farther into the future, the present value factor decreases—meaning the future payment is worth less today. *Time and the value of money are inversely related.* For example, if your relative pays you today, it doesn't matter what the discount rate is—the value is $100. If you don't really expect the $100 for five years, the present value factor is where row n = 5, intersects with column r = 10%—equal to 0.6269. The $100 promise is worth $62.69 today. Likewise, as the discounting rate, *r*, increases, the present value factor decreases—meaning that the future payment is worth even less today. If time to payment increases or risk increases, the present value of an investment decreases.

The general equation for a discount factor for the payment of $1 to be received *n* years from now with a discounting rate of *r* is:

Discount Factor Equation-One Payment, Multiple Periods
Discount Factor = $1/(1 + r)^n$ *(Eq.9-9)*

Let's see what happens when r = 8%, and n = 3. The number 1/(1 + .08) = .9259. And (.9259) * (.9259) * (.9259) = 0.7938—just as the present value factor table promised. You can use the present value schedules that we include in Section 9.2.3 below, or use a financial calculator as we show in Section 9.2.4 to make this calculation.

9.2.2   Discounting Multiple Cash Flows

So far we only have considered calculating the present value of one payment that is expected either one or more periods into the future. Financial instruments, such as loans, mortgages, and annuities have a number of payments that an individual will either pay or receive over time. This section will deal with discounting and valuing instruments with multiple cash flows. Discounted cash flow (DCF) valuation is considered to be the most accurate way to value an investment or security.

Discounted Cash Flow Valuation *calculates the present value of a stream of expected future cash flows to value an investment.*

Let's examine an example in which Gary wins the Pennsylvania lottery and receives $1,000 per year at the end of each of the next five years. If the interest rate on a five-year investment is 8%, what is the present value of Gary's five lottery payments?

We can value this example in one of three ways, by discounting each of the five cash flows at the appropriate discount factor and summing the results—which we do in this section; by checking the present value annuity tables—which we examine in Section 9.2.3; and by using a financial calculator—which we check in Section 9.2.4.

If Gary receives $1000 at the end of year 1, and $1000 at the end of years 2, 3, 4, and 5, what is the present value, today at time 0, of the cash flow stream? Equation-wise, Gary's annuity looks like this:

PV=(1000/1.08^5) + (1000/1.08^4) + (1000/1.08^3) + (1000/1.08^2) + (1000*1.08^1)

And if we factor out the $1000 from each term we arrive at:

PV = $1000 * (1/1.08^5 + 1/1.08^4 + 1/1.08^3 + 1/1.08^2 + 1/1.08^1)
PV = $1000 * (0.6806 + 0.7350 + 0.7938 + 0.8573 + 0.9259)

PV = $1000 * 3.9926 = <u>$3,992.60</u>

A present value annuity factor is the present value of receiving $1 per year based on an assumed interest rate, r, for a specified number of periods, n. For example, the multiplier of 3.9926 in Gary's case is the present value annuity factor for a payment of $1 per year at the end of 5 years discounted at a rate of 8%.

9.2.3 Present Value Annuity Tables

Table 9-6 lists the present value of a single payment, based on interest rates between 1% per period and 14% per period, with the periods ranging from 1 to 50. It is assumed that a single payment is made at period *n* in the future.

Table 9-6
Present Value of a Single Payment
(Present Value of $1 today at time 0 if it is received at period n in the future)

Rate=r Period=n	1%	2%	3%	4%	6%	8%	10%	12%
1	0.9901	0.9804	0.9709	0.9615	0.9434	0.9259	0.9091	0.8929
2	0.9803	0.9612	0.9426	0.9246	0.8900	0.8573	0.8264	0.7972
3	0.9706	0.9423	0.9151	0.8890	0.8396	0.7938	0.7513	0.7118
4	0.9610	0.9238	0.8885	0.8548	0.7921	0.7350	0.6830	0.6355
5	0.9515	0.9057	0.8626	0.8219	0.7473	0.6806	0.6209	0.5674
6	0.9420	0.8880	0.8375	0.7903	0.7050	0.6302	0.5645	0.5066
7	0.9327	0.8706	0.8131	0.7599	0.6651	0.5835	0.5132	0.4523
8	0.9235	0.8535	0.7894	0.7307	0.6274	0.5403	0.4665	0.4039
9	0.9143	0.8368	0.7664	0.7026	0.5919	0.5002	0.4241	0.3606
10	0.9053	0.8203	0.7441	0.6756	0.5584	0.4632	0.3855	0.3220
11	0.8963	0.8043	0.7224	0.6496	0.5268	0.4289	0.3505	0.2875
12	0.8874	0.7885	0.7014	0.6246	0.4970	0.3971	0.3186	0.2567
13	0.8787	0.7730	0.6810	0.6006	0.4688	0.3677	0.2897	0.2292
14	0.8700	0.7579	0.6611	0.5775	0.4423	0.3405	0.2633	0.2046
15	0.8613	0.7430	0.6419	0.5553	0.4173	0.3152	0.2394	0.1827
20	0.8195	0.6730	0.5537	0.4564	0.3118	0.2145	0.1486	0.1037
25	0.7798	0.6095	0.4776	0.3751	0.2330	0.1460	0.0923	0.0588
30	0.7419	0.5521	0.4120	0.3083	0.1741	0.0994	0.0573	0.0334
35	0.7059	0.5000	0.3554	0.2534	0.1301	0.0676	0.0356	0.0189
40	0.6717	0.4529	0.3066	0.2083	0.0972	0.0460	0.0221	0.0107
45	0.6391	0.4102	0.2644	0.1712	0.0727	0.0313	0.0137	0.0061
50	0.6080	0.3715	0.2281	0.1407	0.0543	0.0213	0.0085	0.0035

Present Value of Single Payment Examples:

Present Value of a Single Payment: Let's use Table 9-6 to calculate the present value of a single payment. Suppose George wants to have $1,000 in the bank at the end of 10 years. What amount does he deposit today as a single payment with an expected interest rate of 8% compounded annually to receive $1,000 in ten years?

Our equation for this example looks like this:

Present Value Equation-Single Cash Flow, Multiple Periods
$$PV = FV * 1/(1.0 + r)^n \qquad (Eq. 9\text{-}10)$$

If FV = $1,000, and r = 8%, n = 10, we find the present value factor for r = 8%, n = 10 years in Table 9-6 to be 0.4632. The equation then becomes:

$$PV = \$1,000 * 0.4632 = \$463.20$$

So George would need to deposit $463.20 at an annual compounding rate of 8% for the $463.20 to grow to $1,000 in 10 years. Remember, we are not taking the effect of taxes into the analysis. If George were investing his funds in a Roth IRA, the investment would increase tax-free. If George were investing in a fully taxable account, George would pay taxes annually on the interest that he receives. The taxes would reduce George's after-tax return.

Let's assume that the interest rate on a 20-year bond is 12%. What is today's value of a U. S. Government Bond that makes a single payment (known as a zero-coupon or stripped bond) of $5,000 in 20 years?

If FV = $5,000, r = 12%, and n = 20, we find the present value factor in Table 9-6 for r = 12%, n = 20 years to be 0.1037. The present value is:

$$PV = \$5,000 * 0.1037 = \$518.50$$

What happens if a compounding rate *r* or a period *n* is not shown in the present value table? How should you handle that situation? The answer is extrapolation or estimation as we discussed in section 9.1.4 above.

Calculate the Discount Rate r on a Single Payment: Let's take the same $1,000 one-time investment that Ainsley made in 1990 in a growth stock mutual fund that grew to $3,105.80 ten years later in 2000. This time let's use the present value tables to find out the average rate of return that she earned over this period. We'll see how this calculation is the mirror image of how we approached Ainsley's problem in section 9.1.4 above.

Our present value equation for this example looks like this:

$$PV = FV * 1/(1.0 + r)^n$$

If FV = $3,105.80, PV = $1000, and n = 10, we know everything but r. Let's solve for the present value discount factor and then find what interest rate in Table 8-6 corresponds to that factor when n = 10. The equation then becomes:

$$\$1,000 = \$3,105.80 * 1/(1.0 + r)^{10}$$

Divide both sides of the equation by $3,105.80

$$\$1,000/\$3,105.80 = 1/(1.0 + r)^{\wedge}10$$
$$0.3220 = 1/(1.0 + r)^{\wedge}10$$

When we examine Table 9-6 along the row where n = 10, we find that the factor 0.3220 corresponds to the row where **r = 12%**. This rate of return or discount rate is the same result from Ainsley's investment that we calculated in section 9.1.4.

Find the Number of Periods n for a Single Payment: Let's visit with Claire again. You may remember that Claire wants to purchase a car but she does not want to go into debt. Her bank is paying interest at the rate of 10% compounded annually and Claire has saved $2,000 from her babysitting job. She figures that she'll buy a cheap car for about $4,287.20 for the sole purpose of getting her from point (a) to point (b). How long will it take for Claire's $2,000 savings to compound to $4,287.20 at a rate of 10%?

If FV = $4,287.20, PV = $2,000, and r = 10%, we know everything but n. We solved Claire's problem in section 9.1.4 by calculating the future value factor and finding the period that corresponded to that factor in Table 9-3. Now, let's solve for the discount factor and then find what period n in Table 9-6 corresponds to that factor when r = 10%. The equation then becomes:

$$\$2,000 = \$4,287.20 * 1/(1.0 + .1)^{\wedge}n$$

Divide both sides of the equation by $4,287.20

$$\$2,000/\$4,287.20 = 1/(1.1)^{\wedge}n$$
$$0.4665 = 1/(1.1)^{\wedge}n$$

When we examine the column in Table 9-6 where r = 10%, we find that the factor 0.4665 corresponds to the column where **n = 8**.

Table 9-7 lists the present value of multiple payments of $1, based on interest rates of between 1% per period and 14% per period, with the periods ranging from 1 to 25. It is assumed that the first dollar is received at the end of the first period at n = 1, and $1 is received at the end of each subsequent period.

Table 9-7
Present Value of Multiple Payments
(PV of $1 per period received at n = 1, and at end of each subsequent period)

Rate=r Period=n	1%	2%	3%	4%	6%	8%	10%	12%
1	0.9901	0.9804	0.9709	0.9615	0.9434	0.9259	0.9091	0.8929
2	1.9704	1.9416	1.9135	1.8861	1.8334	1.7833	1.7355	1.6901
3	2.9410	2.8839	2.8286	2.7751	2.6730	2.5771	2.4869	2.4018
4	3.9020	3.8077	3.7171	3.6299	3.4651	3.3121	3.1699	3.0373
5	4.8534	4.7135	4.5797	4.4518	4.2124	3.9927	3.7908	3.6048
6	5.7955	5.6014	5.4172	5.2421	4.9173	4.6229	4.3553	4.1114
7	6.7282	6.4720	6.2303	6.0021	5.5824	5.2064	4.8684	4.5638
8	7.6517	7.3255	7.0197	6.7327	6.2098	5.7466	5.3349	4.9676
9	8.5660	8.1622	7.7861	7.4353	6.8017	6.2469	5.7590	5.3282
10	9.4713	8.9826	8.5302	8.1109	7.3601	6.7101	6.1446	5.6502
11	10.3676	9.7868	9.2526	8.7605	7.8869	7.1390	6.4951	5.9377
12	11.2551	10.5753	9.9540	9.3851	8.3838	7.5361	6.8137	6.1944
13	12.1337	11.3484	10.6350	9.9856	8.8527	7.9038	7.1034	6.4235
14	13.0037	12.1062	11.2961	10.5631	9.2950	8.2442	7.3667	6.6282
15	13.8651	12.8493	11.9379	11.1184	9.7122	8.5595	7.6061	6.8109
16	14.7179	13.5777	12.5611	11.6523	10.1059	8.8514	7.8237	6.9740
17	15.5623	14.2919	13.1661	12.1657	10.4773	9.1216	8.0216	7.1196
18	16.3983	14.9920	13.7535	12.6593	10.8276	9.3719	8.2014	7.2497
19	17.2260	15.6785	14.3238	13.1339	11.1581	9.6036	8.3649	7.3658
20	18.0456	16.3514	14.8775	13.5903	11.4699	9.8181	8.5136	7.4694
21	18.8570	17.0112	15.4150	14.0292	11.7641	10.0168	8.6487	7.5620
22	19.6604	17.6580	15.9369	14.4511	12.0416	10.2007	8.7715	7.6446
23	20.4558	18.2922	16.4436	14.8568	12.3034	10.3711	8.8832	7.7184
24	21.2434	18.9139	16.9355	15.2470	12.5504	10.5288	8.9847	7.7843
25	22.0232	19.5235	17.4131	15.6221	12.7834	10.6748	9.0770	7.8431

Present Value of Multiple Payments Examples:

Present Value of Multiple Payments: Let's use Table 9-7 to calculate the present value of multiple payments. Suppose George borrows money from his local bank to buy a used car. The bank charges George 8% per year and requires repayment of the loan in 3 equal annual payments. George believes that he can afford to make payments of $1,000 per year. Based on these payments, how much can George borrow to purchase the car?

Our equation for this example looks like this:

Present Value Equation-Multiple Cash Flow, Multiple Periods
$$PV = PMT * PV \text{ Annuity Factor } (r,n) \qquad (Eq. 9-11)$$

If PMT = $1,000, and r = 8%, n = 3, we find the PV Annuity Factor for r = 8%, n = 3 years in Table 9-7 to be 2.5771. The equation then becomes:

$$PV = \$1,000 * 2.5771 = \$2,577.10$$

What happens if a compounding rate r or a period n is not shown in the present value of multiple payments table? How should you handle that situation? You guessed it—extrapolation or estimation.

Let's again examine Ali's account and assume that her bank makes a loan to her at 9% interest rate compounded annually, and that Ali can afford to pay $1000 per year. How much can Ali borrow and repay in 4 years?

In Table 9-7 the present value of an annuity factor corresponding to $n = 4$, $r = 8\%$, is 3.3121, and the present value of an annuity factor for $n = 4$, $r = 10\%$, is 3.1699. The factor for $n = 4$, $r = 9\%$ would be midway between these two factors and a simple averaging procedure will give us the approximate factor. In this case the average is equal to: $(3.3121 + 3.1699)/2 = 3.2410$. Ali's $1000 per year payment would amortize a loan equal to:

$$\$1,000 * 3.2410 = \$3,241$$

Calculate the Rate of Return r on Multiple Payments: Suppose Ginger goes to the bank and wants to borrow $5,000 to buy kitchen cabinets and make other kitchen improvements. The bank agrees to lend her the money if she makes annual payments of $1,387 per year for 5 years. What rate of return is the bank earning on its loan to Ginger?

The equation that links present value and annual payments is:

$$PV = PMT * PV \text{ Annuity Factor}(r,n)$$
$$\$5,000 = \$1,386 * PV \text{ Annuity Factor } (r,5)$$

We know that the annual PMT = $1,386, that PV = $5,000, $n = 5$, we find the PV Annuity Factor by dividing both sides of the above equation by the annual payment of $1,386. The equation then becomes:

$$\$5,000/\$1,386 = 3.607 = PV \text{ Annuity Factor } (r,5)$$

When we examine Table 9-7 along the row where $n = 5$, we find that the factor 3.607 corresponds to the column where **$r = 12\%$**.

9.2.4   Calculating Present Value Using a Financial Calculator

The comments that we made relating to financial calculators and future values in section 9.1.5 hold for present values also. The five most important keys are: PV = present value; FV = future value; PMT = the periodic payment; n = number of periods; and r or i

= the interest rate or rate of return on the asset. Recall the rule of calculators and computers—Garbage in, Garbage out! Make sure that you understand the inputs and where they should go. Also, remember to clear your calculator before every calculation.

Present Value Examples:

Present Value of a Single Payment: David is 25 years old and wants to retire at age 65 with a million dollars in his account. He wants to make one lump-sum payment and he does not intend to make any more payments to this retirement account. He believes that he can earn an average of 9% per year after taxes and transactions costs by trading stocks in his online stock brokerage account. How much does he need to invest today to achieve his goal?

Clear your calculator! Inputs are: FV = $1,000,000, PMT = 0, n = 40, i = 9%, **solve for PV.** We plug these numbers into the HP-12c, which spits out that **PV = - $31,837.58**.

Present Value of Multiple Payments: When David reaches age 65, he has succeeded in reaching his $1,000,000 goal. He decides that he wants to purchase an annuity that pays him $50,000 per year for 20 years. He reasons that at the end of 20 years and at the age of 85, he either will be dead or will be committed to a nursing home and be supported by welfare. The rate of return or yield on an annuity is 6%. Based on the 6% rate of return, what will be the cost of David's annuity?

Inputs are: FV = 0, PMT = $50,000, n = 20, i = 6%, **solve for PV**. With these inputs, **PV = -$573,496.07**. This means that David can use the remaining $426,503 from his million to buy a nice condo on Florida's West Coast, attend a lot of Phillies spring training games in Clearwater, and feast daily (and before 5:00 PM) on the early-bird specials at the Florida restaurants that cater to the silver-haired crowd.

Using Present Value to Calculate Annual Loan Repayments: Jilly just got married and she and her husband want to buy a new house. She's concerned about the annual loan repayments and whether they will be able to afford them. The cost of the house is $300,000 and Jilly and her husband can make an upfront payment of $50,000 to reduce the mortgage to $250,000. The interest rate quoted by the bank is 7% and it will be repaid in 30 annual payments. Jilly wants to determine the annual payment on the mortgage.

Inputs are: PV = $250,000, FV = 0, n = 30, i = 7%, **solve for PMT**. With these inputs, **PMT = -$20,146.60**.

Using Present Value to Calculate Monthly Loan Repayments: Jilly and her husband think that a new BMW would look awfully good in the driveway of their new home. The model that they like most has a price tag of $50,000, which includes taxes, title and tags. Dealer financing is available for 4 years at a 6% interest rate, ***payable***

monthly. What would Jilly's *monthly payments* be if she and her husband finance the entire $50,000 purchase price?

This is a little tricky. The inputs need to be adjusted to reflect the monthly payments. The 6% annual interest rate needs to be converted to a monthly rate by dividing by 12, which yields a 0.5% monthly rate. We multiply the 4 years by 12 to give us 48 monthly payments. The inputs are: PV = $50,000, FV = 0, i = 0.5%, n = 48, **solve for PMT**. With these inputs, <u>**PMT = -$1,174.25**</u>. So Jilly's payments will be a *cash outflow*, hence the negative sign of (–)1,174.25 per month.

Rate of Return r on a Single Payment: Justin wants to buy an IBM bond that promises to make a single payment of $1,000 in 20 years. That bond is trading in the secondary market at a price of $380. What is the interest rate or yield associated with the bond?

Inputs are: PV = -$380, FV = $1,000, PMT = 0, n = 20, **solve for i**. With these inputs, <u>**i = 4.9569%**</u>.

Rate of Return r on Multiple Payments: Kathleen's banker offers her a loan of $100,000, which she would repay over 20 years with equal annual installments of $12,000. What is the yield or rate of return on this loan?

Inputs are: PV = $100,000, PMT = -$12,000, FV = 0, n = 20, **solve for i**. With these inputs<u>, i = 10.3156%</u>.

A Simple Way to Value a Bond—a Present Value Example: Five years ago, Nick bought a corporate bond with a 25-year maturity that pays annual interest of $100 per year (10% interest) and principal of $1000. Since Nick's purchase five years ago, interest rates have dropped. Today's interest rate for a similar bond that matures in 20 years (at the same time that Nick's bond matures) is 8%. Based on these simple assumptions, what is the present value of Nick's bond?

Bond pricing is very important in the real world. Bonds usually pay interest semi-annually and may have payment and redemption characteristics that make valuation complex. To simplify this example we assume Nick's bond pays interest annually. Since interest rates have declined to 8% in the bond market, a bond with a relatively high rate, in this case—10%, will be worth more than bonds with lower rates that reflect a lower current interest rate environment. In this case Nick's bond has a 10% rate in an environment where interest rates for comparable bonds are 8%. So this bond will trade at a price above its maturity value, a market environment in which the bond is *trading at a premium*.

Clear your calculator for this one! Inputs: n = 20, i = 8, PMT = $100, FV = $1000, solve for present value or market value, which in this case is equal to: **PV=-$1,196.36**— So $1,196.36 is the fair market value of a 20-year, 10% bond today in an 8% interest rate environment. The reason the financial calculator computes a negative value is because an investor would be required to pay (a cash outflow for the investor) that amount to purchase the bond in an 8% bond market.

9.3 Summary

If you are interested in finance or serious about investing, it is essential that you understand how to properly value projects, alternative investments, and stocks and bonds. This requires that you know the basics regarding the time value of money—the math underlying compounding and discounting.

The math is not difficult but does require that you understand the relationship between present and future values, how to use exponents, and how to compound to future value and discount to present value. Inexpensive calculators have built-in financial programs that quickly churn out future and present values. We strongly recommend that you take the time necessary to understand compounding and discounting, and that you learn how to use a financial calculator to perform those functions. When you master the time value of money, you will be able to estimate:

- The future value of a single investment that compounds at a given rate of return over a specified period of time;
- The future value of multiple investments that compound at a given rate of return over a specified period of time;
- The rate of return that you earn on an investment;
- Today's value (present value) of a single cash flow to be received in the future;
- Today's value of a multiple cash flows that you expect to receive in the future;
- The value of stocks and bonds, given expected rates of return.

List of Terms:

1. Compounding
2. Discounting
3. Positive Interest Rates
4. Risk Aversion
5. Present Value
6. Future Value
7. Compound Interest
8. Compound Rate, Growth Rate, Interest Rate, Yield
9. Compounding Frequency
10. Future Value Factor
11. Simple Interest
12. Rule of 72
13. Single Period Investment
14. Multiple Period Investment
15. Rate of Return
16. Effective Annual Rate
17. Annual Percent Rate
18. Marginal Tax Bracket
19. After-Tax Rate of Return
20. Discount Rate
21. Discount Factor
22. Discounted Cash Flow Valuation
23. Annuity Tables
24. Single Payment
25. Multiple Payment
26. Trading at Premium

Questions

1. Why does money have time value?
2. What does the rate of interest represent in time value analysis?
3. What is the relationship between Present Value and Future Value?
4. How does increasing the interest rate and lengthening the time affect Present Value and Future Value? Why? Is the relationship direct or inverse?
5. What is the difference between Annual Percent Rate and Effective Annual Rate?
6. What happens to the Effective Annual Rate of Interest as the frequency of compounding increases?
7. What effect does tax have on Present Value and Future Value of investments?

Problem Sets

1. Ben deposits $1,000 into a savings certificate today that will pay 7% annual interest for 10 years.
   (a) What will the savings certificate be worth in 10 years?
   (b) How much interest has Ben earned in 10 years?
   (c) If Ben withdrew interest each year and spent it immediately, how much will the savings certificate be worth in 10 years?
   (d) If Ben withdrew interest each year, how much interest would he have withdrawn in 10 years?
   (e) Explain why interest in (b) is higher than total interest in (d).

2. If Amy wants to double her current deposit balance of $2,000 in 8 years, what interest should she earn on her deposit? Suppose the deposit earns an interest rate of 6%, how long will Amy have to wait before the deposit doubles?

3. If Eduardo deposits $1,000 at the end of every year for the next 5 years, in a bank account that pays 6% compound interest, how much would he have at the end of 5 years?

4. If Jane has a choice of depositing $5,000 in either bank A that offers interest at 8.4% (APR) compounded monthly of bank B that offers interest at 8.6% (APR) compounded semi-annually, which bank should she choose?

5. If Kathy takes out an $8,000 car loan that calls for 48 monthly payments of $225 each, calculate the APR and EAR of the loan.

6. Bill's bank savings was $72,430. He had deposited $5,000 every year for the last 10 years. How much interest did Bill earn on his savings?

7. Barry purchased a new car for $27,000 and has to make equal monthly payments for the next 6 years, with the first payment due one month from now. If Barry's time value of money is 6%, what is the monthly payment that Barry has to make?

8. Aretha invests $2,000 in a savings account that pays her 8% per year compounded annually. She falls in the 30% tax bracket. If Aretha uses a portion of the interest earnings to pay her taxes, how much money will she have in her account at the end of eight years?

9. Tom will receive a $5,000 gift from his aunt after 5 years. What is the present value of the gift if Tom's time value of money is 7% per year?

10. Given an interest rate of 6%, what would you prefer (a) receiving $1,000 a year for next 10 years, or (b) receiving $800 a year for next 15 years? Would your decision change if the interest rate was 20% instead of 6%?

11. George wants to purchase a house when he retires in 20 years. For the next 10 years George can save $3,500 per year and can earn interest at 12% compounded annually. Given that for the next 10 years George can earn interest at 8% on saved balance at that time and on any new deposit, how much must George save from year 11 through 20 so that he has exactly $300,000 at the time he retires? Suppose George can continue to earn 12% on the amount saved in the first 10 years and will earn 8% on new deposits from year 11, how much should he deposit every year from year 11 through 20 so that he has exactly $300,000 at the time he retires?

12. Chris is 35 years old and wants to save for retirement. Suppose Chris invests $1,000 per year at an effective rate of 5% per year for the next 25 years, with the first deposit beginning one year hence. Beginning at age 60, Chris starts withdrawing an equal amount every year for the next 20 years. How much can Chris withdraw in order to use up all the funds at the end of 20 years?

13. James has to save for his daughter's college education. His daughter will be attending college at the end of 6 years from today. James estimates that the college fee (which has to be paid in the beginning of the year) will be $7,000 in the first year, $6000 in the second year and $5,000 in the 3rd and 4th year. James expects to earn 8% interest compounded annually on his savings. How much must James save every year for the next 5 years to fund his daughter's education?

14. Suppose Harry wants to start saving money for a trip across Europe and estimates it to cost $15,000. He wants to take the trip 8 years from today. His bank offers interest at 8%, compounded semi-annually.
    (a) How much will Harry have to deposit at the end of each year starting one year from now such that his last deposit is made on the day of the trip?
    (b) How much will Harry have to deposit at the end of each year starting one year from now such that his last deposit is made one year prior to the day of the trip?
    (c) How much will Harry have to deposit if he already has $4,000 in his savings account and his last deposit will be made one year prior to the day of his trip

15. Suppose Jeremy wants to buy a sail boat and wants to fund it entirely by taking a loan from a bank which will be repaid in equal annual installments over the next 5 years. Jeremy can make payments up to $2,500 a year for the next 5 years starting one year from now. Based on these payments, within what price level should Jeremy look for a sail boat if the bank charges an interest rate of
    (a) 6%
    (b) 8%
    (c) 10%

Assignment #9-1:

1. John invests $10,000 in a bank account that offers interest of 6% per year compounded monthly. How much interest will John have earned in 5 years?
   (a) $2,986
   (b) $3,382
   (c) $3,486
   (d) $3,643

2. Jane has $5,000 in a deposit account that offers interest at 8% per year compounded annually. How long will it take for Jane's money to double?
   (a) 6 years
   (b) 7 years
   (c) 8 years
   (d) 9 years

3. Jill has $4,000 in her bank account that offers interest at 10% per year compounded monthly. How many months will it take for Jill's balance to increase to $10,000?
   (a) 111
   (b) 104
   (c) 100
   (d) 96

4. Jack currently has $2,000 in his bank account. Jack wants to buy a car for $5,000 after 3 years. Jack can deposit $650 every year, first deposit starting from today. How much interest should he earn per year for him to be able to buy the car after 3 years?
   (a) 8.25%
   (b) 9.75%
   (c) 10.50%
   (d) 11.75%

5. Sam wants to start saving for a vacation he wants to take one year from today. He expects the vacation to cost him $5,000. How much should he save every month for next 12 months if his bank pays interest at 6% per year compounded monthly?
   (a) $390.33
   (b) $405.33
   (c) $410.66
   (d) $416.67

6.   Sunny wants to purchase a ring that costs $1,200. He can either pay in 3 equal monthly installments of $400 (starting one month from today) or pay cash up-front and avail a discount. How much should the discount be so that Sunny is indifferent between both the options? (Assume Sunny's opportunity cost is 10% per year.)
(a) $14.56
(b) $15.33
(c) $19.73
(d) $20.94

7.   What amount should George deposit today as a single payment if he wants to have $8,000 in his bank account at the end of 8 years with the bank offering interest at 8% per year compounded quarterly?
(a) $4,245
(b) $4,525
(c) $4,425
(d) $5,425

8.   If Greg deposits $1,000 every year in his bank account for the next five years, how much will Greg have at the end of five years if bank pays an interest of 8% per year compounded annually?
(a) $5,690.33
(b) $5,758.33
(c) $5,802.66
(d) $5,866.60

9.   If Gary deposits $500 in his bank account at the end of every quarter for next 3 years (first deposit starting after 3 months) and has $6,897.77 in his account at the end of 3 years from today, what APR did the bank pay on Gary's deposit?
(a) 2.5%
(b) 3.0%
(c) 10.0%
(d) 12.0%

10.   If John deposits $1,000 in his bank account and uses a portion of his interest earnings to pay taxes (John has 35% tax rate) and has $1,466 in his account at the end of ten years, what interest rate did John's bank offer?
(a) 5.5%
(b) 6.0%
(c) 6.5%
(d) 7.0%

Assignment #9-2:

1. If a bank charges interest of 12% per year compounded monthly for a loan, how much is it actually charging (EAR)?
    (a) 12.42%
    (b) 12.68%
    (c) 12.76%
    (d) 12.84%

2. For positive interest rates is $FV_{k,n}$?
    (a) Less than 1
    (b) Equal to 1
    (c) Greater than 1

3. For positive interest rates is $PV_{k,n}$?
    (a) Less than 1
    (b) Equal to 1
    (c) Greater than 1

4. If Joan wishes to accumulate $6,000 by the end of 4 years by making annual end of year deposits over the next four years in a bank that offers 8% interest per year compounded annually, how much must she deposit at the end of each year
    (a) $1,231.52
    (b) $1,331.52
    (c) $1,431.52
    (d) $1,531.52

5. If Julie has $1,500 to invest today at 7% interest compounded semi-annually, how much will Julie have at the end of 2 years and 6 years?
    (a) $1,717.35, $2,251.10
    (b) $1,606.84, $1,843.88
    (c) $1,721.28 , $2,266.60
    (d) $1,832.52 , $2,435.45

6. If Carla has been depositing $2,500 every year in his savings account every December for the last four years and is planning to deposit $3,000 for the next 4 years, how much will she have at the end of 8 years (since first deposit) if the bank pays interest at 6% per year compounded annually?
    (a) $23,430.98
    (b) $25,545.56
    (c) $26,930.98
    (d) $28,235.52

7. If you owe $30,000 at the end of five years, how much should your creditor accept in payment immediately if he could earn 10% interest per year on his money?
    (a) $12,310.52

(b) $13,531.75
(c) $16,431.59
(d) $18,627.64

8. If Joe has borrowed $24,838 and is required to pay back the loan in eight equal annual installments of $5,000, what is the interest rate associated with the loan?
   (a) 12.00%
   (b) 12.50%
   (c) 13.00%
   (d) 13.50%

9. If Shirley borrows $50,000 from the bank at 8% interest per year, compounded annually over the eight-year life on the loan, what equal annual payments must be made to discharge the loan, plus pay the bank its required rate of interest?
   (a) $8,250
   (b) $8,500
   (c) $8,700
   (d) $8,950

10. What is the value of $500 deposit made every year for 10 years where for the last 3 years interest rate is decreased from 10% to 8% per year compounded annually?
    (a) $7,175.24
    (b) $7,598.75
    (c) $7,718.76
    (d) $7,954.23

CHAPTER 10

DISCOUNTED CASH FLOW VALUATION

How much is a stock or a bond or another investment really worth? This seemingly simple question actually is not very simple. If you win the Powerball lottery with payments of $1,000,000 per year for 20 years, is the value of those payments ($1,000,000 * 20) simply equal to $20 million? No, it is worth less!

Is the true value of the baseball contract of Alex Rodriquez, formerly the shortstop for the Texas Rangers and currently the third baseman for the New York Yankees, equal to the simple addition of yearly payments that total over $100 plus million that an incredibly optimistic (or stupid) general manager of a major league team has committed to pay to him over the next 20 years? No, it is worth much less.

Recall from Chapter 2 the principle relating to investment valuation—**Value Equals the Sum of Expected Cash Flows Discounted for Time and Risk**. In this chapter we examine how to discount those expected cash flows. This chapter helps you to understand how to value bonds, stocks, investments, projects, and contracts that have multiple cash flows that pay out over a number of years. You will learn how to:

- Calculate the future and present values of level cash flow streams;
- Calculate the future and present values of uneven cash flow streams;
- Learn how to calculate loan payments, effective interest rates, and amortization schedules; and
- Learn how to value financial assets by using the discounted cash flow valuation approach.

10.1   Introduction to DCF Valuation

Before making an investment in a bond or the stock of a company, do some research! Do you understand the company's business? What is the growth potential of the industry in which the company operates, and how is the company positioned? Who are the company's top competitors? What is the quality and stability of the company's management?

Let's assume that you've answered these questions to your satisfaction. What should you do next? If you like the company, its products and prospects, you can use a discounted cash flow valuation approach to help you decide if the company is *undervalued, overvalued,* or *fairly-valued.* Stock of even the best-managed company is a poor investment if its price is too high.

Your investment decision should be based **solely** on *price versus value.* If your analysis shows that the price of a bond or a stock is greatly below its value—consider buying it. If you believe that an investment is worth much less than its current price in the market, you can sell it if you own it; or you can patiently follow its price and acquire it when and if it moves to a more attractive price range. The DCF approach, which we explain in this chapter, empowers you with the information relating to the **value** of financial assets so that you can buy and sell wisely.

10.1.1 Definitions Relating to DCF Valuation

The *value of a financial investment* (stock, bond, mortgage, money market account, etc.) equals the present value of its expected future cash flows, discounted (reduced) for the risk and timing of those cash flows. This basic valuation relationship underlies the theory of finance. It's so basic and important that it warrants more description and some valuation-related definitions.

Expected cash flows are the **most likely** cash payments (dividends, interest, capital gain or loss) that you can **expect** (not hope) to receive from an investment that you own. They also are moneys that you are expected to pay under a debt that you owe, such as scheduled payments relating to your car loan or home mortgage.

To *discount* means to multiply a number by less than one. The *discount rate* that you should use in any valuation depends upon the timing of the expected cash flows and the risks associated with receiving the expected cash flows. The discount rate is a function of both time and risk: *discount rate = f (time, risk).* The discount rate should increase for securities with a greater default risk (WorldCom bonds) and decrease for securities with a lower default risk (U.S. Treasury Bonds) associated with the expected cash payments.

Similar to the discount rate, the *discount factor* takes into account both the discount rate and the timing of the expected cash flow. The discount factor is a function of both time and the discount rate: *discount factor = f (time, discount rate).* For example, the discount factor for a 1-year cash flow, whose discount rate is 6%, is simply equal to (1.0) divided by (1.06) which in equation form looks like this: $1/(1.06) = .9434$. The discount factor for a 2-year cash flow, whose discount rate is also 6%, is equal to one divided by (1.06) = .9434, that amount divided again by (1.06) = $.9434/(1.06) = .8900$. This process for a 3-year cash flow continues with a third division by (1.06). And so on, ad infinitum. The discount factor decreases with increasing time to the payment of a cash flow and decreases with an increasing discount rate.

The value of an investment, known as the *present value (PV),* is found by taking the sum of the investment's expected cash flows multiplied by their respective discount factors. For example, using a 6% discount rate, a discount factor of (.9434), and an expected $100 cash flow in 1 year, the present value of that cash flow would be $100 times (.9434): $100 * (.9434) = $94.34. Using a 6% discount rate, a $100 cash flow expected in 2 years, and a discount factor of (.8900), the present value of that cash flow would be: $100 * (.8900) = $89.00. The value of an investment is the sum of the present values of all of the expected cash flows. The present value of the two cash flows described above is: PV = $94.34 + $89.00 = $183.34.

Present Value of an Investment = Σ Discounted Expected Cash Flows (Eq.10-1)

10.1.2 Gary's Mortgage: A DCF Valuation Example

To better understand the DCF process, let's examine a home mortgage. Gary wants to purchase a new house, so he borrows $100,000 from a bank and is the obligor on an 8%, 30-year mortgage. If we put the proper inputs into a financial calculator—(n = 360, i = 8%/12 = .6667% because of monthly payments, pv = $100,000—the amount of the mortgage, fv = 0—the loan amortizes down to 0) and **solve for pmt,** we find that the monthly mortgage payment is $733.77. We round the payment off to $734 for 360 months, as shown in Exhibit 10-1.

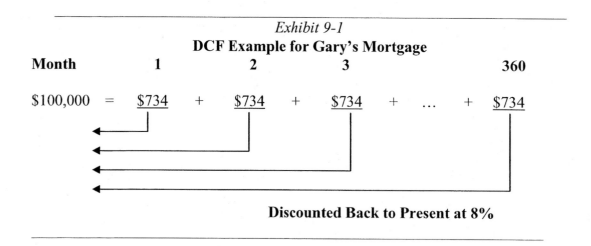

Exhibit 9-1
DCF Example for Gary's Mortgage

Month	1	2	3		360
$100,000 =	$734 +	$734 +	$734 +	... +	$734

Discounted Back to Present at 8%

Gary's $734 monthly payments are the cash flows that he is obligated to pay for the next 360 months under his mortgage loan and that the bank expects to receive for lending him the money. Over the life of the mortgage (assuming that he doesn't prepay it), Gary will pay a total of $264,240 ($734 * 360 months) to the bank—$100,000 is the return of principal and $164,240 is the payment of interest. The initial mortgage amount of $100,000 represents the present value to the bank of the 360-monthly payments of $734—each discounted using a rate of 8% and the appropriate discount factor.

The 8% mortgage rate is the *discount rate*, or *yield*, that the bank requires to lend Gary the money. The discount rate is a function of the general level of interest rates in the economy, as represented by the yield on a United States Treasury Bond with a similar maturity, plus a *risk premium* for the bank to compensate it for the possibility that Gary may not make his payments. United States Treasury Bonds are risk-free because Uncle Sam can always print more money to repay its loans!

The interest or discount rate that the bank requires on Gary's mortgage depends upon the market interest rate at the time he gets his loan. If interest rates change, the present value of the mortgage could increase or decrease. Consider these two scenarios:

- *If mortgage interest rates rise*, the bank will increase its lending rates on new mortgage loans in order to cover the higher market interest rates the bank offers to attract deposits. For example, if interest rates rise 1% (also known as 100 basis points), the present value of Gary's 360 mortgage payments of $734 (discounted now @ 9%) decreases to $91,223. A new mortgage made by the bank in the higher rate scenario would have monthly payments increased to $805 (a monthly payment difference of $71) so that its present value, discounted at 9%, would equal $100,000.
- *If mortgage interest rates fall*, the bank must decrease its lending rates in order to compete for new loans. Due to the declining interest rates, the bank's cost of deposits also drops. For example, if interest rates fall 1%, the present value of Gary's 360 mortgage payments of $734 (discounted now @ 7%) increases to $110,326. A new mortgage made by the bank in the lower rate scenario would have monthly payments decreased to $665 (a payment difference of $69) so that their present value, discounted at 7%, equals $100,000.
-

10.1.3   The DCF Approach to Valuation

The DCF approach is a valuation technique that is employed by investors and traders to value all types of financial instruments such as U.S. Government bonds, preferred and common stocks, corporate bonds, and mortgage-backed securities. Investment bankers use DCF models to value mergers and acquisition (*M&A*) targets, leveraged buyout transactions (*LBOs*), and initial public offerings (*IPOs*) of stock. DCF is Wall Street's preferred valuation method.

DCF is also the valuation approach that's favored by Main Street. Corporations from Maine to California use DCF techniques to analyze capital budgeting and investment decisions. Corporate managers who use the DCF approach understand how their operating and financing decisions will affect their company's stock value and the managers' real bottom lines—the value of their stock options.

The DCF method follows a three-step approach to valuation:

- First, we develop a set of future cash flows that we expect the asset to generate.
- Second, we estimate an interest rate to discount the expected cash flows. The discount rate is a function of the expected timing and risk associated with the cash

flows. We calculate discount factors, which are a function of the discount rate and the time that the cash flows are expected to be received.

- Third, we multiply the expected cash flows by the appropriate discount factors and total them to calculate the **_value_** of the asset.

The characterization of the cash flows of an investment depends upon the classification of the asset:

- If the asset is a _bond_, the future cash flows are the payments of periodic interest, and the repayment of principal at maturity.
- If the asset is a _mortgage_, such as in the example above, the monthly payments consist of both the payment of interest on the mortgage and the repayment of a portion of the principal.
- If the asset is a _stock_, the future cash flows are the payments of dividends, if any, and the appreciation—capital gains, or depreciation—capital losses associated with the movement in the price of the stock.

Once we estimate the _value_ of an asset, we can then compare the value to the asset's price to determine which assets are undervalued or overvalued and which assets to buy, sell, or hold. For example, if we determine that the value of the common stock of McDonald's Corporation is $40 per share and its current price is $30 per share, we believe that the stock is undervalued and we will buy McDonald's stock. This is what portfolio managers and investors do when they value and trade stocks.

If you believe the value of a stock is greater than the stock's current price by some margin, you should buy the stock. If you believe that the value of a stock is less than its current price, you should sell it or, at least, not buy any more stock. We discuss stock valuation later in this chapter, and we describe in depth how to use the DCF method to value stocks in Chapter 15.

10.2 Valuing Level Cash Flows

Have you ever received emails or junk mail offering you a credit card, or a loan to purchase a car or a mortgage to purchase a home? Have you ever seen an advertisement in a financial newspaper that warns about the future cost of college tuition for your children or the costs associated with your retirement? The implication of the advertisement is that if you don't start saving funds today with that excellent financial institution—The First and Foremost National Secure Investment and Savings Insured and Guaranteed Bank—to provide for your retirement in X (20 to 50) years, you'll wind up bankrupt and in the county nursing home like your Aunt Gertie. This chapter teaches you how to value investments and use that skill to keep yourself out of that nasty county nursing home.

10.2.1 Valuing Loans, Mortgages, and Annuities

In this section we value loans and contracts that have level payments or cash flows that are associated with the contract, such as car loans, mortgage loans, and annuities. First, we discuss the general aspects of loans, mortgage loans, and annuities and show you typical amortization schedules. We assume that the interest payments and cash flows associated with the loans, mortgages, and annuities that we value are fixed at the time the obligations are entered into and that the interest rates do not change. We then show you how changing yields and discounting rates in the debt market affect the value of these investments.

A *loan* is an obligation under which an obligor, such as you, borrows money from a lender, such as your local bank. You can use the money to pay your college tuition, to buy a computer or a high definition TV, to purchase a car, or for any other purpose that you desire. The lender will require security—a *lien* on the car or television, or a guarantee from your parents—for its loan. Under the terms of the loan, there will be an interest rate that either will be fixed (e.g., a 10% fixed-rate loan) or floating (for example, a loan in which the interest rate floats at the Treasury bill rate plus 5%) and a repayment schedule associated with the loan. Typically the loan will be fully paid off in three or four years. When you repay the loan, the lender will release any claim it had against the loan, such as a lien on the car, and you will own that property free and clear.

You can then trade that car in for a new one, go back into debt, and begin to make another set of car loan payments. Because the security associated with a loan often is of questionable value—you can easily trash a new car and computers depreciate quickly as new models are introduced—the interest rates on loans usually are significantly higher than the rates on Treasury bonds, corporate bonds, and home mortgages.

Example—Randy's Car Loan:

Randy likes Budweiser and expensive cars. Let's suppose that he purchases a new BMW for $50,000 and finances it through his local bank with a four-year loan and an interest rate of 10%. Car loans usually pay principal and interest on a monthly basis, but for simplicity let's assume that Randy's car loan pays annually at the end of each year.

The bank officer tells Randy that his annual payment will be $15,774 and the amortization of the loan will be as shown in Table 10-1. Column 1 shows the year, column 2 shows the principal outstanding of the car loan at the beginning of the year, column 3 shows the interest that will accrue during the year and is equal to the beginning principal times the interest rate of 10%, column 4 is the amount of principal paid during the year, column 5 is the annual payment of $15,774 on the loan, column 6 is the discount factor and is calculated by the equation: *discount factor = [1/(1 + discount rate)^t]*, column 7 shows the discounted cash flow for the particular payment and is equal to the annual payment (column 5) times the discount factor (column 6), and column 8 shows ending principal, which is equal to the beginning principal (column 2) minus the principal payment (column 4).

Table 10-1
Randy's Car Loan Amortization

| | | | | | Interest Rate | | 10.00% |
| | | | | | Discount Rate | | 10.00% |

Year	Beginning Principal	Interest Payment	Principal Payment	Annual Payment	Discount Factor	DCF	Ending Principal
1	$50,000	$5,000	$ 10,774	$ 15,774	0.9091	$ 14,340	$39,226
2	$39,226	$3,923	$ 11,851	$ 15,774	0.8264	$ 13,036	$27,375
3	$27,375	$2,737	$ 13,037	$ 15,774	0.7513	$ 11,851	$14,338
4	$14,338	$1,434	$ 14,340	$ 15,774	0.6830	$ 10,774	
Totals		$13,094	$50,002	$63,096		**$ 50,001**	

Example—Gary's Home Mortgage:

A *home mortgage* is an obligation under which an obligor, such as you and your spouse or significant other, borrows money from a financial institution and uses the proceeds to purchase a house, a condominium, or single family dwelling. A home mortgage loan is a loan that is secured by a *lien*—a claim on a specific piece of property. Usually, that lien is secured by a first mortgage. When a financial institution makes a mortgage loan, they inspect and appraise the property to make sure that the value of the property exceeds by some margin the amount of the loan. The financial institution will also be concerned that the financial resources—the savings or income of the obligors—are sufficient to make the payments under the mortgage.

Let's take a closer look at Gary's $100,000 home mortgage. Because the loan is secured by a lien on a single family home and the value of the home has been appraised at more than the amount outstanding on the mortgage, a home loan is more secure that a car loan or consumer loan, and generally has a lower interest rate—8%. Home loan payments are made on a monthly basis. For simplicity, let's assume that Gary's mortgage has annual payments that are due at the end of each year, and the loan is amortized on a level payment basis over 30 years. The annual payment is $8,883 per year. The present value of the annual payments of $8,883 per year, discounted at 8%, is equal to the principal amount of the loan—$100,000, and the amortization schedule is shown in Table 10-2.

Table 10-2
Gary's Mortgage Payment

| | | | | | Interest Rate | | 8.00% |
| | | | | | Discount Rate | | 8.00% |

Year	Beginning Principal	Interest Payment	Principal Payment	Annual Payment	Discount Factor	DCF	Ending Principal
1	$100,000	$8,000	$ 883	$ 8,883	0.9259	$ 8,225	$99,117
2	$99,117	$7,929	$ 954	$ 8,883	0.8573	$ 7,616	$98,163
3	$98,163	$7,853	$ 1,030	$ 8,883	0.7938	$ 7,052	$97,133
4	$97,133	$7,771	$ 1,112	$ 8,883	0.7350	$ 6,529	$96,021
5	$96,021	$7,682	$ 1,201	$ 8,883	0.6806	$ 6,046	$94,820
6	$94,820	$7,586	$ 1,297	$ 8,883	0.6302	$ 5,598	$93,522
7	$93,522	$7,482	$ 1,401	$ 8,883	0.5835	$ 5,183	$92,121
8	$92,121	$7,370	$ 1,513	$ 8,883	0.5403	$ 4,799	$90,608
9	$90,608	$7,249	$ 1,634	$ 8,883	0.5002	$ 4,444	$88,973
10	$88,973	$7,118	$ 1,765	$ 8,883	0.4632	$ 4,115	$87,208
11	$87,208	$6,977	$ 1,906	$ 8,883	0.4289	$ 3,810	$85,302
12	$85,302	$6,824	$ 2,059	$ 8,883	0.3971	$ 3,528	$83,243
13	$83,243	$6,659	$ 2,224	$ 8,883	0.3677	$ 3,266	$81,020
14	$81,020	$6,482	$ 2,401	$ 8,883	0.3405	$ 3,024	$78,618
15	$78,618	$6,289	$ 2,594	$ 8,883	0.3152	$ 2,800	$76,025
16	$76,025	$6,082	$ 2,801	$ 8,883	0.2919	$ 2,593	$73,224
17	$73,224	$5,858	$ 3,025	$ 8,883	0.2703	$ 2,401	$70,199
18	$70,199	$5,616	$ 3,267	$ 8,883	0.2502	$ 2,223	$66,931
19	$66,931	$5,355	$ 3,528	$ 8,883	0.2317	$ 2,058	$63,403
20	$63,403	$5,072	$ 3,811	$ 8,883	0.2145	$ 1,906	$59,592
21	$59,592	$4,767	$ 4,116	$ 8,883	0.1987	$ 1,765	$55,477
22	$55,477	$4,438	$ 4,445	$ 8,883	0.1839	$ 1,634	$51,032
23	$51,032	$4,083	$ 4,800	$ 8,883	0.1703	$ 1,513	$46,231
24	$46,231	$3,698	$ 5,185	$ 8,883	0.1577	$ 1,401	$41,047
25	$41,047	$3,284	$ 5,599	$ 8,883	0.1460	$ 1,297	$35,447
26	$35,447	$2,836	$ 6,047	$ 8,883	0.1352	$ 1,201	$29,400
27	$29,400	$2,352	$ 6,531	$ 8,883	0.1252	$ 1,112	$22,869
28	$22,869	$1,830	$ 7,053	$ 8,883	0.1159	$ 1,030	$15,816
29	$15,816	$1,265	$ 7,618	$ 8,883	0.1073	$ 953	$8,198
30	$8,198	$656	$ 8,227	$ 8,883	0.0994	$ 883	
Totals		$166,461	$100,029	$266,490		**$100,003**	

The amortization schedule for Gary's mortgage loan is set up similarly to the amortization schedule associated with Randy's car loan, only the interest rate on the mortgage loan is at 8% and is amortized over a period of 30 years. We see from the amortization schedule that the present value of the expected cash flows associated with a $100,000 mortgage with an interest rate of 8%, discounted at a rate of 8%, is equal to $100,000—no surprise here. We'll see what happens to the present value of this mortgage when we use different discounting rates.

Example—Katie's Retirement Annuity:

The last example that we'll examine is an *annuity*. An annuity is a financial contract that is sold by pension funds and life insurance companies that pays a specified amount of money per month or per year to the purchaser of the annuity, his beneficiary, or the owner of the annuity contract. Typically, an investor will make either a lump-sum payment or a series of periodic payments, which will be invested in an annuity contract with a financial institution. The principal amount of the annuity will compound over a period of time at a pre-determined interest rate. At a point in time, usually upon the retirement of the investor, the annuity will generate periodic payments to the annuity owner.

The interest rates and yields associated with annuities—*savings*, generally are lower that the rates associated with loans or mortgages—*borrowings*. You'll recall from Chapter 8 relating to financial intermediation and financial institutions, this is how intermediaries make money—they create secondary securities that are desired by small investors and savers, such as savings accounts and annuities. Financial institutions borrow money at a lower rate (e.g., the yield on the annuity) and invest that money in primary securities that have higher rates (e.g., the yield on loans and mortgages) of return.

Let's suppose that Katie is 55 years old and has $100,000 that she would like to invest in anticipation of her retirement in ten years. She is considering the purchase of an annuity that will accrue at the rate of 6% per year over the ten years until Katie's retirement, and then will pay out over a twenty-year period in the amount of $15,613 per year. Is this a good deal for Katie?

The cash flows associated with annuities are more complex than the cash flows associated with a loan or a mortgage. In Katie's case she spends $100,000 today and it will compound or grow at the rate of 6% per year over a 10-year period. At the end of that ten-year period, the annuity payments will begin. In most cases annuity payments are made on a monthly basis but to keep things simple we'll assume annual annuity payments. Let's set up a cash flow schedule that shows Katie's initial $100,000 cash outflow, its accrual over ten years at a 6% per year annual compounding rate, and then its annuity payment in the amount of $15,613 per year over twenty years. The cash flow schedule is shown in Table 10-3.

Table 10-3
Katie's Annuity Payments

| | | | | | Interest Rate | | 6.00% |
| | | | | | Discount Rate | | 6.00% |
Year	Beginning Principal	Interest Payment	Principal Payment	Annual Payment	Discount Factor	DCF	Ending Principal
1	$100,000	$6,000	$ (6,000)	$ -	0.9434	$ -	$106,000
2	$106,000	$6,360	$ (6,360)	$ -	0.8900	$ -	$112,360
3	$112,360	$6,742	$ (6,742)	$ -	0.8396	$ -	$119,102
4	$119,102	$7,146	$ (7,146)	$ -	0.7921	$ -	$126,248
5	$126,248	$7,575	$ (7,575)	$ -	0.7473	$ -	$133,823
6	$133,823	$8,029	$ (8,029)	$ -	0.7050	$ -	$141,852
7	$141,852	$8,511	$ (8,511)	$ -	0.6651	$ -	$150,363
8	$150,363	$9,022	$ (9,022)	$ -	0.6274	$ -	$159,385
9	$159,385	$9,563	$ (9,563)	$ -	0.5919	$ -	$168,948
10	$168,948	$10,137	$(10,137)	$ -	0.5584	$ -	$179,085
11	$179,085	$10,745	$ 4,868	$ 15,613	0.5268	$ 8,225	$174,217
12	$174,217	$10,453	$ 5,160	$ 15,613	0.4970	$ 7,759	$169,057
13	$169,057	$10,143	$ 5,470	$ 15,613	0.4688	$ 7,320	$163,587
14	$163,587	$9,815	$ 5,798	$ 15,613	0.4423	$ 6,906	$157,790
15	$157,790	$9,467	$ 6,146	$ 15,613	0.4173	$ 6,515	$151,644
16	$151,644	$9,099	$ 6,514	$ 15,613	0.3936	$ 6,146	$145,130
17	$145,130	$8,708	$ 6,905	$ 15,613	0.3714	$ 5,798	$138,224
18	$138,224	$8,293	$ 7,320	$ 15,613	0.3503	$ 5,470	$130,905
19	$130,905	$7,854	$ 7,759	$ 15,613	0.3305	$ 5,160	$123,146
20	$123,146	$7,389	$ 8,224	$ 15,613	0.3118	$ 4,868	$114,922
21	$114,922	$6,895	$ 8,718	$ 15,613	0.2942	$ 4,593	$106,204
22	$106,204	$6,372	$ 9,241	$ 15,613	0.2775	$ 4,333	$96,963
23	$96,963	$5,818	$ 9,795	$ 15,613	0.2618	$ 4,087	$87,168
24	$87,168	$5,230	$ 10,383	$ 15,613	0.2470	$ 3,856	$76,785
25	$76,785	$4,607	$ 11,006	$ 15,613	0.2330	$ 3,638	$65,779
26	$65,779	$3,947	$ 11,666	$ 15,613	0.2198	$ 3,432	$54,113
27	$54,113	$3,247	$ 12,366	$ 15,613	0.2074	$ 3,238	$41,747
28	$41,747	$2,505	$ 13,108	$ 15,613	0.1956	$ 3,054	$28,639
29	$28,639	$1,718	$ 13,895	$ 15,613	0.1846	$ 2,881	$14,744
30	$14,744	$885	$ 14,728	$ 15,613	0.1741	$ 2,718	$16
Totals		$212,276	$ 99,984	$312,260		$ 99,997	

Table 10-3 is set up in a manner similar to Table 10-1 and Table 10-2 but the cash flows are more complex. We see that the principal value of Katie's annuity grows through the adding of the interest that accrues each year at the annual compounding rate of 6%, from $100,000 to $179,085 over the 10-year accrual period. In year 11, the annuity payments kick in at the rate of $15,613 per year for the next twenty years. The initial cash outflow was $100,000, and the value of the cash inflows that Katie receives from year 11 to year 30, discounted at the rate of 6%, is also equal to $100,000. What a coincidence! We'll see how the value of the annuity changes when we use different discounting rates in the section below.

10.2.2 Valuing Level Cash Flows Using a Spreadsheet

In this section we look again at the cash flows in Tables 10-1, 10-2, and 10-3. We keep the same cash flows for Randy's loan, Gary's mortgage, and Katie's annuity, and examine how the present values of those cash flows change as the discounting rates change. We have programmed these cash flows into Excel spreadsheets, and it is easy to change a discount rate and see the effect of that change on the annuity of loan's value and discounted cash flows.

Let's first take a look at Randy's car loan. Let's assume that interest rates for high-end cars such as Randy's BMW have increased by 1%. What is the current value of Randy's loan to the bank that made the loan and still owns it? Let's examine Table 10-4.

Table 10-4
Randy's Car Loan
11% Discounting Rate

					Interest Rate		10.00%
					Discount Rate		11.00%
	Beginning	Interest	Principal	Annual	Discount		Ending
Year	Principal	Payment	Payment	Payment	Factor	DCF	Principal
1	$50,000	$5,000	$ 10,774	$ 15,774	0.9009	$ 14,211	$39,226
2	$39,226	$3,923	$ 11,851	$ 15,774	0.8116	$ 12,803	$27,375
3	$27,375	$2,737	$ 13,037	$ 15,774	0.7312	$ 11,534	$14,338
4	$14,338	$1,434	$ 14,340	$ 15,774	0.6587	$ 10,391	
Totals		$13,094	$50,002	$63,096		**$ 48,938**	

Let's discuss again where these numbers come from. The beginning principal of $50,000 was the original amount of the loan that Randy used to buy his BMW. The interest payment that is shown in column 3 is the beginning principal of column 2 times the interest rate on the loan of 10%. The principal payment in column 4 is the amount of principal that Randy pays on the car loan for that year. It is equal to the annual payment in column 5 minus the interest payment in column 3. The *discount factor* shown in column 6 is calculated using the following equation: $[1/(1 + discount\ rate)^{\wedge}t]$, where the discount rate is now 11%, and t is the time period shown in column 1. The discounted cash flows are shown in column 7 and are equal to the discount factor times the annual payment of $15,774. **The sum of the discounted cash flows equals the value of the investment—in this case $48,938.** Ending principal is equal to beginning principal (column 1) minus the annual principal payment (column 4).

The cash flows associated with interest payments, principal payment, ending principal, and annual payments in Table 10-4 are the same as in Table 10-1. The change in the value of the loan is due to the higher discount rate—increasing from 10% to 11%—and the discount factors, which have decreased. The value of the loan is equal to the sum of the discount factors times the annual payment. The reduction in discount factors also reduces the discounted cash flows. The total discounted cash flow of the loan has been reduced to $48,938 from $50,000. This underscores an important relationship in finance. **When interest rates and discounting rates increase, the value of a financial asset decreases. When interest rates and discounting rates decrease, the value of financial assets increases.**

Once you program a loan amortization schedule into a spreadsheet, changing parameters such as interest rates, principal amortization, or discounting rates can be easily accommodated. Let's look at the case in which interest rates drop and the discounting rate for a car loan that is equally as risky as Randy's declines from 10% to 9%. How does this drop in market interest rates affect the value of the loan? Let's adjust old Table 10-1 by substituting a 9% discount rate for the 10% rate. The result is Table 10-5.

Table 10-5
Randy's Car Loan
9% Discounting Rate

| | | | | | Interest Rate | | 10.00% |
| | | | | | Discount Rate | | 9.00% |
Year	Beginning Principal	Interest Payment	Principal Payment	Annual Payment	Discount Factor	DCF	Ending Principal
1	$50,000	$5,000	$ 10,774	$ 15,774	0.9174	$ 14,472	$39,226
2	$39,226	$3,923	$ 11,851	$ 15,774	0.8417	$ 13,277	$27,375
3	$27,375	$2,737	$ 13,037	$ 15,774	0.7722	$ 12,180	$14,338
4	$14,338	$1,434	$ 14,340	$ 15,774	0.7084	$ 11,175	
Totals		$13,094	$50,002	$63,096		**$ 51,103**	

Based on a lower discount rate of 9%, the discount factors uniformly increase. This result is an increase in discounted cash flows and an increasing value of Randy's loan. Based on a 9% discounting rate, the value of Randy's car loan has increased to $51,103.

If we examined Gary's mortgage we would find similar reaction to a change in the discount rate. When we increase the discounting rate to 9% from 8%, the present value of the mortgage—the sum of the discounted cash flows—decreases from $100,000 to $91,258. And when we decrease the discounting rate to 7% from 8%, the present value of the mortgage increases from $100,000 to $110,226. This brings up an important point when we value a debt instrument. In most loans and mortgages, the obligor is permitted to repay the amount of the loan or mortgage at any time. **This prepayment ability gives a valuable option to the obligor.** For example, if Gary takes out a home mortgage loan at 8% and interest rates drop substantially to 6%, Gary can refinance his loan at the lower 6% interest rate and take advantage of the prepayment option. By reducing the interest rate on his loan, he can reduce his yearly annual payments from $8,883 to $7,264. This effectively negates any benefits for a drop in interest rates to increase the mortgage value for owners of mortgages or mortgage-backed securities.

Let's take a closer look at the cash flows associated with Katie's annuity. If interest rates on annuities with a similar payment schedule rise, how does that affect the value of Katie's annuity? Let's assume that interest rates on annuity contracts increase from 6% to 7%. Will Katie's annuity increase or decrease in value? Let's take a look at Table 10-6.

Table 10-6
Katie's Annuity
7% Discounting Rate

| | | | | | Interest Rate | | 6.00% |
| | | | | | Discount Rate | | 7.00% |
Year	Beginning Principal	Interest Payment	Principal Payment	Annual Payment	Discount Factor	DCF	Ending Principal
1	$100,000	$6,000	$ (6,000)	$ -	0.9346	$ -	$106,000
2	$106,000	$6,360	$ (6,360)	$ -	0.8734	$ -	$112,360
3	$112,360	$6,742	$ (6,742)	$ -	0.8163	$ -	$119,102
4	$119,102	$7,146	$ (7,146)	$ -	0.7629	$ -	$126,248
5	$126,248	$7,575	$ (7,575)	$ -	0.7130	$ -	$133,823
6	$133,823	$8,029	$ (8,029)	$ -	0.6663	$ -	$141,852
7	$141,852	$8,511	$ (8,511)	$ -	0.6227	$ -	$150,363
8	$150,363	$9,022	$ (9,022)	$ -	0.5820	$ -	$159,385
9	$159,385	$9,563	$ (9,563)	$ -	0.5439	$ -	$168,948
10	$168,948	$10,137	$(10,137)	$ -	0.5083	$ -	$179,085
11	$179,085	$10,745	$ 4,868	$ 15,613	0.4751	$ 7,418	$174,217
12	$174,217	$10,453	$ 5,160	$ 15,613	0.4440	$ 6,932	$169,057
13	$169,057	$10,143	$ 5,470	$ 15,613	0.4150	$ 6,479	$163,587
14	$163,587	$9,815	$ 5,798	$ 15,613	0.3878	$ 6,055	$157,790
15	$157,790	$9,467	$ 6,146	$ 15,613	0.3624	$ 5,659	$151,644
16	$151,644	$9,099	$ 6,514	$ 15,613	0.3387	$ 5,289	$145,130
17	$145,130	$8,708	$ 6,905	$ 15,613	0.3166	$ 4,943	$138,224
18	$138,224	$8,293	$ 7,320	$ 15,613	0.2959	$ 4,619	$130,905
19	$130,905	$7,854	$ 7,759	$ 15,613	0.2765	$ 4,317	$123,146
20	$123,146	$7,389	$ 8,224	$ 15,613	0.2584	$ 4,035	$114,922
21	$114,922	$6,895	$ 8,718	$ 15,613	0.2415	$ 3,771	$106,204
22	$106,204	$6,372	$ 9,241	$ 15,613	0.2257	$ 3,524	$96,963
23	$96,963	$5,818	$ 9,795	$ 15,613	0.2109	$ 3,294	$87,168
24	$87,168	$5,230	$ 10,383	$ 15,613	0.1971	$ 3,078	$76,785
25	$76,785	$4,607	$ 11,006	$ 15,613	0.1842	$ 2,877	$65,779
26	$65,779	$3,947	$ 11,666	$ 15,613	0.1722	$ 2,688	$54,113
27	$54,113	$3,247	$ 12,366	$ 15,613	0.1609	$ 2,513	$41,747
28	$41,747	$2,505	$ 13,108	$ 15,613	0.1504	$ 2,348	$28,639
29	$28,639	$1,718	$ 13,895	$ 15,613	0.1406	$ 2,195	$14,744
30	$14,744	$885	$ 14,728	$ 15,613	0.1314	$ 2,051	
Totals		$212,276	$ 99,984	$312,260		$ 84,083	

When the interest rate on comparable annuities increases from 6% to 7%, the sum of the discounted cash flows of Katie's annuity drops from $100,000 to **$84,083**—a significant decrease in value—much more significant on a percentage basis than the decrease in value associated with the increase in discount rate for Randy's car loan and even for Gary's mortgage loan. Because of the structure of the annuity payment and accrual, the annuity contract has a **longer average maturity or duration** than the other two loans. With a longer duration, the change in value of a debt obligation increases in proportion to the increase in average life or duration. We discuss the concept of duration in greater depth in Chapter 14 relating to bonds and bond valuation.

Let's look at what the value of Katie's annuity becomes when interest rates decrease by 1%. We revisit our spreadsheet and input 5% as our discounting rate. The present value of the discounted cash flows of the annuity is **$119,451**—a significant increase of almost 20% over the original value of $100,000.

Table 10-7
Katie's Annuity
5% Discounting Rate

| | | | | | Interest Rate | | 6.00% |
| | | | | | Discount Rate | | 5.00% |
Year	Beginning Principal	Interest Payment	Principal Payment	Annual Payment	Discount Factor	DCF	Ending Principal
1	$100,000	$6,000	$ (6,000)	$ -	0.9524	$ -	$106,000
2	$106,000	$6,360	$ (6,360)	$ -	0.9070	$ -	$112,360
3	$112,360	$6,742	$ (6,742)	$ -	0.8638	$ -	$119,102
4	$119,102	$7,146	$ (7,146)	$ -	0.8227	$ -	$126,248
5	$126,248	$7,575	$ (7,575)	$ -	0.7835	$ -	$133,823
6	$133,823	$8,029	$ (8,029)	$ -	0.7462	$ -	$141,852
7	$141,852	$8,511	$ (8,511)	$ -	0.7107	$ -	$150,363
8	$150,363	$9,022	$ (9,022)	$ -	0.6768	$ -	$159,385
9	$159,385	$9,563	$ (9,563)	$ -	0.6446	$ -	$168,948
10	$168,948	$10,137	$(10,137)	$ -	0.6139	$ -	$179,085
11	$179,085	$10,745	$ 4,868	$ 15,613	0.5847	$ 9,129	$174,217
12	$174,217	$10,453	$ 5,160	$ 15,613	0.5568	$ 8,694	$169,057
13	$169,057	$10,143	$ 5,470	$ 15,613	0.5303	$ 8,280	$163,587
14	$163,587	$9,815	$ 5,798	$ 15,613	0.5051	$ 7,886	$157,790
15	$157,790	$9,467	$ 6,146	$ 15,613	0.4810	$ 7,510	$151,644
16	$151,644	$9,099	$ 6,514	$ 15,613	0.4581	$ 7,152	$145,130
17	$145,130	$8,708	$ 6,905	$ 15,613	0.4363	$ 6,812	$138,224
18	$138,224	$8,293	$ 7,320	$ 15,613	0.4155	$ 6,488	$130,905
19	$130,905	$7,854	$ 7,759	$ 15,613	0.3957	$ 6,179	$123,146
20	$123,146	$7,389	$ 8,224	$ 15,613	0.3769	$ 5,884	$114,922
21	$114,922	$6,895	$ 8,718	$ 15,613	0.3589	$ 5,604	$106,204
22	$106,204	$6,372	$ 9,241	$ 15,613	0.3418	$ 5,337	$96,963
23	$96,963	$5,818	$ 9,795	$ 15,613	0.3256	$ 5,083	$87,168
24	$87,168	$5,230	$ 10,383	$ 15,613	0.3101	$ 4,841	$76,785
25	$76,785	$4,607	$ 11,006	$ 15,613	0.2953	$ 4,611	$65,779
26	$65,779	$3,947	$ 11,666	$ 15,613	0.2812	$ 4,391	$54,113
27	$54,113	$3,247	$ 12,366	$ 15,613	0.2678	$ 4,182	$41,747
28	$41,747	$2,505	$ 13,108	$ 15,613	0.2551	$ 3,983	$28,639
29	$28,639	$1,718	$ 13,895	$ 15,613	0.2429	$ 3,793	$14,744
30	$14,744	$885	$ 14,728	$ 15,613	0.2314	$ 3,612	
Totals		$212,276	$ 99,984	$312,260		**$119,451**	

10.2.3 Valuing Level Cash Flows Using a Financial Calculator

Financial calculators are preprogrammed to calculate present values, future values, rates of return, discount factors, payment factors, and many other financial functions. Some calculators are even preprogrammed to value options and other complex equations. We're going to use our financial calculator to value Randy's loan, Gary's mortgage, and Katie's annuity—all examples of equal annual payments, based on the inputs that we discussed above.

The five most important financial function keys on a financial calculator are usually labeled, *n—number of periods, r or i—interest rate or yield, PV—present value, PMT—payment*, and *FV—future value*. When you know four of these inputs, the financial calculator will solve the equation for the fifth input. It is a good idea to always input each of the other four known inputs, even if that input is zero.

Randy's Car Loan—Valuing a four-year, 10% Loan @ 11% and 9%:

Discounted Present Value of Multiple Payments: The particulars of Randy's car loan is that is has a term of 4 years, a fixed interest rate of 10%, a principal amount of $50,000, and annual payments of (-$15,773.54). Assume interest rates for a comparable loan have increased to 11%. What is the current value of Randy's loan?

Clear your calculator! Inputs are: n = 4, i = 11, PMT = -15,773.54, FV = 0, **solve for PV**, which is equal to **$48,936.55**. At a 9% discounting rate, inputs are: n = 4, i = 9, PMT = (-15,773.54), FV = 0, **solve for PV,** which is equal to **$51,101.85**.

Gary's Mortgage Loan—Valuing a 30-year, 8% Mortgage Loan @ 9% and 7%:

Discounted Present Value of Multiple Payments: Gary's mortgage is for a principal amount of $100,000 amortized over 30 years with a fixed 8% interest rate. The annual payments are (-$8,882.74). Initially assume that interest rates on a comparable mortgage increases to 9%. What is the current value of Gary's mortgage?

Inputs are: n = 30, i = 9, PMT = (-8,882.74), FV = 0, **solve for PV**, which is equal to **$91,258.23**. At a 7% discounting rate, inputs are: n = 30, i = 7, PMT = (-8,882.74), FV = 0, **solve for PV,** which is equal to **$110,226.32**.

Katie's Annuity—Valuing a 6% Annuity at 7% and 5%:

Compounded Future Value of a Single Payment for 10 Years, and Discounted Present Value of Multiple Payments for 20 Years: Katie invests a lump-sum of $100,000 in an annuity that compounds at a rate of 6% per annum for 10 years, and then pays an annuity stream at a rate of 6% per annum for 20 years. First, we must solve for the annuity payments. Inputs are: n = 10, I = 6, PMT = 0, PV = (-100,000), **solve for FV**, which is equal to $179,084.76. Then inputs are: n = 20, I = 6, PV = (-179,084.77), FV = 0, **solve for PMT**, which is equal to $15,613.42.

Assume that discounting rates for comparable annuities have increased to 7%. What is the value of Katie's annuity based on a discount rate of 7%? Inputs are a little tougher this time. We are only concerned about discounting the relative cash flows that are promised by the annuity contract. Katie paid $100,000 for the contract and expects to receive no cash flows for the first ten years, and then receive $15,613.42 for the next twenty years.

We do not have uniformly even cash flows in this problem. The initial ten periods have no cash inflows and the next twenty periods have a cash inflow of $15,613.42. Most popular financial calculators, such as the models that are produced by Texas Instrument, Sharpe, and Hewlett-Packard, have their own specific systems for entering uneven sequential cash flows, and then discounting those cash flows at a uniform discount rate. We take you through the process of entering these cash flows into our own HP-12C model to give you the general idea.

First, we input the number of periods and press the *n* button. Then we input the discounting rate and press the *i* button. The HP-12C model then follows a procedure in which we enter the cash flows associated with time 0, press the blue *g* button, and press the *CFo* button. We then enter the next cash flow, press the blue *g* button, and press the *CFj* button. If a set of cash flows are equal, such as our first ten entries of zero, we can press the blue *g* button, press 10 for the 10 equal payments, and press the *Nj* button. We continue this process until all thirty annual cash flows are entered. Finally, we press the yellow *f* button and then press the *NPV* button to calculate the discounted present value associated with the cash flows.

Here goes! First we clear our calculator. Then our inputs are: *n* = 30, *i* = 7. The incremental cash flows associated with the project are show on the column 5, the annual payment, of Table 10-7. If we were calculating the net present value of an investment, which we describe in Chapter 10, our input for time 0 would be -$100,000. In this chapter we are concerned with only present values of the future cash flows associated with the investment—not the investment amount itself. We assume a 0 initial outlay at time 0, so our entry is 0, blue *g* button, *CFo* button. Our next entry follows the pattern of 0, blue *g* button, *CFj* button, 10, blue *g* button, *CFj* button. The next entry is 15613.42, blue *g* button, *CFj* button, 20, blue *g* button, *CFj* button. Finally, we press the yellow *f* button and hit the *NPV* button. Our financial calculator spits out the result of **$84,085.44**.

To find out the value of Katie's annuity when the cash flows are discounted at a rate of 5%, since all of the cash flows are still input in sequence into the calculator, we press *5* and the *i* button—this changes the discounting rate, and then press the yellow *f* button and hit the *NPV* button—the result is **$119,453.84**.

10.3 Valuing Uneven Cash Flows

In the previous section we valued contracts that have cash flows that are essentially level payment streams, and we discounted those cash flows at a uniform discounting rate. In the real world most projects—such as those that are analyzed by a corporation for potential investment under the capital budgeting process, and investments in stocks and bonds that you may be considering to purchase for your own account, do not have level expected cash flows associated with them.

In this section we value investments that have cash flow streams that are not level. We got a taste of the complications that may arise in valuing different cash flows when we valued Katie's annuity, which consisted of zero cash flows for the first ten years and then a level cash flow of $15,613.42 for years 11 through 30. So let's delve a little deeper into valuing uneven cash flows.

10.3.1 Valuing Investment Projects, Bonds, and Stocks

In this section we value projects or assets that have uneven payments or cash flows associated with the assets, such as investment projects, bonds, and stock. First, we discuss the general aspects of projects, bonds, and stocks and show you typical cash flow examples. We assume that the cash flows associated with the projects, bonds, and stocks that we value are fixed at the time the investments are entered into and that they do not change. We then show you how changing yields and discounting rates in the market affect the value of these investments.

A *project* or venture is an investment by a firm that produces a product or provides a service in hopes that the investment of money today will generate more money in the future. Most investments in the real world do not adhere to a single cash flow or equal periodic cash flows that we discussed in the beginning of this chapter and in Chapter 9. When a company invests in a project or a venture the cash flows often will increase over time as marketing of the product ramps up, or as prices increase due to the effect of inflation; or revenues will decrease due to the effect of competitors entering the marketplace and driving down prices and profit margins. We value a corporate investment in the section below and discuss how to value projects and corporate investments in Chapter 11.

A *bond* is a debt instrument that is similar to a loan. Corporations, the United States Government and its agencies, municipalities such as cities and states, and other entities issue bonds. Bonds are payable from certain revenue sources of the issuer, such as taxes by the U.S. Government or municipal issuer, or the general revenues of a corporation. A bond usually pays interest every six months (twice a year) and a principal payment, usually in the amount of $1,000 or a multiple thereof, that is payable at the maturity date of the bond. We value a bond in the section below and discuss more about bonds and their valuation in Chapter 14.

A *stock* represents an ownership interest in a corporation, and it is a tough asset to value. The cash flows associated with a stock are difficult to predict and are subject to a wide range of outcomes, which introduce substantial volatility and variability. Unlike a bond there is no maturity associated with a stock—the life of a stock is infinite. The risk of a stock is difficult to quantify, meaning it is hard to determine the proper discounting rate. We make some simplifying assumptions and value a stock of a hypothetical company in the section below. We'll visit stock valuation in greater depth in Chapter 15.

10.3.2 Valuing Uneven Cash Flows Using a Spreadsheet

In Chapter 11 we will look at the cash flows associated with the investment in new paper machinery by the Lemont Pulp and Paper Company. Here, we briefly discuss one of the scenarios and show how to calculate the discounted cash flow associated with a project.

Using a Spreadsheet to Value the Investment Project:

Managers of the Lemont Pulp and Paper Company are considering the purchase of a new machine to process high quality paper from pulp. It is Bill's (the financial manager's) responsibility to recommend whether this investment is a good one—and should be accepted by the company, or a bad one—and should be rejected by the company. Bill's first order of business is to develop a set of cash flows that he expects the project to generate if it is accepted. Cash inflows will be the result of additional revenues coming into the company from the sale of additional products that are produced by the new machinery. Cash outflows will be the result of additional expenses involved with the manufacturing and sale of the new products. The difference between cash inflows and outflows are the net cash flows.

Bill expects that if the company invests in the new machinery its incremental revenues from paper sales initially will be $3,000,000 per year, and that the cost of the raw pulp for the additional paper will be $2,500,000 per year. The operation and maintenance of the new machinery requires the hiring of two additional workers. Bill estimates that the annual costs for each worker, including salary, insurance, health, and retirement benefits, will be $50,000. Bill estimates that revenues will increase at the rate of 6% per year and that costs will increase at a lower rate of 4% per year. The machinery is expected to last 8 years and is expected to have no salvage value at the end of this period. What are the discounted cash flows associated with this project if management of the company believes that comparable risk investments have a discounting rate of 14%?

Bill's first step in analyzing this investment project is to develop a financial spreadsheet detailing his estimates. As a first cut, he keeps the analysis simple and ignores the incremental income taxes that the project may generate, the depreciation (a non cash item) charges that also would affect taxes, and any incremental working capital effects that the investment may have. Bill initially looks only at the hard cash flows of the project. Those cash flows are represented in Table 10-8.

Table 10-8
Lemont Pulp and Paper Company
Investment in New Machinery
(In Thousands of Dollars)

				Discount Rate =		14%
Year	Cash Inflow	Cash Outflow	Net Cash Flow	Discount Factor	DCF	
1	$3,000	$(2,600)	$400	0.8772	$351	
2	$3,180	$(2,704)	$476	0.7695	$366	
3	$3,371	$(2,812)	$559	0.6750	$377	
4	$3,573	$(2,925)	$648	0.5921	$384	
5	$3,787	$(3,042)	$746	0.5194	$387	
6	$4,015	$(3,163)	$851	0.4556	$388	
7	$4,256	$(3,290)	$966	0.3996	$386	
8	$4,511	$(3,421)	$1,089	0.3506	$382	
Total			$5,735		$3,021	

Based on Bill's initial assumptions, the project has expected gross cash inflows of $5,735,000 and a discounted cash flow valuation base on a 14% discount rate of $3,021,000. What exactly does this mean? Based on Bill's risk assessment, the project is **worth** $3,021,000 to Lemont Pulp and Paper. The company should accept this project if the present value of the up-front costs associated with the project is less than $3,021,000. Lemont should reject the project if the costs are greater than $3,021,000. If the costs were exactly $3,021,000, Lemont would be indifferent to the project.

When Bill creates the spreadsheet for Lemont's proposed investment, he builds a powerful tool in which he can examine a number of *what if* scenarios. The spreadsheet is programmed so that Bill can change the discounting rate and immediately see how that change will affect the projects discounted cash flows and its values. For example, if Bill believes the risk is actually far lower than 14%, perhaps 8%. When bill plugs 8% into the discount rate slot, the spreadsheet calculates that the $5,735,000 in net cash flow has increased in value to $3,895,000 in discounted cash flow. And if Bill thinks the risk has increased to 20% and plugs that number into the discount rate slot, the discounted cash flow of the $5,735,000 in raw cash flow drops to $2,408,000 in discounted cash flow. He can also use the spreadsheet to change the assumptions relating to the growth in revenues or expenses—but those changes would effect the gross cash flows.

Using a Spreadsheet to Value a Bond:

Let's use the discounted cash flow technique to value a bond. For example, let's assume that the United States Government has issued a Bond that has an 8% interest rate, five years remaining to the maturity of the Bond, and a principal payment of $1,000. The Bond pays interest in the amount of $40 dollars (equal to $1,000 * 8% * ½ year) two times per year (April 1 and October 1), plus the $1,000 repayment of the principal at maturity. Let's also assume that the interest rates associated with this type of bond has increased to 10% in today's market. What is the current value of this Bond?

Let's call up our Excel spreadsheet and develop the cash flows for the Bond. Every six months for the next five years—10 periods, the Bond will pay its owner $40. At the end of the five years, the Bond will repay the $1,000 in principal. Based on today's discount rate for similar securities, we discount those cash flows at the rate of 10% on an annual basis—5% on a semi-annual basis. We value this Bond in Table 10-9.

Table 10-9
U.S. Government Bond Valuation

		Semi Annual Rate =	5%
Period	Cash Flow	Discount Factor	DCF
1.0	40	0.9524	38.10
2.0	40	0.9070	36.28
3.0	40	0.8638	34.55
4.0	40	0.8227	32.91
5.0	40	0.7835	31.34
6.0	40	0.7462	29.85
7.0	40	0.7107	28.43
8.0	40	0.6768	27.07
9.0	40	0.6446	25.78
10.0	1040	0.6139	638.47
Total	$1,400.00		$ 922.78

The value today for the $1,400 in cash flows associated with an 8% U.S. Government Bond that matures in five years (ten semi-annual periods), discounted at the rate of 10%, is **$922.78**. If interest rates for comparable securities were to drop to 6%, the value today for the Bond would rise—remember the inverse relationship between the movement in yields or discounting rates and the value of a financial asset? The total of the discounted cash flows—the value of the bond, based on a discount rate of 6% per annum—3% semi-annual, is **$1,085.30**, and is shown below in Table 10-10.

Table 10-10
U.S. Government Bond Valuation

		Semi Annual Rate =	3%
Period	**Cash Flow**	**Discount Factor**	**DCF**
1.0	40	0.9709	38.83
2.0	40	0.9426	37.70
3.0	40	0.9151	36.61
4.0	40	0.8885	35.54
5.0	40	0.8626	34.50
6.0	40	0.8375	33.50
7.0	40	0.8131	32.52
8.0	40	0.7894	31.58
9.0	40	0.7664	30.66
10.0	1040	0.7441	773.86
Total	**$1,400.00**		**$1,085.30**

Using a Spreadsheet to Value a Stock:

The basic approach to valuing a stock is the same as that used by the bank in making a fixed-rate mortgage loan, or the approach that we used above when we valued the U.S. Government Bond. When it comes to estimating the future cash flows associated with a stock versus the cash flows of a bond or mortgage, there are two important exceptions:

- *First*, the Bond and the mortgage have cash flows that are known with certainty, while the range of future cash flows for a stock can be enormous. In this example we make some simplifying assumptions regarding expected cash flows to use the DCF approach to value a stock.
- *Second*, common stock represents ownership shares in a corporation, which is a legal entity with an infinite life. So the stock valuation procedure must address the problem of valuing cash flows to infinity.

If we make some simplifying assumptions relating to the cash flows associated with the stock, valuing an infinite stream isn't a difficult as it sounds. Remember from Chapter 9 that we can value a series of level cash flows as an annuity. An asset that has a stream of even cash flows that continues to infinity is known as a *perpetuity*.

> ***Perpetuity*** *is an asset that has a stream of even cash flows that continues to infinity.*

The value of a perpetuity is calculated by dividing the level annual cash flow associated with the perpetuity by the discounting rate:

Value of a Perpetuity = Annual Cash Flow/Discounting Rate (Eq.10-2)

Let's assume that ABC Utility Company produces and distributes electric power to an urban rustbelt area that has limited growth potential, and little competition. Expected revenue for the current year is $1 billion and profits and cash flows after taxes are expected to be $200 million per year and remain at 20% of revenue. ABC expects revenue and profits to grow at the compound rate of 3% per year for five years and then to remain exactly the same for the foreseeable future. Further, the company pays out its entire profits and cash flows to its shareholders in the form of dividends and intends to do so in the future. Also assume that ABC is financed solely with common stock, and that the return or discount rate required by common stockholders for stocks similar to the common stock of ABC Utility is 10%. What is the discounted cash flow valuation of the common stock of the shares outstanding of ABC Utility?

This question essentially is asking what amount of market equity ABC's underlying business and operations can support in today's market environment.

Let's first figure out the expected cash flows associated with the valuation of the stock. ABC pays all of its profits and cash flows out in dividends so we don't need to debate whether it's better to discount profits or free cash flow or dividends—in this case they are one and the same. So, we expect the net cash flows to be at $200 million for next year and increase at the rate of 3% per year, to $206 million to $212.18 million to $218.54 million to $225.1 million. To calculate ABC's market equity associated with year six and above, we calculate the value of a perpetuity by *capitalizing* (capitalize means to divide an amount by a number between zero and one) ABC's expected annual cash flows in year five at the yield required by the market.

Capitalize *means to divide an amount by a number between zero and one.*

If ABC's cash flows are $225.1 million in year five and its cost of capital is 10%—and there are no expectations of growth, the market value of the perpetuity that the operations of ABC at that time can support is: [$225.1 million/(.10)] = $2.251 billion. To get today's value of the company, we discount all of these cash flows back to today at a discounting rate of 10%. We show this calculation in Table 10-11.

Table 10-11
ABC Utility Common Stock Valuation
(In millions of dollars)

Year	Cash Flow Profits	Value of Perpetuity	Total Cash Flow	Discount Rate =	10%
				Discount Factor	DCF
1	200.00	0	200.00	0.9091	181.82
2	206.00	0	206.00	0.8264	170.25
3	212.18	0	212.18	0.7513	159.41
4	218.55	0	218.55	0.6830	149.27
5	225.10	2251.02	2476.12	0.6209	1537.48
Total DCF					**$2,198.22**

The total value of the common stock of ABC Utility is $2.198 billion, which we'll round up to $2.2 billion to keep the numbers simple. Because ABC has no debt or preferred stock outstanding, this $2.2 billion is also ABC's *enterprise value* or *market capitalization* or *market equity*—terms you may hear when investors talk about the value of a company.

> ***Enterprise value*** or ***market capitalization*** *means the total value (debt plus stock) of a company.*

> ***Market equity*** *means the total common stock value of a company.*

That $2.2 billion in equity can be divided in many ways: 2 billion shares @ $1.10 per share; or 200 million shares @ $11 per share; or 20 million shares @ $110 per share; or 2 million shares @ $1100 per share—you get the idea. This price/share tradeoff is similar to what happens when a stock splits (for example, the company issues two shares for every share that a shareholder owns—a 2 for 1 split). It's easy to change the number of shares and per share intrinsic value, but the aggregate values of the underlying shares should always add to $2.2 billion.

How about interest rates? Do changing interest rates or discounting rates affect ABC's stock value? Let's assume that interest rates in the market have increased and the discounting rate associated with the risk of ABC Utility increases from 10% to 12%. When we revisit our trusty Excel spreadsheet, we plug 12%—an increase of 2% in rate into the cell for the discounting rate. The result is Table 10-12. Let's take a look at the discounted cash flows associated with a 12% discounting rate.

Table 10-12
ABC Utility Common Stock Valuation
(12% Discounting Rate)
(In millions of dollars)

			Discount Rate =		12%
Year	Cash Flow Profits	Value of Perpetuity	Total Cash Flow	Discount Factor	DCF
1	200.00	0	200.00	0.8929	178.57
2	206.00	0	206.00	0.7972	164.22
3	212.18	0	212.18	0.7118	151.03
4	218.55	0	218.55	0.6355	138.89
5	225.10	1875.85	2100.95	0.5674	1192.14
Total DCF					**$1,824.84**

The cash flows associated with profits of ABC Utility are the same, but the value of the perpetuity at the end of year 5—now calculated by the equation [225.1/(.12)] = $1.875 billion, decreases due to the higher 12% discounting rate. We see that the market equity associated with the same cash flows discounted at 12% has dropped from $2.198 billion to $1.824 billion—a steep drop of over 17% of its discounted value at 10%.

How about a decrease in interest rates? If increasing interest rates have a negative effect on stock prices, will decreasing interest rates have a positive affect? Let's revisit our spreadsheet and plug 8%—a decrease of 2% in rates, into the cell for the discounting rate. Table 10-13 is the result of that decrease.

Table 10-13
ABC Utility Common Stock Valuation
(8% Discounting Rate)
(In millions of dollars)

			Discount Rate =		8%
Year	Cash Flow Profits	Value of Perpetuity	Total Cash Flow	Discount Factor	DCF
1	200.00	0	200.00	0.9259	185.19
2	206.00	0	206.00	0.8573	176.61
3	212.18	0	212.18	0.7938	168.44
4	218.55	0	218.55	0.7350	160.64
5	225.10	2813.77	3038.87	0.6806	2068.21
Total DCF					**$2,759.08**

Yes! As the discount rate is reduced from 10% to 8%, the discounted cash flow and value of the stock of ABC Utility increases from $2.198 billion to $2,759 billion—an increase of approximately 20%. The value of the perpetuity portion has increased due to the division of the cash flow in year 5 by a lower discounting rate. So the value of a financial asset, such as a stock or a bond, moves inversely to the movement of interest rates and discounting rates. **As interest rates go up—the value of financial assets goes down. As interest rates go down—the value of financial assets goes up.**

In this simple example we see that the market equity level of a stock is crucially dependent upon two variables: the amount of future *profits* or *cash flows* that the firm is expected to generate—**greater profits increase a stock's market value and lower profits decrease value**; and the *interest rate* or required yield level that is expected from the investment—**lower yields and interest rates increase market value, and higher yields and interest rates reduce market value**.

10.3.2   Valuing Uneven Cash Flows Using a Financial Calculator

Using a Financial Calculator to Value an Investment Project:

Let's value the cash flows associated with the Lemont Pulp and Paper Company and its investment in new machinery. The cash flows over an eight-year period that the company expects to generate (in 000's) are: $400, 476, 559, 648, 746, 851, 966, and 1,089.

In this chapter we are concerned with only present values of the future cash flows associated with the investment—not the cost of the investment itself. Clear the calculator! If we want to use our HP-12c to value these cash flows at a discounting rate of 14%. Our inputs are: $n = 8$, $i = 14$, we assume a 0 initial outlay at time 0, so our entry is 0, blue g button, *CFo* button. Our next eight entries follow the pattern of (400, 476, 559, 648, 746, 851, 966, 1089) blue g button, *CFj* button. Finally, we press the yellow f button and hit the *NPV* button. Our financial calculator spits out the result of **$3,021.08**.

We also want to value these same cash flows at discount rates of 8% and 20%. The cash flows are already stored in the calculator. The only entry that we have to alter is the discounting rate. To do this, our initial input is $i = 8$, and when we press the yellow f button and hit the *NPV* button, our financial calculator comes up with the value of **$3,894.51**—very close to the value that was determined via our spreadsheet. We make this same type of adjustment to solve for a discounting rate of 20%, where $i = 20$. We press the yellow f button and hit the *NPV* button and our value is **$2,407.54**—again very close to the value that was determined by the spreadsheet.

Using a Financial Calculator to Value a Bond:

Let's value the cash flows associated with the 5-year United States Government Bond, that pays $40 in interest on a semi-annual basis and is discounted at a rate of 10% annually—5% semi-annually. The cash flows over ten six-month periods that are promised on the Bond are: $40 for the first nine periods and $1,040 for the tenth period. Our inputs are $n = 10$, $i = 5$ (semi-annual compounding), we assume a 0 initial outlay at time 0, so our entry is 0, blue g button, *CFo* button. Our next entry follows the pattern of 40, blue g button, *CFj* button, 9, blue g button, *CFj* button. The next entry is 1040, blue g

button, *CFj* button. Finally, we press the yellow *f* button and hit the *NPV* button. Our financial calculator spits out the result of **$922.78**.

We then want to value the discounted cash flows when the annual discount rate is 6% (semi-annual discount rate of 3%). The cash flows are still in the calculator so our entry is $i = 3$. Then we press the yellow *f* button and hit the *NPV* button. Our financial calculator gives us the value of **$1,085.30**.

Using a Financial Calculator to Value a Stock:

Let's value the cash flows associated with the stock of ABC Utility Company. The cash flows associated with profits over the five-year period that the company expects to generate (in 000's) are: $200, 206, 212.18, 218.54, and 225.10. Based on a 10% discounting rate, the cash flow associated with the value of the perpetuity in year five is 2,251.02, bringing the total cash flow in year five to 2,476.12.

Clear your calculator! Our inputs are: $n = 5$, $i = 10$, we assume a 0 initial outlay at time 0, so our entry is 0, blue *g* button, *CFo* button. Our next five entries follow the pattern of (200, 206, 212.18, 218.54, 2,476.12) blue *g* button, *CFj* button. Finally, we press the yellow *f* button and hit the *NPV* button. Our financial calculator spits out the result of **$2,198.22**—which is the exact value produced by our spreadsheet.

When we discount the cash flows at 12%, the changes we make are: $i = 12$, and the change in value of the perpetuity, which equals (225.12/.12) = 1,876. This changes the fifth cash flow to 2,101.12. When we input the changes into our HP12-c and press the yellow *f* button and hit the *NPV* button, our discounted cash flow of the value of the stock of ABC Utility is **$1,824.93**—very close to the value produced by the spreadsheet.

When we discount the cash flows at 8%, the changes we make are: $i = 8$, and the change in value of the perpetuity, which equals (225.12/ .08) = 2,814. This changes the fifth cash flow for the 8% discounting rate scenario to 3,039.12. When we input these changes into our calculator and press the yellow *f* button and the *NPV* button, the result is **$2,759.24**.

10.4 Summary

How much is a stock or a bond or another investment really worth? This not so simple question is answered best by using the discounted cash flow approach to valuing an investment. In this chapter we showed you how to value a project—the Lemont Pulp and Paper Company's investment in new machinery, and we also showed you how to value bonds and stocks using some simplifying assumptions. And if we had a copy of Alex Rodriquez's ridiculous contract, we also could have determined its value.

The DCF technique is the basis for the valuation approach that is most often used by corporations in capital budgeting and by Wall Street in valuing stocks, mergers and acquisitions, and leveraged buy-outs. It is a technique with which you will want to be familiar as you wade into the next few chapters on capital budgeting and measurement of investment return, and in the chapters relating to valuation.

Is the true value of the contract of Alex Rodriquez equal to the simple addition of the $100 plus million that a major league baseball team has committed to pay to him over the next 20 years? No! Because of risk and the time value of money, the process of discounting makes the value of the contract much less. This chapter helps you to determine how much less and how to value investments, projects, and contracts that have multiple cash flows that pay out over a number of years. You learned how to:

- Calculate the future and present value of level cash flow streams;
- Calculate the future and present value of uneven cash flow streams;
- Calculate loan payments, effective interest rates, and amortization schedules; and
- Value projects, bonds, and stocks using the discounted cash flow valuation approach.

Let's now use what we learned in the last two chapters to wade into understanding the process of capital budgeting and learn how to use the discounted cash flow technique to measure investment returns.

List of Terms

1. Discounted Cash Flow Valuation
2. Value of Financial Investment
3. Expected Cash Flows
4. Discount
5. Discount Rate
6. Discount Factor
7. Present Value
8. Risk Premium
9. Loan
10. Mortgage
11. Annuity
12. Level Cash Flows
13. Loan Amortization
14. Uneven Cash Flows
15. Project/Venture
16. Bond
17. Stock
18. Perpetuity
19. Enterprise Value or Market Capitalization or Market Equity

Problem Set

1. Suppose John's father promised to give him $500 every year for the next five years starting at the end of this year. What is the present value of money that John will receive if his opportunity cost is 8 percent per year?

2. Suppose Jane will receive annual payments of $20,000 for a period of 8 years. The first payment will be made 4 years from now. If the interest rate is 6 percent per year, what is the present value of Jane's future stream of payments?

3. George's bank sends him a check for $20,000. If George cashes the check he will have to pay the bank $500 every month for the next 50 months starting one month from the date of cashing the check. What rate of interest is the bank charging for the arrangement?

4. Puja wants to purchase a laptop that has a cash price of $1000. Under the installment plan Puja will have to pay $100 up-front and 24 monthly installments of $47.58. What annual interest rate is Puja paying for the monthly installment plan?

5. Calculate the price of a 10-year bond paying semi-annually a 6% annual coupon on a face value of $1,000 if investors can earn 8% per year on alternative investments.

6. What is the present value of cash flows of $100 per year forever
   (a) Assuming an interest rate of 8 percent per year?
   (b) Assuming an interest rate of 10 percent per year?
   (c) Assuming an interest rate of 12 percent per year?

7. Kathy has leased out her property for a rental of $10,000 per year forever. If Kathy estimates that its value is $125,000, what must be the discount rate?

8. British government 2½ percent perpetuities pay €2.50 interest each year forever. What is the value of the perpetuity if the long term interest rate is 6%? What would be the value of the perpetuity if it was a 5 percent perpetuity paying €5 interest every year?

9. John's bank offers a deal that will pay John or his beneficiaries $100 a year forever if John pays the bank a $100 a year for 10 years. Advise John if this is a good deal if the interest rates available on other deposits are 8 percent per year.

10. ABC Finance Company offers you a $5,000 loan. The repayment is structured to be in four annual payments of $1416. The first payment will be deducted from the loan amount; the second payment is due one year from now, etc. What is the approximate effective annual rate of interest on this loan?

11. Tom has borrowed $5,000 from his bank at an interest rate of 10 percent per year. Repayment is due in four equal annual year end installments. Prepare amortization schedule showing annual payments, year end loan outstanding balance, interest payment, and principal payment.

12. Jim takes out a 30 year $100,000 mortgage loan with an APR of 8% and monthly payments. In 12 years he decides to sell the house and pay off the mortgage. What is the principal balance on the loan?

13. XYZ Annuity Corp. offers a lifetime annuity to retiring employees. For a payment of $80,000 at age 65, the firm will pay the retirees $600 a month until death.
   (a) If a retiree's remaining life expectancy is 15 years, what is the monthly rate on this annuity? What is the effective annual rate?
   (b) What is the effective annual rate if the retiree's remaining life expectancy is 20 years?
   (c) If the monthly interest rate is 0.5 %, what monthly annuity payment can the firm offer to the retiree, if remaining life expectancy is 15 years and 20 years?

14. Chris wants to buy a car, but he can make an initial payment of only $2000 and can afford monthly payments of at most $500.
   (a) If the interest rate for an auto loan is 12 percent per year, what is the maximum price Chris can pay for the car if he finances the purchase over 48 months?
   (b) If the interest rate falls to 10 percent, how much can Chris pay for the car?
   (c) If the interest rate increases to 14 percent per year and Chris decides to finance the purchase over 60 months, how much can Chris pay for the car now?

15. Jack is considering buying a property that is on sale for $3 million. He expects to sell it after 5 years for $4 million. If his opportunity cost is 8 percent, advise Jack if this is a good investment decision if the property is not expected to earn any rental income. Would your advice change if the property is expected to earn a rental income of $200,000 per year?

16. A store will give you 3 percent discount on the cost of your purchase if you pay cash today. Otherwise you will be billed the full price with payment due in 1 month. What is the implicit borrowing rate being paid by customers who choose to defer payment for the month?

17. Your company can lease a piece of equipment for $8000 a year (paid at year end) for 6 years. It can instead buy the equipment for $40,000. The equipment will be valueless after 6 years. If the interest rate your company can earn is 7%, is it cheaper to buy or lease?

18. Carlos wants to buy a refrigerator. The department store offers two payment plans. Under the installment plan, he pays 25% down and 25% of the purchase price in each of the next 3 years. Under a cash payment plan, if Carlos pays the entire bill immediately, he can avail a 10% discount from the purchase price. Which is a better deal if Carlos can borrow or lend funds at a 6% interest rate?

19. A factory costs $400,000. You forecast that it will produce cash inflows of $120,000 in year 1, $180,000 in year 2, and $300000 in year 3. Is the factory a good investment if the interest rate is
    (a) 8 percent per year?
    (b) 10 percent per year?
    (c) 12 percent per year?

20. Consider cash flows of $1000 at the end of year 1, $3000 at the end of year 2, $ 2000 at the end of year 3, and $1500 at the end of year 4. Assuming an interest rate of 10% per year, calculate the present value of remaining payments to be received
    (a) Today
    (b) At the end of year 1
    (c) At the end of year 2
    (d) At the end of year 3

Assignment #10-1:

11. James borrowed $100,000 loan from his bank to start a business. The bank terms require a repayment of $159,229 in five years. How much interest rate is the bank charging James?
    - (a) 8.75%
    - (b) 9.25%
    - (c) 9.75%
    - (d) 10.25%

12. Jerry invested in a business that is expected to give a cash flow of $50,000 for the next 5 years. What is the present value of the business if cost of capital is 8% per year?
    - (a) $182,345
    - (b) $189,463
    - (c) $194,975
    - (d) $199,635

13. Tom is planning to buy a land and construct a building to be rented out. The initial investment for land and building construction is expected to be $1,000,000. Tom expects to earn a rent of $100,000 per year for the next 20 years. What is Tom's return on this investment?
    - (a) 6.15%
    - (b) 6.95%
    - (c) 7.25%
    - (d) 7.75%

14. Suppose Harry plans to buy a truck for $8000 and leases it out for a rental. What rental should Harry charge per year if his opportunity cost is 12% per year and the truck is expected to last for 6 years?
    - (a) $1,945
    - (b) $2,165
    - (c) $2,355
    - (d) $2,625

15. Jim is planning to save $1000 every year for the next 15 years. He deposits his savings in an account that gives interest of 6% per year compounded annually. How much would Jim's savings be worth at the end of 15 years?
    (a) $21,615
    (b) $23,275
    (c) $25,725
    (d) $27,775

16. Kathy wants to make equal annual deposits in a savings account that offers interest at 7% per annum so that she will have $100,000 at the end of 15 years. How much should Kathy save every year if she already has $12,000 in her savings account?
    (a) $2,362.95
    (b) $2,465.42
    (c) $2,661.93
    (d) $2,862.56

17. Jack has won a lottery that promises to pay $1000 every year forever. If Jack's opportunity cost is 8%, what is the lottery worth today?
    (a) $8,000
    (b) $10,000
    (c) $12,500
    (d) $16,000

18. What is the present value of the following stream of cash flows received at the end of each year, at an opportunity cost of 9% per year?

    Year 1: $10,000
    Year 2: $16,000
    Year 3: $17,500
    Year 4: $15,000
    Year 5: $5,000

    (a) $50,030
    (b) $48,265
    (c) $42,680
    (d) $38,805

19. George is planning to purchase and install equipment which would cost him $50,000. George expects to receive cash inflows of $20,000, $25,000 and $ 15,000 at the end of years 1, 2 and 3. At the end of year 4 George expects to incur $2000 in dismantling the equipment before scrapping it. What is the present value of the project, if George's opportunity cost is 6%?
    (a) $1,027.90
    (b) $2,127.90
    (c) $2,017.90
    (d) $2,710.90

20. Jason has $20,000 in the bank earning interest of 0.5% per month. He needs $30,000 to make a down payment on a house. He can save an additional $100 per month. How long will it take for Jason to accumulate the $30000?
    (a)   1.5 years
    (b)   2.6 years
    (c)   3.1 years
    (d)   3.8 years

Assignment #10-2:

21. Chris borrowed $100,000 from another bank to start a business. This bank required a repayment of $25,000 at the end of each year for the next five years. How much interest rate is the bank charging Chris?
    (a)   7.93%
    (b)   8.14%
    (c)   8.87%
    (d)   9.13%

22. Suppose Chris negotiates with the bank to repay $15,000 at the end of each year for the next 10 years for the loan of $100,000 he borrowed today. How much interest rate is Chris paying for the loan now?
    (a)   7.93%
    (b)   8.14%
    (c)   8.87%
    (d)   9.13%

23. Tom is planning to buy land and plant trees that will be cut and sold for $5,000,000 after 25 years. If Tom's opportunity cost is 8% per year, beyond what amount should Tom not invest today, in purchase of land and planting trees?
    (a) $615,970
    (b) $730,090
    (c) $752,560
    (d) $797,540

24. Suppose Harry wants to buy a laptop and notices an advertisement that offers a Toshiba laptop for a cash price of $2,400. The advertisement also talks about an installment plan that requires a monthly payment of $127 that includes interest of 2% per month. For how many months would Harry have to pay $127 before the entire laptop is paid for and there are no dues?
    (a)   20 months
    (b)   22 months
    (c)   24 months
    (d)   26 months

25. Tom wants to plan for a vacation 2 years from now that is expected to cost him $15,000. How much should Tom deposit every month in his savings account that offers him interest of 6% per year compounded monthly, so that Tom will have an additional $2000 at the end after withdrawing for his vacation expense?
    (a) $669
    (b) $721
    (c) $764
    (d) $803

26. Kathy has a house that gives her a rental income (net of maintenance expenses) of $6000 per year. Kathy expects to receive this rental income forever and estimates the value of the house to be $50,000. What is Kathy's opportunity cost of capital?
    (a)   12.0%
    (b)   13.5%
    (c)   14.0%
    (d)   14.5%

27. Jack purchases an annuity by paying a lump sum amount today. Jack will receive $500 at the end of every year. If the interest rate is expected to stay at 6% and Jack is expected to live for another 25 years, how much would Jack have to deposit for the annuity?
    (a) $4,866
    (b) $5,236
    (c) $5,894
    (d) $6,392

28. John purchases equipment for $10,000 and expects to earn cash of $4,200, $5,300, $2,000 in years 1, 2, and 3 respectively. If John's opportunity cost is 9% per year, what is the net preset value of John's investment?
    (a) $10,141.50
    (b) $141.50
    (c) $(141.50)
    (d) $(10,141.50)

29. George has purchased a house that cost $250,000. George has entered into a contract to lease the house for an annual rent of $20,000 for the next 5 years. If George's opportunity cost is 8% and the house has an estimated life of 35 years, for how much should George lease the house for in the remaining years to break even?
    (a) $20,170.80
    (b) $22,206.86
    (c) $15,113.60
    (d) $27,100.50

30. If Jason has to invest in an annuity in annual equal installments over the next 20 years before his retirement and then start receiving $6,000 every year after his retirement for the next 30 years, how much should Jason's annual installment be before his retirement if the interest rate is 8%?
    (a) $1,067.55
    (b) $1,274.35
    (c) $1,378.03
    (d) $1,476.05

CHAPTER 11

CAPITAL BUDGETING AND MEASURES OF INVESTMENT RETURN: NPV, IRR, AND MORE

Corporations and organizations have opportunities to invest large sums of money today in hopes of receiving financial rewards in the future. Capital budgeting is the process of evaluating these opportunities and deciding which projects are worthwhile and which ventures are trash. When we refer to the capital budgeting process of a firm or a corporation, a successful investment will increase the value of the corporation by increasing the price of its stock.

Your objectives for this chapter are to:

- Learn the process of capital budgeting and how to estimate incremental cash costs and benefits associated with projects, ventures and investments;
- Learn how to apply the standard techniques for measuring investment returns including net present value (NPV), internal rate of return (IRR), and other approaches for measuring returns for capital budgeting problems;
- Understand the contribution of capital budgeting towards increasing the stock price of a company and maximizing shareholder value.

11.1   Capital Budgeting

11.1.1 What is Capital Budgeting?

As we discussed in Chapter 4, *capital budgeting* is the process of planning and managing a firm's long-term investment in projects and ventures. The financial management team tries to identify investment opportunities that are worth more than they cost, so that the present value of the future cash flows generated by a project exceeds the cost of building or acquiring the project.

Regardless of the specific project, financial managers must be concerned with how much (amount) in the way of cash flows they expect the project to generate, when (timing) they expect to receive the cash flows, and how likely (risky) is the receipt of the cash flows. Valuing the amount, timing, and risk of future cash flows is the essence of capital budgeting. In fact, whenever you value any investment, the cash flow related factors of amount, timing, and risk should be your most important considerations.

Capital budgeting decisions are the most critical financial decisions that the management team of a corporation makes. The financial decisions relating to capital structure and working capital management, though also important, do not define the business. The capital budgeting decisions relate to the fixed assets of the firm—what it does, what it makes, and the industries in which the firm is involved. For example, when we think of IBM we think of a computer company and a high-tech consulting company. The projects in which IBM invests relate to computers and software. When we think of BMW we think of a luxury car company. The projects in which BMW invests relate to cars and trucks.

Capital budgeting decisions are often complex. A company may have dozens of investment possibilities, some of which are mutually exclusive. By mutually exclusive, we mean that if one investment is chosen, an alternative investment opportunity must be excluded. For example, should a real estate development firm build an office building or a shopping mall on a specific piece of property that it owns?

Also, it may be difficult to estimate the incremental cash flows associated with investing in a project. *Incremental cash flows* are the changes in the company's future cash flows that result directly from the company undertaking the investment. Another set of concerns relating to incremental cash flows that the firm faces when considering investing in a project are the financing costs associated with the project and any increase in net working capital that will require the firm to finance inventories and accounts receivable that will be associated with the project. We consider these questions, along with others, in the sections that follow.

11.1.2 Examples of Capital Budgeting Projects

Each of the examples below involves a firm investing a sum of money now in hopes of making more money in the future or lowering operating expenses over time. Many of the costs and cash outflows associated with a project are known and payable today, while the benefits and cash inflows of a project are uncertain and will be received in the future. Some examples of capital budgeting related decisions are:

- In order to assemble personal computers and sell them in East Asia, IBM is evaluating whether to build a new plant in Hong Kong. Construction of the plant will cost $500 million. IBM believes it can earn an extra $50 million per year from incremental computer sales in East Asia. Will this investment be profitable and increase the share price of IBM?
- BMW is planning to hire an engineering team to design a new car. The salaries and equipment for the team will total about $50 million per year. If the team is successful in its design efforts, BMW expects to earn an extra $10 million a year above their annual incremental costs from sales of the new model. Will this create value for BMW shareholders?
- A retail sales mail order company is considering installing a new phone system at an up-front cost of $2 million. The company estimates that the new phone system

will save about $100,000 a year in labor costs since fewer phone operators will be needed. Should this investment increase the company's stock price?

11.1.3 Capital Budgeting Procedures

Once an asset, project, or venture has been identified as a possible investment candidate, the first step in any financial analysis is to estimate the incremental cash flows—the costs and benefits—of accepting or rejecting the project. The basic unit of time that the cash flows are usually segmented into and analyzed is a month or a year, but it could be a day, a quarter, or some other unit of time. Once the estimated cash flows and their expected timing are identified, we create a time line of future cash flows. We identify the incremental cash flows associated with the project, and then we compare the present value of the cash flows to the costs of purchasing the asset or acquiring or building the project.

After we identify the incremental cash flows, we can use a number of different investment techniques to compare the benefits—uncertain and spread over several future periods—associated with accepting the project, with the costs of the project, which most likely will be incurred at a much earlier time than when the benefits are received. The capital budgeting techniques that we use to analyze projects are: *net present value, internal rate of return, payback period, book rate of return*, and *profitability index*.

11.2   Net Present Value (NPV)

11.2.1 What is it?

In Chapter 10 you learned how to value the cash flows associated with an investment or loan by using the discounted cash flow (DCF) method. Using the DCF method, the accept/reject decision should be based on the price of the investment versus the value of the investment as determined by its discounted cash flow. The value of any project, venture or investment is equal to the present value of its expected cash flows, discounted for their risk and timing. The goal of the financial managers of a firm is to create additional value for stockholders by investing in projects or ventures that are worth more than they cost.

> ***Net present value*** *of an investment is the difference between the value of an investment and its cost.*

The net present value of a project or investment is the difference between the value of an investment and its cost. Theoretically, the value of a company's stock should increase by the net present value associated with an investment. Therefore, a goal for the financial manager in the capital budgeting process is to fund only those investments that have a positive net present value.

11.2.2 How to Calculate NPV

How do we calculate net present value? As we discussed in Chapter 10, we value an investment by using a three-step approach to calculate its discounted cash flow. The three steps are:

- To develop a set of expected future cash flows associated with the project;
- To estimate a discount rate for the cash flows associated with the project—the discount rate should be based on the risk associated with the project's expected cash flows; and
- To discount the expected cash flows at the appropriate discount rate, and total the discounted cash flows to calculate the value of the project or investment.

This three-step process determines the present value of the cash flows. We then compare the value of the investment with its cost. The investment decision should be based on cost versus value. If our analysis shows that a project is worth significantly more than its cost, we should take the plunge and fund it. If the cost is greater than the projects value, we should avoid it.

$$NPV = \text{Present Value of Cash Flows} - \text{Cost of Investment} \quad \text{(Eq. 11-1)}$$

Let's examine a simple example. We assume that the Lemont Pulp and Paper Co. is considering the purchase of a new machine to process high quality paper from pulp. The company expects that its incremental revenues from paper sales would be an additional $3,000,000 a year while the cost of the raw pulp for the additional paper will be $2,500,000 a year. The operation and maintenance of the new machine will require the hiring of two additional workers. It is estimated that each worker will cost $50,000 a year for salary, insurance, health, and retirement benefits. The up-front cost of the paper machinery and installation is $2,000,000. The machinery is expected to last 8 years and has little or no salvage value at the end of this period. Calculate the NPV of the investment using a discount rate of 6%.

Table 11-1

Lemont Pulp and Paper Company						**Discount Rate =**		6.00%		
Investment in New Paper Machinery										
(In Thousands of Dollars)										

Year	0	1	2	3	4	5	6	7	8
Inflow	0	3000	3000	3000	3000	3000	3000	3000	3000
Outflow	-2,000	-2600	-2600	-2600	-2600	-2600	-2600	-2600	-2600
Net Flow	-2,000	400	400	400	400	400	400	400	400
Discount Factor	1	0.9434	0.8900	0.8396	0.7921	0.7473	0.7050	0.6651	0.6274
Discounted Cash Flow	-2000.00	377.36	356.00	335.85	316.84	298.90	281.98	266.02	250.96
NPV									**$483.92**

We programmed the incremental cash flows for the Lemont Pulp and Paper project into an Excel spreadsheet, which is shown in Table 11-1. The year is shown on the first input line of the spreadsheet. Yearly cash inflow, outflow, and net cash flows are shown on the next three lines. The company pays $2,000,000 up-front to purchase and install the paper machinery. Incremental cash flows in the amount of $3,000,000 per year flow into the company from the sale of additional paper that is produced by the new machinery. The $2,500,000 cost of raw pulp and the $100,000 in salaries and benefits total the $2,600,000 in yearly cash outflows. The cash inflows and outflows are totaled on a yearly basis to calculate the net cash flow over the eight-year period. The present value discount factors are shown in the spreadsheet and are calculated in the manner that we described in Chapter 9:

$$\text{PV Discount Factor} = 1/(1 + r)^n \quad \text{(Eq. 9-7)}$$

The discounted cash flow is the product of the net cash flow times the relevant present value discount factor. And the net present value equals the total of all of the discounted cash flows. In this case, based on the assumed cash flows and using 6% as the discounting rate, the net present value of the investment equals **$483,920**.

Based on the above analysis, the financial managers of Lemont Pulp and Paper should invest in the new paper machinery. The acceptance of the project should make the shareholders of the firm richer to the tune of $483,920 and the stock price per share of Lemont Pulp and Paper should rise by an amount equal to: [$483,920 / (number of shares outstanding)].

What if investors and the financial markets believe that the cash flows associated with Lemont's new paper project are considerably more risky than 6%? Let's assume that the market assesses the risk of the project at 14%, significantly higher than the internal estimate of 6% by the financial manager of Lemont. How does this assessment affect the projects net present value and the value of Lemont's stock?

We assume that the raw expected cash flows are the same for both the 6% and 14% scenarios. The only assumption that we've changed is the discounting rate—due to the market's different perception of risk associated with the project. When we substitute 14% for the 6% discounting rate, the discounted cash flows that result are shown in Table 11-2.

Table 11-2

Lemont Pulp and Paper Company   **Discount Rate =**   14.00%

Investment in New Paper Machinery

(In Thousands of Dollars)

Year	0	1	2	3	4	5	6	7	8
Inflow	0	3000	3000	3000	3000	3000	3000	3000	3000
Outflow	-2,000	-2600	-2600	-2600	-2600	-2600	-2600	-2600	-2600
Net Flow	-2,000	400	400	400	400	400	400	400	400
Discount Factor	1	0.8772	0.7695	0.6750	0.5921	0.5194	0.4556	0.3996	0.3506
Discounted Cash Flow	-2000.00	350.88	307.79	269.99	236.83	207.75	182.23	159.85	140.22

| **NPV** | | | | | | | | | **-$144.45** |

This example shows how important interest rates and the discounting rate are when we compute net present value. Based on a risk assessment of 14%, the net present value of the project is reduced from positive $483,920 to a negative number (-$144,450). Based on a 14% discounting rate, Lemont Pulp and Paper should reject the investment in the new paper machinery. If they accept the project, the total stock value of Lemont should *decrease* by $144,450.

The participants in the stock market frequently believe that investments have a higher risk and a lower net present value than the values assumed by the financial managers of the firm. Often we see the price of a stock react negatively to the announcement of a merger or acquisition by the company. Mergers and acquisitions by companies often are the result of weeks of secret negotiations and endless financial analysis by the managers of the companies that are involved. The merger or acquisition would not occur if the financial managers did not believe that the transaction would increase the value of the merged or acquiring firm. However, when the acquisition is announced, the market price of the acquiring firm often drops significantly. The stock market makes its own assessment of the risks and expected cash flows and instantly records its assessment in the way of a change in the stock's price.

Note on taxes, depreciation and other adjustments:

In a real-world setting, a project such as the investment by Lemont Pulp and Paper would have cash flow adjustments relating to depreciation—which does not involve the payment of cash but affects the income taxes that the company pays, and to additional working capital that is needed to support the project. Any project is going to affect the firm's income before taxes and, therefore, will affect the firm's tax payments. A complete capital budgeting analysis would address depreciation, taxes, incremental working capital requirements, and any other incremental cash flows that would be affected by investing in a project.

11.2.3 The NPV Rule

The goal of the management of a company is to make decisions that increase the value of the company's stock. Given this goal, the appropriate criterion for the capital budgeting decision is:

Invest if the net present value of the project is positive. Do not
invest if the net present value is negative.

This rule seems simple enough to follow, however, in a world of uncertainty there always are complications. The expected cash flows are estimates—best guesses—and the actual results could diverge significantly from those estimates. The discount rate that is used in the calculation should reflect the risks of the cash flows associated with the project. Not all investments have equal degrees of risk, and the discounting rate that is used could greatly underestimate or overestimate the risk involved. However, even with these caveats the NPV approach, along with the net present value rule, is the best method for companies to use when making capital budgeting decisions because it relates the investment to the net change in value of the corporation.

11.2.4 NPV, Uneven Cash Flows, and Financial Calculators

In Chapter 9 we discussed how to calculate future values and present values for either a single cash flow or equal multiple cash flows. In those situations, we showed how five input buttons on a financial calculator are used to calculate present and future values, rates of return, and periodic payments. However, most investments in the real world will not adhere to single or equal expected cash flow restrictions. When a company invests in a project or venture, often the cash flows will increase over time as the marketing of a product ramps up, or will increase in price simply due to the effect of inflation, or could decrease as similar products from competitors eat into market share. How do we handle these types of varying cash flow situations when we analyze a project?

Spreadsheets and Uneven Cash Flows:

Let's revisit our Lemont Pulp and Paper example of Table 11-2 and assume that the revenue associated with the project will increase 6% per year, and that expenses will increase by a lesser annual amount of 4% per year. If these growth patterns occur, what is the NPV of the project?

We reprogram our Excel financial spreadsheet for the revenues to compound at the rate of 6% per year over the eight-year period (compound the inflows at 6% per year by multiplying sequentially by 1.06), and for expenses to increase at the rate of 4% per year (compound the outflows by 4% per year). We continue to use a discounting rate of 14%. The cash flows associated with this scenario are shown in Table 11-3.

Table 11-3
Lemont Pulp and Paper Company   **Discount Rate = 14.00%**
Investment in New Paper Machinery
(In Thousands of Dollars)

Year	0	1	2	3	4	5	6	7	8
Inflow	0	3000	3180	3371	3573	3787	4015	4256	4511
Outflow	-2,000	-2600	-2704	-2812	-2925	-3042	-3163	-3290	-3421
Net Flow	-2,000	400	476	559	648	746	851	966	1,089
Discount Factor	1	0.8772	0.7695	0.6750	0.5921	0.5194	0.4556	0.3996	0.3506
Discounted Cash Flow	-2000	351	366	377	384	387	388	386	382
NPV									**1021**

When we examine the numbers associated with this scenario, we find the annual cash inflow increasing by 6% per year and the cash outflow increasing by 4%. The increase in net cash flow is sufficient to cause the net present value of the project to turn positive. Based on these assumptions, the net present value of the project is **$1,021,000**. Acceptance of the project should increase the value of the company by the amount of the project's net present value, and financial management should invest in the project.

How difficult is it to use a calculator to replicate the cash flows and the results that we show in Table 11.3? Not very difficult, but you need to understand how to properly use a financial calculator.

Most popular financial calculators, such as the models that are produced by Texas Instrument, Sharpe and Hewlett-Packard, have their own specific systems for entering uneven sequential cash flows, and then discounting those cash flows at a uniform discount rate. We take you through the process of entering these cash flows into our own trusted (and ancient) HP-12C model to give you the general idea. The HP-12C model follows a procedure in which we enter the cash flows associated with time 0, press the blue *g* button, and press the *CFo* button. We then enter the next cash flow, press the blue *g* button, and press the *CFj* button. We continue this process until all eight annual cash flows are entered. Once all of the cash flows are entered, we input the discounting rate and press the *i* button. Finally, we press the yellow *f* button and then press the *NPV* button to calculate the net present value associated with the discounted cash flows.

Here goes! First we clear our calculator. The incremental cash flows associated with the project are show on the net flow line of Table 10-3. The initial outlay at time 0 is –2000, so our entry is *–2000*, blue *g* button, *CFo* button. Our next entry follows the pattern of *400*, blue *g* button, *CFj* button. With the next seven entries being the following numbers—(*476*, *559*, *648*, *746*, *851*, *966*, *1089*)—each of them followed by the blue *g* button, and *CFj* button. Our next input is the *n* = *8* button, and then the discounting rate of *14* percent input into the *i* button. Finally, we press the yellow *f* button and hit the *NPV* button. Our financial calculator spits out the result of *1,021.08*, and since our numbers were all input in thousands of dollars, the answer is that the net present value of the project is **$1,021,080**.

If we wanted to see what the net present value of the net cash flows of Table 11-3 at the 6% discounting rate that we used in Table 11-1, we can simply input *i* = 6, and press the yellow *f* button and hit the *NPV* button. The projects NPV based on a 6% discounting rate is **$2,266,694**.

11.3   Internal Rate of Return (IRR)

11.3.1 IRR—What is it?

Along with the net present value approach, corporations frequently use the internal rate of return (IRR) as the measure of capital budgeting to determine whether or not to invest in a project. The IRR calculates the actual rate of return that we expect a project to earn. The procedure for calculating the IRR is to determine the exact rate at which the present value of the net cash flows associated with a project are equal to its cost. The IRR is also known as the *rate of return* on an investment.

> ***Internal rate of return*** *is the rate of return that a project is*
> *expected to earn. It is the discounting rate that makes*
> *the net present value of an investment equal to 0.*

Suppose that the Boalsburg Memorial Grave Marker Company is deciding whether to purchase a dozen blank tombstones today for $10,000. The company expects to spend $2,000 in labor and costs to engrave and deliver the tombstones, and then resell them for a total of $15,000 by the end of the year. Let's simplify the cash flows and assume that Boalsburg pays $10,000 at time 0 and receives a net inflow of $13,000 (the sale price of $15,000 minus the $2,000 in costs) at time 1. The internal rate of return on this project, in which Boalsburg pays $10,000 and then receives $13,000—a profit of $3,000, one-year later is 30%, a nice 30% return on its investment.

11.3.2 How to Calculate IRR

The IRR for a one-period investment such as the project considered by the Boalsburg Memorial Grave Marker Company is fairly easy to calculate. The expected internal rate of return on the one-year investment is equal to:

$$IRR = Profit/Investment$$
$$IRR = (Cash\ Flow - Investment)/Investment$$
$$IRR = (\$13,000 - \$10,000)/\$10,000 = 30\%$$

Let's now calculate the IRR for the Lemont Pulp and Paper Project with the cash flows that we used in Table 11-3. You'll recall that the NPV associated with that project, when discounted at the rate of 14%, was $1,021,080. We know that the IRR associated with a project is the rate that makes the net present value equal to zero. In this case, because NPV is positive at a discount rate of 14%, the IRR must be in excess of 14%. Let's look again at our Excel spreadsheet that we captured in Table 11-3.

Table 11-3

Lemont Pulp and Paper Company **Discount Rate =** 14.00%
Investment in New Paper Machinery
(In Thousands of Dollars)

Year	0	1	2	3	4	5	6	7	8
Inflow	0	3000	3180	3371	3573	3787	4015	4256	4511
Outflow	-2,000	-2600	-2704	-2812	-2925	-3042	-3163	-3290	-3421
Net Flow	-2,000	400	476	559	648	746	851	966	1,089
Discount Factor	1	0.8772	0.7695	0.6750	0.5921	0.5194	0.4556	0.3996	0.3506
Discounted Cash Flow	-2000	351	366	377	384	387	388	386	382
NPV									1021

If we go to the cell that contains the discounting rate and begin to increase the rate from 14% to 20% to 24% to 25%, we notice that the net present value declines towards 0. At 25.5%, the net present value is negative. And at 25.45%, the net present value equals 0. So we can calculate IRR by an iterative process associated with changing the discount rate as shown in Table 11-4.

Table 11-4

Lemont Pulp and Paper Company   Discount Rate =   25.45%

Investment in New Paper Machinery

(In Thousands of Dollars)

Year	0	1	2	3	4	5	6	7	8
Inflow	0	3000	3180	3371	3573	3787	4015	4256	4511
Outflow	-2,000	-2600	-2704	-2812	-2925	-3042	-3163	-3290	-3421
Net Flow	-2,000	400	476	559	648	746	851	966	1,089
Discount Factor	1	0.7971	0.6354	0.5065	0.4038	0.3218	0.2566	0.2045	0.1630
Discounted Cash Flow	-2000	319	302	283	262	240	218	197	178
NPV									0

It is possible to reprogram the spreadsheet to calculate the internal rate of return—Excel has an IRR calculation in its financial function repertoire. When we use that function to calculate the IRR associated with the net cash flows of (-2000, 400, 476, 559, 648, 746, 851, 966, 1089), we find an exact IRR of 25.44% and the program output is shown in Table 11-5.

Table 11-5

Lemont Pulp and Paper Company   IRR =   25.44%

Investment in New Paper Machinery

(In Thousands of Dollars)

Year	0	1	2	3	4	5	6	7	8
Inflow	0	3000	3180	3371	3573	3787	4015	4256	4511
Outflow	-2,000	-2600	-2704	-2812	-2925	-3042	-3163	-3290	-3421
Net Flow	-2,000	400	476	559	648	746	851	966	1,089
Discount Factor	1	0.7972	0.6355	0.5066	0.4038	0.3219	0.2566	0.2046	0.1631
Discounted Cash Flow	-2000	319	302	283	262	240	218	198	178
NPV									0

Using a Financial Calculator for IRR:

The approach to finding an IRR on a financial calculator is similar to the approach that we took in Section 11.2 to calculate the NPV of a project. We take you through the process of entering these cash flows into our HP-12C model. The initial investment is the cash outflow (-2000) associated with time 0, we press the blue *g* button, and press the *CFo* button. We then enter the number of periods, 8 in this case, and press the *n* button. We then enter the cash flow for period 1 (400), press the blue *g* button, and press the *CFj* button. We continue this process until all eight annual cash flows are entered. We then press the yellow *f* button and then the *IRR* button to calculate the internal rate of return associated with the cash flows.

First we clear our calculator. The incremental cash flows associated with the project are show on the net flow line of Table 11-5. The initial outlay at time 0 is –2000, so our entry is –2000, blue *g* button, *CFo* button. We then enter the number of periods, 8, and press the *n* button. Our next entry follows the pattern of 400, blue *g* button, *CFj* button. With the next seven entries being the following numbers—(476, 559, 648, 746, 851, 966, 1089)—each of them followed by the blue *g* button, and *CFj* button. Finally, we press the yellow *f* button and hit the *IRR* button. Our financial calculator whirs for a long time and then spits out the IRR of **25.4436%**.

11.3.3 The IRR Rule

The investment rule that is based upon the calculation of an internal rate of return is:

> ***If the IRR is higher than some predetermined required rate of return, accept the investment. If the IRR is lower than the required rate of return, reject the investment.***

We stated that the goal of management of a company is to make decisions that increase the value of the company's stock. The IRR Rule does not specifically address an increase in shareholder value. Rather it bases its accept/reject decision on an arbitrary rate.

This rule seems simple enough to understand. However, the IRR of an investment is not all that easy to calculate. IRR is also subject to most of the same caveats that we discussed in using the NPV Rule. In a world of uncertainty there always are complications. The expected cash flows are estimates—best guesses—and the actual results could diverge significantly from those estimates. We discuss some of the problems associated with calculating and using IRR in the sections below.

11.3.4 Relationship of IRR and NPV

The IRR is the discount rate that makes the NPV of an investment equal to 0. The relationship between NPV and IRR is direct and the use of the IRR rule and NPV rule often results in the same accept/reject decision. Let's revisit our Lemont Pulp and Paper example to see just how closely NPV and IRR are related.

Let's use the same assumptions of cash flows associated with Table 11-5, but let's alter the discounting rate, *r*, and see how that affects the NPV of the project. Let's start with a discounting rate of 0—that yields an NPV of $3,735,000, see Table 11-6.

Table 11-6

Lemont Pulp and Paper Company					**R =**		**0.00%**		
Investment in New Paper Machinery									
(In Thousands of Dollars)									
Year	**0**	**1**	**2**	**3**	**4**	**5**	**6**	**7**	**8**
Inflow	0	3000	3180	3371	3573	3787	4015	4256	4511
Outflow	-2,000	-2600	-2704	-2812	-2925	-3042	-3163	-3290	-3421
Net Flow	-2,000	400	476	559	648	746	851	966	1,089
Discount Factor	1	1.0000	1.0000	1.0000	1.0000	1.0000	1.0000	1.0000	1.0000
Discounted Cash Flow	-2000	400	476	559	648	746	851	966	1089
NPV									3735

And as we increase the discounting rate by 4% we get the following pairings:

Discount Rate	0%	4%	8%	12%	16%	20%	24%	25.44%	28%
Net Present Value	3,735	2,691	1,895	1,278	793	408	92	0	-156

11.3.5 Pros and Cons Regarding Internal Rate of Return

While the IRR rule is easy to state and easy to understand, it is often difficult to calculate. Problems arise if the cash flows are complex—if more than one cash flow is negative. Specifically, a problem that has complex cash flows can have multiple rates of return. With multiple rates of return, there is no convenient or easy way to interpret the solution to the capital budgeting problem.

The IRR rule also comes up short when it is used to determine alternatives between two mutually exclusive investments. Taking an investment that has a higher rate of return is not always optimal for the shareholders of a company. When choosing between two mutually exclusive investments, the preferred measure should be the investment that creates the most value for the company. That is not necessarily the investment with the highest rate of return.

11.4 Other Measures Relating to Capital Budgeting

Most corporations use the net present value or the internal rate of return rule as the primary measure to accept or reject a project. Sometimes financial managers also use other measures of return that are more simplistic or focus on a measure that is not oriented to a change in value of the corporation or a measure of investment return. These methods include: payback period, book accounting return, and the profitability index.

11.4.1 The Payback Period

We often hear comments about how an investment will pay for itself in a certain period of time. The payback period is the length of time for the return on an investment to cover the cost of the investment.

Suppose the Lincoln Doormats—a perennial loser NBA team—signs the red-hot high school basketball player LeBron Jones to a long-term contract that has a total cost of $50 million. Let's assume that when Jones signed the contract, season ticket sales of Doormat increased, and along with additional concession revenues, television revenues, and the sales of LeBron Jones bobblehead dolls and numbered jerseys, the revenues and net profits of Doormat increases by $15 million in year 1. In year 2, Doormat's investment in Jones really pays off when he leads the Doormats to the NBA title and creates a $35 million incremental profit in year 2.

> *Payback period is the length of time for the return on an investment*
> *to cover the cost of the investment.*

The $15 million incremental profit from year 1 plus the $35 million incremental profit in year 2 pays the $50 million cost associated with LeBron's contract, and the *payback period* for this investment is 2 years. When a corporation uses the *payback rule* as an investment criterion, they:

> *Invest if the payback period is less than a predetermined number of*
> *years. **Reject the investment if its payback period is greater***
> ***than the predetermined number of years.***

The payback rule is a simplistic rule that involves only the gross cash flows—no discounting of cash flows is involved. Because there is no discounting process, there also is no consideration of risk. The rule doesn't differentiate between safe cash flows and extremely risky cash flows. What if LeBron Jones tears his ACL? Really bad investment! Also, the rule does not take into account the cash flows associated with the project that are expected to be received after a predetermined payback cutoff date. Because of its simplicity, many corporations use the payback rule for small investment decision. It has its drawbacks, but it is a popular capital budgeting criterion in the real world.

11.4.2 Book Rate of Return

Some corporations are concerned about certain accounting ratios relating to their long-term investment. One such ratio is the book rate of return. The book rate of return is calculated by dividing the company's accounting profits by the book value of the company's assets:

Book Rate of Return = Accounting Profits/Book Asset Value

As an example, let's assume that David, the pizza delivery man who is also a freshman in college, is considering the purchase of a used 1994 Nissan Pathfinder with four-wheel drive that he can drive around Buffalo, New York, to make deliveries in snowy, messy bad weather and the good weather that Buffalo experiences for two months per year. The Nissan has almost 200,000 miles and its owner is willing to sell it for $3,000. David feels that if he babies the Pathfinder, he can get three years of service that will get him through college. He believes that he can earn $2,000 per year in excess of the costs of gas, insurance, maintenance, and operation of the car. He intends to fully depreciate the car over the three-year period.

The pizza delivery business is a cash business and a deliveryman sometime will ignore the bothersome concern of declaring income and paying taxes to the federal government. So to keep things simple, we will ignore the effect of taxes. Table 11-7 shows what the financial statements of David's pizza delivery business would look like, and calculates the book rate of return on a yearly basis.

Table 11-7
David's Pizza Delivery Business

Book Value Beg. Year	Net Income per Year	Book Income Year End	Book Rate of Return
$3,000	$2,000	$2,000	2000/3000 = 66.7%
$2,000	$2,000	$1,000	2000/2000 = 100%
$1,000	$2,000	0	2000/1000 = 200%

Table 11-7 shows that the book rate of return for David's Pizza Delivery Business increases over time as the book value of its only asset—the Nissan Pathfinder depreciates from $3,000 to $2,000 to $1,000 to 0. As the book value of the company decreases, the book rate of return increases—from 66.7% to 100% to 200%. Because of this somewhat irrational movement, many corporations take an average of the expected book rate of return over a period of years. In this case the average would be (66.7% + 100% + 200%)/ 3 = 122%.

When a corporation uses the *book rate of return rule* as an investment criterion, it will:

> *Make the investment if its book rate of return exceeds a predetermined target ratio. It will reject the investment if its book rate of return is less than a target return.*

Like the payback period, the book rate of return ignores the time value of money. Since there is no discounting of cash flows, there is no differentiation between safe cash flows and risky ones. There also is no consideration given to the value of the company and whether accepting or rejecting an investment will positively or negatively affect the company's stock price.

11.4.3 Profitability Index

The profitability index is usually defined as the net present value of an investment, divided by its cost:

Profitability Index = NPV/Project Cost

The goal of this criterion is to rank projects in a manner that shows financial managers the projects that will receive the best return associated with the amount of dollars invested. For example, let's assume that we are considering investing in the following three ventures: Venture 1, which has a present value of $100 and a cost of $80; Venture 2, which has a present value of $1,000 and a cost of $900, and Venture 3, which has a present value of $10,000 and a cost of $9,500. Table 11-8 shows the profitability index for these three examples.

Table 11-8
3 Venture Sample

Venture	Present Value	Cost	NPV	Profitability Index
1	$100	$80	$20	20/80 = .25
2	$1,000	$900	$100	100/900 = .111
3	$10,000	$9,500	$500	500/9500 = .052

When a corporation uses the *profitability index* as a criterion for ranking its investments, the rule is:

> *Accept the project with the highest profitability index first. Sequentially accept ventures with lower positive profitability indices, until the projects expend the capital budget. Reject projects with a negative profitability index.*

The profitability indices for the three ventures shown in Table 11-8 rank from .25 to .111 to .052. Using the profitability index rule, Venture 1 would be accepted first, then Venture 2 and then Venture 3. If management were making decisions in a manner that maximized the value of the firm, management would first accept the project with the greatest net present value—Venture 3, then Venture 2, and finally Venture 1. If the firm's capital is constrained and is insufficient to invest in all three projects, or if they are mutually exclusive projects, accepting projects according to the profitability index rule would result in suboptimal capital budgeting decisions that did not maximize shareholder value.

11.5 Summary

If you are interested in working in a finance department of a company, it is important that you understand the capital budgeting process, and how to properly value projects, investments, and stocks and bonds. This requires that you know the basics regarding the time value of money—the math underlying compounding and discounting, and the different measures of investment returns.

The math underlying investment returns is not difficult but does require you to understand the relationship between present and future values that we discussed in Chapter 9, and how to calculate the present value of an investment, which we discussed in Chapter 10. Using your knowledge of the basic time value of money—compounding to future values and discounting to present values, you will be able to program and use Excel spreadsheets and inexpensive financial calculators to compute net present values and internal rates of return—the two most important measures relating to the capital budgeting process. When you master this chapter, you will be able to calculate:

- The net present value associated with an investment project and use the NPV rule to accept or reject a project;
- The internal rate of return associated with a project and use the IRR rule to accept or reject a project;
- The payback period and whether to accept or reject the project according to the payback rule;
- The book rate of return associated with an investment and whether to accept or reject the investment according to the book rate of return rule;
- The profitability index of an investment and whether to accept or reject an investment based on the profitability index rule.

List of Terms

1. Capital Budgeting
2. Mutually Exclusive
3. Incremental Cash Flows
4. Discounted Cash Flow
5. Investment
6. Net Present Value (NPV)
6. NPV Rule
7. Internal Rate of Return (IRR)
8. IRR Rule
9. Payback Period
10. Payback Rule
11. Book Rate of Return
12. Profitability Index

Questions:

1. Define capital budgeting and explain why capital budgeting is important for a company.
2. Define Net Present Value and explain what it means if the NPV of a project is positive.
3. Define Internal Rate of Return. Under what circumstances do NPV and IRR give conflicting results.
4. Define Payback Period and explain shortcomings of this method.
5. Explain Book Rate of Return and explain its shortcomings.
6. How does Profitability Index enable financial managers to choose among projects?

Problem Sets

1. Explain how the NPV of a project is impacted by a change (increase/decrease) in
   (a) Cash inflows from the project
   (b) Timing of the cash inflows
   (c) Duration of expected cash flows
   (d) Initial Investment
   (e) Discount Rate

2. A company is planning to invest $100,000 in a project which is expected to generate the following cash flows
   Year 1 : $35,000
   Year 2 : $45,000
   Year 3 : $25,000
   Year 4 : $20,000
   Calculate the following given that the discount rate is 10% per year
   (a) NPV
   (b) Profitability Index
   (c) Payback Period

3. A firm is evaluating an investment that requires an initial capital outlay of $500,000 at the end of year 1; $200,000 at the end of year 2. The project is expected to generate a cash flow of $350,000 in year 3; $450,000 in year 4; and $200,000 in year 5.
   (a) Calculate the NPV of the project if the firm's opportunity cost is
       (i) 10% per year
       (ii) 14% per year
       (iii) 18% per year
   (b) Calculate the IRR of the project
   (c) If the initial investment increases by $50,000 in year 2, what is the revised IRR?

4. Tools Inc. receives an offer of $300,000 for its old product line that is expected to generate cash flows of $120,000 in year 1; $110,000 in year 2; $100,000 in year 3; and $70,000 in year 4. If Tools Inc.'s required rate of return for the product line is 12%, should it accept the offer?

5.   The projected cash flows from a project are as follows:

End of Year	Cash Flows
1	$ 450,000
2	$ 350,000
3	$ 250,000
4	$ 150,000
5	$ 50,000

(a) If the required rate of return is 15%, what is the minimum the firm can afford to invest in the project?

(b) If the firm incurs $800,000 initial capital outlay, what is the firm's IRR?

6.   Real Estate Inc. has a property and is contemplating building either a mall or executive apartments. The construction of the mall will involve an initial outlay of $100 million and is expected to generate cash flows of $12 million every year for 20 years. The apartments will require an outlay of $80 million and will generate cash flows of 12 million for 15 years. If the cost of capital is 15%, calculate the NPV and IRR of both the plans. Advise Real Estate Inc. as to what it should construct.

7.   Transistors Inc. has a product that is expected to generate $100,000 in year 1; $75,000 in year 2; $50,000 in year 3; and $25,000 in year 4. Transistors Inc. has received an offer for $200,000 for the product line. Transistors Inc. can alternatively modernize the line by spending $50,000 that will increase the estimated cash flows every year by an additional $25,000. What should Transistors Inc. do if its discount rate is 10%.

8.   A firm has $1,000,000 and is considering investing in one project that will serve to enhance shareholders' value. It has two projects to choose from; Project A and Project B, both of which require an initial outlay of $1,000,000. The expected cash flows from the projects are given below.

End of Year	Project A	Project B
1	$350,000	$600,000
2	$350,000	$400,000
3	$350,000	$300,000
4	$350,000	$200,000
5	$350,000	$100,000
Total	$1,750,000	$1,600,000

(a) Which project should the firm choose if its cost of capital is 15% per year?

(b) Calculate the IRR and Payback periods for both the projects.

9.   Toys Inc. has to choose between 2 different models of molding machines. Machine 1 costs $300,000 and will generate a cash flow of $50,000 for the next 10 years. Machine 2 costs $200,000 and will generate a cash flow of $40,000 for the next 8 years; it has a resale value of $25,000 at the end of 8th year. Which machine should Toys Inc. choose if its discount rate is 10%?

10.   Leathers Inc. is considering constructing a new manufacturing plant for bleaching and dyeing. The new facility requires an initial outlay of $250,000 and is expected to generate cash flows of $90,000 for the next 5 years. At the end of sixth year, Leathers Inc. should clean the immediate environment and is expected to incur $50,000 for the restoration process. Calculate the Net Present Value of the project if the discount rate is 15% per year.

11.   Chemicals Inc. has found two new chemicals, Chem A and Chem B. To start production, each of the chemicals requires a separate new plant and since Chemicals Inc. has limited funds of $3,000,000, it cannot undertake both the projects at the same time.
      (a) Calculate IRR and advise Chemicals Inc. what project it should undertake, if initial outlay and the cash flows of the project are as given below:

End of Year	Chem A Plant	Chem B Plant
Initial Outlay	($ 1,750,000)	($ 2,750,000)
2	$600,000	$1,000,000
3	$550,000	$900,000
4	$500,000	$700,000
5	$450,000	$600,000

      (b) Calculate NPV for both the projects. Does your answer change after calculating NPV?

12.   The Machine Tool Company is considering replacing its existing equipment with a new one that is expected to cost $500,000. The new equipment is automated and will generate savings of $165,000 in labor cost every year. The equipment requires annual maintenance which is expected to cost $25,000 per year. Calculate NPV of the project:
      (a) If the life of the equipment is 6 years and Machine Tool Company's cost of capital is 15%.
      (b) If the life of the equipment increases to 8 years and cost of capital is 20%.
      (c) If the life of the machinery remains at 6 years but equipment has salvage value of $75,000 at the end of 6 years and Machine Tool Company's cost of capital is 18%.
      (d) If the savings generated decreases by 20% i.e. to $132,000 and the remaining stays the same as (a).
      (e) If maintenance costs increase by 20% to $30,000 and the remaining stays the same as (c).

13. Clothing Inc. has two projects, both requiring a capital outlay of $200,000, in the pipeline. The projected cash flows of the project as are given below:

End of Year	Project A	Project B
1	$ 100,000	$ 70,000
2	$ 80,000	$ 70,000
3	$ 60,000	$ 70,000
4	$ 40,000	$ 70,000

(a) Calculate NPV of both the projects if Clothing Inc.'s cost of capital is 13%.

(b) Calculate the IRR of both the projects.

(c) If the projects are independent, should Clothing Inc. choose both?

(d) Which project should be selected if the projects are mutually exclusive?

Assignment #11-1:

1. What is the net present value of the following streams of cash flows, if the discount rate is 10% and initial cash outlay is $25,000; Year 1 - $10,000, Year 2 - $12,000, Year 3 - $15,000, Year 4 - $ 6,000
    (a) $9,376?
    (b) $8,642?
    (c) $7,794?
    (d) $7,234?

2. What is the net present value of the following streams of cash flows, if the discount rate is 8% and initial cash outlay is $50,000; Year 1 - $25,000, Year 2 - $18,000, Year 3 - $12,000, Year 4 - $ 8,000 and year 5 has a cash outflow of $ 10,000?
    (a) $4,346
    (b) $2,643
    (c) ($1,596)
    (d) ($2,819)

3. What is the internal rate of return for a project requiring an initial capital expenditure of $1,000,000 and generating cash flows of $100,000 for the next 20 years?
    (a) 15.25%
    (b) 16.50%
    (c) 17.75%
    (d) 18.25%

4. What is the payback period for a project that requires a capital investment of $200,000 today and which generates a future stream of cash flows as follows; Year 1 - $25,000, Year 2 - $50,000, Year 3 - $75,000, Year 4 - $60,000 and Year 5 - $30,000?
    (a) 3 years, 8 months
    (b) 3 years, 10 months
    (c) 4 years, 2 months
    (d) 4 years, 4 months

5. If the required rate on a project is 20%, what cash flow must a company earn at the end of the 5th year of operations from the project that requires a capital expenditure of $500,000 today and generates a cash flow of $250,000 in Year 1, $125,000 in Years 2 and 3, and $100,000 in Year 4?
    (a) $45,850
    (b) $51,350
    (c) $54,650
    (d) $58,250

6.   If a project requires an immediate investment of $838,000 and will generate a cash flow of $250,000 every year, for how many years should cash flows be generated for the project to break even if the discount rate is 15%?
     (a) 6 years
     (b) 7 years
     (c) 8 years
     (d) 9 years

7.   If a project requires a capital outlay of $1 million today, what equal cash flows should it generate every year for the next five years so that the firm earns a rate of return of 20%?
     (a) $334,380
     (b) $362,640
     (c) $381,590
     (d) $402,810

8.   What is the net present value (if discount rate is 15%) and internal rate of return for a project requiring an initial capital expenditure of $750,000 and generating cash flows of $100,000 in Year 1, $150,000 in year 2, $175,000 in year 3, $200,000 in year 4, $125,000 in year 5 and $100,000 in year 6?
     (a) $42,084, 17.26%
     (b) $45,065, 17.26%
     (c) $42,084, 16.54%
     (d) $45,065, 16.54%

9.   ABC Corp. is considering expanding its existing plant in 2 phases. Phase I requires a capital outlay of $2,000,000 and will start generating cash flows of $500,000 from year 1 to year 4. At the end of 4 years, ABC Corp. will implement the second phase that will require an additional capital expenditure of $3,000,000. This will increase cash flows for the next 12 years to $800,000 per year. Calculate the NPV of the project if the discount rate is 15%.
     (a) $132,084
     (b) $145,065
     (c) $191,635
     (d) $214,167

10. XYZ Corp. is acquiring new equipment that requires a capital outlay of $1,000,000. The cash flows from the new equipment is expected to be as follows: Year 1 – $400,000, Year 2 – $300,000, Year 3 – $200,000, Year 4 – $200,000 and Year 5 – $100,000. What should the terminal value of the equipment be at the end of five years so that XYZ Corp earns a return of 12% on the investment?
     (a) $102,084
     (b) $114,043
     (c) $124,088
     (d) $136,385

Assignment #11-2:

1. Calculate the net present value of the project that requires an initial capital outlay of $125,000 and generates $50,000 for 5 years if the discount rate is 12%.
   (a) $49,376
   (b) $55,239
   (c) $57,794
   (d) $63,234

2. Calculate the IRR of the project that requires a initial cash outlay of $50,000 and generates cash flows as follows; Year 1 - $25,000, Year 2 - $18,000, Year 3 - $12,000, Year 4 - $ 8,000.
   (a) 10.26%
   (b) 11.32%
   (c) 12.34%
   (d) 17.38%

3. What is the NPV of a project requiring an initial capital expenditure of $800,000 and generating cash flows of $100,000 for the first 5 years, $200,000 for the next 3 years and $50,000 for the last 2 years, if the discount rate is 10%?
   (a) $71,611
   (b) ($71,611)
   (c) $132,821
   (d) ($132,821)

4. What is the payback period for a project that requires a capital investment of $500,000 today and which generates a future stream of cash flows as follows: Year 1 - $125,000, Year 2 - $250,000, Year 3 - $175,000, and Year 4 - $120,000
   (a) 2 years, 8.5 months
   (b) 2 years, 10 months
   (c) 3 years, 2 months
   (d) 3 years, 4 months

5. If the required rate on a project is 15%, what cash flow must a company earn at the end of the 5th year of operations from the project that requires a capital expenditure of $5,000,000 today and generates a cash flow of $2,250,000 in Year 1, $2,125,000 in Year 2, $1,200,000 in Year 3 and $1,000,000 in Year 4?
   (a) $145,850
   (b) $150,350
   (c) $152,662
   (d) $158,250

6. If a project requires an immediate investment of $800,000 and requires a rate of return of 18%, what cash flows should the project generate for the next five years?
   (a) $240,780
   (b) $255,850
   (c) $260,770
   (d) $285,320

7. If a project requires a capital outlay of $1 million today, and can generate cash flows of $250,000 for the next 3 years, what equal cash flows should it generate for the following 3 years so that the firm earns a rate of return of 20%?
   (a) $130,300
   (b) $190,400
   (c) $210,600
   (d) $215,500

8. Calculate NPV (if discount rate is 12%) and IRR for a project requiring an initial capital expenditure of $600,000 and generating cash flows of $100,000 in Year 1, $125,000 in year 2, $155,000 in year 3, $200,000 in year 4, 125,000 in year 5, and $100,000 in year 6?
   (a) ($55,044), 8.96%
   (b) ($45,065), 7.26%
   (c) $45,065, 13.22%
   (d) $55,044, 15.54%

9. Electronics Corp. is considering modernizing its existing plant in 3 phases. Phase I requires a capital outlay of $1,000,000 and will start generating cash flows of $400,000 from year 1 to year 3. At the end of 3 years, Electronics Corp. will implement the second phase that will require an additional capital expenditure of $1,500,000. This will increase cash flows for the next 6 years to $500,000 per year. The last phase will require a capital expenditure of $500,000 at the end of 6 years and it will increase the cash flows to $600,000 for 2 years. Calculate the NPV of the project if the discount rate is 20%.
   (a) $122,076
   (b) $135,060
   (c) $140,905
   (d) $156,162

10. Computers Corp. is building a new plant that requires a capital outlay of $5,000,000. The cash flows from the new project are expected to be as follows: Year 1 – $3,400,000, Year 2 – $1,300,000, Year 3 – $1,300,000, and Year 4 – $1,000,000. What is the IRR of the project?
    (a) 16.70%
    (b) 19.60%
    (c) 20.30%
    (d) 22.10%

The Beaver Stadium Expansion Project

10-A.1 General

The Penn State football program is one of the top programs in the country, based on win-loss performance and in attendance per game. During the late 1990's, the seats to all of the home games were sold out and there was a significant waiting list for season tickets for Beaver Stadium's 96,000 seats.

The football program and athletic department at Penn State wanted to upgrade the stadium to provide for luxury boxes, and to also increase its seating capacity. The athletic department has proposed an expansion project to add about 10,000 end-zone seats and 58 Lion Suites to the east stands. Each Lion Suite can accommodate up to 16 fans. The Athletic Director believes that the construction project will be self-supporting—the incremental revenues associated with the sale of the seats will be more than sufficient to pay for the cost of the construction project. The role of capital budgeting is to assess the financial viability of proposals. The Athletic Director submits this plan to the finance department staff of the University and they are responsible for running the numbers on the project.

Costs:

The estimated construction costs total $84 million and last over a two-year period. The construction will be suspended during the football season to allow home games to be played, even during the construction program. Although the construction contracts call for periodic payments (construction companies have cash flow needs), we will assume for cash flow purposes that the entire $84 million is due at the time 0, and that the project will begin generating cash flows at time 1.

Benefits:

The benefits will come from sales of the additional end-zone seats and Lion Suites. There will be additional benefits, such as additional concession and parking revenues, and additional costs, such as personnel to work in the new sections of the stadium. We assume that those incremental revenues and costs offset each other. Based on a marketing survey, Penn State believes that they can charge the following amounts for the tickets and the Lion Suites:

Lion Suites:

The anticipated annual suite rental will be between $45,000 and $65,000 per suite depending on location (50 yard line is most expensive) for each of the 58 suites. In addition, each suite comes with the option to buy up to 16 tickets for each game although there only are twelve (12) fixed-back seats per suite.

Cash Flow Estimates for Lion Suites:

Suite rental at $55,000 x 58 suites..................................	$3,190,000 per year
12 seats * 6 games * $44 per ticket * 58 suites.................	183,744 per year
Total suite revenue	$3,373,744 per year

Club-level Seats:

About 4,000 of the proposed 10,000 end zone seats will be Club-level seats. All Club-level seats will be chair backs and seat holders will have access to a large lounge with food services and a spectacular view of Mount Nittany. The anticipated annual fee per seat will be between $1,200 and $1,500. The cost of game tickets is extra.

Cash Flow Estimates for Club-level Seats:

$1,350 annual fee * 4,000 seats....................................	$5,400,000 per year
4,000 seats * $44 a ticket * 6 games a year......................	1,056,000 per year
Total Club-level seat revenue	$6,456,000 per year

End Zone Seating:

Cash Flow Estimates for End Zone Seating:

6,000 seats * $39 a ticket * 6 games a year......................	$1,404,000 per year
Total End Zone Seating	$1,404,000 per year

Total Annual Incremental Cash Inflows......................	***$11,233,744 per year***

Time Line of Cash Flows:

Year	0	1	2	3	....	20

- 390 -

| Cash Flow | -$84,000,000 | $11,233,744 | $11,233,744 | $11,233,744 | $11,233,744 | $11,233,744 |

The minus sign in front of the first cash flow indicates that the $84,000,000 will be spent at time 0 and the cash flows will be received in the periods shown. We perform the analysis assuming that the project will generate cash flows over a 20-year period. In all likelihood, the suite and ticket sales at Beaver Stadium will last longer than the 20-year period.

Project Financing:

A municipal entity will issue municipal revenue bonds on behalf of The Pennsylvania State University. A municipal bond issue in the amount of $84 million with a final maturity of 20 years will be issued to pay for construction of the stadium improvements. The interest payments on the bonds that are part of this bond issue are exempt from federal and Pennsylvania income taxation and the average interest rate on the bond issue is 6%.

11-A.2 Applying Capital Budgeting Methods to the Beaver Stadium Project

11-A.2.1   The Net Present Value Method

Calculation of NPV:

NPV= PV of future cash flows - Initial Cost

What do we know about the Beaver Stadium Project? We know that t = 20 years, i = 6%, the present value cost of building the project is -$84,000,000, and we expect incremental cash inflows of a level $11,233,744 per year for 20 years. To calculate the net present value of the Beaver Stadium Project we go to our HP-12C and input: 20 and the *n* button; 6 and the *i* button; the cost of the project at -84,000,000 and the blue *g* button and the *CFo* button; 11,233,744 and the blue *g* button and the *CFj* button; 20 and the blue *g* button and the *Nj* button to signify that there are 20 identical cash flows. Finally, we press the yellow *f* button and the *NPV* button and the calculator whirs and spits out the number **$44,850,158**—the number we want to know.

Good or bad project?

Any project with a positive NPV is deemed a good project (at least financially) and is an investment that should increase the value of the entity. The Beaver Stadium Project with a net present value of $44,850,158 should be accepted.

NPV—what does it mean?

In the Beaver Stadium Project, the annual incremental cash flows are $11,233,744 per year for 20 years. The inputs into a financial calculator to find the present value for these cash flows are: *n* = 20, *I* = 6%, *PMT* = $11,233,744, *FV* = 0. When you punch these inputs into the calculator and solve for PV the answer is $128,850,158. This means that Penn State can borrow up to $128,233,744 and still be able to payoff the loan (at 6%) using the cash benefits of $11,233,744 a year for 20 years. Since the project only requires $84 million, the project is generating a surplus income to the Penn State community. In theory, Penn State could borrow $128,233,744, use $84 million to pay for the stadium expansion, and still have $44,849,920 left over to pay for other needs.

Penn State is $44,849,920 richer (or wealthier) due to the stadium expansion. Penn State is not likely to borrow more than is needed to pay for the expansion ($84 million) but the extra cash flow from the expansion is more than enough to pay off an $84 million loan and have extra cash flow for other needs. The PV of this extra cash flow is $44,849,920. NPV measures the PV of the surplus after paying off the funds required to meet the initial cost.

Another interpretation of NPV involves the concept of *economic profit*. Any cash flow in excess of what is needed to pay off the suppliers of capital for a new project is called economic profit. In the Beaver Stadium example, Penn State could borrow $84 million at 6% and repay the loan with 20 equal annual payments of $7,323,502 (this loan calculation might be good practice for you). Since we estimate that the expansion project will pull in an extra $11,233,744, the annual economic profit is $3,910,242 (the difference between $11,233,744 and $7,323,502). The present value of $3,910,242 a year for 20 years at 6% is $44,850,084 or the same as NPV.

In corporate finance, NPV has the same interpretations. NPV measures the increase in the wealth of the firm's shareholders due to accepting the investment. Share price is higher by NPV divided by number of shares outstanding. If investors have no idea that a project is under consideration and a firm announces the project, share price should rise by the NPV associated with the investment divided by the number of shares outstanding.

Sensitivity Analysis or What If … …

Often, managers like to ask questions such as what if cash flows are 10% lower than expected or what if construction costs are 15% higher than anticipated or what if the project delivers cash flows for fewer years than planned. An easy way to handle these questions is to compute an NPV under these different possibilities. In the following sections, we look at some less desirable cash returns for the Beaver Stadium Project.

Case 1: Lower cash flows than originally expected:

Here, we ask what happens to NPV if cash flows are 10% below our forecasted levels, then 20% below, and so on. Cash flows could be lower because the estimated prices for suites and club seats were too high or because not all available seats could be sold at the estimated prices. Whatever the reason, we ask what happens to NPV assuming cash flows are lower.

Cash flow shortfall	10%	20%	30%	40%	50%
NPV	$31,964,928	$19,079,936	$6,194,944	-$6,690,048	-$19,575,040

From this exercise, we see that even if actual cash flows fall short of what was expected by as much as 30%, this project will be able to pay off the bond issue and deliver a surplus to the Penn State community.

Case 2: Fewer years of benefits than expected

Properly maintained, these extra stadium seats might last for a hundred years. The real question involves how many years the University is exposed to the risk of a serious decline in attendance. Below are NPVs for 20 years, 16, years, 12 years.

Number of years	20 years	16 years	12 years	8 years
NPV	$44,849,920	$14,181,463	$2,681,479	-$14,240,697

From this exercise, you can see that the stadium expansion project needs more than 8 years but less than 12 years to pay for itself including the 6% capital cost. To satisfy your curiosity, NPV is very near zero at 10 years. This calculation effectively is a calculation of the *payback period*, which we described in Section 10.4.1.

11-A2.1   The Internal Rate of Return Method (IRR)

Calculation of IRR:

IRR is the Rate of Return that makes the NPV = 0

The IRR method calculates the rate of return that is expected for the project. The procedure for calculating the IRR is to determine the rate at which the PV of cash flows equals the initial cost.

In the Beaver Stadium expansion project, we know that the cost of the project is -$84,000,000, that it is expected to generate $11,233,744 per year for 20 years. Based on these numbers, we can calculate the IRR of the project with the aid of our HP-12c. Our inputs are: 20 and the *n* button; -84,000,000 and the blue *g* button and the *CFo* button; 11,233,744 and the blue *g* button and the *CFj* button and 20 and the blue *g* button and the *Nj* button to signify the 20 identical cash inflows. Finally, we push the yellow *f* button and the *IRR* button and the calculator generates an answer of **11.9828%**.

Good or bad project?

The IRR (12%) is compared with the cost of capital (6%). If the IRR exceeds the cost of capita, the project is acceptable. The cost of capital generally depends on the risk of the project.

What does IRR mean?

To say that the IRR is 12% (or, more precisely, 11.98%) means that if the $84,000,000 were deposited in a bank, the bank would need to pay 12% interest to enable Penn State to withdraw $11,233,744 a year for 20 years. Since the PV of the cash flows equals the initial cost when 12% is used, that is the rate of return earned.

Investing money in the stadium project is just as good as investing money in a bank at 12%. Penn State needs only to decide if a 12% return is attractive or not. Since investors are willing to finance this project at 6%, the Penn State community captures the extra return.

When IRR is used for corporate finance decisions, the idea is that the corporate manager should identify investments that offer a return better than what shareholders can earn on their own. If shareholders can earn 10% on their money by investing in stocks or bonds, then managers would not be doing a good job if they invested the firm's money (really the shareholders' money) at 8%. Of course, this is on a comparable risk basis. In capital budgeting, more risky projects should offer higher returns just like more risky stocks and bonds offer higher returns.

(Many thanks to Professor James Miles of The Pennsylvania State University for developing and contributing The Beaver Stadium capital budgeting example.)

CHAPTER 12

RISK AND RETURN AND THE CAPITAL ASSET PRICING MODEL

This chapter addresses what determines the required and expected rates of return associated with an investment. The principle relating to return versus risk, the first principle we discuss in Chapter 2—**Higher Returns Require Taking More Risk,** shows the direct trade-off between the expected rate of return on an asset and its risk. We represent that trade-off by the diagonal line in Exhibit 12-1.

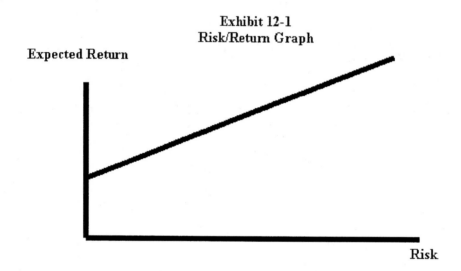

Exhibit 12-1
Risk/Return Graph

Expected Return

Risk

Finance theory assumes that a rational investor prefers to receive a higher percentage return on an investment to a lower return, and would rather accept less risk than more risk in earning that return. However, the proverbial free lunch does not exist in the investment world. A trade-off occurs between a higher expected return and greater risk of an investment. Safe investments have low returns. High returns require investors to take big risks.

It's important that we all start on the same page when discuss expected returns and risk. In this section, we define some terms that relate to the calculation of returns on an asset. We then tackle the thorny issue of understanding risk.

The objectives of the chapter are to:

- Demonstrate the risk/return relationship;
- Show that historic returns are consistent with that risk/return relationship;
- Define and explain the capital asset pricing model;
- Define the systematic and nonsystematic risk and how CAPM deals with them;
- Show the benefits associated with diversification; and
- Use the risk/return relationship to evaluate investment performance.

12.1 A Review of Investment Returns

Suppose you buy a share of IBM for \$90 on December 31st and sell that share on December 31st of the following year for \$104. During the year, you receive \$4 in cash dividends. What is the annual return on your investment in IBM stock?

Return = (Change in Price + Cash Payment) / Purchase Price   (Eq.12-1)

Return = (\$14 + \$4) / \$90 = 0.20 or 20%

The returns that you receive on a stock consist of dividends, if dividends are paid by the company, plus the appreciation (capital gain) or minus the depreciation (capital loss) in the price of the stock. The returns that you receive on a bond consist of periodic (usually every six months) interest payments and the repayment of principal. Additionally, you may have capital gains or losses associated with a bond if you sell it prior to its maturity.

In the United States, *dividends* paid on stocks and *interest* paid on bonds are typically classified as *ordinary income* and are added to the taxpayer's salary to get total ordinary income for the year.

In the United States, a *capital gain* is defined as a positive change in price of a stock, bond or other asset. In the IBM example, the capital gain was \$14. Since the stock was sold during the tax year, we say the capital gain was *realized* and a payment of a tax on the capital gain may be due. If the stock price had gone to \$104 but you did not sell the stock, the capital gain is *unrealized*. Generally, only realized gains are taxed in the United States.

> **Capital gain** *is a positive change in price of a stock, bond or other asset.*

To encourage longer-term investment, U.S. tax laws sometimes differentiate among the length of time an asset is held. For example, if an asset is held for one year or longer, it may be categorized as a *long-term capital gain*. If an asset is held for less than a year (or some other period), it may be categorized as a *short-term capital gain*. Long-term capital gains are usually taxed at a lower rate than short-term capital gains and ordinary income. Tax rates may be revised frequently—usually with a change of administration in the White House. In some years, ordinary income, short-term capital gains, and long-term capital gains may all be taxed at the same rate.

Suppose you buy a bond for $980 and sell that bond one year late for $920. You receive an interest payment on the bond of $35. What is your return?

Return = (-$60 + $35) / $980 = -.0255 or -2.55%

In this example, the change in price is negative and you incur a *capital loss*. Capital losses can offset capital gains and portions of ordinary income, and capital losses may reduce the federal and state income taxes that you pay.

> ***Capital loss*** *is a negative change in the price of a stock, bond or other asset.*

12.2 Definitions Relating to Returns and Risk

12.2.1 Definitions Relating to Returns

Expected Return on a Risky Asset—$E(R_i)$ is the rate of return an investor expects to receive on a risky asset over a period of time. The expected return consists of interim cash flow payments, such as dividends on a stock or interest on a bond, plus or minus any changes in the price of the asset over time. When we discuss the Capital Asset Pricing Model later in this chapter, we describe how to calculate the expected return on a risky asset by using a very simple equation.

Expected Return on a Portfolio of Risky Assets is the expected rate of return on each risky asset in a portfolio, multiplied by its portfolio weight. The portfolio weight is the percentage of the total portfolio's value that is invested in each risky asset. We discuss this calculation later in this chapter

Expected Return on the Market—$E(R_m)$ is the rate of return an investor expects to receive on a diversified portfolio of common stock. The expected return on the market is usually measured by the recent average return on the stock market or a return associated with a stock market index. Many investors use the rate of return on the S&P 500 Index or on the Wilshire 5000 Index as a measure of market performance for stocks in the United States.

Return on the Risk-Free Asset—R_f is the rate of return that an investor receives on a safe asset—free from credit risk. Obligations of the U.S. Treasury are assumed to be risk-free because it is believed that the U.S. Government will always meet its financial obligations. To meet those obligations, the government has powers that companies and individuals do not have—it can borrow money, increase taxes, or print more money.

12.2.2 Definitions Relating to Risk

Risk reflects the uncertainty associated with the expected future returns of an asset. Buying Treasury Bills is a low-risk investment. You are assured of receiving your original principal plus interest when the T-bill matures. On the other hand, the risk of investing in a high-flying biotech stock is high. The return that you receive depends upon the future price of the company's stock. Often the stock price may depend on the company receiving FDA approval on a new drug, or a set of other uncertain events occurring. Many things could go wrong and torpedo the stock's price. Or everything can go right and the stock price could multiply. *Risk is the part of an asset's price movement that is caused by a **surprise or an unexpected event**.* Risk is measured by the standard deviation of the return on the asset as discussed below.

The risk of a stock is subdivided into two categories: unsystematic risk and systematic risk.

- *Unsystematic risk* or *firm specific risk (FSR)* is the risk caused by a surprise event that affects one company, such as an accounting irregularity, new drug discovery, or a patent expiration. Unsystematic risk is unique to a stock. The effects of unsystematic risks for an investor are greatly reduced by proper diversification of the assets in a portfolio. The stock market does not reward investors for unsystematic risk because that risk can be minimized or eliminated through proper diversification.
- *Systematic risk* is the risk caused by a surprise event that affects the entire economy and all assets to some degree, such as an increase in interest rates, a terrorist attack, or the declaration of war. The level of systematic risk for an asset can not be reduced by diversification. In the stock valuation approach that we use, the expected return on an asset depends *only on an asset's systematic risk*.

Beta—($ß_i$) is a measure of the systematic risk of an asset. The market has a beta of 1.0. The beta of a stock with the same price movement as the market also has a beta of 1.0. A stock that generally has a price movement that is greater than the price movement of the S&P 500 Index, such as a technology or internet stock, has a beta greater than 1.0. A stock with a below average price movement, such as the stock of a public utility, has a beta less than 1.0. We discuss beta in greater depth below.

Market Risk Premium—[$E(R_m) - R_f$]: is equal to the expected return on the stock market (e.g., the expected return on the S&P 500 Index—$E(R_m)$) minus the rate of return on the risk-free asset (R_f). It is the additional return that investors expect to receive if they buy a stock of average risk (beta = 1.0), as opposed to a Treasury bond. Assume McDonald's stock has a beta of 1.0. If investors require an 8% return on McDonald's stock, and 10-year Treasury yields are 5%, the market risk premium is: (8% - 5%) = 3%. Market risk premiums increase when investors become more risk-averse, and decrease when investors become less risk-averse.

Standard Deviation of Return—(σ): Overall risk on an asset is usually measured by the variability of returns. The standard deviation is the statistic that is normally used to measure how wildly or tightly the observed stock returns cluster around the average stock return. A higher standard deviation means wilder fluctuations and greater risk.

It is not difficult to calculate a stock's standard deviation. Here's how to do it for a distribution of stock returns:

1. Take the simple average return of the distribution of returns;
2. Take each individual observed return and subtract the average of the returns;
3. Square the resulting difference and add the squares to get the sum of the squares;
4. Divide the sum of the squares by (the total number of observations minus 1)—the result is the variance of the distribution;
5. Finally, take the square root of the variance to get the standard deviation of the returns.

While this may seem complicated to read and explain, it is easy to compute using any standard spreadsheet program like Excel, or a hand held calculator. Furthermore, the interpretation of the standard deviation is much simpler than its calculation.

An example may be helpful. Assume that we observe that ABC stock over a four-year period has the following annual returns: 9%, 15%, -3%, and 21%, as shown in Table 12-1.

Table 12-1
Standard Deviation of ABC's Stock Return

Year	Observed Return	Average Return	Deviation of Return	Squared Deviation
1	9.00%	10.50%	-1.50%	0.000225
2	15.00%	10.50%	4.50%	0.002025
3	-3.00%	10.50%	-13.50%	0.018225
4	21.00%	10.50%	10.50%	0.011025
Totals	42.00%		0.00%	0.0315

The distribution of returns for the four-year period is shown in column 2 of Table 12-1. The average annual return over the four years is 10.5% as shown in column 3. The sum of the deviations around an average is always equal to zero, as shown at the bottom of column 4. The sum of the squares of the deviations divided by (n − 1) yields the *variance* of the returns—in this case it is equal to [.0315/(4 − 1)] = 0.0105. The square root of the variance is the *standard deviation* of the distribution, in this case $(0.0105)^{(1/2)} = 10.25\%$.

The standard deviation measures the expected spread of the observations around the average of the returns. A high standard deviation means a big spread of returns and a high risk that the actual return will not equal the expected return. In finance and economics, risk has both positive and negative implications.

Normal Distribution: You may remember the grading curve that turned your high school D's into B's. The curve is called a *bell curve* and is a classic example of a *normal distribution*. Most theories regarding the pricing of financial assets assume that the distribution of returns for an asset follows a normal distribution. The normal distribution is a bell-shaped symmetrical curve. The shape of the curve is determined by two key variables: the *mean* or *average* of the observations, and the *standard deviation* of the observations.

In a normal distribution, about two-thirds of the observations will be in a range of plus and minus one standard deviation around the average, and 95% of the observations will range between plus or minus two standard deviations of the average. In the case of the stock of ABC, the average or expected return is 10.5% and the standard deviation is 10.25%. We expect that two-thirds of the observations will be in the range between 10.5% plus or minus 10.25%—generating a high of 20.75% to a low of 0.25%. We also expect that 95% of the observations will be between 10.5% plus or minus two standard deviations—(2 * 10.25%), or a high of 31% to a low of –10.0%.

If the distributions of the returns of ABC stock over time are normal, they would appear as in Exhibit 12-2:

Exhibit 12-2

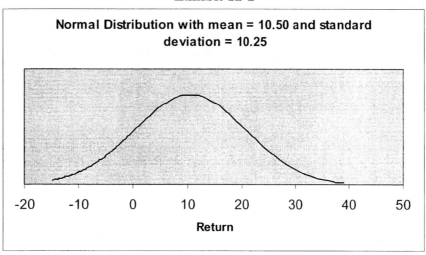

12.3   *Simple Average Returns Versus Compound Average Returns*

The section deals with the somewhat perverse math underlying the calculation of investment returns that treats percentage investment gains more favorably than comparable investment losses. For example, let's assume that Martha the portfolio manager tells you that she has achieved good investment performance over the past two years. Two years ago her portfolio skyrocketed 100%. This year hasn't been as good, with her stocks losing 80%. She says that her average yearly return over the past two years is 10%—a pretty respectable showing in a tough stock market.

Is Martha correct, or is she a pathological liar?

Let's closely examine her claim of a two-year average return of 10%.

First, let's figure the average of her returns. Her average yearly return over the past two years is: [+ 100% (year 1 return) + (-80%) (year 2 return)] / 2 = *(100%-80%)/2 = 10%,* as she alleges.

For fun let's verify her claim by injecting some real numbers into the equation. We keep this example simple. Let's assume her portfolio consists of one stock, Stock A, which she bought two years ago for $10/share. Her timing and analysis were impeccable and Stock A went up 100% to $20 at the end of the first year. The next year was a bad year for the stock market and Stock A, because Stock A tanked and dropped 80% to $4/share.

When we look at real dollars as opposed to averages, it's apparent that her actual 2-year return is negative. A $10 portfolio went up to $20 and then down to $4, a 2-year loss of 60%—a $10 portfolio was reduced to $4. This is a far more dire result than one would suspect from the positive 10% average performance that Martha is touting. How can there be two such different results?

The problem is embedded in the calculation of simple averages. In fact, if there is a negative percentage return in the distribution of returns, the calculation of a simple average percentage return is **biased upward**. For example, look again in Chapter 2 at Table 2-1, which shows the returns and risks for five asset classes. In each case the compound annual return, also known as a geometric rate of return, is lower than the simple average return. The compound average return is a correct measure of the dollar return you would have received from holding an investment over multiple time periods. Sometimes, as in the case of Martha's investment performance, the differences between simple and compound averages are substantial.

Table 12-2 shows how Martha's investments performed over the past two years. The simple average annual return, or arithmetic mean, is easy to calculate and is equal to the sum of the annual returns (20%) divided by the number of returns (2) equal to **10%**. The total percentage return over the two-year period is also easy to calculate. Martha's investment started at $10 and fell to $4, a loss of 60% over the two-year period. Below, we show how to calculate the compound average return.

Table 12-2

	Martha's Investment Performance Simple & Compound Average Returns		
Year	**Beginning Value**	**Ending Value**	**Annual Return**
1	$10	$20	100%
2	20	4	-80%
			20%
Simple Average Return			**10%**
Compound Average Return			**-36.75%**

The compound average return is calculated by:

- Dividing the most recent value—(A) ($4 at the end of Year 2) by the beginning value—(B) ($10 at the beginning of Year 1);
- Taking the resulting ratio to the (1/T) power, where T is the number of years in the compounding period; and
- Subtracting 1.0 to bring it into percentage terms. In math terms, the previous sentence looks like this: $[(A/B)^{(1/T)} - 1.0]$. The calculation of the compound annual return above is:

$$[(\$4/\$10)^{(1/2)} - 1.0] = [(.4)^{(1/2)} - 1.0] = [0.6325 - 1.0] = \underline{\textbf{\textit{-36.75\%}}}$$

Many investment managers and advisors use simple averages to portray their historic performance. Simple averages are a misleading way to assess investment returns—compound or geometric averages are far more representative of actual investment performance. Be careful when you read advertising material that bases performance records upon simple average returns.

With simple averages, a larger percentage gain is required to offset a given percentage loss. Let's take a real life example of the investment performance of a highly focused mutual fund that specialized in investing in Internet stocks. The Pro-Funds Ultra OTC Mutual Fund incurred a drop of 94.71% between the NASDAQ high in March 2000 and April 4, 2001. Let's assume that you invested $1,000 in the Ultra OTC Fund in March 2000. Thirteen months later it would have dropped to $52.90. A market rally occurred between April 4, 2001, and May 2, 2001, and the Ultra OTC Fund rose an enormous 95.6% in less than a month. Jim's $52.90 investment increased by 95.6% to $103.50—a very nice increase. However, you still find yourself down 89.65% below the March 2000 high—the point at which you invested in the mutual fund. The average return for these two unequal time periods is: (-94.71% + 95.6%) / 2 = 0.45%. The true return for your fifteen-month holding period is negative (-89.65%).

The following equation (Equation 12-2) yields the percentage gain required to make an investment whole again after suffering a loss:

Percentage Gain to Break Even = 1 / (100% - % drop)   *(Eq.12-2)*

In the example above, the equation looks like this:

1 / (100% - 94.71%) = 1 / (.0529) = 1,890%.

So your investment would need to increase by almost nineteen hundred percent for you just to break even. The likelihood that you will ever breaking even on this investment appears to be somewhat remote.

12.4   Historic Returns and Risk by Asset Class

To get a sense of the types of returns that we should expect in the future from an investment, let's look at historic average returns on different classes of financial assets. We want to observe if lower risk investments generally have offered lower returns and higher risk investments have offered higher returns. Let's again look at the results of the Ibbotson and Sinquefield study shown in Table 12-3 that we first discussed in Chapter 2. Their compound and simple average returns by asset class over the past 76 years are shown below:

Table 12-3
Ibbotson & Sinquefield Study

Asset Class	Compound Average Annual Return	Simple Average Annual Return	Std. Dev. of Return
U.S. Treasury Bills	3.70%	3.80%	3.10%
U.S. Treasury Bonds	5.40%	5.80%	9.40%
Corporate Bonds	5.90%	6.20%	8.60%
Large Company Stocks	10.40%	12.40%	20.40%
Small Company Stocks	12.70%	17.50%	33.30%

Do the average returns rank in the same order that you would rank the risk of the investments? Most of us would answer yes. Treasury bills are virtually risk-free. Long-term government bonds have price risk and interest rate risk but no default risk. Corporate bonds have price risk and interest rate risk and they also carry the risk that the corporation could default on its interest and principal payments. Interestingly, the standard deviation of corporate bonds is slightly lower than government bonds. Common stocks are by far the most risky of the five investment classes, with small company stocks exceeding the returns and risks of large company stocks. The standard deviation of return is how we measure price volatility and risk, associated with the five asset categories.

The results of the I&S study are important and show the direct relationship between the expected return of an asset and the risk associated with receiving that return. An investment in a Treasury bill with no default risk and little price volatility has a lower expected average return (3.8%) than a large cap stock (10.7%). The Treasury bill also has a lower risk measure of 3.2% relative to a portfolio of large company stocks with a standard deviation of 20.2%. A graphical representation of the expected returns and risks associated with these asset classes is shown below in Exhibit 12-3.

Exhibit 12-3

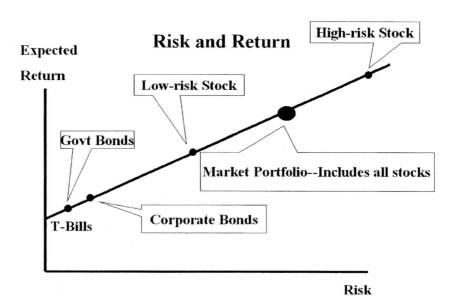

Returns on individual stocks can swing even more wildly than the standard deviations of returns that were calculated on the portfolios of large stocks and small stocks. We discussed previously that the price of Internet Capital Group fell from $200.94 per share at the height of the Internet era to $0.36 per share in a brief period of time—a dramatic and very painful swing, if you happened to be a shareholder. However, on average, investing in common stocks and accepting risk have increased returns significantly.

12.5   The Capital Asset Pricing Model

12.5.1   CAPM—a Simple Explanation

The *capital asset pricing model* (CAPM) is a theory about the pricing of assets and the tradeoff between the risk of the asset and the expected returns associated with the asset. In the CAPM two types of risk are associated with a stock: firm-specific risk or unsystematic risk; and market or systematic risk, measured by a firm's beta. CAPM or the *market model* is an expression of how expectations of stock returns are generated. No law says that stock returns must follow this model but there is some evidence that the predictions associated with CAPM generally hold.

The common sense behind CAPM is so basic that many investors have come to use the model. The model makes use of the following:

- $E(R_i)$ represents the *expected rate of return on risky asset i*;
- $E(R_m)$ represents the return an investor would expect to earn by placing her money in a *well diversified portfolio of stocks*. Frequently, the return associated with the S&P 500 Index is called the market return, although the S&P 500 ignores many U.S. firms and most foreign firms;
- (R_f) represents the *rate of return on the risk-free asset*;
- $[E(R_m) - (R_f)]$ represents the *expected market risk premium*—the excess return that you expect to receive above the risk-free rate for investing in a diversified portfolio of risky stocks;
- *Beta*—(ß_i) is a measure of the market related *systematic risk of an asset*;
- *FSR* is the abbreviation for firm specific return and is a measure of *unsystematic risk of an asset*. It represents the extra return received by a firm due to some event affecting only that firm.

We explain CAPM with a simple example. We've talked about the trade-off between risk and return. As a base rate of return, the return on every risky asset should be at least that of the risk-free rate of return. How much higher the expected return should be above the risk-free rate is a function of the risk associated with the asset. Below, $E(R_{ibm})$ is the expected annual rate of return for the stock of IBM. Of course, we won't know the actual rate of return until the end of the year but the market model says this about $E(R_{ibm})$:

$$E(R_{ibm}) = (R_f) + \text{ß}_{ibm} * [E(R_m) - (R_f)] + FSR \qquad \textit{(Eq. 12-3)}$$

According to CAPM, if we multiply the market risk premium, $[E(R_m) - (R_f)]$, by IBM's beta, ß_{ibm}, and add in the risk- free rate and the extra return for any firm-specific event, we get IBM's expected return for the year.

Firm specific return represents the *extra return* received by a firm due to some event affecting only that firm. For example, if IBM announced the award of a new and important patent, or that sales would be much higher than expected, or that it discovered a way to reduce manufacturing costs by 30%, then IBM's stock price would jump. The

FSR of IBM might be 5%, 10%, or even 20% to reflect the good news, but the news should not significantly affect the rest of the stock market. Of course, if IBM announced that profits will fall or that they are being sued for billions of dollars or that their costs will rise, then the share price will fall and FSR will be negative. The key to firm specific returns is this—the FSR for any company is just as likely to be positive as it is to be negative, and **averages 0%.**

Let's pop some numbers into the IBM equation shown above. Let's assume that the risk-free rate is 5%, that the expected return on the market is 10%, that the beta for IBM is 1.25, and that the expectation of FSR for IBM is 0. Here is our expected return for IBM stock:

$$E(R_{ibm}) = 5\% + 1.25 * [10\% - 5\%] + 0$$

$$E(R_{ibm}) = 5\% + 1.25 * [5\%] = 12.5\%$$

That wasn't so tough!

12.4.2 What is Beta?

In Equation 12-3 above, what does it mean that the estimate of IBM's beta is 1.25?

If IBM's beta is 1.25, it means that on average when the excess market return is up 10%, IBM is up 12.5% (1.25 * 10%), (before adding FSR). When the excess market return is down 20%, IBM, on average, is down by (1.25 * 20%) 25%. Beta indicates how responsive IBM's return is to changes in the excess market return. Excess market returns are *magnified* by IBM's beta of 1.25.

Suppose some other company had a beta of 3 (they seldom are this large). This company's returns would triple the excess market returns before the FSR is included. If the excess market return is 10%, this firm's excess market return would be 30% on average (since FSR is zero on average) and if the excess market return is -5%, this firm would be down 15% on average. The larger a firm's beta, the more responsive is that firm's return to excess market returns. Conversely, if a company had a beta of only 0.50, then that firm would not see such wild swings in its return over time as the market goes up or down.

The uncertainty about a firm's return that is caused by not knowing what the market return will be is called *market risk. The amount of market risk for a given firm depends on that firm's beta.*

How do we measure a firm's beta? To estimate beta in the real world, investment professionals will use 60 or more pairs of monthly or weekly returns for the performance of a stock versus the performance of a stock market index (e.g. S&P 500 Index). They will have the stock market index return on the horizontal axis and the firm's returns on the vertical axis. They plot these 60 or more points and use regression analysis to fit the line through them. *The slope of this line is the estimate of beta.*

Below is a graph (Exhibit 12-4) that may help you to understand the concepts of calculating beta. For both IBM and the overall market, ten months (the 10 dots shown on the graph) of returns were observed and plotted. Then a regression line was fitted to those points. If IBM did not have any firm specific risk, each point would be on the regression line. For each point, the vertical distance from the point to the line measures IBM's firm specific return for that particular month. If the point is above the line, IBM experienced a good firm specific return, and if the point is below the line, IBM experienced a bad firm specific return. The slope of the regression line is IBM's beta. A steeper line means IBM's return is more sensitive to the return on the overall market. For example, if IBM has a greater beta it has more market risk. A less steep line indicates a lower beta and less market risk.

Exhibit 12-4

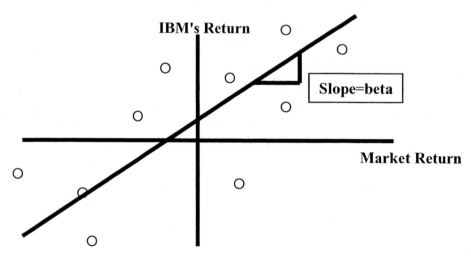

Calculation of IBM's Beta

12.5.3 CAPM and Portfolios

The term *portfolio* refers to the specific securities (stocks, bonds, mutual funds) owned by an investor. Just as each stock has a beta and a firm-specific component to its return, so each portfolio has a beta and what is called a portfolio specific return component.

Suppose you invest 40% of your money in IBM and 60% of your money in AT&T. The return on your portfolio can be written as:

$$R_{portfolio} = 0.40 * R_{ibm} + 0.60 * R_{att}$$

We say the portfolio return is a weighted average of the returns on IBM and AT&T. The weights are the fractions invested in each security. Since IBM and AT&T each have a beta and an FSR component to their returns, we could work out that the portfolio with 40% invested in IBM and 60% invested in AT&T, which also has a beta and an FSR, so that:

$$E(R_{portfolio}) = (R_f) + [(.4 * \beta_{ibm}) + (.6 * \beta_{att})] * [E(R_m) - (R_f)]$$
$$+ (.4 * FSR_{ibm} + .6 * FSR_{att})$$

The expression above is simpler than it looks. It just tells us that the portfolio's beta is a weighted average of the betas for IBM and AT&T; the FSR part for the portfolio is just a weighted average of FSRs for IBM and AT&T.

Suppose we change our portfolio by adding General Motors (GM) stock. We invest 40% of our money in IBM, 30% in AT&T, and 30% in GM. Then

$$E(R_{portfolio}) = (R_f) + [(.4 * \beta_{ibm}) + (.3 * \beta_{att}) + (.3 * \beta_{ge})] * [E(R_m) - (R_f)]$$
$$+ (.4 * FSR_{ibm} + .3 * FSR_{att} + .3 * FSR_{ge})$$

Even with three securities, the portfolio's beta is a weighted average of the individual betas for IBM, AT&T, and GM, and the portfolio's FSR is a weighted average of FSR(IBM), FSR(AT&T), and FSR(GM). Mutual funds, retirement funds, and other large portfolios may invest in the shares of several hundred companies. No matter how many companies are involved, each of these large portfolios has a beta and an FSR that are just weighted averages of the betas and FSR for the individual companies.

Our portfolio containing IBM, AT&T, and GM has *four* sources of uncertainty affecting the return for this portfolio. First, there is the market return, (R_m). The market return affects the return of every stock in the portfolio, and the effect of the market return for each stock depends on that stock's beta. Additionally, there are the three FSRs. Each FSR is caused by independent events that are specific to the individual firm, so the FSRs are not connected to one another in any way.

12.5.4 Beta, Firm Specific Returns, and Diversification

Suppose half of your money is in General Electric (GE) and half is in General motors (GM). Then your portfolio FSR is:

$$FSR_{portfolio} = 0.50 * FSR_{ge} + 0.50 * FSR_{gm}$$

Remember that the FSR of GE is just as likely to be positive as negative—the firm-specific news for GE is as likely to be good as it is to be bad no matter what the market return might be. The same is true for the FSR of GM. It's like tossing a coin twice to determine the FSR for the portfolio. There is some chance that one of the FSRs is positive and the other is negative so that they come close to canceling each other out.

This is the essence of *diversification*. A portfolio's firm specific return component can be made small by investing in a large number of companies.

Suppose you had the shares of 100 different firms in your portfolio. The FSR component of your portfolio will be practically insignificant. Think of 100 tosses of the coin to get the 100 FSRs that are in the portfolio. Your money is spread evenly among them, each of which is multiplied by 0.01. The number of FSRs that are positive will very likely be near 50, as will the number that are negative. The small return that remains after the positives and negatives cancel one another is multiplied by 0.01. This leads to the following belief that underlies modern portfolio theory:

> *Investors who hold large portfolios are NOT concerned about firm-specific return or risks. The process of **diversification** involves investing in enough firms that the FSRs of the individual companies tend to cancel out one another.*

A *well-diversified portfolio* is one whose FSR component is so small as to be insignificant. Suppose you select companies at random and spread your money equally across companies. How many companies do you need before your portfolio becomes well diversified? In the principle relating to diversification that we discussed in Chapter 2, we found that **Asset Diversification Will Reduce Risk**. We further discuss the benefits of diversification in Chapter 16. Academic studies have found that twenty unrelated stocks seem to be sufficient for a fairly well-diversified portfolio.

12.5.5 CAPM and Well-diversified Portfolios

Are well-diversified portfolios free of risk? Absolutely not! Diversified portfolios have reduced their unsystematic risk to close to zero, but still have market or systematic risk. CAPM and modern portfolio theory assume that Rational Investors Are Risk Averse (see Chapter 2) and assumes that all investors own a well-diversified portfolio. The CAPM equation looks as follows for a well-diversified portfolio:

$$E(R_{portfolio}) = (R_f) + \beta_{portfolio} * [E(R_m) - (R_f)] \qquad (Eq. 12\text{-}4)$$

What happened to the FSRs? By definition, a well-diversified portfolio has enough firms in it that the aggregate of the FSRs is virtually zero, so they drop out of the equation. There is only one source of uncertainty for a well-diversified portfolio, and that is uncertainty over the performance of the market in general.

Portfolios that are composed of high-risk stocks have a high beta and portfolios composed generally of low-risk stocks have a low beta. A high-risk portfolio has mostly high-beta companies, like the Pro Funds Ultra OTC Fund that we discussed earlier in this chapter, while a low-risk portfolio might be composed of mostly low-beta companies such as a utility fund.

Well-diversified portfolios are identical to one another except for their betas. They have no firm-specific risk. They simply follow the market, magnifying the market return if the portfolio beta is greater than one, and dampening the swings of the market if the portfolio beta is less than one.

Most money is invested in well-diversified portfolios, such as pension funds, mutual funds, and funds managed by financial institutions. When an individual investor considers a single stock such as IBM for her portfolio, the key question is how much additional risk that stock will contribute to the portfolio. We already saw that firm-specific risk disappears through the inclusion of a large number of companies in the portfolio. However, if IBM is added to the portfolio, IBM affects the portfolio's beta—which is a weighted average of all of the stocks in the portfolio. The sole contribution that one company makes to the risk of a well-diversified portfolio is through its beta. High beta companies make well-diversified portfolios more risky while low-beta companies lower the risk of a portfolio.

Here is another way to look at beta. Investors are attracted to investments that have their biggest payoff when financial conditions are bad. Insurance is a good example of this. People pay premiums for fire insurance that pay off when money is needed to rebuild a house. Life and health insurance contracts also pay off when money is needed. High beta stocks are just the opposite. They have their biggest payoff when the market is up, meaning their biggest payoffs come when investors already have lots of money. High beta stocks provide their biggest losses when the market is down and investors don't have as much money. Therefore, investors are only willing to buy high beta stocks when the price falls to the point where the expected return compensates them enough. Low beta stocks are more desirable in this regard and so investors are content to accept a lower expected return.

For any investment, beta is the relevant measure of risk.

12.6   The Risk and Return Trade-off

The standard example of a risk-free asset is the short-term Treasury bill. If you expect to own a T-bill to its maturity, the return on the T-bill is known with certainty at the time it is purchased and its return in no way depends on the market return. Therefore, T-Bills have a beta of zero.

Suppose you invested in the entire stock market. You could do this by putting a little of your money in the stock of each and every company. An easier way to do this is to invest in a stock index fund—a mutual fund that invests in all companies that make up a particular index. Some mutual funds invest in the stocks that make up the Wilshire 5,000, a stock index that tracks the performance of all United States stocks, or invests in the stocks in the S&P 500. Your index fund investment gives the same return as the return on the market so its beta is 1.0.

Suppose you want an investment with a beta of 0.75. One way to do this is to put 75% of your money in the overall stock market, and put the remaining 25% of your money in T-Bills. The beta of this portfolio is just a weighted average of the two individual investments or

$$R_{portfolio} = (0.25 * 0.00) + (0.75 * 1.00) = 0.75$$

You can have a portfolio with a beta equal to any number you prefer just by allocating your money between T-Bills and the overall market in the proper proportions.

Suppose the T-Bill rate is 4% (approximately the average for the 20th century) and the expected return on the overall market is 12% (approximately the average for the 20th century). Then you can have a portfolio with a beta equal to any number you want just by investing some money in T-Bills and some in the overall market as shown in Table 12-4 below:

Table 12-4
Expected Portfolio Returns

Beta	% in T-Bills	% in Market	Exp. Ret. Portfolio
0.00	100.00%	0.00%	4.00%
0.25	75.00%	25.00%	6.00%
0.50	50.00%	50.00%	8.00%
0.75	25.00%	75.00%	10.00%
1.00	0.00%	100.00%	12.00%
1.25	-25.00%	125.00%	14.00%

Note the following about Table 12-4:

- The portfolio beta is just a weighted average of the beta for T-Bills (that's 0) and the beta for the overall market (that's 1.0);
- The expected return is just a weighted average of the return for T-Bills and the expected return for the overall market;
- As the risk of the portfolio increases (remember that beta measures risk), the expected return increases.

What does it mean to invest (-25%) of your money in T-bills, as shown in Table 12-4? It means you borrow some money at 4% (actually shorting T-bills) and combining the borrowed money with your own to invest in the overall stock market. As an example, suppose you had $100 to invest in stocks. Let's assume that you borrow $25 at 4%, add it to the $100 that you have, and invest the entire $125 in the overall market. If the overall market returns 20% for the year, you have $150. However, you must pay back $25 plus $1—representing the interest on $25 @ 4%, so the $150 falls to $124. The return on your own $100 is 24%. The overall market returned 20% but through borrowing, you levered your return to 24%. Of course, borrowing to invest in the stock market won't look so good if the market falls.

The betas and expected returns can be used to construct a risk-return line. Beta is on the horizontal axis and expected return in on the vertical axis. Since beta is the only measure of risk, any and all investments should lie somewhere on this risk-return line.

The graph representing the CAPM is shown in Exhibit 12-5:

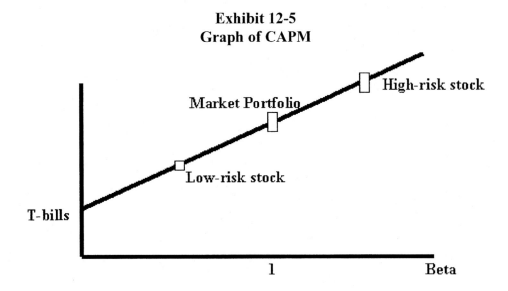

Exhibit 12-5
Graph of CAPM

12.7   Using CAPM to Evaluate Investment Performance

Suppose you want to evaluate the performance of a mutual fund or of investment advisors that manage pension fund money. One way might be to compare their average annual returns. However, some managers invest primarily in bonds and others in stock. Just because the managers picking stocks have higher average returns than those picking bonds doesn't mean they are better investment managers. Fund managers who invest in higher risk securities should be expected to earn higher average returns because of the increased risk. To properly evaluate investment performance, we must adjust for the risk associated with a portfolio.

As an example, let's suppose that during the past five years, a portfolio manager held a portfolio with an average beta of 0.50. This manager could easily hold a portfolio of this risk level by investing half of her money in T-Bills and the other half in the overall market without making even an attempt to decide which stocks are good investments and which stocks are bad investments. Did the manager do better picking stocks than she could have done by pursuing the no-brainer alternative strategy of holding a portfolio consisting of ½ T-Bills and ½ of an overall stock index fund.

- 413 -

Let's assume that Meredith managed a $2 billion portfolio over the past five years. The portfolio's beta was 0.50 and its average annual return was 15%. Over this same period of time, T-Bills averaged a 6% per year return and the overall market averaged a return of 18% a year. How did Meredith's performance compare with the markets?

Any investor could have split her money equally between T-Bills and a stock index fund and have earned an average portfolio return of:

$$Average\ return = (0.50 * 6\%) + (0.50 * 18\%) = 12\%$$

Another way to get that 12%, if we assume that the expected return on the market was also equal to the observed return of 12%, is to use the CAPM form of the equation to get:

$$E(R_{portfolio}) = (R_f) + ß_{portfolio} * [E(R_m) - (R_f)] \qquad (Eq.12\text{-}5)$$

$$E(R_{portfolio}) = 6\% + 0.5 * [18\% - 6\%] = 12\%$$

Meredith, for the same level of risk, earned an average return of 15%—so she outperformed our benchmark no-brainer strategy by 3%. This 3% is called the *alpha* of her performance. A positive alpha means an investor outperformed the returns expected under the CAPM benchmark, while a negative alpha means the investor performed worse than the returns expected under CAPM.

$$Alpha = Observed\ Return - Expected\ Return \qquad (Eq.12\text{-}6)$$

Exhibit 12-6
Measuring Investment Performance

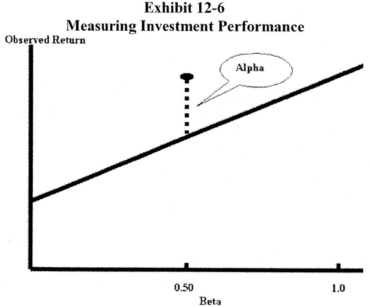

- 414 -

A positive alpha is the vertical distance above the risk-return line. For this problem, Meredith's $2 billion portfolio had a beta of 0.50 and an average return of 15%. Her return was 3% higher than the 12% return that was expected for a beta of 0.5 using the CAPM. Meredith had a positive alpha of 3%—a very strong performance. An investor who performs below the CAPM risk/return line has a negative alpha.

12.8 Summary

This chapter addresses the issues relating to what determines the required and expected rates of return associated with an asset or an investment. There is a direct trade-off between the expected rate of return on an asset and its risk. It's important that we all start on the same page when discuss expected returns and risk. We defined terms that relate to the calculation of returns on an asset and we tackled the thorny issue of understanding risk.

This chapter:

- Demonstrated the risk/return relationship;
- Showed that historic returns are consistent with that risk/return relationship;
- Defined and explained the capital asset pricing model;
- Defined the systematic and nonsystematic risk and how CAPM deals with them;
- Showed the benefits associated with diversification; and
- Used the risk/return relationship to calculate alpha and evaluate investment performance.

List of Terms

1. Ordinary Income
2. Realized Capital Gain
3. Unrealized Capital Gain
4. Long-Term Capital Gain
5. Short-Term Capital Gain
6. Expected Return on a Risky Asset
7. Expected Return on a Portfolio of Risky Assets
8. Expected Return on the Market
9. Return on the Risk-Free Asset
10. Market Risk Premium
11. Risk
12. Unsystematic Risk or Firm Specific Risk
13. Systematic Risk
14. Beta
15. Market Risk
16. Standard Deviation of Return
17. CAPM
18. Portfolio
19. Well-Diversified Portfolio
20. Performance Evaluation
21. Positive Alpha
22. Negative Alpha

Questions

1. What is the risk/return relationship?
2. How do you calculate annual return on your investment in a stock or in a bond?
3. Do you pay interest on the dividends earned for the stock or the interest received for the bonds that you are holding?
4. How do you define Expected Return on a Risky Asset and Expected Return on a Portfolio of Risky Assets?
5. What do we mean by Expected Return on the Market and Return on the Risk-Free Asset?
6. What are the two types of risk associated with a stock? How do you differentiate them?
7. How do you calculate Market Risk Premium and Standard Deviation of Return?
8. What is the reason that small company stocks have an average annual return of 12.5% compared to just 3.8% for Treasury bills?
9. What is the formula for CAPM and how does it take care of systematic and unsystematic risk of a stock?
10. What is a beta of a firm and that of a portfolio?
11. How does a well-diversified portfolio reduce the unsystematic risk to near zero?
12. How does the investment performance of a mutual fund or of an investment advisor evaluated? What is Positive Alpha and what is Negative Alpha?

Assignment #12-1:

1. Ted Turner bought Bank of America stock on 1st January at a price of $63 and sold it at $70 exactly after a year. In between he earned a dividend of $0.60 each quarter. What is his return on investment?
    (a) 11.11%
    (b) 14.67%
    (c) 13.20%
    (d) 3.80%

2. In the example above, did he make a capital gain or capital loss?

3. Jack Welch bought a bond at $980 and sold it at $950 after a year. He earned an interest of $30 in that year. How much profits or loss did he make?
    (a) 3.0%
    (b) 5.0%
    (c) -2.4%
    (d) 0.0%

4. Find the market risk premium for a stock which is expected to give a return on market of 10%. The beta of the stock is 1.0. [Hint: Use www.marketguide.com to find out the return on T-Bills]

5. Find out the Standard Deviation of Returns for a stock with annual returns of 3%, 5%, 9% and -7% over the last four years.

6. Consider a utility company stock with an annual return of 8% and a standard deviation of 10%. Assuming a normal distribution and two standard deviations, what can we expect as the maximum and minimum return on the stock?
    (a) 18% and 2%
    (b) 18% and -6%
    (c) 26% and -6%
    (d) 26% and 2%

7. Use CAPM model to find out expected return on the stock of Dell Computers for an expected return on market of 12%. [Hint: Get the value of beta for Dell and the value of Risk free rate of return for T-bills from www.marketguide.com or from www.finance.yahoo.com]

8. If a company has a beta of 1.5 and the expected return on market is 10%, what is the firm's expected return with firm specific risk equal to zero?
    (a) 15%
    (b) 11.5%
    (c) 5%
    (d) 25%

9. Use 3 yrs monthly data for IBM and the market return to plot a graph of market return versus that of IBM. Find the slope of the regression line to get beta of IBM.

10. You want to maintain a portfolio of stocks with IBM as 40%, Dell 40% and rest Microsoft. Use return on market as 12% and the firm specific rates of return as zero for all three firms and find out the rate of return of the portfolio.

11. You want to have a portfolio with a beta of 0.85. You have decided to invest partly in the S&P 500 index and the rest in T-bills. How much will you invest in Index and how much in T-Bills?
   (a) 85% and 15%
   (b) 15% and 85%
   (c) 50% and 50%
   (d) 70% and 30%

12. A top investment manager at Lehman Brothers managed a portfolio of over $5 billion and earned annual return of 15% (with a beta of 0.5 over last 3-year period). During that period, T-bills averaged 4.5% and the market averaged 16%. How did he perform compared to the market? Did he have a positive Alpha or negative Alpha?
   (a) Positive Alpha of 5.25%
   (b) Negative Alpha of 5.25%
   (c) Positive Alpha of 4.75%
   (d) Negative Alpha of 4.75%

CHAPTER 13

EFFICIENT CAPITAL MARKETS AND RANDOM WALKS

The focus of this chapter is on a basic principle that underlies modern portfolio theory—**Efficient Capital Markets are Tough to Beat**. We first discussed the existence of efficient capital markets in Chapter 2. If a market is efficient, all investments are properly priced and have a zero net present value, meaning that the cost or value of an investment is equal to its current price. In terms of the discussion relating to risk and return and the CAPM in Chapter 12, a market is efficient if the return and risk characteristics of all investments in that particular market lie on the risk-return line. This risk/return relationship is shown in Exhibit 13-1 below.

Exhibit 13-1
CAPM Graph

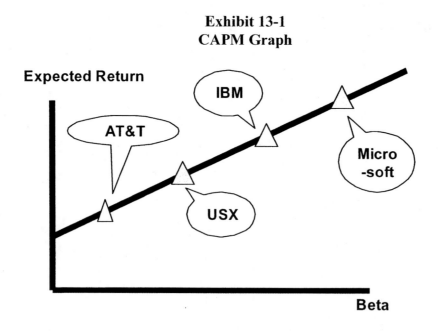

According to the CAPM graph, is Microsoft a better investment than AT&T? Not necessarily! An investor in Microsoft expects a higher rate of return than AT&T because Microsoft has a higher beta. But a higher beta means that Microsoft has more *risk* or volatility associated with owning it. The concept of an efficient market means that no investment is either a good investment or a bad investment. Every investment should be priced in such a manner that its expected return is consistent with its level of risk.

The objectives of the chapter are to:

- Understand how prices and returns of financial assets adjust quickly to new information;
- Understand the different forms of market efficiency;
- Examine the implications of market efficiency for investing in assets; and
- Discuss the results of research that shows that some trading rules seem to work to identify undervalued and overvalued assets.

13.1 What is an Efficient Capital Market?

13.1.1 Theory of Efficient Capital Markets

According to the theory of *efficient capital markets* (ECM), the stock market is brutally efficient. Current stock prices reflect all publicly available information, and stock prices adjust and react completely, correctly, and almost instantaneously to incorporate the receipt of new information.

- If the stock market is efficient, it would be useless to analyze patterns of past stock prices and trading volume to forecast future prices—which are what market technicians do in *technical analysis*.
- It also would be useless to analyze the economy, industries, and companies, and study financial statements in an effort to find stocks that are undervalued or overvalued—which are what most research analysts do in *fundamental analysis*.

Many of Wall Street's investment professionals think that the concept of efficient capital markets is just the musing of some ivory tower academicians and that the theory doesn't properly describe the real life action of the stock market. Many academics disagree and point to studies that support the notion that the stock market is efficient. The good news for Wall Street professionals is that some chinks exist in the armor of the proponents of efficient capital markets.

Efficient capital markets, along with the *random walk hypothesis* of stock prices and the *capital asset pricing model*, form the cornerstone of modern portfolio theory (*MPT*). The development and championing of efficient capital markets is identified closely with the finance faculty at the University of Chicago, particularly Dr. Eugene F. Fama. According to Professor Fama, an *efficient capital market* (ECM) is a market that efficiently processes information. Prices of securities fully reflect available information and are based on an accurate evaluation of all available information.

Let's look at the risk-return line shown in Exhibit 13-2 below. Is every stock on the risk-return line? No! In this example, IBM is assumed to be offering an abnormally high rate of return for its level of risk. Can this skewed relationship exist for a long period of time? In the real world, markets are so competitive that when IBM begins to offer an abnormal return due to its stock price being too low, smart market participants will buy

IBM shares. This excess demand for IBM shares will cause IBM's share price to rise immediately. As an investor pays more for an asset, the lower the return he will receive. Competition will drive IBM's share price to the correct price, at which point it will be at the level where it will reside again on the risk-return line. At that point IBM will offer the expected return for its level of risk, its particular beta.

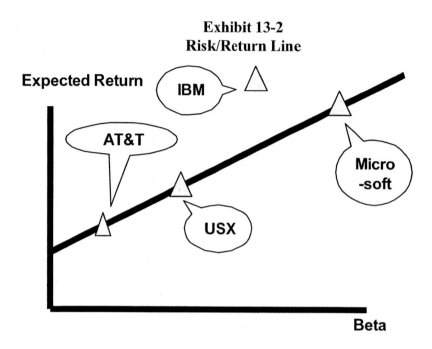

Exhibit 13-2
Risk/Return Line

13.1.2 What Causes Share Prices to Change?

According to efficient capital markets, the receipt of *new information* by the market causes stock prices to change. For example, let's assume that IBM is selling for $50 a share and IBM's CEO announces at 11:00 AM that IBM's earnings for the last quarter will be 10% higher than was previously expected. Obviously, IBM's stock price will rise with this good news because the estimated present value of IBM's profit and dividend streams are now higher. Because of this good news, let's assume that the true value of a share of IBM price goes from $50 to $60. How will IBM's stock price react to the news?

Below in Exhibit 13-3 is a hypothetical chart of IBM's share price for the day of the earnings announcement with two possible paths shown. The path labeled *immediate adjustment* shows what happens if IBM's share price reacts immediately to new information. If share price slowly reacts to the news, the line labeled *gradual adjustment* may be a reasonable picture of IBM's share price over time.

Exhibit 13-3
Stock Price Reaction to Information

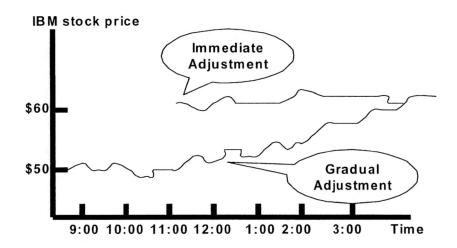

The immediate adjustment path describes how share price responds to news in an **efficient market**. If the price adjustment occurs gradually from 11:00 in the morning until about 3:30 in the afternoon, then IBM would have been a good investment for most of the day. If IBM was undervalued during that time (it was worth about $60 and was selling for less), then IBM was offering an unusually high rate of return. For example, if you buy at IBM @ $55/share and IBM goes to $60, that's a $5/$55 = .091 or 9.1% return over a period of just a few hours. Efficient markets do not allow that type of abnormally high return to persist. The price of IBM would adjust almost instantaneously and completely.

What will cause the next big change in IBM's share price? The market's receipt of the next important piece of news relating to the value of IBM's shares will cause the stock price to change. The next price-affecting event could be news of a new product, a lawsuit, higher than expected sales, lower than expected sales, or labor trouble at a factory. Price changes could also be caused by changes in broad economic variables such as interest rates, unemployment rates, war, peace, acts of terrorism, and other news.

Can we as investors predict the next bit of news? Not unless we're clairvoyant. Otherwise, it wouldn't be news. For example, suppose investors were expecting a 15% increase in sales and IBM announces a 15% increase in sales. Will that announcement have a big effect on IBM's share price? No! But if investors were expecting a 15% increase in revenue and IBM announced a 25% increase, IBM's share price would probably increase significantly. And if IBM announced a 5% increase in revenue when the market expected 15%, IBM's share price would drop like a stone.

13.1.3 What is a Random Walk?

A *random walk* is a path that a variable takes, such as the observed price of a stock, where the future direction of the path (up or down, right or left) can not be predicted solely on the basis of past movements. As far as the stock market is concerned, a random walk means that it is impossible to predict short-run changes in stock prices by looking at past price patterns and trading volume. In short, successive price changes are *independent* of each other, and the best estimate of tomorrow's stock price is today's stock price. In the long-run, research has found that most stock prices move in tandem with a stock's long-term growth of earnings and dividends. After adjusting for this growth trend, the random walk hypothesis assumes that the paths of stock prices are, in fact, *random*.

The odds associated with the movement of a variable that exhibits a random walk is similar to the results associated with a coin toss. If we assume that if the coin turns up heads, the price of a stock will increase. And if the coin comes up tails, the stock price will drop. If the price or the return of an asset follows a random walk, such as in the results of a coin toss, the previous price or return performance of the asset (the result of the coin toss) has no effect on the present or future price or return performance of the asset.

*In efficient capital markets, share price changes are **random**.* Share prices react immediately to news so that we don't have the predictable trend implied by a more gradual share price adjustment. Also, the next news event leading to the next immediate adjustment cannot be predicted. Therefore, in an efficient market, share price changes are random.

Even in efficient markets, you can get lucky and earn abnormally high returns. Using CAPM, suppose IBM's expected return is 16%. Let's assume you buy IBM and a week later IBM announces an unexpected sales increase for the last quarter and its price jumps immediately. Nobody expected this sales increase until the announcement by IBM, or else IBM's share price would have reflected this information. Lucky you! The firm-specific return from Chapter 12 worked in your favor here. Of course, the FSR could have just as likely been negative and reduced your returns also.

A summary of life in the ideal world of efficient markets and random walks:

- Share prices react almost immediately when investors receive new information. Therefore, buying or selling stock on the basis of news events will not produce superior returns (a positive *alpha* as described in Chapter 12).
- Since news events cannot be predicted in advance, stock price changes cannot be predicted in advance. Stock price changes are random.

13.2   Types of Market Efficiency

Empirical tests of stock market efficiency have examined whether stock prices reflect information about securities. Tests of market efficiency have may be classified into three categories:

- *Weak Form Efficiency: The information in past stock prices and trading*—The first category of testing is aimed at the *weak form* of the efficient market hypothesis to determine if trends exist in day-to-day stock price changes, or if daily stock price movements are independent. This is the well-known *Random Walk Hypothesis*.

- *Semi-Strong Form Efficiency: Public information and stock prices*—The second category of testing addresses the *semi-strong form* of the efficient market hypothesis to see whether stock prices reflect all publicly available information. One way this proposition has been assessed is to see how quickly public information disclosures, such as earnings reports or takeover announcements, are reflected in stock prices. Another method of evaluating public information and stock prices has been to examine whether future stock returns have been associated with available public information such as stock price to earnings (P/E) ratios.

- *Strong Form Efficiency: All information and stock prices*—The final category of testing addresses the *strong form* of the efficient market hypothesis. This involves assessing whether stock prices reflect even non-public information, information that is not yet available to the investment community. This would include information such as the trades of corporate managers and directors who clearly know more about a firm's prospects than the investing public.

If the stock market is efficient in pricing stocks, the implications are rather ominous for stock investors. If there are no trends in daily stock price movements and daily stock price changes are independent, then technical trading rules such as 200-day moving averages and point-and-figure charts are of no use to investors. If stock prices react so quickly to corporate news announcements that this information cannot be used to earn abnormal stock returns, then buying on news of good earnings or a takeover offer will not be beneficial to investors.

This also implies that the recommendations of stock market analysts who appear nightly on CNN and CNBC are likewise fruitless since their stock opinions are based on the same public information that other investors have. And finally, if the stock trades of corporate officers and directors do not yield abnormally good results, then we may presume that the stock market is exceptional in its ability to use information to price securities.

13.2.1 Weak Form Efficiency

Weak form efficiency means that stock prices reflect the information contained in the history of past stock prices and trading volume. This notion implies that daily stock price changes are independent and thus it is useless for investors to try to detect and exploit trends in stock prices. This is the random walk hypothesis, according to which stock prices are random and unpredictable.

Why might we expect stock prices to follow a random walk? One reason is that the stock market is full of knowledgeable and aggressive investors who attempt to find simple schemes to make money in the market. If a particular trend were to prove successful in predicting future prices, then other investors would attempt to exploit the scheme, which would be self-defeating, since such activity would cause stock prices to reflect the scheme, thereby eliminating the trend.

For example, consider the coin toss experiment highlighted in the well-known MBA corporate finance textbook by Richard Brealey and Stewart Meyers.[v] Consider the two graphs in Exhibit 13-4. One represents the movement of the S&P 500 over a sixty-month period and the other is the result of sixty repeated coin tosses where the index increases by 5% on a head and declines 4.5% on a tail. Which is the S&P 500? If you said the graph on the left is the S&P 500, you are correct. Nonetheless, it is not an obvious choice.

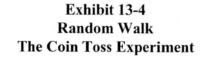

Exhibit 13-4
Random Walk
The Coin Toss Experiment

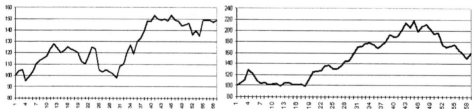

13.2.2 Semi-Strong Form Efficiency

Semi-strong form efficiency indicates that stock prices should reflect all publicly available information. This includes economic information such as inflation and GNP growth, industry information such as growth and prospects, and company-specific information such as the balance sheet and earnings, management, product/service prospects, and so on.

According to this proposition, stock prices react very, very quickly to new economic, industrial, and company disclosures. For example, suppose that Exxon announces that it has made a major oil find in China. Based on information in the report, stock analysts indicate that the oil find will add $10 to Exxon's stock price.

Exhibit 13-5 provides two alternative ways the stock price may adjust to the new information. According to Scenario 1, the price adjusts instantly to $80 and then goes back to a random walk. Under Scenario 2, the stock price adjusts to the new equilibrium price of $80 over a period of time, which allows investors to profit from buying at the announcement. In a semi-strong form efficient market, the stock price follows Scenario 1 and adjusts very quickly to the news announcement thereby prohibiting investors from earning abnormal returns.

Exhibit 13-5
The Reaction of Stock Prices to Public Information

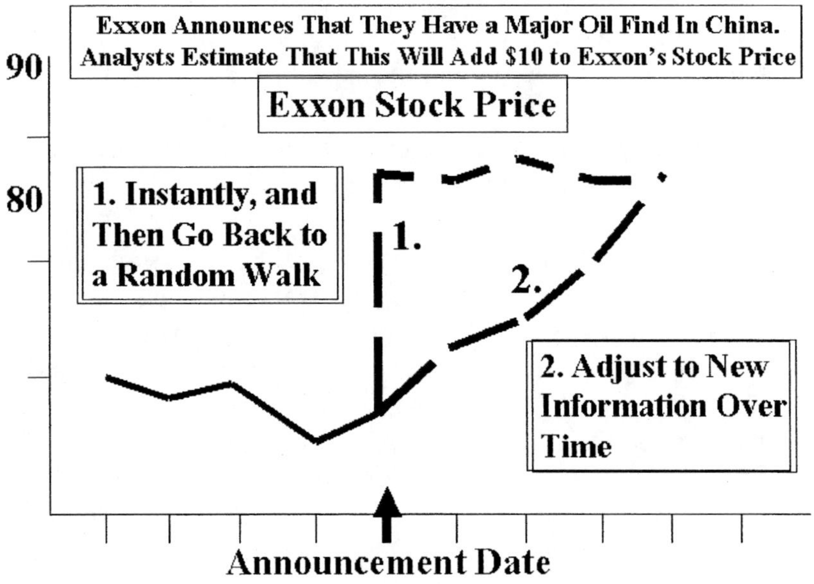

13.2.3 Strong-Form Efficiency

According to strong-form efficiency, stock prices reflect all information, including information not available to the investment community. This idea is usually tested by examining the returns earned by corporate managers and directors, who clearly have information not available to investors, on trades in their own company shares. While these corporate insiders are presumed to have a fiduciary responsibility to shareholders, their privileged position provides them with the potential to profit at shareholders' expense. As such, Rule 10b-5 of the Securities Exchange Act of 1934 limits the trading activities of corporate officials and directors in their own stock and requires these insiders to report all trades.

13.3   Tests of Market Efficiency

Hundreds of doctoral dissertations and academic papers are based on various event studies that test the efficient capital market hypothesis. The studies attempt to find exceptions, or anomalies, to the predictions associated with market efficiency. An *event study* examines the movement of stock prices for a certain number of days prior to an event, such as an earnings announcement, until a certain number of days after the event. The goal of an event study is to understand and capture any unusual stock price reaction to the event and to determine how quickly and completely the price of the stock reacts to the event. The stock returns typically are adjusted for the general movement of prices in the stock market.

The goal of many of the studies has been to find an investment strategy or trading rule that consistently produces investment returns, adjusted for risk, that are greater than the returns associated with a long-term buy-and-hold strategy for a diversified portfolio of stocks. A proxy for the buy and hold strategy is usually the return associated with a broad stock market index such as the S&P 500 Index.

Some of the studies have found that certain trading rules produced higher gross returns than a buy-and-hold strategy. However, when trading costs were incorporated into the study, the net returns declined and the excess returns vanished. Other studies found that a certain investment approach worked for a specific period of time and generated excess returns. However, once the strategy was touted and known to the general public, the excess returns disappeared. Too many intelligent investors hopped on the bandwagon. The excess profits were arbitraged away. The majority of studies have shown that new information is quickly incorporated into stock prices and the excess returns that are associated with certain stock selection strategies are arbitraged away. In market lore, there is empirical evidence that the stock market is relatively efficient, or at least semi-efficient.

A number of assumptions about investor behavior and the structure of capital markets underlie modern portfolio theory and the efficient capital market hypothesis. Investors are assumed to be rational and calculating, to have identical beliefs and expectations of how the market works, and to have equal access to new information. Investors are assumed to be intelligent and so well informed that the prices they establish, based on new information, are correct (equilibrium) prices.

13.3.1 Enter Behavioral Finance

In recent years the assumptions underlying MPT have been challenged by academicians who specialize in the field of behavioral finance, a branch of finance that examines human decision-making and behavioral patterns while interjecting sociology and psychology into the mix. Modern portfolio theory assumes rational, calculating, intelligent investors who focus on stock prices. Behavioral theorists have conducted studies that show that investors do not behave in that manner at all.

The 2002 Nobel Prize in Economics was awarded to behavioral finance specialists Dr. Daniel Kahneman, a professor of psychology at Princeton University, and Dr. Vernon Smith of George Mason University. Kahneman, in collaborating with the late Dr. Amos Tversky, challenged the assumption that consumers are rational and that markets behave rationally. He showed that individuals make errors in judgment, the direction and magnitude of which can be predicted with some accuracy. Dr. Smith in the late 1980s conducted mock stock market experiments with students and showed that stock markets were not efficient. He found that people and markets, at times, behave irrationally.

Today's active proponents of behavioral finance, notably Professors Richard Thaler, Robert Shiller, and Robert Haugen, have published studies and books[vi] that also call into question the assumptions of rational investor behavior that underlie efficient capital markets and modern portfolio theory. Their studies find the following:

- Investors hate to lose, which causes them to hold on to losing stocks much longer than they should.
- Investors often are ill informed and tend to overreact or under-react to new information.
- Investors love patterns (technical analysis is based on observing patterns in prices and trading volumes) and tend to find them even where they don't exist.
- They also find that investors are overconfident in their stock-picking abilities and tend to be overoptimistic. Overconfidence causes investors to think they are smarter than they are, and leads them to underestimate risk.

In short, they find that investors are human, exhibiting all of the associated flaws of humanity. Investors are not the cold, calculating, completely rational automatons that are assumed in MPT.

13.3.2 The Fama and French Study

One set of anomalies, however, has been identified as very promising in attacking modern portfolio theory. Ironically, Dr. Eugene F. Fama, the leading proponent of ECMs, and Dr. Kenneth R. French, another professor from the University of Chicago conducted this breakthrough research.[vii] The study was published in the June 1992 issue of the *Journal of Finance*, the world's most prestigious academic publication that specializes in the field of finance.

The study compares the performance of the returns associated with portfolios of stocks that have certain similar characteristics. For example, Fama and French grouped stocks by book value to market value ratios (BV/MV) and studied their return performance over time. They also grouped stocks by earnings to price (E/P) ratios, and by the size of their stock market capitalization.

The study showed, among other things, that portfolios of stock with a high book value (BE) to market value (ME) ratio consistently outperformed portfolios with low

(BE/ME) ratios. The study also found that stocks with high earnings to price ratios (low price to earnings ratios) consistently outperformed portfolios of stocks with low earnings to price ratios (high price to earnings ratios) and that stocks with small market capitalization outperformed stocks with large market capitalization. This study called to question the validity of efficient capital.

The F&F study examines monthly stock returns during the period from July 1963 until December 1990 and includes nearly all of the non-financial stocks traded on the New York Stock Exchange, American Stock Exchange, and NASDAQ. The portion of the study that examines (BE/ME) ratios was designed so that at the beginning of July stocks are divided into ten portfolios based on their (BE/ME) ratios. Portfolio 1 consists of the stocks with the lowest (BE/ME) ratios, portfolio 2, 3, 4...9 consist of groups of stocks with increasing (BE/ME) ratios, with portfolio 10 consisting of the stocks with the highest (BE/ME) ratios.

The monthly returns for each of the ten portfolios were measured over a twelve-month period. The following July, each stock's (BE/ME) ratio was recomputed and stocks were reassigned to the ten portfolios based on their new (BE/ME) ratios, ranging from lowest to highest. Depending on their relative return performance, stocks moved from one portfolio to another. The returns for the portfolios were again measured over the ensuing twelve months. The return calculation and sorting process occurred again and again over the 26-year period, and an average return of each of the 10 portfolios was computed. Fama and French further subdivided portfolios 1 and 10 into two portfolios each, resulting in a total of twelve portfolios. Table 13-1 presents a summary of their findings:

Table 13-1
1992 Fama and French Stock Return Study
Portfolios Based on Ascending Book Equity/Market Equity Ratios

Portfolio	Monthly Return	Annualized Return	Avg. Number of Stocks	Weighted Avg.Return	Difference in Return
1A	0.30%	3.60%	89	14.99%	-11.39%
1B	0.67%	8.04%	98	14.99%	-6.95%
2	0.87%	10.44%	209	14.99%	-4.55%
3	0.97%	11.64%	222	14.99%	-3.35%
4	1.04%	12.48%	226	14.99%	-2.51%
5	1.17%	14.04%	230	14.99%	-0.95%
6	1.30%	15.60%	235	14.99%	0.61%
7	1.44%	17.28%	237	14.99%	2.29%
8	1.50%	18.00%	239	14.99%	3.01%
9	1.59%	19.08%	239	14.99%	4.09%
10A	1.92%	23.04%	120	14.99%	8.05%
10B	1.83%	21.96%	117	14.99%	6.97%
			2261		

Exhibit 13-6
Fama-French Study

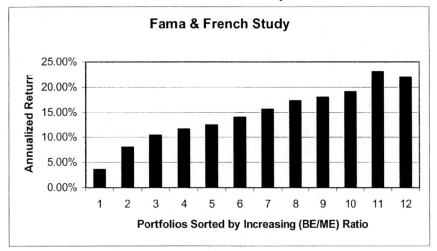

The results of the study are significant. The efficient capital market hypothesis predicts that the returns of each of the portfolios should be about equal to the average stock return in the sample, approximately 15%. This certainly is not the case when the size of (BE/ME) ratios acts as the basis for the formulation of portfolios. As we move from portfolios with stocks that have lower (BE/ME) ratios to higher (BE/ME) ratios, we observe an almost uniform increase in monthly and annualized returns. The investment strategy that purchased stocks with the highest (BE/ME) ratios had a return that exceeded the average annualized return (14.99%) of the 2,261 stocks in the study by approximately 7% per year—a huge number. The strategy of buying the stocks with the highest BE/ME ratio had a return that exceeded the average return of stocks in the lowest (BE/ME) portfolio by almost 20% per year.

The F&F study also examined the relationship between earnings/price ratios and found a similar result. Portfolios of stocks that have high E/P ratios (low P/E ratios) had consistently higher actual returns than portfolios of stocks with low E/P ratios (high P/E ratios).

Other researchers have conducted studies based upon the F&F study with roughly the same results. In 1997, Fama & French studied stocks that were traded in thirteen international stock markets and found similar results. Stocks with high (BE/ME) ratios significantly out performed stocks with lower ratios in twelve of the international markets. The Italian stock market was the lone exception.

13.3.3 Less Technical Evidence from the Real World

Much evidence indicates that absent the effect of the few anomalies discussed above, stock price changes are independent. We often say that stock prices follow a random walk. This means that the next price change is completely unrelated to the sequence of past price changes. What's this mean in the real world?

If IBM stock rose 55% over the past six months, is it time to sell IBM stock? Not necessarily. According to the random walk hypothesis, IBM's next share price change is unrelated to its past price changes. The fact that IBM rose substantially over the past six months is not relevant to IBM's next change in share price. This is the theory. Some investors might argue that a 55% run-up in share price is likely to be the result of overvaluation, and the price of IBM is more likely to drop in the future.

Most evidence indicates stock prices react immediately to news announcements. For example, ShowBiz Pizza announced at 11:00 A.M. that same-store sales were down substantially for the last quarter. By 11:15 A.M., their stock price had fallen from nearly $30 per share to around $20. Very few investors were fast enough to avoid this loss by selling their shares at $30. To sell their shares, these investors needed to find people willing to buy at $30. There weren't many buyers, especially after the sales announcement.

If Apple Computer announces that it believes next year's sales will be up 45%, does this make Apple a good buy for investors? Not necessarily! The evidence is that Apple's share price will rise immediately to reflect this higher level of expected sales. Perhaps a few investors who sit beside their computer terminals waiting for big news announcements might be able to buy Apple shares before the price run-up. For them, Apple is a good investment but very few buy orders will be executed before the price of Apple rises to reflect this new information. After all, each buyer needs to find a seller, and there will not be many sellers who will transact at the price in the market that existed before the release of favorable news about sales. If investors believe the announcement, the average investor will not be able to trade Apple to capitalize on this information.

Evidence From Mutual Funds:

Let's look at how mutual funds have performed in the market. Mutual funds are managed by finance professionals who focus their efforts to out perform the market. We can look at the performance of about 10,000 mutual funds over the past twenty years or so.

The following definitions relate to the performance of mutual funds:

- *Gross Return*—the return a fund earns on its investments before fees are subtracted;
- *Net Return*—the return a fund earns after subtracting all fees from the gross return.

We want to know if professional managers of mutual funds are good investors that earn high returns on their investments. If we calculate the alpha for each mutual fund using gross returns, we can get some idea of how they perform. For a given risk measure (beta) of a fund, alpha measures the performance of the return of a fund by the distance above or below the expected return as captured by the CAPM risk-return line. Studies indicate that about half of the funds have positive alphas, base on gross returns, and about half of the funds have negative alphas over most time periods (e.g., see Malkiel, J., in *Finance*, June 1995). One way to interpret this is that on average, mutual funds do no better than to lie on the risk-return line.

Half of the observations of gross returns plot above the line and half plot below, which could mean that some fund managers are lucky and some are unlucky. In efficient markets, we would expect the observations to plot on the risk-return line, and returns would only be above the line due to good luck or below the line due to bad luck. When a large number of mutual fund managers are evaluated, we would expect half of them to have good luck and half of them to have bad luck. We did not observe 70% of mutual fund managers above the line and 30% below. The split is close to 50-50, which would be expected if luck is used to explain these alphas.

Those who choose not to believe in efficient markets might argue that the funds that plot above the risk-return line, funds that have positive alphas, are run by good investment managers who really know how to pick good stocks. However, studies indicate that if we pick some time period (say 1980-1985) and identify those funds that had positive alphas over that time period, those funds will have an average alpha of zero over the next five-year period. This result is more in line with luck than with good investment skills. The idea is that no group of managers consistently shows abnormally good investment returns. When an investor is lucky once, she is no more likely to do well the next time than to do poorly the next time.

Let's assume markets are efficient. If a mutual fund has done well over the past five years (experienced a positive alpha), what would you expect that mutual fund's alpha on the basis of gross returns to be over the next five years? Zero! In efficient markets, we always expect an alpha of zero regardless of past performance.

Mutual fund customers receive the net return, not the gross return. If mutual funds offer an average alpha of zero when gross returns are used, what is their average alpha when net returns are used? Net returns are smaller than gross returns since fees are deducted to arrive at net returns. Therefore, the average alpha using net returns will be negative (approximately equal to the average fees).

If markets are efficient, what strategy will allow a mutual fund customer to earn (on average) the highest alpha? Chose the funds with the lowest fees since alpha will, on average, be zero before fees are deducted. There are other considerations, of course, including the risk level of the fund. If the fund is well diversified (has no firm-specific event risk), then the beta of the fund is one measure of the risk the investor is exposed to.

Evidence on Individual Investors:

Brad Barber and Terrance Odean, two professors of finance from the University of California at Davis, studied the investment performance for 60,000 individual and household accounts at a major discount brokerage firm. The time period was February of 1991 through December of 1996. Over this period of time, the average stock return was 17.1% a year (the overall stock market averaged 17.1% a year). For those 60,000 accounts, the average gross return was 17.7% a year. If the stock market is efficient, you would guess that the average beta for the stocks held in these 60,000 accounts was slightly higher than the beta of the overall market, which happens to be 1.0. These 60,000 accounts, on average, tended to be invested more in higher beta stocks, and their average beta is slightly above 1.0.

Professors Barber and Odean looked at the effect of trading costs on investment performance. For example: Suppose you have $10,000 in your account with a discount broker and the standard charge is $15 a trade. If you have 100 shares of McDonald's and you want to sell those shares and buy 100 shares of Cisco, you would be charged for two trades. The first trade is when you sell McDonald's shares, and the second is when you buy Cisco shares. Selling shares of one company and then buying shares of another company is called a *round-trip* in the vernacular of the stock market. With your $10,000 account, suppose you make six round-trips in one year. What is the affect of trading fees on your annual return? Each round-trip is two trades costing $30, so six round-trips will cost $180. That $180 is 1.8% of your initial account balance. Therefore, trading fees would have lowered your annual return by 1.8%. That's a significant percentage, even when transacting at a discount broker.

Professors Barber and Odean divided those 60,000 households into five groups of 12,000 each, based on how many trades were made. Group 1 had the most trades, then came Groups 2, 3, 4, and 5. How do you think these groups compared based on the average annual gross return for each group? We would expect all groups to lie on or near the risk-return line. If the groups invested in stocks of similar risk, the groups should have average returns that are about the same. That is what was observed for these five groups.

How about net returns? Referring to the five groups ranked on number of trades, how did their net returns compare? The answer is shown in the small Table 13-2 that follows.

Table 13-2

	Average Annual Net Return
Stock Market	**17.1%**
Avg. Account	**15.3%**
Group 1 Result	**10.0%**

Professors Barber and Odean found evidence that trading costs negatively and significantly affect the returns of market participants. The most frequent traders had the highest trading costs and the lowest net return. The results of this study reinforce the principle that we discussed in Chapter 2 relating to minimizing the cost of investing—**Transaction Costs, Taxes and Inflation are your Enemies**. Reduce transactions costs to the lowest level possible!

13.4   Summary

This chapter introduces you to the concept of market efficiency. The chapter also provides evidence that in the real world, markets are mostly efficient. However, reality never is quite so simple. Finance academicians, such as Fama and French, have uncovered evidence on a number of fronts that contradict the notion of completely efficient markets. Stock price changes are not quite random, accounting ratios may provide some modest help in predicting stock price changes, corporate insiders seem to be able to predict changes in the prices of their companies' shares using publicly available information, and finance professionals sometimes exploit their instantaneous access to new information in ways that produce high returns. Nevertheless, many believe that most investors will benefit from acting as if markets are efficient. It is very difficult for any investor to systematically earn abnormally high returns.

If markets are efficient, what types of stocks are currently good investments that will generate abnormally high returns? None of them! All investments lie on the CAPM risk-return line, so you should make your choices based on the amount of risk you can bear. Which stocks are currently bad investments? Same answer. All investments lie on the risk-return line so you should make your choices based on the amount of risk you desire.

Another question that we frequently hear is, how can an investor identify good mutual funds? Since it is unlikely that any fund can consistently produce consistent *gross* returns that are above the CAPM risk-return line, the best approach is to find a well-diversified fund that matches your preferred risk level and *charges low fees*. An alternative is to invest some of your money in a low-fee index fund and place some of your money in a low-risk money market fund. You control your risk level by the proportions you chose to invest in each.

What is a good wealth-building strategy? If markets are efficient, there are neither good nor bad investments. Pick a risk level with which you are comfortable, and try to reduce your transaction costs to the lowest amount possible.

How about some questions relating to corporate finance? If the capital market is efficient, when is good time for a firm to sell new shares? In an efficient market a firm's shares are always properly priced. Therefore, it makes no sense to try to sell shares when they are overvalued. Should one firm acquire another because it believes that the shares are undervalued? In an efficient capital market, No! Don't acquire a firm for that reason. In efficient markets, a firm sells for exactly what it is worth.

List of Terms

1. Efficient Capital Markets
2. Random Walk Hypothesis
3. CAPM
4. Modern Portfolio Theory
5. Risk/Return Line
6. Immediate Adjustment
7. Gradual Adjustment
8. Abnormally High Returns
9. Weak Form of Efficient Market
10. Semi-Strong Form of Efficient Market
11. Strong Form of Efficient Market
12. Gross Return
13. Net Return

Questions

1. What is an efficient capital market?
2. What are the implications of efficient market in terms of the risk and return characteristics of an investment?
3. What are the three things that you would need to know to understand *Modern Portfolio Theory (MPT)?*
4. How does (or how quickly does) the market react to new information in the case of a) an efficient market and b) an inefficient market?
5. What is a *random walk* in relation to stock price? What do we mean by successive price changes are *independent*?
6. What are the underlying assumptions of the weak form of efficient markets?
7. What are the underlying assumptions of the semi-strong form of efficient markets?
8. What are the underlying assumptions of the strong form of efficient markets?
9. In efficient market is it possible to earn abnormally high returns under any circumstances?
10. How does an event study examine market efficiency?
11. What are the main aspects and results of the F&F study?
12. What is the difference between gross returns and net returns? How does the trading cost affect the net returns and the investment performance in general?

Assignment #13-1:

1. If I have two stocks; one (stock A) with a return of 8% and the other (stock B) with a return of 12%, can I say that the stock B is a better investment?

2. Theory of efficient capital markets claims that the market reflects new information immediately. Look at the market fluctuation in indices on 09/11/01 when the disaster of WTC happened. Did the market crash immediately after the attack?

3. How would the market react to better than expected annual or quarterly results of any company? Would the price (given no other factors exist to affect the market)
   (a) Go up
   (b) Go down
   (c) Wouldn't move
   (d) Can't say

4. According to the weak form of efficiency theory, stock price changes are random and don't follow a pattern. Look at the historical prices of Bank of America stock and see if you can find any pattern in the price changes.

5. Do you think that if a company declares its dividends more than expected, there will be an immediate rise in its share price? If yes, why and if no, why? Can you site any recent example?

6. Corporations and managers are not allowed to use insider information. Do you know of any real time example where the managers are being questioned by SEC for insider trading?

7. Look at two groups of stocks; one with a high BV to MV ratio and the other with a lower BV/MV ratio. Look at their past performance and see which group performed better.

8. Repeat the procedure above for two different groups, this time with earnings to price as the grouping mechanism.

9. Repeat the procedure above for two different groups, this time with market capitalization as the grouping mechanism.

10. Take a mutual fund and look at its gross return. Compare this return with net return. The difference will tell us the impact of an increase in the number of transactions and the increase in fees.

CHAPTER 14

BOND VALUATION AND INTEREST RATES

In this chapter we delve more deeply into understanding bonds—a financial contract issued by the U.S. Government, corporations, municipalities, agencies, or other entities. Bonds are debt securities that are sold to investors in order to raise long-term funds for the issuer. A bond is a contract in which the issuer borrows money from investors and promises to make periodic payments of interest, and repay the principal amount of the debt when the bond matures.

In Chapter 9, we introduced you to a simple way to value a bond by using a present value example. In this chapter we examine different types of bonds, the risks associated with bonds, how bonds are traded in the market, how to value a bond, and the effect of interest rates on bond valuation.

The learning objectives for this chapter include an understanding of:

- Bonds—their structure and risks;
- How bonds are issued in the primary market and traded in the secondary markets;
- How to value a bond;
- Interest rates and how interest rates affect bond valuation.

14.1   Bonds—In General

A bond is a debt financial contract under which the issuer is obligated to make periodic interest payments and repay the principal at some predetermined time. Common terms for securities that are classified as debt include: bonds, debentures, loans, commercial paper, secured debt, unsecured debt, promissory notes, senior-lien bonds, junior-lien bonds, etc.

There are many different types of bonds. The most common type of bond has a fixed interest rate (a fixed-coupon bond) and a known maturity. Other bonds have interest payments that change or float based on some type of economic factor or interest rate index. Other bonds pay little or no interest prior to maturity, and are sold at a discount to their principal payment at maturity. We describe all of these types of bonds and how to value them in the following sections.

14.1.1 Terms of the Bond Issue

Bonds are issued under a financing document known as an *indenture*, which is the legal agreement between the issuer (a corporation, government, agency or municipality) of the bond and an entity or trustee that represents the investors that own the bonds. Usually, a major commercial bank acts as the trustee under the indenture. The trustee monitors the terms of the bond, determines whether the issuer is in violation of any of the legal agreements of the indenture, and collects the interest and principal payments from the issuer, and distributes those payments to investors.

The indenture determines the terms of the transaction and the structure of the bond. A bond has what is known as a *principal value*, *par amount* or *maturity value*, which is the amount that is repaid when the bond matures and the principal payment is due. Various types of bonds are issued with different principal amounts. Corporate and government bonds usually are issued with maturities of $1,000 denominations. Municipal bonds usually are issued with maturities of $5,000 denominations. Some types of bonds have maturities of $100,000 or even $1,000,000 denominations. Associated with the principal amount is the periodic payment of interest on the amount borrowed. We describe the different types of interest payments and structures below.

The terms of the indenture specify the security associated with the bond issue—the monies that the issuer pledges to pay the interest and principal on the bonds, how the investors will be protected, and what rights the investors will have if the issuer fails to make scheduled payments on the bonds. The indenture also specifies if the issuer has a right to repay the principal of the bonds prior to their specified maturity date. This prepayment or call right is a valuable option and is described later in this chapter.

14.1.2 Structure of Interest Payments on Bonds

The mechanism by which interest rates and payments are set can sometimes be complicated and cause confusion for investors. In this section we describe the different types of interest rate setting structures and how these structures affect the value of a bond. The *interest rate* or *coupon rate* on a bond is the annual interest, expressed on a percentage basis, which accrues or is paid by the issuer to the owner of the bond.

Fixed-Rate Structures:

Fixed-rate or fixed-coupon bonds with interest payments every six months are the most common type of bonds that are issued and traded in the United States bond markets. The interest rates and payments are fixed over the life of the bond and the payments do not change. Fixed-rate bonds may be issued at face value or par value—when the coupon rate is equal to the offering yield on the bonds, at a discount to face value, or at a premium to face value.

The *fixed-rate par bond* is the most popular and most often-used form in which bonds are issued in the primary market. The issuer, along with its investment banker, determines the interest rate (for example, 6%) associated with the credit quality (for example, a AAA-rated bond) and maturity (for example, 30 years) of the bond that results in a market value of 100%, or par value, at the time of the marketing of the bond. In this case the issuer, through the investment bankers, offers 6% bonds to investors at a price of 100% and the issuer receives 100% less the underwriting discount. The issuer pays the annual coupon of 6 percent (3 percent paid every six months) on predetermined semi-annual interest payment dates (for example, April 1 and October 1). At the maturity date of the bond (for example, October 1, 2035) the issuer pays the maturity amount of 100% of par value, plus the final semi-annual interest payment.

The *fixed-rate discount bond* is another popular bond in the market, particularly in the municipal bond market. In a discount offering the issuer will market a bond through its investment bankers to investors with a coupon and interest rate (for example, a 4% coupon rate) that creates a market value of less than 100% at the time of pricing, and an offering yield (for example, a 6% market environment) that is higher than the coupon rate. We discuss how to value discount bonds in Section 14.5 below. An extreme example of a discount bond is a zero-coupon bond. These deeply discounted bonds are offered with no current interest payment—the current coupon is 0 percent. The value of a zero-coupon bond is simply the discounted present value of the maturity value of the bond, as we show in Section 14.5.

Finally, a *fixed-rate premium bond* is another way to market bonds to investors. In a premium offering, the issuer will market a bond through its investment bankers with a coupon and interest rate (for example, an 8% coupon rate) that creates a market value of more than 100% at the time of pricing, and an offering yield (for example, in a 6% market environment) that is higher than the coupon rate. We also value a premium bond in Section 14.5.

Floating Rate Structures:

Floating interest rate structures take advantage of the upward sloping nature of the yield curve, which we discuss later in this chapter. Initially, interest rate setting mechanisms for floating rate bonds were based upon some interest rate index or level of a risk free security such as Treasury bills or long-term Treasury bonds. Over the years, rate setting mechanisms using remarketing agents or the use of a periodic auction rate-setting system have been developed that are designed to create a bond that always trades at or near par value. The benefit of floating rate bonds is that, historically, the interest rates that investors accept for these types of bonds has generally been significantly lower than the rates on fixed-coupon bonds.

The bad news for issuers of floating rate bonds is that the interest rate associated with the bonds increases as interest rates in the bond market increases. This means that the issuer retains the *interest rate risk* inherent in a bond issue. We discuss interest rate risk along with other risks associated with bonds in Section 14.3.

14.1.3 Security for Bond Issues

Bond investors are very concerned about the source of repayment of their interest and principal and the collateral that is pledged to secure those payments. The sources of security on a bond issue will affect the credit rating and creditworthiness of the issue. Let's examine the security and repayment sources associated with different bond issues.

Securities that are issued by the U.S. Government are usually deemed to be *risk-free* because they are assumed to have no credit risk. This means that investors believe that the U.S. Treasury will not default on its obligations. The security underlying U.S. Government bonds is the power to levy taxes, to borrow additional money, and to print money in order to pay obligations.

Municipal bonds by way of default ratios are the next most secure class of bonds. Municipal bonds, issued by cities, states, municipalities, and their agencies, may be secured in a variety of ways:

- General obligation bonds are secured by the issuer's taxing power, which may be limited or unlimited, and other revenues of the issuer.
- Revenue bonds are payable principally from revenues generated by the facility or system constructed with the proceeds of the bonds.
- Additionally, municipal bonds often are secured by credit enhancement devices, such as municipal bond insurance and commercial bank letters of credit.

Examples of revenue bonds and their primary security sources are:

- Gas and electric revenue bonds—user charges.
- Bridges, tunnel, and turnpike revenue bonds—toll collections, gas taxes, and driving-related fees.
- Airport revenue bonds—landing fees, terminal rentals, and concession fees.
- Mortgage revenue bonds—mortgages and mortgage-loan repayments.
- Hospital revenue bonds—patient payments, third-party commercial payers, and federal and state reimbursement programs.
- Resource recovery bonds—garbage and tipping fees, revenues from sales of scrap, electricity, or steam.
- Sewer and water revenue bonds—user charges.

Corporate bonds are more likely to default than Treasury or municipal bonds. Whereas the U.S. Treasury and municipalities have taxing power and the ability to control the delivery and pricing of essential services, such as water and sewer, trash collection and electric power, corporations are at the mercy of the marketplace.

The source of security for corporate bonds most often is an unsecured promise by the corporation to pay its debts. When a corporation issues debt, often it makes promises or *covenants* that are specified in the indenture for it to perform certain actions or prohibit it from certain activities. For example, the corporation may promise to maintain assets in good condition; or maintain a minimum ratio of working capital; and provide audited and independent financial statements to bondholders. The firm may not be able to merge with another firm, issue additional debt, limit the amount of dividends that it pays to shareholders, or pledge its assets and cash flows in a senior position to other lenders. Sometimes the obligation to pay debt service on the bonds will be secured by collateral or a mortgage on a particular property or piece of equipment.

Asset-backed debt is another type of debt that is marketed and traded in the bond market. The assets backing this type of debt can be a portfolio of mortgages on single-family homes, or a portfolio of car loans, or a portfolio of consumer loans or credit card loans. These securities are created by a sponsor, usually a large financial institution which has originated the loans and is responsible for monitoring and servicing the loans. The sponsor structures the financing, usually purchases credit enhancement in the way of insurance or a letter of credit, and markets asset-backed debt to sophisticated investors. Most of the time these transactions have very strong security features and are rated in the highest rating category by the bond rating agencies. We discuss bond ratings in Section 14.2.

14.1.4 Optional Redemption

In many bond issues, the issuer reserves the option (the *call option*) to redeem bonds prior to their stated maturity, at a predetermined price above par value. The amount that the call price is above the par value is the *call premium*. The call option can be exercised on or after a predetermined date—usually at least five to ten years from the date of the original issuance of the bonds.

The call option has a quantifiable cost to the issuer, which is paid in the form of a higher interest rate or yield. *Investors will require a higher yield on callable bonds than on otherwise comparable non-callable bonds*. The optimal time for an issuer to exercise the call option is when it becomes financially desirable to do so—when interest rates drop and the issuer can refinance at a lower rate. Therefore, an investor that owns a callable bond is subject to considerable uncertainty about the cash flows on its callable bonds. This uncertainty exacts a price that is measured by higher required yields.

Included in the issuance of many asset-backed securities and municipal bond issues are unusual mandatory or extraordinary call features that are the result of circumstances that are beyond the control of the issuer. This cuts short the life of the cash flows and can reduce the value of a bond. The most complex extraordinary redemption provisions are associated with pooled asset-backed revenue bonds, such as mortgage revenue bonds or student loan bonds. These issues have a number of mandatory redemption features such as: unexpended proceeds, prepayments, excess revenues, mortgage defaults and foreclosure, etc. These features make valuations of these types of bonds very difficult because of the uncertainty of when the cash flows will be received.

14.2 Bonds and Risk

There are four types of risk involved when you invest in fixed-rate or fixed-coupon debt obligations:

- *Default risk*—the risk that the bond will not pay interest or principal when due;
- *Reinvestment risk*—the unknown rate at which cash inflows may be reinvested;
- *Prepayment risk*—when an issuer calls a bond prior to its maturity; and
- *Interest rate risk*—the risk that a change in market interest rates will adversely affect the value of the bond.

We describe each of these risks in the sections below. As we have discussed in Chapter 2, there is a trade-off between risk and return in the bond market, just as there is that trade-off in the stock market. **Higher Returns Require Taking More Risk.** To the extent that you reduce or eliminate risks, you probably will reduce your overall returns. Your reward will be lower risk and less price and return volatility.

14.2.1 Default Risk and Bond Ratings

Companies issue corporate bonds to finance their working and fixed capital needs. Asset-backed bonds are issued to finance a portfolio of less liquid primary securities such as home mortgages, student loans, or credit card receivables. These bonds typically are initially issued as fixed-rate par bonds and have maturities of anywhere from five to thirty years.

All taxable fixed-rate debt that is issued or traded in the United States capital markets is priced at what is called a *spread to Treasuries*. Because Treasuries bonds are risk-free, are free from state income taxes, and are actively traded in the capital market and very liquid, all other types of taxable debt has a higher yield (effective interest cost) than the yield associated with comparable maturity U.S. Treasury Bonds. The spread to Treasuries measures the difference in current yields. This spread will change over time, depending on economic conditions and the relative default risk associated with the specific debt security.

The interest rate, or *yield*, of all debt is vitally dependent on the risk-free rate associated with the comparable maturity U.S. Treasury debt. For example, the 10-year Treasury rate is the risk-free rate that we use as our starting point for the calculation associated with finding the weighted average cost of capital for a company.

The spread to Treasuries is the *measure of default risk* on an asset-backed transaction or a specific company's debt. For a large company with little operating risk and low financial leverage (low percentage of debt in the company's market capitalization), the spread to Treasuries might be quite small (0.75% to 1.0%). For companies with considerable operating risk or high leverage, the spread to Treasuries might be quite large (5.0% to 9.0%).

Corporate bonds trade at a spread to U.S. Treasury securities that is dependent upon the default risk and *rating* of the bond issue. Three rating agencies—Moody's Investors Services, Standard & Poor's Corporation, and Fitch Ratings, Ltd.—specialize in rating the default risk and credit worthiness of a bond issue and of general default risk of corporate, municipal, and even sovereign government issuers. Corporate issuers pay standard fees to the rating agencies to have the agencies independently analyze the default risk associated with a bond issue. The agencies then assign the issue with a default risk rating that ranges from the equivalent of AAA, the highest grade with only a very remote chance of default, down to CCC, the lowest grade and currently in default. The ratings have significant bearing on what the required yield is on a bond when it sells in the bond market. For example, a 10-year corporate bond that is rated AAA, may trade at a rate of 1.5% above the rate of the 10-year Treasury bond. And a 10-year BBB rated bond may trade at a rate of 3.5% above the 10-year Treasury bond.

Many financial institutions, such as mutual funds, are restricted from investing in bonds that are rated by the rating agencies at a level lower than *investment grade*. The market generally defines investment grade to be at a level of BBB-, or higher. Once a bond falls to a rating level below BBB-, far fewer investors may buy the bond and the offering yield increases significantly.

Beyond the general corporate credit risk rating is the risk classification specific to a particular bond issue of the company. *Senior debt* is usually the most secure debt issued by a company. The level of seniority is used to determine claims on assets in the event of the liquidation of the firm. If a company is healthy, the level of seniority is not very important other than to determine the level of risk associated with the bond, hence its spread to Treasuries. However, in the event of liquidation in bankruptcy, the most senior debt is paid first and whatever is left over is distributed to the rest of the debt holders. *Subordinated debt* is debt that follows senior debt in line for claims on cash flows and assets upon liquidation. Theoretically, all senior debt is paid off prior to any proceeds going to subordinate debt holders. This junior claim on assets makes subordinated debt more risky than senior debt, meaning that investors will demand a higher interest rate for subordinated debt.

14.2.2 Reinvestment Risk

Reinvestment risk arises from the periodic interest payments associated with fixed-rate bonds. Since payments are received over the life of a current interest bond, an investor faces the risk of reinvesting interest payments at uncertain future interest rates that may be lower than the offering yield on the bond. Most graphs of the yield curve depict the yield, y, of par full-coupon bonds (assume the yield on a full coupon bond = 8%) as a function of the bond's term to maturity, t (e.g. 10 years). This depiction assumes that each of the semi-annual interest or coupon payments, $C/2$ (8%/2 = 4%), will be reinvested in a manner that will give an amount at maturity such that the bond yields y (8%).

In effect, the yield to maturity on coupon bonds depends significantly on the reinvestment rates. Because of this reinvestment dependency in calculating yield, there is significant reinvestment risk associated with coupon bearing bonds. *Zero coupon bonds do not have reinvestment risk.* The zero coupon yield is the yield to maturity, or discount rate, on a bond with only one cash flow, which occurs at maturity.

14.2.3 Prepayment Risk

Prepayment risk is the risk that a bond will be retired or redeemed at a time earlier than its maturity date. For instance, a municipal or corporate bond that matures in 30 years may include an option for the issuer to call or retire the bond at a price that includes a *call premium*—a price that is added to the face value of the bond—100%, after a certain period of time, usually 10 years or longer. Call premiums usually range from 2% to 5%.

The call option has considerable value to the issuer of the bond. If interest rates in the bond market drop, the value of non-callable high coupon bonds can rise substantially. A call option gives the issuer the ability to call the bonds at a price that can be significantly below the value of a non-callable bond, and the issuer will call the bonds if it's advantageous to do so. However, the call option has a cost to the issuer, which is paid in the form of a higher borrowing rate. Investors require a higher yield on callable bonds than on otherwise comparable non-callable bonds.

If the issuer has a call option, the price of the bond will rise far less, due to the fact that investors will price the bond with the assumption that it will be redeemed at the earliest opportunity and the cash flows after the optional call date will not be paid. We price a callable bond later in this chapter. Most bonds that are issued by the U.S. Government do not have an optional call or early redemption feature.

Many corporate and municipal bonds have a maturity date and are subject to an annual call in accordance with a pre-specified retirement schedule. This redemption schedule is referred to as a *sinking fund redemption*, and even otherwise non-callable bonds may be subject to this redemption schedule. This redemption feature increases the uncertainty of the cash flows and also retards the upward price movements of a bond in the event that interest rates drop.

Extraordinary redemptions in the municipal and asset-backed bond markets are a source of great confusion about the expected life of bond cash flows. Different types of bonds have provisions that, in the event of certain occurrences, present the possibility of an unexpected mandatory redemption and a truncation of cash flows. Mortgage-related bonds typically include the following redemption events: unexpended proceeds, mortgage prepayment redemptions, and foreclosure redemptions.

These redemption features introduce uncertainty into the expected cash flows. This uncertainty has a cost, in the way of a higher rate of interest on the bonds. Remember the first principle of finance relating to valuation—the trade-off between return and risk, with higher returns requiring more risk. With a greater risk of early redemption of a bond, investors will require a higher yield or interest rate.

14.2.4 Interest Rate Risk

We come now to the risk that often is the most difficult to assess and address—interest rate risk. Interest rate risk relates to a change in market interest rates that will adversely affect the value of a bond. We can handle default risk by buying U.S. Government bonds, or bonds that are rated AAA by rating agencies. We can overcome reinvestment risk by buying zero-coupon bonds. We can avoid prepayment risk by buying only non-callable bonds. Interest rate risk is a tougher nut to crack.

The price volatility of a bond is the extent to which the price of a bond changes with fluctuations in market levels of interest rates. Bond prices and yields move in opposite directions. As interest rates go up, the price of fixed-rate bonds goes down. However, the magnitude of price movements will differ based on specific bond characteristics. For example, the price volatility of a bond is directly related to its maturity: a longer maturity bond will experience a sharper price adjustment for a given change in interest rates than an otherwise identical shorter maturity bond.

Table 14-1 demonstrates the price volatility of three non-callable bonds with maturities of 10, 20, and 30 years to fluctuations in market interest rates. The three bonds have an identical coupon rate of 6%. Table 14-1 shows the price changes that correspond to a 1% decrease and a 1% increase in yield. For a given change in market rates, the price of the 30-year bond changes the most, followed by the price of the 20-year bond. The 10-year bond exhibits the least price volatility. This table effectively shows that *the longer the maturity of a bond, the higher the volatility of bond prices.*

Table 14-1
Price Volatility Versus Maturity for 6% Coupon Bond

Maturity	Coupon	Yield	Price	%	Yield	Price	%
n	c	y	P	Change	y	P	Change
10	6%	5%	$107.79	7.79%	7%	$92.89	-7.11%
20	6%	5%	$112.55	12.55%	7%	$89.32	-10.68%
30	6%	5%	$115.45	15.45%	7%	$87.53	-12.47%

Let's now take a look at the relationship between the fixed-rate on a bond and its price volatility. Table 14-2 shows the relationship for three non-callable 30-year bonds: a zero coupon bond, a 6% bond, and a 12% bond. It measures the price and the percentage change in price for the three bonds, based on an initial offering yield of 6%, with price changes that correspond to a 1% decrease in yields to 5% and a 1% increase in yields to 7%. For a given change in market rates, we see that the percentage price of a zero coupon bond changes the most, followed by the percentage change in the 6% bond. The 12% bond exhibits the least price volatility. This table effectively shows that the lower the coupon on a bond, the higher the price volatility.

Table 14-2
Price Volatility Versus Coupon for 30-Year Bond

Coupon c	Yield y	Price P	Yield y	Price P	% Change	Yield y	Price P	% Change
0%	6%	$ 16.97	5%	$ 22.74	34.00%	7%	$ 12.69	-25.23%
6%	6%	$100.00	5%	$115.45	15.45%	7%	$ 87.53	-12.47%
12%	6%	$183.02	5%	$208.18	13.74%	7%	$162.36	-11.29%

When market professionals talk about measures of price volatility for debt issues, they often use a measure called *duration*. Duration measures the weighted average maturity of a bond's cash flows. The duration of a bond is measured in units of time (for example, 7.3 years). In the simplest case, the duration of a zero coupon bond is equal to its current time to maturity. A coupon bearing bond has a duration that is somewhat less than that of a zero coupon bond of the same maturity, since interest payments are received throughout the life of the bond. *The higher the current coupon payments, the lower the price volatility and the shorter the duration.*

> **Duration** *measures the weighted average maturity of a bond's Cash flows. Duration also is a measure of price volatility.*

Duration is also defined as a percentage change in the price of an asset, divided by a change in interest rates, and can be represented by the following equation:

$$D = \frac{-\Delta P / P}{\Delta y} \qquad\qquad (Eq.14\text{-}1)$$

where: D = Duration, P = dollar price of a bond, ΔP = change in dollar price of a bond, y = market yield, and Δy = change in market yield.

We can reduce the price volatility and the duration of a bond through the use of hedging techniques and derivative securities. However, as we previously have discussed in the principle relating return and risk, there is a cost in reducing risk. It is the cost of the hedging instrument and the yield that is sacrificed when you hedge positions in the market. It is possible to use hedging instruments such as futures and options contracts to lessen or even eliminate the duration and interest rate risk associated with a portfolio consisting of a bond and a derivative security. We describe this type of hedging activity in Chapter 16.

After a bond is initially issued and marketed to investors either directly through the issuer or through an investment banker, the bond trades in the over-the-counter market for that particular type of bond issue. The bond's price fluctuates daily in response to changes in interest rates and the economy. There is an inverse relationship between interest rate movements and bond prices. For the fixed-rate bond, if interest rates increase, the price will fall so that the resulting yield on the bond will increase to be in line with yields on similar investments. Likewise, if interest rates decrease, the price will increase so that the resulting yield on the bond will decrease to be in line with other interest rates.

The relationship between the yields and the maturities on Treasury securities is called the yield curve. The yield curve is published daily in the financial press and shows the required yield on Treasury securities of different maturities.

The yield curve usually is positively sloped, which means that investors require higher returns for longer maturity Treasury securities. This is because the prices of longer maturity bonds are more volatile and therefore are viewed as being riskier than shorter maturity securities.

14.3   Types of Bonds and Trading Activity

14.3.1 *Treasury Securities and the Treasury Market*

The largest securities market in the world with the greatest daily trading activity is the market for U.S. Treasuries. In 2005, over $7 trillion in Treasury securities were outstanding. U.S. Treasury Notes and Bonds are interest-bearing notes and bonds with initial maturities that range from one to thirty years. Treasury notes have maturities of one to seven years, and bonds have maturities of over seven years. The most common maturities are one, two, five, and ten years. These securities pay interest on a semi-annual basis over the life of the issue, and then the investor receives the repayment of principle at maturity. For example, a $1,000, 8%, 10-year Treasury bond pays interest of $40 every six months (semi-annually), and the investor then receives the $1,000 back after ten years.

The market for U.S. Treasury securities is the largest and most liquid of any financial market. The interest payments on a Treasury obligation that are received by a resident of the United States is exempt from state income taxation. The risk-free nature of the interest payments makes them a highly desirable investment with relatively low rates of return.

After a U.S. Note or Bond is initially offered in the primary market through an auction conducted by the U.S. Treasury, it trades in the secondary over-the-counter market for Treasury securities. Its price fluctuates daily in response to changes in interest rates and the economy. There is an inverse relationship between interest rate movements and bond prices. For the 10-year bond listed above, if interest rates increase, the price will fall, so that the resulting yield on the bond will increase to be in line with other interest rates. Likewise, if interest rates decrease, the price will increase, so that the resulting yield on the bond will decrease to be in line with other interest rates. The relationship between the yields and the maturities on Treasury securities is called the yield curve. The yield curve is published daily in the financial press and shows the required yield on Treasury securities of different maturities.

14.3.2 Municipal Bonds and the Municipal Market

Municipal bonds are debt instruments issued by states, cities, municipal authorities, and other entities. The overwhelming attraction of municipal bonds for investors is the exemption of interest income on the bonds from federal and certain state and local income taxation. Because of this exemption, an investor's decision to invest in tax-exempt bonds is based upon an after-tax income comparison with other fixed-income securities, taking into account the investor's marginal tax bracket.

Investors are willing to accept lower interest yields on municipal bonds than on corporate and Treasury bonds because of this federal income tax exemption. It is possible to calculate the comparable taxable yield on municipal bonds so that the investor can relate this to current market interest rates and other comparable maturities. The taxable equivalent yield (*TEY*) for an investor in the 28% tax bracket for a municipal bond that pays a tax-exempt interest rate of 5% is calculated as follows:

$$\text{Taxable Equivalent Yield} = \frac{r}{1-t} = \frac{5.00}{1-0.28} = 6.94\% \qquad \text{(Eq. 14-2)}$$

Municipal entities generally issue debt for two purposes: to fund longer-term capital expenditures through the issuance of long-term bonds; and to fund short-term operating expenses through the issuance of short-term notes. The municipal bond market is a huge, diverse, and extremely complicated. There are almost 40,000 municipal issuers and the outstanding aggregate face value of bonds outstanding was over $2 trillion as of 2005. The security underlying municipal bond issues range in complexity from a general obligation pledge with unlimited taxing power to revenues from garbage facility tipping fees. The variety of security structures makes credit analysis difficult. In addition, unusual redemption features associated with municipal bonds often make the timing of expected cash flows uncertain further complicating valuation.

Municipal bonds are initially marketed to investors in the primary market by an investment bank or an underwriting syndicate composed of a number of investment banks, which have either negotiated the purchase of the bonds from the issuer, or which have purchased the bonds through a competitive bidding process. Secondary trading in the municipal bond market is though a network of financial institutions and dealers in the over-the-counter market who specialize in certain sectors of the municipal market.

14.3.3 Corporate Bonds and the Taxable Bond Market

Corporations typically issue bonds to finance their long-term capital needs and to take advantage of the tax deduction associated with the interest payments on debt. Corporations in capital-intensive and stable industries, such as manufacturing and electric utilities, are more likely to issue debt than industries that are subject to technological changes and substantial competition, such as the high-tech industry.

Corporations will issue bonds in the primary market through an investment banking syndicate, at a yield based on the spread to Treasuries that is required for an issue with the appropriate default risk and bond rating, prepayment aspects, and liquidity considerations. In the secondary market, some corporate bonds are traded in the bond section of the stock exchanges, but the vast majority of bonds are traded in the over-the-counter market among financial institutions and dealers that specialize in corporate bond trading.

The market for mortgage-backed bonds and the asset-backed bonds—secured by car loans, credit card receivables, and other structured bond issues—has grown considerably in the last two decades. These types of bonds are usually created and sponsored by financial institutions that originate the loans that are then pooled and marketed to institutional investors. These bonds are sold to investors in the primary market through an investment banking syndicate and are traded in the secondary over-the-counter market.

Convertible bonds are bonds that are issued by a corporation that usually pays a fixed rate of interest, and after a certain period of time, can be converted into a fixed number of shares of the issuing corporation. This conversion option is valuable and attractive to investors. Because of this option, convertible bonds have lower interest rates than comparable bonds without the conversion feature. The particular aspects associated with the conversion option makes a convertible bond more difficult to value as a financial asset.

14.4 Interest Rates, Default Risk, Other Factors and Bond Yields

The yield or return that an investor should expect to receive on a financial asset such as a bond is a function of a number of factors, the most important of which are as follows:

- The *time value of money*, which we have discussed in Chapter 9 and which is represented by the yields on risk-free Treasury securities known as the term structure of interest rates;
- The *default risk* associated with a particular security, which is measured by the rating category for the security and the measure of its spread to Treasuries;
- The *liquidity premium and other factors* specific to the financial asset, such as call provisions, which we have discussed previously in this chapter.

14.4.1 The Term Structure of Interest Rates

The *yield curve*, also known as the *term structure of interest rates*, describes the relationship between the *yield* on a security and its maturity. In constructing a yield curve, it is important that the securities represented differ only in the maturity and not other factors—particularly not in risk. Typically, the shape of the taxable yield curve is determined by yields on non-callable, risk-free, highly liquid U.S. Treasury securities. Yield curves exist for all types of debt instruments but we will focus on the Treasury yield curve in this section.

> *The **yield curve** describes the relationship between the yield on a bond and its maturity.*

The Treasury yield curve for Saturday, January 1, 2005 as captured from the website of www.bloomberg.com is depicted in Exhibit 14-1 below. As you can see, the interest rates and yields associated with the yield curve on this date generally increase with the time to maturity of the bond.

Exhibit 14-1
U.S. Treasury Yield Curve

U.S. TREASURIES

Bills

	COUPON	MATURITY DATE	CURRENT PRICE/YIELD	PRICE/YIELD CHANGE	TIME
3-Month	N.A.	03/31/2005	2.17/2.21	0.02/-.009	12/31
6-Month	N.A.	06/30/2005	2.51/2.57	0.02/.006	12/31

Notes/Bonds

	COUPON	MATURITY DATE	CURRENT PRICE/YIELD	PRICE/YIELD CHANGE	TIME
2-Year	3.000	12/31/2006	99-28/3.07	0-00/-.008	12/31
3-Year	3.000	11/15/2007	99-12/3.22	0-02/-.022	12/31
5-Year	3.500	12/15/2009	99-16/3.61	0-03/-.021	12/31
10-Year	4.250	11/15/2014	100-08/4.22	0-09/-.037	12/31
30-Year	5.375	02/15/2031	108-03/4.82	0-24/-.048	12/31

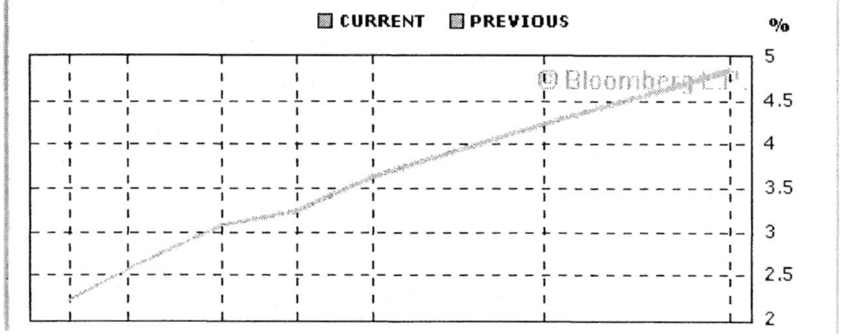

The shape of the yield curve depends on the rate of inflation or deflation, the economy, and monetary policies among other things. The shape can be upward sloping—which is the most common, downward sloping—when a significant slowdown in inflation is anticipated, or flat or humped. Several academic hypotheses attempt to explain the term structure of interest rates and the information that it conveys to the market. The three most common explanations of the shape of the yield curve are the *pure expectations hypothesis,* the *liquidity preference hypothesis,* and the *market segmentation hypothesis.*

The Pure Expectations Hypothesis:

The pure expectations hypothesis explains the yield curve as a function of a series of expected future or forward short-term interest rates. According to the theory, the yield curve can be analyzed as a series of expected future short-term interest rates that will adjust in a way such that investors will receive equivalent holding period returns. So the expected average annual return on a long-term bond is the compound average of the expected short-term interest rates. For example, the two-year interest rate can be thought of as a product of the one-year interest rate and the one-year rate that we expect to observe one year from now.

Under this theory, an upward-sloping yield curve means that investors expect higher future short-term interest rates, whereas a downward-sloping yield curve implies expectations of lower future short-term rates. Since expected short-term rates are implied in the yield curve associated with the expectations hypothesis, investors are assumed to be indifferent about whether they hold a 20-year investment, a series of 20 consecutive 1-year investments, or 2 consecutive 10-year investments. Based on this theory, we can calculate the series of expected short-term (one-year) spot rates, which over any given period will reproduce the observed market rates expressed in the yield curve. This set of forward rates is known as the *implied forward yield curve* (which is beyond the scope of this book) and is the basis for the valuation of derivative securities, which we examine in Chapter 16.

The Liquidity Preference Hypothesis:

Under the liquidity preference hypothesis, long-term rates are composed of expected short-term rates plus a *liquidity premium.* This theory posits that most investors prefer to hold short-term maturity securities. In order to induce investors to hold bonds with longer maturities, the issuer must pay a higher interest rate as a liquidity premium. For example, an investor who prefers a bond with a two-year maturity can purchase a bond with a three-year maturity and sell the bond after two years. This strategy involves some risk—the investor doesn't know at what price he can sell the bond after two years. The liquidity premium is compensation for investors to accept the risk in purchasing longer maturity securities, whereas they would prefer investing in shorter maturity securities. The amount of the liquidity premium is the extra yield demanded by the market to stretch its maturity preference by a specified number of years.

The liquidity premium increases with time to maturity. The observed yield curve under the liquidity preference hypothesis is always higher than the yield curve predicted solely by the pure expectations hypothesis. It assumes that investors are risk-averse. This theory implies an upward sloping yield curve even when investors expect that short-term rates will remain constant. An upward sloping yield curve is consistent with the majority of observations of the Treasury yield curve over the last four decades.

The Market Segmentation Hypothesis:

The market segmentation hypothesis, also known as the *preferred habitat hypothesis*, recognizes that the market is composed of diverse investors with differing investment requirements. Some investors, such as corporations with short-term funds to invest, prefer to invest in bonds at the short end of the yield curve. Others, such as insurance companies and pension funds, desire bonds with longer maturities, the term and cash flows of which coincide with their obligations under life insurance policies and pension programs. Most investors prefer to invest so that the life of their assets matches the life of their liabilities.

In order to induce investors to move away from their preferred position on the yield curve, an issuer must pay a premium. For this reason, the market segmentation hypothesis predicts that any maturity that does not have a balance of supply and demand will sell at a premium or discount to their expected yields. Under this hypothesis, there is no formal relationships between expected future short-term spot rates and implied forward rates; and the shape of the yield curve is a function of the supply and demand for the underlying maturities.

The Yield Curve as a Predictor of Short-Term Rates:

To our knowledge, no market participants or even ivory-tower academicians truly believe that the yield curve, or the term structure of interest rates, accurately predicts the future course of short-term interest rates. Studies have shown evidence of the existence of liquidity premiums in the yield curve. The ability to quantify these liquidity premiums and to determine how they shift over time and over different interest rate scenarios has eluded academicians and practitioners.

Based on empirical evidence, the yield curve has been a particularly poor predictor of future short-term interest rates. Professor Eugene Fama compared the forecasting ability of forward rates implied by the yield curve with a simple forecasting model—the assumption that short-term rates will remain constant for the next observation period.[viii] Fama observes that the assumption that short-term rates will remain constant provided forecasts superior to the results obtained by using the forward rates implied by the yield curve. He notes that implied forward rates probably overestimate expected future short-term rates. If Fama's observation is correct, why do we concern ourselves with and use the rates implied by the pure expectations model of the yield curve? Here are reasons for their importance:

- Trading activity can effectively lock in forward and zero coupon rates that are implied in the yield curve and incorporated in the pricing of bonds in the market;
- The yield curve provides the yield or discount rates used to value the cash flow associated with bonds; and
- The pricing model used by market participants in valuing any derivative security incorporates the forward rates implied by the pure expectations model of the yield curve.

The Yield Curve, Inflation and Deflation:

The price of goods and services change over time. The price of a candy bar and other items we enjoy seems to continually increase. Inflation is defined as the average increase in the general level of prices. An increase in prices means that the purchasing power of money has decreased. The price of certain high -tech products, such as computers, has declined over time. If prices decline over a period of time, we experience *deflation*—a period of generally falling prices that last occurred in the United States during the Great Depression of the early 1930s.

In our discussion of interest rates, we have focused on *nominal interest rates,* the actual rate of return or yield associated with an investment. We have not discussed the effect of inflation or deflation on the purchasing power of an asset. When we take about nominal rates or yields, we mean the face rate or percentage amount that will be paid on the investment. If you deposit $10,000 in a bank with a nominal rate of interest of 5%, you will have $10,500 at the end of the year. If the rate of inflation during that period of time was less than 5%, the purchasing power of your money has grown over time. If the rate of inflation was greater than 5%, your purchasing power has declined over time.

The real rate of interest is defined as the difference between the nominal rate of interest and the rate of inflation:

Real Rate of Interest = Nominal Rate of Interest – Inflation Rate   (Eq. 14-3)

For example, if inflation has averaged 3% per year during the 1990's and the nominal interest rate associated with a 10-year Treasury bond has averaged 6% during the same period, the real rate of interest = 6% - 3% = 3%.

14.4.2 *Default Risk*

The risk that an issuer of bonds will not pay interest or principal on its bonds is known as *default risk*. Bonds issued by the U.S. Treasury do not have default risk but corporations, municipalities, agencies, and asset-backed securities do. Because of this risk, corporations and issuers of securities with the risk of default must offer investors a greater return to compensate them for accepting additional risk. Remember our risk/return tradeoff—a higher risk security requires the expectation of a greater return.

The difference between the yield on a non-callable United States Treasury bond and the yield on a non-callable corporate bond with an identical maturity is called the *spread to Treasuries* and is a measure of the *default premium* associated with the corporate bond. The spread to Treasuries is a function of the type of industry the issuer belongs to (bank, financial, utility, or industrial), the credit rating of the corporate bond—the lower the credit rating, the greater the spread to Treasuries; and is a function of the time to maturity of the bond—the longer the term to maturity, the higher the spread to Treasuries. Exhibit 14-2 shows the spread to Treasuries as captured from the Web site www.bondsonline.com/ on Saturday, January 1, 2005, for a group of corporate bonds in the banking sector with ratings ranging from AAA to CCC, and terms to maturity ranging from 1 year to 30 years.

Exhibit 14-2
Spread to Treasuries—a Measure of Default Risk

Rating	1 yr	2 yr	3 yr	5 yr	7 yr	10 yr	30 yr
Aaa/AAA	12	14	25	31	47	59	81
Aa1/AA+	21	29	30	42	57	70	92
Aa2/AA	23	36	38	47	60	73	96
Aa3/AA-	24	38	39	51	64	76	102
A1/A+	42	47	51	58	72	86	110
A2/A	45	50	53	60	74	88	114
A3/A-	49	53	56	64	77	91	117
Baa1/BBB+	60	70	78	85	114	136	163
Baa2/BBB	63	78	86	90	121	144	170
Baa3/BBB-	70	83	88	95	126	151	175
Ba1/BB+	175	185	195	205	225	245	265
Ba2/BB	185	195	205	215	235	255	275
Ba3/BB-	195	205	215	225	245	265	285
B1/B+	265	275	285	315	355	395	445
B2/B	275	285	295	325	365	405	455
B3/B-	285	295	305	335	375	415	465
Caa/CCC	465	475	485	510	520	530	560

Source: www.bondsonline.com website

The exemption from United States income taxation relating to the interest payments on municipal bonds make them a very attractive asset for individual and institutional investors in high tax brackets. So the nominal interest rate associated with municipal bonds often is below the nominal interest rate associated with U.S. Treasury bonds with a comparable maturity. The default risk of a municipal bond is measured by the difference between its tax-equivalent yield and the rate on a comparable maturity Treasury bond.

The taxable equivalent yield is equal to the nominal interest rate on a municipal bond, divided by (1 – maximum income tax rate). If the rate on a municipal bond is 5% and the maximum federal income tax rate is 34%, the T.E.Y. is equal to:

Taxable Equivalent Yield = 5% / (1 - .34) = 5% / (.66) = 7.576%

14.4.3 Call Features and Other Factors

The last consideration relating to yield level on a bond are aspects associated with its liquidity, call features and other factors. U.S. Treasuries are highly liquid securities that are traded round the clock by dealers and brokers around the world, and the bid/ask spreads associated with these securities is very small. Conversely, many municipal, corporate, and asset-backed bonds are traded by a very few number of broker dealers and the bid/ask spread for these securities can be very significant. With greater liquidity the bonds are more marketable and there is less of a liquidity yield premium associated with the bond.

We discussed call provisions and optional and extraordinary calls previously in this chapter. When investors analyze a corporate, municipal, or asset-backed bond, they closely analyze the optional and extraordinary call provisions and assign a premium in the way of a higher interest rate to reflect those provisions. For example, let's assume that a 30-year AAA-rated non-callable corporate bond was worthy of a 6% interest rate and yield if it is marketed in a particular economic environment. If the bond is callable at the option of the issuer after a period of 10 years at a call price of 105% of par value, that bond may need to bear an interest rate of 6.25% to be sold at par in the same interest rate environment. So the issuer will have to pay another 0.25% per year in interest rate to purchase the particular call option.

14.4.4 Putting it all Together to Arrive at a Required Yield

When market participants value a bond in the marketplace, they will discount cash flows associated with a bond at the yield level that is required by securities of comparable maturity, risk, liquidity and call features. Therefore, the computation of a required yield level is a function of all of these factors. The time value of money is best represented by the term structure of interest rates for United States Treasury securities. The default risk on a security is best represented by its spread to Treasuries. Finally, the liquidity and call features of a bond are best represented by an analysis of the bond specific call features and bid/ask spreads.

So we find that the yield on a risky security can be represented by the yield on a comparable maturity risk-free security, plus a measure of the spread to Treasuries for default risk, plus a bond specific spread.

Bond Yield = R_f + Spread to Treasuries + Bond Specific Spread **_(Eq.14-4)_**

14.5 Valuing a Bond

Now that we've examined many of the features of bonds, let's discuss some important aspects associated with valuing them. Two important facts associated with valuation and bond prices in the marketplace are:

- Bond prices and changes in interest rates move in opposite directions—when interest rates go up, bond prices go down. When interest rates go down, bond prices go up.
- Investors and traders value bonds based on a *price to worst* call feature scenario. We discuss what we mean by that below.

When bond traders and investors value the cash flows associated with a bond, they assume that the issuer of the bond will act in its own best interest in calling or managing the bond's call features. Let's assume that ABC Company issued 10% bonds at a time in the market when comparable maturity U.S. Treasury bond rates were 8%. So ABC's Bonds traded at a 2% spread to Treasuries. Rates have fallen and an interest rates are now 7% for a bond, the maturity and credit risk of which is similar to the bonds of ABC Company. If ABC Company has the ability to call its 10% bonds and replace them with 7% bonds, it will do so. Such a call will be advantageous to ABC Company and act to the disadvantage of owners of the outstanding 10% bonds. *Price to worst* will price the bonds in such a way as to assume that ABC calls its 10% bonds at the first available opportunity that is economically advantageous to ABC.

The principal relating to investment valuation states that **Value Equals the Sum of Expected Cash Flows Discounted for Time and Risk**. When we value an asset, two basic sources of uncertainty come to mind—the amount of the expected cash flows, and the discounting rate that we use in calculating the present value of those cash flows. With bonds, the most cash flow that we can expect to receive are the promised interest payments and the repayment of principal at maturity, or the payment of a redemption price, which may include a call premium, prior to maturity. The discounting rate that we should use to value a bond is the **Bond Yield** that we calculate in Equation (14-4) above, that consists of a risk-free rate component, a default-risk component, and a bond specific component.

It's now time to value a bond. In the United States most bonds are structured such that interest only is paid on the bonds on a semi-annual basis (every six months on May 1 and November 1, or on February 1 and October 1, or some other dates) and the lump sum principal is paid at maturity. If a bond is called prior to maturity on a call date, the issuer pays a redemption price for the bond (usually 105% of the principal down to 100% of the principal value) plus the interest on the bond that has accrued to the redemption date.

Let's value the bonds of ABC Corporation and we'll see how the value of the bond changes as the required yield for the bond changes. Assume that ABC's bonds were issued when interest rates for a 10-year bond of comparable risk were at 10%. Each

$1,000 bond has a semi-annual coupon payment of 5%—equal to $50 paid every six months on April 1 and October 1. Also assume that the bonds are not callable at this time. The expected cash flows associated with this bond consist of 20 semi-annual payments of the $50 coupon, plus the repayment of principal ten years after issuance. Let's value this bond using various current market interest rate scenarios.

14.5.1 Valuing ABC Discount Bond

A *discount bond* is a bond in which its coupon is lower than the yield required by the market to sell a bond with a comparable maturity, credit rating, and other features. Therefore, the market price for the bond is below, or at a *discount* to, its face value.

Let's assume that for some unusual reason, such as a terrorist attack or an economic crisis, interest rates for bonds similar to ABC's in credit risk and maturity move immediately from 10% to 12%. Let's use what we learned in Chapter 9 about present value to price ABC's bond, which should be at a discount because market interest rates have risen above the level of ABC's coupon. The bond is a 10% bond with $50 semi-annual coupon payments and a 10-year maturity offered at a discount rate or yield of 12%. How much would an investor be willing to pay for the stream of cash flows associated with ABC's bond, discounted at a rate of 12%?

When we value a bond, we can think of the interest payments as an annuity stream and the principal or redemption payment as a lump sum payment at maturity. Therefore, we can value a bond as a combination of a 20-period annuity stream for its $50 coupons, and a single $1,000 payment for its principal. We can value these cash flows by using present value tables or by valuing the present value of an annuity and the present value of a single payment lump sum on a calculator.

Using Present Value Tables:

We can value the bond by adding the present value associated with its coupon stream to the present value associated with its lump sum principal. In equation form the valuation looks like this:

PV = Present Value (Annuity Coupon Stream) + Present Value (Principal)

PV = (Annuity Factor (n,r) * Coupon) + (PV Factor * $1000)

We revisit the Present Value of Multiple Payments Table 9-7 to find our annuity factor. The entry in which the number of semi-annual periods is 20 (10 years * 2), and the semi-annual discounting rate is 6% (12%/2), is equal to 11.4699. The coupons are $50. The Present Value of a Single Payment Factor Table 9-6 gives us a factor of 0.3118 for the period n = 20, and discount rate of r = 6%. So if we plug in the numbers into the equation above, we have:

PV = (11.4699 * $50) + (0.3118 * $1,000)

$$PV = \$573.49 + \$311.80 = \$885.29$$

Using a Financial Calculator:

For ABC's bonds the principal value is \$1,000, the coupon payment is \$50, the discounting rate is 12% or 6% for each semi-annual period, and the number of periods is 20. We value these cash flows by adding together the two calculations, just as we did above. First, we value the annuity where our inputs are: n = 20, i = 6, PMT = 50, FV = 0, **solve for PV**. With these inputs, PV = $\underline{\$573.49}$.

Next we solve for the present value of the lump sum principal payment. Our inputs for this calculation are: n = 20, i = 6, PMT = 0, FV = 1,000, **solve for PV**. With these inputs PV = $\underline{\$311.80}$.

The total value for the discount ABC Bond is simply the sum of the present values of the interest component and the principal component:

$$\$573.49 + \$311.80 = \underline{\textbf{\$885.29}}$$

14.5.2 Valuing ABC Par Bond

A *par bond* is a bond in which its coupon is lower than the yield required by the market to sell a bond with comparable maturity, credit rating, and other features. Therefore, the market price for a par bond is equal to its face value.

Let's assume that interest rates for bonds similar to ABC's in credit risk and maturity stay at 10%. The bond is a 10% bond with semi-annual \$50 coupon payments and a 10-year maturity offered at a discount rate or yield of 10%. How much would an investor be willing to pay for this stream of cash flow?

Using Present Value Tables:

We revisit the Present Value of Multiple Payments Table 9-7 to find our annuity factor, in which the number of periods is 20 and the semi-annual discounting rate is 5%. We find that there is no column in Table 9-7 to correspond to r = 5%, but we can extrapolate between the values for r = 4%, factor = 13.5903, and r = 6%, factor = 11.4699, to get an approximate factor. If we average the two factors—((13.5903 + 11.4699)/2), our resulting factor is 12.530. The coupon is \$50. The Present Value of a Single Payment Factor Table 9-6 does not contain r = 5% either. We extrapolate between the factor for r = 4%, factor = 0.4564, and r = 6%, factor = 0.3118. Again averaging the two factors ((0.4564 + 0.3118)/2), our resulting factor is 0.3841, for the period n = 20, and discount rate of r = 5%. So if we plug in the numbers into the equation above, we have:

$$PV = (12.530 * \$50) + (0.3841 * \$1,000)$$

$$PV = \$626.50 + \$384.10 = \$1,010.60$$

The answer of $1,010.60 is a good bit above the answer of par value, or $1,000, that we expected for this example. The reason for this difference is due to the extrapolation process, which at best gives an approximate answer. For a more accurate answer, the use of a financial calculator as we show below is strongly suggested.

Using a Financial Calculator:

For ABC's bonds the principal value is $1,000, the coupon payment is $50, the discounting rate is 10% or 5% for each semi-annual period, and the number of periods is 20. We value these cash flows by adding together the two calculations, just as we did above. First, we value the annuity where our inputs are: n = 20, i = 5, Pmt = 50, FV = 0, **solve for PV**. With these inputs, PV = $623.11.

Next we solve for the present value of the lump sum principal payment. Our inputs for this calculation are: n = 20, i = 5, PMT = 0, FV = 1,000, **solve for PV**. With these inputs PV = $376.89.

The total value for the par ABC Bond is simply the sum of the present values of the interest component and the principal component:

$$\$623.11 + \$376.89 = \underline{\textbf{\$1,000}}$$

14.5.3 Valuing ABC Premium Bond to Maturity

A *premium bond* is a bond in which its coupon is higher than the yield required by the market to sell a bond with comparable maturity, credit rating, and other features. Therefore, the market price for a premium bond is greater than its face value.

Let's assume that interest rates for bonds similar to ABC's in credit risk and maturity drop to 8%. The bond is a 10% bond with semi-annual $50 coupon payments and a 10-year maturity offered at a discount rate or yield of 8%. Let's also assume for now that ABC does not have the right to call bonds in the market prior to their maturity. How much would an investor be willing to pay for this stream of cash flows?

Using Present Value Tables:

We revisit the Present Value of Multiple Payments Table 9-7 to find our annuity factor. The entry in which the number of semi-annual periods is 20, and the semi-annual discounting rate is 4% (8%/2)—is equal to 13.5903. The coupon is $50. The Present Value of a Single Payment Factor Table 9-6 gives us a factor of 0.4564 for the period n = 20, and discount rate of r = 4%. So if we plug in the numbers into the equation above, we have:

$$PV = (13.5903 * \$50) + (0.4564 * \$1,000)$$

$$PV = \$679.51 + \$456.40 = \underline{\pmb{\$1,135.91}}$$

Using a Financial Calculator:

For ABC's bonds, the principal value is $1,000, the coupon payment is $50, the discounting rate is 8% or 4% for each semi-annual period, and the number of periods is 20. We value these cash flows by adding together the two calculations, just as we did above. First, we value the annuity where our inputs are: n = 20, i = 4, PMT = 50, FV = 0, **solve for PV**. With these inputs, PV = $\underline{\$679.52}$.

Next we solve for the present value of the lump sum principal payment. Our inputs for this calculation are: n = 20, i = 4, PMT = 0, FV = 1,000, **solve for PV**. With these inputs PV = $\underline{\$456.39}$.

The total value for the par ABC bond is the sum of the present values of the interest component and the principal component:

$$\$679.52 + \$456.39 = \underline{\pmb{\$1,135.91}}$$

14.5.4 Valuing ABC Premium Bond to Call Date

A *callable bond* is a bond that can be optionally called by the issuer of the bond prior to its stated maturity. *Premium callable bonds* are priced by market participants on the *price to worst* scenario, which usually assumes that the issuer will call the bond at the first available opportunity in which it makes economic sense. Because the market price for a premium bond is greater than its face value, pricing of a bond assumes that the bond will be called at the issuer's earliest economic opportunity and that the premium coupon payments no longer will be paid after that date.

Let's assume that interest rates for bonds similar to ABC's in credit risk and maturity are at 8%. The bond is a 10% bond with semi-annual $50 coupon payments and a 10-year maturity offered at a discount rate or yield of 8%. ABC has the right to call bonds in the market after a period of 5 years at a price of 101% of par value. The price to worst scenario means that an investor will assume that ABC will call those bonds in 5 years at the first call date at a price of 101%. How much would an investor be willing to pay for this stream of cash flows?

Using Present Value Tables:

We revisit the Present Value of Multiple Payments Table 9-7 to find our annuity factor. Our price to worst scenario assumes that the entry in which the number of semi-annual periods is 10, and the semi-annual discounting rate is 4% (8%/2), is equal to 8.1109. The coupon is $50. The Present Value of a Single Payment Factor Table 9-6 gives us a factor of 0.6756 for the period n = 10, and discount rate of r = 4%. The redemption price is 101% of par value or $1,010. So if we plug in the numbers into the equation above, we have:

$$PV = (8.1109 * \$50) + (0.6756 * \$1,010)$$

$$PV = \$405.54 + \$682.35 = \underline{\mathbf{\$1,087.89}}$$

Using a Financial Calculator:

For ABC's bonds the redemption price is $1,010, the coupon payment is $50, the discounting rate is 8% or 4% for each semi-annual period, and the number of periods is 10. We value these cash flows by adding together the two calculations, just as we did above. First, we value the annuity where our inputs are: n = 10, i = 4, PMT = 50, FV = 0, **solve for PV**. With these inputs, PV = $405.54.

Next we solve for the present value of the lump sum principal payment. Our inputs for this calculation are: n = 10, i = 4, PMT = 0, FV = 1,010, **solve for PV**. With these inputs PV = $682.32.

The total value for the par ABC bond is the sum of the present values of the interest component and the principal component:

$$\$682.32 +-\$405.54 = \underline{\mathbf{\$1,087.86}}$$

The important thing to note regarding valuation in this section is that the value of a premium callable bond—*$1,087.86*—is much lower in this example that the value of a premium non-callable bond—$1,135.91.

Below in Table 14-3 is a summary of the valuations that we performed in this section. The table shows how the price of a bond changes inversely with the market interest rates. As interest rates and discounting rates increase, bond values decrease. As interest rates and discounting rates decrease, bond values increase. This table also shows the importance of the call feature. A callable bond is priced on a price to worst basis. The price of the premium callable bond was significantly lower than the price of an otherwise comparable non-callable bond.

Table 14-3
ABC 10%, 10-Year Bond Values

	Interest Rate	Discount Rate	Call Feature	Bond Price
Discount Bond	10%	12%	Non-callable	$885.29
Par Bond	10%	10%	Non-callable	$1,000.00
Premium Non-Call	10%	8%	Non-callable	$1,135.91
Premium Callable	10%	8%	5 yrs @ 101%	$1,087.86

14.6 Summary

In this chapter we focused on understanding bonds—a very important type of financial contract issued by the United States Government, corporations, municipalities, agencies, or other entities. Bonds are debt securities that are sold to investors in order to raise long-term funds for the issuer. A bond is a contract in which the issuer borrows money from investors, and promises to make periodic payments of interest and repay the debt at some time in the future.

In Chapter 9, we introduced you to a simple way to value a bond by using a present value example. In this chapter we examined different types of bonds, the risks associated with bonds, how bonds are traded in the market, and the effect of interest rates, default risk, and call features on bond valuation.

The learning objectives for the chapter included an understanding of:

- Bonds—their structure and risks;
- How bonds are issued in the primary market and traded in the secondary markets;
- How to value a bond;
- Interest rates and how interest rates affect bond valuation.

List of Terms

1. Fixed coupon bond
2. Indenture
3. Principal value
4. Par amount
5. Maturity value
6. Zero coupon bond
7. Fixed-rate par bond
8. Fixed-rate discount bond
9. Fixed-rate premium bond
10. Asset-backed debt
11. Optional redemption
12. Call premium
13. Default risk
14. Prepayment risk
15. Interest rate risk
16. Spread to Treasuries
17. Senior debt
18. Subordinated debt
19. Sinking fund redemption
20. Duration
21. Yield curve
22. Taxable bonds
23. Term structure of interest rates
24. The pure expectations hypothesis
25. The liquidity preference hypothesis
26. The market segmentation hypothesis
27. The preferred habitat hypothesis
28. Implied forward yield curve
29. Inflation
30. Deflation
31. Default premium

Questions

1. What are the various risks associated with the bond? Explain.
2. What is the coupon rate and required return on a bond? Explain the differences.
3. Explain the effect of interest rate changes on bond prices.
4. Explain the relationship between coupon rate and yield to maturity for premium bonds, discount bonds, and bonds selling at par.
5. A company has two bonds with same coupon rate and maturity, but one bond is callable whereas the other one is not. Explain the price, duration, and yield relationships between these two bonds.
6. What are the characteristics of asset-backed debt?
7. Define the following terms:
   (a) Spread to treasuries.
   (b) Call premium.
   (c) Sinking fund redemption.
   (d) Duration.
   (e) Yield curve.
8. Discuss the three hypotheses that explain the term structure of interest rates.

Problem Set:

1. Jason Co. bond has an 8 percent coupon rate and a $1,000 face value. Interest is paid semi-annually, and the maturity of the bond is 30 years. If the required rate on this kind of bond is 10 percent, what is the value of bond?

2. Joseph Corporation bond has a coupon rate of 10 percent, paid semi-annually. The face value of the bond is $1,000 and it will mature in 8 years. If the bond currently sells at $1,100, what is the yield to maturity?

3. David Industries has 8 percent coupon bonds selling in the market. These bonds have 10 years left for maturity. If the yield to maturity on these bonds is 10%, what is the current price of the bond?

4. Thomas Tool Factory's bonds are selling for $965 in the market. These bonds have seven years left for maturity and coupon payments are made semi-annually. If the YTM on these bonds is 9.2 percent, what must be the coupon rate on these bonds?

5. Bond X and bond Y have 7 percent coupons, selling at par and paying interest semi-annually. Bond X has five years for maturity and bond Y has 16 years to maturity. If the interest rate suddenly increases by 2 percent, what is the percentage change in bond X and bond Y?

6. Michael Technologies has 5 percent bonds on the market with 10 years to maturity. This bond currently sells for 85 percent of the par and the interest payments are made semi-annually. What is the yield to maturity on this bond?

7. Anderson Chemical's 8 percent coupon bond that matures in 9 years is currently selling for $1,070. Anderson Chemical is planning for a new bond issue to fund a major R&D project. If they want to sell the bond at par, what should be the coupon rate on the new bond issue?

8. Toni Enterprise has 9 percent coupon bonds with interest payments made annually. The yield to maturity on this bond is 8.25 percent. If the bond is currently selling at $1,025, how many years do these bonds have left until they mature?

9. Bond ABC has a coupon rate of 6 percent and bond XYZ has a coupon rate of 10 percent. Both bonds have eight years left for maturity and have a yield to maturity of 8 percent. If the YTM remains same for next year at 8 percent, what is the rate of return on each bond?

10. Consider four bonds with 7 percent coupon rates. All these bonds are selling at par today. The maturity of these bonds is 4, 6, 8, and 10 years respectively. Calculate the change in price for each bond, if their yield increases to 9 percent.

Assignment #14-1:

1. Suppose you buy a 7 percent coupon, 10-year bond at par. After you bought the bond, interest rates suddenly increases to 9 percent. What will happen to the bond price?
   (a) Increase
   (b) Decrease
   (c) Stay the same
   (d) None of the above

2. You buy a bond for $1,095 in the market and it has 8 years left for maturity. If the yield to maturity on this bond is 8 percent. What is the coupon rate on this bond?
   (a) 8.42 percent
   (b) 9.63 percent
   (c) 10.17 percent
   (d) 11.49 percent

3. A 10-year bond pays interest of $100 annually and sells for $1,050. What is the coupon rate of the bond?
   (a) 9.2 percent
   (b) 10.0 percent
   (c) 11.4 percent
   (d) 12.3 percent

4. When ABC Corporation issued a 6 percent 12-year maturity bond, it was sold for $950. One year later, this bond is selling for $1,050. What is the new yield to maturity?
   (a) 4.12 percent
   (b) 4.99 percent
   (c) 5.39 percent
   (d) 5.86 percent

5. If expectations of inflation increase, what is the likely effect on the yield to maturity on bonds?
   (a) Increase
   (b) Decrease
   (c) Stay the same
   (d) Interest rate has no effect on yield

6. If bond A has a coupon rate of 7% and yield to maturity of 8%. Which of the following is true for the price of the bond?
   (a) More than par
   (b) Less than par
   (c) At par
   (d) Yield does not have any effect on price

7. When the bond issue creates a market value of more than 100% at the time of pricing, which of the following type of bond is this?
   (a) Zero coupon bond
   (b) fixed-rate par bond
   (c) fixed-rate discount bond
   (d) fixed-rate premium bond

8. A municipal bond has a coupon rate of 6 percent. If an investor is in the 32 percent tax bracket, what is the taxable equivalent bond yield?
   (a) 8.82 percent
   (b) 8.68 percent
   (c) 8.42 percent
   (d) 8.34 percent

9. Company X has a default risk of 2 percent and a bond specific risk of 3 percent. If the yield on a 10-year Treasury bond is 4 percent, what should be the yield on a 10-year bond issued by company X?
   (a) 5.0 percent
   (b) 6.0 percent
   (c) 7.0 percent
   (d) 9.0 percent

10. Company ABC issued an 8 percent coupon bond with 10 years for maturity. ABC has the right to call this bond at a premium of 102 percent of par value after 5 years. If the required interest on bonds similar to ABC's risk and maturity is 6 percent, what is the yield to call on this bond?
    (a) 2.98 percent
    (b) 3.92 percent
    (c) 4.96 percent
    (d) 5.94 percent

Assignment #14-2:

1. A 6 percent coupon bond was sold at par today. Suppose three years from now the required return on this bond changes to 8 percent. What is the coupon rate of the bond now?
   (a) 4 percent
   (b) 6 percent
   (c) 8 percent
   (d) 10 percent

2. Johnson Corporation has 11% coupon bonds in the market that mature in 12 years. Interest on these bonds is paid semi-annually. If the bonds currently sell for $1,115, what is the yield to maturity of them?
   (a) 6.44 percent
   (b) 7.96 percent
   (c) 8.69 percent
   (d) 9.38 percent

3. Sam Corporation has 4 percent bonds on the market with 7 years to maturity. This bond currently sells for $890 and the interest payments are made semi annually. What is the yield to maturity on these bonds?
   (a) 5.94 percent
   (b) 6.38 percent
   (c) 7.02 percent
   (d) 7.98 percent

4. A 12-year bond pays interest of $95 annually and sells for $1,080. What is yield to maturity of the bond?
   (a) 6.78 percent
   (b) 7.92 percent
   (c) 8.43 percent
   (d) 9.61 percent

5. If the credit rating of a bond is decreased by Moody's, what is the likely effect on the bond price?
   (a) Decrease
   (b) Increase
   (c) Stay the same
   (d) Ratings do not have any effect on price

6. Jason Consulting Company has 8 percent coupon bonds selling in the market. These bonds mature in 20 years. What is the current price of the bond, if the present yield to maturity is 6%?
   (a) $1,094.32
   (b) $1,106.46
   (c) $1,182.98
   (d) $1,231.15

7. Brian Corporation issued a 15 year, 12 percent coupon bond at par. If the bond can be called after 6 years for $1,050, what is the bond's yield to call?
   (a) 11.42 percent
   (b) 12.58 percent
   (c) 13.64 percent
   (d) 14.26 percent

8. Which of the following type of bond does not have reinvestment risk?
   (a) Zero coupon bond
   (b) fixed-rate par bond
   (c) fixed-rate discount bond
   (d) fixed-rate premium bond

9. If the nominal interest rate on a 10-year Treasury bond is 6 percent, and the inflation during this period is 2 percent, what is the real rate of interest?
   (a) 3.50 percent
   (b) 3.80 percent
   (c) 4.00 percent
   (d) 4.32 percent

10. When the coupon rate on a bond is less than the yield required by the market, which of the following best represents this bond?
   (a) zero coupon bond
   (b) fixed-rate par bond
   (c) fixed-rate discount bond
   (d) fixed-rate premium bond

CHAPTER 15

STOCK VALUATION

Chances are that you already know that a company's growth rate, earnings, risk, and interest rates influence a stock's price. But you might not understand how all of these factors are interrelated.

You may be wondering:
- How does the market come up with a stock's price?
- What's driving stock market valuations?
- Why does a stock's price react so violently to small quarterly earnings surprises?
- Why and how do interest rate changes affect a stock's value?
- And how can you make money by buying and selling stock?

We'll explore these questions, introduce you to an easy-to-use approach to value a stock, and teach you how to value common stock without pain, anxiety, or astrology. However, we are going to present an approach to stock valuation that may be considered a bit advanced for an introductory text book in finance. The stock valuation approach will be introduced in conjunction with a stock valuation computer program called ValuePro that is included on the compact disk that comes with this book.[ix]

15.1   Introduction to Stock Valuation

Common stock represents a proportionate ownership interest in a corporation. Stockholders have a *residual claim on corporate assets* and are subject to *limited liability*. Limited liability means that the maximum amount that a shareholder can lose in the event of the failure of a corporation is the cost of her shares. If the corporation does well financially and its revenues and profits increase, the value of the common stock should also increase and generate a positive return for its shareholders. From the year 1926 to 2001, investors in large common stocks in the United States earned a compound average annual rate of return of 10.7 percent—significantly higher than the rates of return associated with corporate or government bonds or Treasury bills.

We saw in the simple stock valuation example of Chapter 10 that the value of a stock is crucially dependent upon two variables:

- The amount of future *profits* or *cash flows* that the firm is expected to generate—greater profits increase a stock's market value and lower profits decrease value; and

- The *interest rate* or required *yield* that is expected from the investment—with lower interest rates increasing market value, and higher interest rates reducing market value.

We believe that a stock should be valued in the same manner as other financial assets, such as bonds and mortgages—using a discounted present value technique. As we discussed in Chapter 2 in the principle relating to investment valuation, a stock's **Value Equals the Sum of its Expected Cash Flows Discounted for Time and Risk**.

There are two important differences when we compare the *expected cash flows of a stock* with the cash flows of a fixed income security such as a bond or a mortgage:

- First, unless there is a default or prepayment, the bond and the mortgage have cash flows that are known with certainty and will not be more than what is promised by contract. The range of future cash flows for a stock can be enormous, and the cash flows can be higher or lower than expected.
- Second, common stock represents ownership shares in a corporation, which is a legal entity itself with an infinite life. So the stock valuation procedure must address the problem of valuing cash flows to infinity.

If we make some simplifying assumptions regarding the cash flows associated with the stock, valuing an infinite stream isn't as difficult as it sounds. Remember from Chapter 9 that we can value a series of level cash flows as an annuity. An asset that has a stream of even cash flows that continue to infinity is known as a *perpetuity*. The value of a perpetuity is calculated by dividing the level annual cash flow associated with the perpetuity by the discounting rate:

Value of a Perpetuity = Annual Cash Flow/Discounting Rate   *(Eq.15-1)*

We use the value of a perpetuity stream when we calculate the *residual value* of the stock of Microsoft later in this chapter.

15.2 Return to Stockholders

The stock price of Internet Capital Group (ICGE), a high-flying Internet stock, fell from $200.94 per share in early 2000 to under a dollar in less than two years—a painful negative 99.9 percent return. Because of a favorable newspaper article in *The New York Times*, the stock price of EntreMed—a biotech firm that had never shown a profit—jumped from a closing price of under $13 per share on Friday May 1, 1998, to open on the following Monday at a price of over $84 per share—a three-day return of over 600 percent. Dozens of initial public offerings during the Internet heyday more than doubled or tripled in price on the day that they were first marketed to the public. The volatility of the returns associated with individual stocks is very high, with an annual average 49 percent standard deviation of return.

Stock returns fluctuate significantly because they depend on random future events and states of the economy that are impossible to predict. Forecasting returns accurately is extremely difficult. Your principal concern with a stock should be the investment return or cash flows that you expect to receive. Does the stock pay dividends? Has the stock price gone up according to your expectations? What is your total rate of return? The bottom line is that you should be interested in stock performance measures that relate to your pocketbook and whether you've gained or lost money on your investment.

15.2.1 Calculation of Return to Stockholders

Return to stockholders includes any dividend payments plus the increase (or minus the decrease) in stock price that investors experience during an investment holding period. The market's focus is on yearly or annualized returns to stockholders, as measured by percentage gains or losses, and usually uses the calendar year as the calculation period. Return to stockholders refers to an annual return, which is equal to the sum of the dividends paid plus the net change in a stock's price, divided by the beginning price of the stock.

$$\textbf{\textit{\% Return to Stockholders}} = \frac{\textbf{\textit{(Dividends + Change in Stock Price)}}}{\textbf{\textit{Beginning Stock Price}}} \textbf{\textit{(Eq.15-2)}}$$

For example, if a stock's price started the year at $100, the stock paid $1 in dividends during the year, and it ended the year at $109, its percentage annual return to stockholders equals: ($1 + $9) / $100 = 10%. This is not a complex calculation.

The stock market, however, sometimes acts in funny ways. The return on a stock may be negative even if the company had a successful year from an operations or earnings perspective. The stock market may have plummeted due to macroeconomic concerns like higher interest rates, lower earnings forecasts, inflation or deflation fears, or corporate governance or accounting scandals. Or the stock market could have fallen due to geopolitical concerns such as the 9/11 terrorist attacks, the perennial deterioration in Middle East relations, or an economic and currency crisis in Argentina. The market downdraft may have pulled your stock with it, and there may have been nothing the company's management could have done to change the adverse stock price movement.

Conversely, the return to stockholders may be very positive, even though the company had mediocre or poor operating performance. The stock market may have skyrocketed due to positive economic events like the settlement of a major labor strike, or a breakthrough technology such as computers in the 1980s or the Internet in the 1990s that increases productivity, or reduced inflation fears. Poor company performance or a legal scandal may put a company into the takeover candidate category, and the increase in price may be the result of a tender offer for the company's stock.

15.2.2 Stock Value and Dividend Policy

Does the current value of a stock depend on its dividend policy?

NO!

Dr. Merton H. Miller and Dr. Franco Modigliani are two Nobel Laureates in economics who have written extensively about corporate capital structure and dividend policy. In their 1961 article, "Dividend Policy, Growth and the Valuation of Shares," in the *Journal of Business*, they proved that the dividend policy of the firm should **not** affect the current value of a stock. However, the expected future value of a stock is greatly affected by dividend policy.

Here's an example that illustrates their Dividend Irrelevance Hypothesis—the relationship between dividend policy and stock price.

Assume XYZ Dividend Company has an invested capital base of $1 billion, is financed solely by equity, and has 100 million shares of stock outstanding. It operates in a competitive industry in which the cost of equity capital is 10%, and the marginal after-tax return on new investment is also 10%. Assume that XYZ earns $100 million per year after taxes and net investment and pays all of its earnings to shareholders in the form of dividends. Based on its cost of capital, XYZ's operations support market equity of: [$100 million/(.10)] = $1 billion, or $10 per share based on 100 million shares outstanding. XYZ expects to generate $100 million after-tax per year forever and pay all of its earnings in dividends. If its required yield in the market remains at 10%, it will have a $1 billion—$10 per share—constant stock market value.

Let's see how XYZ's stock will perform over a three-year time period by looking at Table 15-1:

Table 15-1
XYZ Dividend Company-Stock Price Change
100% Dividend Payment

Year	Market Equity	Earnings	Required Return	Dividend	Net Invest	Stock Price
1	$1 billion	$100 million	10%	$100 million	0	$10
2	$1 billion	$100 million	10%	$100 million	0	$10
3	$1 billion	$100 million	10%	$100 million	0	$10

The stockholders of XYZ Dividend Company receive $100 million per year in dividends, equal to $1 per share in stock outstanding—a 10% return on the company's market equity of $1 billion. The stock price remains stable at $10 per share because the shareholders are receiving their required 10% in the form of the $1 per share dividend. Our hypothetical performance of XYZ Dividend Company is similar to the actual performance of an electric utility in the stock market.

A company that is identical to XYZ Dividend Company—let's call it UVW Growth Company—operates in the same industry and has the same initial $100 million per year earnings after taxes. UVW is financed 100% by equity, has 100 million shares outstanding, and faces the same marginal after-tax return on new investments of 10%. Instead of paying dividends to its shareholders, UVW invests all of its earnings back into its business and receives a return on its new investments of 10% per year. So, the earnings of UVW increase from $100 million in year 1, to $110 million in year 2, to $121 million in year 3. Based on a 10% cost of equity capital, the market equity that UVW Company can support increases from $1 billion (equal to $10/share) in year 1, to [$110 million/(.10)] = $1.1 billion (equal to $11 per share) in year 2, to [$121/(.10)] = $1.21 billion (equal to $12.10 per share) in year 3. Shareholders of UVW receive their 10% rate of return through an increase in UVW's share price. See Table 15-2.

Table 15-2
UVW Growth Company-Stock Price
0% Dividend Payment

Year	Market Equity	Earnings	Required Return	Dividend	Net Invest	Stock Price
1	$1 billion	$100 million	10%	0	$100 million	10.00
2	$1.1 billion	$110 million	10%	0	$110 million	11.00
3	$1.21 billion	$121 million	10%	0	$121 million	12.10

Shareholders of UVW Growth Company receive no current dividend payment, but they expect to receive an increase in stock price as UVW reinvests its earnings in investment projects that earn 10% per year.

Shares of both *XYZ and UVW are each worth $10 per share today*—the year 1 price. *Their **current** stock prices do not depend on their respective dividend policies.* What does change is the future path of the price of stocks XYZ and UVW: a flat $10 per share for XYZ, because it pays its 10% earnings to shareholders as dividends; and an expected 10% per year increase in the price of the shares of UVW, because its earnings are reinvested at an after-tax return of 10% per year. The Modigliani and Miller Dividend Irrelevance Hypothesis shows that the current stock price is independent of the company's dividend policy.

15.3 Stock Valuation Approaches: Fundamental, Technical, and MPT

The economics underlying the movements and price levels of the stock market are a mystery to most people. At the end of trading each day, stock analysts on CNNfn, CNBC, and other financial news networks attribute stock price movements to any number of factors: government reports on consumer or wholesale prices; changes in interest rates and the bond market; the increasingly bullish or bearish sentiment of investors; statements by Federal Reserve Chairman Alan Greenspan; or company earnings reports exceeding or falling short of expectations.

Even more puzzling for many market players is what factors determine the absolute price of a stock. Why is the Dow Jones Industrial Average at 10,783.01? Why does McDonald's sell for $32.06 per share? We contend that over time stock prices will gravitate to their underlying intrinsic values. The valuation of common stock is no different from the valuation of any other asset. Asset valuation—be it a financial, real, or human asset—is a generic exercise.

Today's economic value of any asset is simply the total of cash flows that it expects to generate, discounted back to the present at a rate that reflects both the time value of money and the degree of risk or uncertainty associated with those expected cash flows. Cash flows for common stocks can come from dividends, from the sale or merger of a company, from repurchase of stock by the company (Microsoft and Intel have large share repurchase programs), or from the sale of the stock at market prices.

The DCF valuation approach applies to all assets: financial assets such as bonds, mortgages, and stock; real assets such as buildings and real estate, art and antiques, and rare coins; and human assets such as a college education and the economic value of a person's life. For financial assets with fixed payments such as bonds and mortgages, it's relatively simple to apply the DCF approach. Adapting this approach to common stocks is more difficult.

Professional stock market participants practice a number of investment approaches and techniques. These philosophies range from the conservative buy-and-hold companies you know strategies of individual investors to the aggressive long/short, risk-neutral strategies employed by sophisticated hedge fund managers playing the international markets. In general terms, the different stock market investment and valuation strategies can be classified as fitting into one of three camps—fundamental analysis, technical analysis, and modern portfolio theory (MPT). The three philosophies have different beliefs about the relationship between the stock prices that we observe in the markets and underlying intrinsic stock values. These different beliefs are summarized in Exhibit 15-1.

Exhibit 15-1
Valuation Strategies

How to Value a Share?

	Technical Analysis	Fundamental Analysis	Portfolio Theory
What Drives Stock Prices?	Psychology Technical Cosmic	Earnings Dividends	Risk & Return
How to Value A Share?	Trends Waves Factors	Forecast Dividends & Earnings	Risk & Return
Relationship Between Value and Prices?	P ✗ V	P will Eventually Equal Value	P = V

An example of fundamental analysis is the discounted cash flow valuation approach we discussed earlier in Chapter 10. According to this approach, the company's current and future operating and financial performance determine the value of a company's stock. Fundamental analysts use other approaches to assess value as well—primarily target stock price and relative valuation—which we discuss below. To assess a company's prospects, fundamental analysts evaluate overall economic, industry, and company data to estimate a stock's value. The assumption underlying fundamental analysis is that a company's stock price over time will gravitate to its intrinsic value.

Technical analysts believe that short-term stock price movements are influenced primarily by changes in market psychology—the supply and demand considerations that we described in the principle in Chapter 2—**Supply and Demand Drive Asset Prices in the Short-run**. True technicians are not concerned with a company's balance sheet and income statement but instead believe that stock prices reflect the greed versus fear mentality of investors. Underlying technical analysis, there is no necessary relationship between a stock's price and its underlying intrinsic value.

The followers of modern portfolio theory (MPT) believe that competitive forces in the stock market result in stock prices that always reflect underlying intrinsic values. In MPT terminology, the market is efficient because new information is very quickly incorporated into stock prices and there never are any undervalued or overvalued stocks. We explain some of the theories associated with MPT in Chapters 12 and 13.

15.3.1 Fundamental Analysis

Fundamental analysis starts with the assumption that a stock has a true or intrinsic value to which its price is anchored. Price may diverge from this value in the short run, but over time price and intrinsic value will converge. The more famous advocates of fundamental analysis include investors Benjamin Graham, Warren Buffett, and Peter Lynch.

We estimate that more than 80% of Wall Street's analysts primarily use fundamental valuation techniques to base their buy/sell recommendations and to estimate a company's *intrinsic value*. In this analytical style, value is a function of revenue, growth, earnings, dividends, cash flows, profit margins, risk, interest rates, and other factors. Fundamental stock analysts assess a company's stock price versus value using one or more of the three methods that we describe below.

Target Stock Price Analysis:

This popular technique begins with a forecast of a firm's future earnings per share (EPS). This figure is then multiplied by a projected price/earnings (P/E) ratio to arrive at a target stock price. A typical target stock price analysis would conclude in this manner: "With a 2006 EPS estimate of $2.50/share, and assuming a market P/E ratio of 18, our target stock price for McDonald's is $45 per share. Given the current price of $32, we recommend buying the stock."

Relative Value Analysis:

Relative value measures are often used in conjunction with the target stock price approach. Relative value analysis employs a measure of value—most commonly the P/E ratio—for a company and similar stocks and industry peers. In addition to the price/earnings ratio, relative value measures include price/book value (*P/BV*), price/sales (*P/S*), or the price/earnings/growth (*PEG*) ratios as yardsticks for comparisons of different companies with varying characteristics.

Because it's simple to compute and understand, the P/E ratio is the relative value measure quoted most frequently by the media. The P/E ratio for the company is compared to P/E ratios of the company's peers in conjunction with other fundamental factors—most notably earnings per share growth, net operating profit margin, and risk—to ascertain if a stock is overvalued or undervalued. The PEG ratio for the valuation of growth stocks has been a popular metric among investors recently because it is a favorite measure used by The Motley Fool in its publications and Website.

A relative value analysis may read as follows: "McDonald's current P/E of 15.8 is below the P/Es of other fast food restaurant chains. Given that the company's growth (5% for sales and earnings) is in line with industry peers, and its risk profile (as measured by earnings volatility and debt levels) is below that of its competitors, we conclude that McDonald's is undervalued."

Discounted Cash Flow Analysis:

We use DCF analysis as our principal valuation method in this book. While DCF analysis is used to value all types of fixed income investments (bonds, mortgages, etc.), it receives much less attention as a method to value common stocks. In the DCF approach a stock's value is the sum of the expected cash flows of the company, discounted at an appropriate interest rate. The most basic DCF approach is the *dividend discount model (DDM),* under which the value of a stock is the present value of the dividends that an investor expects to receive. Using the DDM approach, the analyst estimates future dividend growth and the required rate of return on the stock, and then discounts those expected dividends to arrive at a stock's value.

Another DCF approach is the *free cash flow to equity (FCFE)* model, which measures the cash flow left over after payments for working capital, capital expenditures, the interest and principal on debt, and dividends on preferred stock. These cash flows are then discounted at the company's cost of equity to arrive at the stock's value. The final DCF approach is the *free cash flow to the firm (FCFF) approach.* It is the approach that we describe herein at length.

Analysts who use DCF analysis tend to provide a simple value statement, as opposed to detailed assessments to investors, such as: "On a cash flow basis, we estimate that McDonald's fair value is $42 per share. Given the current price of $32, we rate MCD as a strong buy."

Many market participants use fundamental analytic techniques as the basis for long-term buy/sell decisions. The basic investment rule associated with fundamental analysis is: if a stock price is well below its intrinsic value, buy the stock; if the stock price is well above its value, sell the stock.

15.3.2 Technical Analysis

Technical analysts chart historic stock price movements, volume of trading activity, and the price/volume aspects of related equity and debt markets to predict or anticipate the stock buying behavior of other market participants. The emotions of other market players are more important to technical analysts than to fundamental analysts. Technical analysts believe that stock prices are influenced more by investor psychology and the emotions of the crowd than by changes in the underlying fundamentals of the company. And the actions of the crowd of investors in the stock markets are driven by *fear* on the downside and *greed* on the upside.

Recall the principle relating to supply and demand—**Supply and Demand Drive Stock Prices in the Short-run**. Technical analysts focus on how market participants will behave in the near-term and how stock market pessimism or optimism affects their behavior. To a technical analyst, when a stock's price trends upward, it is not necessarily because of better operating aspects of the company, but because of increasing demand for the stock and momentum in the company's stock price. Investors who use technical analysis generally have a shorter-term stock holding orientation and more frequent trading activity than investors who employ only fundamental analysis.

Many market participants use technical analytical techniques as the basis for short-term buy/sell decisions. The basic investment rule associated with technical analysis is: if your indicators signal that a stock's price will rise, buy the stock. If your indicators signal that a stock's price will fall, sell the stock.

15.3.3 Modern Portfolio Theory

The notion of efficient capital markets (see Chapter 13) is a cornerstone of MPT. It is the belief that stock prices ALWAYS reflect intrinsic value, and that any type of fundamental or technical analysis is already embedded in the stock price. To support this claim, advocates of efficient markets cite academic studies showing, among other things: daily stock price changes are random (the *random walk hypothesis*); stock prices react very quickly to new company disclosures about earnings, dividend changes, and other corporate news; and that investment funds run by professional money managers (mutual and pension funds), on average, tend to underperform a buy-and-hold overall stock market strategy, as measured by owning an S&P 500 Index Fund.

As a group, these findings suggest that investors cannot use past stock price information or public news releases of firm-specific information to find undervalued stocks; and that even investment fund managers, on average, cannot find a way to detect undervalued stocks. An important exception to these studies is the research performed by Fama and French, and similar research by others, which we discussed in Chapter 13. These studies show that investors can consistently outperform the market by buying undervalued value stocks and selling overvalued growth stocks.

MPT practitioners sometimes express disdain for technical or fundamental analysis. As such, MPT devotees tell investors not to bother to search for undervalued stocks but instead to pick a risk level that they can live with and diversify holdings among a portfolio of stocks (see the principle relating to asset diversification).

MPT presumes that fundamental and technical analysis will get you nowhere in the investment world, since all this information already is reflected in the stock's price. While academics tend to believe this notion, investment professionals do not. Some empirical evidence is beginning to turn against the idea that stock prices always reflect intrinsic stock values. The Fama and French article that we have described previously is the most obvious and best study showing that markets may not be efficient or semi-efficient. Other academic studies using the F&F approach have had similar results.

Since 1990, *The Wall Street Journal* has tested the notion of stock market efficiency in its Investment Dartboard column. The *Journal* compares the six-month total return performance of four stocks, one selected by each of four different investment professionals, with the performance of four stocks picked through the random method of tossing darts at the stock listings pages of the *Journal*. Beginning in 1999, four different amateur investors that read the *Journal* also were invited to participate in each contest. The final contest ended on September 11, 2002. The aggregate performance strongly supports the pros over both the darts and the amateurs. In the 147 contests over the twelve-year period, the pros have beaten the darts in 90. On a relative return basis, the pros have earned an average 6-month return of 9.6% over the period, compared to 5.1% for the DJIA, and 2.9% for the randomly-selected dart stocks,[x] creating a significant difference in returns.

In the 35 contests since 1999 when amateurs were first invited to participate, the professionals have averaged a six-month profit of 4.7%, while the picks of the amateurs lost 5.4%, the dart stocks lost an average of 2.4%, and the Dow Jones Industrial Average fell by an average of 1.7%—a resounding victory for Wall Street and the proponents of fundamental analysis.

We believe strongly that there is value to careful stock selection. We also believe that an investor should own a diversified portfolio of assets. Within that portfolio, the investor should value each stock or asset individually using the DCF technique that we have described. When a stock's price is *overvalued* and it exceeds its intrinsic value by more than X% (the investor picks that percentage, e.g. 15%), the investor should sell that stock and replace it with another stock that is *undervalued* by more than X% (e.g. 15%). This approach allows an investor to benefit from the diversification that is advocated by modern portfolio theory, while also making the value play in her investments.

15.4 The Discounted Free Cash Flow to the Firm Valuation Approach

15.4.1 The Discounted Cash Flow Process

The discounted free cash flow to the firm valuation approach and the ValuePro stock valuation program use a four-step process to value the stock of a company. In this section we value the common stock of Microsoft as of January 1, 2005. If you follow along with us closely, you'll quickly learn the basics about valuing a stock.

Forecast Expected Cash Flow:

The first order of business is to forecast the expected cash flows for the company. We use the most likely assumptions regarding the company's growth rate, net operating profit margin, income tax rate, fixed investment requirement, and incremental working capital requirement. It's easier than it sounds. We describe these cash flow inputs below. The expected cash flows are separated into two time periods: the excess return period—in which the corporation generates cash flows from operation; and the residual value period—the time period after the excess return period in which the corporation is under competitive pressures from rivals and is not able to create additional free cash flows.

Estimate the Weighted Average Cost of Capital:

Next, we estimate the company's weighted average cost of capital (WACC). Its weighted average cost of capital is the discounting rate that we use in the valuation process. We show how to estimate a company's WACC later in this chapter.

Calculate the Enterprise Value of the Corporation:

We then use the company's WACC to discount the expected cash flows during the excess return period to get the aggregate of the corporation's cash flow from profitable operations. We calculate the company's residual value, which usually represents 60% to 90% of the corporation's total value, by dividing the company's net operating profit after taxes (*NOPAT*) at the end of the excess return period by its WACC. We then discount that future value back to today also at a discount rate equal to the company's WACC. We add the cash flow from operations, the residual value, and the short-term assets to get today's value of the corporation as a whole—the corporate or enterprise value. We describe this procedure in greater depth later in this section.

$$\textbf{\textit{Corporate Value = Cash Flow Operations + Residual Value +}}$$
$$\textbf{\textit{Short-term Assets}} \qquad \textbf{\textit{(Eq.15-3)}}$$

The ValuePro Software shows this calculation at the top of the General Pro Forma Page. Again, this simple spreadsheet program does the work automatically.

Calculate Intrinsic Stock Value:

We subtract the value of the company's senior liabilities—debt and preferred stock—from the enterprise value to get value to common equity, as shown below.

$$\textbf{\textit{Value to Common Equity = Corporate Value - Debt - Preferred}}$$
$$\textbf{\textit{- Short-term Liabilities}} \qquad \textbf{\textit{(Eq.15-4)}}$$

We then divide value to common equity by shares outstanding to get the per share intrinsic value of common stock.

Where do we get all this information for a valuation? You can get most of the information for a valuation through a free stock valuation Website:

www.valuepro.net/

that the authors of this book own and operate. But before we jump ahead, let's now spend a little time discussing the theory of competitive advantage that underlies the calculation of cash flow from operations described in Step 3 above.

15.4.2 Excess Return Period and Competitive Advantage

Because of a competitive advantage enjoyed by the firm, the company is able to earn returns on new investments that are greater than its cost of capital during the *excess return period*. Examples of companies that experienced a significant period of big-time competitive advantage are IBM in the 1950s and 1960s, Apple Computer in the 1980s, and Microsoft, Intel, and Cisco in the 1990s.

Success invariably attracts competitors with their own lower-cost versions of the product or service, and whose aggressive practices cut into market share and revenue growth rates. The pricing and marketing activities of competitors also drive down net operating profit margins. A lower NOPM reduces return on new investments to levels that approach the corporation's WACC. When a company loses its competitive advantage and the return from its new investments just equals its WACC, the corporation is investing in business strategies in which the aggregate net present value is 0. Worse yet, companies can generate negative returns and destroy shareholder value—witness IBM in the 1980s, Apple in the 1990s, and the telecom companies in the 2000s.

As a company increases in size it attracts additional competition. As industries develop and market sectors grow, companies serving those sectors can have relatively small revenue—$10 to $100 million—and not make the radar screens of competitors to attract their interest. However, when a company hits the $100 million revenue threshold, potential competitors start to notice and begin to enter the sector space, cutting into growth and profit margins. So small-cap firms initially may have very little competition in a specialty market sector, so they can make some hay and generate abnormal profits from operations.

The length of time over which a company can earn abnormal profits depends on the particular products being produced, the industry in which the company operates, and the barriers for competitors to enter the business. Markets that have a high barrier to entry, such as products with patent protection, strong brand names, or unique marketing channels, might have an excess return period that is quite long—10 to 15 years or longer. More typically, the excess return period for most companies will be 5 to 7 years or shorter. All else equal, a shorter excess return period results in a lower stock value.

What happens after the excess return period? Does the company dry up, shrivel, or go bankrupt? NO! For valuation purposes, the company loses its competitive advantage over its competitors. The loss of competitive advantage means that the company's stock value may still grow, but only at the market's required rate of return for the stock—not at an abnormally high growth rate level. For example, if the common stock price of RST Company (which does not pay dividends) is $10, and its required rate of return is 12%, its stockholders expect it to grow to ($10 * 1.12) = $11.20 after year 1; ($11.20 * 1.12) = $12.54 after year 2; ($12.54 * 1.12) = $14.03 after year 3; ad infinitum. Once the excess return period ceases and the company has no more profitable new investments, the company should pay all of its free cash flow to shareholders through dividends or share repurchases.

When return on investment equals a company's WACC, investors are only compensated for the risk that they are taking in owning the company's stock and no additional value is created from new business investments. The stock price is still growing in value, but its growth does not exceed its risk-adjusted market expectation (or match investors' hopes). At that point in time, the after-tax earnings of the company can be treated and valued as what is known as a cash flow perpetuity—equal to the company's net operating profit after tax divided by its WACC (NOPAT/WACC). This number is discounted to the present, also at the company's WACC.

This discounted value is called the company's *residual value*—a very important number that generally represents 60% to 90% of the total value of the company. The residual value is very sensitive to projections of the company's NOPAT and its WACC, as described below. What is our preferred excess return period? This is a judgment call. We use the 1-5-7-10 Rule.

We group companies into one of four general categories and excess return periods. We then value them using a ten-year excess return period to calculate what we consider to be their maximum value, and a more conservative one or five or seven-year excess return period to calculate a reasonable or minimum value.

Here are the criteria we use to determine the lower, more conservative excess return period:

- *Boring companies* are those that operate in a highly competitive, low-margin industry in which they have nothing special going for them—a one-year excess return period;
- *Decent companies* that have a recognizable name, decent reputation and perhaps a regulatory benefit (e.g., a utility like Consolidated Edison), but don't control pricing or growth in their industry—a five-year excess return period;
- *Good companies* with good brand names, large economies of scale, good marketing channels, and consumer identification (e.g., McDonald's)—a seven-year excess return period; and
- *Great companies* with great growth potential, tremendous marketing power, brand names, and in-place benefits (e.g. Intel, Microsoft, Coca Cola, and Disney)—a ten-year excess return period.

We do not believe in going out more than 10 years with an excess return period. Some fundamental stock valuation models, like the dividend discount model, incorporate earnings and dividend growth in excess of the company's WACC, out to an infinite time period. Cash flows in these models are discounted until the hereafter. We think that ten years is a reasonable amount of time to incorporate the product cycles of today's markets.

Does a corporation really lose its competitive advantage and the benefit of its excess return period? For well-managed corporations, the answer is probably not. Most well run companies will continue to innovate, to reduce operating costs and increase efficiency, and to create new business strategies so that they will maintain their competitive advantage for a long time. Some will go bankrupt. Some will be acquired or merge. But the concept of an excess return period or forecast period is one that should result in a more conservative, less aggressive, stock valuation. When we invest, we would rather err on the side of conservatism than overpay for a stock.

15.4.3 The Three Valuation Categories

In calculating corporate or enterprise value, the FCFF approach and the spreadsheet software that we use segments corporate assets and liabilities, and discounts cash flows into three categories and time periods:

- *Cash Flow From Operations.* First, during the excess return period, we calculate free cash flow to the firm. This is the difference between operating cash inflows and cash outflows. The free cash flows are then discounted. The discount factors are a function of the firm's WACC and the timing of the expected cash flows.
- *Corporate Residual Value.* Second, we find the corporation's residual value. This is the value calculated by taking the company's NOPAT at the end of the excess return period, dividing it by the company's WACC, and discounting it (also at the WACC) to today's value. At the end of the excess return period, we assume that the corporation is just receiving a return on investment equal to its WACC. Therefore, the net present value (*NPV*) of additional investment by the corporation is zero and no additional value is created for stockholders.[xi]
- *Short-term Assets.* Third, we add the firm's short-term assets to the mix. We include only real current assets that could be sold or liquidated at close to face value, such as investment securities, inventories, accounts receivable, and other current corporate financial investments. We do not include intangible assets, such as goodwill, which would be difficult to sell or value, or long-term assets such as property, plant, and equipment, which are essential to generating the company's cash flow from operations. Here the current balance sheet of the firm comes into play. These assets have no business operating risk and should not be discounted in the valuation procedure.

Corporate value is the sum of the discounted cash flow from operations, plus discounted corporate residual value, plus short-term assets.

Corporate Value = Cash Flow Operations + Residual Value
+ Short-Term Assets

Once total corporate value is calculated, we subtract the amount of short-term liabilities and the market value of debt and preferred stock, and then divide that amount by the shares of stock outstanding to get the per share intrinsic stock value.

Intrinsic Value = (Corporate Value – Debt – Preferred – S.T. Liabilities)
Shares Outstanding   **(Eq.15-6)**

Mathematically, this is as difficult as the DCF approach gets. No calculus, no differential equations—just addition, subtraction, multiplication, and division. And through the magic of a microprocessor, the computations occur instantaneously.

15.5   Microsoft—A Simple DCF Example

So how complex is it to value stocks like a pro? To illustrate the valuation process, we now take you through a simplified valuation of Microsoft. The four steps are: forecast expected cash flow; estimate the required rate of return (the WACC); discount the expected cash flow by the WACC; and calculate per share intrinsic value.

15.5.1 Forecast Microsoft's Expected Cash Flow

Expected cash flow to shareholders includes cash dividends, if any, and the expected increase (or decrease) of the stock's price during the investor's holding period of the stock. As we showed in Chapter 10, it's easy for the bank to estimate the expected cash flow from Gary's mortgage because he agrees to pay the bank exactly $734 per month. Accurate estimations of cash flow for common stock are more challenging. Here we describe ways to help you overcome the complications associated with cash flow estimation.

The DCF valuation analysis that we use estimates expected free cash flow to the firm. Free cash flows are cash amounts that are available to be paid to stockholders. Earnings-per-share is an accounting measure and an accountant's way of measuring corporate performance. Discounted free cash flows are an investor's way of measuring potential returns to shareholders. DCF is more wallet-oriented, hence more meaningful to an investor.

The discounted free cash flow approach uses corporate performance measures that focus solely on real cash dollars flowing into and out of the company. Corporate activities that produce additional net cash inflows to the company, such as increased revenue growth or increased net operating profit margins, have a positive effect on stock value. These are good activities.

Corporate activities that produce net cash outflows from the company, such as higher income tax rates, higher capital investment or working capital requirements, or lower net operating profit margins due to increasing labor costs or other costs of production, have a negative effect on stock value. These payments may be necessary from the corporation's perspective but they are not particularly good activities for the stock's value.

Exhibit 15-2
Microsoft Stock Price Chart

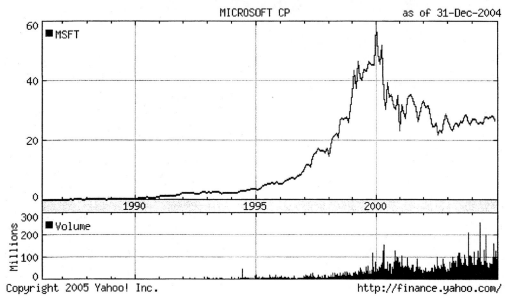

Microsoft has been a darling of Wall Street for many years. Since it's initial public offering in March of 1986, Microsoft produced an average annual return of almost 50% per year to investors until 2000 (see Exhibit 15-2 above as taken from the Yahoo Finance Website). With the bursting of the high-tech bubble in 2000, Microsoft's return dropped into negative figures.

The cash flow measures that are most important for valuation and the initial estimates for Microsoft are: the revenue growth rate—10%; the net operating profit margin—40%; the net fixed capital investment rate; the incremental working capital investment rate—12.47%; and the company's income tax rate—33. Briefly, these may be described as:

Revenue Growth Rate	=	Annual Growth in Revenue
Net Operating Profit Margin	=	Operating Income/Revenue
Tax Rate	=	Taxes/Pre-tax Income
Working Capital Investment	=	Change in Working Capital/Revenue
Fixed Capital Investment	=	Net Capital Investment/Revenue

To compute net capital investment, we have provided the depreciation rate—3.22% depreciation divided by revenue, and the investment rate—3.01%, capital expenditures divided by revenue.

Exhibit 15-3

ValuePro 2002 - [VP2002.BWB]

File Edit ValuePro Window Help

Valuation Date 01/02/2005

ValuePro 2002
General Input Screen
Intrinsic Stock Value $26.16
General Inputs

Company Ticker.....	MSFT		
Excess Return Period (years)	10	Depreciation Rate (% of Rev.)	3.22
Revenues ($mil)	36835	Investment Rate (% of Rev.)	3.01
Growth Rate (%)	10.00	Working Capital (% of Rev.)	12.47
Net Operating Profit Margin (%)	40.00	Short-Term Assets ($mil)	40301
Tax Rate (%)	33.00	Short-Term Liabilities($mil)	14843
Stock Price($)	26.72	Equity Risk Premium (%)	3.00
Shares Outstanding (mil)	10865	Company Beta	1.21
10-year Treasury Yield (%)	4.25	Value of Debt Out. ($mil)	0
Bond Spread to Treasury (%)	0.00	Value of Pref. Stock Out. ($mil)	0
Preferred Stock Yield (%)	0.00	Company WACC (%)	7.87

We performed analysis of the historic ratios for Microsoft and used them in calculating the sample inputs listed above. We used analyst consensus estimates for Microsoft's projected growth rates. We show our sample inputs in Exhibit 15-3, the general input screen of the ValuePro software program. Our valuation spreadsheets will become more meaningful to you as we progress through this example.

Net operating profit (NOP) for Microsoft during the excess return period is projected to grow more than 2.5 times, from $13,207 million in 2006 to $38,216 million in the year 2015. To convert from net operating profit to free cash flow to the firm, we must: (1) add depreciation (a non-cash expense), and (2) subtract income taxes, incremental working capital, and fixed capital investment. Free cash flow (FCFF) projections for Microsoft (in millions of dollars) are:

Year	**2006**		**2007**		**2008**		**2009**		**.....**		**2015**
FCFF	$10,485	+	$11,533	+	$12,687	+	$13,955	+	.....	+	$24,722

See the projected annual free cash flows to Microsoft as shown in Column 11 of Exhibit 15-4 below.

Exhibit 15-4
Microsoft General Pro Forma Screen

ValuePro 2002 - [VP2002.BWB]

File Edit ValuePro Window Help

| Valuation Date | 01/02/2005 |

ValuePro 2002
General Pro Forma Screen
10-year Excess Return Period
MSFT

Disc. Excess Return Period FCFF	$106,291	Total Corporate Value	$299,033
Discounted Residual Value	$152,441	Less Debt	$0
Short-Term Assets	$40,301.0	Less Preferred Stock	$0
Total Corporate Value	$299,033	Less Short-Term Liabilities	($14,843)
		Total Value to Common Equity	$284,190
		Intrinsic Stock Value	**$26.16**

(2)	(3)	(4)	(5)	(6)	(7)	(8)	(9)	(10)	(11)	(12)	(13)
12 Months Ending	Revenues	NOP	Adj. Taxes	NOPAT	Invest.	Deprec.	Change in Invest.	Change in Working Capital	FCFF	Discount Factor	Discounted FCFF
01/02/2005	36,835										
01/02/2006	40,518	16,207	5,348	10,859	1,220	1,305	-85	459	10,485	0.9270	9,720
01/02/2007	44,570	17,828	5,883	11,945	1,342	1,435	-94	505	11,533	0.8594	9,911
01/02/2008	49,027	19,611	6,472	13,139	1,476	1,579	-103	556	12,687	0.7967	10,107
01/02/2009	53,930	21,572	7,119	14,453	1,623	1,737	-113	611	13,955	0.7385	10,306
01/02/2010	59,323	23,729	7,831	15,899	1,786	1,910	-125	673	15,351	0.6846	10,509
01/02/2011	65,255	26,102	8,614	17,488	1,964	2,101	-137	740	16,886	0.6347	10,717
01/02/2012	71,781	28,712	9,475	19,237	2,161	2,311	-151	814	18,574	0.5883	10,928
01/02/2013	78,959	31,584	10,423	21,161	2,377	2,542	-166	895	20,432	0.5454	11,143
01/02/2014	86,855	34,742	11,465	23,277	2,614	2,797	-182	985	22,475	0.5056	11,363
01/02/2015	95,541	38,216	12,611	25,605	2,876	3,076	-201	1,083	24,722	0.4687	11,587
	95,541	38,216	12,611	25,605	3,076	3,076	0	0	325,244	0.4687	152,441

15.5.2 Estimate Microsoft's Discount Rate—The WACC

What is the appropriate rate to use to discount Microsoft's uncertain (but expected) cash flow? There are several discounted cash flow methods used in the capital market. The method used in this book calculates *the after-tax weighted average cost of capital* (WACC) of the company and uses that WACC to discount the company's after-tax free cash flow. Again, we show you how to estimate a company's WACC longhand, and if you use the ValuePro software it automatically does all the work based on the inputs that you feed it.

How do you calculate a WACC? Finance theory (as we discussed in the principle relating to investment valuation) tells us that a company's WACC discounting rate is a function of three general categories of risk/return adjustments required by the market:

- As a *base rate of return* for any investment, use the market's current long-term risk-free rate of interest (which incorporates expectations of inflation). We use the current 10-year (the maturity coincides with the maximum length of the excess return period) United States Treasury bond yield.
- For the expected return associated with the company's debt and preferred stock, a spread above the risk-free rate that reflects the company's *risk of default.*
- For the expected return associated with the company's common stock, we use the market's assessment of the current equity risk premium, in general, and the *specific risk* (*beta*) associated with the company's stock.

To arrive at the company's WACC, the cost of capital inputs described above must be adjusted for two factors: the tax deductibility of interest payments; and the percentage of debt, preferred stock, and common stock employed by the company in financing its operations. While this calculation may seem complex, it is actually quite simple with a calculator or software such as ValuePro.

The discount rate that is used in the valuation process, and the general movement of interest rates, can have an enormous effect on the market value of the stock.[xii] The discount rate that is used to value a stock reflects the three risk factors described above. Investments with similar risks should have similar discount rates.

Factors that reduced the discount rate, such as a decrease in interest rates due to expectations of lower inflation, or a decrease in the equity risk premium due to the fall of communism and an increase in free trade among nations, greatly increased stock market valuations in the 1990s. An important reason for the percentage increases in general stock market valuations, in excess of the growth rate of corporate earnings during the 1990s, was due to the significant reduction of interest rates and their related lowering of corporate WACCs. A lower WACC increases a stock's value.

Conversely, factors that increase the discount rate, such as expectations of higher inflation, concerns about corporate accounting, and government policies that restrict free trade, or an increasing equity risk premium due to terrorist attacks, currency/trade crises, production bottlenecks, or other reasons, will have a significant negative effect on stock market prices. A higher WACC reduces a stock's value.

The WACC for Microsoft is easier to compute than for most firms since the company is financed completely by common stock. Microsoft has no debt or preferred stock outstanding. In this simple example, the WACC for Microsoft was entirely a function of its cost of common stock. The capitalization and the WACC for Microsoft looked like this:

Capital Source	Capital Amount	Discounting Rate
Debt	*0*	*0*
Preferred Stock	0	0
Common Stock	$290,312 million	7.87%
WACC		**7.87%**

At one point during 1999, Microsoft had a market capitalization of almost $600 billion. Microsoft's stock price was reduced by more than one-half. Market capitalization is defined as the market value of debt, preferred stock and common stock outstanding. Since Microsoft had no debt or preferred stock outstanding, its market capitalization was equal to the number of common shares outstanding times the stock price per share. Microsoft's market cap (on January 1, 2005) was as follows:

Common Shares Outstanding	*	Stock Price	=	Market Equity
10,865 million	*	*$26.72*	=	*$290.312 billion*

The cost of common stock for Microsoft is a function of the level of interest rates (the 10-year U.S. Treasury—4.25% on the valuation date), the risk of Microsoft relative to the overall stock market (its beta—estimated to be 1.2075), and the equity risk premium (estimated to be 3%). Based on Equation 12-5 using the CAPM pricing model, Microsoft's cost of equity (and weighted average cost of capital since it has no debt or preferred stock) is:

Cost of Equity = Risk Free Rate + Risk Premium
Cost of Equity =   4.25% + 1.2075 * (3%)
Cost of Equity = 7.87%

15.5.3 Calculate Microsoft's Total Corporate Value

Step 3 discounts the expected cash flow by the required rate of return. In the DCF approach, the required rate of return is the firm's WACC. Recall Gary's mortgage example from Chapter 10. This concept is the same.

Two stages are involved:

- Calculate the discounted value of the expected cash flows over the 10-year excess return period; and
- Calculate the value of Microsoft beyond this 10-year period—its residual value— the value of the cash flow stream as a perpetuity.

Column 12 of Exhibit 15-4 shows the discounted expected cash flows for 2006-2015 for Microsoft. The sum of the discounted cash flows over the ten-year excess return period is $106,291 million.

Exhibit 15-4 also shows the total corporate value calculation. We start with the sum of the discounted free cash flows ($106,291 million) and add the present value of the expected cash flows beyond the end of the excess return period (year 2015). Residual value equals net operating profit after tax (NOPAT) divided by the WACC. The residual value for Microsoft is [$25,605 million/(.0787)] = $325,244 million. Since this is the value at a point in time 10 years from today, we discount it at the 10-year discount factor of 0.4687 to get its present value of $152,441 million.

To calculate the enterprise value of the corporation, we sum the discounted free cash flow over the 10-year excess return period ($106,291 million), the discounted residual value ($152,441 million), and the short-term assets ($40,301 million) associated with the firm's balance sheet and come up with a value of $299,033 million for Microsoft.

15.5.4 Calculate Microsoft's Intrinsic Stock Value

The final step involves computing the total value to common equity by subtracting the market value of the firm's liabilities and dividing that amount by shares outstanding. Microsoft has no debt or preferred stock outstanding, and its total short-term liabilities are $14,843 million. Exhibit 15-4 shows the total value to common equity calculation. The estimated market value of Microsoft's common stock is $284,190 million. Dividing this figure by the number of shares outstanding (10.865 billion shares) on January 1, 2005, gives an estimated stock value per share of $26.16.

Notice that the $26.16 intrinsic value was about 2% less than that date's stock price of $26.72. We would be indifferent to owning Microsoft if we owned it, and would refrain from purchasing it until the price declined to a lower level. And we haven't adjusted the intrinsic value for the dilution associated with stock options—an adjustment that would have resulted in a further decrease in the value of Microsoft.

15.6   Valuepro.net Online Stock Valuation Website

Recently, several free websites that specialize in DCF stock valuation models have become popular with investors. The website *www.valuepro.net* is near and dear to our hearts. We created the site in concert with the original 1999 publication of *Streetsmart Guide to Valuing a Stock,* and we have administered the site since that time. The site is devoted to the DCF method of stock valuation and has links that explain the approach in great detail.

In 2000, we introduced a free online valuation service that has become popular with users. Type a stock symbol into the slot on the home web page, see Exhibit 15-6, click on the <u>Get Baseline Valuation</u> button, and the online valuation program accesses data sources for information relating to the company that you are valuing. The program calculates twenty variables, puts them into our valuation algorithm, and calculates the intrinsic stock value—our estimate of that day's value of the shares of the company. Our valuation algorithm uses a simple discounted cash flow model.

Exhibit 15-5
Valuepro.net Home Web Page

ValuePro

- Home
- Learn the ValuePro Approach
- Buy Valuing a Stock 2 - 10 Principles
- Buy Streetsmart Guide 1
- Buy ValuePro Software
- Guide to the ValuePro Software
- Buy Running With the Bulls
- Frequently Asked Questions
- Message Board
- Contact Us
- Terms of Service
- About the Online Valuation

Announcing Valuing a Stock 2 - 10 Principles of Finance!!

Buy ValuePro Stock Valuation Software!!

ValuePro is our new easy-to-use stock valuation program that interacts with our online valuation service. Now you can download data from our web site to your computer and use ValuePro to analyze your investments. The price is only $44.95. Please see our Guide to the ValuePro Software for an in-depth description.

Try our online stock valuation service. Enter the stock symbol, click on the Get Baseline Valuation button, and we do the rest. The inputs used to value the stock are updated periodically. You can change any input and recalculate a stock value. Learn more about using the online valuation by clicking here.

Enter Stock Symbol: [   ]   **Get Baseline Valuation**

We are developing a stock value/stock price screening program which will rank stocks based upon a value-to-price ratio and a portfolio valuation program.

Value Screening   **Portfolio Valuation**

ValuePro.net was founded by three financial engineers/finance professors to develop and distribute inexpensive, easy to use and understand valuation tools.

3232374 hits since June 1, 2001

The online valuation screen of the Valuepro.net website shows each valuation input, see Exhibit 15-6 below. You can go to any or all of the input cells, put your own estimates into the cells, and hit the Recalculate button. The online valuation program calculates a new intrinsic stock value based on the inputs that you have provided. If you want to see the detailed pro forma statement associated with the valuation, click on the Cash Flows button and a cash flow schedule based on the underlying inputs appears. You can then click the Value Another Stock button and begin the process anew. There is no limitation to the number of valuations you may perform and the valuations are free.

The strengths of the website and the online valuation program are that it is easy to use and understand, is completely interactive, and is totally transparent. Just type the symbol into the slot and the program does the rest. With the exception of the WACC input, which is a calculated number, you can change any input that you desire and the new intrinsic value based on your inputs pops up on the computer screen. You can see each input and each assumption and follow the cash flows to verify that the intrinsic value is consistent with the inputs. Another nice feature is that there (currently) is no advertising or annoying banner or pop-up ads on the site.

The weakness of the website is that it is a bare bones site. There is no symbol look up feature and no ancillary information aspects to the stocks that are being valued. The singular focus is on intrinsic stock value. It is also a very low budget operation. Data is updated weekly and there is no effort to comb the data to find inputs that are highly implausible or wrong. The online valuation service does not yet work well for some highly levered stocks, such as REITs and financials, nor does it work well for portfolio companies, such as ICGE or Berkshire Hathaway.

Exhibit 15-6
Valuepro.net Online Valuation—Cisco

ValuePro.net Online Valuation

| VP Home | Cash Flows | Download Baseline Data |

Online Valuation for CSCO - 1 / 1 / 2005

Intrinsic Stock Value `27.66` | Recalculate | | Value Another Stock |

Excess Return Period (yrs)	10	Depreciation Rate (% of Rev)	4.34
Revenues ($mil)	22045.0	Investment Rate (% of Rev)	2.78
Growth Rate (%)	16.5	Working Capital (% of Rev)	10.77
Net Oper. Profit Margin (%)	33.62	Short-Term Assets ($mil)	12476.0
Tax Rate (%)	27.995	Short-Term Liab. ($mil)	9229
Stock Price ($)	19.32	Equity Risk Premium (%)	3
Shares Outstanding (mil)	6591.0	Company Beta	1.5225
10-Yr Treasury Yield (%)	5	Value Debt Out. ($mil)	0
Bond Spread Treasury (%)	1.5	Value Pref. Stock Out. ($mil)	0
Preferred Stock Yield (%)	7.5	Company WACC (%)	9.57

We show the inputs associated with the Valuepro.net online valuation of Cisco on January 1, 2005. The stock price of Cisco closed at $19.32 per share and the online service estimated the intrinsic stock value of Cisco to be $27.66. Since the intrinsic value is greater than the price, an investor might have wanted to consider buying Cisco at this price level.

15.7   Summary

Valuing common stocks is a mystery to many investors. Recent extreme volatility in the stock market no doubt has added to the mystique. Indeed, many market observers insist that these gyrations support the notion that stock valuation is less art and science and more magic. This chapter's focus is on the art and science of stock valuation and how you can profitably use it in your investment decisions. We explain how you can apply solid stock valuation principles and techniques to value stocks.

The crucial concept we attempt to hammer home throughout this book is that the value of a stock—like the value of any other financial instrument—is equal to the discounted value of its expected cash flows, adjusted for risk and timing. For many investors, there are two general sources of confusion in the stock valuation process. First, how do we estimate future cash flows? Second, what is the appropriate rate to discount uncertain cash flows? This book and the principles that we describe herein teach you how to address these questions and use your answers to value stocks.

In this chapter we used a discounted cash flow technique to value Microsoft and found that it was overvalued. On January 1, 2005, we estimated that the value of Microsoft was $26.16 per share. Its closing price that day was $27.72. Based on this type of analysis, we would make decisions on whether to buy or sell the shares of a stock. In this case, we would be relatively indifferent about owning shares of MSFT. We also described the stock valuation website www.valuepro.net and valued the stock of Cisco using the inputs for valuation that were automatically downloaded from the site.

List of Terms
1. Limited Liability
2. Perpetuity
3. Residual Value
4. Return to Stockholders
5. Dividend Irrelevance Hypothesis
6. Fundamental Analysis
7. Intrinsic Value
8. Primary Target Stock Price
9. Relative Valuation
10. Discounted Cash Flow Analysis
11. Dividend Discount Model
12. Free Cash Flow to Equity
13. Free Cash Flow to Firm
14. Technical Analysis
15. Modern Portfolio Theory
16. Efficient Capital Markets
17. Weighted Average Cost of Capital
18. Corporate Value
19. Cash Flow from Operations
20. Value to Common Equity
21. Excess Return Period
22. Working Capital Investment
23. Fixed Capital Investment
24. Base Rate of Return
25. Risk of Default
26. Specific Risk (Beta)

Questions

1. What drives the value of a stock?
2. How does the dividend policy of a company influence the current value of its stock, according to Dr. Miller and Dr. Modigliani?
3. Explain the three basic strategies used to value stock.
4. What is fundamental analysis? Explain the approaches used by fundamental analysts to value stocks.
5. How do technical analysts value stock? Do technical analysts believe in the stock price reflecting its intrinsic value?
6. What is Modern Portfolio Theory?
7. How is intrinsic stock value calculated under Discounted Cash Flow method?
8. What is Excess Return Period? What are the categories into which companies are grouped and what is the excess return period for each category?
9. Explain Residual Value. How is it calculated?
10. What is WACC? How is it calculated?

Problem Set

1. Latifa purchased 100 shares of Tech Inc for $3000 a year before. Tech Inc paid a dividend of $1 per stock. If the stock is currently trading at $35 per share, what return did Latifa earn on his investment?

2. John purchased 10 shares of Drug Inc for $370 a year before. Today the stocks of Drug Inc are trading at $30.5 per share. If John received a dividend of $4.50 per share last year, what is his return on investment?

3. Given the P/E of different companies and the projected earnings per share, estimate the target common stock value of the companies:

Company	Projected EPS	P/E
Wal-Mart	$2.32	31.26
McDonald's	$1.31	21.65
Lockheed Martin	$2.29	40.69
Pfizer	$1.77	20.50

4. If ABC Utility's common stock will always pay a dividend of $2.00 per year, what is the value of its stock if investors required rate of return is 8 percent?

5. Electronics Corp. will pay a year end dividend of $1.50 per share. Investors expect the dividend to grow at a rate of 2 percent indefinitely. If the stock currently sells for $20 per share, what is the required rate of return on the stock?

6. What is the stock price of Foods Inc., if the company will pay a year end dividend of $2.50 per share which is expected to grow forever at 3 percent and if the required rate of return is 12 percent?

7. Instruments Inc.'s common stock currently pays an annual dividend of $2.10 per share. If required return on common stock is 8 percent, calculate the value of Instruments Inc.'s common stock when
    (a) Dividends are expected to remain constant forever.
    (b) Dividends are expected to grow at a constant annual rate of 3 percent to infinity.
    (c) Dividends are expected to grow at 5 percent for the first 5 years and grow at 3 percent constant rate from year 6 to infinity.

8. Tool Inc. paid a stock dividend of $2.00 per share and future dividend payments are expected to remain constant. Calculate the value of common stock of Tool Inc., if
    (a) Investors required rate of return is 8 percent.
    (b) If investors risk perception towards the company increases and required rate of return increases to 15 percent.

9. If Grocery Inc. paid a dividend of $3.00 and dividend is expected to grow by 5 percent forever, what would you pay for the stock of Grocery Inc., if
   - (a) you can earn 12 percent on investments with similar risk?
   - (b) you can earn only 8 percent on investments with similar risk?

10. Chocolates Inc. paid a dividend of $1.50 per share last year and future dividend payments are expected to grow at a rate of 4 percent per year indefinitely.
   - (a) If the price of the stock of Chocolates Inc. is $32, what is the required rate of return?
   - (b) If the price of the stock increases to $40, what is the required rate of return?

11. If a firm's discounted cash flow from operations is estimated to be $10,364 million, its residual value $42,368 million, and it has short term assets of $896 million, calculate the value of the firm.

12. If James calculates the corporate value of XYZ Inc. to be $88,784 million, what is the intrinsic value per share of XYZ Inc., if the company has debt with a market value of $8,344, has no preferred stock or short term liabilities, and the number of shares outstanding is 4,575 million?

13. ABC Inc. is expected to earn free cash flow of $500 million in the current year and free cash flows are expected to increase by 5 percent every year for the next 5 years, after which it is expected to remain constant. Calculate the value of ABC Inc. if the WACC is 10 percent and the company has no debt.

14. XYZ Inc. earned a free cash flow of $380 million. The free cash flows of XYZ Inc are expected to grow at 8 percent for the next 10 years, after which it continues to grow indefinitely at 2 percent. What is the value of XYZ Inc.'s stock, if the market value of its debt as of today is $1,400 million, the required rate of return is 12 percent, and XYZ Inc. has 150 million shares outstanding?

Assignment #15-1

1. Sarah purchased 1,000 shares of ABC Inc for $42,000 a year before and today it is worth $45,800. What return did Sarah earn on her investment, if she also received a dividend of $2.50 per share?
   - (a) 10 percent
   - (b) 12 percent
   - (c) 15 percent
   - (d) 17 percent

2. If Rosa earned a return of 18 percent on 10 shares of XYZ Inc. that she purchased a year ago for $250, what is the value of per share of XYZ Inc. if the company had paid a dividend of $1.50 per share?
   - (a) $25
   - (b) $28
   - (c) $30
   - (d) $32

3. If John earned a return of 20 percent on his investment in the stock of MNO Corp. which he purchased for $28 last year and is currently trading for $31.50, what dividend did MNO Corp pay during the previous year?
   - (a) $1.80
   - (b) $1.90
   - (c) $2.00
   - (d) $2.10

4. Litao holds stock of Z Inc., which is currently trading at $45. He received a dividend of $1.75 per share during the previous year. If Litao calculates his return on investment to be 13.80 percent, how much did he purchase the shares for last year?
   - (a) $39.50
   - (b) $40.00
   - (c) $41.50
   - (d) $42.00

5. If the P/E ratio of Exxon Mobil is 16.07 and the earnings estimate is $2.13 per share, what is the target stock price of Exxon Mobil?
   - (a) $34.23
   - (b) $35.15
   - (c) $35.84
   - (d) $36.12

6. If Jose calculates the target stock price of ConEd to be $37.35 using a P/E multiple of 12.66, what earnings estimate did he use?
   - (a) $3.07
   - (b) $2.98
   - (c) $2.95

(d) $2.64

7. T Inc. paid a dividend of $1.75 last year. If dividends are expected to remain constant indefinitely, and if the required rate of return is 8 percent, what is the stock price of T Inc.?
   (a) $20.78
   (b) $21.88
   (c) $22.44
   (d) $22.86

8. M Inc. paid a dividend of $3.20 in the current year. Its dividend is expected to grow by 5 percent in the next year. If the required rate of return is 12 percent, what is the stock price of M Inc.?
   (a) $25.0
   (b) $26.2
   (c) $28.0
   (d) $28.8

9. If Z Inc. paid a dividend of $2.20 last year and dividend is expected to grow at 3 percent indefinitely, what is the stock price of Z Inc., given that the required rate of return is 15 percent?
   (a) $13.42
   (b) $16.68
   (c) $18.88
   (d) $20.34

10. If after tax cash flows of G Corp was $750 million last year and they are expected to grow at 2 percent per year for the next 5 years after which there is no growth, what is the intrinsic stock value of G Corp if the market value of its debt today is $2,500, it has 200 million shares outstanding, and the required rate of return is 12 percent?
    (a) $20.48
    (b) $23.86
    (c) $25.78
    (d) $26.96

Assignment #15-2

1. If Laurel earned a return of 12 percent on her investment in the stock of Zee Corp., which she purchased for $23.00 last year and is currently trading at $22.80, what dividend did Zee Corp. pay during the previous year?
   (a) $2.64
   (b) $2.96
   (c) $3.12
   (d) $3.68

2. If Jack estimates the earnings of SW Airlines to be $0.32 and calculates the target stock price (using P/E multiple) to be $17.02, what P/E multiple did Jack use?
   (a) 45.67
   (b) 53.20
   (c) 55.46
   (d) 56.89

3. M Corp. paid a dividend of $2.30 last year. If dividends are expected to remain constant indefinitely, what required rate of return gives a share price of $15.33?
   (a) 12 percent
   (b) 13 percent
   (c) 14 percent
   (d) 15 percent

4. If investors' required rate of return on common stock of N Inc. is 12 percent and N Inc. shares are traded at $32, what is the dividend that investors expect from N Inc. assuming that the company has paid constant dividends in the past and is expected to do the same in future?
   (a) $2.86
   (b) $2.94
   (c) $3.34
   (d) $3.84

5. If P Corp. paid a dividend of $1.20 last year and the dividend is expected to grow at 5 percent indefinitely, what is the required rate of return if the stock is being traded at $23 today?
   (a) 10.5 percent
   (b) 11.5 percent
   (c) 12.5 percent
   (d) 13.5 percent

6. Toys Inc. paid a dividend of $2.25 last year and the dividend is expected to grow at a constant rate in the future. If the required rate of return is 11 percent and the stock is being traded at $25.52, what is the constant growth rate of dividend?
   (a) 1.75 percent
   (b) 2.00 percent
   (c) 2.25 percent

(d) 2.75 percent

7. If Tech Inc. paid a dividend of $2.0 last year and its dividend is expected to grow at 5 percent for the next 2 years and after that at 2 percent indefinitely, what is the stock price of the company if the required rate of return is 13 percent?
   (a) $14.24
   (b) $15.76
   (c) $16.24
   (d) $17.76

8. If Machine Inc. is a debt free stable company and is expected to generate free cash flows of $200 million forever, what is its stock value when the required rate of return is 8 percent and the number of shares outstanding is 125 million?
   (a) $18
   (b) $20
   (c) $22
   (d) $24

9. Tools Inc has a debt of $1600 million and 200 shares outstanding today. Tools Inc. generated a free cash flow of $850 million last year and its future cash flow is expected to grow at a constant rate of 1 percent indefinitely. If investors expect a rate or return of 9 percent, what is the value of Tools Inc.'s stock?
   (a) $38.34
   (b) $42.90
   (c) $45.66
   (d) $47.82

10. Icecream Inc., which is currently being traded at $26, generated a free cash flow of $375 million last year and is expected to generate future cash flows that grow at a constant rate. If the number of shares outstanding is 125 million and investors' required rate of return is 16 percent, what is the expected constant cash flow growth rate?
    (a) 1 percent
    (b) 2 percent
    (c) 3 percent
    (d) 4 percent

CHAPTER 16

MANAGING RISK: DIVERSIFYING, HEDGING, INSURING, AND DERIVATIVE SECURITIES

In this section we explore managing risk, a sometimes difficult to understand function of the financial markets. Some of the concepts that we address in this chapter, such as derivative securities and option valuation, are advanced for a first text in finance, and we will not be able to do them justice in the space provided. However, we do want to introduce you to this very important area of finance.

In everyday life we are exposed to many different types of risk:

- The risk of an unexpected illness or disability to a household family member and the cost of treatment that will require the expenditure of scarce resources;
- Premature death of a family member in a car accident;
- Losing a job because of the closure of a plant or facility;
- Being sued by an acquaintance for the broken arm he sustained in an accident jumping on your family's trampoline while he was under the influence of too much Yuengling lager; and,
- The risk associated with the returns of financial assets.

We assume that you will address most of the risks that we list above, among others, through the purchase of insurance—health and disability, life and accident, and home and liability insurance. Purchasing insurance coverage is costly and requires the payment of a premium. We discuss insurance later in this chapter. However, the risk that we are most interested in assessing in this chapter is the last risk listed in the bullet points above—the risk associated with the returns of financial assets.

We discussed risk earlier in the book when we examined the principle of risk versus return and how this trade-off is described and quantified through the use of the capital asset pricing model. Our goals in this chapter are to better understand:

- The risk of financial assets and how that risk can be managed;
- The process of diversification;
- Hedging and how it can be done effectively;
- Derivative securities and how they may be used to reduce risk.

16.1 The Management of Risk

The risk upon which we will focus reflects the uncertainty associated with the expected future returns of an asset. A rational investor favors a higher return on an asset over a lower return, and prefers investments with less risk rather than more risk. We measure the risk of an asset by the volatility and variability of its rate of return as measured by its standard deviation.

In the principle relating to risk and return and in Chapter 12 we saw the direct trade-off between higher expected returns on an investment and greater risk: **Higher Returns Require Taking More Risk**. Safe investments such as Treasury bills have little or no risk—if an investor holds a T-bill until its maturity (usually 3 months) the rate of return is known with certainty. But T-bills also have a lower expected rate of return than common stock. The rate of return for a risky asset such as a stock can fluctuate enormously. The compound average annual rate of return for a portfolio of small company stocks over a 76-year period was 12.5%, and the standard deviation of those returns was 33.2%—a very significant number. We revisit the expected returns and risks of five asset classes, as determined in the Ibbotson and Sinquefield Study, in Table 16-1 below:

Table 16-1
Ibbotson & Sinquefield Study

Asset Class	Compound Annual Return	Simple Average Annual Return	Std. Dev. of Return
U.S. Treasury Bills	3.80%	3.90%	3.20%
U.S. Treasury Bonds	5.30%	5.70%	9.40%
Corporate Bonds	5.80%	6.10%	8.60%
Large Company Stocks	10.70%	12.70%	20.20%
Small Company Stocks	12.50%	17.30%	33.20%

The I&S Study demonstrates the direct trade-off between return and risk. An investment in a Treasury bill with no default risk and little price volatility has a lower expected compound average return (3.8%) than a portfolio of large cap stocks (10.7%). The Treasury bill also has a lower risk measure of 3.2% relative to a portfolio of large company stocks with a standard deviation of 20.2%. Returns on individual stocks can swing more wildly than the standard deviation of portfolio returns shown in Table 16-1.

In the principle relating to risk preference we saw that **Rational Investors are Risk Averse**— meaning that investors are willing to sacrifice higher returns in order to reduce exposure to risk. As we saw in Chapter 2, in choosing between two assets with the same expected return, a risk-averse investor always prefers the asset with lower risk. On average, investing in common stocks and accepting risk have increased the returns on investment portfolios significantly. The key to increasing returns is for investors to understand risk and how to manage it.

There are a number of ways to reduce the risk associated with owning a financial asset. For marketable securities, if you feel that the future returns associated with a particular investment are too volatile for your risk profile, the simple approach is to sell the asset. Other ways to reduce or transfer your financial risk are:

- *Diversification*—instead of concentrating your wealth in one risky financial asset, spread the risk around by investing in a number of risky assets;
- *Hedging*—you reduce risk by using techniques that attempt to lock-in a price or a return associated with a risky asset;
- *Insurance*—you pay a premium to purchase a contract or asset that will protect you for a period of time against adverse price movements.

We explore these risk transfer mechanisms in the sections that follow and discuss how to use certain securities and contracts to reduce risk.

16.2   Diversification—The Costless Way to Reduce Risk

Diversification means to spread your wealth equally among a number of different asset classes and investments. And we saw from the principle relating to diversification that **Asset Diversification Will Reduce Your Risk**. The goal of diversification is to invest in a group of assets that provides you with the highest return possible for a given level of risk. We saw in Section 2.9 that the standard deviation of annual returns for an average stock was about 49%—significantly greater than the average annual standard deviation of a portfolio of large cap stocks of 20.2% as shown in Table 16-1 above.

The reason that the risk of a portfolio is lower than the risk of a single stock is because the diversification provided by a portfolio of assets decreases return volatility, thereby reducing risk. And it reduces risk without any out-of-pocket costs. You'll see in the sections below that there are costs associated with risk reduction using hedging and insurance techniques. Diversification works because the returns and prices associated with different stocks do not move in lockstep. When one company does well and its price increases, another company may be doing poorly and its price may decrease. As long as the returns of companies are not perfectly correlated, diversification acts to reduce risk.

The key to diversification and its corresponding reduction of risk is in the *correlation* of the returns of the assets that make up the portfolio. Correlation measures the degree to which the movements of variables are related. Correlation is measured on a scale of -1.0 to $+1.0$. If the returns of two stocks have a correlation coefficient of $+1.0$, then when one stock is up 10%, the other stock is also up 10%. Conversely, a correlation coefficient of -1.0 means that when one stock is up 5%, the other stock is down 5%. Assets that are highly correlated offer less risk reduction from diversification than assets that have a lesser degree of correlation.

Buying stocks in the same industry generally does not greatly increase the diversification of a portfolio. For instance, if you purchased two business-to-business

Internet incubators, such as Internet Capital Group and CMGI, in late 1999, that two stock portfolio probably didn't provide you much of a benefit in the way of diversification. Both stocks plummeted over 95% when the Internet bubble popped in early 2000. Likewise, the diversification provided by the Pro-Funds Ultra OTC Fund didn't cushion the performance of this investment—which dropped by 94.7% over a thirteen-month period. ICGE and CMGI, along with the companies that were in the portfolio of Pro-Funds Ultra OTC Fund, all benefited and suffered from many of the same macroeconomic forces that inflated and then popped the Internet bubble. It is important to consider the correlation of assets when you construct a portfolio.

Achieving the highest return for each level of risk is known as investing on the *efficient frontier*. This type of investing is normally accomplished by investing in different asset classes. The most general asset classes for stocks are value and growth stocks, and large and small capitalization stocks. If you have decided to increase your expected return on your assets by investing a portion of your portfolio in common stock, how should you diversify to reduce your risk?

Stockholders face two types of risk: systematic risk and unsystematic risk. Systematic risk represents the risk of the stock market. Stock prices are affected by surprises in the economy, taxes, and other market factors. When these factors change, they impact the performance of the entire market. Although systematic changes in the market affect each stock to a different degree, all stocks are impacted. As discussed in Principle 1, we measure the systematic or market risk of a stock by its beta.

Unsystematic risk is specific to a company. It is risk inherent to a particular stock due to decisions made by a corporation relative to the industry in which it operates. While unsystematic risk is unique for all firms, it can be similar for firms in related industries. As we saw in Chapter 2:

Total Risk = Systematic Risk + Unsystematic Risk   *(Eq.16-1)*

Diversification reduces the unsystematic risk of a portfolio. Remember that on average, the negative stock-specific surprises affecting companies in a diversified portfolio will usually be offset by positive surprises to other companies.

Table 16-2, summarizes the results of a study performed by Meir Statman that we discussed in Chapter 2. The study looked at randomly grouped portfolios of stocks of various sizes to determine the marginal amount of diversification achieved by adding additional stocks to a portfolio. Volatility of individual stocks is measured by the standard deviation of their returns. The average standard deviation for an individual stock was found to be 49.24%—a significant amount of volatility and risk. According to the findings, if ten randomly selected stocks are combined in equal amounts, the volatility and risk of this portfolio averaged 23.93%—less than half the risk of the average stock in the portfolio.

Based on these results, we see that diversification is easy to obtain in a portfolio. It does not require hundreds of stocks to adequately diversify a portfolio—most studies suggest that 20 to 25 stocks are sufficient. Proper diversification does, however, require that stocks within a portfolio be selected from different industries to reduce correlation among the assets. Diversification occurs in a portfolio only if the stocks selected have different types of unsystematic risk, that is, the prices of the stock do not move in lockstep because they are all in the same or highly-related industries.

Table 16-2
How Many Stocks Make a Diversified Portfolio?

Number of Stocks in Portfolio	Average Standard Deviation of Annual Portfolio Returns	Ratio of Portfolio Standard Deviation of a Single Stock
1	49.24%	100%
10	23.93%	49%
50	20.20%	41%
100	19.69%	40%
300	19.34%	39%
500	19.27%	39%
1000	19.21%	39%

Diversification, while limiting your risk by spreading your investments over a number of securities, also limits the gains you would have received if you had concentrated your investments in a few stocks that turned out to be incredible winners. However, could you stomach investing the bulk of your fortune in a risky stock that may either climb to the moon or go bankrupt? What are the odds that you will identify a start-up that will perform similarly to Microsoft, Dell, or Cisco in the 1990s? Diversifying your portfolio may not make you the next Bill Gates or Warren Buffet (who became rich by focusing their investments), but if you're risk-averse and feel more pain from losing than pleasure from winning diversification is the way to go.

16.3 Hedging—Sacrifice Gain to Protect Against Loss

Hedging is the process of reducing your exposure to a decrease or an increase in the price of an asset, or the return associated with an investment. Farmers that engage in the production of an agricultural commodity, such as wheat or oats or soybeans, frequently try to reduce the risk associated with the price of the commodity at harvest time. The farmer may hedge that risk by entering into a contract to deliver the commodity at a time in the future for a price that is determined today. This contract fixes the price on the products that the farmer will deliver at a certain date in the future.

These types of contracts are called forward or futures or swaps contracts—an agreement to exchange a commodity at some certain time or dates in the future at a predetermined price. A *futures contract* is a forward contract with standardized terms that trades on an organized exchange, such as the Chicago Board of Trade or the New York Mercantile Exchange. A specialized form of a futures contract is a *forward contract*, which usually is a written agreement between two parties that is not traded on an organized exchange. A *swap*, most notably interest rate or currency swaps, is a contract between two parties where a series of cash flows are made (or swapped) over a predetermined time period. A swap effectively consists of a multiple number of forward contracts, and the payments that are made under a swap are based upon a *notional amount*—an agreed upon principal amount, similar to the *size* of the forwards contract discussed below, on which the financial calculations and swap payments are based.

There are certain characteristics of forward, futures, and swap contracts that make them desirable as assets that can be easily structured and traded in the financial markets to manage and transfer risk. Investors who use these instruments to reduce risk are called *hedgers*. Investors that use these instruments to increase risk are called *speculators*. Characteristics of forward and futures contracts are:

- The future *delivery date* of the commodity is determined when the contract is entered into.
- The purchase price (the *forward price*) of the commodity is determined when the contract is initially entered into.
- The *spot price* of the commodity is the current market price of the commodity for immediate delivery; it changes from minute to minute, much as the price of any commodity. The spot price and futures price of a commodity are equal on the delivery date.
- The *size* of the contract is the amount of the commodity that will be delivered.
- The *value* of the contract is the size of the contract times the forward price.
- Forward contracts are entered into between two parties—the party who agrees to buy the commodity is *long* the position; the party who agrees to sell the commodity is *short* the position.
- The value of the contract fluctuates minute to minute as a function of the change in the spot price of the commodity and its time to delivery.
- The forward contract is usually structured with a forward price determined so that the value of the contract initially is $0.

Billions of dollars of futures contracts relating to agricultural commodities, such as soybeans, corn, oats, and wheat trade daily on the Chicago and Kansas City Boards of Trade. Cattle, hogs, and pork belly futures trade on the Chicago Mercantile Exchange. Crude oil, heating oil, gasoline, and natural gas futures trade on the New York Mercantile Exchange. Futures contracts relating to interest rates such as Fed Funds, Eurodollars, LIBOR, 13-week Treasury Bills, Euroyen trade on numerous exchanges. Even futures relating to stock index prices, such as the Dow Jones Industrial Average, S&P 500 Index, NASDAQ 100, Nikkei 225, and many other indices, trade on various exchanges.

Remember the principle of finance relating to the trade-off between risk and return—**Higher Returns Require Taking More Risk**. When the farmer hedges his risk through a forward or futures contract, the futures price on many contracts is likely to be lower than the spot price on the commodity. There are adjustments in the pricing of futures contracts that incorporate costs of storage and transportation of the commodity and costs known as a *cost of carry* to compensate for the time value of money associated with futures contracts. All of these costs are embedded in the futures price and effectively make a hedger receive a lower price for the commodity to pay for shifting the risk to another entity.

For example, on Monday April 28, the spot price of oats was $1.72 per bushel. The price for the December futures contract for 5,000 bushels was $1.44 cents per bushel, considerably lower than the spot price. The hedger also will lose the potential for any upside gain associated with the movement of commodity prices due to scarcity or excess demand. When an investor hedges, he fixes the sales price for the asset and gives up any upside gain for offloading the risk of loss.

Hedging Example:

Suppose that today with the spot price of oats at $1.72 per bushel, farmer Randy sold a futures contract—5,000 bushels of December oat futures at $1.44 per bushel—locking in that price (5,000 * $1.44) of $7,200 for the 5,000 bushels. Farmer Randy calculates that he can eke out a profit at a sales price of $1.44 per bushel, but would incur a catastrophic loss if he sold the oats for a price lower than $1.40 per bushel. Suppose the spot price of oats in December one day before the delivery date is still at $1.72 per bushel that it was on April 28. On the day before the delivery date the futures price for the delivery of the 1-day contract will be very close to $1.72/bushel. To close out his futures position, farmer Randy buys the oat December futures contract for $1.72/bushel. He loses $.26 per bushel on the sale and repurchase of the futures contract, and he sells the 5,000 bushels of oats at the spot price of $1.72 per bushel—giving him a net price of $1.44 per bushel. His futures contract has allowed Randy to fix the price of his oats at $1.44 per bushel. However, he gave up the upside through hedging the price risk.

16.4   Insurance—Pay a Premium to Protect Against Loss

Hedging involves giving up the potential for gain in exchange for reducing or eliminating the risk of loss. Hedging is done most effectively through the use of forward, futures, and swaps contracts, and fixes the price of an asset for delivery in the future. Insuring is another type of risk transfer device that has a payment profile and outcome that is different from that of a hedging instrument. Under an insurance contract, you pay a premium to insure against specific losses and you do not surrender the possibility of a gain.

Insurance contracts are complex contracts and often involve some limitations. For example, some types of insurance limit the amount of money that can be paid under a claim. This limitation is called a *cap*. A typical cap is included in a car insurance policy when it relates to liability insurance. For example, a liability insurance cap often is $300,000—meaning that if the insured party is sued and the plaintiff is awarded benefits that exceed the cap, the insurance company is limited to a payment only up to the cap. Automobile insurance and home ownership insurance policies often also have *deductibles* associated with the policy. For example, a collision deductible for a car may be $500. The owner of the car is responsible for paying the first $500 in damages and the insurance company will pay for any damages over the deductible. Some insurance policies may also have exclusions—events that are specifically excluded from triggering a payment under a policy. A typical exclusion in a life insurance policy is suicide. If the insured party takes his own life within a certain period of time, the insurance company may not be required to make a payment under the policy.

As we said in the beginning of this chapter, the risk in which we are most interested is the risk associated with the returns of financial assets. Financial assets that have characteristics similar to insurance contracts are *options*. An option represents the *right* to either sell an asset or purchase an asset at a fixed price and at a fixed time in the future. An option gives its owner the right, not the obligation, to do something. If an option can only be exercised at a certain date or time period in the future, it is called a *European* option. If the option may be exercised at any time up to and including the exercise date, it is called an *American* option. Characteristics of option contracts are:

- The *strike price* on the option is the price at which the option may be exercised and is determined when the contract is entered into;
- The *expiration date* of the option is the date after which the option can no longer be exercised and is determined when the contract is initially entered into;
- The contract that enables its owner to buy an asset at a fixed price and on or before a certain date is called a *call option*. The contract that enables its owner to sell an asset at a fixed price and on or before a certain date is called a *put option*.
- The *size* of the option contract is the amount of the asset that will be delivered.
- An option contract prior to its expiration has a *positive value* for its owner. The value of the option contract fluctuates minute to minute as a function of the change in the spot price of the asset, its time to delivery, and the volatility of the underlying price movement of the asset.

Put and call options on individual stocks are the most familiar types of options in the market. Option contracts relating to interest rates such as caps and floors are popular among financial institutions. Many types of options trade on exchanges. Options relating to stock index prices, such as the Dow Jones Industrial Average, S&P 500 Index, Nasdaq 100, and even on volatility itself trade on various exchanges.

Option Example:

A call option is the right to buy an underlying asset, such as a share of stock, a Treasury bond, or a futures contract on a Treasury bond, at a predetermined price—the *strike* or *exercise price*, for a predetermined time—the *term* of the option. The buyer of the call option—the *call owner*, pays a fee—the *call premium* to the entity that sells the call option—the *call writer*. Let:

$$S = current\ market\ price\ of\ security\ underlying\ the\ option$$
$$X_c = exercise\ price\ or\ strike\ price\ on\ the\ call\ option$$

A call option is *in the money* if the current price of the underlying security, S, is greater than the exercise price, X_c. For example, if you own an IBM call option with a strike price of \$75, and IBM is trading at a current price of \$80, then your IBM call is in the money in the amount of \$5.

A put option is the right to sell or put an underlying asset at the strike price on or prior to the exercise date. The put owner—or buyer, pays a fee—the *put premium* to the entity that sells the put option—the put writer. Let:

$$X_p = exercise\ price\ or\ strike\ price\ on\ the\ put\ option$$

A put option is in the money if the current price of the underlying security, S, is less than the exercise price, X_p. For example, if you own an IBM put option with a strike price of \$75 and IBM is trading at a current price of \$65, then your IBM put is in the money in the amount of \$10.

The price or value of a put or a call option has two components. The first, called the *intrinsic value,* is the amount the option is in the money and is the difference between the current asset price and the strike price of the option.

$$\textbf{\textit{Intrinsic Value}} = \textbf{\textit{S}} - \textbf{\textit{X}}_c \qquad \textbf{\textit{(Eq.16-2)}}$$

In the IBM call example above:

$$Intrinsic\ Value = \$80 - \$75 = \$5$$

The second component of an option's price or value is called the *time value* and reflects expectations of an option's profitability associated with exercising it at some future point in time. Whereas the option's intrinsic value is easily observed, we calculate the option's time value by subtracting the intrinsic value from the market price of the option.

$$\textbf{\textit{Time Value of Option} = \textit{Market Price of Option} - \textit{Intrinsic Value} \quad (Eq.16\text{-}3)}$$

For example, if McDonald's stock is trading at $20 per share and the strike price of an option that expires in six months is $18, and the option is trading at a price of $3.80, the intrinsic value and time value of the option is:

$$\textit{Intrinsic Value} = S - X_c = \$20 - \$18 = \$2$$

$$\textit{Time Value of Option} = \$3.80 - \$2 = \$1.80$$

16.5   Derivative Securities

16.5.1 General Description

Simple securities are stocks issued by corporations and non-callable bonds issued by corporations, governments and authorities, and municipalities. A *derivative security* is a financial instrument, the value of which is *derived* from or is based upon either the value of a simple security, or the level of an interest rate, interest rate index, or stock market index. For example, a call option on a stock is an equity-based derivative security—its value is dependent upon, among other things, the value of an underlying share of common stock. In the debt market, a LIBOR-based interest cap is a debt-based derivative security—its value is dependent upon, among other things, the present and expected levels of LIBOR rates and their relationship to the cap rate.

In the stock and bond markets, the delivery of a stock or bond upon purchase or sale occurs a few days after the trade is made. The trade is based on current market prices for the financial assets and these markets are known as *spot* or *cash* markets. In the derivatives markets, the delivery sometimes occurs many years into the future and the buyer or seller can initiate offsetting transactions, which enables it to close out its position without requiring the delivery of the asset. Trades in these markets are based on future prices, which are influenced by the commodities spot price and other things.

Many securities that trade in the stock and bond markets have features embedded in them that make them derivative securities. For example, the 30-year callable corporate bond that we discussed in Section 14.1.4 is a debt-based derivative security—its value is dependent upon the value of a 30-year non-callable bond of the corporate issuer minus the value of the 10-year call option that the issuer has retained as part of the bond structure.

Let's assume that the 30-year bond that is callable in 10 years issued by ABC Company is trading at 100% and has an 8% coupon. Let's also assume that the yield for a non-callable 30-year bond of a company with default risk similar to ABC Company is 7%. What's the value of the call option?

Value Callable Bond = Value NonCallable Bond–Value Call Option (Eq.16-4)

The observed value of the callable bond is 100%. We can value the non-callable bond by pricing a 30-year 8% bond at a discount rate of 7%, similar to what we did in Section 14.5.3 when we valued a premium bond to maturity. We calculate the value of the annuity stream of coupon payments associated with the bond using semi-annual discounting on our HP-12c calculator by inputting: n = 60, PMT = 40, i = 3.5, FV = 0, **solve for PV**. With these inputs, PV = $997.79. Next we solve for the present value of the lump sum principal payment. Our inputs for this calculation are: n = 60, PMT = 0, i = 3.5, FV = 1,000, **solve for PV**. With these inputs, PV for the principal payment = $126.93. The total value of a non-callable bond of ABC Company is the sum of the present values of the annuity interest components and the lump-sum principal components:

Value Non-Callable Bond = $997.79 + $126.93 = $1,124.72

Rearranging the above equation, the value of the call option is equal to:

Value Call Option = Value Callable Bond – Value Non-Callable Bond
Value Call Option = $1,000 - $1,124.72 = -$124.72

Effectively, the value of the call option to ABC Company is **-$124.72**, a negative number. ABC could have raised an additional $124.72 per bond if they had issued non-callable debt.

Some corporations issue bonds that are convertible into common stock. These complex derivative securities have cash flows that depend upon both the debt of the issuer and the performance of the stock of the issuer, and both the debt and equity components should be analyzed and valued in determining the value of the derivative security.

Derivative securities generally are designed in a way that make their cash flows and market values more dependent upon changes in short or long-term interest rates or yield levels, or on stock prices or market indexes. This price or yield sensitivity or *leverage* amplifies the change in value of a derivative security and makes them attractive when they are used as a hedging instrument to hedge exposure to certain risks. However, if derivatives are used for speculation, this leverage feature also can backfire due to the adverse price consequences of leverage.

During the mid-1990s, a number of financial scandals occurred that were associated with the inappropriate use of derivatives to speculate in financial markets. One scandal focused on inappropriate derivatives trading by Orange County, California, with financial institutions and resulted in significant financial penalties. Another scandal was the abuse of derivatives by Proctor and Gamble in a transaction with Banker's Trust Company, which contributed to the consolidation and sale of Banker's Trust to a foreign financial institution.

16.5.2 Types of Derivative Securities

Derivative securities have been developed which allow current levels of interest rates, stock index values, currency rates, and commodity prices, in general, to be locked in for a certain period of time—usually for a price. These financial instruments consist of different types of forwards, futures, swaps, and options contracts.

Complex derivative securities can be analyzed and valued as a package of simpler, more basic securities or building blocks. We saw this when we valued the call option for our simple callable bond. Each type of derivative security has differing characteristics, payoff profiles, and costs; and combinations of these instruments can be used to custom tailor a hedging solution for a market participant.

These building blocks can be broken down into four broad categories: *equity components* (stock-like instruments) and *debt components* (bond-like instruments); *hedging* or price-fixing components (forwards, futures, and swaps instruments); and *option components* (interest rate caps and floors, and stock call and puts).

- *Equity and Debt Components*: a derivative security embedded with the characteristics of a simple stock or bond. The bond component can be fixed-rate, zero-coupon, or amortizing.
- *Hedging or price-fixing components*: forward and futures contracts and interest rate and currency swap contracts. The value of these components may be positive or negative, depending on movements and shifts in yields, currency levels, or spot prices. These components usually are designed and priced such that their relative value at the time of issuance of the derivative security is zero.
- *Option or price insurance components*: interest rate floors and caps, call and put options. Zero or positive values are associated with these components for the *owner* of the option. Zero or negative values are associated with these components for the *writer* of the option.

Forwards, futures, and swaps are known as price-fixing hedging contracts, where the price of an asset or an interest rate associated with a liability are fixed at the time of entering into the contract. Examples of price-fixing hedging contracts are Treasury bond futures contracts and LIBOR forward starting interest rate swaps. These contracts generally have few upfront costs and are usually the most efficient type of hedging contract. If interest rates move in favor of the investor that is long the derivative, money will be received by the investor. If interest rates move against the investor in the future, payments are made to fulfill the investor's obligation under the hedge contract. To protect against the cost of adverse price movement in a price-fixing derivative contract, the investor theoretically gives up any upside benefits. The most popular forms of interest rate hedging instruments are: Treasury bond and Treasury note futures contracts,

Eurodollar futures contracts, LIBOR-based interest rate swap contracts, and option contracts based upon Treasury bonds, notes and LIBOR and Eurodollar futures contracts.

The most popular types of option contracts are put and call options on stocks and bonds. Most corporate and municipal bonds are embedded with a call option that permits the issuer of the bond to call it after a certain period of time at a predetermined price. We value a callable bond in the previous section. Call and put options on stocks are traded actively on financial exchanges. For example, on April 30, 2003, a call option that expires in January of 2005 to purchase shares of Microsoft at a price of $32.50 per share traded at a price of $2.90 per share. The closing price of Microsoft on that date was $25.56 per share. The option was out of the money by almost $7 per share ($32.50 - $25.56), but the option had a time value of almost $10 per share.

16.5.3 Relationship between Cash and Derivative Markets

There are several ways in which the prices of assets for immediate delivery in the cash market are related to the prices of assets in the futures market. Two concerns and costs associated with futures and forwards is the cost of storage and delivery. If you transact in the futures market for a commodity such as oats, that product must be stored somewhere prior to its delivery, and costs are involved in both storage and delivery. These costs are embedded in the futures prices.

An even more important relationship is involved in the concept of arbitrage and the law of one price. Financial participants constantly check markets to compare the prices of financial assets to see if an asset is priced differently in various markets. They are looking for *arbitrage* opportunities. If a difference exists, they will but the asset where the price is relatively low and sell the asset where the price is relatively high, taking the difference as an arbitrage profit. For example, if the stock of XYZ Company is trading on the New York Stock Exchange at $10 per share and on the London Stock Exchange at $11 per share, *arbitrageurs* will buy shares on the NYSE and immediately sell them in London. The action of increasing demand will drive the price of ABC stock higher in New York and increasing supply will drive the price of ABC stock lower in London, until the price in New York equals the price in London.

The activity of arbitrage is the basis for a valuation approach that is known as the *Law of One Price*, which states that equivalent combinations of securities that result in identical cash flows in all scenarios, in aggregate, must have the same cost or price. The Law of One Price is an important concept in the pricing and valuation of derivative securities. Using combinations of different derivative securities, it is possible to replicate the cash flows associated with other securities. The Law of One Price states that the total costs associated with all packages of securities that result in equivalent cash flow payouts should be the same. So if two financial assets have equivalent outcomes in all states of the world, they must have equal prices.

*Law of One Price—equivalent combinations of securities
that result in identical cash flows in all scenarios
must have the same aggregate cost or price.*

The Law of One Price dictates that the futures price of an asset and the spot price of the asset must be the same on the day the futures contract expires. Therefore, we should expect to see the price of futures contracts converge to the spot price as the contract approaches maturity. This is an important linkage that, along with storage and delivery costs and the time value of money, helps to determine exactly what the relationship should be between spot and futures prices.

16.5.4 Valuation of Derivative Securities

The value of a derivative security depends upon the value of the underlying simple securities or building blocks. And the value of the underlying simple securities, like any financial asset, is based upon the expected cash flows associated with the asset. For purposes of valuing derivative securities, we value each of the debt, equity, hedging, and option components and total the value to come up with the total value of the derivative security. The value of the different components may be either positive or negative, depending upon whether the derivative security is long or short the component. The value of derivative securities, particularly the option components, is beyond the scope of an initial finance text, but we can briefly describe some of the basics.

The value of the derivative security will be based on the value of the underlying components. If you are long a debt-based derivative security and interest rates fall, the present value of the cash flows associated with that security increases, and the derivative will increase in value. Likewise, if you own an equity-based derivative and the value of the underlying equity increases, the value of the derivative should increase. So the value of a long position in a derivative should vary directly with the price of the underlying bond or stock. The values of futures, forward, swap and option contracts embedded in the derivative will be dependent upon the time to expiration or maturity. Whether this relationship is direct or inverse will depend on the structure of the cash flows associated with the derivative security.

Generally, the value of any derivative security is crucially dependent on four (if it's a forward, future or swap) or five (if it's an option) inputs:

- The *spot price* and movement of the underlying asset;
- The *amount of time* to the delivery date or expiration date of the derivative contract;
- The *exercise price* on the contract and the relationship of the spot price to the exercise price;
- The *risk-free rate of interest* that corresponds to the amount of time to the delivery date; and
- For option components—the *volatility* associated with the return or price of the underlying asset.

16.5.5 Role of Derivative Markets

Derivative markets, such as the futures markets for commodity contracts, have existed for many years. Derivative markets relating to financial assets have grown exponentially in recent years and have become even more important to the efficient functioning of international markets.

Derivative markets, particularly the futures and options exchanges, often have greater liquidity than the spot markets and permit investors to sell assets short by selling a contract, much more easily than the spot markets do. Often transactions costs in derivative markets are much lower than in the spot markets, and since delivery is not required until the delivery date, less capital is required to take positions.

Derivatives markets are often more efficient than the spot markets and their existence encourages arbitrageurs to participate and drive prices to equilibrium. It also is possible to use derivative markets to replicate other security packages. This replication invokes the Law of One Price and insures asset pricing that will not allow arbitrage opportunities to exist for a very long period of time.

The derivatives markets can be used to manage risk or to speculate. If you buy a Treasury bond and simultaneously sell a Treasury bond future, you reduce your risk position. If interest rates rise, the value of your Treasury bond will fall, and the decrease should be offset by the increase in the value of your Treasury bond future. Using the derivative markets to establish an offsetting risk position to an investment in a financial asset is hedging. Derivatives markets also allow investors to take positions that increase their risks rather than decreasing it. Using derivative markets to increase risk is called speculation.

16.6 Summary

In this section we discussed the management of risk—a sometimes difficult to understand function of the financial markets. Some of the concepts that we addressed in this chapter, such as derivative securities and option valuation, are too advanced to explore in depth in a first text in finance, and we could not do them justice in the space provided. However, we introduced you to this very important area of finance and hope that we whetted your appetite enough that you will learn more about the management of risk.

The risk that we were most interested in assessing in this chapter is the risk associated with the returns of financial assets. We discussed risk earlier in the book when we examined the principle of risk versus return and how this trade-off is described and quantified through the use of the capital asset pricing model. We discussed three risk transfer mechanisms: diversification, hedging, and insurance.

We found that diversification is a costless way to reduce risk, and that proper diversification efficiently reduces the risk associated with owning stocks. We saw that hedging reduces risk exposure and recognized that hedging has a cost, by way of a reduced return or price and the forfeiture of upside return potential if prices were to move in our favor. We discussed forwards, futures, and swap contracts and their characteristics. We saw that hedge instruments exist for numerous types of commodities and financial assets.

Insurance reduces risk for a period of time and has an explicit cost—the insurance premium. Options are financial assets that have features similar to insurance, and we discussed the characteristics of options. We also visited the topic of derivative securities and showed how to value a call option on a bond. And we briefly touched on the Law of One Price and its importance when it comes to valuing derivative securities.

In the beginning of this chapter we stated that our goals were to better understand:
- The risk of financial assets and how that risk can be managed;
- The process of diversification;
- Hedging and how it can be done effectively;
- Derivative securities and how they may be used to reduce risk.

We hope that we accomplished these goals, among others, and we wish you good luck in finance and in life.

List of Terms
1. Risk-averse
2. Diversification
3. Hedging
4. Insurance
5. Correlation
6. Systematic Risk
7. Beta
8. Unsystematic Risk
9. Futures Contract
10. Forward Contract
11. Swap
12. Notional Amount
13. Hedgers
14. Speculators
15. Delivery Date
16. Forward Price
17. Spot Price
18. Size of Contract
19. Value of Contract
20. Long
21. Short
22. Cost of Carry
23. Cap
24. Deductibles
25. Options
26. European Option
27. American Option
28. Strike Price or Exercise Price
29. Expiration Date
30. Call Option
31. Put Option
32. Size of Option Contract
33. Call or Put Owner
34. Call or Put Writer
35. Premium
36. In the Money
37. Intrinsic Value of Option
38. Time Value of Option
39. Derivative Security
40. Spot or Cash Markets
41. Equity Components
42. Debt Components
43. Option Components
44. Arbitrage
45. Law of One Price

Questions

1. Discuss some of the ways in which you can reduce or transfer your financial risk.
2. Explain diversification. Define systematic and unsystematic risk and explain what risk is addressed by diversification.
3. Define and explain the difference between a futures contract and a forward contract. What are their main characteristics?
4. Why are the future prices on many future contracts lower than the spot prices? What costs are embedded in the futures price?
5. How does insurance differ from a hedging instrument such as futures?
6. What are options? Explain the characteristics of an option instrument.
7. Define intrinsic value and time value with regard to options.
8. What is a derivative security? What influences the market value of a derivative security?
9. How can the components of a complex derivative be broadly divided? Briefly explain each component.
10. Explain the Law of One Price and the role it plays in the valuation of derivative securities.

Assignment #16-1

1. An investor who is currently holding long-term treasury bonds is concerned about volatility in interest rates and wants to hedge his risk using futures. He can hedge his risk by buying treasury bond futures
   - (a) True
   - (b) False

2. A two-stock portfolio is most diversified when correlation between the returns of the two stocks are
   - (a) Perfectly positive
   - (b) Positive
   - (c) Zero
   - (d) Negative

3. If you own a ConEd call option with a strike price of $45 and if the stock is currently trading at $38, you option is currently in the money.
   - (a) True
   - (b) False

4. The value of a call option increases when
   - (a) Stock volatility is higher
   - (b) Period till expiration is higher
   - (c) Strike price is lower
   - (d) All of the above

5. Which of the following is a false statement?
   - (a) A call option is in the money when the strike price is lower than the current stock price.
   - (b) A call option is out of money when the strike price is higher than the current stock price.
   - (c) A put option is out of money when the strike price is higher than the current stock price.
   - (d) A put option is in the money when the strike price is higher than the current stock price.

6. The value of a put option increases when
   - (a) Volatility decreases
   - (b) Strike price increases
   - (c) Current stock price increases
   - (d) All of the above

7. If you own an ABC Inc. call option with a strike price of $35 and if the stock is currently trading at $42, the intrinsic value of your option is
    (a) $7
    (b) $35
    (c) $42
    (d)   None of the above

8. If you own a call option having a strike price of $25 and expiring in 3 months, what is the time value of option if the current stock price is $31 and the option is trading for $3.80?
    (a) $2.20
    (b) $3.80
    (c) $6.00
    (d)   None of the above

9. Z Corp. issues a 10-year bond callable in 5 years at par with a coupon rate of 7%. If the yield for a 10-year non-callable bond of a company with a similar risk is 6%, the value of call option is
    (a) $74.39
    (b) $84.35
    (c)   -$74.39
    (d)   -$84.35

10. If you are a long debt based derivative security and interest rates fall, the value of the derivative
    (a)   Is not affected
    (b)   Decreases
    (c)   Increases

Assignment #16-2

1. On adding a stock whose return has a low correlation with the return of stocks in the portfolio, the portfolio's risk
   (a) Increases
   (b) Decreases
   (c) Is not impacted

2. The value of a call option increases when
   (a) Stock volatility is lower
   (b) Period till expiration is shorter
   (c) Strike price is higher
   (d) None of the above

3. The value of a put option decreases when
   (a) Stock volatility increases
   (b) Strike price increases
   (c) Current stock price increases
   (d) All of the above

4. If you own an ABC Inc. call option with a strike price of $42 and if the stock is currently trading at $35, the intrinsic value of your option is
   (a) $7
   (b) $35
   (c) $42
   (d) None of the above

5. A Corp. issues a 30-year bond callable in 20 years at par with a coupon rate of 9%. If the yield for a 30-year non-callable bond of a company with a similar risk is 8%, the value of the call option is
   (a) $74.39
   (b) $113.12
   (c) -$74.39
   (d) -$113.12

6. If the intrinsic value of your call option that expires in six months is $5.60 and its time value is $2.30, what is your option trading at?
   (a) $2.30
   (b) $3.30
   (c) $5.60
   (d) $7.90

7. If you own a call option having a strike price of $40 and expiring in 3 months, what is the time value of option if the current stock price is $44 and the option is trading for $1.65?
   (a) $4.00

(b) $3.80

(c) $2.35

(d) $1.65

8. If the call option you own is currently trading at $4.30 and you have calculated the time value of your option to be $2.70, what is the current stock price of the stock, if the strike price is $58?

   (a) $59

   (b) $61

   (c) $63

   (d) $65

9. If the call option you own is currently trading at $1.10 and you have calculated the time value of your option to be $1.90, what is the exercise price under the option, if the current stock price is $44?

   (a) $41

   (b) $43

   (c) $44

   (d) $45

10. If you own an equity-based derivative and if the value of the equity decreases, the value of your derivative increases.

    (a) True

    (b) False

---

[i] The material in this chapter was first presented by the authors in chapter 2 of the text, *Streetsmart Guide to Valuing Stock Second Edition* (McGraw-Hill), 2003. The authors of this text book, along with Patrick J. Cusatis, are the authors of *Streetsmart Guide.*

[ii] See Ibbotson Associates, *The Stocks, Bonds, Bills and Inflation 2004 Yearbook,* Chicago, 2004.

[iii] Gary P. Brinson, L. Randolph Hood, and Gilbert L. Beebower, "Determinants of Portfolio Performance," *Financial Analysts Journal,* (July/August 1986). And "Brinson, Gary P., Brian D. Singer, and Gilbert L. Beebower, "Determinants of Portfolio Performance II: An Update," *Financial Analysts Journal*, (May/June 1991).

[iv] Meir Statman, "How Many Stocks Make a Diversified Portfolio?" *Journal of Financial and Quantitative Analysis* 22 (September 1987), pp. 353–64.

[v] Brealey, Richard and Stewart Meyers, *Principles of Corporate Finance* (McGraw Hill), 1996.

[vi] See Robert A. Haugen, *The New Finance: The Case Against Efficient Markets,* Prentice Hall, Upper Saddle River, NJ, 1999; Robert J. Shiller, *Irrational Exuberance*, Broadway Books, New York, NY, 2000; and Werner DeBondt and Richard H. Thaler, "Does the Stock Market Overreact?" *Journal of Finance,* 40 (3) (1985): 793-805.

[vii] Fama, Eugene F., and Kenneth R. French. "The Cross Section of Expected Stock Returns," *Journal of Finance,* 47 (1992): 427-466.

[viii] See Fama, E., "Short-Term Interest Rates as Predictors of Inflation," *American Economic Review,* June 1975, pp. 269-82.

[ix] A book that focuses on the discounted cash flow method of valuing stocks and acts as the basis for much of what is included in the chapter is: Gray, G., P. Cusatis, and J. R. Woolridge, *Streetsmart Guide to Valuing a Stock Using the Ten Principles of Finance*, McGraw-Hill 2003. Two of the authors of *Streetsmart Guide* are the authors of this book.

[x] Georgette Jasen, "Investment Dartboard," *The Wall Street Journal*, September 12, 2002, p.C9.

[xi] In calculating the Residual Value of the corporation, it is assumed that there is no net new investment, i.e. investment = depreciation, and there is no additional working capital required. As an example, at the end of an Excess Return Period of 10 years, if the company's NOPAT = $1million and its WACC = 10%, the company's future residual value = $1million/(.10) = $10 million, which amount would be discounted to the present at the discount factor equal to 1.0 divided by (1.0 plus the company's WACC), that sum taken to the tenth power = $1.0/(1.0 + .1)^{10} = (.3855)$. Residual Value = $10 million * .3855 = $3,855,000.

[xii] Burton G. Malkiel explains how the stock market drop of 508 points (22.6%) on October 19, 1987 could have been caused solely by an increase in both interest rates and the equity risk premium *A Random Walk Down Wall Street,* W.W. Norton & Co., New York, 1990, (pp. 203-206).